CONTENDING PERSPECTIVES IN COMPARATIVE POLITICS

CONTENDING PERSPECTIVES IN COMPARATIVE POLITICS

Edited by
Lawrence Mayer, Dennis Patterson, and Frank Thames
Texas Tech University

A Division of SAGE
Washington, D.C.

CQ Press
2300 N Street, NW, Suite 800
Washington, DC 20037

Phone: 202-729-1900; toll-free, 1-866-4CQ-PRESS (1-866-427-7737)

Web: www.cqpress.com

Cover design: Jeff Hall
Composition: Judy Myers

♾ The paper used in this publication exceeds the requirements of the American National Standard for Information Sciences—Permanence of Paper for Printed Library Materials, ANSI Z39.48-1992.

Printed and bound in the United States of America

12 11 10 09 08 1 2 3 4 5

Library of Congress Cataloging-in-Publication Data

Contending perspectives in comparative politics / edited by Lawrence Mayer, Dennis Patterson, Frank Thames.
p. cm.
Includes bibliographical references and index.
ISBN 978-0-87289-925-4 (pbk. : alk. paper) 1. Comparative government. I. Mayer, Lawrence C. II. Patterson, Dennis Patrick. III. Thames, Frank. IV. Title.

JF51.C629 2008
320.3—dc22

2008048871

CONTENTS

PREFACE

The task of compiling a general reader for comparative politics is primarily one of selectivity. Only a very small proportion of the important literature in so broad a field can be represented, let alone included, if the book is to be confined to a manageable length. Such a reader will have more coherence and distinguish itself more clearly from other readers if the process of selecting works for inclusion and organizing them is carried out according to clearly explicated criteria.

At the core of our selection criteria is our definition of comparative political inquiry. We define the field in terms of its goals or purposes: the establishment of empirically testable, explanatory generalizations with cross-national or cross-cultural validity. This definition clearly stresses the comparative implications of comparative politics; hence, we selected literature in which propositions are applied or are logically applicable to more than one context. Our definition also led us toward literature in which propositions are subject, in principle, to falsification in terms of sensory data. This does not mean we believe it desirable or possible to eliminate human interpretation or inference from scientific inquiry. It does mean that we have eschewed a large body of theoretically interesting literature that is framed in such broad, ambiguous terms as to render it inherently untestable.

In vigorous discussions among the editors in the early stages of compiling and constructing this volume, it became apparent that despite the apparently successful revolution in the field in the 1950s and 1960s, there remained strong disagreement as to what we, as comparativists, are or should be doing. We decided to attempt something different from other readers: to reflect this lack of consensus in the field by organizing the chapters and our selections around these scholarly points at issue. Thus we would more clearly show the student the extent to which comparative politics is still in a state of flux, and in the process we could get across our point more strongly than by merely stating that fact.

We have tried to include the major issue areas—the ones most frequently covered in courses in the field in recent decades—and to choose literature that has been frequently cited and discussed. In doing so, we also strived to strike a balance between including some "classic" pieces of research and being up to date with the most current research. Thus, in addition to the well-established discussions of pan-national integration and globalism, we have included commentary on the recent rejections of the EU's proposed constitution.

Our efforts focused on coherence in the order in which the readings and our discussions of them are placed. To that end, we preceded our discussion of democratic institutions and processes with the literature on alternative models of democracy and the ideological context of democracy. However, we present each chapter in such a way that it could stand by itself, thereby giving the instructor the flexibility of arranging the material in whatever way suits his or her needs.

While a collection of readings from the research literature in the field, as opposed to a textbook, presents a challenge to many undergraduate students, we have tried to aid students in interpreting the meaning and significance of the literature with our introductions to each chapter and the headnotes for each reading. In these introductions and headnotes, we have also tried to suggest questions for the students to ponder as they tackle the readings. Although the reading level of some of our selections may be challenging, we feel that the point of a comparative politics reader is to provide students with the experience of confronting the richness and complexity of the actual literature that currently shapes the field of comparative political analysis.

From the start of this project to its eventual conclusion, we have been supported and guided by the skilled editorship of Charisse Kiino at CQ Press. The editorial work of Allison McKay, Allyson Rudolph, and Lorna Notsch played a major role in producing a better organized and better written work than this volume otherwise would have been. We are grateful for the patience and skill they displayed in enhancing the quality of our efforts. We are of course grateful to the scholars who have offered useful suggestions and critiques of our work in the planning stages of this project: Annabelle Conroy, University of Central Florida; Andrea Stevenson Sanjian, Bucknell University; Boyka Stefanova, University of Texas at San Antonio; and Joel Wolfe, University of Cincinnati. We are also grateful to our families and friends who encouraged us and patiently allowed us the freedom to complete this project. Of course, it goes without saying that we assume the responsibility for whatever shortcomings remain in this project.

Lawrence Mayer
Dennis Patterson
Frank Thames
Lubbock, Texas
November 2008

Chapter 1

DOES THE COMPARATIVE METHOD CONTRIBUTE TO BUILDING A BODY OF EXPLANATORY THEORY ABOUT POLITICAL OUTCOMES?

Those of us in the field of comparative politics conceive of it in terms of its goals and purposes. Rather than merely aspiring to accurately describe political structures and events, we seek to identify their causes and more accurately predict their occurrence. To that end, comparative analysis—the framing of generalizations about political phenomena applied to a variety of contexts—has emerged as one of the main methods of explaining political phenomena. As preeminent comparative political scientist Arend Lijphart put it, however, the comparative method is concerned with "the *how* but does not specify the *what* of the analysis"; this chapter explores both the advantages and limitations of this process. Thus, the comparative method is one set of procedures for constructing explanations.

Comparative politics was transformed in the 1950s and 1960s from a field that defined itself in terms of countries and geographic areas to a field delineated by its explanatory purpose. Before this transformation, the field was usually called "comparative government" and was defined by its subject matter: governments other than that of the United States. This traditional field was ironically noncomparative and instead emphasized the uniqueness of each country. The reasoning for this? Every political phenomenon was seen as a product of a unique configuration of factors in each country, and so it was held as foolish to generalize from one country to another. Using this logic, the former noncomparative school would argue that France's Socialist Party cannot be meaningfully compared to Germany's Social Democratic Party because each party is the product of the unique configuration of all the attributes that comprise each of these countries. Advocates of this perspective therefore argued that one cannot compare phenomena that are essentially different; yet the essence of comparison is the identification of what phenomena that are otherwise different have in common. You *can* compare apples to oranges. They may look and taste different, but they are both fruits, grow on trees, and contain vitamin C.

Before the field underwent transformation in the 1950s, it was also narrowly ethnocentric, limiting itself to the major powers of Europe and virtually ignoring the vast world of Asia, Africa, and Latin America, as well as the smaller countries of Europe. This ethnocentrism was possibly exacerbated by the existence of the Western colonial empires, which made the importance of the Afro-Asian and Latin worlds less apparent. Since the field was noncomparative, it did not seek to produce testable explanations in the modern scientific sense; rather, the primary purpose of the field was descriptive—to set forth the constitutionally designated structures of government, such as heads of government and representative assemblies. Scholars were not pursuing systematic explanations, so they were able to ignore factors that had causal impact, such as the society in which a government is situated. Accordingly, these practitioners of traditionally defined comparative government, stressing a clear distinction between the study of government and other fields of social inquiry such as sociology, anthropology, and psychology, focused on the structures of the state while avoiding an analysis of the social or cultural context in which political behavior occurred.

Modern comparativists, by contrast, discovered the analytic utility of such contextual factors as culture, social structure, history, geography, demography, and economics almost to the neglect of the constitutional formats and processes on which they had formerly focused, practicing what Roy Macridis referred to as "the fallacy of inputism." [1] That is, these scholars focused on the impact of contextual factors on the state while neglecting the state itself. (A later section of this volume includes calls to rediscover the state in political analysis.) Nevertheless, one of the major tasks of the modern comparative method is to generalize about the impact of contextual factors because scholars in behavioral sciences cannot isolate their explanatory theories from them. To account for the impact of these contextual factors, comparativists seek the broadest possible cross cultural applicability of our explanatory principles. Thus, a statement about the impact of gender on political orientations varies with the importance of religion in that nation's culture: we can say that women are more conservative than men because women are more religious and religious people tend to be more conservative. However, this difference disappears in highly secularized societies in which few people of either sex are religious.

Modern political analysis, therefore, must operate on two levels. On the one hand, we need to construct explanatory principles based on the relationship among the attributes of individuals or groups found within political systems, looking in particular at such attributes as attitudes or other mental dispositions, ethnicity, religious affiliation (or lack thereof), and behaviors. On the other hand, we generalize about attributes of the entire political system, including its historical patterns of nation building, its social structure, its geography, its demography, and its culture, what we call the context of politics. When an explanatory proposition about the relationship among individual-level attributes holds true in one setting differently than in other settings, we can conclude that something about the settings—the whole system level of analysis—affects that relationship.

What is commonly called the comparative method, generalizing about the attributes of whole systems, is therefore beset with the problem of the small number of cases. Hence, one cannot validly use statistical techniques and probability theory that presume a large N (number of cases). Thus, while Lawrence Mayer focuses on the utility of the comparative method, the second reading by Peter Hall addresses the limitations of the comparative method in seeking explanations, especially the problem of the small N.

Whatever method used, all theories in political science infer causal relations from direct observations or make predictions with the implicit qualifier "other things being equal." The term *infer* means to go from what can be directly observed to using a degree of mental interpretation to draw a conclusion. We can see that two variables, such as class and political attitude, occur together, but we can only conclude a causal relationship by inference; the joint occurrence could be accidental. Contextual factors are among the most important elements comprising the other things being equal qualifier that render explanations incomplete and predictions inaccurate. By taking into account previously ignored contextual factors, political scientists are able to reduce the scope of the other things that are not equal and render increasingly complex and complete explanations and evermore accurate predictions. Theory in this view is cumulatively built over time through numerous pieces of research. This is what Mayer, in this chapter's first reading, means by "Theory Building with the Comparative Method." The second reading by Peter Hall addresses the limitations of the comparative method in seeking explanations, especially the problem of drawing conclusions based on a small number of cases.

The definition of comparative political inquiry offered here also reveals a methodological bias toward an empirical approach, a method that relies on observable data for reaching conclusions. Scientifically useful inquiry then is inquiry directed toward the construction of explanatory principles with predictive power that must be unambiguously falsifiable. What this means is that we try to develop generalizations that could be found inconsistent with relevant observable data,[2] which gives us intersubjective criteria for accepting or rejecting truth claims. Two people, seeing the same relevant observations, would have to reach the same conclusions regardless of their biases or preconceptions. For example, the statement "working-class people tend to vote for parties on the left" is not falsifiable because it logically allows an indefinite number of exceptions. However, the statement "a majority of working-class people vote for parties on the left" is falsifiable if one assumes the concept of "working-class" is precisely defined. People who claim that such observable data constitute the only acceptable source of knowledge are called positivists. Most scholars today theorize and infer to build knowledge while still insisting that truth claims are empirically falsifiable. Members of this school are qualified positivists.

One consequence of using qualified positivist criteria in our selection process for this volume is the relative absence of selections from the voluminous body of literature written in the Parsonian tradition, a tradition based on impressionistic truth claims that achieved great prominence, if not predominance, in the 1960s. The influence of sociologist Talcott Parsons, the leading advocate of this tradition, can be found in the writings of such leading scholars of the time as Gabriel Almond, Lucien Pye, and David Apter. A much-heralded seven-volume series on various aspects of "political development," authored by members of this group during this period and published by Princeton University Press, contains a wealth of impressionistic theorizing but not a single testable hypothesis.[3] A notable example of such impressionistic theorizing among followers of the Parsonian tradition is the so-called systems analysis, the much-celebrated and oft-cited work of David Easton, of which the core proposition is that the breakdown of political systems is a function of a loss of equilibrium between inputs and outputs. In other words, such breakdowns are failures to process issues (convert demands from society into policy outcomes) generated by a new level or new types of demands. While this might partially account for events that have already occurred, such as the collapse of Germany's Weimar Republic or the inability of the post–Saddam Hussein regime in Iraq to acquire widespread acceptance, this idea cannot yield a precise prediction about the future persistence or collapse of any particular system unless the magnitude of stress caused by a specific set of demands or the relief of such stress generated by a particular set of outputs could be measured. Moreover, there would have to be a precise set of indicators for distinguishing system collapse from system change or adaptation.

To yield testable theory, the explanatory principles developed in comparative analysis must not only be broadly theoretical but also must be comprised of concepts that can be precisely indicated or measured by observable phenomena. To that end, the specification of indicators, observable phenomena that tell whether or to what extent a concept is presumed to be present, is *the* key component of testable theory. Unless such theory is in fact rendered testable, inquiry cannot resolve questions of what is actually known, and without such resolution, the task of cumulatively building a body of knowledge becomes impossible: instead, we would eternally be inquiring about the same questions.

Thus, "modern" political theorists, such as John Rawls, grapple with the same questions—such as what is the nature of justice—raised by Plato millennia ago.

For this reason, modern comparative analysis must concern itself with the specification of indicators for and the measurement of the concepts employed. This concern raises special problems in cross-national or cross-cultural research in which an explanatory principle is applied to more than one national or cultural context. The essence of the problem is that the meanings of behaviors or terms are affected by the cultural contexts in which they are found. For example, protest behavior might signify one thing in a context characterized by an activist culture but something else entirely in a context characterized by widespread apathy, and so different indicators or measures might be required in different contexts to maintain a consistent meaning of a concept, what has been called the problem of "equivalence." [4]

A criterion of testability may be required in explanatory theory, but imposing it with inflexible rigor can be counterproductive. In building a science of politics, inquiry should not be limited to those few areas in which rigorously quantified data are available to the exclusion of questions that are theoretically interesting or politically important. As will become apparent from the selections offered in this chapter, measures are frequently inferential, requiring a degree of interpretation in moving from the raw observations to the formation of the concepts or ideas. This means that findings can vary with the predispositions of the scholar in question, thereby weakening their consistency and objectivity.

Moreover, it remains true that the phenomena in which we are interested remain massively overdetermined, meaning they are the product of far more factors than any given study can encompass. Despite comparativists' best efforts or pretensions at scientific inquiry, our explanations remain incomplete and our predictions probabilistic. Yet we believe the range of selections presented in this volume shows progress. Modern comparative politics continues to gain precision and reflects a continuing evolution in the range of phenomena with which the field must cope and in the rigor and sophistication of the tools at our disposal to take on these challenges.

Notes

1. Roy Macridis, "Political Systems and Comparative Politics," in *Comparative Politics: Notes and Readings,* 5th ed., eds. Roy Macridis and Bernard Brown (Homewood, Ill.: Dorsey Press, 1977), 9ff.
2. A generalization is testable if it expresses or implies precisely which data would be incompatible with it. Karl Popper, *The Logic of Scientific Discovery* (New York: Harper Torchbooks, 1958). Chapters 1 and 4 present the best discussion of this. See Section III for a full treatment of culture and its impact.
3. Gabriel Almond, "Introduction," in *The Politics of the Developing Areas,* eds. Gabriel Almond and James Coleman, eds. 1–64. This is as good an example of the work of this school as any. See also *Political Culture and Political Development,* eds. Lucien Pye and Sidney Verba, 1965; *Political Parties and Political Development,* eds. Joseph LaPalombara and Myron Weiner, 1966; *Bureaucracy and Political Development,* ed. Joseph LaPalombara, 1963; *Communications and Political Development,* ed. Lucien Pye, 1963; and *Education and Political Development,* ed. James Coleman, 1965. All of these texts were published by Princeton University Press in Princeton, New Jersey.
4. Adam Przeworski and Henry Teune, *The Logic of Comparative Social Inquiry* (New York: Wiley, 1970), 133ff.

1.1

THE EPISTEMOLOGY OF SOCIAL SCIENCE AND THE COMPARATIVE METHOD

Lawrence Mayer

In this essay, Lawrence Mayer of Texas Tech University describes and defends the explanatory focus of political science in general and the usefulness of the comparative method in particular for constructing scientifically valid explanations and theories about political phenomena. The comparative method is one of three methods in social science used to address the inexorable problem of unanalyzed variables, the other two being the statistical and experimental methods. By comparing very similar or very different cases, the comparative method allows political scientists to propose relationships between independent and dependent variables (such as A causes B). With that in mind, be aware of the criteria for the tentative acceptance of a proposed relationship between two variables and of the difference between a scientifically valid proposition and a metaphysical one.

The revolution in comparative politics discussed in the introductory chapter was part of a broader revolution in the field of political science itself. This broader revolution was clearly intended by its progenitors to bring political science in line with what they perceived to be the attributes of other respected academic disciplines, especially the natural sciences. Specifically, the architects of the revolution in political science endeavored to transform the field from an essentially descriptive enterprise that emphasized the idiographic attributes of social and political phenomena to an enterprise that could explain and predict such phenomena through the formulation of general laws. Comparative political analysis should, in this view, be seen as a method that, if not coterminous with the effort to build a science of politics, is at least one of the useful tools in this effort. This reconceptualization of the comparative field from a geographical focus on foreign government to a method of building a science of politics presumes that such a science is a possible and desirable goal. While this presumption is increasingly widely accepted among political scientists, it is by no means universally accepted.

* * *

Lawrence Mayer, "The Epistemology of Social Science and the Comparative Method," in *Redefining Comparative Politics: Promise versus Performance* (Thousand Oaks, Calif.: SAGE Publications, Inc., 1989), chapter 2, 1–20.

A Science of Politics

Despite pockets of resistance, there is a widespread consensus entrenched in the natural sciences and growing in the social and behavioral sciences that a scientific method exists to explain the phenomena with which that discipline is concerned. Description or narratives have a valuable role to play in the data collection enterprise; however, they do not constitute ends in themselves. Description and narration are of value to the extent that they contribute to the explanatory process.

Explanations in the social or behavioral sciences differ from those in the natural sciences with respect to their completeness and to the accuracy of the predictions they generate. However, the structure of scientific explanation remains the same regardless of the subject matter. The standards of what does or does not constitute a scientifically adequate explanation does not vary with the subject matter.

A scientific explanation consists of a principle, a general statement of a relationship among two or more concepts, that logically entails either the certainty or the probability of the specific phenomenon to be explained such that if the principle were true, then the phenomenon to be explained, the *explicandum,* should occur, given the stipulated preconditions. An explanatory principle is more than a statement of an empirical relationship; it further implies why the relationship should exist. This principle thus becomes a theory that itself accounts for the observed relationship.

For instance, in the violence literature, it was shown that there is a correlation between indices of want formation in relation to indices of want satisfaction on the one hand and a composite index of violent political behavior on the other, or between indices of economic and political discrimination and political separatism on the one hand and measures of civil strife on the other. The correlations obtained have the status of scientific propositions (the probabilistic social science counterpart to scientific laws). However, the question of why these relationships should be observed is answered by a theoretic principle that the psychological states of frustration, anger, or "relative deprivation"—the relationship between what one thinks he or she deserves and what one expects to be able to obtain—lead to aggression. One does not directly observe the psychological states, of course. However, if the theory were true, the observed relation logically should be observed in stipulated circumstances. A theory is thus only indirectly testable.

Theory thus compromises the epistemological criteria of crude positivism which hold that we only know that which is directly observable. B. F. Skinner, for instance, advocates the eschewal of all innerman or personality constructs as a reversion to metaphysics. It is enough to know that certain behaviors do recur when reinforced by certain stimuli, he claims; the inference of causation is unnecessary. By definition, theoretical constructs, as well as any inference, involve a measure of subjectivity. Skinner and other positivists implicitly raise the question of why it is useful to infer a theoretic construct to logically account for observed patterns and thus interject an element of subjectivity into scientific analysis. Knowing that directly observed patterns of behavior do occur will afford the ability to predict and, in some measure, to control such behavior; hence, it is unnecessary to speculate on why such patterns exist.

Scientific theory is not true or false. Rather, it is more or less useful with respect to the number and variety of empirical relationships for which it can account and the extent to which empirical relationships can be derived from it, thereby expanding our knowledge.

In a deterministic science (such as physics), we may say that if the principle were true the explicandum must follow. In the behavioral sciences, we are only able to say that it is more likely to follow than if the preconditions did not exist. The precise probability of the occurrence of the explicandum can frequently be stipulated through the statistical method. Thus, the explicandum must be shown to be a specific case of a more generic concept that is systematically related to another concept. Therefore, explanation is, by definition, a generalizing activity that inexorably involves the method of comparison.

While a scientific explanation consists of a principle that entails the explicandum, such an explanation also implies that the relationship between the explicandum and the factor that putatively accounts for the explicandum, the *explicans*, is causal in nature. When we predict that an observed relationship will continue to exist, the only logical basis for making such a prediction is the assumption that some causal factor is operating.

However, the mere fact of any imperfect relationship does not necessarily entail causation. A conclusion of causation always involves inference, the process of moving from a body of data to a conclusion with a certain amount of interpretation. The imperatives for the necessary conclusion that a given relationship is causal have been listed by Ernest Nagel as follows: (1) The relationship is invariable. (2) The explicans is both a necessary and a sufficient condition for the explicandum although, rather than list all the sufficient conditions, the practice is to list the event that completes the sufficient conditions. (3) The relationship is between phenomena that are specially contiguous. (4) The explicandum follows the explicans in an invariable temporal sequence, and this relationship is asymmetrical (Nagel, 1962). These conditions are never encountered in the social sciences; therefore, one of the major tasks of social inquiry is causal inference, the attempt to distinguish on an empirical basis which relationships are causal in nature and which ones are not.

This task is rendered difficult in social inquiry by the fact that our explanations imply some but not all of the causes of the explicandum. To this extent, our explanations are incomplete (Brodbeck, 1968; Hempel, 1968). The consequence of this incompleteness is that the explicandum does not invariably follow from the presence of the putatively causal variable, the explicans. It will be shown below that social research has as one of its major concerns the task of rendering explanations relatively more complete and that the comparative method is one major method in accomplishing this task.

Przeworski and Teune cite a famous example of an incomplete explanation, one to which we shall return. M. Rouget, a 24-year-old worker in a large factory, has voted Communist (Przeworski and Teune, 1970). Why did he do so? We know that young, male, industrial workers tend to vote for left-wing parties. M. Rouget's attributes fit the first set of concepts; his vote is a particular instance of left voting, implying that there is something about being young, male, and a worker in a large factory that causes one to vote for left-wing parties. Why did he vote that way? In part, because of the aforementioned attributes.

Of course, knowledge of these attributes does not enable us to predict M. Rouget's vote with certainty. We can only say that of the aggregate of people with those attributes, a significantly greater portion will vote left than the aggregate of people without those attributes. We can predict probabilistically but not with certainty. Why not? Our predictions can only be probabilistic because there are more factors that can and do influence individual votes than any single analysis can encompass. The foregoing analysis, for instance, omits the influence of church affiliation, church attendance, family, peers, and all combinations and permutations of unique individual experiences. By identifying some but not all of the factors that influence the explicandum, our explanations remain incomplete.

Obviously, the more causal factors we can isolate and include in our analysis, the more complete, by definition, our explanation becomes and the more accurate our predictions will be. It is inconceivable that we could isolate and identify more of the causes of an explicandum without enhancing our ability to predict its occurrence. Predictability is not an either/or phenomenon in a probabilistic discipline; rather, the accuracy of predictions in such a discipline is a matter of degree. To the extent that a principle significantly enhances one's power to predict an explicandum over not having the principle, we say the principle affords explanatory power. Principles that appear to account for some phenomena under question without enhancing the ability to predict them possess what Anatol Rapoport has called "explanatory appeal" (Rapoport, 1968).[1] Abraham Kaplan [1964] has referred to this distinction in terms of "seeing an explanation" as opposed to "having" one. . . .

* * *

The fit of the predictions generated by explanatory principles to actual occurrences provides a test of the utility of those principles and renders them accountable. Accountability, one of the major imperatives of scientific epistemology, means that truth claims must be demonstrated, not merely asserted. Scientific epistemology is not concerned with criteria for the formulation of such truth claims or explanatory principles; rather, it is concerned with criteria for the justification of such claims.

Truth claims that do not entail any predictions about the sensory or empirical world remain impressionistically true or false, depending upon the individual. Conclusions are subjective in the sense that they depend on the internal dispositions of each individual drawing them. By imposing criteria for the justification of truth claims in terms of sensory data, scientific epistemology seeks to render conclusions intersubjective—consistent from one subject to another despite their differing internal dispositions.

These criteria of justification demand that explanatory principles logically entail some expectations of what any observer would see under stipulated conditions. Unless such a precise set of expectations is generated, one has no means of assessing the compatibility of truth claims with reality. Truth claims that generate unrealized expectations must accordingly be rejected or revised so as to be compatible with sensory experience. In other words, scientific epistemology demands that truth claims or explanatory principles be stated in such a way that they are intersubjectively falsifiable, that there be some conceivable body of data that would cause one to reject or revise the truth claim.[2]

Statements that do not generate such expectations tell us nothing about the experiential world. Such statements may refer to phenomena outside of our experiential world, such as statements about the nature of heaven, hell, or purgatory. They may refer to events that occurred in the past on a one-time basis without any logical expectation that they would ever occur again under stipulated conditions, events such as the biblical account of creation. To say that such statements are not scientific is not to say that they are false; it is to say that their consistency or the lack thereof with the relevant evidence cannot be demonstrated. Such statements constitute what A. J. Ayer calls metaphysical statements (Ayer, 1952). He calls such statements meaningless in the sense that they tell us nothing about our world of experience.

There are those who assert that the concept of knowledge should extend to such metaphysical statements. Such scholars treat the concept of knowledge as a normative one and seem to resent the implication that their eschewal of the criteria of the scientific method renders their truth claims normatively inferior. For instance, Leo Strauss charges that scientific epistemology denies the status of knowledge to

1. See also Rapoport (1967).
2. This is the criterion of demarcation proposed by Karl Popper (1954) to distinguish scientific from nonscientific propositions.

"prescientific knowledge," by which he presumably means such metaphysical statements as revealed religious truth and intuitive judgments, in other words, those conclusions of which he is subjectively certain (Strauss, 1957). However, what is self-evident to him is not necessarily self-evident to others.

Abraham Maslow similarly advocates humanistic and holistic conceptions of science . . . (Maslow, 1970, p.3).

"Pure science," he declares, "has no more intrinsic value than humanistic science" (Maslow, 1970, p.3). The difficulty is that the concept of knowledge is widely understood to refer to a given class of assertions, thereby distinguishing them from other assertions. That class of assertions may also present certain advantages over other assertions that give those assertions called *knowledge* a certain value. Being demonstrable, scientific propositions generate results that are intersubjectively discernible. By definition, the results of scientific knowledge are there for all to see, regardless of their internal dispositions. The power is generated and the lights go on, or the bomb goes off and it matters little whether the theories about nuclear reactions that formed the bases of these phenomena are essentially true.

When one refers to assertions as knowledge or science even though they do not possess the attributes of scientific propositions, one fails to give these other assertions those desired attributes and renders the concept of knowledge meaningless. If all assertions are knowledge, the terms *knowledge* and *assertion* become synonymous, and one of them becomes redundant.

It is clear, then, that those propositions that we regard as scientific must, by definition, be empirical in the sense of being falsifiable by sensory data. It is also clear, however, that this requirement could be met by probabilistic statements as well as by deterministic ones. It is not necessary to hold that a single deviant case entails the rejection of the theory. It is only necessary to specify in advance of testing a theory which or how many deviant cases would entail its rejection. Hence, the fact that human behavior is overdetermined and impossible to predict with certainty in individual cases does not render a science of such behavior impossible to construct.

The concept of free will is held by many to conflict with the attempt to build a science of human behavior. The concept of free will, a concept fundamental in the Judaic-Christian tradition, entails the human capacity to choose, to control one's behavior. To argue, as is implied by social science, that human behavior is caused, one seems to deny that capacity to choose and, perhaps more significantly, to deny the moral responsibility that presumes this capacity to choose. Hence, the entire enterprise of a science of human behavior seems to be in direct conflict with an important aspect of that Judaic-Christian tradition, the power to choose between right and wrong.

For this reason, B. F. Skinner entitles the book popularizing his theory of the causes of human behavior, *Beyond Freedom and Dignity* (1971). The latter two terms imply the freedom to choose to do right or wrong, the ability to disobey the "laws" of behavior. If one's behavior is determined by factors outside oneself, one cannot be blamed or praised for one's actions.

. . . The argument that people make choices that are completely autonomous of factors external to human will is subject to serious reservation. While it is clear that people do choose, the choices they make are constrained by experiences and by contextual variables. *Will* refers to human desire; *choice* refers to picking from among available alternatives. Clearly, one cannot will states that, because of contextual or other external factors, are not among the available alternatives.

The very fact that human behavior is so predictable supports the working assumption that, while people make choices, the choices are rendered more or less likely by factors external to the actor. While the resolution of the debate between the supporters of free will and the supporters of social causation can never be objectively determined, the working assumption that behavior is caused does, in fact, yield substantial predictive power about many important aspects of that behavior.

The attribution of any given behavior to the internal nature of the actor eschews the inquiry into how the actor acquired such a nature. When you answer the question, "Why did he do that evil thing?" with the explanation, "Because he is vicious," you not only avoid the question of how he became vicious, but you are, in effect, stating a tautology. You know he is vicious because of the behavior that the attribute *viciousness* is adduced to explain. The putative dispositional attribute of the actor, far from referring to any precise set of independently conceptualized phenomena, becomes an undefined repository of all those causes of behavior that cannot be identified and measured.

Actual Limits on the Explanation of Human Behavior

It should be clear from the foregoing that, while the probabilistic propositions of social science are structurally the same as those of natural science, an important difference remains between the two fields of inquiry. While in the natural sciences the variables under analysis can generally be isolated from exogenous variables that could affect the outcome to be explained, such outcomes in the social sciences are usually affected by a nearly limitless array of variables that cannot be effectively isolated one from the other. Hence, all feasible propositions in the social sciences must be qualified that they will hold true only to the extent that these unanalyzed or exogenous variables cancel one another out or, otherwise put, they hold true other things being equal (*ceteris paribus*). Of course, the other things never are equal; they act to produce unexpected outcomes that render social science propositions less than universally true. It is the ubiquitous existence of this *ceteris paribus* qualifier that distinguishes propositions in the social sciences from the deterministic propositions feasible in the natural sciences. The phenomena in which social scientists are interested are almost always over-determined; simplistic propositions to the effect that X causes Y usually constitute a very imperfect description of reality. The outcome Y will not invariably follow the putative cause X, due to the presence or absence of these exogenous variables.

The inability to make deterministic predictions does not render such causal statements untrue. Such statements may well be partial truths, in the sense that they account for some but not all of the causes of the explicandum. It was noted above that most social or political phenomena are overdetermined, meaning that social phenomena are the product of an almost infinite myriad of factors, only a fraction of which can be identified in any manageable study. These unanalyzed factors in any given theory are exogenous to that theory. The impact of such exogenous factors on any given explicandum will generate results in some fraction of the observations that are not entailed by the theory; these factors are those "other things" that the *ceteris paribus* clause assumes will cancel one another out, but they never do so.

The Problem of Exogenous Variables: The Experimental and Statistical Methods

A major problem of social research is to isolate putatively causal relationships from exogenous variables. Several methods are available for this purpose: the experimental method, the statistical method, and the comparative method.[3]

---

3. This classification of methods is delineated in Lijphart (1971).

The experimental method best fits popularized notions of the way scientists actually proceed. This method attempts to effect the actual isolation of the exogenous factors under analysis from exogenous factors that may impact on the phenomenon in question by the consciously selective administration of the putatively causal stimulus to one group (the experimental group) but not to another group (the control group), with both groups selected so as to be as alike as possible in other salient respects. Each group is then measured or tested for the variable that constitutes the explicandum. Since no other relevant stimuli were introduced, it should then be possible to assess the actual impact of the explicandum. Some opportunities for this kind of analysis do exist in political research, for instance, simulations and game theory. However, the complex patterns of human behavior and interaction in which political scientists are interested can rarely be isolated from the context in which they occur; hence, one can rarely be certain that the experimental group (to which the putatively causal factor is administered) and the control group (to which that factor is not administered) are, in fact, alike in all other respects. Moreover, many of the putatively causal phenomena in which political scientists are interested cannot be selectively administered or withheld at will; consequently, the social scientist is forced into the role of a passive observer rather than the active creator of a situation implied by the experimental model. Such phenomena can only be imperfectly simulated in experimental research. Experiments are termed valid to the extent that their findings can be extrapolated from the experimental setting to social and political behavior in general. The artificiality of the experimental setting may impede the validity of experimental findings. Frequently, the putatively causal stimuli may involve hypothetical rather than actual situations. For example, the dispositional sets known as social alienation or frustration thought to generate civil violence cannot be reproduced at will in individuals; hence, experimental research utilizing these variables would have to take on a hypothetical mode.

For example, although they were using survey research rather than the experimental method, the small, parochial nature of their sample forced Grofman and Muller to construct a concept called "the potential for political violence" to represent the likelihood of engaging in actual violence (Grofman and Muller, 1973). This potential-for-violence variable was indicated by responses to a questionnaire constituting an approval-of-political-violence scale and an intention-to-engage-in-violence scale. However, it is one thing to approve of violence on paper; it is quite another thing to actually engage in violence. The empirical connection between the contrived and managed potential-for-violence variable in this study and the variable in which the authors are theoretically interested—violent behavior—remains an open question.

When one moves from the controlled and deliberate administration of artificial stimuli in the experimental situation to the passive observation of natural (i.e., uncontrolled) stimuli in the nonexperimental world, the impact of exogenous variables can no longer be excluded. The impact of such variables can, however, be assessed by one of two methods.

The statistical method can reveal what a stochastic relationship between two variables *would* be if all other relevant variables canceled one another out and thus had no aggregate impact on the explicandum. In the case of contingency relationships, tendencies toward the joint occurrence of the independent and dependent variables, the cases to be tested are divided into those that possess the exogenous variables to be controlled and those that do not. In this "elaboration model," it is then possible to ascertain whether the presence or absence of the control variable changes either the structure or magnitude of the relationship in question. If the putatively causal relationship disappears when the control variable is not present, it is reasonable to conclude that it was the control variable, rather than the independent or test variable, that had the direct causal impact. The control variable in such a case may either be the intervening variable or it may cause both the independent and dependent variables, depending on whether the control variable occurs before the independent variable.

In the case of correlation, the concept of a relationship in which one variable changes proportionally to change in another variable, it is also possible to assess the impact of one or more exogenous variables on the relationship in question. The technique of partial correlations is based upon the Pearsonian product moment correlation coefficient (r), a technique that measures the extent to which the magnitude of the independent variable is predictable from the magnitude of the dependent variable (Blalock, 1964). The coefficient is based upon the square root of the mean squared deviation in the magnitude of the cases of the dependent variable about their mean. As such, it is sensitive to the extent that cases on the dependent variable fall into a linear pattern. It is not sensitive to the magnitude of change in that variable; hence, it does not measure the impact of the independent variable on the dependent variable. In Figure 1, the hypothetical data set indicates a high correlation between the variables although the magnitude of the dependent variable remains virtually unchanged, reflecting that changes in the magnitude of the independent variable have little impact on the magnitude of the dependent variable. Yet, because the magnitude of the dependent variable is highly predictable from knowledge of the magnitude of the independent variable, this hypothetical data set would also yield a very high correlation coefficient. Hence, an inference of causation from a high value of r can be misleading.

The discrep[a]ncy between the predicted magnitude of the dependent variable and the actual magnitude of the dependent variable is known as the residual. A partial correlation involves correlating the independent and the dependent variables respectively with a control variable, then correlating the residuals with one another. Since those residuals reflect that part of the variation in the independent and dependent variables that is not predictable from the control variable, a partial correlation reflects what the value of r would be if the magnitude of the control variable did not vary, a valuable tool in the aforementioned task of distinguishing causal relationships from other forms of relationship.

Figure 1 Hypothetical Regression

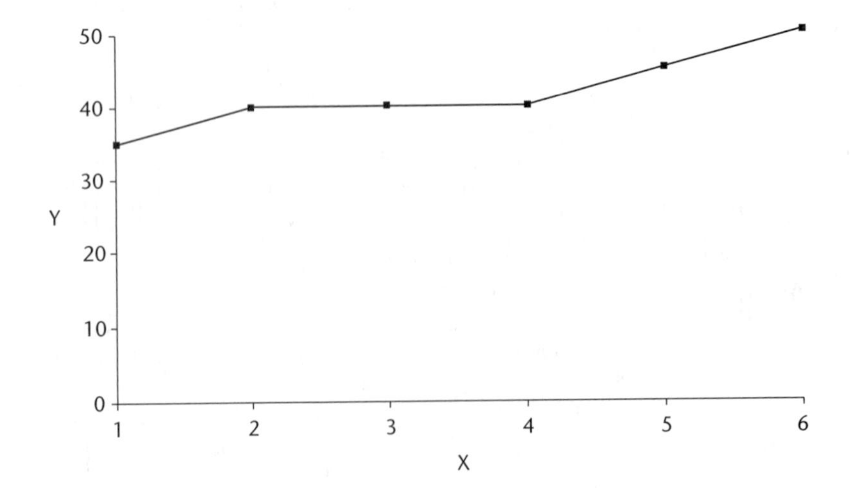

The Comparative Method

The third method of adjusting the imperatives of scientific inquiry to the ubiquitous reality of exogenous variables is the comparative method. Unlike the experimental method, the comparative method does not aspire to isolate the explanatory theory in question from the impact of exogenous variables; rather, like the statistical method, the comparative tries to identify and measure the impact of exogenous variables.

The unique role of the comparative method in building explanatory theory arises from the fact that one may identify two distinct types of objects for analysis: the attributes of individuals and the attributes of whole systems. Przeworski and Teune refer to them as levels of analysis (Przeworski and Teune, 1970). System-level attributes include such phenomena as a nation's political culture, historical experiences, geographical factors (e.g., permeable or insular borders), or demographic factors (e.g., the social stratification system). These system-level attributes constitute the context within which relationships exist among the characteristics of individuals or groups, a context that frequently will affect the magnitude or even the nature of such within-system relationships. It is entirely conceivable, for example, that the relationship between some measure of economic or political deprivations and actual participation in civil violence would be stronger in a system with a history of "successful" violence than in a system in which such violence has been practically nonexistent. In the former class of systems, the experience of accomplishing political goals by violent means would likely render such means more legitimate. The foregoing remains a stochastic theory, however, until the impact of a nation's historical experience with violence on the original relationship is empirically investigated.

When a relationship between within-system concepts differs in structure or significantly in magnitude from one system to another, the reasonable inference is that some system level variable has a causal impact on the original explicandum. This situation constitutes "system level interference" in a within-system relationship (Przeworski and Teune, 1970). Conversely, as a within-system relationship holds true in a greater variety of contexts, one gains more confidence that the relationship is, in fact, causal.

Clearly, the only way that one can empirically determine whether such system level interference exists is by the application of the within-system relationship in as many different contexts as possible. This application of within-system relationships in different contexts constitutes the definition of comparative analysis as a method. This method of assessing the contextual impact on within-system explanatory generalizations is not necessarily cross-national. One may discern differing contexts within complex nations, or one may engage in comparative analysis within a nation in a diachronic sense. The important point is that the method permits one to empirically determine the impact of different contexts on any explanatory generalization.

If, for example, the relationship between economic or political deprivation and violent behavior held true to about the same extent in systems with a violent or revolutionary past and those systems with a history of peaceful evolution, one might reasonably conclude that the variable of a nation's history with respect to violence had little or no effect on the probability of violent behavior in the near future. Przeworski and Teune suggest that comparative analysis is only appropriate when system level interference is present; in the example just given, comparative analysis would be unnecessary. However, it is not possible to establish the absence of system level interference without comparative analysis. A putatively causal relationship among two or more concepts that is derived from data gathered in one context remains conjectural until it is tested against data from other contexts.

An example can be found in the frequent assertion that the economic strength of the United States is due to its particular economic system, a system that places relatively greater reliance on the market for the allocation of economic goods. However, as long as the data supporting this assertion are drawn from this one context, one cannot dismiss the possibility that the joint presence of the two concepts (of economic well-being and policies placing more reliance on the market) is spurious. When one finds that indicators of economic strength are strongly present in other systems with very different economic policies, one may reasonably suspect that the economic strength of the United States is due to other factors.

Theory Building with the Comparative Method

. . . Knowledge is expanded in science by the discovery of deviant cases, by the falsification of explanatory propositions as they are stated. While finding that the data support existing propositions gives one more confidence that such propositions are, in fact, at least partially causal rather than spurious, the tentative confirmation of propositions still serves to consolidate that which is already known or suspected rather than expanding on that knowledge. It is in the process of accounting for disconfirming or anom[a]lous data that one expands on what is already known.

In an illustration discussed earlier, M. Rouget's vote is explained in terms of age, occupation, and sex. Knowing one's age and occupation enables us to predict one's vote with a given probability (substantially above chance); however, knowledge of one's gender substantially improves our ability to predict voting behavior in France. We gain substantially more confidence in our theory as we apply it to a variety of other systems (e.g., Italy, Chile) and find that it still holds true. When we apply the theory to Norway, however, we find that gender difference in voting behavior disappears. Thus, we can now say that men are more likely than women to vote for a left-wing candidate except in Norway.

At this point, explanation ceases as Norway becomes a label for the repository of whatever unidentified factors cause it to be an exception to the theory. In this use of a label, the term *Norway* is a substitute for the analysis of potentially relevant exogenous variables; thus, the proper names of systems in comparative analysis are similar to the "inner man" concepts used by personality theorists to "explain" behavior. To the question, "Why did he do that?" the personality theorist might answer, "Because of his courage, his goodness, his anality," or some other personality concept. However, such concepts not only serve as repositories for the unexplained causes of the behaviors in question, but they constitute essentially tautological reasoning. Why did he risk his life? Because he is courageous. What is a courageous person? Among other things, it is someone who would risk his safety.

Moreover, a proper noun can never serve as the explicans in a scientifically adequate explanation because, referring to a finite phenomenon, such an explanation cannot logically entail any conclusions beyond that phenomenon. It was shown above that explanatory power necessarily entails predictive power, the capacity to logically extrapolate from those patterns directly observed to what would be expected in stipulated preconditions. This capacity becomes possible only when the concepts in the explanatory principle each refer to an infinite category of observations. When the concepts have a finite empirical content, the proposition becomes descriptive.

Thus, the fact that the proposition about sex and voting does not hold true in Norway does not entail any expectations about where else the proposition will not hold true. Our knowledge is not advanced beyond that which is directly observed. A field of inquiry that does not permit us to extrapolate from that which is seen to that which should logically be expected in stipulated circumstances is mere description.

This chapter has argued that it is through the finding of such deviant cases, the falsification of explanatory propositions, that knowledge is advanced. In the foregoing example of a deviant case being an idiosyncratic system identified by a proper noun, knowledge is advanced by the specification of those generic attributes of the system that putatively cause it to be an exception to the theory, or, as Przeworski and Teune put it, by translating the proper names of systems into common noun variables (Przeworski and Teune, 1970). Hence, one should not say that there is a sex difference in voting except in Norway; rather, one should say that there is a sex difference in voting except in those systems in which religion has a diminished political salience, of which Norway happens to be one case. One would then logically expect sex differences in voting also to disappear in other systems in which religion has a low political salience. The theory purporting to explain voting behavior has now become more complex with the addition of the salience-of-religion variable, more narrowly applicable (there are now fewer instances that would entail the prediction of particular vote) but more complete and more accurate with respect to the predictions derived from it.

The cumulative addition of relevant variables by accounting for deviant cases is what is meant by building theory. Theory building in this sense is not the product of a single, grand creative insight so much as the incremental process of cumulating knowledge bits over time. A major argument of this chapter is that the unique potential of comparative analysis lies in the cumulative and incremental addition of system-level attributes to existing explanatory theory, thereby making such theory progressively more complete.

Clearly, there are logistic constraints on the number and variety of contexts to which an explanatory theory may be applied in any given project. At today's prices, many thousands of dollars are required to execute cross-national surveys, and grant money for social research is becoming rather more scarce than in the past. As our knowledge of social reality expands, multivariate analysis is becoming the norm; hence, given the pressure to "complete" and publish a number of research projects within a given time frame, the trend is toward fewer cases with more variables.

Accordingly, the strengths of the comparative method would be best utilized if research were more truly cumulative, if more effort were directed to the testing of existing explanatory theory in a wider variety of settings. Unfortunately, the incentive structure (the kinds of manuscripts most likely to be published) serves to encourage the formulation of new explanatory principles and frequently to urge others to undertake the mundane task of submitting such principles to empirical tests. If such principles are tested, the testing usually occurs in a single setting or in very few settings (Sigelman and Gadbois, 1983). Clearly, more academic prestige is attached to the role of theorizer than to the role of replicator of existing theory.

Yet, at the current state of development of comparative politics, the replication function may be the most crucial one for expanding the corpus of what we can say that we know. The journals are replete with innovative theoretic insights that cry out for testing, falsification, and modification. It is through falsification that knowledge is expanded; yet, rarely does one find a published study in which the null hypothesis is accepted.

The literature in epistemology stresses the conflicting criteria of "parsimony" and accuracy for explanatory theory. However, the value of parsimony has frequently been extolled at the expense of the conflicting imperative of accuracy. *Parsimony,* in this sense, refers to the goal of having theories unencumbered with numerous qualifying variables. Obviously, there are advantages in the ability to explain much of the variation in any given phenomena with one or two factors. The more exogenous factors exist of which one need take account, the more difficult the research task becomes.

Rarely, however, do such "parsimonious" theories explain much of the variation in the complex phenomena in which political scientists tend to be interested. Such phenomena are, as was noted above, nearly always overdetermined. Hence, parsimonious theories frequently generate inaccurate predictions because they are so incomplete. The value of parsimony needs to be balanced against the conflicting value of increasing a theory's predictive power. The value of parsimony has, in the social sciences, the impact of producing very large unexplained residuals. The task of more completely explaining and more accurately predicting reality is inexorably a task of rendering explanatory theories more complex through the addition and analysis of formerly exogenous variables. The more of the unexplained residuals that are specified and incorporated into one's theory, the more accurate will be the predictions deductively entailed by the theory. Theory building consists of the specification and analysis of factors that were part of the unexplained residuals in existing explanatory theory.

The identification of factors in the unexplained residual begins with the falsification of the theory as stated. When a theory that had been supported by the data in several other settings is falsified in a given system, the task at hand is to delineate in generic terms those attributes in which the deviant-case system differs from the systems in which the theory was supported, attributes that could logically account for the deviant-case results.

For example, shortly after the Second World War, a parsimonious theory that purported to explain the instability and collapse of parliamentary governments throughout Europe in the prewar years gained widespread credence. The complex phenomena of the instability and collapse of these parliamentary regimes was putatively traced to one institutional factor, the type of electoral system used by the nation in question. This explanation, most notably associated with the work of F. A. Hermans and Maurice Duverger (Hermans, 1951; Duverger, 1963),[4] suggested that a category of electoral systems collectively known as proportional representation (P.R.) promotes fragmented party systems which, in turn, enhance the probability of cabinet instability. This causal model would look like this: P.R. → party fragmentation → cabinet instability → system collapse. The proponents of this theory were able to offer both empirical and logical support for it. Empirically, it was shown that European parliamentary systems that had been beset by cabinet instability and an inability to govern had both fragmented party systems and a proportional type of electoral system. Logically, it was shown how that type of electoral system should encourage the proliferation and persistence of small parties and how the fragmentation of a party system should encourage dogmatic extremism, thus impeding the compromises necessary to form stable governing coalitions.

Despite the *prima facie* persuasiveness of the case made by the anti-P.R. crusaders, a growing number of anomalies began to be noticed in the decades immediately following World War II: nations that combined proportional representation with cabinet stability. (The converse putative relationship between the Anglo-American single-member district, plurality-electoral system, and a high degree of party aggregation approximating a two-party system, on the other hand, still appears to hold true universally.) Party systems did not necessarily fragment when P.R. was adopted. Moreover, systems consisting of more than two parties did not generate either political extremism or cabinet instability. The Scandinavian democracies and the Low Countries constitute the most obvious anom[a]lies to the P.R. → instability theory.

4. See also Milnor (1969) for the most recent and most naive example of a true believer in the single-factor (electoral system) explanation of cabinet stability.

The tendency of the leading scholars of the discipline, in the face of such contradictory evidence, was to reject outright the electoral-system–cabinet-stability theory as spurious. The existence of anom[a]lous or deviant cases to social theory, however, does not entail the conclusion that the explicans is completely without causal impact on the explicandum. A more useful strategy in the face of anom[a]lies to a theory that did appear to account for a range of other phenomena would be to ascertain those attributes common to the deviant cases and absent in those cases in which the theory held true, attributes that could logically account for the observed anom[a]lies. Thus, in the case of Hermans' theory, it is one thing to say that the explanation that purported to account for differences in cabinet stability among Great Britain, Weimar Germany, Italy, and France does not hold true in Scandinavia, the Low Countries, and Israel. It would be theoretically more useful to delineate the attributes common to the disconfirming or anom[a]lous group of systems in terms of generic variables.

In the example under discussion, the deviant cases are systems in which P.R. produced neither the party fragmentation nor the cabinet instability entailed by the electoral-system theory. These systems all seem to lack those cultural attributes that generate fissiparous tendencies in their stratification system. In those systems, the "interest aggregation" function, in the language of Gabriel Almond, has been inadequately performed. Thus, the theory must now hold that P.R. *permits* the fragmentation of party systems and the representation of extremist positions in those cultural contexts whose fissiparous tendencies discourage the formation of broad and stable political coalitions and otherwise promote extremist politics.

To give another illustration, observers of the American political scene have discerned a growing tendency in the 1980s for women to vote in a more liberal direction than do men (Holbert, 1982). This tendency appears to contradict the conventional wisdom among students of Western democracies, especially of Western Europe, that women act as a conservative political force. This author and others are involved in research to determine in which systems sex predicts voting choice at all and in which systems women tend to vote one way rather than another (Mayer and Smith, 1983). The task of the research is ultimately to specify how cultural or other contextual factors act as intervening variables between gender and voting behavior. Preliminary findings suggest that the salience of religiosity in a nation affects the impact of sex on voting behavior. Religious women tend to be more conservative than men; secularized women tend to be either more liberal or not significantly different in their voting behavior from males, depending on other individual level factors.

Thus, it is suggested that the contribution of comparative analysis to the building of explanatory theory is to distinguish the type of context in which a given explanation holds true and those types of contexts in which it does not. This identification of contextual qualifications as intervening variables to explanatory theory increases the complexity of such theory as well as its predictive accuracy and explanatory completeness.

[A discussion of problems of measurement in comparative analysis is omitted.]

Conclusions

The central theme of this chapter is that comparative analysis should be considered as a method that plays a central role in the explanatory mission of political science itself. It is assumed that political science is an enterprise with the goal of any other scientific enterprise: to develop theories that explain and predict the phenomena with which it is concerned. In pursuing this goal, all scientific enterprises employ certain criteria in the justification of truth claims. These criteria of justification constitute the essence of the distinction between science and what A. J. Ayer calls "metaphysics" (Ayer, 1952, p. 33) or, in Karl Popper's words, "the criterion of demarcation." (Popper, 1954, pp. 34–37, 42–44, Popper, 1963, chapt. 11) The application of these criteria in analysis is what we call the scientific method.

This chapter has argued that there is one such scientific method that can be applied, with appropriate modifications in the area of technique, to all forms of inquiry including the study of social and political phenomena. The claim made here, that the same epistemological criteria apply to the social and behavioral sciences as to the natural sciences, must be qualified by the almost inevitable presence of a large unexplained residual in the explanation of social and political phenomena. Such residuals are attributable to a repository of variables, variables that impact upon the phenomena with which we are concerned but are un-analyzed by and, hence, exogenous to all explanatory theory in political science.

Such exogenous variables frequently constitute attributes of the political or social system itself: the social, cultural, or historical context in which political behavior takes place. It was shown how cross-contextual analysis constitutes the best available method for ascertaining the impact of such contextual variables on the phenomena to be explained. Hence, the function of comparative analysis as a method is best fulfilled, *ceteris paribus*, when explanatory theory is applied to as wide a variety of contexts as possible.

Accordingly, analysis becomes comparative when explanatory theory is framed in such a way that it could be applied to data in two or more distinct contexts. These contexts may or may not involve more than one political system; however, the contexts must differ from one another with respect to at least one important attribute that may affect the magnitude or quality of the explicandum. This book recognizes that explanatory theory may be created based upon data from one context or one political system and that theory entails expectations about data from other systems or contexts. In this way, single-system or single-case analysis may serve as a *means* to comparative analysis. However, such single-system or single-case analysis as an *end* in itself, even if derived from a foreign government, is not *comparative politics* as that term is used in this book. The analysis of foreign governments as an end in itself does not serve the methodological function of comparative politics. Hence, data from foreign governments are useful only insofar as they have theoretic and comparative relevance.

The *ceteris paribus* qualifier referred to above implies a value conflict with cross-contextual generality. This conflicting value is that explanatory theory shall have empirical content. That is, the concepts that comprise such a theory should either be defined in terms of sensory data (operationalized) or assigned indicators that unambiguously determine the extent to which the concept is presumed to be present.

Since the meaning of actions or phenomena varies from context to context, it is rarely possible to operationalize many of the important concepts in political analysis. Moreover, the rules of inference from data to concept vary from one context to another. Hence, the maintenance of a consistent meaning for concepts becomes one of the difficult tasks of cross-contextual analysis.

The contextual relativity of the meaning or the measures of indicators constitutes the most serious impediment to the cross-contextual validity of empirically testable explanatory theory. Yet, this chapter argues that the building of such theory constitutes the *raison d'être* of comparative political analysis. Compromises must inevitably be made, it was argued, in the validity of measures used and in the geographical scope of theory in order to balance these important and conflicting imperatives. Subsequent chapters will examine the success and prospects of scholarship in comparative politics in filling this key theory-building role.

References

Ayer, A. J. 1952. *Language, Truth and Logic.* New York: Dover Publications.

Blalock, Hubert M. 1964. *Causal Inferences in Non-Experimental Research.* Chapel Hill: University of North Carolina Press.

Brodbeck, May. 1968. "Explanation, Prediction, and Imperfect Knowledge." In *Readings in the Philosophy of Social Science.* New York: Macmillan.

Duverger, Maurice. 1963. *Political Parties*, translated by Barbara and Robert North. New York: John Wiley.

Grofman, Bernard and Edward N. Muller. "The Strange Case of Relative Gratification and Potential for Political Violence: The V-Curve Hypothesis." *American Political Science Review* LXVII (2, June): 514–539.

Hempel, Carl. 1968. "Explanatory Incompleteness." In *Readings in the Philosophy of Social Science*, edited by May Brodbeck. New York: Macmillan.

Hermans, F. A. 1951. *Europe Under Democracy or Anarchy.* South Bend, IN: University of Notre Dame Press.

Holbert, Ann. 1982. "What Gender Gap?" *New York Times* (Dec. 10):35.

Kaplan, Abraham. 1964. *The Conduct of Inquiry.* San Francisco: Chandler Publishing Company.

Lijphart, Arend. 1971. *American Political Science Review* LXV(3, Sept.): 682–693.

Maslow, Abraham. 1970. *Motivation and Personality*, 2nd ed. New York: Harper and Row.

Mayer, Lawrence and Roland Smith. 1983. "The Impact of Gender on Electoral Choice in Western Democracies." Paper delivered to the annual meeting of the American Political Science Association.

Milnor, A. J. 1969. *Elections and Political Stability.* Boston: Little, Brown.

Nagel, Ernest. 1962. *The Structure of Science.* New York: Harcourt, Brace, and World.

Popper, Karl. 1954. *The Logic of Scientific Discovery.* New York: Harper and Row.

Popper, Karl. 1963. *Conjectures and Refutations.* New York: Harper and Row.

Przeworski, Adam and Henry Teune. 1970. *The Logic of Comparative Social Inquiry.* New York: John Wiley.

Rapoport, Anatol. 1968. "Explanatory Power and Explanatory Appeal of Theories." Unpublished paper prepared for a conference on explanatory theory in political science, University of Texas at Austin, February.

Rapoport, Anatol. 1967. *Operational Philosophies.* (pp. 53–64). New York: John Wiley. (Reprinted from New York: Harper and Row, 1953).

Sigelman, Lee and George Gadbois. 1983. "Contemporary Comparative Politics: An Inventory and Assessment." *Comparative Political Studies* 16(3, Oct.): 275–307.

Skinner, B. F. 1971. *Beyond Freedom and Dignity.* New York: Knopf.

Strauss, Leo. 1957. "What Is Political Philosophy?" *Journal of Politics* 19(3, Aug.): 352ff.

1.2

BEYOND THE COMPARATIVE METHOD

Peter Hall

Whereas the previous selection by Lawrence Mayer considered the utility of the comparative method in building a body of explanatory theory in political science, in this reading, Peter Hall, a Harvard University professor and specialist in the comparative politics of Western Europe, addresses the method's limitations. When generalizing about the attributes of whole systems, these limitations center on the small-N problem: too many variables drawn from too few cases. There are, for example, only a few cases of a particular constitutional type in a given cultural setting. This small number of cases limits the validity of mathematical research techniques that presume a large number of cases.

Hall explores alternatives to a strict adherence to the comparative method, including increasing the number of cases analyzed or seeking more data from each case. These alternatives further comparative and explanatory work, while acknowledging the shortcomings of the comparative method. However, does Hall's strategy accommodate the need to generalize about the impact of contextual factors, which is at the heart of the comparative method? Consider how process verification—comparing the process of formulating causal inferences described in the explanatory theory to the unfolding sequence of events in successive cases—bolsters the confidence we have in small-N research.

There is a paradox at the heart of comparative politics. The field is closely associated with a specific method—the "comparative method" inspired by [John Stuart] Mill, elegantly defined by Lijphart (1971; 1975a) and elaborated in many texts (cf. Smelser 1976; Collier 1991). When I was a graduate student, this method was presented as virtually synonymous with the field. But even its most prominent exponents admit that it provides a weak basis for assessing the causal claims crucial to political explanation. "If at all possible," noted Lijphart (1971: 685), "one should generally use the statistical (or perhaps even the experimental) method instead of the weaker comparative method."

The limitations of the comparative method are well known. As conventionally defined, it is oriented to a particular type of explanation focused on finding a few key variables said to be the principal causes of a specific kind of outcome. Like the statistical method, it is essentially correlational, assessing the validity of an explanation by inspecting the correspondence between the values of the explanatory vari-

---

Peter Hall, "Beyond the Comparative Method." *APSA-CP, The Comparative Politics Section of the American Political Science Association* 15, no. 2 (Summer 2004): 1–4.

ables and those of the dependent variable or outcome. What distinguishes it from the statistical method is the small number of cases examined.

With few cases, however, it is difficult to secure wide ranges of variation on all potentially relevant variables. For many years, the problem of "too many variables, too few cases" obsessed the field. Ingenious attempts were made to control for the effects of other variables, by selecting cases said to be similar in all relevant respects except on the outcome and explanatory variables of interest or cases different in all respects except for a correspondence between the values of the explanatory variables and outcomes (cf. Przeworski and Teune 1970). Scholars scoured the world for the "critical cases" in which, on current knowledge, their findings could be presented as least likely to hold and hence likely to be valid elsewhere (cf. Eckstein 1975). But, since the "laws" of social science were often thought to be probabilistic, one could never be sure whether one was finding the relevant regularities or encountering the exceptions to them. Despite the prominence of the comparative method, we all knew we were swimming upstream.

How then is the success of comparative politics to be explained? Few would deny that the field has vastly increased our knowledge of the world. No respectable department of political science would be without scholars of comparative politics. There is much to be learned from the leading journals of the field and causal explanation is the currency in which they deal. How can a field so closely associated with such a weak methodology have accomplished so much?

On reflection, I think the answer is that relatively few scholars of comparative politics have ever relied heavily on the comparative method, at least as conventionally defined. Instead, the success of the field rests largely on the ways it has moved beyond that method. Four steps, taken by many scholars, seem important.

The first step was to broaden the object of inquiry. Instead of establishing the causal impact of a few key variables, many comparativists have seen their task as one of mobilizing the power of comparative inquiry to develop new theoretical perspectives on politics. Lijphart's (1975) work on democracy in divided societies is an early example; more recent ones range from Scott's (1998) rumination on the organizing vision of states to the efforts of Swenson (2002) and Mares (2003) to explain how business groups approach social policy. Such works draw their insights from comparison across time and space but rarely rely heavily on the conventional comparative method. Instead, their methods are closer to what Verba (1967) called "disciplined," configurative inquiry—efforts to explore the similarities and differences in political phenomena across nations with a view to identifying new concepts, typologies or causal processes whose import has not hitherto been delineated. Moore's (1966) classic study of the origins of dictatorship and democracy is a good example. With some crudeness, one can reduce his analysis to a comparative study focused on a few key variables, but the principal contribution of the book was to illuminate the types of long-term historical processes that sow the seeds for regime change. Comparative politics has made its mark partly by painting new portraits of the world.

The second move is a shift toward alternative conceptions of what can be explained and in what causal explanation consists. Influenced by logical positivism, conventional presentations of the comparative method assumed that a good explanation was one that identified a few causal variables, operating independently of most others, with consistent effects in all cases and, if possible, attached to precise parameter estimates reflecting the relative influence of each. Occam's razor was the weapon of choice and parsimonious explanation highly valued (cf. Shively 1974).

This approach to explanation was well-suited to the modernization perspectives of the 1960s and 1970s that located the critical determinants of many political outcomes, ranging from the stability of democracy to political attitudes, in socioeconomic developments. Readily measurable social or economic variables were expected to have powerful effects across contexts. In recent decades, however, comparative politics has embraced theories that associate political outcomes with more complex causal processes, such as sequences of strategic interactions or the feedback effects of path dependence (Pierson 2004). Compare recent accounts of the transition to democracy as a strategic interaction between reformers and established elites to the hydraulic theories of democratization of previous eras (Lipset 1959; Colomer 2000).

Partly as a result, prevailing views about what it means to give a good explanation of political outcomes are shifting. Influenced by critical realism, many scholars have moved away from the search for a few key causal variables toward the view that explanation consists in identifying the causal processes that lie behind political outcomes (cf. Yee 1996). Some see this as a problem of modeling complex interactions in which the sequencing of events matters and context effects condition action (cf. Scharpf 1997; Sewell 1996). Others advocate a search for the "mechanisms" that feed into causal processes, conceived as recurrent dynamics with social or psychological roots (McAdam et al. 2001). On the premise that different combinations of variables can produce similar outcomes, others move from variables-oriented explanations toward "case-oriented" explanations aimed at identifying such combinations (Ragin 1987; 2000).

In each of these inquiries, comparison remains central, but the object of inquiry has shifted toward the identification of a range of causal patterns that the conventional comparative method does not anticipate. Although debate about what kind of causal patterns political science should look for is continuing, the achievements of the field cannot be appreciated without acknowledging that it comprehends a wide range of views about what can be explained and what a good explanation embodies.

* * *

Many comparativists have followed Lijphart's advice to make increasing use of statistical methods. Two developments have encouraged this step. One is the growth in cross-national data sets, fueled by interest in comparative political economy, political institutions, and democratization. The other has been the refinement and growing popularity of pooled-cross-sectional time-series analysis. Although it has more limitations than are sometimes acknowledged, by exploiting variation across time as well as space, such techniques allow scholars to apply regression analysis to propositions about nations even when the number of nations available for examination is small (cf. Beck and Katz 1995; Wallerstein 2000). As a result, the study of comparative politics is a much more statistical enterprise than it was in 1970.

Other scholars are using the innovative techniques Ragin (1987; 2000) has devised to apply the logic of the comparative method to a wider range of variables and cases than might otherwise be possible. Using Boolean algebra rather than the partial correlations of regression analysis, his methods yield different kinds of results, but ones that can be highly revealing about the necessary and sufficient conditions for cross-national political phenomena.

If such techniques expand the number of cases examined, the other step long taken by many scholars to bolster their causal claims entails more intensive analysis of each case. Here, the crucial move has been to go beyond the assumption, implicit in most formulations of the comparative method, that the most important information to be secured from a set of cases is about the correspondence between the values of a few key explanatory variables and the value of the dependent variable or outcome in those cases. Campbell (1975) paved the way many years ago, by noting that each case (defined as a unit of analysis displaying one value on the dependent variable) can yield many types of observations pertinent to assessing the validity of a causal theory.

There are interesting divergences of view about how to use the intensive examination of cases to improve causal inference. McKeown (1999) argues that intensive case studies should move beyond the "statistical worldview." Bates et al (1998) advocate iterative procedures in which a theory is reassessed and revised as new pieces of information about the case are uncovered (cf. Elster 2000). Mahoney (2000) outlines a technique of "causal narrative" in which the adequacy of a causal theory is tested by asking whether the causal process it describes fits the unfolding sequence of events observable in successive cases. Pioneers in this area, Bennett and George (1997; George and McKeown 1985) propose a similar method of "process verification."

My own preference is for a relatively positivistic approach in which two or more causal theories are compared to one another, predictions are derived from each theory about key facets of the causal chain leading up to the outcomes, including the sequence in which events are likely to occur and the positions actors are likely to take, and observations are drawn from the cases and inspected to see how well they conform to the predictions of each theory (Hall 2003). We need more debate about precisely how process analysis should be done.

However, the key point is that many of the most fruitful studies in comparative politics employ some version of it, often in combination with the comparative method. The comparison of a small number of cases is and should remain central to work in comparative politics. But the trust placed in such studies often rests as much on the effectiveness of their process tracing, whether described as such or not, as on the correlations they find between the ultimate independent and dependent variables.

It is striking, however, how rarely this dimension of comparative inquiry is discussed. Mesmerized by the comparative method and its statistical analogues, the field has been slow to acknowledge how important some version of process tracing is to most comparisons of a small number of cases. Fortunately, such issues are receiving more attention in the wake of the debates inspired by the efforts of King et al. (1994) to specify a unified approach to research design and the interest aroused by more complex theoretical accounts of the causal processes behind politics (cf. Brady and Collier 2004).

Today, the field is better defined not as one that makes preeminent use of a comparative method but as one that utilizes many methods to compare politics across nations. However, the attempts made to identify a distinctive comparative method have been valuable. Like the grit that sets an oyster in motion, they inspired a series of interchanges that have turned the field of comparative politics into one of the most lively sites for methodological debate in the discipline. That, in turn, has encouraged reflection about how conclusions are to be drawn about the political world, which ultimately strengthens the discipline.

References

Bates, Robert et al. 1998. *Analytical Narratives*. Princeton: Princeton University Press.

Beck, Nathaniel and Jonathan Katz. 1995. "What to do (and what not to do) with Time-Series Cross-Section Data in Comparative Politics," *American Political Science Review*, 89, 3 (September): 634–47.

Bennett, Andrew and Alexander George. 1997. "Process Tracing in Case Study Research." Available at: www.georgetown.edu/faculty/bennetta/PROTCG.htm

Brady, Henry and David Collier. Eds. 2004. *Rethinking Social Inquiry*. New York: Rowman and Littlefield.
Campbell, Donald T. 1975. "Degrees of Freedom and the Case Study," *Comparative Political Studies* 8: 178-93.
Collier, David. 1991. "The Comparative Method: Two Decades of Change," in D. Rustow and K. Erickson, eds., *Comparative Political Dynamics*. New York: Harper Collins: 7–31.
Colomer, Josep M. 2000. *Strategic Transitions*. Baltimore: Johns Hopkins University Press.
Eckstein, Harry. 1975. "Case Study and Theory in Macro-Politics," in F. Greenstein and N. Polsby, eds., *Handbook of Political Science*. Reading, Ma.: Addison-Wesley: 79–139.
Elster, Jon. 2000. "Review Essay: 'Analytical Narratives,' " *American Political Science Review*, 94: 685–95.
George, Alexander and Timothy J. McKeown. 1985. "Case Studies and Theories of Organizational Decision-Making," *Advances in Information Processing in Organizations* 2: 21–58.
Hall, Peter A. 2003. "Aligning Ontology and Methodology in Comparative Research," in J. Mahoney and D. Rueschemeyer, eds., *Comparative Historical Analysis in the Social Sciences*. New York: Cambridge University Press: 373–404.
King, Gary, Robert Keohane and Sidney Verba. 1994. *Designing Social Inquiry*. Princeton: Princeton University Press.
Lijphart, Arend. 1971. "Comparative Politics and the Comparative Method," *American Political Science Review* 64 (September): 682–93.
Lijphart, Arend. 1975a. "The Comparable-Cases Strategy in Comparative Research," *Comparative Political Studies* 8, 2 (July): 158–177.
Lijphart, Arend. 1975. *The Politics of Accommodation*. Berkeley: University of California Press.
Lipset, Seymour Martin. 1959. "Some Social Requisites of Democracy: Economic Development and Political Legitimacy," *American Political Science Review* 53 (March): 69–105.
Mahoney, James. 2000b. "Strategies of Causal Inference in Small-N Analysis," *Sociological Methods and Research* 28, 4 (May): 387–424.
Mares, Isabela. 2003. *The Politics of Social Risk*. New York: Cambridge University Press.
McAdam, Doug et al. 2001. *Dynamics of Contention*. New York: Cambridge University Press.
McKeown, Timothy J. 1999. "Case Studies and the Statistical Worldview," *International Organization*, 53, 1 (Winter): 161–90.
Moore, Barrington, Jr. 1966. *Social Origins of Dictatorship and Democracy*. Boston: Beacon Press.
Pierson, Paul. 2004. *Politics in Time*. Princeton: Princeton University Press.
Przeworski, Adam and Henry Teune. 1970. *The Logic of Comparative Social Inquiry.* New York: Wiley.
Ragin, Charles C. 1987. *The Comparative Method*. Berkeley: University of California Press.
———. 2000. *Fuzzy-Set Social Science*. Chicago: University of Chicago Press.
Scharpf, Fritz. 1997. *Games Real Actors Play*. Boulder: Westview.
Scott, James C. 1998. *Seeing Like a State*. New Haven: Yale University Press.
Sewell, William. 1996. "Three Temporalities: Toward an Eventful Sociology" in T. J. McDonald, ed., *The Historic Turn in the Human Sciences*. Ann Arbor: University of Michigan Press: 245–80.
Shively, W. Phillips. 1974. *The Craft of Political Research*. Englewood Cliffs, N.J.: Prentice-Hall.
Smelser, Neil. 1976. *Comparative Methods in the Social Sciences*. Englewood Cliffs, N.J.: Prentice-Hall.
Swenson, Peter. 2002. *Capitalists Against Markets*. New York: Oxford University Press.
Verba, Sidney. 1967. "Some Dilemmas of Comparative Research," *World Politics* 20 (October): 111–28.
Wallerstein, Michael. 2000. "Trying to Navigate between Scylla and Charybdis: Misspecified and Unidentified Models in Comparative Politics," *APSA-CP: Newsletter* 11, 2 (Summer): 1–21.
Yee, Albert S. 1996. "The Causal Effects of Ideas on Politics," *International Organization*, 50, 1 (Winter): 69–108.

Chapter 2

WHAT IS THE UTILITY OF FORMAL THEORY IN COMPARATIVE ANALYSIS?

Formal theory, or the rational choice approach, is used to describe political actors—individual politicians, political parties, or nation-states—and how they orient their behavior in political situations. To be a rational actor, an individual must have a single goal to which his or her behavior is directed, know all possible ways to achieve that goal, evaluate each of these alternatives, and ultimately select the one that achieves the goal in the most cost-effective manner and maximizes the benefits the actor will receive.

This conceptual basis has its critics, especially when scholars try to apply it to the study of political phenomena. Some criticize the whole theory on procedural grounds, arguing that assumptions of rational behavior describe the cognitive abilities of actors in unrealistic ways; in other words, political actors cannot possess all the cognitive abilities that the rational choice framework says they must necessarily possess.

In many ways this is a legitimate criticism, but does the assumption of rational behavior (rather than the established, quantifiable fact of its presence) really undermine the entire approach? Consider politicians in democratic countries. Given that such political actors are defined by the pursuit and achievement of elective office, rational choice theory assumes that not only will they be focused on this goal more than any other but also that they will achieve it as efficiently as possible and in a way that gains them the maximum support available. Moreover, by making such assumptions and extrapolating the outcomes of such office-seeking behavior, rational choice theory allows scholars to explain more thoroughly the patterns that such behavior produces in the aggregate.

Even as some rational choice theorists agree that the cognitive demands of the approach are seemingly unrealistic, they counter that the effectiveness of the approach must be evaluated not in terms of the reality of its assumptions but rather in terms of the explanations it produces. Other rational choice theorists are less apologetic and argue that the logic and intuitive appeal of this approach become even clearer when you step back and explore more fully what it assumes about the behavior and the cognitive abilities of political actors. This is the position taken by University of Michigan political scientist George Tsebelis in reading 2.2. Tsebelis argues that the assumptions about human behavior and the cognitive abilities of political actors that have been attributed to rational choice have been caricatured and presented inaccurately. He then posits that, if portrayed accurately, the assumptions of rational choice theory are not only intuitive but also accurate in how they capture the cognitive processes that guide actors in their political behavior. In other words, while some scholars who use the rational choice approach concede that actors do not in fact behave as the model's assumptions posit, Tsebelis argues that such assumptions do describe the way that political and economic actors actually behave in their respective roles.

Criticisms of the rational choice model have also been advanced on substantive grounds, that is, on the assertion that the approach's framework provides no intellectual value-added to the explanations its proponents offer. This criticism is based on the observation that scholars using this approach have devoted much more attention to advancing rational choice theory than to applying the approach to substantive problems and subjecting their results to empirical testing. This in turn has led such critics as Donald Green and Ian Shapiro to assert, as they do in reading 2.1, that the rational choice approach has not lived up to its promise.

Despite such criticisms, these assumptions are made because the goal of rational choice analysis, like the overall goal of all research in political science, is to explain outcomes at the aggregate level. The approach accomplishes this by making the explicit assumption that individuals behave rationally—in other words, by assuming that political behavior has a systematic basis—and then comparing the outcomes that one would expect from this rational behavior with what is actually observed at the aggregate level. Consequently, by making the assumption that political actors are goal oriented, the outcomes of their behavior can be determined and evaluated. For example, knowing that politicians pursue the goal of elected office and then reelection, it can be predicted that policies designed to provide benefits to voters and help politicians get reelected—like additional spending for social programs—will be timed close to an upcoming election, whereas announcements about belt-tightening or cutbacks will most likely be dealt with after an election. If political outcomes were entirely random and without a systematic basis, there would be no aggregate patterns to explain.

What is interesting about the substantive criticism made by Green and Shapiro is that it is based almost entirely on political science literature in American politics. While it is true that scholars focused primarily on American politics have been responsible for developing the theory of rational choice, it is scholars in comparative politics who have been responsible for its most successful and insightful empirical applications. For example, in post-independence Africa, many governments went bankrupt after they held elections. Numerous explanations were offered for this, but most stated that the African governments behaved irrationally, which led to their fiscal and economic problems. Robert Bates, on the other hand, noted in his innovative study of the political economy of sub-Saharan Africa that, given that it was rational for governments to wish to remain in power, the African governments studied used whatever financial resources available to stay in power, and this led them to bankruptcy. The rational choice perspective used by Bates tells us that we should have expected this because it was rational for governments to use whatever resources they had to stay in power.

It is well known that humans do things from time to time that appear inexplicable; because of this, individuals often say that such behavior is not rational. This may be an accurate description of inexplicable behavior, but it is not the sense in which political scientists use the term "rational." As the readings and explanation provided here have shown, rationality is an analytic concept that political scientists use to explain certain political patterns at the aggregate level. The debates over this approach will most likely continue, but the rational choice approach will remain a very useful tool to analyze and understand political phenomena.

2.1

METHODOLOGICAL PATHOLOGIES

Donald P. Green and Ian Shapiro

Donald Green and Ian Shapiro are both professors of political science at Yale University who have done considerable scholarly work on the scope and methods of political science. The book from which this reading is taken is the first comprehensive criticism of the rational choice approach to studying political processes and outcomes. The reading provided here offers a clear summary of their criticism of what rational choice scholars do when applying rational choice theory. Specifically, Green and Shapiro argue that, while many advances have been made in rational choice theory itself, very little has been accomplished in terms of applying it to the real world of politics. The result is that rational choice scholarship now includes many precisely specified models and a technically advanced body of theory but still enjoys little empirical success. As you read this selection, keep in mind that Green and Shapiro's discussion is entirely from research done on American politics; they did not look at examples in which rational choice theory was applied successfully to problems in international relations and comparative politics.

Whatever may be said on behalf of the analytic elegance or heuristic value of rational choice theories, empirical applications have tended to suffer from two classes of methodological infirmities. The first encompasses what may be described as pedestrian methodological defects. Scholars working within the rational choice tradition from time to time misapply statistical techniques, overlook problems of measurement error, or rely excessively on inferences drawn from a small number of case studies. Although potentially serious, methodological shortcomings of this kind come with the territory in political science and are not the main focus of our critique.

More interesting is the syndrome of fundamental and recurrent methodological failings rooted in the universalist aspirations that motivate so much rational choice theorizing. These concern the ways hypotheses are conceptualized, the manner in which they are transformed into testable propositions, and the interpretation of empirical results when tests are conducted. We contend that these (often mutually reinforcing) mistakes stem from a method-driven rather than problem-driven approach to research, in which practitioners are more eager to vindicate one or another universalist model than to understand and explain actual political outcomes. More than anything else, it is this aspiration that leads to the errors that we describe here as the pathologies of rational choice theory. . . . In this chapter we describe

---

Donald P. Green and Ian Shapiro, "Methodological Pathologies," in *Pathologies of Rational Choice Theory* (New Haven, Conn.: Yale University Press, 1994), chapter 3, 33–46.

and illustrate these methodological failings, explaining why they are at odds with basic requirements of sound empirical research.[1]

Post Hoc Theory Development

Many of the methodological failings of applied rational choice scholarship are traceable to a style of theorizing that places great emphasis on the development of post hoc accounts of known facts. Can a rational choice hypothesis explain the existence of seniority systems in Congress? The growth of deficit spending by governments? Why people vote for third parties? To answer such questions the theorist engages in a thought experiment designed to generate an explanation of a given phenomenon that is consistent with rational choice assumptions, somehow specified. Fiorina and Shepsle (1982, 63) offer a lucid description of this approach:

> Our position is that scientific progress reflects (1) the scholarly *choice* of models that (2) possess equilibria that (3) correspond to observed regularities. This entails neither constructing equilibrium models *ex ante*, generalizing and refining subject to the constraint that equilibrium be preserved. . .nor retaining disequilibrium models only to be tongue-tied when asked to say something positive about the world. . . . To travel the first path is to say little that applies to the world of phenomena, and to travel the second is to say little, period. Instead, we recommend a third path, one termed "retroduction.". . . Put simply, the retroductive process begins with an empirical regularity X and poses the question, "How might the world be structured so that X is an anticipated feature of that world?" The answers (and there should be several) are models, all of which have in common the regularity X as a logical implication.

To be sure, striving to explain observed empirical regularities is preferable to fashioning theories according to the dictates of "neatness, or other aesthetic criteria" that otherwise guide rational choice theorizing in both political science and economics (Fiorina and Shepsle 1982, 63). But given the lack of specificity about what it means to be a rational actor, it is not obvious what sorts of behaviors, in principle, could fail to be explained by some variant of rational choice theory. Rational choice theorists have at their disposal a variety of assumptions about actors' objectives (wealth, power, moral satisfaction, etc.) and the extent to which individuals derive utility from the well-being of others, as well as the sorts of information and beliefs actors possess, their tastes for risk, the rate at which they discount future rewards, whether their decisions are informed by reasoning about strategic behavior of others, and, if so, the decision rules used when actors face conditions of uncertainty.[2] As Ordeshook (1993, 95) points out, those who craft post hoc explanations have not necessarily achieved much: "Even if such models fit the data up to an acceptable level of statistical accuracy, we must contend with the fact that we can establish nearly any reasonable outcome as an equilibrium to some model, provided only that model is sufficiently complex. . . . Designing assumptions so that a model's predictions fit the data is, in fact, little more than an exercise in curve fitting, albeit of a slightly more complicated sort than the type we generally hold in disrepute."

---

1. It is not our position that every attempt to test rational choice models empirically goes awry. But. . . , in those rare cases when appropriate tests are appropriately conducted, the results seldom sustain any novel or counterintuitive propositions.
2. Although rational choice theory is often advertised as a unified approach to the study of social, economic, and political behavior, . . .there seem to be few constraints on the assumptions that underlie empirical accounts, and sometimes quite contradictory motives are imputed to agents, depending on the domain of application (Mueller 1979).

One indication of the ease with which post hoc accounts may be generated is that a great many sufficient explanations arise to explain phenomena such as nonzero voter turnout or differences between the platforms of the two American parties. Another indication is that sufficient explanations pop up to explain certain "stylized facts" that, on reflection, are not facts at all. McKelvey and Riezman (1992, 951), for example, set for themselves the task of explaining both why incumbent legislators tend to be reelected by wide margins and why legislatures have seniority systems. But neither of these premises holds for legislators or legislatures generally. The reelection rates of U.S. senators and representatives contrast sharply, and the strength of the seniority system in Congress has varied over time. Furthermore, statistical studies of Congressional elections (Feldman and Jondrow 1984; Ragsdale and Cook 1987) detect no evidence of the putative causal connection between seniority and incumbent electoral fortunes. Under these circumstances, it is difficult to know what to make of McKelvey and Riezman's analytic result that in equilibrium legislators adopt a seniority system and voters unanimously reelect all incumbents.[3]

One might at this point object that what we are calling post hoc theorizing might well be characterized as puzzle-solving, a legitimate scientific activity. It could be argued, for example, that the fact that voters go to the polls in large numbers despite the theoretical prediction that rational citizens abstain leads to the discovery of civic-mindedness. Our reservation about such "discoveries" (if they may be described as such) is that retroduction merely establishes the proposition that it is not impossible that some rational choice hypotheses might be true. Often rational choice theorists seem to regard this as the end of the exercise; that the post hoc account they propose indeed vindicates the approach of looking at politics as though it were populated by actors who approach "every situation with one eye on the gains to be had, the other eye on costs, a delicate ability to balance them, and a strong desire to follow wherever rationality leads" (Downs 1957, 7–8). Data that inspire a theory cannot, however, properly be used to test it, particularly when many post hoc accounts furnish the same prediction. Unless a given retroductive account is used to generate hypotheses that survive when tested against other phenomena, little of empirical significance has been established.

For example, many rational choice theorists have sought to explain why, as Schumpeter (1942, 261) put it, "normally, the great political questions take their place in the psychic economy of the typical citizen with those leisure-hour interests that have not attained the rank of hobbies." The hypothesis of "rational ignorance" (Downs 1957) holds that citizens know little beyond what they can learn costlessly, because they have no incentive to expend resources to become knowledgeable about political affairs. In light of the small probability that any voter's ballot will prove decisive in an election, the rational citizen reasons that the benefits of casting a well-informed vote will not offset the expenditure of time and money spent gathering information. . . . [T]his argument is widely touted as a successful explanation of what is taken to be widespread voter ignorance. But since other post hoc explanations for voter ignorance are imaginable, one must ask: Why should we put stock in *this* explanation? What else does this account tell us about the conditions under which voters will or will not invest in costly information?

Post hoc theories are not only tested inadequately, the manner in which they are developed tends to be in tension with the enterprise of empirical testing. To the extent that theorists exploit the ambiguity in the meaning of rationality to transform successive disconfirming instances into data consistent with

3. McKelvey and Riezman (1992, 958) caution that their model implies more than one equilibrium. An alternative equilibrium is one in which "seniority is rejected by the legislature and all legislators are defeated for reelection."

a newly recast theory, one must question whether the succession of theories is susceptible to empirical evaluation in any meaningful sense. . . . [R]ational choice theorists seldom set forth a clear statement of what datum or data, if observed, would warrant rejection of the particular hypotheses they set forth or, more generally, their conviction that politics flows from the maximizing behavior of rational actors.[4]

These problems of empirical evaluation are compounded by the fact that rational choice models of a given phenomenon are difficult to evaluate vis-à-vis alternative theoretical perspectives that are not rooted in the assumption of utility maximization. In principle as well as in practice, rational choice models may be constructed from a wide assortment of assumptions about beliefs, tastes, and environmental constraints. Not surprisingly, rational choice models may generate diametrically opposing predictions. Some rational choice accounts, for example, predict that collective political action will collapse under the weight of the free-rider problem; others suggest that such movements may be sustained by solidary incentives. Some variants of rational choice theory predict that candidates in a two-party system will adopt identical platforms, while others assert that candidates will adopt divergent political stances. That constructions of rational choice theory predict X and Not-X creates vexing problems for those seeking to compare the performance of rational choice models against competing perspectives. The predictions of one rational choice model will invariably overlap with those derived from another kind of theory.

Alternative theoretical accounts, it should be noted, occupy a small pedestal in the rational choice pantheon. The drive for sufficient accounts of political phenomena often impels rational choice theorists to focus instead on what the theory *does* seem to explain. As Russell (1979, 11) notes, this style of analysis is often accompanied by a striking disregard for alternative explanations, leaving open the question of whether the data conform equally well to the predictions of competing theoretical accounts. Sometimes the failure to consider the relative strength of rational choice versus alternative explanations stems from mere sloppiness or parochialism. More often, however, it results from a faulty approach to theorizing that stresses the formulation of sufficient explanations. Ironically, the insistence on pressing one form of explanation to the exclusion of others has the effect of diminishing the persuasiveness of rational choice accounts.[5]

Because of the lack of interest in competing explanations, research is seldom designed with an eye toward rejecting a credible null hypothesis, a conjecture accorded presumption of truth by the researcher, in favor of a rational choice-derived alternative. The null hypothesis that the researcher seeks to reject is frequently rather prosaic—for example, the hypothesis that experimental electors vote randomly (McKelvey and Ordeshook 1984) or that behavior is unresponsive to changes in price (Wittman 1975).[6]

4. It is not hard to understand why rational choice theorists might be reluctant to relinquish the propositions that they advance. Leaving aside rare instances in which theorems rest on flawed proofs (e.g., Austen-Smith and Riker 1987), these propositions *are* true as analytic statements. Rational choice theorists, therefore, often regard empirical setbacks as indicating a given theorem's limited range of application. . . . [T]heorists in this position often cling to the notion that the forms identified in a theorem are fundamental and operative even if they are offset in specific applications.

5. Olson's rational choice explanation for the economic decline of Britain (1982), for example, surely would have been more compelling had he compared (or even mentioned) any of the more than half-dozen competing explanations (see Cameron 1988). Much the same may be said of the large literature that places the blame for inflation and the growth of government at the doorstep of democratic institutions and the incentives they engender (see Barry 1984; Mueller 1989, chap. 17).

6. Wittman (1975, 738) offers (though does not test) the hypothesis that those given paid time off work in order to vote will be more likely to do so. He also suggests that turnout will be higher, all things being equal, among citizens in good health.

Just as overcoming an adversary like Grenada does little to attest to the military might of the United States, one's views of politics are not much influenced by the fact that a rational choice proposition vanquishes a trivial or implausible null hypothesis. This is not a critical failing, but we should accord explanatory power to rational choice theories in proportion to the credibility of the null hypotheses over which they triumph. More often than not, rational choice scholars consider either untenable alternative explanations or none at all.

In sum, when post hoc theorizing is used to come up with possible rational choice explanations of observed phenomena or to reformulate rational choice hypotheses in ways that evade or appear to account for anomalous instances, the rational choice theorist may believe that the theoretical approach has in some significant way been "saved." In reality, the specific hypotheses in question have yet to be tested.

This critique of post hoc theorizing is not meant to foreclose the possibility of genuine theoretical innovation. Our point is not that theoretical predictions can never be changed to accommodate new evidence. Rather it is that the "innovations" that typically emerge do not involve new predictions as such; they involve mere redescription of the processes by which a previously known outcome obtains. Having recast their hypotheses to encompass known facts—and, in particular, anomalies—rational choice theorists typically fail to take the next step: proposing a coherent test to gauge the empirical adequacy of the newly revised hypothesis. Even less often do they take the step after that: gauging the empirical power of their preferred theoretical formulation against that of alternative explanatory accounts.

Formulating Tests

To test a theory, one needs to know in advance what the theory predicts. From time to time, certain rational choice theorists have expressed discomfort with the lack of attention devoted to this aspect of applied rational choice scholarship. For instance, in 1978 Fiorina and Plott observed that "game theoretic and social choice-theoretic models. . .are developed and advocated without a hint of possible operational definitions—one can find proof upon proof, but one searches in vain for a detailed discussion of exactly how and when a model should be applied" (575–76). Concerns of this kind, however, have had surprisingly little impact on the evolution of rational choice scholarship, and the imbalance between analytic exposition and application remains marked.

Those who seek to derive testable propositions from rational choice models frequently find, moreover, that these theories are constructed in ways that insulate them against untoward encounters with evidence. This problem turns up in various forms. Those who advance models so parsimonious or abstract that recognizable features of politics are all but absent (for example, models of policy making that omit mention of political parties and treat each branch of government as unitary actors [Banks and Kiewiet 1989; Spiller and Spitzer 1992]) deflect empirical scrutiny by describing their theories as simplifications or first cuts at thorny theoretical issues. Others assert that their models capture general truths that need not coincide with specific applications, as when Calvert (1985, 87) defends a model of candidate strategy "because it reveals the properties that underlie all electoral competition, even though these properties may be counteracted by the particular conditions of a real world situation" (see also Strom 1990, 11).

Arguably the most important source of slipperiness in model building is the multiplication of unobservable terms, which causes the complexity of a theory to outstrip the capacity of the data to render an informative test. This general problem is compounded by the specific difficulties that attend the ambiguous translation from equilibrium models to empirical tests.

Slippery Predictions

Rational choice explanations typically comprise an array of unobservable entities. Tastes, beliefs, decision rules, and, at a higher order of abstraction, equilibria, form the essential ingredients of most rational choice models. The problem is not the positing of unobservable terms per se, but rather the ratio of latent constructs to observable measures in rational choice accounts.[7] As this ratio grows, it becomes increasingly difficult to establish whether a set of data confirms or disconfirms a rational choice explanation.

Consider, by way of illustration, a game in which two players must divide $14 between them. If the players can agree on how to allocate the money, then that agreement becomes binding; if no agreement is reached, then player 1 receives $12, and player 2 receives nothing. "Cooperative game theory," note Hoffman and Spitzer, "predicts that the subjects will cooperate and divide the rewards $13 to $1 (the Nash bargaining solution: an even division of the $2 gain from trade). Under no circumstances should [player 1] settle for less than $12, according to game theory" (1985, 259). Suppose that after repeated observations of this game actually being played, one encountered a substantial number of resolutions in which the players divided the $14 evenly.[8] What may be inferred from this pattern of results? That the dollar amounts were too small to induce preferences over and above preexisting tastes for fairness? That despite the proscription of threats, player 1 feared physical retaliation from player 2? Mistaken understanding of the game? A temporary departure from equilibrium that would be rectified through greater exposure to the real world of cutthroat negotiations?

As this example indicates, rational choice hypotheses that meet with unanticipated facts may be resuscitated by recourse to a variety of unobservable thought processes for which there are insufficient direct or indirect measures. When faced with discordant results, it may be difficult, therefore, to distinguish empirically among three different claims about the principal unobservable term, equilibrium:

- The preferences assumed by the model are accurately represented in the setting one observes, but some or all of the actors lack the strategic acumen to play the game as rational choice recommends, and hence predicts.
- The model accurately captures the actors' objectives, but, perhaps owing to the particular characteristics of the equilibrium itself, there is a temporary departure from this predicted outcome.[9]
- The model does not capture one or more features of the observed game, and the outcomes conform to the equilibria (or lack thereof) associated with some other game.

7. The problem is exacerbated to some degree by the skepticism with which rational choice scholars regard "psychological" measures of tastes and beliefs. Although tastes and beliefs figure prominently in rational choice explanations, many scholars working within this tradition question the validity of measures other than behavior—actual choices—as indications of preference. . . . [H]owever, this skepticism about soft data has not prevented rational choice theorists from voicing speculations about psychological processes based on no data.
8. Indeed, Hoffman and Spitzer (1985, 260) report that all of their experimental subjects do precisely that when the roles of players 1 and 2 are assigned by coin flip. Under these conditions, the subject in the role of player 1 always "agreed to take $5 *less* than the $12 that he could have obtained *without* the other subject's cooperation." See also Hoffman and Spitzer 1982.
9. Fiorina and Shepsle (1982) offer a lucid typology for various kinds of equilibria. Some, like "black holes," attract and retain outcomes in a social system. Others are retentive but not attractive, or vice versa. In the latter cases, it may be impossible to determine empirically whether a system is temporarily or permanently out of equilibrium.

The propagation of theoretical terms that are either unmeasurable or difficult to measure creates a situation akin to underidentification in statistical models involving latent variables (Bollen 1989). Under these circumstances, data cannot furnish a convincing test. When any hypothesis fails, the researcher is always in a position to argue that a successful prediction was thwarted by an offsetting tendency or temporary aberration. In this respect, empirical discussions in rational choice scholarship are reminiscent of debates about the declining rate of profit that once preoccupied Marxists. Having convinced themselves by analytic argument that the rate of profit in capitalism must fall over time but failing to find evidence to support this contention, Marxists for decades devoted their energies to identifying masking, fleeting, and countervailing tendencies that obscure this alleged phenomenon. Declining profitability was believed to be going on just beneath the surface on the strength of a theory that insisted that this must be so (compare Roemer 1979; Van Parijs 1980).

The underidentification problem may be addressed in two ways. One is to set limits on the range of theoretical arguments that may be used in the construction or resuscitation of a theory. This kind of restriction, however, proves difficult to maintain against the impulse to defend the universal applicability of the rational choice approach. Often these restrictions are endorsed by such figures as Downs (1957) and Olson (1965), who introduce rational choice inquiry into a given domain of politics. But over time these constraints are relaxed by subsequent authors seeking to preserve a model in the face of discordant evidence. Another approach is to gather additional data so as to give the number of measures a sporting chance to catch up with the number of theoretical terms. Rational choice scholars tend to shy away from this approach, perhaps a tacit admission that the formal precision of rational choice models greatly outstrips political scientists' capacity to measure.

Vaguely Operationalized Predictions

A second common pathology related to hypothesis testing concerns the fit between the hypotheses advanced and the empirical tests used to evaluate them. Since equilibrium analysis is at the heart of much rational choice scholarship, many rational choice propositions are stated in the form of point predictions. Sometimes that point prediction is a rate or proportion, as in the case of Olson's conjecture that in the absence of selective incentives or coercion, members of large groups will not engage in collective action to advance their joint interests (1965). In other cases, the point prediction involves a particular outcome, as in the case of a specific majority rule equilibrium point in a cooperative bargaining game. Such propositions are invariably false to some degree; strategic blunders sometimes occur, producing nonequilibrium outcomes. The argument then shifts to the often expressed "hope that enough people act rationally enough of the time in their political behavior for economic theories of politics to yield descriptions, explanations, and predictions which are frequently useful approximations to the truth" (Kavka 1991, 372).[10]

It is unclear whether a rigorous test of a point prediction can be constructed in the form of an approximation. If several millions of dollars in small contributions are collected by referendum campaigns, is that evidence in support of the free-rider hypothesis (Lowenstein 1982, 572–73), given the paltry ratio of contributions to public concern over the outcome of these elections, or against it (Tillock

10. . . .[W]hen empirical failures occur, this "approximation" notion accompanies attribution of anomalies to the behavior of an irrational few.

and Morrison 1979), given the presumed irrationality of absorbing personal costs on behalf of a broadly diffused public good?

The match between theory and evidence becomes more ambiguous when rational choice hypotheses move seamlessly between point predictions and marginal predictions. The former concerns the location of an equilibrium under static conditions; the latter—derived from "comparative statics" analysis—concerns the direction in which an equilibrium is expected to move in response to exogenous changes in goals, beliefs, or environmental constraints. It is logically possible that only one sort of prediction will survive empirical testing, but the availability of two standards of evaluation affords defenders of a model more opportunity to claim support for its predictions. In particular, predictions at the margin are often hailed when static predictions fall into trouble. Whatever the defects of rational choice explanations of why citizens bother to go to the polls, Grofman (1993) argues, rational choice theory does predict correctly that people are less inclined to vote in bad weather.

We have no objection to the use of comparative statics to generate hypotheses. To the contrary, we find tests that focus on change at the margin much more amenable to traditional quasi-experimental methodology than those involving point predictions. Our concern is with the notion that the rationality of certain actions can be rescued on the grounds that the actors are to some degree responsive to changes in costs or benefits. Take, for example, the study of why politically inexperienced candidates challenge incumbent members of the House of Representatives. The behavior of these challengers is something of a mystery, since their chances of defeating an incumbent are nothing short of dismal. Like most puzzles of this sort, the behavior of challengers may been explained by reference to such ancillary factors as self-delusion, eagerness to promote legal practices while on the campaign trail, belief that *somebody* should contest the incumbent, and so forth. Banks and Kiewiet (1989, 1007) try to salvage the notion that rational, election-seeking behavior accounts for the decisions of weak challengers by arguing that "weak challengers can maximize their probability of getting elected to Congress by running now against the incumbent" rather than waiting for an open-seat contest in which they may have to defeat other strong opponents in both the primary and general elections. As the authors note dryly, "This probability may not be very high, but they are maximizing it." The study of whether weak challengers are *more* attracted to races against incumbents or to open-seat contests may be a worthy endeavor in its own right, but it is unclear how the results speak to the question of whether weak challengers are rational to oppose House incumbents, so long as rationality requires that the benefits of doing so outweigh the costs (1000).

Selecting and Interpreting Evidence

Another set of characteristic pathologies concerns the manner in which rational choice hypotheses are tested. The first has to do with the biased fashion in which evidence is selected. The second deals with subtler ways in which evidence is projected from theory rather than gathered independently from it. The last involves the strategic retreat from domains in which the theory is found to perform poorly. All three methodological defects undermine the theoretical claims they are intended to support, as it is the structured search for disconfirming evidence that is essential to scientific testing.

Searching for Confirming Evidence

When reading applied rational choice scholarship, one is struck by the extent to which advocates of rational choice models permit their theoretical commitments to contaminate the sampling of evidence.

The procedure of adducing instances that confirm a hypothesis is perhaps most transparent in such domains as regulation and bureaucratic politics, where the ideological stakes are high. This practice, reminiscent of advertisements that show one brand's achievements while mentioning neither its failings nor the comparable achievements of its competitors, is not limited to these ideologically charged domains, however. In its more qualitative manifestations, rational choice scholarship tends to ruminate over confirming illustrations combed from the political landscape, memorable moments in history, and biblical texts (Brams 1980, 1993; Riker 1982, 1986). Elsewhere, this pathology leads researchers to dwell on instances of successful prediction, be they the phenomena of strategic counteramendments by committee leaders on the House floor (Weingast 1989, 810) or the suboptimal provision of collective goods (Olson 1965). The tendency to adduce confirming instances also manifests itself, though in subtler form, in quantitative research that goes through the motions of contrasting treatment and control conditions en route to a conclusion that follows trivially from the research design. McCubbins (1991, 107), for example, finds that time-series analyses of federal data for the period 1929 to 1988 "strongly support" his game theoretic account of how divided party control of Congress leads to budget deficits. Granted, his statistical estimates suggest that "since 1929, divided government has yielded sizable increases in the national debt" (102), but the period studied contains just two such episodes: the advent of supply-side economics under Ronald Reagan, and the drought of federal revenues during the waning days of the Hoover administration.

A variant of this methodological problem surfaces in studies that use laboratory behavior to support rational choice propositions but fail to build a control group into the experimental design. . . . [S]uccessful experiments of this sort at most suggest that a laboratory setting can be constructed to approximate the conditions presupposed by a theorem; a researcher seeking to defend a rational choice hypothesis need only engineer a confirming illustration. Generated without a control group, the results give no indication of whether the observed outcome would have obtained anyway for reasons unrelated to the theory in question, nor does the experiment tell us whether this theory predicts successfully under other circumstances. Experiments crafted in this way illustrate rather than test.

Projecting Evidence from Theory

A profound desire to establish rational choice theory's breadth of application from time to time opens the door to a tendentious reading of the empirical record. Sometimes this is a simple matter of authors imagining a datum consistent with economic logic (for example, bad weather depresses voter turnout) and assuming this datum to be empirically verified. At other times, one finds rational choice theorists asserting almost by way of afterthought that some eccentric feature of a model mirrors reality. For example, McKelvey and Riezman's legislative model (1992) hinges on the assumption that those with seniority are more likely to be recognized on the floor in the initial round of voting but not in subsequent rounds. The authors insist that this characterization provides a "realistic description of the seniority system for the U.S. Congress" because seniority-influenced committees get first crack at making proposals, and "once the bills go to the floor, the committees lose most of their power" (958). Suffice it to say that this is a rather sparse depiction of the process by which legislation is proposed and amended in Congress (Weingast 1989).

Even when a full-blown empirical study is undertaken, the theoretical convictions of the authors may guide what they infer from a set of observations and how they reconstruct the data for presentation. For example, an obscure set of House votes on the Powell Amendment to a 1956 measure authorizing school construction has been offered up time and again as evidence of how legislators vote to strengthen a proposal they dislike in an effort to make the amended bill unpalatable (Riker 1965, 1982, 1986; Denzau, Riker, and Shepsle 1985). A dispassionate examination of the historical record, however, shows that the facts surrounding the Powell Amendment are at best ambiguous with respect to the phenomenon of strategic voting (Krehbiel and Rivers 1990). Indeed, the omissions and factual distortions that Krehbiel and Rivers detect in previous accounts (556–60, 574) suggest that earlier writers were unable to assimilate data that did not conform to their theoretical expectations.

Arbitrary Domain Restriction

On occasion, rational choice theorists will concede that there are domains—such as voter turnout and organized collective action—in which no plausible variant of the theory appears to work. Some theorists are then inclined to withdraw, choosing to concentrate on applications in which these theories appear to have better success. For instance, in trying to make the case that his wealth-maximization hypothesis explains the evolution of the criminal law, Posner (1985) is forced to come to accept that he cannot explain the existence of laws against such "victimless crimes" as prostitution and drug abuse. He therefore abandons this domain, insisting nonetheless that wealth-maximization provides a powerful explanation of the rest of the criminal law.

Such a move might at first sight seem reasonable, even modest, but there is more at stake here than meets the eye. Suppose it transpired one day that red apples did not fall to the ground as other heavy bodies do. One would not be much impressed by the physicist who said of the theory of gravity that, though it seems not to work for red apples, it does a good job of explaining why other things fall to the ground and that consequently from now on he was going to restrict his attention to those other things when using the theory.

What we are calling arbitrary restriction to domains where a theory seems to work is not to be confused with two nonarbitrary forms of domain restriction that scientists engage in routinely. First, as Moe points out (1979, 235), testing of all scientific theories involves the insertion of ceteris paribus clauses designed to exclude omitted factors, so that a proper test of the hypothesis that objects of unequal mass fall to earth at the same rate presupposes wind resistance to be held constant.[11] Second, theories may properly include an account of what are conventionally termed "interaction effects," factors that limit or enhance the influence of the independent variables of theoretical interest. Indeed, the value of a theory in the eyes of those who wish to understand and influence politics may hinge on a clear account of the conditions under which it is held to apply. Arbitrary domain restriction occurs when an empirically testable set of limiting conditions is lacking but retreat is sounded anyway. There is, in other words, a critical difference between specifying the relevant domain in advance by reference to limiting conditions and specifying as the relevant domain: "wherever the theory seems to work."[12]

---

11. It is important to note that ceteris paribus provisos must refer to confounding factors, such as wind resistance, whose effects are in principle testable. One cannot take the position that only when all the logical assumptions of a theorem are satisfied empirically do the theorem's empirical predictions follow.

12. In much the same vein, arguments about when and where to apply a theory must be advanced in a consistent fashion. For example, in an effort to bolster their claim that House "leaders will be chosen in such a fashion that their personal reelection is not too incompatible with the duties of office," Cox and McCubbins (1993, 130) point out that one rational choice argument, based on the idea of the "uncovered set"..., predicts "definite limits to the policy platforms that those seeking leadership positions will adopt" and, in particular, rules out successful bids by non-

The problem of arbitrary domain restriction is thus the obverse of the tendency to adduce confirming instances. The latter involves fishing for supportive evidence; the former, draining lakes that contain problematic data. While the practice of adducing confirming instances produces misleading tests, arbitrary domain restriction renders problematic the enterprise of testing. If the appropriate domain within which a theory is to be tested is defined by reference to whether the theory works in that domain, testing becomes pointless.

Posner, in our example, pushes the case for wealth-maximization as far as he can and cuts and runs when he has to. Yet he neither considers any alternative explanation nor sees the need to offer an account of why the theory breaks down in the domain of victimless crimes. For domain restriction to be adequate, the relevant domain must be specified independently of whether the theory explains the phenomenon within it. Furthermore, the hypothesis about the limiting conditions of rational choice explanations must itself stand up to empirical testing.... [R]ational choice theorists such as Brennan and Buchanan, Fiorina, and Satz and Ferejohn have suggested some hypotheses about the conditions under which rational choice explanations are likely to apply. It will become plain in subsequent chapters, however, that these recommendations have not yet had much impact on the design and application of rational choice models.

* * *

References

Austen-Smith, David and William H. Riker. 1987. Asymmetric Information and the Coherence of Legislation. *American Political Science Review* 81: 897–918.

Banks, Jeffrey S. and D. Roderick Kiewiet. 1989. Explaining Patterns of Candidate Competition in Congressional Elections. *American Journal of Political Science* 33: 997–1015.

Barry, Brian M. 1984. Does Democracy Cause Inflation? Political Ideas of Some Economists. In *The Politics of Inflation and Economic Stagnation: Theoretical Approaches and International Case Studies,* ed. Leon N. Lindberg and Charles S. Maier. Washington, D.C.: Brookings Institution.

Bollen, Kenneth A. 1989. *Structural Equations with Latent Variables.* New York: John Wiley & Sons.

Brams, Steven J. 1980. *Biblical Games: A Strategic Analysis of Stories in the Old Testament.* Cambridge: MIT Press.

———. 1993. *Theory of Moves.* Cambridge: Cambridge University Press.

Calvert, Randall L. 1985. Robustness of Multidimensional Voting Model: Candidate Motivations, Uncertainty, and Convergence. *American Journal of Political Science* 29: 69–95.

Cameron, David R. 1988. Distributional Coalitions and Other Sources of Economic Stagnation: On Olson's *Rise and Decline of Nations. International Organizations* 42: 561–603.

Cox, Gary W. and Mathew D. McCubbins. 1993. *Legislative Leviathan: Party Government in the House.* Berkeley: University of California Press.

---

centrist candidates (130). Although Cox and McCubbins wish to embrace this prediction, they note that it is open to the objection that decisions enacted by majority rule are inherently unstable, that "there will always be some majority, all of [w]hose members could be made better off if its policies were changed" (131). Cox and McCubbins respond that this objection about the inherent vulnerability of House speakers rests on the assumption that actors incur no transaction costs when identifying or forming new majority coalitions. When these costs are taken into account, they contend, the instability problem no longer applies to the choice of speaker. They neglect to mention, however, that their preferred predictions based on the uncovered set also presuppose the absence of transaction costs.

Denzau, Arthur T., William H. Riker, and Kenneth A. Shepsle. 1985. Farquharson and Fenno: Sophisticated Voting and Home Style. *American Political Science Review* 79: 1117–34.

Downs, Anthony. 1957. *An Economic Theory of Democracy.* New York: Harper & Row.

Feldman, Paul and James Jondrow. 1984. Congressional Elections and Local Federal Spending. *American Journal of Political Science* 28: 147–63.

Fiorina, Morris P. and Charles R. Plott. 1978. Committee Decisions Under Majority Rule: An Experimental Study. *American Political Science Review* 72: 575–98.

Fiorina, Morris P. and Kenneth A. Shepsle. 1982. Equilibrium, Disequilibrium, and the General Possibility of a Science of Politics. In *Political Equilibrium,* ed. Peter C. Ordeshook and Kenneth A. Shepsle. The Hague: Kluwer-Nijhoff.

Grofman, Bernard. 1993. Is Turnout the Paradox that Ate Rational Choice Theory? In *Information, Participation, and Choice,* ed. Bernard Grofman. Ann Arbor: University of Michigan Press.

Hoffman, Elizabeth and Matthew L. Spitzer. 1982. The Coase Theorem: Some Experimental Tests. *Journal of Law and Economics* 25: 73–98.

Hoffman, Elizabeth and Matthew L. Spitzer. 1985. Entitlements, Rights, and Fairness: An Experimental Examination of Subjects' Concepts of Distributive Justice. *Journal of Legal Studies* 14: 259–97.

Kavka, Gregory S. 1991. Rational Maximizing in Economic Theories of Politics. In *The Economic Approach to Politics: A Critical Reassessment of the Theory of Rational Action,* ed. Kristen Renwick Monroe. New York: Harper Collins.

Krehbiel, Keith and Douglas Rivers. 1990. Sophisticated Voting in Congress: A Reconsideration. *Journal of Politics* 52: 548–78.

Lowenstein, Daniel H. 1982. Campaign Spending and Ballot Propositions: Recent Experience, Public Choice Theory and the First Amendment. *UCLA Law Review* 29: 505–641.

McCubbins, Mathew D. 1991. Government on Lay-Away: Federal Spending and Deficit Under Divided Party Control. In *The Politics of Divided Government,* ed. Gary W. Cox and Samuel Kernell. Boulder, Colo.: Westview.

McKelvey, Richard D. and Peter C. Ordeshook. 1984a. An Experimental Study of the Effects of Procedural Rules on Committee Behavior. *Journal of Politics* 46: 182–205.

———. 1984b. Rational Expectations in Elections: Some Experimental Results Based on a Multidimensional Model. *Public Choice* 44: 61–102.

McKelvey, Richard D. and Raymond Riezman. 1992. Seniority in Legislatures. *American Political Science Review* 86: 951–65.

Moe, Terry M. 1979. On the Scientific Status of Rational Choice Theory. *American Journal of Political Science* 23: 215–43.

Mueller, Dennis C. 1979. Public Choice in Practice: A Comment. In *Collective Decision Making: Applications from Public Choice Theory,* ed. Clifford S. Russell. Baltimore: Johns Hopkins University.

———. 1989. *Public Choice II.* Cambridge: Cambridge University Press.

Olson, Mancur, Jr. [1965] 1971. *The Logic of Collective Action.* Cambridge: Harvard University Press.

———. 1982. *The Rise and Decline of Nations: Economic Growth, Stagflation, and Social Rigidities.* New Haven: Yale University Press.

Ordeshook, Peter C. 1993. The development of contemporary political theory. In *Political Economy: Institutions, Competition, and Representation,* ed. William A. Barnett, Melvin J. Hinich, and Norman J. Schofield. Cambridge: Cambridge University Press.

Posner, Richard A. 1985. An Economic Theory of the Criminal Law. *Columbia Law Review* 85: 1193–1231.

Ragsdale, Lyn and Timothy E. Cook. 1987. Representatives' Actions and Challengers' Reactions: Limits to Candidate Connections in the House. *American Journal of Political Science* 31: 45–81.

Riker, William H. 1965. Arrow's Theory and Some Examples of the Paradox of Voting. In *Mathematical Applications in Political Science,* ed. John M. Claunch. Vol. 1. Dallas: Southern Methodist University Press.

———. 1982. *Liberalism Against Populism.* San Francisco: Freeman.

———. 1986. *The Art of Political Manipulation.* New Haven: Yale University Press.

Roemer, John E. 1979. Continuing Controversy on the Falling Rate of Profit: Fixed Capital and Other Issues. *Cambridge Journal of Economics* 3: 379–98.

Russell, Keith. 1972. Why Do High Income People Participate More in Politics? A Response. *Public Choice* 13: 113–14.

Schumpeter, Joseph A. 1942. *Capitalism, Socialism, and Democracy.* New York: Harper & Row.

Spiller, Pablo T. and Matthew L. Spitzer. Judicial Choice of Legal Doctrines. *Journal of Law, Economics, and Organization* 8, no. 1, 8–44.

Strom, Gerald S. 1990. *The Logic of Lawmaking: A Spatial Theory Approach.* Baltimore: Johns Hopkins University Press.

Tillock, Harriet and Denton E. Morrison. 1979. Group Size and Contribution to Collective Action: A Test of Mancur Olson's Theory on Zero Population Growth, Inc. *Research in Social Movements, Conflict, and Change* 2: 131–58.

Van Parijs, Phillipe. 1980. The Falling-Rate-of-Profit Theory of Crisis: A Rational Reconstruction by Way of Obituary. *The Review of Radical Political Economics* 12: 1–16.

Weingast, Barry. 1989. Floor Behavior in the U.S. Congress: Committee Power Under the Open Role. *American Political Science Review* 83: 795–815.

Wittman, Donald. 1975. Determinants of Participation in Presidential Elections: A Comment. *Journal of Law and Economics* 18: 735–41.

2.2

IN DEFENSE OF THE RATIONAL CHOICE APPROACH

George Tsebelis

George Tsebelis is one of the leading game theorists in the field of political science; as a result, he is also one of the discipline's most vocal proponents of the rational choice approach in the study of comparative politics. After spending most of his career in the Political Science Department at the University of California, Los Angeles, he recently relocated to the University of Michigan. His book from which this reading is taken is not only a clear statement of the essential components of the rational choice approach, but also a collection of examples of how this approach explains certain problems in comparative politics better than other, more traditional approaches. In the reading provided here, Tsebelis not only sets out the technical basics of rational choice theory, he also shows how its assumptions are not as unrealistic as many procedural critics assert. In fact, he demonstrates how the assumptions that underpin rational choice form a very intuitive and realistic way to analyze the behavior of actors in certain political contexts. For example, it is well known that politicians must be elected to accomplish anything in the policy arena, and much of their behavior is centered on getting elected or reelected for this reason. This may sound like an oversimplification, but rational choice theorists have shown that making just such an assumption is central to any analysis of politician behavior and offers interesting explanations for a variety of often disparate behaviors. For instance, by placing vote-getting as the primary behavior of elected officials, rational choice theorists are better able to understand why politicians are most visible and vocal during an election cycle and why popular policies are discussed during that time, whereas such unpopular policies as raising taxes and cutting budgets are most often brought up after an election. As students read this selection, they should try to come up with their own examples of how the need of politicians to be elected or reelected influences their behavior with respect to the content and timing of different public policies.

* * *

II. What the Rational-Choice Approach *Is*

The task here is to derive the implications of the means/ends correspondence with respect to the definition of rationality. I distinguish between two different sets of requirements for rationality: *weak re-*

George Tsebelis, "In Defense of the Rational Choice Approach," in *Nested Games: Rational Choice in Comparative Politics* (Berkeley: University of California Press, 1990), chapter 2, 18–47.

quirements of rationality and *strong requirements of rationality*. The first assures the internal coherence of preferences and beliefs; the second introduces requirements for external validity (the correspondence of beliefs with reality). Even the weak requirements of rationality are sometimes difficult to meet, which raises the important question of the feasibility and/or fruitfulness of assuming that political actors are indeed rational, a question I answer in Section III.

Weak Requirements of Rationality

I discuss the following requirements for rationality: (1) the impossibility of contradictory beliefs or preferences, (2) the impossibility of intransitive preferences, and (3) conformity to the axioms of probability calculus. The first two refer to rational actor behavior under certainty; the third regulates rational actor behavior under risk.

Defending an axiomatic system (in this case, the combination of requirements that define rationality) usually entails demonstrating the plausibility of these requirements (axioms). However, a better argument can be developed by elucidating the undesirable consequences of violating such requirements; the more catastrophic these consequences, the more persuasive the argument. In the demonstrations that follow, I use money to demonstrate undesirable or catastrophic consequences. The advantage of using money to measure the desirability of consequences is the immediate understanding that choices have "objective" consequences for the welfare of individuals. However, one can replicate all my arguments with abstract units of utility (utiles) or some other nonmonetary *numeraire* of satisfaction.

(1) The impossibility of contradictory beliefs or preferences.

There are two relevant propositions in formal logic: the first claims that the conjunction of a proposition and its negation is a contradiction.[1] The second claims that anything can follow from a false antecedent. If a proposition is a belief, these two laws of logic indicate that anything follows from contradictory beliefs. Therefore, if an actor holds contradictory beliefs, she cannot reason.[2] If a proposition is a preference, the combination of the two laws indicates that anything follows from contradictory preferences. Thus, if an actor holds contradictory preferences, she can choose any option.

Note here that contradiction refers to beliefs or preferences *at a given moment in time*. The impossibility of contradictory beliefs or preferences excludes neither changing beliefs or preferences over time nor holding one preference in one context and a different one in another. It is therefore weaker than the "independence of irrelevant alternatives" axiom in which an actor is assumed to make the same choice between two alternatives whether or not other alternatives exist (Arrow 1951).

(2) The impossibility of intransitive preferences.

The "transitivity of preferences" axiom states that if an actor prefers alternative a over alternative b, and b over c, she necessarily prefers a over c.[3] It has been demonstrated that one can create a "money pump" (make a lot of money) from a person with intransitive preferences (Davidson, McKinsey, and Suppes 1954). This demonstration is as follows: suppose a person prefers a over b, b over c, and c over

1. It is, in fact, Aristotle's law of the excluded middle, which can be stated formally as $p \& (-p) = F$, where F stands for "false."
2. Popper (1962) uses this argument to reject dialectical reasoning (which accepts contradictions) as impossible.
3. A similar principle of transitivity in logic assures the possibility of reasoning.

a. If she holds a, one could persuade her to exchange it for c provided she pays a fee (say $1). One could also persuade her to exchange c for b for an additional fee (say another dollar). Furthermore, one could persuade her to exchange b for a for an additional fee (say another dollar). Observe that she is in exactly the same situation as before (she holds a); only now she is $3 poorer. In each transaction, she improved her holdings according to her preferences. Because of the intransitivity of her preferences, however, she found herself monetarily worse off. If this money pump continues to function, she could "improve" her situation to the point of starvation.

These two requirements of rationality are part of any rational-choice account because they assure actors' capacity to maximize. The third requirement of weak rationality deals with the objective function that rational actors seek to maximize.

(3) Conformity to the axioms of probability calculus.

This proposition is the most counterintuitive and most difficult to argue; the proof is presented in the appendix to this chapter. One has to introduce the objective function that a rational agent maximizes. In this book, I assume that rational actors maximize their expected utility, that is, the product of the utility they derive from an event, multiplied by the probability that this event will occur.[4]

The proposition asserts that if a person is willing to make bets in the belief that the probability of winning multiplied by the prize is equal to the probability of losing multiplied by the fee,[5] *and if in her calculations, she does not obey the rules of probability calculus, she will definitely lose money.*[6]

For our purposes, this proposition indicates that any individual whose calculus does not conform to the axioms of probability calculus is certain to pay a price (regardless of whether some particular events happen or not) for the inconsistency of her beliefs. For the time being, it does not matter whether an individual's probability estimates correspond to objective frequencies. She may overestimate or underestimate probabilities; she may be optimistic or pessimistic. The only restriction in the proof is that she be willing to accept fair bets, that is, bets with expected utility equal to zero.

In the previous cases, individuals were penalized for deviations from rules of consistency. Some of these rules, of noncontradiction and transitivity, for instance, may seem intuitively pleasing and clear. Others, such as conformity to the axioms of probability calculus, may seem counterintuitive and/or unrealistic. Nevertheless, any deviation from these rules is a deviation from the weak requirements of rationality and will result in a loss of money.

In all the cases, events in the real world were not considered: beliefs had to be (internally) consistent but did not necessarily have to correspond to situations in the real world; in addition, penalties were

---

4. Strictly speaking, there is no reason the decision rule should be part of the definition of rationality. Indeed, one can use different decision rules and derive different predictions. For example, Ferejohn and Fiorina (1974) use the minimax regret criterion to explain why people vote (see *American Political Science Review* [1975] 69:908–60) for an extended discussion generated by their article). Other criteria would be the maximin criterion (Luce and Raiffa 1957) or mixed (Tsebelis 1986) or multiple stage criteria (Levi 1980). However, the overwhelming majority of rational-choice studies assumes that rational actors maximize their expected utility, and this book is no exception.
5. In technical terms, bets with expected utility equal zero. Such bets win $1 if a fair coin comes up heads and lose $1 if it comes up tails, or win $5 if you guess correctly the result of the throw of an unloaded die and pay $1 if you lose. Note that the odds of a fair bet are by far more favorable than the odds that people accept when participating in lotteries or playing in casinos.
6. In this chapter's appendix, I demonstrate that if an individual is willing to make a series of fair bets and her plausibility values do not obey the rules of probability calculus, a Dutch Book can be made against her. . . .

imposed independently of the state of the world. For example, there is no penalty for the belief in an imminent invasion from Mars as long as the person who has this belief acts consistently with it, that is, prepares herself for the invasion. In order to rule out such possibilities, we must now turn to the external requirements of rationality.

Strong Requirements of Rationality

The strong requirements of rationality establish a correspondence between beliefs or behavior and the real world. The following discussion concerns the distinctions among beliefs, probabilities, and strategies, leading to proof of three strong requirements of rationality:

1. Strategies are mutually optimal in equilibrium, or in equilibrium, the players conform to the prescriptions of game theory.
2. Probabilities approximate objective frequencies in equilibrium.
3. Beliefs approximate reality in equilibrium.

It is easier to develop these requirements in reverse order. First, attention must be drawn to the qualifier "in equilibrium," which is present in all three requirements. There are two reasons for this qualification. The first is negative: rational-choice theory cannot describe dynamics; it cannot account for the paths that actors will follow in order to arrive at the prescribed equilibria.[7] The second is positive: equilibrium is defined as a situation from which no actor has an incentive to deviate. Therefore, no matter how equilibrium is achieved, rational actors will remain there.

(1) Conformity to the prescriptions of game theory.

The Nash equilibrium concept is the fundamental concept of game theory.[8] Players use *mutually optimal strategies* in equilibrium: they have achieved a strategy combination from which no one has an incentive to deviate. According to this definition, there may be more than one equilibrium in a game. The problem then becomes selecting the most reasonable one.[9] If there is more than one reasonable equilibrium, coordination between players becomes a problem. If coordination fails, each player will choose an equilibrium strategy, but these strategies will correspond to different equilibria: the outcome will not be an equilibrium.[10] A player could also deviate from her equilibrium strategy without being penalized.[11] This deviation, however, may induce other players to change their strategies, either because they

7. In iterated games, one or more equilibrium *paths* can be computed so that the actors change their behavior over time, but they are technically always at equilibrium.
8. Nash (1951). John Nash is one of the founders of game theory.
9. This is the problem of refinements of the Nash equilibrium concept. Several solutions have been proposed: perfect equilibria (Selten 1975), proper equilibria (Myerson 1978), sequential equilibria (Kreps and Wilson 1982b), and stable equilibria (Kohlberg and Mertens 1986). Some of these concepts are discussed in Chapter 3. However, the interested reader should refer to the original articles as well as to Van Damme (1984) for the relationships among these subspecies of Nash equilibria.
10. A simple example is a chicken game, in which both players drive straight toward each other because they believe the opponent will yield, or else both yield because they believe the opponent will drive straight. . . .
11. She would not be rewarded for such a deviation. In this case, the original position would not have been an equilibrium; she is simply indifferent between the equilibrium strategy and some other strategy. In games with mixed strategy equilibria, indifference between strategies is the rule.

are now worse off than in equilibrium or because they can do even better. In both cases, deviation from equilibrium may generate a series of mutual adjustments, leading to the previous equilibrium or to another Nash equilibrium.

Thus, the concept of Nash equilibrium is a necessary (but not sufficient) condition for stability of outcomes. An observer should not expect a situation to be stable if it is out of equilibrium because one of the players will have an incentive to modify her actions. In this sense, the concept of equilibrium is tautological in the context of rational choice.[12] Equilibria are by definition the only combinations of mutually optimal strategies.

(2) Subjective probabilities should approximate objective frequencies.[13]

This requirement also depends on equilibrium analysis. In game theory, beliefs along the equilibrium path are updated according to Bayes's rule. That is, every player makes the best use of his previous probability assessments and the new information that he gets from the environment. If probability estimates do not approximate objective frequencies, rational actors will be able to improve their results in the long run by revising their probability estimates. Suppose, for example, that one adopts the belief that flipping a coin is a fair bet for heads (it has a one-half probability of landing heads). Suppose also that the coin is biased in such a way that the probability of heads is one-third. After it becomes apparent that losses are more frequent than gains, the player will revise his probability estimates and alter his bets.

(3) Beliefs should approximate reality.

The argument supporting this requirement is also an equilibrium argument. All beliefs of rational players along an equilibrium path are updated according to Bayes's rule; thus, the actor at any point can cho[o]se her optimal strategy given her beliefs. The mutual optimality of the players' strategies (given their beliefs) provides each player information about the beliefs of the opponent. If in the process of the game an actor does not update her information, she may be vulnerable to exploitation by the opponent: the opponent may realize that her situation can be improved given the mistaken beliefs of the first actor. In such a situation, either one of the players would modify her beliefs, or the other would modify her strategy. So such a situation is not an equilibrium.[14]

Consequently, according to the strong requirements of rationality, beliefs and behavior not only have to be consistent, but also have to correspond with the real world (at equilibrium). The penalty for deviations from strong rationality will be a reduced level of welfare.[15]

---

12. This is the dominant position among game theorists. For a proof that only Nash equilibria can be rational solutions to simultaneous games, see Bacharach (1987). For dissenting views concerning sequential games, see Bernheim (1984), Pearce (1984), and particularly Bonanno (1988). The reason for the disagreement is that in sequential games, the calculation of equilibria involves counterfactuals that, by definition, have no truth conditions. For an intermediate position concerning the concept of perfect equilibrium, see Binmore (1987).
13. This assumption is similar to what in the economics literature is known as *rational expectations* (see Muth 1961; Lucas 1982).
14. One more situation exists, characterized by beliefs that have no impact on behavior; thus, there is no reason to modify them. I consider such beliefs innocuous and do not deal with them. The belief in God (without moral imperative supplements) comes as close as possible to such beliefs.
15. I remind the reader that all the proofs can be replicated with utiles instead of money; in this case, one would speak of a reduction in utility instead of welfare.

All arguments concerning both weak and strong rationality are normative. They claim that behavior *should* reflect the prescriptions of expected utility or game theory; otherwise, the actor will pay a price. One could agree with the normative value of these arguments and still not believe that rational choice has any descriptive value. The argument would go as follows: it is true that in an ideally rational world, people should and would behave according to the rational-choice prescriptions, but the real world is very different from such a rational-choice world. In the real world, people are willing to pay the price for their mistakes or for their beliefs; even if real people would like to conform to these prescriptions, they are simply incapable of making all the required calculations and computations; calculating Nash equilibria even for simple games is not easy, and the level of complexity increases astronomically when approximating realistic situations.[16]

Is there any reason to believe that the rational-choice approach is, in Keynes's terminology, not only normative but also positive?[17] In other words, are we to believe that real people not only *should* but also *do* behave according to rational-choice requirements? These are the questions I examine in the next section.

III. Is the Rational-Choice Approach Realistic?

A frequent answer to the above question is, "It does not matter; people behave 'as if' they were rational." The full explanation of this particular view is offered in Friedman's seminal article, "The Methodology of Positive Economics." Friedman (1953, 14) claims, "Truly important and significant hypotheses will be found to have 'assumptions' that are *wildly inaccurate* descriptive representations of reality, and, in general, the more significant the theory, the more unrealistic the assumptions (in this sense).... To be important....a hypothesis must be descriptively false in its assumptions" (emphasis added).

Friedman offers three different examples to support the "F-twist," as economist Paul Samuelson (1963) calls the "as if" thesis. The first concerns expert billiard players who execute their shots "as if" they knew the complicated mathematical formulae describing the optimal path of the balls. The second deals with firms that behave "as if" they were expected utility maximizers. The third concerns the leaves on a tree; Friedman (1953, 19) suggests "the hypothesis that the leaves are positioned as if each leaf deliberately sought to maximize the amount of sunlight it receives."

A similar argument can be made using Hempel's (1964) concept of "potential explanation"—an explanation that is correct if all its premises are true. Nozick (1974) developed this concept in his discussion of the "fundamental potential explanation." He claims that a fundamental potential explanation is important even if it is not true because it reveals important mechanisms that influence the phenomenon under examination. According to these arguments, an explanation may be important even if its premises are not true. So the question of the truth of a theory's assumptions becomes irrelevant.

The "as if" argument claims that the rationality assumption, regardless of its accuracy, is a way to model human behavior. This epistemological position of rationality-as-model is not only partial and un-

16. The issue of complexity of strategy calculations has only recently become the object of serious investigation. See Kalai and Stanford (1988), Rubinstein (1986), and Abreu (1986).

17. Keynes (1891, 34-35) distinguishes between "A positive science...a body of systematical knowledge concerning what is; a normative or regulative science...a body of systematized knowledge discussing criteria of what ought to be."

satisfactory, but also to a large extent responsible for the following situation: on the one hand, several rational-choice explanations use the "as if" argument to justify wildly unrealistic assumptions; on the other hand, empirical scientists mistrust rational-choice explanations for being irrelevant to the real world.

The "rationality-as-model" argument is not satisfactory for the following reason: the assumptions of a theory are, in a trivial sense, also conclusions of the theory. It follows that a scientist who is willing to make the "wildly inaccurate" assumptions Friedman wants him to make admits that "wildly inaccurate" behavior can be generated as a conclusion of his theory. So any scientist who is interested in the realism of the conclusions and explanations of a theory should be concerned with the realism of the assumptions as well. With respect to the rational-choice approach, it is inconsistent to use false assumptions as the basis for explanations after arguing, as I have done, that from false assumptions, anything follows.

I propose a different answer to the realism question. Instead of the concept of rationality as a model of human behavior, I propose the concept of rationality as a subset of human behavior. The change in perspective is important: I do not claim that rational choice can explain every phenomenon and that there is no room for other explanations, but I do claim that rational choice is a better approach to situations in which the actors' identity and goals are established and the rules of the interaction are precise and known to the interacting agents. As the actors' goals become fuzzy, or as the rules of the interaction become more fluid and imprecise, rational-choice explanations will become less applicable. Norton Long (1961, 140–41) provided a similar argument:

> Here we deal with the essence of predictability in social affairs. If we know the game being played is baseball and that X is a third baseman, by knowing his position and the game being played we can tell more about X's activities on the field than we could if we examined X as a psychologist or a psychiatrist. If such were not the case, X would belong in the mental ward rather than in a ball park. The behavior of X is not some disembodied rationality but, rather, behavior within an organized group activity that has goals, norms, strategies, and roles that give the very field and ground for rationality. Baseball structures the situation.

I submit that political games (or most of them) structure the situation as well and that the study of political actors under the assumption of rationality is a legitimate approximation of realistic situations, motives, calculations, and behavior. I present five arguments to demonstrate why individuals attempt the calculations described in Section II or why they adopt the behavior prescribed by such calculations or why the aggregate outcome of individual actions can be approximated by such calculations.

Argument 1. Salience of issues and information.

Following from the normative properties of the rational-choice approach, people prefer to conform with the behavior prescribed by the theory (otherwise they may have to pay a price). This tendency varies directly with the size of the stakes: for example, candidates try to obtain more information about people's choices in a district with a close race than in a "safe" district; parties spend more resources trying to calculate the consequences of a constitutional modification as opposed to the consequences of a simple law.

Moreover, when information is available, people will be able to approximate the calculations required by rational choice better than when payoffs are not well known or approximate. Indeed, some of the most successful applications of the rational-choice approach concern the institutions, norms, and behaviors of the Congress and bureaucracy of the United States (that is, the study of well-structured situations) (Fenno 1978; Ferejohn 1974; Fiorina 1974; Hammond and Miller 1987; Miller and Moe 1983; Shepsle and Weingast 1981).

Argument 2. Learning.

The normative properties of the rational-choice model suggest that people engaging in repeated activities approximate optimal behavior through trial and error. In fact, subjective probabilities will converge to objective frequencies as additional information becomes available through iteration. Consequently, the final outcome becomes almost indistinguishable from rational-choice calculations. This case is described in one of Friedman's examples: the expert billiard players. The billiard players do not understand the laws of geometrical optics, but they are very sensitive to the implications of such laws for their game. Similarly, voters are able to use retrospective evaluations and vote unsuccessful incumbents out of office in two-party systems even though they may not remember the platforms of the different candidates or be able to discriminate between them (Fiorina 1981; Key 1968).

Learning is not independent of the salience of issues and information. One would expect a correlation between the speed of learning and the salience of the issue, as argument 1 indicates. Moreover, convergence to optimal behavior is faster as the frequency of the decision-making problem increases.

Learning is a conscious activity; it presupposes that the decision maker is able to discover past mistakes. An explanation based on the concept of learning produces the same outcomes as the rational-choice approach but uses much weaker assumptions.

Argument 3. Heterogeneity of individuals.

Suppose that instead of adopting the assumption that all individuals can make rational-choice calculations or that all individuals are capable of learning in repeated trials, we make the more realistic assumption that most individuals are not sophisticated, although a small proportion is capable of making these calculations. What will the equilibrium be?

To simplify matters further, assume that a cohort of individuals has to select career paths. Suppose that most have a very simplistic perception of reality and incorrect expectations, but a small percentage is capable of rational-choice calculations. Although the nonsophisticated individuals will make uninformed (and sub-optimal) decisions, the most informed will anticipate this behavior and compensate by having their behavior biased in exactly the opposite manner. For example, if there is an excess of doctors, the sophisticated individuals will become engineers or lawyers. So the social outcome will approximate the equilibrium that would prevail if all agents were sophisticated.

This argument has been made by Haltiwanger and Waldman (1985), who prove that equilibria with some sophisticated agents will tend toward equilibria where all agents are sophisticated in the case of "congestion effects," that is, where each agent is worse off the higher the number of other agents who make the same choice as he.[18]

---

18. The opposite case, in which each agent is better off the more times other agents choose the same behavior as his own (such as buying computer software), is called *synergistic effect*. Haltiwanger and Waldman (1985) prove that in this case, the sophisticated agents imitate the behavior of the nonsophisticated ones, so the latter have a disproportionate effect on the equilibrium.

Most economic goods exhibit properties of congestion effects because an increase in demand raises the price and makes additional buyers worse off. I cannot claim that political phenomena demonstrate properties of congestion more frequently than economic ones. However, the number of cases of congestion effects is already large, and in all these cases, an equilibrium with a small number of sophisticated agents is practically indistinguishable from an equilibrium where all agents are sophisticated.

Argument 4. Natural selection.

The same behavioral outcomes can be supported, however, by even weaker assumptions. Suppose that there are different "populations" of people defined by their different reactions when faced with the same situation. Furthermore, suppose that when decisions are made and rewards or penalties are distributed, the less successful individuals are eliminated. In the long run, the most successful behaviors are reinforced, and the outcome approximates the optimal choice without any conscious means/ends calculation by those involved.[19] In Friedman's example, firms maximize their expected returns as the result of such an evolutionary process. Similarly, if long-term considerations (as in consistency over time and/or ideology) are excluded, politicians who try to maximize their votes will have a higher survival rate than those who do not. In the long run, the latter population will be eliminated.

This evolutionary approach adopts the weakest assumptions about individuals' motivations and calculations. In fact, it attributes the entire explanation to environmental factors. For this reason, the explanation is open to the following criticism: a particular behavior is not necessarily optimal because the reason for its natural selection may not have been the behavior under investigation, but some other characteristic. Consequently, evolutionary arguments can be used to support the optimality of behavior only after eliminating alternative explanations.

Argument 5. Statistics.

This argument involves the properties of the population mean. Assume the following: only a very small proportion of a population uses rational calculations; only a very small proportion is capable of learning; and evolutionary arguments apply only to a restricted segment of the population. In addition, suppose that the largest remainder of the population makes decisions at random or by some roughly equivalent process. Assume, for example, some are optimists and others pessimists, some are risk prone and others risk averse, and some are influenced positively or negatively in their decisions by opinion leaders (e.g., Ronald Reagan or Jane Fonda).

To make matters more concrete, suppose that rationality is a small but systematic component of any individual, and all other influences are distributed at random. The systematic component has a magnitude x, and the random element is normally distributed with variance s. Under these assumptions, each individual of the population will execute a decision in the interval $[x - (2s), x + (2s)]$ 95 percent of the time. If, however, we consider a sample of a million individuals, the average individual will make a decision in the interval $[x - (2s/1000), x + (2s/1000)]$ 95 percent of the time. This can be verified by the statistical properties of the mean: the rational decision assumed to be only a "systematic although very small component" was approximated by the average individual of our sample at a factor of one thou-

19. The outcome approximates the optimal choice provided that the population with the optimal choice exists in the beginning of the experiment.

sand times that of the random individual. Therefore, the rational-choice analysis can be completely inaccurate concerning a specific individual but very accurate concerning the average individual.[20]

There are two possible objections to this statistical argument. First, the problem of aggregation was assumed out. That is, I have assumed aggregation is equivalent to an arithmetic summation. However, as Arrow's (1951) seminal work demonstrates, aggregates (much like societies) can demonstrate properties that are completely divergent from the properties of their constituent parts (individuals). Second, I have arbitrarily equated the systematic component of a decision with rationality. Nonetheless, exactly the same argument can be made if one substitutes any other decision-making rule as a systematic component.

Both objections have merit: if questions of aggregation resembling those described in Arrow's theorem are important, the statistical argument is invalid. Moreover, if any other systematic component is shown to be part of the decision-making process, the decision will gravitate toward this systematic component regardless of its nature. If, for example, people are shown to be risk averse systematically, then risk aversion should be included in the statistical calculations, and the behavior of the aggregate will demonstrate very strong risk aversion.

If the objection concerning the statistical argument in favor of rational choice is essentially correct, why is this argument presented? First, to my knowledge, there are no other claims for *systematic* components of decision making.[21] Second, the reliability of the rational-choice approach does not rest on the statistical argument alone; it rests on all five arguments presented. Each argument is more general but weaker than the previous one. However, taken together, they delineate the range of cases in which the rational-choice approach is legitimate. Validity increases when elites are involved (except when we can use the statistical argument for masses). Validity is practically guaranteed by the existence of small proportions or rational agents in the case of congestion effects. In addition, the results are more likely to be correct in iterated situations in which people learn or are naturally selected than in noniterated games.

To summarize, the rational-choice approach has an indisputable normative appeal. I have also demonstrated that it has a positive value. Contrary to the dominant justification among rational-choice

---

20. The difference between this argument and argument 3 is that here agents are deciding independently; in argument 3, some agents were able to anticipate the behavior of others and change their choice accordingly. Moreover, in argument 3, the nonsophisticated agents were assumed to be biased; here all agents are normally distributed around some central value.

21. I emphasize the word *systematic* because otherwise theories of national culture or political socialization would be exceptions. There are two directions that systematic dispute of rationality has taken. The first is associated with Tversky and Kahneman (1981), and Kahneman and Tversky (1979), and Kahneman, Slovic, and Tversky (1984) and concerns the framing of decisions. Experiments have indicated important deviations from expected utility-maximizing rules when probabilities are very small or utilities are very large (such as questions of life or death). The second is the satisficing approach associated with Simon (1957), March (1978), and Nelson and Winter (1982), in which people are supposed to choose not the best option among different alternatives but one that is "good enough" or above some threshold of acceptability. The crucial question with respect to this second approach is whether or not people will stick with their choice if some better alternative comes along. In the first case, there is a correspondence between rational choice and satisficing: optimizing refers to the whole set of alternatives, and satisficing refers to a restricted set. But the two methods produce the same outcomes when applied to the same set of alternatives (Riker and Ordeshook 1973). In the second case, however, the outcomes are different, and there is no possibility of translation from one research program to the other. These two programs (framing and satisficing) have the advantage of empirical accuracy but have been presented so far as objections to specific claims of the rational-choice program and not as theoretical alternatives.

sympathizers, which claims that the validity of the rational-choice approach stems from good predictions, I claim that it is a legitimate approximation of real processes. People will approximate the rational-choice prescriptions when the issues are important, and the degree of approximation will vary with information. Furthermore, there are learning, evolutionary, and statistical reasons why the assumption of optimizing (rational) behavior is appropriate.

The arguments presented here constitute what Musgrave (1981) calls "domain assumptions": necessary conditions for the rational-choice approach. For example, actions taken in noniterative situations by individual decision makers (such as in crisis situations) are not necessarily well suited for rational-choice predictions. Nevertheless, such an approach could have an important heuristic role; it could indicate the realm of possibilities for different actors, demonstrating why certain decisions were or were not made. Rational choice cannot claim to explain all human behavior. Only behavior in situations covered by my five arguments can be the domain of reasonable rational-choice applications.

These arguments further demonstrate that inside the domain of applicability of rational choice, the rationality assumption constitutes a very good approximation of reality. In Musgrave's (1981) terms, for the kinds of cases covered by my five arguments, the rationality assumption is a "negligibility assumption": an assumption that approximates reality so well that it is worth making.

IV. The Advantages of the Rational-Choice Approach

Even if we assume that actors try to do their best under given circumstances, why push the argument to its extreme logical consequences and make the assumption of rationality? Why push the argument to such extremes and then consider it a reasonable approximation of reality? Why try to avoid at all costs explanations including irrational factors or mistakes?

In particular, with respect to the subject of this book, why be surprised when people make suboptimal choices and then try to explain such choices through the use of nested games? Why not simply conclude that the actor is nonrational or that she made a mistake whenever the observer disagrees with her as to the optimal course of action? What is the reason behind this obsession with the rational-choice approach? Why not perform a crucial experiment regarding the rationality assumption and reject rationality if actors choose suboptimally, as is done in experimental psychology? After all, this is the usual treatment of any hypothesis in the social sciences. Put boldly: "why bother inventing epicycles in order to save the rational-choice approach?" [22] There are several reasons.

The social scientist who assumes actors behave rationally makes a reductionist move and at the same time formulates a statement of purpose. She makes a reductionist move because she replaces a series of processes, such as learning, cognition, or mechanisms of social selection, with their outcomes. She does not claim that the actual processes that people use in order to arrive at their rational decisions are the mathematical formulae used in decision theory or in game theory, but that these formulae lead the scientist in a simple and systematic way to the same outcomes. She makes a statement of purpose because the focus of the study will be on other factors influencing or determining social phenomena.

The rational-choice approach focuses its attention on the *constraints* imposed on rational actors—the institutions of a society. That the rational-choice approach is unconcerned with individuals or ac-

---

22. Epicycles were continuously invented to explain the anomalies of the Ptolemaic system. A similar phenomenon occurred before the invention of the theory of relativity. Astronomers were trying to explain anomalies by inventing "hidden planets," that is, planets whose existence would have accounted for the observed anomalies.

tors and focuses its attention on political and social institutions seems paradoxical. The reason for this paradox is simple: individual action is assumed to be optimal adaptation to an institutional environment, and the interaction between individuals is assumed to be an optimal response to each other. Therefore, the prevailing institutions (the rules of the game) determine the behavior of the actors, which in turn produces political or social outcomes.

This approach presents four major advantages over its rivals: theoretical clarity and parsimony, equilibrium analysis, extensive use of deductive reasoning, and interchangeability of individuals.

(1) Theoretical clarity and parsimony.

Perhaps the most obvious comparative advantage of my approach is in its theoretical clarity and parsimony. Explanations are cast in institutional terms, as opposed to psychological or cognitive process terms. Outcomes are explained as deliberate choices rather than as mistakes. As a consequence, ad hoc explanations are eliminated. If the theoretically predicted behavior does not occur, the notion of mistakes cannot be invoked to explain the actual outcome. Inconsistency between theory and reality is attributed to the inadequacy of the theory rather than to mistaken actors. As a result, the rational-choice approach lends itself to stricter empirical tests than most other theoretical approaches. It also means that the range of potential applications of the theory is limited by its refusal to accept mistakes as explanations of behavior.[23] Although there are phenomena that cannot be explained in rational-choice terms, what rational choice can explain, it explains extremely well because of its parsimony and theoretical clarity.

(2) Equilibrium analysis.

One important methodological consequence of the rational-choice approach that is a recurring theme throughout the book is *comparative statics*. Recurring social or political phenomena are considered to be in equilibrium, and the properties of these equilibria are studied and compared. Behavior "in equilibrium" means that the actors involved in a recurring course of action are considered as not having any incentives to deviate from this course. This assumption is a straightforward corollary of the rationality assumption: if a rational actor had an incentive to deviate (that is, improve her condition) from her previous behavior, that behavior was by definition not optimal.

Equilibrium arguments are used in three different ways. First, they are used to discover the optimal behavior of actors. For example, the Socialists in my brief account of Finnish electoral history did not use an equilibrium strategy in the arena of the presidential election; this observation led to the discovery of a nested game in which internal party considerations played an important part. The Socialists' behavior was then explained as an equilibrium (optimal) strategy in this nested game.

Second, equilibrium arguments are used to answer conditional questions and lead to empirically testable predictions. If one of the parameters of the model changes, then one actor may modify her behavior in response to this change; this change in strategy may lead the opponent to a change in her strategy; and this will lead the first actor to further modification; . . . Equilibrium analysis helps us predict the final outcome of this infinite process. Sometimes the prediction is counterintuitive because without

23. In some game theoretic papers, "mistakes" or small perturbations are used as a means to discover stability properties of Nash equilibria (Selten 1975).

the help of mathematical tools the human mind is unable to make the infinite number of calculations required to provide the answer to conditional statements of the form: what would happen if the value of parameter x increased?[24] To use one example, what would happen if the size of the penalty for a particular crime increased? Pure intuition would lead us to expect the frequency of that crime to decline. However, game theoretic analysis leads to the conclusion that modifying the criminals' payoffs does not affect their behavior at equilibrium; on the contrary, it affects the behavior of the police.[25]

Third, equilibrium arguments are used to eliminate alternative explanations. Consider theoretical arguments that claim to explain recurring patterns as mistakes, such as the money illusion in Keynesian economics; as habits and rituals, as is often done in cultural anthropology; or as having symbolic meaning, as is often the case in political science. According to rational-choice theory, any explanation that rests on suboptimal behavior is incomplete in the best case and wrong in the worst.

(3) Deductive reasoning.

The arguments presented in a rational-choice analysis are formal, that is, made according to the rules of mathematics or logic. The advantage of this process is that formal arguments (assuming they are correct) are truth preserving. The conclusions of the models presented carry with them the truth of the assumptions that generated them. In other words, one cannot argue with a theorem (although one can effectively dispute its assumptions). Using provocative terminology, one might say that all rational-choice models are tautological. This tautological quality, far from being trivial, is difficult to achieve. Probably the most important and unambiguous lesson derived from the development of rational-choice "paradoxes" has been that using nonrigorous reasoning frequently leads to wrong conclusions.[26]

Because rational-choice models are tautological, they have two distinctive characteristics. The first is that if a rational-choice model leads to predictions that turn out to be false, the assumptions have to be modified. This is because the methods of derivation of the conclusions are rigorous and truth preserving; there is nothing more in the conclusions than in the assumptions. Logical rigor is not an exclusive property of formal models, but in these models, the calculations are mechanical and therefore easy to verify. False predictions lead immediately to modification of the assumptions of a model, as opposed to discussions about the logic of the argument.

The second characteristic stemming from the tautological character of rational-choice models is that they permit the cumulation of knowledge. This is because even the models that lead to false predictions are essentially "correct." Once a model has been formulated, it becomes common knowledge that a particular set of assumptions leads to specific results and that a modification of the assumptions or addi-

24. The legitimate question at this point is, "if game theory is necessary for the analyst to find the counterintuitive solution, then how is it possible for the actors to solve the problem?" The answer provided in Section III is that actual game theoretic calculations are only one of the ways to arrive at an aggregate result. Evolutionary, learning, or statistical averaging arguments would lead the actual actors to the same outcome.

25. See Tsebelis (1989), where a simple and plausible game between police and criminals is presented and solved. In equilibrium, modification of a player's payoffs affects the opponent's behavior. In particular, an increase in penalties decreases the frequency of police patrols.

26. People were surprised by Arrow's (1951) possibility theorem because they had never imagined the incompatibility of five restrictions that seemed so trivial and innocuous. McKelvey's (1976) result indicating the omnipresence of majority rule cycles had a similar surprising impact. Many game theoretic results have an important surprise value because the interactions between rational players generates unpredicted outcomes.

tional assumptions are needed to produce a fit between theory and reality. This is why Arrow's and McKelvey's results stimulated an important stream of research on the importance of institutions.[27]

I believe that the use of deductive reasoning will have an important and lasting influence on political science. Up to now, a common procedure in political science scholarship has been to observe an empirical regularity, then to establish it through statistical methods, and finally to produce a plausible argument consistent with the regularity. The deductive arguments of rational choice have demonstrated conclusively that the last part of this procedure (the presentation of plausible arguments supporting empirical regularities) is not equivalent to theoretical reasoning. Each step of a plausible inductive argument is not completely truth preserving, so by the end of the argument, what is left out may be as or even more important than what was preserved.

(4) Interchangeability of individuals.

Because the only assumption regarding actors is their rationality, they lack any other characteristic or identity. They are interchangeable.[28] How can a French Communist be considered interchangeable with an Italian Christian Democrat? What happened to history? What happened to culture? What happened to local tradition? What kind of explanation seems to exclude everything that matters?

It is true that historical, temporal, cultural, racial, or other qualifiers do not enter directly into any rational-choice explanation. However, "The bridge between historical observations and general theory is the substitution of variables for proper names of social systems in the course of comparative research" (Przeworski and Teune 1970, 25). The rational-choice research program is not the only one that tries to replace ethnic or racial characteristics or behaviors with the goals of the actors or the institutions that produce them. If Italians are cynical, Germans obedient, and Mexicans distrustful of government, as *Civic Culture* indicates, it is not because they are Italians, Germans, or Mexicans. Section III gave examples of how some of Almond and Verba's findings can be explained in terms of existing institutions and the assumption of rationality.

I now focus on one particular interchangeable actor: the reader. In the rational-choice approach, outcomes are explained as the optimal choices of actors in a given situation. A successful rational-choice explanation describes the prevailing institutions and context in which the actor operates, persuading the reader that she would have made the same choice if placed in the same situation.

---

27. See Arrow (1951) and McKelvey (1976). For more recent work on institutions, see Shepsle (1979), Shepsle and Weingast (1984), Riker (1980), and Schwartz (1985).

28. They are interchangeable provided they have the same tastes. As I have already argued, tastes are considered exogenous in rational-choice explanations. One could use the degrees of freedom generated by exogeneity of tastes and provide a "rational-choice" explanation of any phenomenon. For example, one can provide a rational-choice explanation of voting by arguing that there is an intrinsic satisfaction from the act of voting (Riker and Ordeshook 1968). For an argument that this approach is tautological, see Barry (1978). I try to avoid the trap of attributing the essential part of my explanation to tastes by attributing "standard" tastes to my actors. One such standard taste for political actors is reelection because it is a necessary condition for achieving any other political goal. For example. . . Labour party activists are considered to have ideological preferences, but not to the point of sacrificing their party's candidate; Belgian elites have preferences over outcomes, but not to the point that it will cost them reelection; and French parties want to improve their electoral position without hurting the electoral chances of their coalition.

References

Abreu, D. 1986. "Extremal Equilibria of Oligopolistic Supergames." *Journal of Economic Theory* 39: 191–225.

Arrow, K. J. 1951. *Social Choice and Individual Values.* New Haven, Conn.: Yale University Press.

Bacharach, M. 1987. "A Theory of Rational Decision in Games." *Erkenntnis* 27: 17–55.

Barry, B. 1978. *Sociologists, Economists, and Democracy.* Chicago: University of Chicago Press.

Bernheim, B. D. 1984. "Rationalizable Strategic Behaviour." *Econometrica* 52: 1007–28.

Binmore, K. 1987. "Modeling Rational Players: Part I." *Economics and Philosophy* 3: 179–214.

Bonanno, G. 1988. "The Logic of Rational Play in Sequential Games." Mimeo, University of California, Davis.

Davidson, D., McKinsey, J. C. C., and Suppes, P. 1954. "Outline of a Formal Theory of Value, I." *Philosophy of Science* 22: 140–60.

Fenno, R. F. 1978. *Home Style.* Boston: Little, Brown.

Ferejohn, J. A. 1974. *Pork Barrel Politics.* Stanford, Calif.: Stanford University Press.

Ferejohn, J. A., and Fiorina, M. P. 1974. "The Paradox of Non-Voting: A Decision-Theoretic Analysis." *American Political Science Review* 68: 525–36.

Fiorina, M. P. 1974. *Representatives, Roll Calls, and Constituencies.* Lexington, Mass.: Lexington Books.

———. 1981. *Retrospective Voting in American Elections.* New Haven, Conn.: Yale University Press.

Friedman, M. 1953. "The Methodology of Positive Economics." In M. Friedman (ed.), *Essays in Positive Economics.* Chicago: University of Chicago Press.

Haltiwanger, J., and Waldman, M. 1985. "Rational Expectations and the Limits of Rationality: An Analysis of Heterogeneity." *American Economic Review* 75: 326–40.

Hammond, T. H., and Miller, G. J. 1987. "The Core of the Constitution." *American Political Science Review* 81: 1155–74.

Hempel, C. G. 1964. *Aspects of Scientific Explanation.* New York: Free Press.

Kahneman, D., and Tversky, A. 1979. "Prospect Theory: An Analysis of Decision Under Risk." *Econometrica* 47: 263–91.

Kahneman, D., Slovic, P., and Tversky, A. 1984. *Judgment Under Uncertainty.* Cambridge: Cambridge University Press.

Kalai, E., and Stanford, W. 1988. "Finite Rationality and Interpersonal Complexity in Repeated Games." *Econometrica* 56: 397–410.

Key, V. O., Jr. 1968. *The Responsible Electorate.* New York: Vintage.

Keynes, J. M. 1891. *The Scope and Method of Political Economy.* London: Macmillan.

Kohlberg, E., and Mertens, J.-F. 1986. "On the Strategic Stability of Equilibria." *Econometrica* 54: 1003–37.

Kreps, D. M., and Wilson, R. 1982. "Sequential Equilibria." *Econometrica* 50: 863–94.

Levi, I. 1980. *The Enterprise of Knowledge: An Essay on Knowledge, Credal Probability, and Chance.* Cambridge, Mass.: MIT Press.

Long, N. 1961. *The Polity.* Chicago: Rand McNally.

Lucas, G. 1982. *Studies in Business-Cycle Theory.* Cambridge, Mass.: MIT Press.

Luce, R. D., and Raifaa, H. 1957. *Games and Decisions.* New York: Wiley.

March, J. 1978. "Bounded Rationality, Ambiguity, and the Engineering of Choice." *Bell Journal of Economics* 9: 587–608.

McKelvey, R. D. 1976. "Intransitivities in Multidimensional Voting Models and Some Implications for Agenda Control." *Journal of Economic Theory* 12: 472–82.

Miller, G. J., and Moe, T. M. 1983. "Bureaucrats, Politicians, and the Size of Government." *American Political Science Review* 77: 297–322.

Musgrave, A. 1981. " 'Unreal Assumptions' in Economic Theory: The F-Twist Untwisted." *Kyklos* 34: 377–87.

Muth, J. 1961. "Rational Expectations and the Theory of Price Movements." *Econometrica* 29: 315–35.

Myerson, R. B. 1978. "Refinements of the Nash Equilibrium Concept." *International Journal of Game Theory* 7:73–80.

Nash, J. F., Jr. 1951. "Noncooperative Games." *Annals of Mathematics* 54: 289–95.

Nelson, R., and Winter, S. 1982. *An Evolutionary Theory of Economic Change*. Cambridge, Mass.: Harvard University Press.

Nozick, R. 1974. *Anarchy, State, and Utopia*. New York: Basic Books.

Pearce, D. G. 1984. "Rationalizable Strategic Behaviour and the Problem of Perfection." *Econometrica* 52: 1029–50.

Popper, K. R. 1962. *Conjectures and Refutations: The Growth of Scientific Knowledge*. New York: Basic Books.

Przeworski, A., and Teune, H. 1970. *The Logic of Comparative Social Inquiry*. New York: Wiley.

Riker, W. H. 1980. "Implications from the Disequilibrium of Majority Rules for the Study of Institutions." *American Political Science Review* 74: 432–47.

Riker, W. H., and Ordeshook, P. C. 1968. "A Theory of the Calculus of Voting." *American Political Science Review* 62: 25–42.

Rubinstein, A. 1986. "Finite Automata Play the Repeated Prisoners' Dilemma." *Journal of Economic Theory* 39: 83–96.

Samuelson, P. A. 1963. "Problems of Methodology—Discussion." *American Economic Review Papers and Proceedings* 53: 231–36.

Schwartz, T. 1985. "The Meaning of Instability." Paper presented to the American Political Science Association meetings.

Selten, R. 1975. "Reexamination of the Perfectness Concept for Equilibrium Points in Extensive Games." *International Journal of Game Theory* 4: 25–55.

Shepsle, K. A. 1979. "Institutional Arrangements and Equilibrium in Multidimensional Voting Models." *American Journal of Political Science* 23: 27–59.

Shepsle, K. A., and Weingast, B. R. 1981. "Political Preferences for the Pork Barrel: A Generalization." *American Journal of Political Science* 25: 96–111.

———. 1984. "Uncovered Sets and Sophisticated Voting Outcomes with Implications for Agenda Institutions." *American Journal of Political Science* 28: 49–74.

Simon, H. A. 1957. *Models of Man*. New York: Wiley.

Tsebelis, G. 1986. "A General Model of Tactical and Inverse Tactical Voting." *British Journal of Political Science* 16: 395–404.

Tsebelis, G. 1989. "The Abuse of Probability in Political Analysis: The Robinson Crusoe Fallacy." *American Political Science Review* 83: 77–91.

Tversky, A. and Kahneman, D. 1981. "The Framing of Decisions and the Psychology of Choice." *Science* 211: 453–58.

Van Damme, E. E. C. 19984. *Refinements of the Nash Equilibrium Concept*. New York: Springer-Verlag.

Chapter 3

WHY DO SOME DEMOCRACIES EMPHASIZE REPRESENTATION WHILE OTHERS EMPHASIZE RULING?

The question of what constitutes democracy still generates debate among scholars, but most political scientists do agree on which countries have crossed the democracy threshold and which have not. While inclusive of a large variety of countries differentiated in terms of wealth, history, geography, and culture, all democracies possess certain characteristics that distinguish their politics from those countries that are not democratic. First, all democratic countries select their top national leaders in free and fair elections. In this context, "free" means that individual citizens have the right to participate in the process through which a nation's top leaders are selected, and "fair" means that all citizens have the same voting power in this selection process. Second, individuals selected for the top political positions have the power to act on the statements that helped them get elected in those free and fair contests. Without a doubt, an elected official may decide not to act in accordance with statements made during a campaign run, but this decision must not result from any official barrier or coercion from some governmental group like the military.

All democracies are alike in these fundamental ways, yet they are not all the same by any stretch of the imagination. Most of the world's oldest democracies are also its wealthiest, but there are also countries that are far less wealthy, such as India, that have been democratic for decades. The world's democratic nations are also very different in terms of geography and culture—they are found in North America and Europe, as well as Asia, Africa, and South America. Moreover, while many have a Judeo-Christian heritage, others are traditionally Buddhist or Hindu. Finally, democracies are different in terms of the institutions they employ in their respective practices of governing.

How democracies are institutionally different is the topic of the two readings in this chapter, which divide democratic nations into two general categories: majoritarian and consensus. These two types of democracy exist because the countries of the world are socioeconomically different. Some are culturally, linguistically, religiously, and geographically divided. Belgium is good example: the southern part of the country is Walloon and French-speaking, whereas the northern part is Flemish and Dutch-speaking. To ensure that both regions receive adequate representation, Belgian-style democracy is consensus-based in its orientation. This is entirely different than the type of democracy practiced in the United Kingdom's winner-take-all-system, in which each national election produces one winner that becomes the majority party and forms a government and one minority party that then forms the opposition.

As Arend Lijphart makes clear in both of the readings in this chapter, there are several institutional and procedural features that distinguish majoritarian from consensus democracies, and he elaborates on these differences not only by identifying the institutional patterns in each but also by offering specific country examples that typify each type. Majoritarian-type democracies, in which electoral competition is typically between two large political parties, exist in the United Kingdom (UK) and former British colonies that continue to practice Westminster-style parliamentary politics. This list includes New Zealand, which until the constitutional changes of 1996 was the quintessential example of a Westminster, majoritarian-style democracy. For consensus-type democracies such as those that exist in socially divided countries, the examples discussed in the readings include Belgium and Switzerland. Indeed, in many ways, the Swiss confederation is perhaps the quintessential example of a consensus-style democracy.

Lijphart's work is very important in the study of democratic politics because, early in the postwar period, some political scientists saw the British system as the highest form of democracy. As a result, they also saw the democratic systems in other states as being lower in the political development hierarchy. Lijphart dispelled this notion by showing that the different institutional forms that distinguish the two types of democracies discussed above are not accidental; rather, they have been purposely put in place to solve certain problems in these countries' politics.

3.1

THE WESTMINSTER MODEL OF DEMOCRACY

Arend Lijphart

Each of the readings in this chapter comes from a book by University of California, San Diego, political scientist Arend Lijphart, whose early research focused on the politics of the Netherlands and Belgium. Lijphart studied these two countries because he wanted to explore how their democratic practices differed from those of countries like the United Kingdom, which had become the touchstone for developed democratic politics. Lijphart's research allowed him to show that political institutions and practices like those witnessed in the United States and United Kingdom—countries in which two-party systems dominate—do not necessarily represent a more developed form of democracy but rather a style of democratic politics that advances different values. These different values are historically based in each country and can be traced to the overall problems that each country's politics must solve. For example, in the United Kingdom, the prevailing values involve the ability of a political party to form a majority in the House of Commons and form a cabinet that can govern the country. Other democracies are more socially divided, and their politics emphasize the values of representation so that all social groups have a voice in the political process.

The first format Lijphart addresses—and the subject of this particular selection—is majoritarian democracy, or the Westminster-style of parliamentary politics. The reading discusses the philosophy behind this system and the institutional features that make it distinct. Majoritarian democracies emphasize ruling, in that their electoral institutions work so that each election cycle produces a single party that has a majority in the House of Commons and can, thus, form a government that can implement its platform. Consider how this is different from the United States, a country in which elections are staggered, and no single election produces one party that can singly dominate the executive and both houses of Congress.

In this [chapter] I use the term *Westminster model* interchangeably with *majoritarian model* to refer to a general model of democracy. It may also be used more narrowly to denote the main characteristics of *British* parliamentary and governmental institutions (Wilson 1994; Mahler 1997)—the Parliament of the United Kingdom meets in the Palace of Westminster in London. The British version of the Westminster model is both the original and the best-known example of this model. It is also widely admired. Richard Rose (1974, 131) points out that, "with confidence born of continental isolation, Americans

---

Arend Lijphart, "The Westminster Model of Democracy," in *Patterns of Democracy* (New Haven, Conn.: Yale University Press, 1999), chapter 2, 9–30.

have come to assume that their institutions—the Presidency, Congress and the Supreme Court—are the prototype of what should be adopted elsewhere." But American political scientists, especially those in the field of comparative politics, have tended to hold the British system of government in at least equally high esteem (Kavanagh 1974).

One famous political scientist who fervently admired the Westminster model was President Woodrow Wilson. In his early writings he went so far as to urge the abolition of presidential government and the adoption of British-style parliamentary government in the United States. Such views have also been held by many other non-British observers of British politics, and many features of the Westminster model have been exported to other countries: Canada, Australia, New Zealand, and most of Britain's former colonies in Asia, Africa, and the Caribbean when they became independent. Wilson (1884, 33) referred to parliamentary government in accordance with the Westminster model as "the world's fashion."

The ten interrelated elements of the Westminster or majoritarian model are illustrated by features of three democracies that closely approximate this model and can be regarded as the majoritarian prototypes: the United Kingdom, New Zealand, and Barbados. Britain, where the Westminster model originated, is clearly the first and most obvious example to use. In many respects, however, New Zealand is an even better example—at least until its sharp turn away from majoritarianism in October 1996. The third example—Barbados—is also an almost perfect prototype of the Westminster model, although only as far as the first (executives-parties) dimension of the majoritarian-consensus contrast is concerned. In the following discussion of the ten majoritarian characteristics in the three countries, I emphasize not only their conformity with the general model but also occasional deviations from the model, as well as various other qualifications that need to be made.

The Westminster Model in the United Kingdom

1. *Concentration of executive power in one-party and bare-majority cabinets.* The most powerful organ of British government is the cabinet. It is normally composed of members of the party that has the majority of seats in the House of Commons, and the minority is not included. Coalition cabinets are rare. Because in the British two-party system the two principal parties are of approximately equal strength, the party that wins the elections usually represents no more than a narrow majority, and the minority is relatively large. Hence the British one-party and bare-majority cabinet is the perfect embodiment of the principle of majority rule: it wields vast amounts of political power to rule as the representative of and in the interest of a majority that is not of overwhelming proportions. A large minority is excluded from power and condemned to the role of opposition.

Especially since 1945, there have been few exceptions to the British norm of one-party majority cabinets. David Butler (1978, 112) writes that "clear-cut single-party government has been much less prevalent than many would suppose," but most of the deviations from the norm—coalitions of two or more parties or minority cabinets—occurred from 1918 to 1945. The most recent instance of a coalition cabinet was the 1940–45 wartime coalition formed by the Conservatives, who had a parliamentary majority, with the Labour and Liberal parties, under Conservative Prime Minister Winston Churchill. The only instances of minority cabinets in the postwar period were two minority Labour cabinets in the 1970s. In the parliamentary election of February 1974, the Labour party won a plurality but not a majority of the seats and formed a minority government dependent on all other parties not uniting to defeat it. New elections were held that October and Labour won an outright, albeit narrow, majority of the seats; but this majority was eroded by defections and by-election defeats, and the Labour cabinet again became a minority cabinet in 1976. It regained a temporary legislative majority in 1977 as a result of the pact it negotiated with the thirteen Liberals in the House of Commons: the Liberals agreed to support the cabinet in exchange for consultation on legislative proposals before their submission to Parliament. No Liberals entered the cabinet, however, and the cabinet therefore continued as a minority instead of a true coalition cabinet. The so-called Lab-Lib pact lasted until 1978, and in 1979 Labour Prime Minister James Callaghan's minority cabinet was brought down by a vote of no confidence in the House of Commons.

2. *Cabinet dominance.* The United Kingdom has a parliamentary system of government, which means that the cabinet is dependent on the confidence of Parliament. In theory, because the House of Commons can vote a cabinet out of office, it "controls" the cabinet. In reality, the relationship is reversed. Because the cabinet is composed of the leaders of a cohesive majority party in the House of Commons, it is normally backed by the majority in the House of Commons, and it can confidently count on staying in office and getting its legislative proposals approved. The cabinet is clearly dominant vis-à-vis Parliament.

Because strong cabinet leadership depends on majority support in the House of Commons and on the cohesiveness of the majority party, cabinets lose some of their predominant position when either or both of these conditions are absent. Especially during the periods of minority government in the 1970s, there was a significant increase in the frequency of parliamentary defeats of important cabinet proposals. This even caused a change in the traditional view that cabinets must resign or dissolve the House of Commons and call for new elections if they suffer a defeat on either a parliamentary vote of no confidence or a major bill of central importance to the cabinet. The new unwritten rule is that only an explicit vote of no confidence necessitates resignation or new elections. The normalcy of cabinet dominance was largely restored in the 1980s under the strong leadership of Conservative Prime Minister Margaret Thatcher.

Both the normal and the deviant situations show that it is the disciplined two-party system rather than the parliamentary system that gives rise to executive dominance. In multiparty parliamentary systems, cabinets—which are often coalition cabinets—tend to be much less dominant (Peters 1997). Because of the concentration of power in a dominant cabinet, former cabinet minister Lord Hailsham (1978, 127) has called the British system of government an "elective dictatorship." [1]

3. *Two-party system.* British politics is dominated by two large parties: the Conservative party and the Labour party. Other parties also contest elections and win seats in the House of Commons—in particular the Liberals and, after their merger with the Social Democratic party in the late 1980s, the Liberal Democrats—but they are not large enough to be overall victors. The bulk of the seats are captured by the two major parties, and they form the cabinets: the Labour party from 1945 to 1951, 1964 to 1970, 1974 to 1979, and from 1997 on, and the Conservatives from 1951 to 1964, 1970 to 1974, and

1. In presidential systems of government, in which the presidential executive cannot normally be removed by the legislature (except by impeachment), the same variation in the degree of executive dominance can occur, depending on exactly how governmental powers are separated. In the United States, president and Congress can be said to be in a rough balance of power, but presidents in France and in some of the Latin American countries are considerably more powerful. Guillermo O'Donnell (1994, 59–60) has proposed the term "delegative democracy"—akin to Hailsham's "elective dictatorship"—for systems with directly elected and dominant presidents; in such "strongly majoritarian" systems, "whoever wins election to the presidency is thereby entitled to govern as he or she sees fit, constrained only by the hard facts of existing power relations and by a constitutionally limited term of office."

in the long stretch from 1979 to 1997. The hegemony of these two parties was especially pronounced between 1950 and 1970: jointly they never won less than 87.5 percent of the votes and 98 percent of the seats in the House of Commons in the seven elections held in this period.

The interwar years were a transitional period during which the Labour party replaced the Liberals as one of the two big parties, and in the 1945 election, the Labour and Conservative parties together won about 85 percent of the votes and 92.5 percent of the seats. Their support declined considerably after 1970: their joint share of the popular vote ranged from only 70 percent (in 1983) to less than 81 percent (in 1979), but they continued to win a minimum of 93 percent of the seats, except in 1997, when their joint seat share fell to about 88.5 percent. The Liberals were the main beneficiaries. In alliance with the Social Democratic party, they even won more than 25 percent of the vote on one occasion (in the 1983 election) but, until 1997, never more than fourteen seats by themselves and twenty-three seats in alliance with the Social Democrats. In the 1997 election, however, the Liberal Democrats captured a surprising forty-six seats with about 17 percent of the vote.

A corollary trait of two-party systems is that they tend to be one-dimensional party systems; that is, the programs and policies of the main parties usually differ from each other mainly with regard to just one dimension, that of socioeconomic issues. This is clearly the case for the British two-party system. The principal politically significant difference that divides the Conservative and Labour parties is disagreement about socioeconomic policies: on the left-right spectrum, Labour represents the left-of-center and the Conservative party the right-of-center preferences. This difference is also reflected in the pattern of voters' support for the parties in parliamentary elections: working-class voters tend to cast their ballots for Labour candidates and middle-class voters tend to support Conservative candidates. The Liberals and Liberal Democrats can also be placed easily on the socioeconomic dimension: they occupy a center position.

There are other differences, of course, but they are much less salient and do not have a major effect on the composition of the House of Commons and the cabinet. For instance, the Protestant-Catholic difference in Northern Ireland is the overwhelmingly dominant difference separating the parties and their supporters, but Northern Ireland contains less than 3 percent of the population of the United Kingdom, and such religious differences are no longer politically relevant in the British part of the United Kingdom (England, Scotland, and Wales). Ethnic differences explain the persistence of the Scottish National party and the Welsh nationalists, but these parties never manage to win more than a handful of seats. The only slight exception to the one-dimensionality of the British party system is that a foreign-policy issue—British membership in the European Community—has frequently been a source of division both within and between the Conservative and Labour parties.

4. *Majoritarian and disproportional system of elections.* The House of Commons is a large legislative body with a membership that has ranged from 625 in 1950 to 659 in 1997. The members are elected in single-member districts according to the plurality method, which in Britain is usually referred to as the "first past the post" system: the candidate with the majority vote or, if there is no majority, with the largest minority vote wins.

This system tends to produce highly disproportional results. For instance, the Labour party won an absolute parliamentary majority of 319 out of 635 seats with only 39.3 percent of the vote in the October 1974 elections, whereas the Liberals won only 13 seats with 18.6 percent of the vote—almost half the Labour vote. In the five elections since then, from 1979 to 1997, the winning party has won clear majorities of seats with never more than 44 percent of the vote. All of these majorities have been what

Douglas W. Rae (1967, 74) aptly calls "manufactured majorities"—majorities that are artificially created by the electoral system out of mere pluralities of the vote. In fact, all the winning parties since 1945 have won with the benefit of such manufactured majorities. It may therefore be more accurate to call the United Kingdom a *pluralitarian democracy* instead of a majoritarian democracy. The disproportionality of the plurality method can even produce an overall winner who has failed to win a plurality of the votes: the Conservatives won a clear seat majority in the 1951 election not just with less than a majority of the votes but also with fewer votes than the Labour party had received.

The disproportional electoral system has been particularly disadvantageous to the Liberals and Liberal Democrats, who have therefore long been in favor of introducing some form of proportional representation (PR). But because plurality has greatly benefited the Conservatives and Labour, these two major parties have remained committed to the old disproportional method. Nevertheless, there are some signs of movement in the direction of PR. For one thing, PR was adopted for all elections in Northern Ireland (with the exception of elections to the House of Commons) after the outbreak of Protestant-Catholic strife in the early 1970s. For another, soon after Labour's election victory in 1997, Prime Minister Tony Blair's new cabinet decided that the 1999 election of British representatives to the European Parliament would be by PR—bringing the United Kingdom in line with all of the other members of the European Union. PR will also be used for the election of the new regional assemblies for Scotland and Wales. Moreover, an advisory Commission on Voting Systems, chaired by former cabinet member Lord Jenkins, was instituted to propose changes in the electoral system, including the possibility of PR, for the House of Commons. Clearly, the principle of proportionality is no longer anathema. Still, it is wise to heed the cautionary words of Graham Wilson (1997, 72), who points out that the two major parties have a long history of favoring basic reforms, but only until they gain power; then "they back away from changes such as electoral reform which would work to their disadvantage."

* * *

6. *Unitary and centralized government*. The United Kingdom is a unitary and centralized state. Local governments perform a series of important functions, but they are the creatures of the central government and their powers are not constitutionally guaranteed (as in a federal system). Moreover, they are financially dependent on the central government. There are no clearly designated geographical and functional areas from which the parliamentary majority and the cabinet are barred. The Royal Commission on the Constitution under Lord Kilbrandon concluded in 1973: "The United Kingdom is the largest unitary state in Europe and among the most centralised of the major industrial countries in the world" (cited in Busch 1994, 60). More recently, Prime Minister Tony Blair called the British system "*the* most centralised government of any large state in the western world" (cited in Beer 1998, 25).

Two exceptions should be noted. One is that Northern Ireland was ruled by its own parliament and cabinet with a high degree of autonomy—more than what most states in federal systems have—from 1921, when the Republic of Ireland became independent, until the imposition of direct rule from London in 1972. It is also significant, however, that Northern Ireland's autonomy could be, and was, eliminated in 1972 by Parliament by means of a simple majoritarian decision. The second exception is the gradual movement toward greater autonomy for Scotland and Wales—"devolution," in British parlance. But it was not until September 1997 that referendums in Scotland and Wales finally approved the creation of autonomous and directly elected Scottish and Welsh assemblies and that Prime Minister

Blair could proclaim the end of the "era of big centralized government" (cited in Buxton, Kampfner, and Groom 1997, 1).

7. *Concentration of legislative power in a unicameral legislature.* For the organization of the legislature, the majoritarian principle of concentrating power means that legislative power should be concentrated in a single house or chamber. In this respect, the United Kingdom deviates from the pure majoritarian model. Parliament consists of two chambers: the House of Commons, which is popularly elected, and the House of Lords, which consists mainly of members of the hereditary nobility but also contains a large number of so-called life peers, appointed by the government. Their relationship is asymmetrical: almost all legislative power belongs to the House of Commons. The only power that the House of Lords retains is the power to delay legislation: money bills can be delayed for one month and all other bills for one year. The one-year limit was established in 1949; between the first major reform of 1911 and 1949, the Lords' delaying power was about two years, but in the entire period since 1911 they have usually refrained from imposing long delays.

Therefore, although the British bicameral legislature deviates from the majoritarian model, it does not deviate much: in everyday discussion in Britain, "Parliament" refers almost exclusively to the House of Commons, and the highly asymmetric bicameral system may also be called near-unicameralism. Moreover, the Lords' power may well be reduced further. Especially in the Labour party, there is strong sentiment in favor of reforms that range from eliminating the voting rights of the hereditary members to the abolition of the House of Lords. The change from near-unicameralism to pure unicameralism would not be a difficult step: it could be decided by a simple majority in the House of Commons and, if the Lords objected, merely a one-year delay.

8. *Constitutional flexibility.* Britain has a constitution that is "unwritten" in the sense that there is not one written document that specifies the composition and powers of the governmental institutions and the rights of citizens. These are defined instead in a number of basic laws—like the Magna Carta of 1215, the Bill of Rights of 1689, and the Parliament Acts of 1911 and 1949—common law principles, customs, and conventions. The fact that the constitution is unwritten has two important implications. One is that it makes the constitution completely flexible because it can be changed by Parliament in the same way as any other laws—by regular majorities instead of the supermajorities, like two-thirds majorities, required in many other democracies for amending their written constitutions. One slight exception to this flexibility is that opposition by the House of Lords may force a one-year delay in constitutional changes.

9. *Absence of judicial review.* The other important implication of an unwritten constitution is the absence of judicial review: there is no written constitutional document with the status of "higher law" against which the courts can test the constitutionality of regular legislation. Although Parliament normally accepts and feels bound by the rules of the unwritten constitution, it is not formally bound by them. With regard to both changing and interpreting the constitution, therefore, Parliament—that is, the parliamentary majority—can be said to be the ultimate or sovereign authority. In A. V. Dicey's (1915, 37–38) famous formulation, parliamentary sovereignty "means neither more nor less than this, namely, that Parliament. . .has, under the English constitution, the right to make or unmake any law whatever; and, further, that no person or body is recognised by the law of England as having a right to override or set aside the legislation of Parliament."

One exception to parliamentary sovereignty is that when Britain entered the European Community—a supranational instead of merely an international organization—in 1973, it accepted the Community's laws and institutions as higher authorities than Parliament with regard to several areas of policy. Because sovereignty means supreme and ultimate authority, Parliament can therefore no longer be regarded as fully sovereign. Britain's membership in the European Community—now called the European Union—has also introduced a measure of judicial review both for the European Court of Justice and for British courts: "Parliament's supremacy is challenged by the right of the Community institutions to legislate for the United Kingdom (without the prior consent of Parliament) and by the right of the courts to rule on the admissibility (in terms of Community law) of future acts of Parliament" (Coombs 1977, 88). Similarly, Britain has been a member of the European Convention on Human Rights since 1951, and its acceptance of an optional clause of this convention in 1966 has given the European Court of Human Rights in Strasbourg the right to review and invalidate any state action, including legislation, that it judges to violate the human rights entrenched in the convention (Cappelletti 1989, 202; Johnson 1998, 155–58).

* * *

The Westminster Model in New Zealand

Many of the Westminster model's features have been exported to other members of the British Commonwealth, but only one country has adopted virtually the entire model: New Zealand. A major change away from majoritarianism took place in 1996 when New Zealand held its first election by PR, but the New Zealand political system before 1996 can serve as a second instructive example of how the Westminster model works.

1. *Concentration of executive power in one-party and bare-majority cabinets.* For six decades, from 1935 to the mid-1990s, New Zealand had single-party majority cabinets without exceptions or interruptions. Two large parties—the Labour party and the National party—dominated New Zealand politics, and they alternated in office. The one-party majority cabinet formed after the last plurality election in 1993 suffered a series of defections and briefly became a quasi-coalition cabinet (a coalition with the recent defectors), then a one-party minority cabinet, and finally a minority coalition—but all of these unusual cabinets occurred in the final phase of the transition to the new non-Westminster system (Boston, Levine, McLeay, and Roberts 1996, 93–96). The only other deviations from single-party majority government happened much earlier: New Zealand had a wartime coalition cabinet from 1915 to 1919, and another coalition was in power from 1931 to 1935.

2. *Cabinet dominance.* In this respect, too, New Zealand was a perfect example of the Westminster model. Just as during most of the postwar period in the United Kingdom, the combination of the parliamentary system of government and a two-party system with cohesive parties made the cabinet predominate over the legislature. In the words of New Zealand political scientist Stephen Levine (1979, 25–26), the "rigidly disciplined two-party system has contributed to the concentration of power within the Cabinet, formed from among the Members of Parliament. . .belonging to the majority party."

3. *Two-party system.* Two large parties were in virtually complete control of the party system, and only these two formed cabinets during the six decades from 1935 to the mid-1990s: the Labour party (1935–49, 1957–60, 1972–75, and 1984–90) and the National party (1949–57, 1960–72, 1975–84, and after 1990). Party politics revolved almost exclusively around socio-economic issues—Labour represented left-of-center and the National party right-of-center political preferences. Moreover, unlike in

Britain, third parties were almost absent from the New Zealand House of Representatives. In eleven of the seventeen elections from 1946 to 1993, the two large parties divided all of the seats; in five elections, only one other party gained one or two seats; and in 1993, two small parties gained two seats each (out of ninety-nine). New Zealand's two-party system was therefore an almost pure two-party system.

4. *Majoritarian and disproportional system of elections.* The House of Representatives was elected according to the plurality method in single-member districts. The only unusual feature was that there were four special large districts, geographically overlapping the regular smaller districts, that were reserved for the Maori minority (comprising about 12 percent of the population). These four districts entailed a deviation from the majoritarianism of the Westminster model because their aim was to guarantee minority representation. From 1975 on, all Maori voters have had the right to register and vote either in the regular district or in the special Maori district in which they reside.

As in the United Kingdom, the plurality system produced severely disproportional results, especially in 1978 and 1981. In the 1978 election, the National party won a clear majority of fifty-one out of ninety-two seats even though it won neither a majority of the popular vote—its support was only 39.8 percent—nor a plurality, because Labour's popular vote was 40.4 percent; the Social Credit party's 17.1 percent of the vote yielded only one seat. In 1981, the National party won another parliamentary majority of forty-seven out of ninety-two seats and again with fewer votes than Labour, although the respective percentages were closer: 38.8 and 39.0 percent; Social Credit now won 20.7 percent of the popular vote—more than half of the votes gained by either of the two big parties—but merely two seats. Moreover, all of the parliamentary majorities from 1954 on were manufactured majorities, won with less than majorities of the popular vote. In this respect, New Zealand was, like the United Kingdom, more a pluralitarian than a majoritarian democracy.

* * *

6. *Unitary and centralized government.* The "Act to grant a Representative Constitution to the Colony of New Zealand," passed by the British parliament in 1852, created six provinces with considerable autonomous powers and functions vis-à-vis the central government, but these provinces were abolished in 1875. Today's governmental system is unitary and centralized—not as surprising, of course, for a country with a population of less than four million than for the United Kingdom with its much larger population of about sixty million people.

7. *Concentration of legislative power in a unicameral legislature.* For about a century, New Zealand had a bicameral legislature, consisting of an elected lower house and an appointed upper house, but the upper house gradually lost power. Its abolition in 1950 changed the asymmetrical bicameral system into pure unicameralism.

8. *Constitutional flexibility.* Like the United Kingdom, New Zealand lacks a single written constitutional document. Its "unwritten" constitution has consisted of a number of basic laws—like the Constitution Acts of 1852 and 1986, the Electoral Acts of 1956 and 1993, and the Bill of Rights Act of 1990—conventions, and customs.[2] Some key provisions in the basic laws are "entrenched" and can be

2. The Constitution Act of 1852 and Electoral Act of 1956 were superseded by the two later acts.

changed only by three-fourths majorities of the membership of the House of Representatives or by a majority vote in a referendum; however, this entrenchment can always be removed by regular majorities, so that, in the end, majority rule prevails. Hence, like the British parliament, the parliament of New Zealand is sovereign. Any law, including laws that "amend" the unwritten constitution, can be adopted by regular majority rule. As one of New Zealand's constitutional law experts puts it, "The central principle of the Constitution is that there are no effective legal limitations on what Parliament may enact by the ordinary legislative process" (Scott 1962, 39).

9. Absence of judicial review. Parliamentary sovereignty also means, as in Britain, that the courts do not have the right of judicial review. The House of Representatives is the sole judge of the constitutionality of its own legislation.

The form of PR that was adopted and used in the 1996 election was a system, modeled after the German system, in which sixty-five members are elected by plurality in single-member districts—including five special Maori districts—and fifty-five members by PR from party lists; a crucial provision is that this second set of fifty-five seats is allocated to the parties in a way that makes the overall result as proportional as possible. Therefore, although the New Zealand term for this system is the "mixed member proportional" (MMP) system, implying that it is a mixture of PR and something else, it is in fact clearly and fully a PR system.[3]

* * *

The first PR election instantly transformed New Zealand politics in several respects (Vowles, Aimer, Banducci, and Karp 1998). First, the election result was much more proportional than those of the previous plurality elections. The largest party, the National party, was still overrepresented, but by less than three percentage points; it won 33.8 percent of the vote and 36.7 percent of the seats. Second, the election produced a multiparty system with an unprecedented six parties gaining representation in parliament. Third, unlike in any other postwar election, no party won a majority of the seats. Fourth, an ethnic dimension was added to the party system: the New Zealand First party, led by a Maori and winning seventeen seats, including all five of the special Maori seats, became the main representative of the Maori minority (although it was not a specifically Maori party nor supported exclusively by Maori voters). The Christian Coalition almost succeeded in making the party system even more multidimensional by adding a religious issue dimension, but its vote fell just short of the required 5 percent threshold. Fifth, in contrast with the long line of previous single-party majority cabinets, a two-party coalition cabinet was formed by the National and New Zealand First parties.

Because of these significant deviations from the majoritarian model, post-1996 New Zealand is no longer a good, let alone the best, example of the "true British system." Hence, in Kurt von Mettenheim's (1997, 11) words, "the United Kingdom [now] appears to be the only country to have retained the central features of the Westminster model." It should be noted, however, that all of the post-1996 changes in New Zealand have to do with the executives-parties dimension of the majoritarian model, comprising the first five of the ten characteristics of the model, and that, especially with regard to this first di-

3. Each voter has two votes, one for a district candidate and one for a party list. To avoid excessive fragmentation, parties must win either a minimum of 5 percent of the list votes or at least one district seat to qualify for list seats.

mension, several other former British colonies continue to have predominantly Westminster-style institutions. A particularly clear and instructive example is Barbados.

* * *

References

Beer, Samuel. 1998. "The Roots of New Labour: Liberalism Rediscovered." *Economist* (February 7): 23–25.

Boston, Jonathan, Stephen Levine, Elizabeth McLeay, and Nigel S. Roberts, eds. 1996. *New Zealand Under MMP: A New Politics?* Auckland: Auckland University Press.

Busch, Andreas. 1994. "Central Bank Independence and the Westminster Model." *West European Politics* 17, no. 1 (January): 53–72.

Buxton, James, John Kampfner, and Brian Groom. 1997. "Blair Says Scots' Home Rule Vote Will Affect Rest of UK." *Financial Times* (September 13–14): 1.

Cappelletti, Mauro. 1989. *The Judicial Process in Comparative Perspective.* Oxford: Clarendon.

Coombs, David. 1977. "British Government and the European Community." In Dennis Kavanaugh and Richard Rose, eds., *New Trends in British Politics: Issues for Research,* 83–103. London: Sage.

Dicey, A. V. 1915. *Introduction to the Study of the Law of the Constitution,* 8th ed. London: Macmillan.

Hailsham, Lord. 1978. *The Dilemma of Democracy: Diagnosis and Prescription.* London: Collins.

Johnson, Nevil. 1998. "The Judicial Dimension in British Politics." *West European Politics* 21, no. 1 (January): 148–66.

Kavanagh, Dennis. 1974. "An American Science of British Politics." *Political Studies* 22, no. 3 (September): 251–70.

Levine, Stephen. 1979. *The New Zealand Political System: Politics in a Small Society.* Sydney: George Allen and Unwin.

Mahler, Gregory S. 1997. "The 'Westminster Model' Away from Westminster: Is it Always the Most Appropriate Model?" In Abdo I. Baaklini and Helen Desfosses, eds., *Designs for Democratic Stability: Studies in Viable Constitutionalism,* 35–51. Armonk, N.Y.: M. E. Sharpe.

O'Donnell, Guillermo. 1994. "Delegative Democracy." *Journal of Democracy* 5, no. 1 (January): 55–69.

Peters, B. Guy. 1997. "The Separation of Powers in Parliamentary Systems." In Kurt von Mettenheim, ed., *Presidential Institutions and Democratic Politics: Comparing Regional and National Contexts,* 67–83. Baltimore: Johns Hopkins University Press.

Rae, Douglas W. 1967. *The Political Consequences of Electoral Laws.* New Haven: Yale University Press.

Rose, Richard. 1974. "A Model Democracy?" In Richard Rose, ed., *Lessons from America: an Exploration,* 131–61. New York: Wiley.

Scott, K. J. 1962. *The New Zealand Constitution.* Oxford: Clarendon.

von Mettenheim, Kurt. 1997. "Introduction: Presidential Institutions and Democratic Politics." In Kurt von Mettenheim, ed., *Presidential Institutions and Democratic Politics: Comparing Regional and National Contexts,* 1–15. Baltimore: Johns Hopkins University Press.

Vowles, Jack, Peter Aimer, Susan Banducci, and Jeffrey Karp, eds. 1998. *Voters' Victory? New Zealand's First Election Under Proportional Representation.* Auckland: Auckland University Press.

Wilson, Graham. 1997. "British Democracy and Its Discontents." In Metin Heper, Ali Kazancigil, and Bert A. Rockman, eds., *Institutions and Democratic Statecraft,* 59–76. Boulder, Colo.: Westview.

Wilson, Woodrow. 1884. "Committee or Cabinet Government?" *Overland Monthly*, Ser. 2, 3 (January): 17–33.

3.2

THE CONSENSUS MODEL OF DEMOCRACY

Arend Lijphart

Arend Lijphart, originally from the Netherlands, pioneered the study of consensus-style democracies. His work showed that such democracies are typically found in socially divided countries like the Netherlands because such countries need to practice a consensus style of democracy to keep from aggravating existing social divisions. The work from which this reading is taken extended his earlier research to show how consensus-style democracies are institutionally different from their majoritarian counterparts.

Consensus-style democracy is prevalent in non-English speaking countries that are divided along ethnic, linguistic, religious, or regional lines. Such countries have populations composed of many groups, and democratic politics is practiced in a way that emphasizes the representation of these groups. This is done by designing electoral rules that allow more political parties, which represent a nation's social groups, to obtain legislative seats in national elections; the best examples include Belgium, the Netherlands, and Switzerland. This reading includes a discussion of such institutions as PR electoral rules with high district magnitudes, which help consensus-style democracies emphasize the value of representation. With knowledge of consensus-style and majoritarian democracies, students can observe how different institutions fit with certain societal characteristics and help to solve particular societal problems.

The majoritarian interpretation of the basic definition of democracy is that it means "government by the *majority* of the people." It argues that majorities should govern and that minorities should oppose. This view is challenged by the consensus model of democracy. As the Nobel Prize-winning economist Sir Arthur Lewis (1965, 64–65) has forcefully pointed out, majority rule and the government-versus-opposition pattern of politics that it implies may be interpreted as undemocratic because they are principles of exclusion. Lewis states that the primary meaning of democracy is that "all who are affected by a decision should have the chance to participate in making that decision either directly or through chosen representatives." Its secondary meaning is that "the will of the majority shall prevail." If this means that winning parties may make all the governmental decisions and that the losers may criticize but not govern, Lewis argues, the two meanings are incompatible: "to exclude the losing groups from participation in decision-making clearly violates the primary meaning of democracy."

Arend Lijphart, "The Consensus Model of Democracy," in *Patterns of Democracy* (New Haven, Conn.: Yale University Press, 1999), chapter 3, 31–47.

Majoritarians can legitimately respond that, under two conditions, the incompatibility noted by Lewis can be resolved. First, the exclusion of the minority is mitigated if majorities and minorities alternate in government—that is, if today's minority can become the majority in the next election instead of being condemned to permanent opposition. This is how the British, New Zealand, and Barbadian two-party systems have worked. In Barbados, alternation has operated perfectly since independence in 1966: neither of the two main parties has won more than two elections in a row. In Britain and New Zealand, however, there have been long periods in which one of the two main parties was kept out of power: the British Labour party during the thirteen years from 1951 to 1964 and the eighteen years from 1979 to 1997, the New Zealand National party for fourteen years from 1935 to 1949, and New Zealand Labour for twelve years from 1960 to 1972.

Even during these extended periods of exclusion from power, one can plausibly argue that democracy and majority rule were not in conflict because of the presence of a second condition: the fact that all three countries are relatively homogeneous societies and that their major parties have usually not been very far apart in their policy outlooks because they have tended to stay close to the political center. One party's exclusion from power may be undemocratic in terms of the "government *by* the people" criterion, but if its voters' interests and preferences are reasonably well served by the other party's policies in government, the system approximates the "government *for* the people" definition of democracy.

In less homogeneous societies neither condition applies. The policies advocated by the principal parties tend to diverge to a greater extent, and the voters' loyalties are frequently more rigid, reducing the chances that the main parties will alternate in exercising governmental power. Especially in *plural societies*—societies that are sharply divided along religious, ideological, linguistic, cultural, ethnic, or racial lines into virtually separate subsocieties with their own political parties, interest groups, and media of communication—the flexibility necessary for majoritarian democracy is likely to be absent. Under these conditions, majority rule is not only undemocratic but also dangerous, because minorities that are continually denied access to power will feel excluded and discriminated against and may lose their allegiance to the regime. For instance, in the plural society of Northern Ireland, divided into a Protestant majority and a Catholic minority, majority rule meant that the Unionist party representing the Protestant majority won all the elections and formed all of the governments between 1921 and 1972. Massive Catholic protests in the late 1960s developed into a Protestant-Catholic civil war that could be kept under control only by British military intervention and the imposition of direct rule from London.

In the most deeply divided societies, like Northern Ireland, majority rule spells majority dictatorship and civil strife rather than democracy. What such societies need is a democratic regime that emphasizes consensus instead of opposition, that includes rather than excludes, and that tries to maximize the size of the ruling majority instead of being satisfied with a bare majority: consensus democracy. Despite their own majoritarian inclinations, successive British cabinets have recognized this need: they have insisted on PR in all elections in Northern Ireland (except those to the House of Commons) and, as a precondition for returning political autonomy to Northern Ireland, on broad Protestant-Catholic power-sharing coalitions. PR and power-sharing are also key elements in the agreement on Northern Ireland reached in 1998. Similarly, Lewis (1965, 51–55, 65–84) strongly recommends PR, inclusive coalitions, and federalism for the plural societies of West Africa. The consensus model is obviously also appropriate for less divided but still heterogeneous countries, and it is a reasonable and workable alternative to the Westminster model even in fairly homogeneous countries.

The examples I use to illustrate the consensus model are Switzerland, Belgium, and the European Union—all multiethnic entities. Switzerland is the best example: with one exception it approximates the pure model perfectly. Belgium also provides a good example, especially after it formally became a federal state in 1993; I therefore pay particular attention to the pattern of Belgian politics in the most recent period. The European Union (EU) is a supranational organization—more than just an international organization—but it is not, or not yet, a sovereign state. Because of the EU's intermediate status, analysts of the European Union disagree on whether to study it as an international organization or an incipient federal state, but the latter approach is increasingly common (Hix 1994). This is also my approach: if the EU is regarded as a federal state, its institutions are remarkably close to the consensus model of democracy. I discuss the Swiss and Belgian prototypes first and in tandem with each other and then turn to the EU example.

The Consensus Model in Switzerland and Belgium

The consensus model of democracy may be described in terms of ten elements that stand in sharp contrast to each of the ten majoritarian characteristics of the Westminster model. Instead of concentrating power in the hands of the majority, the consensus model tries to share, disperse, and restrain power in a variety of ways.

1. *Executive power-sharing in broad coalition cabinets.* In contrast to the Westminster model's tendency to concentrate executive power in one-party and bare-majority cabinets, the consensus principle is to let all or most of the important parties share executive power in a broad coalition. The Swiss seven-member national executive, the Federal Council, offers an excellent example of such a broad coalition: the three large parties—Christian Democrats, Social Democrats, and Radical Democrats—each of which has held about one-fourth of the seats in the lower house of the legislature during the post-World War II era, and the Swiss People's party, with about one-eighth of the seats, share the seven executive positions proportionately according to the so-called magic formula of 2:2:2:1, established in 1959. An additional criterion is that the linguistic groups be represented in rough proportion to their sizes: four or five German-speakers, one or two French-speakers, and frequently an Italian-speaker. Both criteria are informal rules but are strictly obeyed.

The Belgian constitution offers an example of a formal requirement that the executive include representatives of the large linguistic groups. For many years, it had already been the custom to form cabinets with approximately equal numbers of ministers representing the Dutch-speaking majority and the French-speaking minority. This became a formal rule in 1970, and the new federal constitution again stipulates that "with the possible exception of the Prime Minister, the Council of Ministers [cabinet] includes as many French-speaking members as Dutch-speaking members" (Alen and Ergec 1994). Such a rule does not apply to the partisan composition of the cabinet, but there have only been about four years of one-party rule in the postwar era, and since 1980 all cabinets have been coalitions of between four and six parties.

2. *Executive-legislative balance of power.* The Swiss political system is neither parliamentary nor presidential. The relationship between the executive Federal Council and the legislature is explained by Swiss political scientist Jürg Steiner (1974, 43) as follows: "The members of the council are elected individually for a fixed term of four years, and, according to the Constitution, the legislature cannot stage a vote of no confidence during that period. If a government proposal is defeated by Parliament, it is not necessary for either the member sponsoring this proposal or the Federal Council as a body to resign."

This formal separation of powers has made both the executive and the legislature more independent, and their relationship is much more balanced than cabinet-parliament relationships in the British, New Zealand, and Barbadian cases in which the cabinet is clearly dominant. The Swiss Federal Council is powerful but not supreme.

Belgium has a parliamentary form of government with a cabinet dependent on the confidence of the legislature, as in the three prototypes of the Westminster model. However, Belgian cabinets, largely because they are often broad and uncohesive coalitions, are not at all as dominant as their Westminster counterparts, and they tend to have a genuine give-and-take relationship with parliament. The fact that Belgian cabinets are often short-lived attests to their relatively weak position: from 1980 to 1995, for instance, there were six cabinets consisting of different multiparty coalitions—with an average cabinet life of only about two and a half years.

3. *Multiparty system.* Both Switzerland and Belgium have multiparty systems without any party that comes close to majority status. In the 1995 elections to the Swiss National Council, fifteen parties won seats, but the bulk of these seats—162 out of 200—were captured by the four major parties represented on the Federal Council. Switzerland may therefore be said to have a four-party system.

Until the late 1960s, Belgium was characterized by a three-party system consisting of two large parties—Christian Democrats and Socialists—and the medium-sized Liberals. Since then, however, these major parties have split along linguistic lines and several new linguistic parties have attained prominence, creating an extreme multiparty system: about a dozen parties have usually been able to win seats in the Chamber of Representatives, and nine of these have been important enough to be included in one or more cabinets.

The emergence of multiparty systems in Switzerland and Belgium can be explained in terms of two factors. The first is that the two countries are plural societies, divided along several lines of cleavage. This multiplicity of cleavages is reflected in the multidimensional character of their party systems. In Switzerland, the religious cleavage divides the Christian Democrats, mainly supported by practicing Catholics, from the Social Democrats and Radicals, who draw most of their support from Catholics who rarely or never attend church and from Protestants. The socioeconomic cleavage further divides the Social Democrats, backed mainly by the working class, from the Radical Democrats, who have more middle-class support. The Swiss People's party is especially strong among Protestant farmers. The third source of cleavage, language, does not cause much further division in the Swiss party system, although the Swiss People's party's support is mainly in German-speaking Switzerland, and the three large parties are relatively loose alliances of cantonal parties *within* which the linguistic cleavage is a significant differentiator (McRae 1983, 111–14).

Similarly, the religious cleavage in Catholic Belgium divides the Christian Social parties, representing the more faithful Catholics, from the Socialists and Liberals, representing rarely practicing or non-practicing Catholics. The Socialists and Liberals are divided from each other by class differences. In contrast with Switzerland, the linguistic cleavage in Belgium has caused further splits both by dividing the above three groupings, which used to be Belgium's three dominant parties, into separate and smaller Dutch-speaking and French-speaking parties and by creating several additional small linguistic parties (McRae 1986, 130–48)

4. *Proportional representation.* The second explanation for the emergence of multiparty systems in Switzerland and Belgium is that their proportional electoral systems have not inhibited the translation of societal cleavages into party-system cleavages. In contrast with the plurality method, which tends to

overrepresent large parties and to underrepresent small parties, the basic aim of proportional representation (PR) is to divide the parliamentary seats among the parties in proportion to the votes they receive. The lower houses of both legislatures are elected by PR.

* * *

6. *Federal and decentralized government.* Switzerland is a federal state in which power is divided between the central government and the governments of twenty cantons and six so-called half-cantons, produced by splits in three formerly united cantons. The half-cantons have only one instead of two representatives in the Swiss federal chamber, the Council of States, and they carry only half the weight of the regular cantons in the voting on constitutional amendments; in most other respects, however, their status is equal to that of the full cantons. Switzerland is also one of the world's most decentralized states.

Belgium was a unitary and centralized state for a long time, but from 1970 on it gradually moved in the direction of both decentralization and federalism; in 1993, it formally became a federal state. The form of federalism adopted by Belgium is a "unique federalism" (Fitzmaurice 1996) and one of "Byzantine complexity" (McRae 1997, 289), because it consists of three geographically defined regions—Flanders, Wallonia, and the bilingual capital of Brussels—and three nongeographically defined cultural communities—the large Flemish and French communities and the much smaller German-speaking community. The main reason for the construction of this two-layer system was that the bilingual area of Brussels has a large majority of French-speakers, but that it is surrounded by Dutch-speaking Flanders. There is a considerable overlap between regions and communities, but they do not match exactly. Each has its own legislature and executive, except that in Flanders the government of the Flemish community also serves as the government of the Flemish region.

7. *Strong bicameralism.* The principal justification for instituting a bicameral instead of a unicameral legislature is to give special representation to minorities, including the smaller states in federal systems, in a second chamber or upper house. Two conditions have to be fulfilled if this minority representation is to be meaningful: the upper house has to be elected on a different basis than the lower house, and it must have real power—ideally as much power as the lower house. Both of these conditions are met in the Swiss system: the National Council is the lower house and represents the Swiss people, and the Council of States is the upper or federal chamber representing the cantons, with each canton having two representatives and each half-canton one representative. Hence the small cantons are much more strongly represented in the Council of States than in the National Council. Moreover, as Wolf Linder (1994, 47) writes, the "absolute equality" of the two chambers is a "sacrosanct rule" in Switzerland

The two Belgian chambers of parliament—the Chamber of Representatives and the Senate—had virtually equal powers in prefederal Belgium, but they were both proportionally constituted and hence very similar in composition. The new Senate, elected for the first time in 1995, especially represents the two cultural-linguistic groups, but it is still largely proportionally constituted and not designed to provide overrepresentation for the French-speaking and German-speaking minorities.[1] Moreover, its pow-

1. Most senators—forty out of seventy-one—are directly elected from two multimember districts that are partly defined in nongeographical terms—one comprising Flanders and Dutch-speakers in Brussels and the other Wallonia and French-speaking Bruxellois. The remaining thirty-one senators are indirectly elected or coopted in different ways. The overall linguistic composition is: forty-one Dutch-speakers, twenty-nine French-speakers, and one German-speaker. A further curious provision is that any adult children of the king are "senators by right."

ers were reduced in comparison with the old Senate; for instance, it no longer has budgetary authority (Senelle 1996, 283). Hence the new federal legislature of Belgium exemplifies a relatively weak rather than strong bicameralism.

8. *Constitutional rigidity*. Both Belgium and Switzerland have a written constitution—a single document containing the basic rules of governance—that can be changed only by special majorities. Amendments to the Swiss constitution require the approval in a referendum of not only a nationwide majority of the voters but also majorities in a majority of the cantons. The half-cantons are given half weight in the canton-by-canton calculation; this means that, for instance, a constitutional amendment can be adopted by 13.5 cantons in favor and 12.5 against. The requirement of majority cantonal approval means that the populations of the smaller cantons and half-cantons, with less than 20 percent of the total Swiss population, can veto constitutional changes.

In Belgium, there are two types of supermajorities. All constitutional amendments require the approval of two-thirds majorities in both houses of the legislature. Moreover, laws pertaining to the organization and powers of the communities and regions have a semiconstitutional status and are even harder to adopt and to amend: in addition to the two-thirds majorities in both houses, they require the approval of majorities within the Dutch-speaking group as well as within the French-speaking group in each of the houses. This rule gives the French-speakers an effective minority veto.

9. *Judicial review*. Switzerland deviates in one respect from the pure consensus model: its supreme court, the Federal Tribunal, does not have the right of judicial review. A popular initiative that tried to introduce it was decisively rejected in a 1939 referendum (Codding 1961, 112).[2]

There was no judicial review in Belgium either until 1984, when the new Court of Arbitration was inaugurated. The court's original main responsibility was the interpretation of the constitutional provisions concerning the separation of powers between the central, community, and regional governments. Its authority was greatly expanded by the constitutional revision of 1988, and the Court of Arbitration can now be regarded as a genuine constitutional court (Alen and Ergec 1994, 20–22; Verougstraete 1992, 95).

References

Alen, André, and Rusen Ergec. 1994. *Federal Belgium After the Fourth State Reform of 1993*. Brussels: Ministry of Foreign Affairs.

Codding, George Arthur, Jr. 1961. *The Federal Government of Switzerland*. Boston: Houghton Mifflin.

Fitzmaurice, John. 1996. *The Politics of Belgium: A Unique Federalism*. Boulder, Colo: Westview.

Hix, Simon. 1994. "The Study of the European Community." *West European Politics* 17, no. 1 (January): 1–30.

Lewis, W. Arthur. 1965. *Politics in West Africa*. London: George Allen and Unwin.

Linder, Wolf. 1994. *Swiss Democracy: Possible Solutions to Conflict in Multicultural Societies*. New York: St. Martin's.

McRae, Kenneth D. 1983. *Conflict and Compromise in Multilingual Societies: Switzerland*. Waterloo, Ont.: Wilfrid Laurier University Press.

———. 1986. *Conflict and Compromise in Multilingual Societies: Belgium*. Waterloo, Ont.: Wilfrid Laurier University Press.

2. National laws can, however, be challenged in a different manner: if, within ninety days of the passage of a law, a minimum of fifty thousand citizens demand a referendum on it, a majority of Swiss voters can reject it.

———. 1997. "Contrasting Styles of Democratic Decision-Making: Adversarial versus Consensual Politics." *International Political Science Review* 18, no. 3 (July): 279–95.

Senelle, Robert. 1996. "The Reform of the Belgian State." In Joachim Jens Hesse and Vincent Wright, eds., *Federalizing Europe? The Costs, Benefits, and Preconditions of Federal Political Systems,* 266–324. Oxford: Oxford University Press.

Steiner, Jürg. 1974. *Amicable Agreement Versus Majority Rule: Conflict Resolution in Switzerland.* Chapel Hill: University of North Carolina Press.

Verougstraete, Ivan. 1992. "Judicial Politics in Belgium." *West European Politics* 15, no. 3 (July): 93–108.

Chapter 4

IDEOLOGICAL CHANGE OR IDEOLOGICAL DECLINE?

The transformation of the field of comparative politics from a largely descriptive enterprise to an explanatory one in the early 1950s involved an expanded focus on variables that had previously been dismissed as not relevant to the field. Once the field's purpose of scholarship became the explanation of political behaviors, processes, and events, scholars had to consider the context or setting in which these occurred, because a given constitutional format will operate one way in one society, while the same constitution will produce different outcomes in another.

For this reason, modern comparative analysis has been identified with a focus on cultural and social factors previously dismissed as belonging to such fields as sociology or psychology almost to the neglect of the political and structural factors that once defined the field. With the advent of modern comparative analysis, some of the most prominent bodies of research in the field are concerned with the impact of culture and other contextual factors on political outcomes. In particular, comparativists have been concerned with the nature, causes, and consequences of cultural change.

The central question of the readings in this chapter is whether there is a declining salience of the principles that structured political conflict for much of modern history through the immediate post–World War II period and, if so, whether the world is witnessing a decline in the salience of ideology itself (relatively closed, logically consistent thought systems) or if the principles that guide our conduct are merely changing. In this modern world, which can be characterized by the progressive growth of education, literacy, and complex technology, material well-being increasingly can be taken for granted, and the ideologies defining the classic struggle for material well-being are declining in salience. Meanwhile, the growth of science in the modern world offers answers to questions formerly left to the realm of religion; hence, modernization is linked to the declining salience of religious ideologies and the growth of secularism.

Ronald Inglehart, in some of the most influential and oft-cited research in the last three decades, has been at the cutting edge of this research on cultural change. While accepting and, indeed, corroborating the position that the relevance of the classic ideologies has declined with the advent of modernity, Inglehart argues that, as a result of the postwar prosperity, class-based issues of material well-being have declined in importance and are being supplanted with lifestyle issues such as feminism and environmentalism. This cultural change is not a change in the orientation of individuals over the course of their lifetimes but rather a generational change in which these post-materialist values are derived from the absence of scarcity during the new generation's formative years.

The significance of this "silent revolution" in values among Western publics is that the cleavage system of these societies no longer reflects the political divisions in their party systems. The major parties have traditionally been defined along the lines of class conflict and religiosity (as in the case of Christian democratic parties); both of these factors are allegedly being displaced by Inglehart's post-materialist orientation. Faced with a declining vote share in their respective countries, many of these parties are being driven to redefine themselves. For example, after the British Labour Party had been on the opposition benches for nearly a decade and a half in the early 1990s, it attempted to redefine itself as a party with middle-class appeal by renouncing the party's historic commitment to the nationalization of industry and inserting the word "new" in front of every public use of the party's name.

The case for the finding that value change has occurred in Western societies is strong and widely accepted. The controversy in this literature is in regard to the nature of the post-materialist world. Scott Flanagan, in an article excerpted in this chapter, claims that Inglehart virtually equates post-materialism with the new left (dealing with social and lifestyle issues rather than those that are class-based), and clearly, the examples offered by Inglehart come from that orientation. Flanagan and others point to the emergence of a new right. In this regard, he offers a distinct dimension of values, an authoritarian-to-libertarian dimension that exists alongside the materialist-to-post-materialist dimension offered by Inglehart. Flanagan also challenges the validity of the indicators Inglehart uses to measure cultural change, criticizing the simple four-item instrument on which Inglehart's research is based.

Francis Fukuyama, a well-known U.S. academic, has also theorized on the cultural shift spurred by modernization. His oft-cited essay "The End of History?" exemplifies the tradition that the conflicts that had been such a familiar part of the political landscape are losing their salience as the conflicts that drove them have largely been resolved to the satisfaction of most people.[1] Therefore, he argues, the world will soon enjoy a conflict-free liberal universe as the course of historical evolution will end with the universal achievement of liberal democracy. Unlike Ingelhart, Fukuyama makes no attempt to frame his broad theory of cultural change into a falsifiable proposition. Rather, his claims are what comparativists call impressionistic: they entail no precise predictions of what one should see in given circumstances.

There are, of course, differing ways of conceptualizing the dimensions of political conflict and development. The thread in the literature on which scholars agree is that some kind of cultural change is occurring in the postwar era. This chapter reflects the enduring debate on the nature and content of that change.

Note

1. This tradition had first and most prominently been associated with Seymour Lipset. See his "The End of Ideology," postscript to *Political Man* (New York: Doubleday, 1960).

4.1

THE END OF HISTORY?

Francis Fukuyama

Political scientist Seymour Lipset hypothesized in the 1960s that the issues that generated the great principles and ideologies of political life had essentially been resolved—issues such as the class struggle over the distribution of material well-being or the role of religious institutions in civil life. Given this, these ideologies were no longer salient. In his 1989 article "The End of History?" Francis Fukuyama, writing in the same tradition, argued that after centuries of evolving through the great ideas of political and economic life, the world had reached a consensus on liberal, capitalist democracy as the desirable millennium, thereby ending the incentive for further historical evolution. Fukuyama was writing in the tradition of "historicism"—the idea that history, driven by such impersonal forces as the conflict between the major ideas of capitalism and socialism—is moving inexorably in a linear path toward a golden age; a tradition of thought characterized by Karl Marx and Georg Hegel. Fukuyama, a professor at George Mason University, is known for postulating grand theories while remaining untroubled by considerations of measurement and testability. As such, he is more accessible and, consequently, more popular with the general public than many more rigorous scholars. Writing just before the collapse of the Soviet Union, he presciently argued that the Communist system could not endure, although he specifically did not expect it to implode so soon. Students should ask themselves if Fukuyama is persuasive in finding that even Communist China has been influenced by liberal ideas. Can the country's leaders accept the universal appeal of liberality in light of the rise of militant Islamism and utter rejection of the liberal values of the West? Fukuyama finds it "hard to believe that [Islamic fundamentalism] will take on any universal significance."

In watching the flow of events over the past decade or so, it is hard to avoid the feeling that something very fundamental has happened in world history. The past year has seen a flood of articles commemorating the end of the Cold War, and the fact that "peace" seems to be breaking out in many regions of the world. Most of these analyses lack any larger conceptual framework for distinguishing between what is essential and what is contingent or accidental in world history, and are predictably superficial. If Mr. Gorbachev were ousted from the Kremlin or a new Ayatollah proclaimed the millennium from a desolate Middle Eastern capital, these same commentators would scramble to announce the rebirth of a new era of conflict.

Francis Fukuyama, "The End of History?" *The National Interest* 16 (Summer 1989): 3–18.

And yet, all of these people sense dimly that there is some larger process at work, a process that gives coherence and order to the daily headlines. The twentieth century saw the developed world descend into a paroxysm of ideological violence, as liberalism contended first with the remnants of absolutism, then bolshevism and fascism, and finally an updated Marxism that threatened to lead to the ultimate apocalypse of nuclear war. But the century that began full of self-confidence in the ultimate triumph of Western liberal democracy seems at its close to be returning full circle to where it started: not to an "end of ideology" or a convergence between capitalism and socialism, as earlier predicted, but to an unabashed victory of economic and political liberalism.

The triumph of the West, of the Western *idea*, is evident first of all in the total exhaustion of viable systematic alternatives to Western liberalism. In the past decade, there have been unmistakable changes in the intellectual climate of the world's two largest communist countries, and the beginnings of significant reform movements in both. But this phenomenon extends beyond high politics and it can be seen also in the ineluctable spread of consumerist Western culture in such diverse contexts as the peasants' markets and color television sets now omnipresent throughout China, the cooperative restaurants and clothing stores opened in the past year in Moscow, the Beethoven piped into Japanese department stores, and the rock music enjoyed alike in Prague, Rangoon, and Tehran.

What we may be witnessing is not just the end of the Cold War, or the passing of a particular period of postwar history, but the end of history as such: that is, the end point of mankind's ideological evolution and the universalization of Western liberal democracy as the final form of human government. This is not to say that there will no longer be events to fill the pages of *Foreign Affairs'* yearly summaries of international relations, for the victory of liberalism has occurred primarily in the realm of ideas or consciousness and is as yet incomplete in the real or material world. But there are powerful reasons for believing that it is the ideal that will govern the material world *in the long run*. To understand how this is so, we must first consider some theoretical issues concerning the nature of historical change.

I

The notion of the end of history is not an original one. Its best known propagator was Karl Marx, who believed that the direction of historical development was a purposeful one determined by the interplay of material forces, and would come to an end only with the achievement of a communist utopia that would finally resolve all prior contradictions. But the concept of history as a dialectical process with a beginning, a middle, and an end was borrowed by Marx from his great German predecessor, Georg Wilhelm Friedrich Hegel.

For better or worse, much of Hegel's historicism has become part of our contemporary intellectual baggage. The notion that mankind has progressed through a series of primitive stages of consciousness on his path to the present, and that these stages corresponded to concrete forms of social organization, such as tribal, slave-owning, theocratic, and finally democratic-egalitarian societies, has become inseparable from the modern understanding of man. Hegel was the first philosopher to speak the language of modern social science, insofar as man for him was the product of his concrete historical and social environment and not, as earlier natural right theorists would have it, a collection of more or less fixed "natural" attributes. The mastery and transformation of man's natural environment through the application of science and technology was originally not a Marxist concept, but a Hegelian one. Unlike later historicists whose historical relativism degenerated into relativism tout court, however, Hegel believed that history culminated in an absolute moment—a moment in which a final, rational form of society and state became victorious.

. . .Among. . . modern French interpreters of Hegel, the greatest was certainly Alexandre Kojève, a brilliant Russian émigré who taught a highly influential series of seminars in Paris in the 1930s at the *Ecole Practique des Hautes Etudes.*[1]

* * *

The state that emerges at the end of history is liberal insofar as it recognizes and protects through a system of law man's universal right to freedom, and democratic insofar as it exists only with the consent of the governed. For Kojève, this so-called "universal homogenous state" found real-life embodiment in the countries of postwar Western Europe—precisely those flabby, prosperous, self-satisfied, inward-looking, weak-willed states whose grandest project was nothing more heroic than the creation of the Common Market.[2] But this was only to be expected. For human history and the conflict that characterized it was based on the existence of "contradictions": primitive man's quest for mutual recognition, the dialectic of the master and slave, the transformation and mastery of nature, the struggle for the universal recognition of rights, and the dichotomy between proletarian and capitalist. But in the universal homogenous state, all prior contradictions are resolved and all human needs are satisfied. There is no struggle or conflict over "large" issues, and consequently no need for generals or statesmen; what remains is primarily economic activity. And indeed, Kojève's life was consistent with his teaching. Believing that there was no more work for philosophers as well, since Hegel (correctly understood) had already achieved absolute knowledge, Kojève left teaching after the war and spent the remainder of his life working as a bureaucrat in the European Economic Community, until his death in 1968.

To his contemporaries at mid-century, Kojève's proclamation of the end of history must have seemed like the typical eccentric solipsism of a French intellectual, coming as it did on the heels of World War II and at the very height of the Cold War. To comprehend how Kojève could have been so audacious as to assert that history has ended, we must first of all understand the meaning of Hegelian idealism.

II

For Hegel, the contradictions that drive history exist first of all in the realm of human consciousness, i.e. on the level of ideas[3]—not the trivial election year proposals of American politicians, but ideas in the sense of large unifying world views that might best be understood under the rubric of ideology. Ideology in this sense is not restricted to the secular and explicit political doctrines we usually associate with the term, but can include religion, culture, and the complex of moral values underlying any society as well.

---

1. Kojève's best known work is his *Introduction à la lecture de Hegel* (Paris: Editions Gallimard, 1947), which is a transcript of the Ecole Practique lectures from the 1930's. This book is available in English entitled *Introduction to the Reading of Hegel* arranged by Raymond Queneau, edited by Allan Bloom, and translated by James Nichols (New York: Basic Books, 1969).
2. Kojève alternatively identified the end of history with the postwar "American way of life," toward which he thought the Soviet Union was moving as well.
3. This notion was expressed in the famous aphorism from the preface to the *Philosophy of History* to the effect that "everything that is rational is real, and everything that is real is rational."

Hegel's view of the relationship between the ideal and the real or material worlds was an extremely complicated one, beginning with the fact that for him the distinction between the two was only apparent.[4] He did not believe that the real world conformed or could be made to conform to ideological preconceptions of philosophy professors in any simpleminded way, or that the "material" world could not impinge on the ideal. Indeed, Hegel the professor was temporarily thrown out of work as a result of a very material event, the Battle of Jena. But while Hegel's writing and thinking could be stopped by a bullet from the material world, the hand on the trigger of the gun was motivated in turn by the ideas of liberty and equality that had driven the French Revolution.

For Hegel, all human behavior in the material world, and hence all human history, is rooted in a prior state of consciousness—an idea similar to the one expressed by John Maynard Keynes when he said that the views of men of affairs were usually derived from defunct economists and academic scribblers of earlier generations. This consciousness may not be explicit and self-aware, as are modern political doctrines, but may rather take the form of religion or simple cultural or moral habits. And yet this realm of consciousness in the long run necessarily becomes manifest in the material world, indeed creates the material world in its own image. Consciousness is cause and not effect, and can develop autonomously from the material world; hence the real subtext underlying the apparent jumble of current events is the history of ideology.

Hegel's idealism has fared poorly at the hands of later thinkers. Marx reversed the priority of the real and the ideal completely, relegating the entire realm of consciousness—religion, art, culture, philosophy itself—to a "superstructure" that was determined entirely by the prevailing material mode of production. Yet another unfortunate legacy of Marxism is our tendency to retreat into materialist or utilitarian explanations of political or historical phenomena, and our disinclination to believe in the autonomous power of ideas. A recent example of this is Paul Kennedy's hugely successful *The Rise and Fall of the Great Powers*, which ascribes the decline of great powers to simple economic overextension. Obviously, this is true on some level: an empire whose economy is barely above the level of subsistence cannot bankrupt its treasury indefinitely. But whether a highly productive modern industrial society chooses to spend 3 or 7 percent of its GNP on defense rather than consumption is entirely a matter of that society's political priorities, which are in turn determined in the realm of consciousness.

The materialist bias of modern thought is characteristic not only of people on the Left who may be sympathetic to Marxism, but of many passionate anti-Marxists as well. Indeed, there is on the Right what one might label the *Wall Street Journal* school of deterministic materialism that discounts the importance of ideology and culture and sees man as essentially a rational, profit-maximizing individual. It is precisely this kind of individual and his pursuit of material incentives that is posited as the basis for economic life as such in economic textbooks.[5] One small example will illustrate the problematic character of such materialist views.

Max Weber begins his famous book, *The Protestant Ethic and the Spirit of Capitalism*, by noting the different economic performance of Protestant and Catholic communities throughout Europe and Amer-

4. Indeed, for Hegel the very dichotomy between the ideal and material worlds was itself only an apparent one that was ultimately overcome by the self-conscious subject; in his system, the material world is itself only an aspect of mind.
5. In fact, modern economists, recognizing that man does not always behave as a *profit*-maximizer, posit a "utility" function, utility being either income or some other good that can be maximized: leisure, sexual satisfaction, or the pleasure of philosophizing. That profit must be replaced with a value like utility indicates the cogency of the idealist perspective.

ica, summed up in the proverb that Protestants eat well while Catholics sleep well. Weber notes that according to any economic theory that posited man as a rational profit-maximizer, raising the piece-work rate should increase labor productivity. But in fact, in many traditional peasant communities, raising the piece-work rate actually had the opposite effect of *lowering* labor productivity: at the higher rate, a peasant accustomed to earning two and one-half marks per day found he could earn the same amount by working less, and did so because he valued leisure more than income. The choices of leisure over income, or of the militaristic life of the Spartan hoplite over the wealth of the Athenian trader, or even the ascetic life of the early capitalist entrepreneur over that of a traditional leisured aristocrat, cannot possibly be explained by the impersonal working of material forces, but come preeminently out of the sphere of consciousness—what we have labeled here broadly as ideology. And indeed, a central theme of Weber's work was to prove that contrary to Marx, the material mode of production, far from being the "base," was itself a "superstructure" with roots in religion and culture, and that to understand the emergence of modern capitalism and the profit motive one had to study their antecedents in the realm of the spirit.

As we look around the contemporary world, the poverty of materialist theories of economic development is all too apparent. The *Wall Street Journal* school of deterministic materialism habitually points to the stunning economic success of Asia in the past few decades as evidence of the viability of free market economics, with the implication that all societies would see similar development were they simply to allow their populations to pursue their material self-interest freely. Surely free markets and stable political systems are a necessary precondition to capitalist economic growth. But just as surely the cultural heritage of those Far Eastern societies, the ethic of work and saving and family, a religious heritage that does not, like Islam, place restrictions on certain forms of economic behavior, and other deeply ingrained moral qualities, are equally important in explaining their economic performance.[6] And yet the intellectual weight of materialism is such that not a single respectable contemporary theory of economic development addresses consciousness and culture seriously as the matrix within which economic behavior is formed.

Failure to understand that the roots of economic behavior lie in the realm of consciousness and culture leads to the common mistake of attributing material causes to phenomena that are essentially ideal in nature. For example, it is commonplace in the West to interpret the reform movements first in China and most recently in the Soviet Union as the victory of the material over the ideal—that is, a recognition that ideological incentives could not replace material ones in stimulating a highly productive modern economy, and that if one wanted to prosper one had to appeal to baser forms of self-interest. But the deep defects of socialist economies were evident thirty or forty years ago to anyone who chose to look. Why was it that these countries moved away from central planning only in the 1980s? The answer must be found in the consciousness of the elites and leaders ruling them, who decided to opt for the "Protestant" life of wealth and risk over the "Catholic" path of poverty and security.[7] That change

6. One need look no further than the recent performance of Vietnamese immigrants in the U.S. school system when compared to their black o[r] Hispanic classmates to realize that culture and consciousness are absolutely crucial to explain not only economic behavior but virtually every other important aspect of life as well.
7. I understand that a full explanation of the origins of the reform movements in China and Russia is a good deal more complicated than this simple formula would suggest. The Soviet reform, for example, was motivated in good measure by Moscow's sense of insecurity in the technological-military realm. Nonetheless, neither country [o]n the eve of its reforms was in such a state of material crisis that one could have predicted the surprising reform paths ultimately taken.

was in no way made inevitable by the material conditions in which either country found itself on the eve of the reform, but instead came about as the result of the victory of one idea over another.[8]

For Kojève, as for all good Hegelians, understanding the underlying processes of history requires understanding developments in the realm of consciousness or ideas, since consciousness will ultimately remake the material world in its own image. To say that history ended in 1806 meant that mankind's ideological evolution ended in the ideals of the French or American Revolutions: while particular regimes in the real world might not implement these ideals fully, their theoretical truth is absolute and could not be improved upon. Hence it did not matter to Kojève that the consciousness of the postwar generation of Europeans had not been universalized throughout the world; if ideological development had in fact ended, the homogenous state would eventually become victorious throughout the material world.

* * *

But while man's very perception of the material world is shaped by his historical consciousness of it, the material world can clearly affect in return the viability of a particular state of consciousness. In particular, the spectacular abundance of advanced liberal economies and the infinitely diverse consumer culture made possible by them seem to both foster and preserve liberalism in the political sphere. I want to avoid the materialist determinism that says that liberal economics inevitably produces liberal politics, because I believe that both economics and politics presuppose an autonomous prior state of consciousness that makes them possible. But that state of consciousness that permits the growth of liberalism seems to stabilize in the way one would expect at the end of history if it is underwritten by the abundance of a modern free market economy. We might summarize the content of the universal homogenous state as liberal democracy in the political sphere combined with easy access to VCRs and stereos in the economic.

III

Have we in fact reached the end of history? Are there, in other words, any fundamental "contradictions" in human life that cannot be resolved in the context of modern liberalism, that would be resolvable by an alternative political-economic structure? If we accept the idealist premises laid out above, we must seek an answer to this question in the realm of ideology and consciousness. Our task is not to answer exhaustively the challenges to liberalism promoted by every crackpot messiah around the world, but only those that are embodied in important social or political forces and movements, and which are therefore part of world history. For our purposes, it matters very little what strange thoughts occur to people in Albania or Burkina Faso, for we are interested in what one could in some sense call the common ideological heritage of mankind.

In the past century, there have been two major challenges to liberalism, those of fascism and of communism. The former[9] saw the political weakness, materialism, anomie, and lack of community of the

8. It is still not clear whether the Soviet people are as "Protestant" as Gorbachev and will follow him down that path.
9. I am not using the term "fascism" here in its most precise sense, fully aware of the frequent misuse of this term to denounce anyone to the right of the user. "Fascism" here denotes [any] organized ultra nationalist movement with universalistic pretensions—not universalistic with regard to its nationalism, of course, since the latter is exclusive by definition, but with regard to the movement's belief in its right to rule other people. Hence Imperial Japan would qualify

West as fundamental contradictions in liberal societies that could only be resolved by a strong state that forged a new "people" on the basis of national exclusiveness. Fascism was destroyed as a living ideology by World War II. This was a defeat, of course, on a very material level, but it amounted to a defeat of the idea as well. What destroyed fascism as an idea was not universal moral revulsion against it, since plenty of people were willing to endorse the idea as long as it seemed the wave of the future, but its lack of success. After the war, it seemed to most people that German fascism as well as its other European and Asian variants were bound to self-destruct. There was no material reason why new fascist movements could not have sprung up again after the war in other locales, but for the fact that expansionist ultranationalism, with its promise of unending conflict leading to disastrous military defeat, had completely lost its appeal. The ruins of the Reich chancellery as well as the atomic bombs dropped on Hiroshima and Nagasaki killed this ideology on the level of consciousness as well as materially, and all of the pro-fascist movements spawned by the German and Japanese examples like the Peronist movement in Argentina or Subhas Chandra Bose's Indian National Army withered after the war.

The ideological challenge mounted by the other great alternative to liberalism, communism, was far more serious. Marx, speaking Hegel's language, asserted that liberal society contained a fundamental contradiction that could not be resolved within its context, that between capital and labor, and this contradiction has constituted the chief accusation against liberalism ever since. But surely, the class issue has actually been successfully resolved in the West. As Kojève (among others) noted, the egalitarianism of modern America represents the essential achievement of the classless society envisioned by Marx. This is not to say that there are not rich people and poor people in the United States, or that the gap between them has not grown in recent years. But the root causes of economic inequality do not have to do with the underlying legal and social structure of our society, which remains fundamentally egalitarian and moderately redistributionist, so much as with the cultural and social characteristics of the groups that make it up, which are in turn the historical legacy of premodern conditions. Thus black poverty in the United States is not the inherent product of liberalism, but is rather the "legacy of slavery and racism" which persisted long after the formal abolition of slavery.

As a result of the receding of the class issue, the appeal of communism in the developed Western world, it is safe to say, is lower today than any time since the end of the First World War. This can [b]e measured in any number of ways: in the declining membership and electoral pull of the major European communist parties, and their overtly revisionist programs; in the corresponding electoral success of conservative parties from Britain and Germany to the United States and Japan, which are unabashedly pro-market and anti-statist; and in an intellectual climate whose most "advanced" members no longer believe that bourgeois society is something that ultimately needs to be overcome. This is not to say that the opinions of progressive intellectuals in Western countries are not deeply pathological in any number of ways. But those who believe that the future must inevitably be socialist tend to be very old, or very marginal to the real political discourse of their societies.

One may argue that the socialist alternative was never terribly plausible for the North Atlantic world, and was sustained for the last several decades primarily by its success outside of this region. But it is precisely in the non-European world that one is most struck by the occurrence of major ideological

---

as fascist while former strongman Stoessner's Paraguay or Pinochet's Chile would not. Obviously fascist ideologies cannot be universalistic in the sense of Marxism or liberalism, but the structure of the doctrine can be transferred from country to country.

transformations. Surely the most remarkable changes have occurred in Asia. Due to the strength and adaptability of the indigenous cultures there, Asia became a battleground for a variety of imported Western ideologies early in this century. Liberalism in Asia was a very weak reed in the period after World War I; it is easy today to forget how gloomy Asia's political future looked as recently as ten or fifteen years ago. It is easy to forget as well how momentous the outcome of Asian ideological struggles seemed for world political development as a whole.

The first Asian alternative to liberalism to be decisively defeated was the fascist one represented by Imperial Japan. Japanese fascism (like its German version) was defeated by the force of American arms in the Pacific war, and liberal democracy was imposed on Japan by a victorious United States. Western capitalism and political liberalism when transplanted to Japan were adapted and transformed by the Japanese in such a way as to be scarcely recognizable.[10] Many Americans are now aware that Japanese industrial organization is very different from that prevailing in the United States or Europe, and it is questionable what relationship the factional maneuvering that takes place with the governing Liberal Democratic Party bears to democracy. Nonetheless, the very fact that the essential elements of economic and political liberalism have been so successfully grafted onto uniquely Japanese traditions and institutions guarantees their survival in the long run. More important is the contribution that Japan has made in turn to world history by following in the footsteps of the United States to create a truly universal consumer culture that has become both a symbol and an underpinning of the universal homogenous state. V. S. Naipaul traveling in Khomeini's Iran shortly after the revolution noted the omnipresent signs advertising the products of Sony, Hitachi, and JVC, whose appeal remained virtually irresistible and gave the lie to the regime's pretensions of restoring a state based on the rule of the *Shariah*. Desire for access to the consumer culture, created in large measure by Japan, has played a crucial role in fostering the spread of economic liberalism throughout Asia, and hence in promoting political liberalism as well.

The economic success of the other newly industrializing countries (NICs) in Asia following on the example of Japan is by now a familiar story. What is important from a Hegelian standpoint is that political liberalism has been following economic liberalism, more slowly than many had hoped but with seeming inevitability. Here again we see the victory of the idea of the universal homogenous state. South Korea had developed into a modern, urbanized society with an increasingly large and well-educated middle class that could not possibly be isolated from the larger democratic trends around them. Under these circumstances it seemed intolerable to a large part of this population that it should be ruled by an anachronistic military regime while Japan, only a decade or so ahead in economic terms, had parliamentary institutions for over forty years. Even the former socialist regime in Burma, which for so many decades existed in dismal isolation from the larger trends dominating Asia, was buffeted in the past year by pressures to liberalize both its economy and political system. It is said that unhappiness with strongman Ne Win began when a senior Burmese officer went to Singapore for medical treatment and broke down crying when he saw how far socialist Burma had been left behind by its ASEAN neighbors.

But the power of the liberal idea would seem much less impressive if it had not infected the largest and oldest culture in Asia—China. The simple existence of communist China created an alternative pole

10. I use the example of Japan with some caution, since Kojève late in his life came to conclude that Japan, with its culture based on purely formal arts, proved that the universal homogenous state was not victorious and that history had perhaps not ended. See the long note at the end of the second edition of *Introduction à la Lecture de Hegel*, 462–3.

of ideological attraction, and as such constituted a threat to liberalism. But the past fifteen years have seen an almost total discrediting of Marxism-Leninism as an economic system. Beginning with the famous third plenum of the Tenth Central Committee in 1978, the Chinese Communist party set about decollectivizing agriculture for the 800 million Chinese who still lived in the countryside. The role of the state in agriculture was reduced to that of a tax collector, while production of consumer goods was sharply increased in order to give peasants a taste of the universal homogenous state and thereby an incentive to work. The reform doubled Chinese grain output in only five years, and in the process created for Deng Xiaoping a solid political base from which he was able to extend the reform to other parts of the economy. Economic statistics do not begin to describe the dynamism, initiative, and openness evident in China since the reform began, [although] China could not now be described in any way as a liberal democracy.

* * *

What is important about China from the standpoint of world history is not the present state of the reform or even its future prospects. The central issue is the fact that the People's Republic of China can no longer act as a beacon for illiberal forces around the world, whether they be guerrillas in some Asian jungle or middle class students in Paris. Maoism, rather than being the pattern for Asia's future, became an anachronism, and it was the mainland Chinese who in fact were decisively influenced by the prosperity and dynamism of their overseas co-ethnics—the ironic ultimate victory of Taiwan.

Important as these changes in China have been, however, it is developments in the Soviet Union—the original "homeland of the world proletariat"—that have put the final nail in the coffin of the Marxist-Leninist alternative to liberal democracy. It should be clear that in terms of formal institutions, not much has changed in the four years since Gorbachev has come to power: free markets and the cooperative movement represent only a small part of the Soviet economy, which remains centrally planned; the political system is still dominated by the Communist party, which has only begun to democratize internally and to share power with other groups; the regime continues to assert that it is seeking only to modernize socialism and that its ideological basis remains Marxism-Leninism; and, finally, Gorbachev faces a potentially powerful conservative opposition that could undo many of the changes that have taken place to date. Moreover, it is hard to be too sanguine about the chances for success of Gorbachev's proposed reforms, either in the sphere of economics or politics. But my purpose here is not to analyze events in the short-term, or to make predictions for policy purposes, but to look at underlying trends in the sphere of ideology and consciousness. And in that respect, it is clear that an astounding transformation has occurred.

Émigrés from the Soviet Union have been reporting for at least the last generation now that virtually nobody in that country truly believed in Marxism-Leninism any longer, and that this was nowhere more true than in the Soviet elite, which continued to mouth Marxist slogans out of sheer cynicism. The corruption and decadence of the late Brezhnev-era Soviet state seemed to matter little, however, for as long as the state itself refused to throw into question any of the fundamental principles underlying Soviet society, the system was capable of functioning adequately out of sheer inertia and could even muster some dynamism in the realm of foreign and defense policy. Marxism-Leninism was like a magical incantation which, however absurd and devoid of meaning, was the only common basis on which the elite could agree to rule Soviet society.

What has happened in the four years since Gorbachev's coming to power is a revolutionary assault on the most fundamental institutions and principles of Stalinism, and their replacement by other principles which do not amount to liberalism per se but whose only connecting thread is liberalism. This is most evident in the economic sphere, where the reform economists around Gorbachev have become steadily more radical in their support for free markets, to the point where some like Nikolai Shmelev do not mind being compared in public to Milton Friedman. There is a virtual consensus among the currently dominant school of Soviet economists now that central planning and the command system of allocation are the root cause of economic inefficiency, and that if the Soviet system is ever to heal itself, it must permit free and decentralized decision-making with respect to investment, labor, and prices. After a couple of initial years of ideological confusion, these principles have finally been incorporated into policy with the promulgation of new laws on enterprise autonomy, cooperatives, and finally in 1988 on lease arrangements and family farming. There are, of course, a number of fatal flaws in the current implementation of the reform, most notably the absence of a thoroughgoing price reform. But the problem is no longer a conceptual one: Gorbachev and his lieutenants seem to understand the economic logic of marketization well enough, but like the leaders of a Third World country facing the IMF, are afraid of the social consequences of ending consumer subsidies and other forms of dependence on the state sector.

In the political sphere, the proposed changes to the Soviet constitution, legal system, and party rules amount to much less than the establishment of a liberal state. Gorbachev has spoken of democratization primarily in the sphere of internal party affairs, and has shown little intention of ending the Communist party's monopoly of power; indeed, the political reform seeks to legitimize and therefore strengthen the CPSU's [Communist Party of the Soviet Union's] rule.[11] Nonetheless, the general principles underlying many of the reforms—that the "people" should be truly responsible for their own affairs, that higher political bodies should be answerable to lower ones, and not vice versa, that the rule of law should prevail over arbitrary police actions, with separation of powers and an independent judiciary, that there should be legal protection for property rights, the need for open discussion of public issues and the right of public dissent, the empowering of the Soviets as a forum in which the whole Soviet people can participate, and of a political culture that is more tolerant and pluralistic—come from a source fundamentally alien to the USSR's Marxist-Leninist tradition, even if they are incompletely articulated and poorly implemented in practice.

Gorbachev's repeated assertions that he is doing no more than trying to restore the original meaning of Leninism are themselves a kind of Orwellian doublespeak. Gorbachev and his allies have consistently maintained that intraparty democracy was somehow the essence of Leninism, and that the various liberal practices of open debate, secret ballot elections, and rule of law were all part of the Leninist heritage, corrupted only later by Stalin. While almost anyone would look good compared to Stalin, drawing so sharp a line between Lenin and his successor is questionable. The essence of Lenin's democratic centralism was centralism, not democracy; that is, the absolutely rigid, monolithic, and disciplined dictatorship of a hierarchically organized vanguard Communist party, speaking in the name of the demos. All of Lenin's vicious polemics against Karl Kautsky, Rosa Luxemburg, and various other Menshevik and Social Democratic rivals, not to mention his contempt for "bourgeois legality" and freedoms, cen-

11. This is not true in Poland and Hungary, however, whose Communist parties have taken moves toward true power sharing and pluralism.

tered around his profound conviction that a revolution could not be successfully made by a democratically run organization.

Gorbachev's claim that he is seeking to return to the true Lenin is perfectly easy to understand: having fostered a thorough denunciation of Stalinism and Brezhnevism as the root of the USSR's present predicament, he needs some point in Soviet history on which to anchor the legitimacy of the CPSU's continued rule. But Gorbachev's tactical requirements should not blind us to the fact that the democratizing and decentralizing principles which he has enunciated in both the economic and political spheres are highly subversive of some of the most fundamental precepts of both Marxism and Leninism. Indeed, if the bulk of the present economic reform proposals were put into effect, it is hard to know how the Soviet economy would be more socialist than those of other Western countries with large public sectors.

The Soviet Union could in no way be described as a liberal or democratic country now, nor do I think that it is terribly likely that perestroika will succeed such that the label will be thinkable any time in the near future. But at the end of history it is not necessary that all societies become successful liberal societies, merely that they end their ideological pretensions of representing different and higher forms of human society. And in this respect I believe that something very important has happened in the Soviet Union in the past few years: the criticisms of the Soviet system sanctioned by Gorbachev have been so thorough and devastating that there is very little chance of going back to either Stalinism or Brezhnevism in any simple way. Gorbachev has finally permitted people to say what they had privately understood for many years, namely, that the magical incantations of Marxism-Leninism were nonsense, that Soviet socialism was not superior to the West in any respect but was in fact a monumental failure. The conservative opposition in the USSR, consisting both of simple workers afraid of unemployment and inflation and of party officials fearful of losing their jobs and privileges, is outspoken and may be strong enough to force Gorbachev's ouster in the next few years. But what both groups desire is tradition, order, and authority; they manifest no deep commitment to Marxism-Leninism, except insofar as they have invested much of their own lives in it.[12] For authority to be restored in the Soviet Union after Gorbachev's demolition work, it must be on the basis of some new and vigorous ideology which has not yet appeared on the horizon.

If we admit for the moment that the fascist and communist challenges to liberalism are dead, are there any other ideological competitors left? Or put another way, are there contradictions in liberal society beyond that of class that are not resolvable? Two possibilities suggest themselves, those of religion and nationalism.

The rise of religious fundamentalism in recent years within the Christian, Jewish, and Muslim traditions has been widely noted. One is inclined to say that the revival of religion in some way attests to a broad unhappiness with the impersonality and spiritual vacuity of liberal consumerist societies. Yet while the emptiness at the core of liberalism is most certainly a defect in the ideology—indeed, a flaw that one does not need the perspective of religion to recognize[13]—it is not at all clear that it is remediable through politics. Modern liberalism itself was historically a consequence of the weakness of reli-

12. This is particularly true of the leading Soviet conservative, former Second Secretary Yegor Ligachev, who has publicly recognized many of the deep defects of the Brezhnev period.

13. I am thinking particularly of Rousseau and the Western philosophical tradition that flows from him that was highly critical of Lockean or Hobbesian liberalism, though one could criticize liberalism from the standpoint of classical political philosophy as well.

giously-based societies which, failing to agree on the nature of the good life, could not provide even the minimal preconditions of peace and stability. In the contemporary world only Islam has offered a theocratic state as a political alternative to both liberalism and communism. But the doctrine has little appeal for non-Muslims, and it is hard to believe that the movement will take on any universal significance. Other less organized religious impulses have been successfully satisfied within the sphere of personal life that is permitted in liberal societies.

The other major "contradiction" potentially unresolvable by liberalism is the one posed by nationalism and other forms of racial and ethnic consciousness. It is certainly true that a very large degree of conflict since the Battle of Jena has had its roots in nationalism. Two cataclysmic world wars in this century have been spawned by the nationalism of the developed world in various guises, and if those passions have been muted to a certain extent in postwar Europe, they are still extremely powerful in the Third World. Nationalism has been a threat to liberalism historically in Germany, and continues to be one in isolated parts of "post-historical" Europe like Northern Ireland.

But it is not clear that nationalism represents an irreconcilable contradiction in the heart of liberalism. In the first place, nationalism is not one single phenomenon but several, ranging from mild cultural nostalgia to the highly organized and elaborately articulated doctrine of National Socialism. Only systematic nationalisms of the latter sort can qualify as a formal ideology on the level of liberalism or communism. The vast majority of the world's nationalist movements do not have a political program beyond the negative desire of independence from some other group or people, and do not offer anything like a comprehensive agenda for socio-economic organization. As such, they are compatible with doctrines and ideologies that do offer such agendas. While they may constitute a source of conflict for liberal societies, this conflict does not arise from liberalism itself so much as from the fact that the liberalism in question is incomplete. Certainly a great deal of the world's ethnic and nationalist tension can be explained in terms of peoples who are forced to live in unrepresentative political systems that they have not chosen.

While it is impossible to rule out the sudden appearance of new ideologies or previously unrecognized contradictions in liberal societies, then, the present world seems to confirm that the fundamental principles of sociopolitical organization have not advanced terribly far since 1806. Many of the wars and revolutions fought since that time have been undertaken in the name of ideologies which claimed to be more advanced than liberalism, but whose pretensions were ultimately unmasked by history. In the meantime, they have helped to spread the universal homogenous state to the point where it could have a significant effect on the overall character of international relations.

IV

What are the implications of the end of history for international relations? Clearly, the vast bulk of the Third World remains very much mired in history, and will be a terrain of conflict for many years to come. But let us focus for the time being on the larger and more developed states of the world who after all account for the greater part of world politics. Russia and China are not likely to join the developed nations of the West as liberal societies any time in the foreseeable future, but suppose for a moment that Marxism-Leninism ceases to be a factor driving the foreign policies of these states—a prospect which, if not yet here, the last few years have made a real possibility. How will the overall characteristics of a de-ideologized world differ from those of the one with which we are familiar at such a hypothetical juncture?

The most common answer is—not very much. For there is a very widespread belief among many observers of international relations that underneath the skin of ideology is a hard core of great power national interest that guarantees a fairly high level of competition and conflict between nations. Indeed, according to one academically popular school of international relations theory, conflict inheres in the international system as such, and to understand the prospects for conflict one must look at the shape of the system—for example, whether it is bipolar or multipolar—rather than at the specific character of the nations and regimes that constitute it. This school in effect applies a Hobbesian view of politics to international relations, and assumes that aggression and insecurity are universal characteristics of human societies rather than the product of specific historical circumstances.

Believers in this line of thought take the relations that existed between the participants in the classical nineteenth century European balance of power as a model for what a de-ideologized contemporary world would look like. Charles Krauthammer, for example, recently explained that if as a result of Gorbachev's reforms the USSR is shorn of Marxist-Leninist ideology, its behavior will revert to that of nineteenth century imperial Russia.[14] While he finds this more reassuring than the threat posed by a communist Russia, he implies that there will still be a substantial degree of competition and conflict in the international system, just as there was say between Russia and Britain or Wilhelmine Germany in the last century. This is, of course, a convenient point of view for people who want to admit that something major is changing in the Soviet Union, but do not want to accept responsibility for recommending the radical policy redirection implicit in such a view. But is it true?

In fact, the notion that ideology is a superstructure imposed on a substratum of permanent great power interest is a highly questionable proposition. For the way in which any state defines its national interest is not universal but rests on some kind of prior ideological basis, just as we saw that economic behavior is determined by a prior state of consciousness. In this century, states have adopted highly articulated doctrines with explicit foreign policy agendas legitimizing expansionism, like Marxism-Leninism or National Socialism.

[Fukuyama's discussion of European nationalism and expansionism is omitted.]

. . .The developed states of the West do maintain defense establishments and in the postwar period have competed vigorously for influence to meet a worldwide communist threat. This behavior has been driven, however, by an external threat from states that possess overtly expansionist ideologies, and would not exist in their absence. To take the "neo-realist" theory seriously, one would have to believe that "natural" competitive behavior would reassert itself among the OECD states were Russia and China to disappear from the face of the earth. That is, West Germany and France would arm themselves against each other as they did in the 193Os, Australia and New Zealand would send military advisers to block each others' advances in Africa, and the U.S.-Canadian border would become fortified. Such a prospect is, of course, ludicrous: minus Marxist-Leninist ideology, we are far more likely to see the "Common Marketization" of world politics than the disintegration of the EEC into nineteenth-century competitiveness. Indeed, as our experiences in dealing with Europe on matters such as terrorism or Libya prove, they are much further gone than we down the road that denies the legitimacy of the use of force in international politics, even in self-defense.

---

14. See his article, "Beyond the Cold War," *New Republic*, December 19, 1988.

The automatic assumption that Russia shorn of its expansionist communist ideology should pick up where the czars left off just prior to the Bolshevik Revolution is therefore a curious one. It assumes that the evolution of human consciousness has stood still in the meantime, and that the Soviets, while picking up currently fashionable ideas in the realm of economics, will return to foreign policy views a century out of date in the rest of Europe. This is certainly not what happened to China after it began its reform process. Chinese competitiveness and expansionism on the world scene have virtually disappeared: Beijing no longer sponsors Maoist insurgencies or tries to cultivate influence in distant African countries as it did in the 1960s. This is not to say that there are not troublesome aspects to contemporary Chinese foreign policy, such as the reckless sale of ballistic missile technology in the Middle East; and the PRC continues to manifest traditional great power behavior in its sponsorship of the Khmer Rouge against Vietnam. But the former is explained by commercial motives and the latter is a vestige of earlier ideologically-based rivalries. The new China far more resembles Gaullist France than pre-World War I Germany.

The real question for the future, however, is the degree to which Soviet elites have assimilated the consciousness of the universal homogenous state that is post-Hitler Europe. From their writings and from my own personal contacts with them, there is no question in my mind that the liberal Soviet intelligentsia rallying around Gorbachev have arrived at the end-of-history view in a remarkably short time, due in no small measure to the contacts they have had since the Brezhnev era with the larger European civilization around them. "New political thinking," the general rubric for their views, describes a world dominated by economic concerns, in which there are no ideological grounds for major conflict between nations, and in which, consequently, the use of military force becomes less legitimate. As Foreign Minister Shevardnadze put it in mid-1988:

> The struggle between two opposing systems is no longer a determining tendency of the present-day era. At the modern stage, the ability to build up material wealth at an accelerated rate on the basis of front-ranking science and high-level techniques and technology, and to distribute it fairly, and through joint efforts to restore and protect the resources necessary for mankind's survival acquires decisive importance.[15]

The post-historical consciousness represented by "new thinking" is only one possible future for the Soviet Union, however. There has always been a very strong current of great Russian chauvinism in the Soviet Union, which has found freer expression since the advent of glasnost. It may be possible to return to traditional Marxism-Leninism for a while as a simple rallying point for those who want to restore the authority that Gorbachev has dissipated. But as in Poland, Marxism-Leninism is dead as a mobilizing ideology: under its banner people cannot be made to work harder, and its adherents have lost confidence in themselves. Unlike the propagators of traditional Marxism-Leninism, however, ultranationalists in the USSR believe in their Slavophile cause passionately, and one gets the sense that the fascist alternative is not one that has played itself out entirely there.

The Soviet Union, then, is at a fork in the road: it can start down the path that was staked out by Western Europe forty-five years ago, a path that most of Asia has followed, or it can realize its own

15. Vestnik Ministerstva Inostrannikh Del SSSR no. 15 (August 1988), 27-46. "New thinking" does of course serve a propagandistic purpose in persuading Western audiences of Soviet good intentions. But the fact that it is good propaganda does not mean that i[t]s formulators do not take many of its ideas seriously.

uniqueness and remain stuck in history. The choice it makes will be highly important for us, given the Soviet Union's size and military strength, for that power will continue to preoccupy us and slow our realization that we have already emerged on the other side of history.

V

The passing of Marxism-Leninism first from China and then from the Soviet Union will mean its death as a living ideology of world historical significance. For while there may be some isolated true believers left in places like Managua, Pyongyang, or Cambridge, Massachusetts, the fact that there is not a single large state in which it is a going concern undermines completely its pretensions to being in the vanguard of human history. And the death of this ideology means the growing "Common Marketization" of international relations, and the diminution of the likelihood of large-scale conflict between states.

This does not by any means imply the end of international conflict per se. For the world at that point would be divided between a part that was historical and a part that was post-historical. Conflict between states still in history, and between those states and those at the end of history, would still be possible. There would still be a high and perhaps rising level of ethnic and nationalist violence, since those are impulses incompletely played out, even in parts of the post-historical world. Palestinians and Kurds, Sikhs and Tamils, Irish Catholics and Walloons, Armenians and Azeris, will continue to have their unresolved grievances. This implies that terrorism and wars of national liberation will continue to be an important item on the international agenda. But large-scale conflict must involve large states still caught in the grip of history, and they are what appear to be passing from the scene.

The end of history will be a very sad time. The struggle for recognition, the willingness to risk one's life for a purely abstract goal, the worldwide ideological struggle that called forth daring, courage, imagination, and idealism, will be replaced by economic calculation, the endless solving of technical problems, environmental concerns, and the satisfaction of sophisticated consumer demands. In the post-historical period there will be neither art nor philosophy, just the perpetual caretaking of the museum of human history. I can feel in myself, and see in others around me, a powerful nostalgia for the time when history existed. Such nostalgia, in fact, will continue to fuel competition and conflict even in the post-historical world for some time to come. Even though I recognize its inevitability, I have the most ambivalent feelings for the civilization that has been created in Europe since 1945, with its north Atlantic and Asian offshoots. Perhaps this very prospect of centuries of boredom at the end of history will serve to get history started once again.

4.2

POST-MATERIALISM IN AN ENVIRONMENT OF INSECURITY

Ronald Inglehart

The following article by Ronald Inglehart is one manifestation of what has become one of the most cited bodies of research in the field of comparative politics since the 1980s. In his research, Inglehart addresses cultural change: the changes in the values, attitudes, and principles that define a society. Such changes arguably will redefine the very nature of political conflict. Given the spread of democracy in the past three decades and the efforts of the U.S. government to install democracy in formerly authoritarian societies, it is important to know the changing content of the cultures of advanced democracies and how such cultural changes come about.

Four decades ago, two well-known scholars—Seymour Lipset and Stein Rokkan—proclaimed "the end of ideology," arguing that the cleavages of Western societies were frozen around such class-based and religious-based issues as the distribution of material well-being and public support of religious principles, and that political party systems had evolved to represent these issues. Inglehart, writing in the 1970s, argued that the politics of class had declined with postwar prosperity and the declining importance of a semi-skilled industrial labor force. Class-based issues had been replaced, he argued, with "post-materialist" issues, such as environmental concerns and antinuclear stances. Does this change render traditional party systems less representative of the salient concerns of contemporary society? Students should ask whether Inglehart is clear about which issues constitute post-materialism. In equating post-materialism with the student radicalism of the 1960s, did he miss the mark? Are other scholars justified in critiquing whether he has recognized a post-materialism of the right as well as the left?

Inglehart also addresses the critically important issue of the nature of cultural change. Do people's attitudes and values change over the course of their lifetimes in response to changes in their social, political, and economic circumstances, or is change generational—that is, does change happen as one generation ages and dies and another comes of age? Inglehart argues the latter is usually the case. There are important implications from the answer if readers are looking at efforts to engineer democratic formats in such previously authoritarian systems as postwar Germany and Japan, as well as those in the current Middle East.

Ronald Inglehart, "Post-Materialism in an Environment of Insecurity," *American Political Science Review* 75, no. 4 (December 1981): 880–900.*

---

* The author thanks the following for stimulating comments and suggestions: Samuel Barnes, Russell Dalton, Kenan Jarboe, Max Kaase, Hans D. Klingemann, Shinsaku Kohei, Rex Leghorn, Warren Miller, Ichiro Miyake, Sigeki Nisihira, Tadao Okamura, Jacques-René Rabier, Tatsuzo Suzuki, and Joji Watanuki. The European public opinion surveys

A decade ago it was hypothesized that the basic value priorities of Western publics had been shifting from a Materialist emphasis toward a Post-Materialist one—from giving top priority to physical sustenance and safety, toward heavier emphasis on belonging, self-expression and the quality of life. This shift was traced to the unprecedented levels of economic and physical security that prevailed during the postwar era (Inglehart, 1971). Since this first exploration, the Materialist/Post-Materialist value change hypothesis has been subjected to further analysis by dozens of investigators using field work carried out in the United States, Canada, Australia, Japan and 15 West European nations.[1]. . .

Our data now span a decade. Implications for political change that were suggested by the original cross-sectional analysis can be tested in diachronic perspective. We can begin to distinguish between: (1) intergenerational value change, based on cohort effects; (2) life cycle or aging effects; and (3) period effects; in particular, we can ask: have the economic uncertainty and the deterioration of East-West detente in recent years produced a sharp decline in Post-Materialism? As we will see, the answer is No. Overall there was remarkably little change in the ratio of Materialists to Post-Materialists among Western publics. But, like Sherlock Holmes's dog that did not bark in the night, this lack of dramatic change has crucial implications. Much of the literature on Post-Materialism deals with whether it is a deep-rooted phenomenon having a long-term impact on political behavior, or simply a transient epiphenomenon. We will reexamine this issue in the light of recent evidence. If a society's basic values change mainly through intergenerational population replacement, we would expect them to change at a glacial pace. But though short-term changes may be small, close examination of their societal location can provide valuable insight into their long-term implications. Contrary to what some observers have assumed (Kesselman, 1979), Post-Materialism has not dwindled away in the face of diminished economic and physical security. In most countries its numbers grew, and in some ways its political influence seems greater now than a decade ago; but its character and tactics have changed significantly.

One of the most important changes derives from the simple fact that today, Post-Materialists are older than they were when they first emerged as a major political factor in the 1960s. Initially manifested mainly through student protest movements, their key impact is now made through the activities of young elites. For the students have grown older, and Post-Materialism has penetrated deeply into the ranks of young professionals, civil servants, managers, and politicians. It seems to be a major factor in the rise of a "new class" in Western society—a stratum of highly educated and well-paid young technocrats who take an adversary stance toward their society (Ladd, 1978; Gouldner, 1979; Lipset, 1979; Steinfels, 1979). The current debate between those giving top priority to reindustrialization and rearmament, versus those who emphasize environmentalism and the quality of life, will not be easy to resolve: it reflects persisting value cleavages.

---

were sponsored by the Commission of the European Communities; the American data are from the National Election surveys carried out by the Center for Political Studies, Institute for Social Research, University of Michigan. Interviews with candidates to the European Parliament were sponsored by the European Parliament, the Commission of the European Communities, and the Volkswagen Foundation. The data used in this article are available from the ICPSR survey data archive, the Belgian Archive for the Social Sciences, and the Zentralarchiv für empirische Sozialforschung. This research was supported by grant SOC 79-14619 from the National Science Foundation.

---

1. For representative examples, see Ike, 1973; Kerr and Handley, 1974; Marsh, 1975, 1977; Kmieciak, 1976; Lafferty, 1976; Hildebrandt and Dalton, 1977; Zetterberg, 1977; Watanuki, 1979; Inglehart, 1977; Jennings, Allerbeck and Rosenmayer, 1979; Lehner, 1979; Kaase and Klingemann, 1979; Heunks, 1979; Pesonen and Sankiaho, 1979; Kemp, 1979; Flanagan 1979, 1980; Nardi, 1980.

Reexamining the Theory of Value Change

Before turning to time series evidence, let us re-examine our theoretical framework in the light of recent findings. It is based on two key hypotheses:

1. *A Scarcity Hypothesis.* An individual's priorities reflect the socioeconomic environment: one places the greatest subjective value on those things that are in relatively short supply.
2. *A Socialization Hypothesis.* The relationship between socioeconomic environment and value priorities is not one of immediate adjustment: a substantial time lag is involved, for, to a large extent, one's basic values reflect the conditions that prevailed during one's preadult years.

The *scarcity hypothesis* is similar to the principle of diminishing marginal utility in economic theory. A complementary concept—Abraham Maslow's (1954) theory of a need hierarchy underlying human motivation—helped shape the survey items we used to measure value priorities. In its simplest form, the idea of a need hierarchy would probably command almost universal assent. The fact that unmet physiological needs take priority over social, intellectual or esthetic needs has been demonstrated all too often in human history: starving people will go to almost any lengths to obtain food. The rank ordering of human needs becomes less clear as we move beyond those needs directly related to survival. But it *does* seem clear that there is a basic distinction between the "material" needs for physiological sustenance and safety, and nonphysiological needs such as those for esteem, self-expression and esthetic satisfaction.

The recent economic history of advanced industrial societies has significant implications in the light of the scarcity hypothesis. For these societies are a remarkable exception to the prevailing historical pattern: the bulk of their population does *not* live under conditions of hunger and economic insecurity. This fact seems to have led to a gradual shift in which needs for belonging, esteem and intellectual and esthetic satisfaction became more prominent. As a rule, we would expect prolonged periods of high prosperity to encourage the spread of Post-Materialist values; economic decline would have the opposite effect.

But it is not quite that simple: there is no one-to-one relationship between economic level and the prevalence of Post-Materialist values, for these values reflect one's *subjective* sense of security, not one's economic level *per se*. While rich individuals and nationalities, no doubt, tend to feel more secure than poor ones, these feelings are also influenced by the cultural setting and social welfare institutions in which one is raised. Thus, the scarcity hypothesis alone does not generate adequate predictions about the process of value change. It must be interpreted in connection with the *socialization hypothesis*.

One of the most pervasive concepts in social science is the notion of a basic human personality structure that tends to crystallize by the time an individual reaches adulthood, with relatively little change thereafter. This concept permeates the literature from Plato through Freud and extends to the findings of contemporary survey research. Early socialization seems to carry greater weight than later socialization.

This, of course, doesn't imply that no change whatever occurs during adult years. In some individual cases, dramatic behavioral shifts are known to occur, and the process of human development never comes to a complete stop (Levinson, 1979; Brim and Kagan, 1980). Nevertheless, human development seems to be far more rapid during preadult years than afterward, and the great bulk of the evidence points to the conclusion that the statistical likelihood of basic personality change declines sharply after one reaches adulthood. Longitudinal research following given individuals over periods as long as 35 years shows strong correlations (as high as .70) between people's scores on standardized personality scales from young adulthood to middle age, or even old age (Block, 1981; Costa and McCrae, 1980).

Taken together, these two hypotheses generate a coherent set of predictions concerning value change. First, while the scarcity hypothesis implies that prosperity is conducive to the spread of Post-Materialist values, the socialization hypothesis implies that neither an individual's values nor those of a society as a whole are likely to change overnight. Instead, fundamental value change takes place gradually, almost invisibly; in large part, it occurs as a younger generation replaces an older one in the adult population of a society.

Consequently, after a period of sharply rising economic and physical security, one would expect to find substantial differences between the value priorities of older and younger groups: they would have been shaped by different experiences in their formative years. But there would be a sizeable time lag between economic changes and their political effects. Ten or fifteen years after an era of prosperity began, the age cohorts that had spent their formative years in prosperity would begin to enter the electorate. Ten more years might pass before these groups began to occupy positions of power and influence in their society; perhaps another decade would pass before they reached the level of top decision makers.

The socialization hypothesis complements the scarcity hypothesis, resolving objections derived from an oversimplified view of how scarcity affects behavior. It helps account for apparently deviant behavior: on one hand, the miser who experienced poverty in early years and relentlessly continues piling up wealth long after attaining material security, and on the other hand, the saintly ascetic who remains true to the higher-order goals instilled by his culture, even in the face of severe deprivation. In both instances, an explanation for the seemingly deviant behavior of such individuals lies in their early socialization.

The socialization hypothesis also explains why certain experimental tests of the need hierarchy have found no positive correlation between satisfaction of a given need at one time, and increased emphasis on the next higher need at a later time (Alderfer, 1972; Kmieciak, 1976). For these experiments are based on the implicit assumption that one would find almost *immediate* changes in an individual's priorities. But if, as hypothesized, an individual's basic priorities are largely fixed by the time he or she reaches adulthood, one would not expect to find much short-term change of the kind that was tested for.

This does not mean that an adult's value priorities are totally immutable—merely that they are relatively difficult to change. Normally, the rewards and deprivations employed in experimental psychology are modest, and the treatment is continued for a fairly brief time. . . .

Marsh (1975) finds that Post-Materialists do not express higher satisfaction with their incomes than do Materialists. This is illogical, he argues: presumably, the former are Post-Materialists *because* their material needs are satisfied—so why don't they express relatively high levels of subjective satisfaction with their material circumstances? Once again the confusion is based on the implicit assumption that value change reflects an *immediate* response to one's environment. In the short run, one normally *does* experience a subjective sense of satisfaction when one satisfies material needs. But if these needs have been satisfied throughout one's formative years, one takes them for granted and develops higher expectations. In the long run, the fact that one has enough oxygen, water, food and clothing does *not* produce a subjective sense of satisfaction—which is precisely why the Post-Materialists seek satisfaction in *other* realms.

Because their incomes are higher than those of the Materialists, and yet they are still dissatisfied, Marsh concludes that Post-Materialists are actually *more* acquisitive than Materialists. Their emphasis on nonmaterial societal goals reflects mere lip service to fashionable causes, he argues, not their true personal values. Subsequent findings by Marsh himself refute this interpretation. To test his hypothesis, he developed an index of "Personal Post-Materialism"; he finds a correlation of +.22 between it and my index of societal Post-Materialism (Marsh, 1977, p. 180). While his discussion emphasizes the fact that this correlation is "only" .22, the crucial point is that the correlation is *positive*—and not negative, as he argued earlier. When one is dealing with survey data, a product-moment correlation of +.22 is fairly strong, particularly when it is found between two sets of items that were designed with the expectation that they would show a *negative* correlation.

Time Series Evidence from the Postwar Era

Our hypotheses imply that the unpredecented prosperity prevailing from the late 1940s until the early 1970s, led to substantial growth in the proportion of Post-Materialists among the publics of advanced industrial societies. We would need a time machine in order to go back and test this proposition, using the battery specifically developed to measure Materialist/Post-Materialist values. Though this is impossible, some available data *do* seem to tap the relevant dimension.

Data on the priorities of the German public, for example, cover more than 20 years, from 1949 to 1970. In these surveys, representative national samples were asked, "Which of the four Freedoms do you personally consider most important—Freedom of Speech, Freedom of Worship, Freedom from Fear or Freedom from Want?" In 1949, postwar reconstruction had just begun, and "Freedom from Want" was the leading choice by a wide margin. But in the following years, Germany rose from poverty to prosperity with almost incredible speed. In 1954, "Freedom from Want" was still narrowly ahead of any other choice, but by 1958 "Freedom of Speech" was chosen by more people than all other choices combined (EMNID, 1963, 1970).

These changes in the German population's value priorities seem to reflect the concurrent changes in their economic environment. And there is clear evidence of an age-related lag between economic change and value change. In 1962, 59 percent of the Germans from 16 to 25 years old chose "Freedom of Speech"; the figure declines steadily as we move to older groups; among Germans aged 65 and older, only 35 percent chose "Freedom of Speech." The fact that the young are much likelier to give "Freedom of Speech" priority over "Freedom from Want" fits theoretical expectations neatly. The original data have been lost, and it is not possible to perform an age cohort analysis in order to determine how much of this age difference is due to generational change. But the magnitude of the overall shift is so great that each age group must have *de-emphasized* "Freedom from Want" as it aged during this period: the age differences *cannot* be attributed to life cycle effects. Further persuasive evidence of an intergenerational shift toward Post-Materialist priorities among the German public is found in the massive and definitive analysis of German survey data from 1953 through 1976 by Baker, Dalton and Hildebrandt (1981).

The most dramatic example of economic change in modern history is Japan—a nation that rose from harsh poverty to astonishing prosperity in a single generation. Indicators of the Japanese public's values are available in the Japanese national character studies carried out at five-year intervals, from 1953 through 1978. Analysis of these surveys indicates that Japanese culture changed along *several* different dimensions during this period, with the perceived sacredness of the emperor declining and emphasis on individuation and political participation rising (Ike, 1973; Hayashi, 1974; Nishihira, 1974; Richardson, 1974; Research Committee on [the Study of the] Japanese National Character, 1979; Flanagan, 1979; Inglehart, 1982). One of the changes, it seems clear, was a shift from Materialist to Post-Materialist priorities. Among the available survey questions, the most unambiguous indicator of Materialist versus Post-Materialist priorities is the following: "In bringing up children of primary school age, some think that one should teach them that money is the most important thing. Do you agree or disagree?" In 1953, a strong majority (65 percent) of the Japanese public agreed that financial security was the most important thing. This figure declined steadily in subsequent surveys: by 1978 only 45 percent of the public still took this view. As was true of Germany, the trend is in the predicted direction—but in this case, the original data have been preserved and we can carry out a cohort analysis. Table 1 shows the results.

In any given year, the young are a good deal less likely to emphasize the importance of money than are the old. Does this simply reflect an inherent idealism of youth that will disappear as they grow older? Apparently not—for when we follow given age cohorts as they age during this 25-year period, we find no indication whatever of increasing materialism. Quite the contrary, we find a tendency for a given cohort as it grows older to place *less* emphasis on money: the five cohorts for which we have data throughout the 25-year period show an average shift of six points *away* from giving top priority to money. Almost certainly this was a period effect, with the sharply rising prosperity of the postwar era producing a diminishing emphasis on money within each age cohort, quite independently of generational change or aging effects. As closer examination of Table 1 indicates, this period effect operated rather strongly from 1953 to 1973 and then reversed direction, so that from 1973 to 1978 each age cohort came to place slightly *more* emphasis on the importance of money. This pattern reflects changes in the economic environment rather faithfully: the extraordinary rise in prosperity that took place in Japan from 1953 to 1973 was mirrored in a gradual deemphasis on money within each age cohort; and the economic uncertainty that followed the oil shock of 1973 was accompanied by a partial reversal of this trend.

But these period effects are dwarfed by the intergenerational differences. While period effects seem to account for a mean net shift of 6 percentage points away from emphasizing the importance of fi-

Table 1 Cohort Analysis: Percentage of Japanese Public Agreeing that Financial Security Is Most Important

Age group	1953	1958	1963	1968	1973	1978	Change within given cohort 1953–1978	
20–24	60	—	43	34	22	18		
25–29	66		55	49	36	26		
30–34	63		58	58	42	37		
35–39	62		56	59	43	43		
40–44	65		63	59	46	49		
45–49	66		62	62	46	56	−4	
50–54	72	—	68	65	49	51	−15	Mean: −6
55–59	72	—	72	67	60	56	−7	
60–64	77	—	76	66	59	62	0	
65–69	78	—	72	73	59	62	−3	
Spread between youngest and oldest:	+18	—	+29	+39	+37	+44		

Source: Japanese National Character Surveys carried out by the Institute of Statistical Mathematics, Tokyo.

nancial security, we find a difference of 44 points between the youngest and oldest groups in 1978. Since these data show no evidence whatever that aging leads to increasing emphasis on money, there is a strong *prime facie* case for attributing this 44-point difference entirely to intergenerational change. It is conceivable that a life cycle tendency toward increasing Materialism with increasing age *also* exists, but is totally concealed by stronger period effects working in the opposite direction: the complexities of distinguishing between aging effects, cohort effects and period effects are such that we can not totally exclude this possibility (Glenn, 1976; Knoke and Hout, 1976). But belief in such an aging effect must depend on faith alone; it is totally unsupported by empirical evidence.

Indications of intergenerational change, conversely, seem incontrovertible. In 1953, even the *youngest* group showed overwhelmingly Materialistic priorities—because at that time, *all* adult age cohorts had spent their formative years during World War II or earlier. These cohorts show only modest changes as they age during the ensuing quarter-century. It is only from 1963 on—when the postwar cohorts begin to enter the adult population—that we find a clear rejection of financial security as a value having top priority among the younger cohorts. The shift of the Japanese public from a heavy majority giving money top priority, to a minority doing so, seems to reflect intergenerational population replacement above all, with only a minor component due to period effects. By 1978, there was a tremendous difference between the priorities of younger and older Japanese. As the leading example of economic growth in the postwar era, Japan constitutes a crucial case for testing our hypotheses. The time series data are unambiguous: from 1953 to 1978 there was an intergenerational shift away from Materialism among the Japanese public.

Materialist and Post-Materialist Values from 1970 to 1979

Our data from Western countries cover a shorter period than those from Japan, but they were specifically designed to measure Materialist/Post-Materialist value priorities. It is difficult to measure values directly. But their presence can be inferred from a consistent pattern of emphasis on given types of goals. Accordingly, we asked representative samples of citizens from Western nations what they personally considered the most important goals among the following:

A. Maintain order in the nation
B. Give people more say in the decisions of the government
C. Fight rising prices
D. Protect freedom of speech
E. Maintain a high rate of economic growth
F. Make sure that this country has strong defense forces
G. Give people more say in how things are decided at work and in their community
H. Try to make our cities and countryside more beautiful
I. Maintain a stable economy
J. Fight against crime
K. Move toward a friendlier, less impersonal society
L. Move toward a society where ideas count more than money.

Our earliest survey (in 1970) used only the first four items, in six countries. The full 12-item battery was first used in 1973 in the nine-nation European Community and the United States (Inglehart, 1977).

Both batteries were administered in numerous subsequent surveys. Items A, C, E, F, I and J were designed to tap emphasis on Materialist goals; theoretically, these values should be given high priority by those who experienced economic or physical insecurity during their formative years. The remaining items were designed to tap Post-Materialist goals; they should be emphasized by those raised under relatively secure conditions. If so, certain respondents would favor Materialist items consistently, while others would consistently emphasize the Post-Materialist ones.

* * *

The predicted relationships with social background are also confirmed empirically. Within any given age group, those raised in relatively prosperous families are most likely to emphasize Post-Materialist items, and the predicted skew by age group is manifest. Figure 1 depicts this pattern in the pooled sample of six West European publics interviewed in our initial survey. Significant cross-national differences exist, but the basic pattern is similar from nation to nation: Among the oldest group, Materialists outnumber Post-Materialists enormously; as we move toward younger groups, the proportion of Materialists declines and that of Post-Materialists increases.

A major watershed divides the postwar generation (in 1970, those 15 to 24 years old) from all other age groups. While Materialists are still more than twice as numerous as Post-Materialists among those 25–34 years old, when we move across the World War II watershed, the balance shifts dramatically, with Post-Materialists becoming more numerous than Materialists.

The Materialist and Post-Materialist types have strikingly different opinions on a wide variety of issues, ranging from women's rights, to attitudes toward poverty, ideas of what is important in a job, and positions on foreign policy. Within each age group, about half the sample falls into the mixed value types. On virtually every issue, their position is between the Materialists and Post-Materialists: they seem to be a cross-pressured group that could swing either way.

By 1970, Post-Materialists had attained numerical parity with Materialists *only* among the postwar generation. Furthermore, they were concentrated among the more affluent strata of this age group: among university students, they heavily outnumbered the Materialists. In this light, perceptions of a generation gap in the late 1960s and early 1970s are understandable. Even among the postwar generation, Materialists were about as numerous as Post-Materialists. But in this age group's most articulate and most visible segment—the students—there was an overwhelming preponderance of Post-Materialists. The students lived in a distinct milieu: they had highly developed communications networks with other students but were largely isolated from their non-student peers. The priorities prevailing in this milieu were fundamentally different from those shaping the society as a whole.

The existence of such a milieu can play an important part in the evolution and propagation of a given set of values. Indeed, Habermas (1979) argues that the rise of Post-Materialism is not due to the different formative experiences of different generation units, but to exposure to the specific world views inculcated by distinct communications networks (c.f. Jaeggi, 1979). This explanation seems to complement, rather than substitute for, the one proposed here. It helps account for the spread of values in a given milieu, but provides no explanation why given generation units were disposed to accept given values in the first place, while others rejected them. Nevertheless, it seems clear that in virtually all Western nations, the student milieu of the late 1960s *did* constitute a distinct communications network, propagating a distinctive viewpoint. Given these circumstances, it is not surprising that the student elite

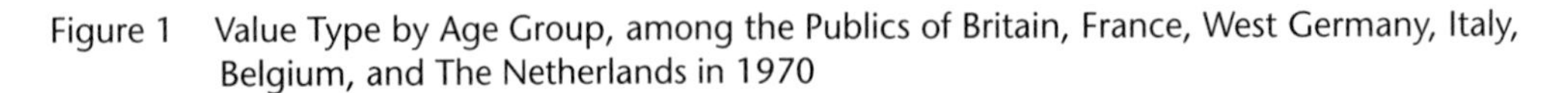
Figure 1 Value Type by Age Group, among the Publics of Britain, France, West Germany, Italy, Belgium, and The Netherlands in 1970

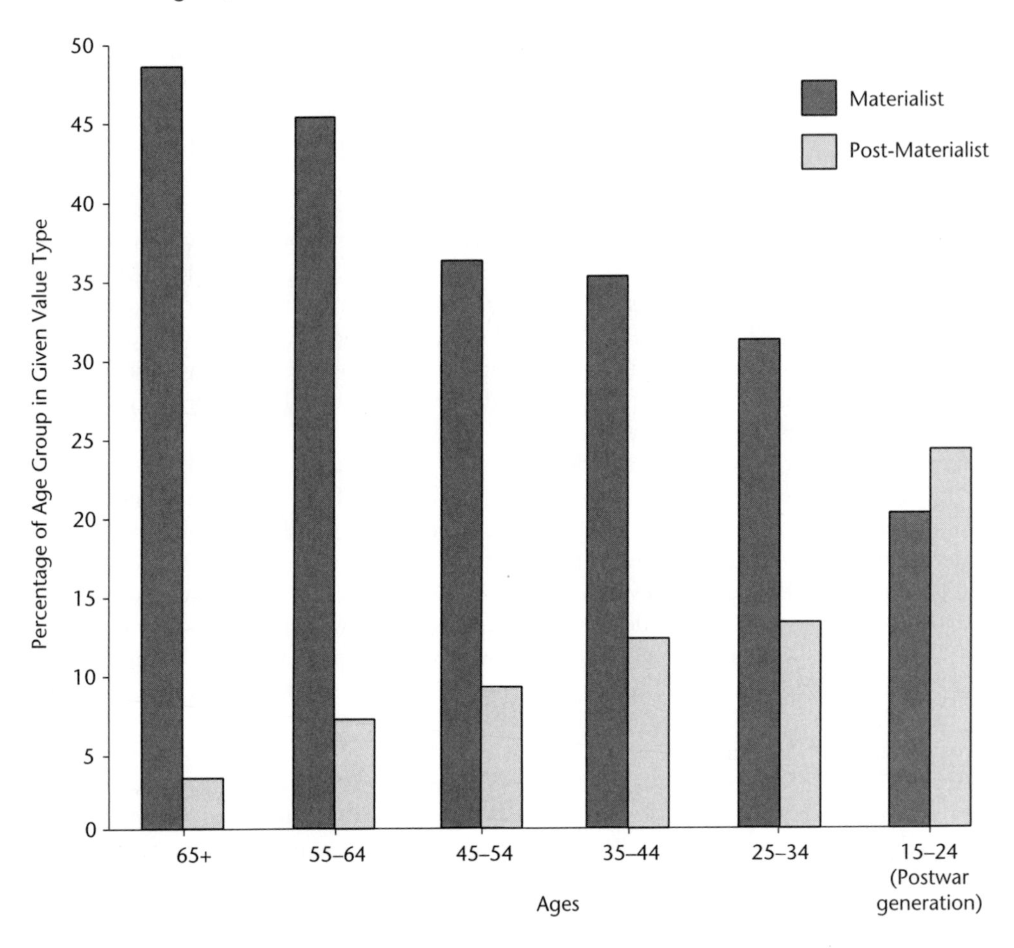

Source: European Community survey carried out in Feb.-Mar. 1970, sponsored by Commission of the European Communities; principal investigators were Jacques-René Rabier and Ronald Inglehart.

saw themselves as part of a counterculture that was engaged in an irreconcilable clash with the culture of an older generation: From their viewpoint, the dictum, "Don't trust anyone over thirty" seemed plausible. Our hypotheses imply that as time went by, the Post-Materialists became older and more evenly distributed across the population. But in 1970, conditions were optimal to sustain belief in a monolithic generation gap, with youth all on one side and older people all on the other.

Clearly, there are large empirical differences between the priorities of younger and older groups in Western Europe (and, as subsequent research revealed, the entire Western world). But one can advance various interpretations concerning the *implications* of this finding. Though our own hypotheses point to intergenerational change based on cohort effects, we must acknowledge that any given pattern of age differences could, theoretically, result from (1) aging effects, (2) cohort effects, (3) period effects, or some combination of all three.

1. Aging Effects versus Cohort Effects. Perhaps the most obvious alternative interpretation is one based on aging effects. It would argue that for biological or other reasons, the young are inherently less materialistic than the old. As they age, however, they inevitably become just as materialistic as their elders; after 50 years, the youngest group will show the same overwhelming preponderance of Materialists that the oldest group now displays. The aging interpretation, then, holds that the pattern found in 1970 is a permanent characteristic of the human life cycle and will not change over time. The cohort interpretation, on the other hand, implies that the Post-Materialists will gradually permeate the older strata, neutralizing the relationship between values and age.

The most dramatic change from one age group to the next, in Figure 1, is the sudden shift in the balance between Materialist and Post-Materialist types that occurs as we move from the second-youngest to the youngest group. Our hypotheses imply the existence of a significant watershed between the postwar generation and the older groups that had experienced the World Wars, the Great Depression and their associated threats to economic and physical security. The gap between the two youngest groups in 1970 fits the historical change theory neatly. But this gap could *also* be interpreted as a permanent feature of the human life cycle. For in 1970, the dividing line between the postwar generation and all older groups happened to coincide with the boundary between those 25 years of age or older, and those who were 24 or younger. Since we know that people tend to get married, have their first child, and begin a permanent career at about this age, it might be argued that what we have identified as an historical watershed between the postwar generation and the older ones, merely reflects the stage in the life cycle when people get married and settle down. Time series data are needed to determine which interpretation is correct.

2. Period Effects. Both the German data and the Japanese data reviewed earlier show period effects: the economic environment of the period up to 1973 apparently induced *all* age groups to become less materialistic as time went by, quite apart from any processes of aging or generational change. These surveys were executed during a period of dramatic improvement in living standards, particularly in Germany and Japan. But even in the United States (where economic growth was much slower) the real income of the American public approximately doubled from 1947 to 1973.

From 1973 on, however, economic conditions changed drastically. Energy prices quadrupled almost overnight; the industrialized world entered the most severe recession since the 1930s. Economic growth stagnated and Western nations experienced extraordinarily high levels of inflation *and* unemployment. By 1980, the real income of the typical American family was actually *lower* than in 1970.

Western publics were, of course, acutely aware of changed economic circumstances, and responded to them. The most amply documented case is that of the American public, whose economic outlook is surveyed each month. In mid-1972, the University of Michigan Survey Research Center's Index of Consumer Sentiment stood at 95, only slightly below its all-time high. By the spring of 1975, the SRC Index had plummeted to 58—the lowest level recorded since these surveys were initiated in the 1950s. With the subsequent economic recovery, consumer confidence revived—only to collapse again in the wake of the second OPEC price shock in late 1979; in April, 1980 consumer confidence had reached a new all-time low, with the SRC Index at 53. Similar patterns of declining confidence in the economic outlook were recorded among West European publics (Commission of the European Communities, 1979).

The sense of physical security has also declined. The Soviet arms buildup, their invasion of Afghanistan, and the Western response to these events led to an erosion of East-West detente. This, too, had a pronounced impact on the outlook of Western publics. In the fall of 1977, the publics of the European Community nations were asked to assess the chances of a world war breaking out within the next ten years. Only 26 percent of the nine publics (weighted according to population) rated the likelihood at 50 percent or greater. This was roughly comparable to the results obtained when a similar question was asked in July, 1971. In April, 1980, however, fully 49 percent of the nine publics rated the danger at 50 percent or greater: such pessimism had almost doubled since 1977 (Euro-Barometer 13, 1980, p. 16).

Clearly (as the scarcity hypothesis implies), the period effects of recent years should inhibit the development of a Post-Materialist outlook. And the socialization hypothesis implies that current conditions would have their greatest impact on the youngest and theoretically most malleable respondents—those aged 15-24, who are still in their formative years.

Which of these three processes was most important during the 1970s? Given the severity of the economic decline and the almost total disappearance of student protest and other dramatic manifestations of a counterculture, one might assume that Post-Materialism has been swept away completely by a new, harsher environment. Or—as the socialization hypothesis suggests—are these priorities sufficiently deep-rooted among the adult population to weather the effects of the current socioeconomic environment?

Table 2 provides part of the answer. It shows the distribution of the two polar value types from early 1970 to late 1979, in the six countries for which we have data covering this entire time span, and in the United States from 1972 to 1980. Of necessity, we use the original 4-item index here. By contrast with the cataclysmic changes that took place in consumer confidence indices and in perceptions of the danger of war, the changes here are remarkably small: for the most part, the shifts from year to year fall within the range of normal sampling error. Moreover, only modest and nonlinear cumulative changes took place from 1970 to 1980, and they vary cross-nationally. In four of the seven countries—Great Britain, Germany, France and The Netherlands—there were fewer Materialists and more Post-Materialists at the end of the decade than at its start. In two countries (Belgium and the United States) there was virtually no change. Only in the seventh country—Italy—do we find a shift toward the Materialist pole.

The fact that Italy is the deviant case is not surprising. During the 1970s Italy not only experienced exceptionally severe economic difficulties, but also severe political disorder. Probably for this reason, there was a substantial net shift toward Materialism among the Italian public. But in the other six countries, the process of population replacement outweighed the effects of economic and physical insecurity. The net result for the seven countries as a whole is that Post-Materialists were slightly *more* numerous at the end of the 1970s than they were at the start.

The impression of remarkable stability that the aggregate national data convey, conceals an extremely interesting underlying pattern. For, as hypothesized, the distribution of values across age groups has changed over time. Table 3 shows this relationship, from early 1970 through late 1979. Figure 2 depicts these data in graphic form. As these data reveal, the overall stability shown in Table 2 is the result of two opposing processes that largely cancel each other.

On one hand, the youngest group shows a substantial *decline* in the ratio of Post-Materialists to Materialists. In 1970, Post-Materialists were 4 percentage points more numerous than Materialists among

Table 2 Changes in Prevalence of Materialist and Post-Materialist Value Types, 1970–1980 (Percentage falling into the two polar types)

	1970	1973	1976	1979
Britian				
Materialist	36	32	36	27
Post-Materialist	8	8	8	11
Germany				
Materialist	43	42	41	37
Post-Materialist	10	8	11	11
France				
Materialist	38	35	41	36
Post-Materialist	11	12	12	15
Italy				
Materialist	35	40	41	47
Post-Materialist	13	9	11	10
Belgium				
Materialist	32	25	30	33
Post-Materialist	14	14	14	14
Netherlands				
Materialist	30	31	32	28
Post-Materialist	17	13	14	19
	1972		1976	1980
United States				
Materialist	35		31	35
Post-Materialist	10		10	10

Source: European Community surveys carried out in Feb.–Mar. 1970; Sept. 1973; Nov. 1976; and Nov. 1979; and Post-Election wave of the U.S. National Election surveys carried out in each respective year by the Center for Political Studies, Institute for Social Research, University of Michigan.

this group: in other words, the group showed a Percentage Difference Index (PDI) of +4. This fell to a PDI of –1 in 1973 and fell further to a PDI of –5 in 1976. Although the trend then reversed itself, with a partial recovery to an index of –3 in 1979, this youngest group showed a net shift of 7 points in the Materialist direction during the 1970s.

But this shift was more than offset by shifts in the *opposite* direction among the older groups. The socialization hypothesis implies that period effects would have their greatest impact on the youngest group. Empirically, it turns out that the youngest group was the *only* group on which period effects had a significant negative net impact: the older ones moved in the Post-Materialist direction. The American data show a similar pattern: younger respondents became more Materialist but the older ones became *less* so. In Europe, this countervailing tendency was especially strong among the second youngest group, which showed a steady rise in the proportion of Post-Materialists even during the depths of the 1970s recession; despite economic uncertainty and the erosion of detente, by 1979 this group had registered a net shift of 8 points toward the Post-Materialist pole.

Table 3 Changes in Prevalence of Materialist and Post-Materialist Values, 1970–1979 by Age Group (Percent) (Combined results from six European nations)

	1970		1973		1976		1979	
Ages	M	P-M	M	P-M	M	P-M	M	P-M
15–24	20	24	21	20	25	20	24	21
25–34	31	13	28	13	29	16	27	17
35–44	35	12	35	9	35	11	33	13
45–54	36	9	39	7	39	8	41	10
55–64	45	7	43	6	47	6	41	8
65 and over	48	3	45	4	52	5	49	5
Total:	35	12	34	10	37	12	35	13
Percent Difference Index:	–23		–24		–25		–22	

Source: Surveys sponsored by the Commission of the European Communities, carried out in Feb.–March, 1970; Sept. 1973; Nov. 1976 and Nov. 1979.

Figure 2 Change in Value Priorities in Six Nations, 1970–1979, by Age Group

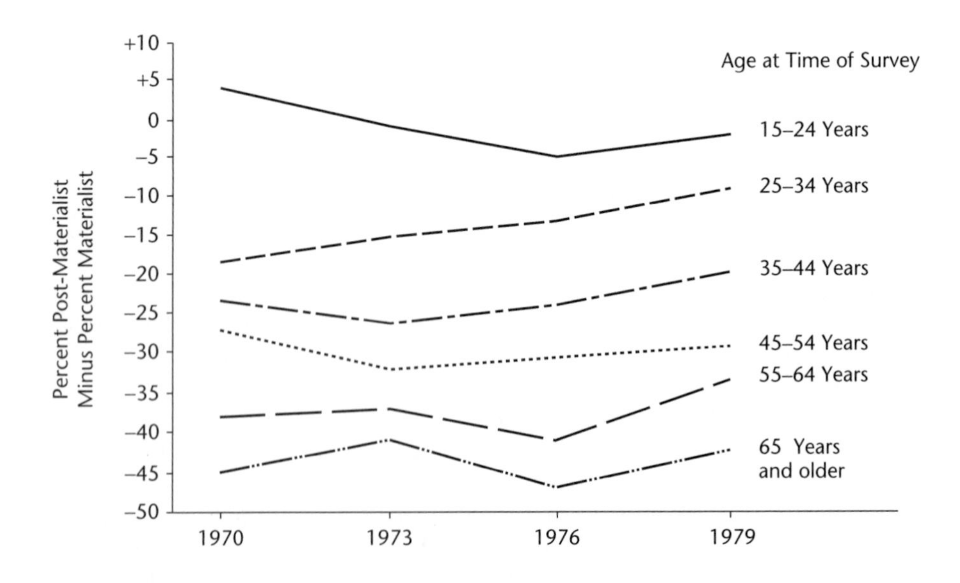

Source: European Community surveys carried out in Feb.-Mar. 1970; Sept. 1973; Nov. 1976 and Nov. 1979 in Britain, Germany, France, Italy, Belgium and The Netherlands: since data from only these nations are available for 1970, only these data are used for the subsequent time points. Surveys were sponsored by the Commission of the European Communities; principal investigators were Jacques-René Rabier and Ronald Inglehart.

This seemingly counterintuitive development reflects changes in the composition of the 25–34-year-old group, due to population replacement. In 1970 this group contained no one born after 1945; but by late 1979 its members were recruited entirely from the postwar generation. The World War II watershed now fell between the *two* youngest groups and all of the older ones.

Let us examine Figure 2 more closely. In 1970, by far the widest gap between adjacent age groups was that between the youngest and second-youngest groups. This gap was a prominent feature of the value distributions in each of the six nations surveyed in that year. At that point, it was unclear whether this gap should be interpreted as a World War II watershed, or as the reflection of a major life-cycle transition that takes place in one's mid-twenties.

That uncertainty has now vanished. During the 1970s, the still-malleable 15–24-year-old group became progressively more Materialist until the recession bottomed out, and then staged only a partial recovery. But the 25–34-year-old group became steadily more Post-Materialist throughout the 1970s. By the end of 1979 the largest gap no longer was located between these two youngest groups, but between the 25–34-year-old group, and those aged 35–44. This accords perfectly with the fact that members of the postwar generation had now reached 34 years of age.

It is virtually impossible to interpret this pattern in terms of aging effects—unless one believes that the human life cycle changed radically between 1970 and 1979: the crucial life stage transition that took place at age 25 in 1970, had somehow shifted to age 35 in 1979. Furthermore, there is no indication that aging has an inherent tendency to produce a Materialistic outlook. Despite the economic uncertainty of this period, only the 15–24-year-old group became significantly more Materialist; among older groups, the downward pressure of period effects was more than offset by the upward pressure of the population replacement process. Furthermore, not even the youngest category showed a *continuous* downward trend: plummeting steeply until 1976, it began to reverse itself with recovery from the recession. It seems far more plausible to attribute this nonlinear pattern to period effects than to the aging process (which presumably is continuous).

The economic and physical uncertainty of the 1970s produced a significant period effect. The net movement toward Post-Materialism that would be expected from population replacement slowed to a crawl. By the decade's end, the 15–24-year-old group was significantly less Post-Materialist than their counterparts a decade earlier had been. This is congruent with impressionistic observations that the student population no longer seems as nonconformist as it once was. For while young people have become more materialistic, those in their thirties and forties have become less so: the notion of a generation gap, already an oversimplification in 1970, was even farther from reality in 1979 due to this convergence.

Post-Materialism and Political Change

The evidence indicates that Post-Materialism is a deep-rooted phenomenon. Despite the recession of recent years, it not only persisted but increased its penetration of older groups. What are the political implications? The remainder of this article will focus on that question.

One would expect that, despite their favored socioeconomic status, Post-Materialists would be relatively supportive of social change, and would have a relatively high potential for unconventional and disruptive political action. The reasons can be summarized as follows: (1) Materialists tend to be preoccupied with satisfying immediate physiological needs; Post-Materialists feel relatively secure about them and have a greater amount of psychic energy to invest in more remote concerns such as politics. (2) As a recently emerging minority whose highest priorities have traditionally been given relatively little emphasis in industrial society, Post-Materialists tend to be relatively dissatisfied with the established order and relatively supportive of social change. (3) The disruption and property damage that sometimes result from unconventional political action seem less negative to Post-Materialists, since they threaten things they value less than Materialists do. In short, Post-Materialists have a larger amount of psychic energy available for politics, they are less supportive of the established social order, and, subjectively, they have less to lose from unconventional political action than Materialists. Consequently, the rise of Post-Materialism has made available a new, predominantly middle-class base of support for the left.

Is it empirically true that Post-Materialists tend to be relatively change-oriented and ready to engage in unconventional political protest? One measure of support for social change is now a standard feature of the European Community surveys carried out twice each year. Representative national samples of the publics of the European Community countries are asked:

> On this card are three basic kinds of attitudes toward the society we live in. Please choose the one which best describes your opinion. (1) The entire way our society is organized must be radically changed by revolutionary action. (2) Our society must be gradually improved by reforms. (3) Our present society must be valiantly defended against all subversive forces.

These alternatives might be described as Revolutionary, Reformist and Conservative.

The Reformists constitute a clear majority—63 percent of those responding—in the European Community as a whole, and this holds true for all value types. But there is a pronounced difference between Materialists' and Post-Materialists' attitudes toward social change. Table 4 shows the relationship between value type and attitudes toward social change among the publics of the European Community as a whole. Among Materialists, only 4 percent endorse the Revolutionary option; nearly ten times as many (38 percent) support the Conservative option. Among Post-Materialists, by contrast, the Revolutionary option draws *more* support than the Conservative one. For both, the Reformist option is the leading choice—but Post-Materialists are only about one-third as likely to hold Conservative views as are Materialists, and about four times as apt to favor radical social change.

Despite their relatively privileged social status, Post-Materialists are markedly more favorable to social change than are other value types. But how far are they ready to go on behalf of their values?

A central feature of an eight-nation survey carried out during 1974–1976 was a scale designed to measure an individual's potential for participation in political protest activities (for details of field work,

Table 4 Support for Social Change versus Resistance to Social Change, by Value Type, 1976–1979 (percent)

Respondent's Value Type	Support for Revolutionary Change	Support for Gradual Reform	Support for Defense of Present Society	N
Materialist	4	57	38	18,292
Mixed	8	62	30	26,694
Post-Materialist	17	69	14	6,098

Source: Pooled data from Euro-barometre surveys, 1976 through 1979, from all nine European Community nations.
Note: Results are weighted according to size of each nation's population.

see Barnes, Kaase et al., 1979). This scale is based on whether the respondent has done, or would do and approves of, a series of acts ranging from circulating petitions to occupying buildings and disrupting traffic. Tested and applied in eight countries, the scale has remarkably good technical characteristics and seems to measure, in a straightforward way, just how far an individual is willing to go in order to carry out his or her beliefs.

Do Post-Materialists show a relatively high propensity for unconventional political activities as measured by the Protest Potential Scale? On one hand, Marsh (1975) has argued that Post-Materialist responses tap nothing more than a form of radical chic among a basically conservative elite. If so, the answer would be No. On the other hand, if our typology reflects basic value differences, the answer should be Yes. The Protest Potential Scale was developed, in part, to test whether Post-Materialist values go no deeper than lip service to fashionable goals, or whether they have behavioral implications. The answer is unequivocal.

Table 5 shows the relationship between protest potential and value type in each of the eight nations surveyed in 1974–1976. A score of "3" is the cutting point for this table: Those scoring below this level are (at most) ready to circulate petitions or to march in peaceful demonstrations; a good many of them have done nothing at all and are not willing to do anything. Those scoring higher are willing to do all of the above *and* engage in boycotts; many are ready to go still farther—to take part in rent strikes, illegal occupation of buildings or to block traffic.

As Table 5 makes clear, people's value priorities have a strong relationship to their level of Protest Potential. In Great Britain (where the relationship is weakest), only 21 percent of the Materialists are ready to engage in boycotts or go beyond them in protest against some form of perceived political injustice; among the Post-Materialists, 55 percent have done so, or are willing to do so. The linkage between values and the potential for protest is particularly strong in Italy, where only 20 percent of the Materialists rank high on protest potential—as compared with 69 percent of the Post-Materialists. In all eight countries Post-Materialists are far readier to engage in political protest than Materialists.

In multivariate analyses, when we control for the effects of age, education, income, and one's level of ideological sophistication, a strong relationship persists between Post-Materialist values and a predisposition for unconventional protest. A relatively high potential to use unconventional and disruptive techniques in order to intervene in the political process seems to be directly linked with the Post-Materialist outlook; it is not merely a spurious correlate, resulting from the fact that Post-Materialists tend to be young and well educated.

Table 5 Protest Potential, by Value Type in Eight Western Nations, 1974–1976 (Percent)

Respondent's Value Type	The Netherlands	Britain	United States	Germany	Austria	Italy	Switzerland	Finland
Materialist	27	21	38	23	17	20	17	20
Mixed	42	31	48	36	21	38	27	34
Post-Materialist	74	55	72	74	48	69	61	58

Source: Eight-Nation survey, carried out 1974–1976; for details of fieldwork and a report of findings from five of these eight nations, see Samuel H. Barnes, Max Kaase, et al., *Political Action* (Beverly Hills, Calif.: Sage, 1979).
Note: Figures represent percent scoring "3" or higher on Protest Potential scale. Values index is based on items A–L cited above.

This might seem paradoxical. On one hand, we have seen that the economic uncertainty of the 1970s did not cause Post-Materialism to disappear—on the contrary, its support seems to have grown in most Western countries. On the other hand, the dramatic political protest movements of the late sixties and early seventies have disappeared in the United States (though not in Western Europe): why did this happen, if a relatively high protest potential characterizes the Post-Materialists?

The main answer is that people don't protest in a social vacuum. The Post-Materialists did not protest for the sake of protesting—they responded to specific issues, above all the war in Indochina. The fact that there no longer is a war in Indochina (or, at least, no *American* war) makes a big difference. Almost nothing can compare with war, in terms of violence, drama and human tragedy, and nothing on the current scene can command sustained mass attention in the way the Vietnam War did. In the absence of any political cause fully comparable to the war, it is only natural that much of the attention and energies of Post-Materialists have been diverted into other channels.

For some, this means seeking self-actualization through development of the inner self, rather than through social action. The human potential movement is an example. For those who remain politically active, this turning inward seems like desertion of the cause; the current crop of youth has been characterized as the Me Generation, practicing a culture of narcissism. There is some truth and even more misapprehension in this view. As we have seen, at the close of the 1970s the 15 to 24-year-old group *was* more materialistic than their counterparts at the start of the decade had been—but the difference was modest. If the potential for political protest generally remained only a potential, it may have been because none of the current political causes were as compelling as those of the earlier decade.

[A discussion of disproportionate Post-Materialist presence among elites has been omitted.]

Post-Materialism and the Rise of the New Class

. . .The relative youth and powerlessness of the Post-Materialists may have dictated a strategy of student protest in the 1960s. But Post-Materialism has moved out of the student ghetto. By 1980, a Post-Materialist outlook had become more common than a Materialist one among young technocrats, professionals and politicians of Western countries. As experts, congressional staffers and members of ministerial cabinets, Post-Materialists had direct access to the command posts of the sociopolitical system. Protest was no longer their most effective tool. The impact of Post-Materialism was no longer symbolized by the student with a protest placard, but by the public interest lawyer, or the young technocrat with an environmental impact statement.

In recent years, a growing number of Western intellectuals have focused their attention on the rise of "The New Class." In contrast with the establishment-oriented New Class of Eastern Europe described by Djilas (1966), the New Class in the West is an elite characterized by its adversary stance toward the existing social order (Podhoretz, 1979; Bruce-Briggs, 1979); by its "culture of critical discourse" (Gouldner, 1979, pp. 28-29); and by a "new liberalism" (Ladd, 1978, pp. 48-49). Broder (1980) describes the emergence of a new generation of political elites have many of these characteristics as a "changing of the guard."

There is no clear consensus on the criteria that define the New Class. Ehrenreich and Ehrenreich (1977) describe it as those in the census categories of "professional and technical," plus "managers and administrators"—precisely the categories we have found to be most heavily Post-Materialist. But Ladd (1978) extends its limits to include anyone with a college education. There is even less consensus concerning *why* this well-paid and increasingly powerful stratum of society is critical of the existing economic and political order and participates in leftist political movements. There is a tendency to view an adversary culture as something *inherent* in higher education or in certain occupations, but the reasons are not altogether clear. Highly educated groups have existed for a long time, but in the past they generally were politically conservative. High levels of education and information are the *resource* that enables the New Class to play an important role—but they do not explain why today, an increasing share of the most highly educated and informed strata take an adversary stance toward their society.

I suggest that the rise of Post-Materialism and its subsequent penetration of technocratic and professional elites has been a major factor behind the emergence of the New Class. For this group is distinctive not only in its occupational and educational characteristics, but also in its values. And the ideology attributed to the New Class reflects Post-Materialist values rather closely (Ladd, 1976, 1978). If this is true, it explains why a New Class having these specific characteristics has emerged at this particular point in history.

For the distinctive values of the New Class reflect an historical change that can not be attributed simply to a changing educational and occupational structure. Rising levels of education and a shift of manpower into the "knowledge industries" have played a major role in the rise of this new elite, as Bell (1973, 1976), Lipset and Dobson (1972), Lipset (1979), and others have argued. But—as Table 6 makes clear—an "adversary culture" is not an *inherent* concomitant of the education or adult role of professionals and technocrats. *Older* professionals and technocrats are preponderantly Materialist; it is only among the younger segments of these groups that Post-Materialist priorities outweigh Materialist ones.

Because both the political environment and the social location of Post-Materialists have changed significantly, their tactics have also changed. Though the war in Indochina no longer plays an important role in Western politics, some of the most important movements on the current scene reflect the clash

Table 6 Materialist versus Post-Materialist Values by Respondent's Occupation and Age Group in Nine European Community Nations, 1976–1979 (percent)

	Age less than 35			Ages 35–49			Age 50 and over		
	M	P-M	N	M	P-M	N	M	P-M	N
Top management + top civil servants	20	30	565	22	22	702	28	16	374
Students	20	25	3,800	—	—	—	—	—	—
Professionals	25	21	280	21	19	218	29	12	162
Nonmanual employees	26	18	4,591	34	13	2,918	38	9	1,569
Unemployed persons	24	16	875	38	9	279	48	6	321
Self-employed business persons	35	13	1,329	41	10	1,109	43	7	855
Manual workers	32	11	4,673	40	8	3,264	44	5	2,255
Housewives	38	9	3,469	46	6	3,763	50	5	4,755
Farmers	42	10	347	44	5	528	48	4	778
Retired persons	—	—	—	—	—	—	51	5	7,018

Source: Based on combined data from the nine-nation European Community surveys carried out from 1976 through 1979.

of Materialist and Post-Materialist world views—among them, the women's movement, the consumer advocacy movement, the environmental movement and the antinuclear movement. These movements involve questions of whether one gives top priority to economic growth, or to the individual's right to self-realization and the quality of life.

[A discussion of environmentalism as a Post-Materialist concern has been omitted.]

Conclusion

. . .A decade's time series data indicate that Post-Materialism is a deep-rooted phenomenon with important political consequences. Persisting in an atmosphere of insecurity, Post-Materialism has come to manifest itself in new ways under new circumstances; what was a student subculture in the 1960s has evolved into the ideology of The New Class. And conflict between those seeking Materialist and Post-Materialist goals has become the basis of a major dimension of political cleavage, supplementing though not supplanting the familiar polarization between labor and management.

There are ironies on both sides. For generations, predominantly Materialistic elites took it for granted that nature had infinite resources to withstand consumption and environmental pollution, for the sake of industrial development. But growth did *not* inaugurate the "Politics of Consensus in an Age of Affluence" (Lane, 1965). Instead, after a certain lag, it led to the emergence of new sources of discontent while a blind emphasis on growth that depended on cheap oil, undermined its own future.

More recently, some Post-Materialist elites adopted a mirror image of this view, taking it for granted that industry had infinite resources to support taxation, and regulation—sometimes in a needlessly punitive spirit. The irony here was that in the long run, Post-Materialism is contingent on material security; the insecurity of recent years arrested its growth and gave impetus to a renewed emphasis on reindustrialization and rearmament.

The rise of Post-Materialism was accompanied by a wave of legislation designed to advance the cause of human equality, raise social welfare standards, and protect the consumer and the environment. There were pervasive changes in national priorities. Prior to 1965, over half of the American federal budget was spent on defense and only about one-quarter on health, education and welfare. By the end of the 1970s, these proportions had been almost exactly reversed. That reallocation of resources is now under attack.

It would be gratifying to be able to identify one side as totally right and the other as utterly wrong. Unfortunately it is not that simple. Both Materialist and Post-Materialist goals are essential elements of a good society, and neither emphasis is automatically appropriate, regardless of circumstances. A healthy economy, and defense forces adequate to deter attack are essential to the realization of *both* Materialist and Post-Materialist goals. But they are not the only legitimate political concerns. Beyond a certain point, a military buildup tends to generate countermeasures. The Soviet Union is militarily stronger than ever before, but faces suspicion and opposition from China, Afghanistan, Poland, the West and much of the Third World. And beyond a certain point, material production produces growing social costs and a diminishing payoff. When there are two cars in every garage, a third adds relatively little; a fourth and a fifth would be positively burdensome. From this perspective, a shift to Post-Materialist priorities, with more time, thought and resources going into improving the social and natural environment, is simply a rational response to changing conditions.

A statesman's task is to seek a reasonable balance between a variety of social goals. That task is complicated in any case, but all the more so if the goals themselves can change.

References

Alderfer, Clayton P. (1972). *Existence, Relatedness and Growth: Human Needs in Organizational Settings*. New York: Free Press.

Baker, Kendall L., Russell Dalton and Kai Hildebrandt (1981). *Germany Transformed*. Cambridge, Mass.: Harvard University Press.

Barnes, Samuel, Max Kaase et al. (1979). *Political Action*. Beverly Hills, Calif.: Sage.

Bell, Daniel (1973). *The Coming of Post-Industrial Society*. New York: Basic Books.

——— (1976). *The Cultural Contradictions of Capitalism*. New York: Basic Books.

Block, Jack (1981). "Some Enduring and Consequential Structures of Personality." In A. I. Rabin et al. (eds.), *Further Explorations in Personality*. New York: Wiley-Interscience.

Brim, Orville G., Jr., and Jerome Kagan, eds. (1980). *Constancy and Change in Human Development*. Cambridge, Mass.: Harvard University Press.

Broder, David S. (1980). *Changing of the Guard*. New York: Simon and Schuster.

Bruce-Briggs, B., ed. (1979). *The New Class?* New Brunswick, N.J.: Transaction Books.

Commission of the European Communities (1979). *Survey of Consumer Confidence in the European Community Countries*. Brussels: European Community.

——— (1980). *Public Opinion in the European Community: Euro-Barometre 13*. Brussels: European Community.

Costa, Paul T., Jr., and Robert R. McCrae (1980). "Still Stable after All These Years: Personality as a Key to Some Issues in Adulthood and Old Age." In Paul B. Bates and Orville G. Brim, Jr. (eds.), *Life-Span Development and Behavior*, Vol. 3. New York: Academic Press.

Dalton, Russell J. (1977). "Was There a Revolution? A Note on Generational versus Life-cycle Explanations of Value Differences." *Comparative Political Studies* 9, No. 4: 459–75.

Davies, James C. (1963). *Human Nature and Politics*. New York: Wiley.

Djilas, Milovan (1966). *The New Class*. London: Unwin.

Ehrenreich, Barbara, and John Ehrenreich (1977). "The Professional-Managerial Class." *Radical American* 2: 7–31.

EMNID (1963). *Pressedienst*, cited in *Encounter* 22: 53.

Flanagan, Scott C. (1979). "Value Change and Partisan Change in Japan: The Silent Revolution Revisited." *Comparative Politics* 11: 253–78.

——— (1980). "Value Cleavages, Economic Cleavages and the Japanese Voter." *American Journal of Political Science* 24, No. 2: 178–206.

Glenn, Norval D. (1976). "Cohort Analysts' Futile Quest: Statistical Attempts to Separate Age, Period and Cohort Effects." *American Sociological Review* 41: 900–04.

Gouldner, Alvin W. (1979). *The Future of the Intellectuals and the Rise of the New Class*. New York: Seabury.

Habermas, Jürgen (1979). "Einleitung." In Jürgen Habermas (ed.), *Stichworte zur "Geistigen Situation der Zeit."* Frankfurt: Suhrkamp.

Harrington, Michael (1979). "The New Class and the Left." In B. Bruce-Briggs (ed.), *The New Class?* New Brunswick, N.J.: Transaction Books.

Hayashi, Chikio (1974). "Time, Age and Ways of Thinking—From the Kokuminsei Surveys." *Journal of Asian and African Studies* 10, Nos. 1-2: 75–85.

Heunks, Felix J. (1979). *Nederlanders en hun Samenleving*. Amsterdam: Holland University Press.

Hildebrandt, Kai, and Russell Dalton (1977). "Die neue Politik: Politischer Wandel oder Schönwetter Politik?" *Politische Vierteljahresschrift* 18: 230–56.

Ike, Nobutaka (1973). "Economic Growth and Intergenerational Change in Japan," *American Political Science Review* 67: 1194–1203.

Inglehart, Ronald (1971). "The Silent Revolution in Europe: Intergenerational Change in Post-Industrial Societies." *American Political Science Review* 65: 991–1017.

——— (1977). *The Silent Revolution: Changing Values and Political Styles among Western Publics*. Princeton: Princeton University Press.

——— (1982). "Value Change in Japan and the West." *Comparative Studies* 14, forthcoming.

———, Jacques-René Rabier, Ian Gordon and Carsten J. Sorenson (1980). "Broader Powers for the European Parliament? The Attitudes of Candidates." *European Journal of Political Research* 8: 113–32.

Jaeggi, Urs. "Drinnen and draussen." In Jürgen Habermas (ed.), *Stichworte zur "Geistigen Situation der Zeit."* Frankfurt: Suhrkamp, pp. 443–73.

Jennings, M. Kent, Klaus R. Allerbeck and Leopold Rosenmayer (1979). "Generations and Families: General Orientations." In Samuel H. Barnes, Max Kaase et al. (eds.), *Political Action*. Beverly Hills, Calif.: Sage.

Kaase, Max, and Hans D. Klingemann (1979). "Sozialstruktur, Wertorientierung und Parteiensysteme." In Joachim Matthes (ed.), *Sozialer Wandel in Westeuropa*. Frankfurt: Campus Verlag.

Kemp, David A. (1979). "The Australian Electorate." In Howard R. Penniman (ed.), *The Australian National Elections of 1977*. Washington, D.C.: American Enterprise Institute.

Kerr, Henry, and David Handley (1974). "Conflits des Générations et Politique Etrangère en Suisse." *Annuaire Suisse de Science Politique*, pp. 127–55.

Kesselman, Mark (1979). Review of "The Silent Revolution." *American Political Science Review* 73: 284–86.

Kmieciak, Peter (1976). *Wertstrukturen und Wertwandel in der Bundesrepublik Deutschland*. Göttingen: Schwartz.

Knoke, David, and M. Hout (1976). "Reply to Glenn." *American Sociological Review* 41: 906–08.

Ladd, Everett C., Jr. (1976). "Liberalism Upside Down: The Inversion of the New Deal Order." *Political Science Quarterly* 91: 577–600.

——— (1978). "The New Lines are Drawn: Class and Ideology in America." *Public Opinion* 1: 48–53.

Lafferty, William M. (1976). "Basic Needs and Political Values: Some Perspectives from Norway on Europe's 'Silent Revolution.' " *Acta Sociologica* 19: 117–36.

Lehner, Franz (1979). "Die 'Stille Revolution': zur Theorie und Realität des Wertwandels in hochindustrialisierten Gesellschaften." In Helmut Klages and Peter Kmieciak (eds.), *Wertwandel und gesellschaftlicher Wandel*. Frankfurt: Campus Verlag, pp. 317–27.

Levinson, Daniel J., et al. (1979). *The Seasons of a Man's Life*. New York: Alfred A. Knopf.

Lipset, Seymour Martin (1979). "The New Class and the Professoriate." In B. Bruce-Briggs (ed.), *The New Class?* New Brunswick, N.J.: Transaction Books, pp. 67-88.

———, and Richard B. Dobson (1972). "The Intellectual as Critic and Rebel." *Daedalus* 101: 137–98.

Marsh, Alan (1975). "The Silent Revolution, Value Priorities and the Quality of Life in Britain." *American Political Science Review* 69: 1–30.

——— (1977). *Protest and Political Consciousness*. Beverly Hills, Calif.: Sage Publications.

Maslow, Abraham H. (1954). *Motivation and Personality*. New York: Harper.

Meadows, Donella H., et al. (1972). *The Limits to Growth*. New York: Universe.

Nardi, Rafaella (1980). "Sono le condizioni economiche a influenzare I valori? Un controllo dell'ipotesi di Inglehart.' *Rivista Italiana di Scienza Politica* 10: 293–315.

Nishihira, Sigeki (1974). "Changed and Unchanged Characteristics of the Japanese." *Japan Echo* 1: 22–32.

Pesonen, Pertti, and Risto Sankiaho (1979). *Kansalaiset je kansanvalta: Soumalaisten kasityksia poliittisesta toiminnasta*. Helsinki: Werner Soderstrom Osakeyhtio.

Podhoretz, Norman (1979). "The Adversary Culture and the New Class." In B. Bruce-Briggs (ed.), *The New Class*. New Brunswick, N.J.: Transaction Books, pp. 19–32.

Research Committee on the Study of the Japanese National Character (1979). *A Study of the Japanese National Character: The Sixth Nation-Wide Survey*. Tokyo: Institute of Statistical Mathematics.

Richardson, Bradley M. (1974). *The Political Culture of Japan*. Berkeley, Calif.: University of California Press.
Steinfels, Peter (1979). *The Neo-Conservatives*. New York: Simon and Schuster.
Watanuki, Joji (1979). "Japanese Politics: Changes, Continuities and Unknowns." In Joji Watanuki, *Japanese Politics*. Tokyo: Tokyo University Press.
Zetterberg, Hans (1977). *Arbete, Livsstil och Motivation*. Stockholm: Svenska Arbetsgivareforeningen.

4.3

VALUE CHANGE IN INDUSTRIAL SOCIETIES

Scott C. Flanagan

This essay is a response and critique of Ronald Inglehart's oft-cited and influential theory of value change presented in selection 4.2. Scott Flanagan, a leading scholar in the field of comparative politics, offered this critique as part of a symposium on Inglehart's work. In it, Flanagan does not question the fact of value change; however, he does argue that Inglehart oversimplifies the post-materialist world as unidimensionally embodying such lifestyle issues as environmentalism, racial tolerance, equality, toleration of alternative lifestyles, and self-actualization.

While these definitely are not materialist or class-based issues, they are all aspects of the political and social left. What Flanagan is proposing is that there is a post-materialism of the right that includes law and order, fighting crime, and national defense; these are neither left-leaning nor class-based economic issues. This post-materialism of the right is often referred to as the "new right," which is distinct from the old right in its concern for the protection of property. Flanagan further takes issue with Inglehart's reliance on his diminishing marginal utility argument—the idea that many of the problems of the industrial world have been solved, thus reducing the demand for policies that address these problems. Flanagan does not reject Inglehart's important theory of value change, but rather paints a more complex and what some regard as a more accurate picture of the post-materialist world. Do you find Flanagan's critique of Inglehart compelling?

This controversy harks back to a debate I started with Ronald Inglehart in 1979 (Flanagan 1979), which has found its clearest expression to date in an exchange of articles in 1982 (Flanagan 1982a, 1982b; Inglehart 1982). . . .

The crux of the debate revolves around my argument that there are two distinct kinds of value change taking place in the advanced industrial democracies and that Inglehart has obscured this distinction by collapsing indicators of both into a single scale. My argument has been that these two kinds of change are not only conceptually distinct but are explained by different causal phenomenon and exhibit different patterns of relationships with key demographic and political variables.

Scott C. Flanagan, "Value Change in Industrial Societies," *American Political Science Review* 81 (December 1987): 1303–1319.

Figure 1 Inglehart's View of Cleavage Structures in Advanced Industrial Democracies

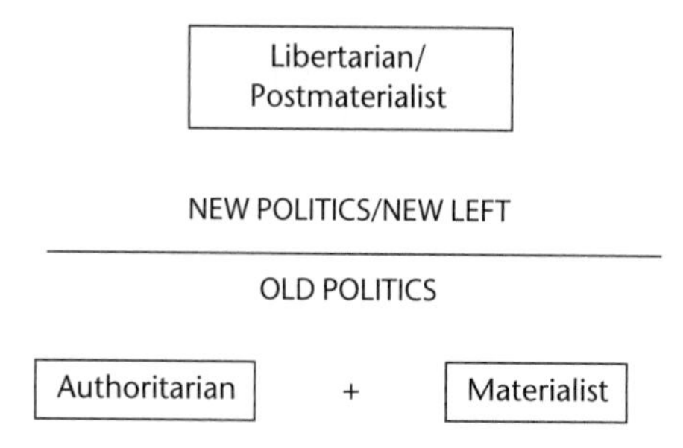

Libertarian-Postmaterialist Values

The distinctions between our respective positions can be confusing because we use overlapping but not identical kinds of indicators to measure our respective scales, and similar labels to identify different conceptual phenomenon. To help clarify the differences, Figures 1 and 2 depict our contrasting conceptualization of value change, with the types of indicator items used to measure the scales presented in boxes. Each line represents the axis of a value cleavage, with labels on either side of the cleavage indicating the political impact of the particular type of value orientation defined by the cleavage.

First it should be noted that our three scales, my two and Inglehart's one, are measured by essentially only three kinds of items. What I call *libertarian* and Inglehart and others label *postmaterialist* items are essentially identical. Looking across the full collection of items that have been designated by these labels, we find they include an emphasis on personal and political freedom, participation (more *say* in government, in one's community, and on the job), equality, tolerance of minorities and those holding different opinions, openness to new ideas and new life styles, environmental protection and concern over quality-of-life issues, self-indulgence, and self-actualization (Calista 1984; Hildebrandt and Dalton

Figure 2 Flanagan's View of Cleavage Structures in Advanced Industrial Democracies

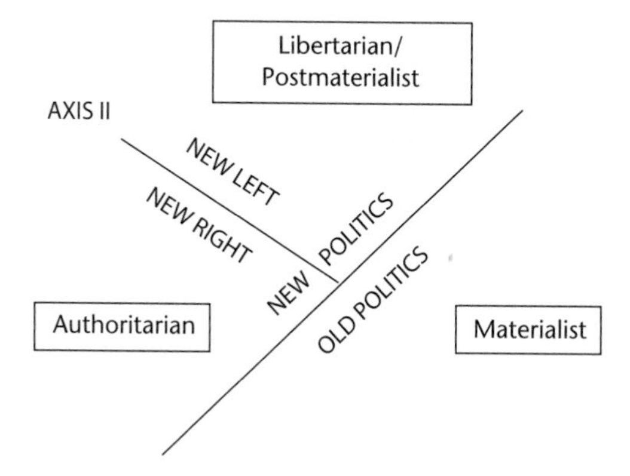

1978; Inglehart 1977; Lafferty and Knutsen 1985). There may be some minor differences over which of the above elements are more or less central to these two concepts, but to the extent that they are all found to cluster, I expect none of the above authors would have trouble accepting any of these elements as part of the concept of *postmaterialism*. I include them all in my notion of *libertarianism*, so we have two different labels representing the same cluster of items. While I believe that Inglehart's term *postmaterialism* is a misnomer as a characterization of either the causes or nature of this value cluster, I will label it here *libertarian-postmaterialist* to clarify that regardless of how we choose to identify these items, we are measuring essentially the same set of values.

The differences emerge at the other end of our scales. I have used the term *materialism* in a more limited sense than Inglehart to identify the emphasis attached to economic concerns, both for oneself and one's society. In my sense of the term, then, *materialists* are those who place a high priority on a stable economy, economic growth, fighting rising prices and, at the more personal level (the private domain), on securing a high-paying job, adequate housing, and a comfortable life. Inglehart includes in his *materialism* concept, however, a second set of noneconomic issues, namely support for a strong defense, law and order, and fighting crime. I label this second set of noneconomic issues as one component of an *authoritarian* value orientation. This *authoritarian* orientation designates a broader cluster of values, which, along with concerns for security and order, includes respect for authority, discipline and dutifulness, patriotism and intolerance for minorities, conformity to customs, and support for traditional religious and moral values. To avoid confusion, I will use the term *materialism* in this discussion to refer to my definition of the term rather than his.

As Figure 1 shows, Inglehart in his original argument presented us with one dimension of value change. Those holding his combination of what I label *materialist* and *authoritarian* value orientations defined the Old Politics for him, while those with the libertarian-postmaterialist orientation the *New Politics* or *New Left*, terms which he used virtually synonymously. He made no mention of a New Right.

This conceptualization encounters difficulty when it attempts to explain realignment. On the one hand we can readily grasp why the younger generation of highly educated, middle-class respondents, whose families have traditionally supported the Right for economic reasons, may now be induced to vote Left as a result of their socialization into libertarian-postmaterialist values. Inglehart's argument breaks down in trying to explain why working-class voters should abandon their historic support of the parties of the Left. Here his argument has rested on a variation of the *embourgeoisement* thesis that he still endorses (Inglehart and Rabier 1986, 458). In his original formulation he wrote that working-class respondents who "have attained a certain level of prosperity relatively recently" will "continue to place a comparatively high value on defending and extending their recent gains" (Inglehart 1971, 992). Because the value priorities of these working-class respondents remained primarily acquisitive or materialist, their growing share of the good life would lead them to become more economically conservative and, hence, potential recruits for the conservative parties.

However, while the working-class Tory phenomenon is well documented, it is capable of explaining the behavior of only a deviant portion of the working class (Goldthorpe et al. 1968; Hamilton 1967). Conservative parties do not defend the economic interests of the working class, and certainly we cannot expect a major realignment of working-class support from Left to Right based on the economic appeals of conservative parties. Moreover, realignment via *embourgeoisement* applies only to the most affluent portion of the working class. However, since affluence in Inglehart's formulation is the primary cause of postmaterialism, these are the very workers most likely to be developing postmaterialist values, which should only reinforce their traditional support for the Left.

In contrast to Inglehart's view, my conceptualization defines two distinct dimensions along which values are changing. The first value cleavage, running along the lower-left-to-upper-right diagonal, taps the priority a respondent attaches to economic issues as opposed to noneconomic, value issues. This cleavage divides materialists from nonmaterialists and the Old Politics from the New Politics. Since materialists attach primary importance to economic concerns, they tend to relate to politics in economic terms, which corresponds to the traditional class politics of the Old Right and the Old Left party alignments. Conversely, the nonmaterialists emphasize the importance of value concerns over economics. This emphasis on value issues defines the New Politics and includes, for example, *both* prochoice and right-to-life alternatives and *both* strong defense and antinuclear positions. Nonmaterialists, then, are those holding either authoritarian or libertarian value preferences, and those who place a higher priority on the kinds of issues defined by these value preferences than on economic issues.

The New Politics is divided by the second value cleavage, which distinguishes the New Left from the New Right. Those falling on the libertarian side of this second value cleavage support for the New Left issue agenda, including liberalizing abortion, women's lib, gay rights, and other new morality issues; protecting the environment, antinuclear weapons, and other quality-of-life issues; and support for protest activities, more direct forms of participation, and minority rights. On the other side of this value cleavage, the authoritarians endorse the New Right issue agenda, which includes right-to-life, anti-women's lib, creationism, antipornography, and support for traditional moral and religious values; a strong defense, patriotism, law and order, opposition to immigration and minority rights, and respect for the traditional symbols and offices of authority.

Figures 1 and 2 are presented to demonstrate the contrasting ways that Inglehart and I have chosen to combine three types of items into our respective scales. Figure 3 depicts the full cleavage structure and its implications for realignment. As in Figure 2, Axis 1 again divides the Old Politics from the New Politics and materialists from nonmaterialists on the basis of the relative salience accorded to economic, as opposed to value, issues. The relevant cleavage on the New Politics side of Axis 1 is Axis 2, which divides the New Left from the New Right and libertarians from authoritarians. The relevant cleavage on the Old Politics side of Axis 1 is Axis 3, which divides the Old Right from the Old Left and the middle class from the working class. As the dotted extension of the New Left-New Right value cleavage into the Old Politics domain in Figure 3 suggests, the Axis 1 value priority distinction and the Axis 2 value preference cleavage are essentially independent of each other. Thus we should expect to find libertarian-materialists as well as authoritarian-materialists. The line is dotted in the Old Politics domain because for the materialist, who places greatest priority on economic concerns, the libertarian-authoritarian distinction will have little effect on his or her voting behavior. Similarly, the Axis 3 class cleavage extends as a dotted line into the New Politics domain, but for nonmaterialists these class distinctions will not be paramount in their voting decisions.

It is important, therefore, to reach an independent determination of a respondent's position on both value dimensions. An authoritarian-libertarian value preferences scale will tell us whether the respondent is likely to support the New Right or New Left issue agenda. A materialist-nonmaterialist value priorities scale will tell us whether these New Politics kinds of value concerns or the Old Politics economic issues will be foremost in the voter's mind when he or she makes a choice. This latter distinction is particularly important for predicting the behavior of cross-pressured voters, who, for example, may

Figure 3 Full Cleavage Structures for Advanced Industrial Democracies

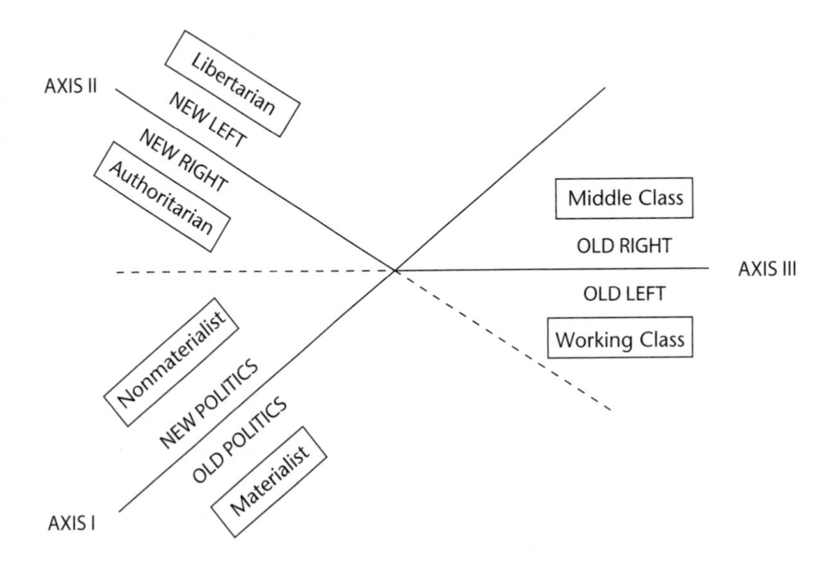

fall on the Left side on the Old Politics cleavage because of their working-class occupations and union memberships but on the Right side of the New Politics cleavage because of their authoritarian values.

The conceptualizations of value change in Figures 2 and 3 can explain the realignment of working-class voters to the Right more effectively than can Inglehart's conceptualization (Figure 1). Across Axis 2 in Figure 3 there has been a long-term shift from authoritarian to libertarian values associated with the changing circumstances under which younger generations are being socialized and the growth of higher education. As the number of libertarians in the advanced industrial democracies reached a critical mass, they began pushing for New Left issues and achieving some successes. The increasing articulation of libertarian values and the protest movements organized to press for the adoption of the New Left agenda mobilized a backlash among authoritarians, who felt that their basic values and way of life were being threatened. This increasing polarization on the New Politics issues in turn heightened their salience in relation to the Old Politics class issues, which were already on the decline due to growing affluence and the success of the welfare state. Thus the shift across Axis 2 from a heavily asymmetric balance in favor of the traditional authoritarian values to a more symmetric balance between authoritarian and libertarian values heightened the salience of New Politics relative to Old Politics issues, thereby inducing movement across Axis I as well. Since education is related to the class and values cleavages in a cross-cutting pattern, associating high education with both the Old Right and the New Left, the combined trends on both dimensions promote the middle-class-to-the-Left and working-class-to-the-Right realignment pattern Inglehart and others have been describing.

One thing that is new in Inglehart's most recent contributions is that he is now beginning to adopt much of the terminology of the Figure 3 conceptualization explicitly. However, he is doing this without in any way revising or altering his scale, which collapses the two dimensions into one and hence treats authoritarian values and the New Right issue agenda as essentially synonymous with materialism. This approach of grafting a new terminology onto his old conceptualization simply adds to the confusion.

Examples of this subtle shift in terminology are abundant in his recent discussions of the value change-realignment phenomenon. In this discussion, Inglehart first reiterates the argument that he and others have made explaining why the New Politics values cleavage is an important phenomenon to study even though there is as yet little evidence that it has induced a realignment of party systems in the advanced industrial democracies. That argument points out that the expression of the New Politics value cleavage in patterns of party support is inhibited by frozen party loyalties and institutionalized interest-group-to-party linkages (Dalton, Flanagan, and Beck 1984; Flanagan and Dalton 1984). Nevertheless the rising salience of the New Politics is increasingly placing these party systems under stress. Perhaps Inglehart's most important contribution in this regard is to demonstrate that the meaning of *Left* and *Right* is changing among the elites and mass electorates of these societies from economic-issue orientations to noneconomic-value-issue orientations (Inglehart 1984). And most recently, he demonstrates that the amount of class-party realignment that can be shown to have already taken place is mostly benefiting New Left and New Right parties rather than the traditional Old Left and Old Right parties and that beyond that, there exists considerable potential support in these electorates for New Left and New Right kinds of parties (Inglehart and Rabier 1987; and the opening to this *Controversy*).

In this discussion of the shift from the Old Politics to the New Politics and its implications for realignment, he seems to buy into many of the distinctions presented in the conceptualizations of Figures 2 and 3. He says that the New Politics issue polarization "primarily reflects the new noneconomic issues" and that "the issues that define Left and Right for Western publics today are not class conflict [issues], so much as a polarization between the goals emphasized by post-materialists, and the *traditional social and religious values* emphasized by materialists" (Inglehart and Rabier 1986, 470, 471; emphasis added). While still using the term *materialists*, the cluster of values and issues preferences that emerge from his own factor analyses reported in his 1984 and coauthored 1986 pieces as being associated with self-placement on the Right end of a Left-Right scale are that the military-defense effort should be stronger, the existing social order should be defended, terrorism should be punished more severely, nuclear power plants are essential, the unemployed don't want to work, there are too many immigrant workers, one should sacrifice oneself for one's country, abortion is wrong, religion is important, and God exists. To apply the label *Materialist* to these New Right issues is clearly a misnomer. Moreover, the New Left issues he identifies (proenvironment, abortion, peace, homosexual rights, etc.) clearly did not "stimulate a materialist reaction" in the sense of an increased concern for economic issues. Quite to the contrary, the New Left issues have helped to crowd the economic issues off the agenda and have rather provoked the emergence of the above New Right set of moral and religious issues.

Here we begin to see the problems inherent in the theoretical arguments and conceptual labels that Inglehart has attached to his value scale. The emergence in his own studies of a New Right cluster of noneconomic value issues around the New Politics cleavage that fit my definition of authoritarian values implies a delinking of the New Right with the concept of *materialism*. The point is that the New Right is as much *nonmaterialist* as the New Left. The program of the National Front, the French example of a New Right party, stresses law and order, restrictions on immigration, opposition to abortion and anticommunism. It is because these issues have little or nothing to do with traditional class issues and material, economic concerns that the New Right parties are able to draw their support disproportionately from the working class, as Inglehart so clearly demonstrates.

A New Theoretical Basis for Materialism

In my view, the most important fresh contribution found in Inglehart's analysis presented above is the new theoretical basis he provides for understanding the shift from materialist to nonmaterialist issue priorities. He labels this argument "the diminishing marginal utility of economic determinism." The diminishing-marginal-utility approach is a much sounder theoretical foundation for explaining the shift from economic to noneconomic value priorities than Maslow's need hierarchy. Maslow presents us with a theory of psychological development and motivation arguing that an individual reared in an environment in which lower-level needs are satisfied will develop into a mature personality, one who as an adult is better able to cope with the deprivation of lower-level needs and hence is insulated from need regression (Maslow 1970). In contrast, Inglehart's items typically tap issue priorities in the domain of public policy. He is, then, dealing with a vastly different phenomenon, and thus the inappropriateness of the Maslowian argument leaves him with no rationale for explaining why respondents would not increasingly place a higher priority on the issue of rising prices when inflation becomes an increasingly serious problem in their country. Indeed the evidence suggests that they will (Flanagan 1982b).

What the *diminishing marginal utility* concept suggests, however, is something quite different than the Maslowian early-childhood-socialization notion. As Inglehart's Table 1 and Figure 3 demonstrate, the higher a nation's GNP per capita, the weaker both the felt need for further reducing income inequality and the other classic economic policies of the Left designed to redistribute the wealth more equally. As Inglehart argues, after a certain level of equality has been achieved, further movement in the direction of perfect equality has a diminishing marginal utility, as there is less and less left to redistribute, and fewer gain and more lose in the process.

Figure 1 in his companion piece (Inglehart and Rabier 1987), most clearly presents the lesson that is to be learned from the diminishing-marginal-utility thesis. As median income goes up in a nation, the ratio of what the respondent views would be the absolutely necessary income to what the actual household income is drops. In other words, more people find themselves with a comfortable surplus. Their basic economic needs are being met, so economic issues become less intensely held and are assigned a relatively lower priority than they were when household income was at or below the level of absolutely necessary income. All other things being equal, the proportion of non-materialists will rise as average household income within a nation rises above a level perceived as necessary to provide the basic necessities of life. As the margin of surplus income increases, the citizen's expenditure of energy in support of economic issues will yield a diminishing marginal utility, and the nonmaterialist is born.

Being a nonmaterialist at time one, however, does not ensure that a respondent will still assign a relatively low priority to economic concerns at time two. As has been shown elsewhere, the relative priority that a respondent attaches to economic issues in relation to other concerns varies across the life cycle as the respondent's economic responsibilities and burdens change (Flanagan 1982a; Milkis and Baldino 1978). A respondent's priorities will also shift in response to short-term changes in perceptions of how well-off he or she is. Aggregate stability in the proportion of materialists, therefore, is a function of national affluence and will remain rather stable so long as economic conditions in the country do not change. Nevertheless, aggregate stability can mask considerable instability at the individual level.

Inglehart claims that his diminishing-marginal-utility (DMU) argument is not new but was implicit in his original value-change thesis. Rather, the logic of the DMU argument as a causal explanation of value change is completely different from his original Maslowian approach. It should be recalled that it was his reference to Maslow's hierarchy of needs that enabled Inglehart to claim that the materialism-postmaterialism value change was the product of early childhood socialization. The Maslowian analogy gave birth to the idea that socialization under conditions of affluence and security create a distinct prioritization of needs that immunizes the individual from regression to lower-level concerns as an adult, even if the conditions of life change. Apparently Inglehart has found that there is a diminishing marginal utility in citing Maslow for his purposes, and indeed we find no references whatsoever to Maslow or the need hierarchy in either of his two current companion pieces. I believe history will show that his Maslowian argument was a clever analogy that did not fit.

In contrast, childhood socialization logically plays no role in the DMU argument. An estimation of the diminishing marginal utility of added increments of income is a rational-choice assessment based on the individual's current level of need and sense of relative deprivation. This assessment, then, is very much a *context-dependent* phenomenon, very similar to the life-context arguments that Milkis and Baldino (1978) and I have made. What is new in Inglehart's notion is that he has changed the relevant context from the individual level, a level at which we would expect to find considerable change across the life cycle, to the societal level. In doing so, he has convincingly made the case that we should find important thresholds in national income and household income, which, once crossed, yield aggregate shifts in the relative priority attached to economic concerns. These thresholds are probably not absolute but rather are likely to shift somewhat in line with changing societal standard-of-living expectations. Still, the notion that at some point a sufficient surplus should lower the priority attached to economic issues and to further increasing one's income, not in every case but in the aggregate, is compelling.

The *diminishing marginal utility* notion provides some legitimacy for using the term *postmaterialist.* I have preferred the term *nonmaterialist* because of my focus on the fluctuation that occurs on the individual level across the life cycle. However, the notion that advanced industrial societies as a whole are moving towards a lower priority ranking for materialistic concerns suggests more of a unidirectional shift, perhaps justifying the *post-* prefix. Still this is clearly not the kind of irreversible phenomenon as suggested by the Maslowian arguments. Indeed we would expect that serious economic problems, such as runaway inflation or depression, would alter the current assessments of many respondents as to the relative priority that should be attached to economic concerns.

Thus, we are dealing with two distinct kinds of value change explained by very different kinds of causal phenomenon. On the one hand we are witnessing an eclipse of the salience of economic issues. This trend is explained by the diminishing-marginal-utility argument. As the affluence of, and equality within, nations increases, the percentage of the population that enjoys a cushion of surplus income above what is needed for the basic necessities of life grows. For these people, noneconomic issues begin to gain in salience relative to material, economic concerns. There may be some variation in the priority accorded to economic issues at the individual level over time, with changes in fortune and life context, and also short-term setbacks at the aggregate level associated with economic down-turns. Over the long haul, however, we should be seeing a net growth in the proportions of *postmaterialists*—as here defined in terms of the relative priority attached to economic issues (Old Politics) as opposed to noneconomic, value issues (New Politics).

The second and distinct trend is the one that defines the change in value preferences. Within the so-called New Politics can be detected a long-term, gradual movement from the New Right to the New Left poles, as a function of age (intergenerational change) and education. Space constraints will not permit a full elaboration here of the causal mechanisms, elaborated elsewhere, behind this pattern of value change (see Flanagan 1979, 1982a, 1984). In brief, the argument is that an intergenerational pattern of value change along the authoritarian-libertarian (A/L) dimension has resulted from four major changes in the basic conditions of life under which successive generations have been socialized—a growing equality in incomes and life styles, the accelerating pace of change, the advance and diffusion of scientific knowledge, and the rise of the "no-risk" society (Aharoni 1981). These changes are increasingly liberating mankind respectively from the constraining conditions of subservience to authority figures, conformity, ignorance, and insecurity, and enabling the individual to pursue more fully the goal of self-actualization. Given the nature of many of these changes in basic life conditions, which are driving the change along the A/L value dimension, it is not difficult to understand why the increasing levels of higher education found in the advanced industrial societies are also playing an important role in diffusing libertarian values.

New Evidence of Dimensional Independence

At this point one might raise the question why—if I am in fact right—it has been so difficult to demonstrate the problems with Inglehart's scale empirically and why he has been able to pile up evidence from an exhaustive number of surveys conducted in 10–15 nations over the past 15 years. For example, Inglehart has consistently claimed that there is no evidence of a life-cycle effect on the proportion of materialist[s] found in given age cohorts over time and that there was no substantial reduction in the proportion of his postmaterialists across a large number of countries despite inflation, recession, and other economic woes in the seventies. Moreover, he seems to have the evidence to make good on those claims.

Such a finding is central to his argument because it supports his notion that the materialist-postmaterialist change is a function of early learning that insulates the individual against later change. However the problem here is that while Inglehart labels his scale *materialist–post-materialist*, 75% of the items used to operationalize the scale rather tap the authoritarian-libertarian dimension. This latter dimension, which measures how respondents divide on the New Politics value cleavage, is not affected by changes in the economy. Changes in one's income, all other things being equal, will not affect one's position on abortion, pornography, or nuclear weapons or one's respect for authority. The relative aggregate stability of Inglehart's scale over time in the face of changes in the economic context, therefore, is derived in large part from the fact that his scale, in essence, is tapping more of the New Left-New Right (libertarian-authoritarian) cleavage than the New Politics-Old Politics (materialist–non-materialist) division.

What further confounds our ability to disaggregate the two dimensions combined within his scale is the format of his value-priority questions, which artificially forces an association between his materialist and authoritarian items. Whether using his original 4-item format or his expanded 12-item version, respondents are typically presented with groups of four alternatives and asked to select their first and second priorities. In each case two items are—to use my terminology—libertarian (e.g., free speech and participation); one item is authoritarian (e.g., defense); and one is materialist (e.g., rising prices). This presents the respondent with a *dilemma of constrained choice*. Libertarians who are also non-materialists will naturally select the two libertarian items. Libertarians who are materialists, placing greater priority on their economic than on their value concerns, will pick the one materialist item and then, having no other materialist item to pick, will select one of the libertarian alternatives, dropping them into Inglehart's mixed category. Authoritarian-materialists, following the same logic, will pick the materialist item first and then select the authoritarian option.

The real problem, however, is confronted by the authoritarian-nonmaterialists. As a nonmaterialist the respondent will be mostly concerned with the non-economic, value issues. But he or she finds only one authoritarian option. As an authoritarian, the respondent is very unlikely to select either of the libertarian options and thus, by default, is most likely to pick up the economic option as a second choice. The result is that the authoritarian-nonmaterialists are classified as *materialists*, which is an incorrect coding for a materialist-nonmaterialist scale but a correct coding if we view Inglehart's scale as a stand-in for the authoritarian-libertarian scale.

This logic explains two important characteristics of Inglehart's scale. First it helps us understand why we always find a heavily skewed distribution with many materialists and typically only 5%–15% postmaterialists, while the authoritarian-libertarian type of scale tends to divide samples much more evenly. Although both types of nonmaterialists are properly sorted, the authoritarian-materialists are classified as materialists while the libertarian-materialists are classified as mixed. Secondly, and more importantly, whatever real association there may be between authoritarian and materialist orientations is greatly exaggerated by the constrained-choice feature, which forces authoritarian-nonmaterialists to select the materialist option.

The answer to this problem is to adopt an item format that allows an independent and unconstrained assessment of the priority of all three types of items identified in Figure 1—libertarian, authoritarian, and materialist. This is a little tricky, due to the inherent differences between value priorities and value preferences. The materialism items are designed to tap the relative importance of economic and value concerns, both of which are presumably positively valued by the respondent. In contrast, authoritarian and libertarian values stand in opposition to each other, with those who stand at one pole typically viewing the opposite set of preferences in a negative light.

* * *

The data to test these conflicting hypotheses comes from a 16-item value question I designed using the above unconstrained format administered in a 1984 nationwide Japanese survey of university-educated respondents.[1] Due to the richness of the value themes tapped by the survey, it was possible to add several more items, bringing the total to 21, with 9 libertarian, 8 authoritarian and 4 materialist items. As shown in Table 1, the *libertarian* items cover the themes of participation, support for minorities, open-mindedness, personal freedom and freedom of speech, improving the quality of life, self-fulfillment, and self-indulgence. The *authoritarian* items include the themes of patriotism, a strong defense, respect for authority and strong leaders, preserving traditional morals and values, conformity, and intolerance of dissenters. The *materialist* priorities were measured by the four items identifying those who place high emphasis on maintaining high economic growth, securing a high-paying job, and working hard and saving for the future and those that do not feel that their society overemphasizes material things.

---

1. This Japan's Successor Generation survey was conducted under the sponsorship of the United States Information Agency in October and November of 1984, yielding 803 completed questionnaires of university-educated Japanese between the ages of 20 and 91. I am greatly indebted to the principal investigator of the study, James S. Marshall of the East Asia and Pacific Branch of the USIA's Office of Research, for including my values battery in the survey and making the data available to me (see Marshall 1985).

As Table 1 shows, the libertarian items all load positively on the first unrotated factor and the authoritarian items all load negatively, while the four materialist items all fall in the middle, closer to a zero loading. Even more dramatically, the table demonstrates that with the exception of two libertarian items and one materialist item that have somewhat ambiguous loadings, the rotated three-factor solution neatly divides the three types of items, with the libertarian items loading on the first factor, the authoritarian items on the second factor, and the materialist items on the third. In discussing the exceptions below, it is important to note that all of the items included in each of the three reported value domains drawn in Table 1 load highly on a first unrotated factor when the analysis is limited to only those items within a given value type. The inclusion of these three items (marked ?) within their identified value domain is only brought into question because of the presence of other factors on which they also load.

Table 1 Factor Loadings for 21 Libertarian, Authoritarian, and Materialist Items on the First Unrotated Factor and for the Three-Factor Rotated Solution, Japan 1984

	Factor Loadings For			
	1st Unrotated	Three-Factor Rotated Solution		
Items by Type	Factor	1st	2nd	3rd
Libertarian items				
Personal freedom	.611	.523	−.293	.267
Freedom of speech	.530	.413	−.292	.279
Giving people more say in government decisions	.475	.548	−.117	−.098
Increasing benefits for disadvantaged	.475	.672	.032	−.047
Improving environment and quality of life	.436	.633	.073	.113
Active citizen participation in local politics	.363	.318	−.185	.040
Being open-minded to new ideas	.309	.421	.015	.040
Seeking personal fulfillment	.309	?.286	−.081	.395
Living for today and enjoying oneself	.281	?.188	−.143	.431
Materialist items				
Securing a high-paying job	.104	.131	.100	.664
Working hard and saving for the future	.002	.299	.390	?.329
Maintaining high economic growth	−.114	−.116	.132	.541
Feel our society is not too materialistic	−.115	−.192	.037	.482
Authoritarian items				
Preserving traditional morals and values	−.197	.150	.468	−.009
Following custom and neighbors' expectations	−.325	.066	.592	.145
A few strong leaders better than parties	−.343	−.131	.380	.044
Respect for authority	−.351	−.106	.419	.029
Providing for strong defense forces	−.491	−.349	.399	.295
No room in Japan for dissenters	−.509	−.103	.633	−.145
Patriotism and loyalty most important	−.631	−.268	.638	−.106
Should increase defense spending	−.637	−.468	.456	.106

Notes: The three-factor solution was derived from a varimax rotation.
The three items marked ? are brought into question because of the presence of other factors on which they may also load.

Table 2 The Association among the Libertarian, Authoritarian, and Materialist Item Scales and between Those Scales and Several Key Demographic and Attitudinal Variables

Scales and Variables	Libertarian	Authoritarian	Combined Authoritarian-Libertarian	Materialist
Authoritarian scale	–.32			
Materialism scale	.13	.23	(–.07)	
Age	–.28	.30	–.37	(–.02)
Right-Left party identification	.28	–.39	.41	(–.04)
Right-Left self-placement	.30	–.41	.44	(–.05)

Note: All correlations are significant at the .001 level except those in parentheses, which are not significant even at the .01 level.

Each type of item was then combined into a scale and the resulting three scales were then correlated with each other and with several key demographic and attitudinal items as shown in Table 2. As expected, a strong inverse correlation was found between the libertarian and authoritarian scales (–.32). Moreover, the libertarian scale is inversely associated with age (–.28) and positively correlated with the Left ends of the Right-Left self-placement and party identification scales (.30 and .28 respectively). Conversely, the authoritarian scale is associated with old age (.30) and the political Right (–.41 and –.39). The strength of these correlations is somewhat further increased when all the libertarian and authoritarian items are combined into a single scale. In marked contrast, the materialism scale yields no significant correlations with either age or political preference. Unfortunately, the relationships with the other key demographic variable, education, could not be tested because the sample was limited to the university educated. However, the relationships reported in Table 2 are precisely those reported in my earlier study (Flanagan 1982a), only now the materialism scale is derived from the kinds of materialism items Inglehart employs (rather than on a post hoc basis from a most-important-problem question), so there can be no question of comparability. The earlier study included education and class, and we can infer that the relationships would be the same here if the sample had not been restricted on those dimensions.

The most important finding in Table 1 is that the security items Inglehart uses to measure materialism cluster with the authoritarian items while the economic items stand alone. The most important finding in Table 2 is that the pattern of relationships supports my argument that the materialism-nonmaterialism and authoritarian-libertarian dimensions of change are explained by different causal phenomen[a] and yield contrasting patterns or relationships with key demographic and political variables.

The most interesting unexpected finding in Table 2 is that materialism is positively correlated not only with the authoritarian scale (.23) but also with the libertarian scale (.13). Since I have viewed materialism as essentially an utilitarian orientation, I expected some significant correlation between the authoritarian and materialist items based on the following logic: The relative importance a respondent will place on the economic issues of the day—inflation, depression, unemployment, further economic growth, etc.—is a function of both the respondent's margin-of-income surplus and the extent to which the respondent perceives that his or her economic interests are being threatened by those issues. Thus new middle-class professionals in the advanced industrial democracies are likely to be nonmaterialists, both because of the substantial cushion their incomes provide them with beyond the basic necessities of life and because the skills they possess are highly valued in postindustrial economies, providing them with great job security. Conversely, the blue-collar worker is more likely to be a materialist, both because of his or her smaller income surplus and because this respondent's skills are increasingly becoming obsolete, thus heightening concern over livelihood.

The finding of positive correlations with both of these opposite value preferences suggests that those lying towards both of the extreme ends of the authoritarian-libertarian value dimension might have other kinds of inducements beyond utilitarian evaluations. It may be that something in the values themselves that are held by the extreme form, or pure type, of authoritarian or libertarian predispose each of them towards materialist priorities. Clues as to what these motivations might be are derived from the three items in Table 1 with ambiguous loadings. The materialism item *working hard and saving for the future* actually loads slightly more heavily on the authoritarian dimensions than on the materialism dimension. Elsewhere I have argued that the values of frugality, discipline, and hard work are part of the traditional authoritarian orientation (Flanagan 1979).

One might just mark this down as a bad item, since it combines the authoritarian orientation towards diligence and the traditional "Confucian" and "protestant" work ethics with the materialist concern with economic well-being. If we look more deeply, however, we may find a *psychological materialism*; that is, the authoritarian's preoccupation with discipline and hard work, in contrast with the self-indulgent libertarian orientations, which place a high priority on leisure activities, may be related to the same heightened need for power and sense of weakness that drive one to identify with established authority figures and symbols. Thus the same insecurities that prompt one to support a strong military and law and order may also motivate hard work, frugality, and a heightened effort to maximize one's economic security to placate anxieties about one's own weaknesses and lack of power. Psychological studies have provided evidence suggesting that such authoritarian needs for power and feelings of weakness and insecurity are the product of child-rearing practices that stress discipline over affective ties, a behavioral distinction that has been shown to correlate with class and education (Adorno et al. 1950; Winter 1973). Thus, a number of lower-class, low-education authoritarians may also be psychological materialists.

Just as revealing is the loading of the two libertarian items, *seeking personal fulfillment* and *living for today and enjoying oneself*, on the materialism factor. This suggests a Yuppie type of *terminal materialism*. Some libertarians who are preoccupied with self-fulfillment and self-indulgence may place an excessive valuation on maintaining a strong economy, acquiring high-paying jobs and surrounding themselves with all the material trappings of affluence. While for some libertarians, materialism may only be a secondary instrumental priority, something to be valued because it makes other life goals possible; for others, materialism may become an end in itself—a terminal value—because of the status, self-esteem, sense of achievement, comfort, self-indulgence and other gratifications that it provides. Some libertarians, then, may be susceptible to a "terminal materialism" in which, notwithstanding their relative affluence, increasing their wealth, possessions, and consumption of the good life comes to be valued more highly than other kinds of libertarian values. Thus, for them, economic issues may take precedence over their support for the New Left issue agenda.

The diminishing-marginal-utility thesis is a powerful one for explaining why there is a higher proportion of nonmaterialists in the United States than in Colombia. However, after reaching and surpassing some level of societal and personal affluence, further gains in affluence will have little effect on altering one's value priorities, and we are left with having to explain why some upper-middle-class respondents are still materialists. Indeed there is some evidence of a countertrend in the United States running against the logic of the diminishing-marginal-utility thesis. The American Council on Education's (1973–86) annual nationwide surveys of roughly two hundred thousand entering college freshmen, which began 20 years ago, have documented a growing emphasis on materialism. In 1966 only 45% of the respondents nationwide selected *money: being well off* as an essential or very important life goal. By 1976 this had increased to 52% and by 1986 to 74%. Undoubtedly for some of these entering freshmen, money is viewed as a strictly secondary instrumental priority. On the other hand, it is likely to be a vital priority for others and the notion of a Yuppie type of terminal materialism may be useful here in explaining the failure of materialism to wither away among some of the affluent.

As shown in Figures 4–5, when the three items with ambiguous loadings are dropped and the remaining 18 items are factored again, the factor plots yield three tightly clustered and distinct value domains. The plot of the first and second factors in Figure 4 depicts a sharp differentiation of the libertarian and authoritarian items along both dimensions while the materialism items fall near the origins of both axes. The plot of the second and third factors show the libertarian and authoritarian items splitting on the second factor but lying close to the origins on the third, while the materialist items load heavily on the third factor but lie close to the origins on the second.

When the value scales are recomputed based on the smaller set of 18 items, the correlation between the libertarian and materialism scales drops from .13 to an insignificant but still positive .04. The correlation between the authoritarian and materialism scales also drops from .23 to .18, and if the two authoritarian items loading below .40 are removed, the correlation declines further to .14. The finding of a higher correlation between authoritarianism and materialism in the case of a class-constrained sam-

Figure 4 Two-Dimensional Plot of the Item Factor Loadings for the 18-Item Three-Factor Varimax Rotated Solution (horizontal axis = factor 1; vertical axis = factor 2)

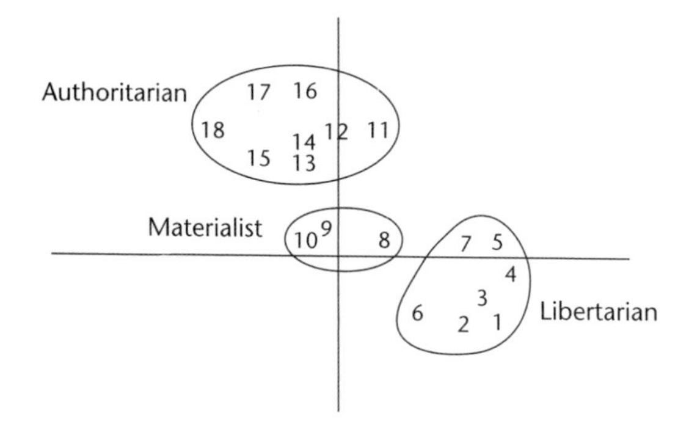

Figure 5 Two-Dimensional Plot of the Item Factor Loadings for the 18-Item Three-Factor Varimax Rotated Solution (horizontal axis = factor 2; vertical axis = factor 3)

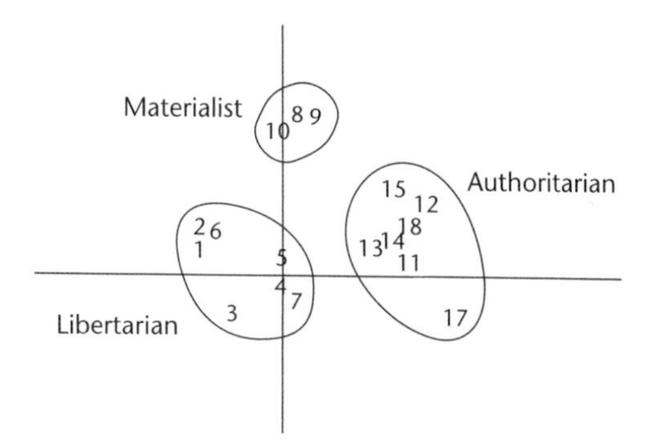

Note: Items 1–7 are respectively the first seven libertarian items listed in Table 1, Items 8–10 are the three materialist items (omitting *working hard*), and Items 11–18 are in order of the Table 1 listing of the eight authoritarian items.

ple of university-educated respondents, where the utilitarian argument discussed above is likely to have less relevance, suggests that even among the highly educated there are still more authoritarians who are psychological materialists than there are libertarians who are terminal materialists.

* * *

References

Abramson, Paul R., John H. Aldrich, and David Rohde. 1985. *Change and Continuity in the 1984 Elections*. Washington, DC: Congressional Quarterly.

Abramson, Paul R., and Ronald Inglehart. 1986. Generational Replacement and Value Change in Six West European Societies. *American Journal of Political Science* 30: 1–25.

Adorno, Teodor, Else Frenkel-Brunswick, David J. Levinson, and R. Nevitt Sanford. 1950. *The Authoritarian Personality*. New York: Harper.

American Council on Education. 1973–86. *The American Freshman: National Norms*. Annual report issued by the Cooperative Institution Research Program. Graduate School of Education. University of California.

Ahroni, Yair. 1981. *The No-Risk Society*. Chatham, NJ: Chatham.

Baker, Kendall, Russell Dalton, and Kai Hildebrandt. 1981. *Germany Transformed*. Cambridge: Harvard University Press.

Books, John W., and Joann Reynolds. 1975. A Note on Class Voting in Great Britain and the United States. *Comparative Political Studies* 75: 360–75.

Boore, O. 1984. Critical Electoral Change in Scandinavia. In *Electoral Change in Advanced Industrial Democracies*, ed. Russell J. Dalton, Scott C. Flanagan, Paul A. Beck. Princeton: Princeton University Press.

Calista, Donald. 1984. Postmaterialism and Value Convergence. *Comparative Political Studies* 16: 529–55.

Chen, Edward K. Y. 1979. *Hyper-growth in Asian Economics*. New York: Holmes & Meier.

Connor, Walter D. 1979. *Socialism, Politics, and Equality: Hierarchy and Change in Eastern Europe and the USSR*. New York: Columbia University Press.

Converse, Philip E., and George Dupeaux. 1962. Politicization of the Electorate in France and the United States. *Public Opinion Quarterly* 26: 1–23.

Converse, Philip E., and Roy Pierce. 1986. *Political Representation in France*. Cambridge: Belknap Press of Harvard University Press.

Dalton, Russell J. 1981. The Persistence of Values and Life Cycle Changes. In *Contributions to Political Psychology*, ed. Hans Klingemann and Max Kaase. Weinheim: Beltz.

Dalton, Russell J. 1984. The German Party System Between Two Ages. In *Electoral Change: Realignment and Dealignment in Industrial Societies*, ed. author, Scott Flanagan, and Paul Beck. Princeton: Princeton University Press.

Dalton, Russell, Scott Flanagan, and Paul Beck. 1984. *Electoral Change in Advanced Industrial Democracies: Realignment or Dealignment?* Princeton: Princeton University Press.

Finer, Samuel. 1980. *The Changing British Party System 1945–79*. Washington, DC: American Enterprise Institute.

Flanagan, Scott C. 1979. Value Change and Partisan Change in Japan: The Silent Revolution Revisited. *Comparative Politics* 11: 253–78.

Flanagan, Scott C. 1982a. Changing Values in Advanced Industrial Societies. *Comparative Political Studies* 14: 403–44.

Flanagan, Scott C. 1982b. Measuring Value Change in Advanced Industrial Societies. *Comparative Political Studies* 15: 99–128.

Flanagan, Scott C. 1984. Electoral Change in Japan: A Study of Secular Realignment. In *Electoral Change in Advanced Industrial Democracies*, ed. Russell Dalton, Scott Flanagan, and Paul Beck. Princeton: Princeton University Press.

Flanagan, Scott C., and Russell J. Dalton. 1984. Parties under Stress: Realignment and Dealignment in Advanced Industrial Societies. *Western European Politics* 7: 7–23.

Goldthorpe, John, David Lockwood, Frank Bechhofer, and Jennifer Platt. 1968. *The Affluent Worker*. Cambridge: Cambridge University Press.

Hamilton, Richard F. 1967. *Affluence and the French Worker in the Fourth Republic*. Princeton: Princeton University Press.

Hibbs, Douglas A., R. Douglas Rivers, and Nicholas Vasilatos. 1982. The Dynamics of Political Support for American Presidents among Occupational and Partisan Groups. *American Journal of Political Science* 26: 312–32.

Hildebrandt, Kai, and Russell J. Dalton. 1978. The New Politics: Political Change or Sunshine Politics. In *Elections and Parties*, ed. Max Kaase and Klaus von Beyme. Beverly Hills: Sage.

Inglehart, Ronald. 1971. The Silent Revolution in Europe: Intergenerational Change in Post-Industrial Societies. *American Political Science Review* 65: 991–1017.

Inglehart, Ronald. 1977. *The Silent Revolution*. Princeton: Princeton University Press.

Inglehart, Ronald. 1982. Changing Values in Japan and the West. *Comparative Political Studies* 14: 445–80.

Inglehart, Ronald. 1984. The Changing Structure of Political Cleavages in Western Society. In *Electoral Change in Advanced Industrial Democracies*, ed. Russell Dalton, Scott Flanagan, and Paul Beck. Princeton: Princeton University Press.

Inglehart, Ronald. 1985a. New Perspectives on Value Change. *Comparative Political Studies* 17: 485–532.

Inglehart, Ronald. 1985b. Aggregate Stability and Individual-Level Change in Mass Belief Systems: The Level of Analysis Paradox. *American Political Science Review* 79: 97–116.

Inglehart, Ronald, and Jacques-René Rabier. 1986. Political Realignment in Advanced Industrial Society: From Class-Based Politics to Quality of Life Politics. *Government and Opposition* 21: 456–79.

Kinder, Donald R., and D. Roderick Kiewiet. 1981. Sociotropic Politics: The American Case. *British Journal of Political Science* 11: 129–61.

Kramer, Gerald H. 1971. Short-term Fluctuations in U.S. Voting Behavior, 1896–1964. *American Political Science Review* 65: 131–43.

Lafferty, William M., and Oddbjorn Knutsen. 1985. Postmaterialism in a Social Democratic State. *Comparative Political Studies* 17: 411–30.

Lewis-Beck, Michael. 1986. Comparative Economic Voting: Britain, France, Germany, Italy. *American Journal of Political Science* 30: 315–46.

Lipset, Seymour Martin. 1981. *Political Man*. 2d ed. Baltimore: Johns Hopkins University Press.

MacRae, Duncan, Jr. 1967. *Parliament, Parties, and Society in France, 1946–1958*. New York: St. Martin's.

Marshall, James S. 1985. Japan's Successor Generation: Their Values and Attitudes. *Research Report* R-15–85. Washington: U.S. Information Agency Office of Research.

Maslow, Abraham. 1970. *Motivation and Personality*. New York: Harper & Row.

Milkis, Sidney, and Thomas Baldino. 1978. The Future of the Silent Revolution. Paper presented at the annual meeting of the Midwest Political Science Association, Chicago.

Przeworski, Adam, and Michael Wallerstein. 1982. The Structure of Class Conflict in Democratic Capitalist Societies. *American Political Science Review* 76: 215–38.

Stephens, John D. 1981. The Changing Swedish Electorate. *Comparative Political Studies* 14: 000–00.

Tufte, Edward R. 1978. *Political Control of the Economy*. Princeton: Princeton University Press.

Winter, David. 1973. *The Power Motive*. New York: Free Press.

Zetterberg, Hans. 1986. *Class Voting in Sweden, 1979–85*. Svenska Institutet Foer Opionionsundersoe Khingar (SIFO). Mimeo.

Chapter 5

REALIGNMENT OR DEALIGNMENT?

As we illustrated in chapter 1, the employment of empirical falsifiability as a guiding principle in modern comparative analysis has led to the importance of measurable data in explaining political phenomena. It is therefore not surprising that the subfield of political behavior has produced one of the largest bodies of literature in the field of comparative political analysis. Behavior, after all, is directly observable, in contrast to the internal or mental dispositions that were the focus of chapter 4 and can be measured only indirectly. Moreover, since developed, Western countries keep reasonably accurate and reliable records of most aspects of political behavior, such data are fairly accessible to most scholars and as such often figure into the selection of research questions.

Researching political behavior may take the form of inquiries into the extent, forms, and causes of political participation. Besides the inherent measurability of these variables, interest in political participation reflects the growing interest in the social requisites of democracy. As we discuss later in this volume, the past three decades have witnessed a wave of transitions to a democratic political format.[1] It is widely assumed that mass political participation supports the establishment and consolidation of democracy while the forms of such participation are undergoing change. Russell Dalton and his associates have produced a widely cited body of literature examining these changes in the forms and extent of participation, the most recent example of which is offered in this chapter as reading 5.1.

Conventional wisdom, supported by cross-national research beginning in the 1950s, held that even in the most advanced and successful democracies such as the United States and United Kingdom, actual participation in public affairs fell far short of the democratic ideal of a rational and activist citizenry.[2] Indeed, Gabriel Almond and Sidney Verba's famous five-nation study in the late 1950s found that it was the widely shared myth of a rational-activist citizenry that was largely responsible for holding the elites in check. Hence, they asserted that the model citizen "is not the active citizen; he is the potentially active citizen." Similarly, Norman Nie and Sidney Verba were merely echoing a broadly held conclusion when they announced that "only a small minority of the citizenry is active beyond the act of voting." [3] Moreover, such participation was not usually guided by a coherent political ideology but instead was based on a paucity of information and driven by nonrational considerations.[4] Thus, political participation was largely through the intermediary of the political party system; direct political behavior was limited to a small segment of the citizenry.

More recent research indicates that political participation and possession of political knowledge have become more widespread in advanced Western democracies, an increase driven in large measure by the increased level of education, which is one of the major predictors of such participation.[5] Access to political information for the essentially nonreading public has been exponentially expanded with the advent of television, and this increased access is a result of both an expansion of television ownership throughout the Western world and the around-the-clock availability of such news and information on cable television and the Internet.

However, this increased level of participation is not found across the spectrum of issues but rather tends to be confined to particular issues of interest to the individuals in question. For example, farmers might be informed about and active regarding agricultural policy, religious conservatives may be active with regard to the issue of abortion, or Jews might be informed about and involved in trying to influence policies toward the Middle East.

In the selection from the 2003 book *Democracy Transformed* offered in this chapter, Dalton and his associates describe and document trends and changes in the forms of participation, changes that are also partly attributable to increased levels of education and feelings of political competence. The recent growth of the direct forms of participation described by Dalton and his associates diminishes the brokerage function of translating citizen needs and demands into manageable electoral choices. For this reason, many former supporters of mainstream parties have not yet formed new political allegiances. These changes have implications for the nature of the democratic process in Western countries, implications that should be carefully considered by students of comparative politics.

The data from the parties and behavior literature reveal two related trends: a widespread decline in the vote share of the major parties that formerly dominated the political landscape of Western democracies and growing electoral support of either new or reemerging categories of parties. This political *realignment* (if indeed that is what is occurring) has been described by Dalton as a movement from *social mobilization,* a form of partisanship based on socioeconomic interests such as class or religion, to *cognitive mobilization* in which partisanship stems from ideas and values.[6] Jeff Justice, Lawrence Mayer, and Alan Arwine have conceptualized this shift as one from the politics of interests (class and religion) to the politics of identity (nation-state patriotism and subcultural defense)[7] driven by a declining importance of social class in this era of sustained material affluence and the subsiding impact of religion due to the secularization of the post-modern world.

We thus find that parties of classic conservatism and Christian democracy—part of whose *raison d'être* (reason for being) has been the protection of property and the free market—and parties of social democracy and trade union–based parties—whose purpose has been economic redistribution and equality—have lost vote share across the Western world (although the extent of this loss has varied with such institutional factors as electoral systems, as discussed in detail in this chapter). Another part of the basis of support for these conservative or Christian democratic parties has been the protection of traditional Christian morality and traditions that have been weakened by the aforementioned secularization of modern society. The weakening vote share of these heretofore major parties has driven many of them to attempt to redefine themselves to accommodate the growing lack of fit between traditional party system cleavages and the realigned social cleavages.[8] Such redefinition, evident in Tony Blair's attempt to recast the formerly trade union–based Labour Party in Britain as "New Labour," a party with middle-class appeal, affects the bases of electoral support for such parties.

In the gap created by the loss of vote share of these former major parties is found the emergence of a category of parties variously conceptualized by comparativists as parties of the extreme right, radical right, or populist right, as exemplified by Piero Ignazi in the second reading in this chapter.[9] The emergence of this category of parties has alarmed many students of politics, especially those concerned with European politics, because they perceive the possible reappearance of the politics of fascism that so devastated that continent in the 1930s and 1940s. Scholars studying the emergence of these parties have attempted to identify the circumstances related to their relative electoral success—for example, rising unemployment among the marginalized strata whose socioeconomic roles are threatened by technology and modernization. These marginalized strata generally resent the attributes of modernity, including urbanization, globalism, and the advance of technology, that have reduced the demand for (if not eliminated) their jobs.[10]

The marginalized strata to whom these emerging populist right parties appeal include unskilled or semi-skilled labor; peasants, or proprietors of small family farms; clerks; artisans; and shopkeepers—that is, the lower middle class and white underclass—and they are quite distinct from the normal electoral clientele of the conservative or Christian democratic parties of the mainstream right. Moreover, the issue agenda of these parties is quite distinct from the mainstream right, which seeks to protect property, the free market, and social institutions; the clientele of these emerging parties tend to exhibit a deep distrust of such institutions and resent the affluence of socioeconomic elites; and it may not be accurate to view these emerging parties as merely a more radical or extreme version of the political right.

What these emerging parties have in common, in addition to a distrust of many sociopolitical institutions, is the defense of an ethnically or culturally defined nation against the perceived threat of culturally or ethnically distinct immigrants. Part of this perceived threat may be a result of the economic uncertainty that leads marginalized strata to resent and fear competing with immigrants and ethnic minorities for a dwindling number of semi- and unskilled jobs. This defense of the nation may take the form of nation-state patriotism, as in the case of such chauvinistic nationalist parties as the Pim Fortuyn List and its current leader Geert Wilders in the Netherlands, whose sole agenda was to limit the size and impact of that country's Muslim population. Defense of the nation may also result in a separatist or secessionist agenda of a subculture, exemplified by the electoral success of *Bloc Québécois* in Canada. Whether at the nation-state or the subcultural level, these parties are essentially about identity. Moreover, while many, if not most, of these parties are seen as sitting on the political right, this is not necessarily the case: they may just as easily appear on the populist left. The *Bloc Québécois* in Canada, for example, has an economic agenda that is clearly leftist.

Thus, the ideological and cultural changes documented in chapter 4 have produced a partial realignment of partisan cleavages. Scholars disagree as to whether the apparent dealignment, indicated by a declining vote share of the major parties, is a temporary phenomenon driven by contemporary economic circumstances or whether it is in fact a permanent realignment, with these emerging parties continuing as a fixture on the new political landscape.

Notes

1. Samuel Huntington, *The Third Wave: Democratization in the Late Twentieth Century* (Norman: University of Oklahoma Press, 1991).
2. Garbriel Almond and Sidney Verba, *The Civic Culture* (Boston: Little Brown, 1961).
3. Norman Nie and Sidney Verba, "Political Participation" in *The Changing American Voter* (Cambridge, Mass.: Harvard University Press, 1979).

4. Angus Campbell et al., *The American Voter* (New York: John Wiley, 1960). See also Philip Converse, "The Nature of Belief Systems in Mass Publics," in *Ideology and Discontent,* ed. David Apter (New York: The Free Press, 1964).
5. Russell Dalton, *Citizen Politics,* 3d ed. (New York: Chatham House, 2002), 19ff.
6. Russell Dalton, "Cognitive Mobilization and Partisan Dealignment in Advanced Industrial Democracies," *Journal of Politics* 46 (February 1984): 264–284.
7. Jeff Justice and Lawrence Mayer, "Populism and The Emerging Politics of Identity: The Transformation of the Canadian Party System," *Nationalism and Ethnic Politics* 6, no. 1 (Spring 2000): 72–102; Mayer and Justice, "A Research Note on Identity Politics in the Older British Commonwealth," *Politics and Policy* 31, no. 1 (March 2003): 152–162; and Alan Arwine and Mayer, "The Changing Bases of Political Conflict in Western Europe: The Cases of Belgium and Austria," *Nationalism and Ethnic Conflict* 14, no. 3 (July 2008): 428–452.
8. Ronald Inglehart, "The Changing Structure of Political Cleavages in Western Societies," in *Electoral Change in Advanced Industrial Democracies,* eds. Russell Dalton, Scott Flanagan, and Paul Allen Beck (Princeton, N.J.: Princeton University Press, 1984).
9. See Pippa Norris, *Radical Right* (New York: Cambridge University Press, 2005), for a comparative discussion of the nature of these emerging parties.
10. Christopher Husbands, "How to Tame the Dragon, or What Goes Around Comes Around: A Critical Review of Some Major Contemporary Attempts to Account for Extreme Right Racist Politics in Western Europe," in *Shadows Over Europe: The Development and Impact of the Extreme Right in Western Europe,* eds. Martin Schain, Aristide Zolberg and Patrick Hossay (New York: Palgrave Macmillan, 2002), 39–59.

5.1

NEW FORMS OF DEMOCRACY? REFORM AND TRANSFORMATION OF DEMOCRATIC INSTITUTIONS

Russell J. Dalton, Susan E. Scarrow, and Bruce E. Cain

Students of democratic politics have witnessed a significant drop in the vote share of the major or mainstream parties in advanced industrial democracies, a drop of around 10 to 25 percent depending on institutional and cultural impediments to the emergence of successful new parties. The contending perspective in this chapter by Piero Ignazi (reading 5.2) exemplifies a body of literature that finds that a significant number of former supporters of these mainstream parties are now supporting an emerging category of parties concerned with such lifestyle issues as identity and environmentalism. This shift, then, signals a period of realignment that raises questions about the extent to which the party system reflects and represents the issues now salient to the voting public. Russell Dalton, a professor at the University of California, Irvine, and one of the leading scholars in the area of the comparative study of public participation in Western democracies, and his associates, however, have argued that many citizens, rather than realigning with new political parties, are finding forms of participation outside the party system, such as protest marches and vigils, a phenomenon known as dealignment. These more direct forms of citizen involvement are driven by the expansion of a formal education among the citizenry and of opportunities to receive from and impart political information and ideas to political elites. This move from representative to more direct democracy would render party systems less salient. Students should consider whether this shift from just voting to wider forms of direct participation will render the government more or less responsive to public needs and demands.

> *Democracy in the full sense of the word will always be no more than an ideal; one may approach it as one would a horizon, in ways that may be better or worse, but it can never be fully attained.*
>
> Vaclav Havel addressing a joint session of the US Congress, 21 February 1990

Over the past quarter century, citizens and political elites in advanced industrial democracies have displayed a growing willingness to question whether a fundamental commitment to the principles and institutions of representative democracy is sufficient to sustain the legitimacy and effectiveness of current mechanisms of self-government. In most of these nations, turnout in elections has declined, as has

Russell J. Dalton, Susan E. Scarrow, and Bruce E. Cain, "New Forms of Democracy? Reform and Transformation of Democratic Institutions," in *Democracy Transformed? Expanding Political Opportunities in Advanced Industrial Democracies* (New York: Oxford University Press, 2003), 1–22.

party membership and various forms of electoral participation (Gray and Caul 2000; Blais 2000; Wattenberg 2002). In addition, the public is increasingly sceptical of politicians, political parties, and political institutions (Dalton 2004; Pharr and Putnam 2000; Norris 1999). These signs point to a spreading dissatisfaction with the institutions and processes of representative democracy.

These trends are often concomitant with increasing demands for political reforms to expand citizen and interest group access to politics in new ways, as well as to restructure the process of democratic decision-making. Public interest in politics is generally growing across the advanced industrial democracies (Dalton and Wattenberg 2000: 57; Putnam 2002).[1] Although electoral participation is generally declining, participation is expanding into new forms of action. Today, more people are signing petitions, joining citizen interest groups, and engaging in unconventional forms of political action (Inglehart 1997; Dalton 2002: ch. 4; Norris 2002: ch. 10). The enormous expansion of public interest groups, social movements, and non-governmental organizations (NGOs) creates new opportunities for action.

Reforms to implement these new demands for citizen participation can have multiple goals and multiple effects: expanding access to politics, increasing citizen control of elites, taking decisions out of the hands of elites, prompting more responsive policy-making, and engaging new groups into the political process. And, given this expanded menu of participation choices, it is perhaps not surprising that some traditional forms of electoral participation are declining.

These trends suggest that the public's preferred mode of democratic decision-making is moving toward new forms of more direct involvement in the political process. Public opinion surveys routinely find that large majorities favour shifting political decision-making from elites to the citizens themselves (Dalton, Buerklin, and Drummond 2001; Bowler, Donovan, and Tolbert 1998). Reflecting these tendencies, contemporary publics and political groups seemingly place greater reliance on referendums as a tool for policy influence and agenda setting (Butler and Ranney 1994; Gallagher and Uleri 1996). For example, as Italian parliamentary politics struggled with scandals and immobilism during the 1990s, referendum usage increased dramatically in that country. Growing interest in the processes of deliberative or consultative democracy is another indication of this trend (Fishkin 1995; Elster 1998). There are also regular calls for greater reliance on citizen advisory committees for policy formation and administration, especially at the local level where direct involvement is possible.

Now a chorus of voices is calling for democracies to reform and adapt to changing political conditions and a changing public. Benjamin Barber's (1984) "strong democracy" and Robert Dahl's (1989) discussion of "transformative democratic reform" raise deeper questions about how democratic institutions can involve the public more directly (also see Habermas 1992*a*,*b*). Mark Warren (2001: 226) writes, "Democracy, once again in favor, is in need of conceptual renewal. While the traditional concerns of democratic theory with state-centered institutions remain importantly crucial and ethically central, they are increasingly subject to the limitations we should expect when nineteenth-century concepts meet twenty-first century realities." The pragmatic American political analyst, Dick Morris (2000), similarly observes: "The fundamental paradigm that dominates our politics is the shift from representative to direct democracy. Voters want to run the show directly and are impatient with all forms of intermediaries between their opinions and public policy." Ralf Dahrendorf (2000: 311) has summarized the

1. The contrary evidence tends to emphasize the U.S. experience (for example, Putnam 2000; Hibbing and Theiss-Morse 2002), but even in the U[nited] S[tates] the increase in non-electoral forms of participation has been generally documented (Dalton 2002: ch. 4; Verba, Schlozman, and Brady 1995: 72).

mood of the times: "representative government is no longer as compelling a proposition as it once was. Instead, a search for new institutional forms to express conflicts of interest has begun."

The same themes are heard in government reactions to these trends. In 1999 the OECD held a symposium: "Government of the Future: Getting from Here to There." The symposium report noted that technological advances and a more knowledgeable citizenry create more demands on contemporary governments. In response, the OECD began a dialogue about how its member states could reform their governments to create new connections to the public (OECD 2000*a*).

Building on this experience, the OECD conducted several studies to assess existing opportunities for citizen access to information and consultation, active participation in policy-making, and "best practice" reforms for expanding these opportunities. The report of these activities begins:

> New forms of representation and public participation are emerging in all of our countries. These developments have expanded the avenues for citizens to participate more fully in public policy making, within the overall framework of representative democracy in which parliaments continue to play a central role. Citizens are increasingly demanding more transparency and accountability from their governments, and want greater public participation in shaping policies that affect their lives. Educated and well-informed citizens expect governments to take their views and knowledge into account when making decisions on their behalf. Engaging citizens in policy making allows governments to respond to these expectations and, at the same time, design better policies and improve their implementation. (OECD 2000*b*: 9)

As this suggests, public officials within the OECD clearly recognize these new citizen demands for greater access, transparency, and accountability. Similarly, the European Union recently issued a white paper on the need to increase citizen involvement in the policy process, to help citizens hold their political leadership to account for the EU's decisions and to guarantee that the EU's system will be opened up to greater public scrutiny and debate (Commission of the European Union 2001).

In summary, there is an apparently growing consensus on the need for political reform to adapt democracy to new conditions; and the cumulative experiments in democratic reform suggest that important new developments may be at hand. The most avid proponents of such reforms conclude that we may be experiencing *the most fundamental transformation of the democratic process* since the creation of mass democracy in the early twentieth century. Yet cycles of democratic reform are a recurring theme in history, and pressures for change in one direction often wane as new problems and new possibilities surface (see next section). So in discussing the impact of reform we must go beyond the rhetoric and ask whether these changes are really transforming the foundations of the democratic process or merely accommodating popular pressures without altering the basic nature of representative democracy.

* * *

The First Wave of Democratic Reform

At one level, there is nothing new about the call to inject more democracy into the institutions of representative government. The history of modern democracies has witnessed repeated waves of debate about the nature of the democratic process, some of which have produced institutional reform (Huntington 1981, 1993; Lipset 1981). These debates have revolved around two questions. First, how does one ensure that democratic processes best represent the views of the governed? This involves the sub-questions of who should be decision-makers and how they should be selected and also raises the more normative question of whether decisions are legitimate if the process for reaching them is not broadly inclusive and equitable (Held 1996). Thus, a first theme in the democratization process is whether to expand and improve the process of representative government as the "democratic compromise" between the rulers and the ruled.

The second question concerns the desirability of direct citizen participation in government as an alternative (or corrective) to representative democracy. Scholars and practitioners repeatedly debate whether it is possible to design procedures that expand citizen participation without overly impairing the efficiency of government. Direct democracy is understandable in small settings such as the New England town hall or the Swiss canton. It is less certain how direct democracy can be applied to large-scale national policy decisions and debates over complex policy matters. Thus, a second theme in the democratization process involves a search for new procedures or technologies that allow more direct citizen input into the political process.

These questions about how to realize democracy are as old as efforts to institutionalize popular government. The patrician framers of the then radically democratic United States Constitution fundamentally rejected the idea of pure democracy. Madison, Hamilton, and others argued that representative structures were better, in part because they made it possible to "refine and enlarge the public views, by passing them through the medium of a chosen body of citizens, whose wisdom may best discern the true interest of their country, and whose patriotism and love of justice will be least likely to sacrifice it to temporary or partial considerations" (*Federalist* 10). Similar views were stated by Edmund Burke in his famous "Address to the Electors of Bristol" in 1774 and by Abbé de Sieyès in describing the events of the French Revolution. In short, this logic called for a system of limited representative government as the basis of the democratic process.

Of course, these views were challenged by others at the time. Jefferson, Paine, and other early American democrats expressed greater faith in the ability of the average citizen to make political decisions. Moreover, Jefferson stressed the educational element of democracy: by participating in the decisions affecting their lives, citizens learned how to become better democrats. From this tradition began the mantra of populist democratic reformers for the next two centuries: the cure for the ills of democracy is more democracy.

Belief in the innate superiority of representatives lost ground during the nineteenth century. By the end of the century an increasing number of reformers questioned both the notion that representatives ought to act as trustees and the idea that public decisions were improved by legislators' independence from the wishes of those who elected them. This change came about because legislators were increasingly seen as captives of parties or of special interests; many people felt that politicians ignored the wishes of their voters for selfish reasons, not because they were honestly working for the common good. This distrust of elected officials stimulated the first waves of pressure for democratic reform in the late nineteenth and early twentieth centuries that defined the Progressive era. Coupled with this dissatisfaction with political elites was a growing trust in the competence of the broader electorate.

In the United States, this wave of democratic discourse had multiple effects (Goodwyn 1976). Progressive-era reforms introduced a variety of changes to strengthen the electoral process, such as the introduction of the secret ballot in the late 1800s or the extension of the franchise to women in the early 1900s. Other reforms, such as the introduction in 1913 of the direct primary and direct elections of U.S.

senators, expanded the citizens' role in the electoral process as a corrective to the corruption of machine politics and special interests. These reforms sought to ensure that democratic elections were more representative, so that the public's wishes would be translated more clearly and directly into governmental action.[2]

Second, many of these same American reformers developed an interest in direct democracy through their new-found attention to constitutional and legislative referendums in Switzerland (Sullivan 1892; McCrackan 1893; Oberholtzer 1900; Wuarin 1895). Populist and later Progressive reformers promoted devices to give citizens a more direct say in politics and portrayed these changes as tools for wresting power back from corrupt politicians and from the powerful economic interests that dominated them (Cree 1892; Croly 1914). These arguments led to the widespread adoption of legislative and constitutional referendums and initiatives at the state level in the United States. Between 1900 and 1920, twenty-two American states adopted the referendum and/or the initiative into their state constitutions (Cronin 1984: 52). Similar arguments were used a little later in the twentieth century in Canada, where populists promoted direct democracy as a means of shaking off the shackles of entrenched interests (Laycock 1990: 37–40).

During this same period there were similar moves to expand democracy in Europe, both by improving the methods of representation and by using direct democracy to circumvent representation. A broadening franchise rapidly expanded democratic participation in the late nineteenth century and early twentieth century. Even after the "democratizing" First Reform Bill of 1832, only 650,000 voters registered for the British election of 1833, at a time when the population of [the] United Kingdom exceeded 16 million (Bentley 1987: 88). By 1921 Britain had nearly universal adult male suffrage. In the wake of expanded manhood suffrage, female suffrage spread across a host of European nations in the first quarter of the twentieth century. At about the same time, many countries witnessed debates about which electoral system would most fairly represent public opinion in elections, debates that eventually led to the adoption of proportional representation electoral systems for most of Europe's lower legislative chambers. These reforms were intended to strengthen the process of representative democracy so that participation yielded equitable and representative results.

* * *

Despite these disagreements on both sides of the Atlantic about exactly what direct democracy would achieve, the first decades of the twentieth century saw a growing acceptance of referendums as a device for ensuring that major political decisions had broad popular support. This was one reason that the victorious Western Allies promoted the use of plebiscites to settle issues of national self-determination at the end of the First World War (Suksi 1993). Several of the new constitutions written in the wake of the First World War also included provisions for referendums.

The twentieth-century advocates of a new science of politics added their voices to these debates about institutional reform. They argued that the defects of representative democracy could not be remedied

2. At the same time, these movements frequently were exclusionary in their definition of "the people." Some of the nineteenth-century electoral reforms, for example, aimed at restricting the electoral participation of foreigners and immigrants. Other democratic reforms increased political inequality by increasing access in ways that require higher levels of political skills and sophistication. Thus the effect of democratic reform is not always egalitarian.

by entrusting more decisions to citizens (Goodnow 1900; Bruce 1924; Lowell 1913). These scholars questioned the claim that the cure for democracy was more democracy. Instead, they suggested that more decisions should be taken by professional policy-makers who could be insulated from parties and electoral politics. Such insulation might include expanding merit-based civil services or establishing life tenure for judges. These analysts were well-aware of the problems of representative democracy, but they rejected the idea that more democracy could solve them, arguing that many issues were just too complicated for the mass of citizens to be able to make informed decisions. Some of those who hailed the virtues of non-partisan professional policy-makers in Third Republic France helped establish the school that became the training ground for generations of French administrators and political leaders: the *École Libre des Sciences Politiques* (Quagliariello 1996).

The various waves of democratic reform had begun to recede by the 1920s, and were in full ebb by the 1930s. The vulnerability of new democracies to populist and fascist movements in the inter-war era and the undemocratic use of plebiscites in this period prompted many observers to revise their ideas about the desirability of allowing "the masses" greater direct access to government. In particular, the failure of the citizenry was widely (if unfairly) cited as the reason for the collapse of democracy in Weimar Germany (Schiffers 1971). The abuse of the referendum by the Third Reich further worsened the image of direct democracy. The fear of "too much democracy" and an unpredictable mass public was thus very prominent as the Second World War came to an end (Kornhauser 1959). As a result, by the middle of the twentieth century many democratic politicians and scholars returned to a more Madisonian view that saw representative institutions as having an elevating influence, and there was more wariness of giving "the masses" too much direct say. This attitude was best exemplified by the (West) German constitution of 1949, which reacted against perceived deficiencies of the Weimar constitution both by eliminating provisions for direct democracy, such as the national referendum, and by restricting the process of representative democracy by eliminating direct elections of the federal president. Among academic theorists and constitutional scholars, corporatist and pluralist paradigms stressed the role of bargaining among groups and group leaders, and downplayed a direct governance role for individual citizens.

The most notable exception during this period is France—but it may be the exception that "proves" the generalization. President de Gaulle resurrected the use of national referendums during the early years of the Fifth Republic, but this reinforced many observers' doubts about direct democracy. De Gaulle's referendums were more reminiscent of the Napoleonic plebiscites of the nineteenth century than the model of direct democracy. These referendums were dictates from on high that the public could (and should) endorse. One plebiscite even went so far as to unconstitutionally revise the constitution.

The Second Wave of Democratic Reform

The democratic tide shifted again as a new wave of democratic debate and rhetoric grew in the last third of the century. The stimulus for change often appeared first among university students and young professionals who pressed the boundaries of the conventional system of representative democracy (Altbach and Laufer 1972). The Free Speech Movement in the United States was an early example of the rejection of traditional political processes and a search for alternative methods of political expression and influence. These sentiments soon broadened to include social protests over race, urban issues, and the Vietnam War. A strikingly parallel wave of student unrest spread across Europe in the late 1960s and the early 1970s: the Provo movement in Dutch politics in the late 1960s, the Alternativ and APO movements in Germany, and the RAF assaults on the Italian government during the 1970s. In France, the revolts of May 1968 marked the apogee of the student movement. Moreover, embedded within the French student movement were clear challenges to the established system of representative democracy.

Although these dramatic protests subsequently waned, the new challenges to democracy that they embodied are still affecting advanced industrial democracies. Calls for reform in recent decades seem to emanate from a complex mix of needs and motivations. One factor may simply be the underlying logic of democracy. Participation and consensus-building are essential characteristics of the democratic process. Once these values become accepted, there may be an inevitable pressure to expand these processes to allow greater citizen access and ensure the effectiveness of democratic participation. For instance, after becoming German Chancellor in the late 1960s, Willy Brandt challenged Germans to "risk more democracy." Democratic expectations may also expand to include other domains, such as Dahl's (1989) emphasis on democratic reforms in the economic sphere. In other words, the logic of democracy may generate its own expectations for the expansion of the democratic process.

Relatedly, the modernization process in advanced industrial democracies also may contribute to calls for democratic reform (Luhmann 1998; Lipset 1981). The dramatic growth of public interest groups in the United States and citizen action groups in Europe has introduced new actors and new styles of action into the democratic process. From the 1960s onwards there was a general expansion of new forms of direct action, used by student protestors but also by environmentalists and other social movements, and eventually by the Gray Panthers, teachers, neighbourhood associations, and a wide spectrum of society. The increasing social and political diversity of interests active in the democratic process may generate pressures to formalize the rules as well as to assure the transparency and legitimacy of the process. In addition, the increasing skills and resources of average citizens may stimulate new demands and expectations about how citizens will influence the decisions affecting their lives (Inglehart 1990; Dalton 2002: ch. 2). Thus, advanced industrial democracies are experiencing a "participatory revolution" in which new forms of political action compete with the traditional participation style of representative democracy.[3]

Another explanation of the changes focuses on Schumpeter's (1943) model of elite competition. The expansion of political actors stimulates a search for new opportunities for political access and influence. Elites try to change the rules of the democratic game to produce a fairer process or more transparent rules, or even to manipulate the rules to their advantage. For example, the electoral primary was introduced by a conservative party in Iceland to create a new basis for attracting voters; in response, this innovation was gradually accepted by the other parties. From this perspective, the changing patterns of democratic institutional structures are part of an ongoing process of political competition between contending forces in a democracy, perhaps accelerated by an increasing number and diversity of actors.

A contrasting view suggests that the congestion of the governance process may stimulate institutional change. In line with the governmental overload approach (for example, Crozier, Huntington, and Watanuki 1975), the claim is made that the demands for access and influence now exceed the ability of democratic governments to respond. This might arise either from increases on the input side or because of restrictions on throughput by party or parliamentary elites (as posited by the cartel thesis of party

3. While we link the beginnings of this democratization wave to groups that often had a New Left orientation, in the 1990s conservative populists raised additional questions about the failures of representative democracy, albeit from a contrasting perspective.

action). Such a development would stimulate attempts to develop new access points through processes of institutional reform and restructuring. Governments themselves decide to delegate authority to administrators or the courts, which leads citizens and elites to try to influence these new decision-making centres.

* * *

Our project focuses on assessing the degree of institutional change in contemporary democracies and the implications of these changes, rather than testing alternative causal explanations for these processes. The analytic chapters demonstrate, however, that a mix of factors is needed to explain the patterns we uncover. But whatever the sources of change, we are particularly interested in the question of how these reforms are affecting the democratic process.

Three Modes of Democracy

The contemporary pressures for democratic reform, as in earlier democratization waves, first appeared in efforts to improve the process of *representative democracy*, in which citizens elect elites who then deliberate on policy matters and ultimately make the policy choices for the nation. U.S. presidential elections are an especially striking example of the trends to reform representative processes. In a thirty-year span there was a dramatic shift toward expanding citizen influence by selecting candidates through primary elections. In 1968 the Democratic Party held seventeen presidential primaries and the Republicans sixteen; in 2000 there were Democratic primaries in forty states and Republican primaries in forty-three. In addition, first the Democratic Party and then the Republican Party instituted reforms intended to ensure that the convention delegates were more representative of the party's supporters (Shafer 1983). Public funding of presidential elections sought to limit the influence of money and thereby ensure the equality of citizens. More recently, reformers have championed devices such as term limits and campaign finance reform as the new populist causes to remove the influence of special interests from the democratic process (Carey, Niemi, and Powell 2000). If Dewey and Truman were brought back to observe the modern presidential election process, they would hardly recognize the system as the same one that nominated them in mid-twentieth century.

The institutionalized system of party government in Europe restrained some of the populist reforms that occurred in the United States, but there are parallels in many nations. On a limited basis, some political parties have experimented with, or even adopted, closed primaries as a means of selecting parliamentary candidates (Scarrow, Webb, and Farrell 2000; Bille 2001; Hopkin 2001). There is some evidence that party members are wielding greater influence in the selection of party candidates (Farrell and Webb 2000). Other reforms apparently increase the number of electoral choices available to voters by transforming appointed positions into elective offices (Scarrow 2001). Suffrage was again expanded, this time to include voters aged 18–20. In summary, these reforms are expanding the realm of representative democracy, and thus implicitly accepting the ultimate premise of democracy by representation.

Second, this democratization wave stimulated calls for new forms of *direct democracy* that bypass (or complement) the processes of representative democracy. With direct democracy, citizens both participate in the discussion and deliberation about policies, and then make the final policy choice: it is unmediated participation in both policy formation and policy decision. For example, referendum usage has increased in the United States and other democracies. The Initiative and Referendum Institute calculates that there were 118 statewide referendums in the U[nited] S[tates] during the 1950s; this figure increased to 378 referendums in the 1990s. Several other nations have amended laws and constitutions to provide greater opportunities for direct democracy at both national and local levels (Scarrow 2001). For instance, Britain had its first national referendum in 1975, Sweden's constitutional reform introduced the referendum in 1980, and Finland adopted the referendum in 1987. In these and other cases, the referendum won a new legitimacy as a basis for national decision-making, one that runs strongly counter to the ethos of representative democracy. There is also mounting interest in expanding direct democracy into new institutional forms, such as citizen juries and methods of deliberative democracy (Matthews 1999; Fishkin 1995).

Third, this democratization wave expanded the participation repertoire to include a new style of *advocacy democracy* in which citizens directly participate in the process of policy formation or administration (or participate through surrogates such as environmental groups and other public interest groups), although the final decisions are still made by elites. In other words, participation of this type seeks to influence the process rather than make outright decisions, as is done with referendums and initiatives. For example, the principle of "maximum feasible participation" became the watchword of the Great Society social service reforms in the United States in the 1960s. As a result, citizen consultation and public hearings are now embedded in an extensive range of legislation, giving citizens new access points to government policy formation and administration (Ingram and Smith 1983; Berry, Portney, and Thomson 1993). Congressional hearings and state government meetings are public events in the U[nited] S[tates], and legislation such as the 1972 Federal Advisory Committee Act even extended open-meeting requirements to advisory committees. This yields, for example, the contrast between the system of Environmental Impact Reviews (EIRs) and public hearings now required by U.S. environmental policy on the one hand and the traditional closed system of British environmental policy-making protected by the Official Secrets Act on the other. In 1970 only a handful of nations had freedom of information laws; now they are almost universal in the OECD nations. It is not difficult to guess what Edmund Burke would think about the "government in the sunshine" provisions that have been enacted in recent years.

Advocacy democracy also includes the new legal rights that citizen groups and individuals have won that give them access to information and influence. The judicialization of the policy process enables citizen groups in most Western democracies to develop class action suits on behalf of the environment, women's rights, or other public interests (Stone Sweet 2000). Virtually every public interest can be translated into a rights appeal, which provides a new avenue of action through the courts. This is a new form of policy participation that was seldom available to individual citizens or interest groups a generation ago.

Britain as an Illustration

Britain's experience in the later twentieth century illustrates the processes we are studying. In 1960 Britain was considered a highly successful democracy. Indeed, the support of the British people for their government and their nation was one factor that sustained them through the Second World War and was a hallmark of British democracy (Almond and Verba 1963). At the same time, however, citizens' actual access to the democratic process was limited in terms of both the processes of representative democracy and direct and advocacy democracy. For most British citizens, their participation focused on electoral involvement. But actual input through the process of representative government was quite limited: a single vote for a Member of Parliament every five years, and perhaps single votes for the local and county councils. Participation beyond elections was quite limited.

Gradually, pressures mounted for greater democratic access. In response, various reforms increased the role of elections. For instance, the creation of the Scottish Parliament and the Welsh National Assembly in the 1990s expanded citizens' electoral input, as did the new direct elections to the European Parliament and the Local Government Act of 2000 allowing cities to institute directly elected mayors. New parties emerged to represent regional interests and for short periods new parties such as the Social Democrats and Greens appeared on the electoral stage. Other reforms sought to increase the citizens' role within the political parties, such as the restructuring of the Labour Party nominating process in the 1980s and the increasing formalization of participatory rights for individual members in all the major parties.

Direct forms of citizen access also expanded during this period. In 1975 Britain held the first national referendum in its history, which was followed by several regional referendums on devolution. Even if referendums are used infrequently, their existence has shifted the content of political debate in Britain, where now the public rather than Parliament is seen as the source of political sovereignty. There are also clear prospects for further national referendums (such as on membership of the eurozone).

Protest and other forms of direct political action increased; in place of the deference of British political culture arose a culture that tolerated and encouraged elite-challenging activities. Membership in the European Union brought new rights of legal standing and citizen rights that were lacking under Britain's unwritten constitution. No longer was parliament supreme, because the public could turn to the European Court of Justice to challenge parliamentary sovereignty. And Britain finally initiated a Freedom of Information Act in 2000, which lifted some of the veil of secrecy that protected governments under the Official Secrets Act. Thus Britain developed new channels for political access as well as participation in elections.

Progress along each dimension is uneven, and likely follows a non-linear course. But gradually Britain has moved from a starting point of limited public access in 1960 towards more opportunities for citizen involvement in the process through representative institutions, direct democracy, and advocacy democracy channels. Our estimate of the degree of change along these dimensions is imprecise as we begin this study, but even at the outset we can see that access has increased on all dimensions. The guiding hypothesis of this study is that the changes illustrated by the British example are far from unique. Although other nations may have different starting points, we posit that they, too, have followed a similar trajectory in developing both representative and direct channels. Determining the degree of change along these three dimensions and the relationship between dimensions is one of the main empirical goals of this project.

The Cross-National Pattern

In Britain as in most other advanced industrial democracies, each wave of democratic reform has brought forth multiple claims about the merits of democratization, only some of which are realized. Calls for democratic reform generally favour changes to strengthen both the system of representative government *and* direct democracy. Thus, the American populists of the early 1900s advocated both electoral reform and institutional changes that took decisions away from the electoral arena. Similarly, many democratic reformers of the late twentieth century pressed for electoral reforms as well as new methods of direct democracy and advocacy. These processes are often intertwined as part of the democratic passion of reformers. The recent democratic reform wave contains all three elements, but we believe it is important to realize the important theoretical and political differences between them.

In addition, history shows that the democratic process is dynamic and complex—so that the consequences of institutional reforms are not always as predicted. Some scholars—including some contributors to this collection—doubt the Jeffersonian logic that the cure for democracy is more democracy. These analysts argue that overly extensive reforms may undermine the democratic process by making governing so complex that accountability and transparency are diluted. Meny and Surel (2002), for instance, claim that constitutionalist expansion of democratic institutions and processes actually reduces the space left for the public (see also Bobbio 1987). Another argument holds that, by eroding governability, democratic reforms may make government less effective (Huntington 1981). One of the strongest critical statements comes from Hibbing and Theiss-Morse (2002), who claim that Americans' current disenchantment with politics actually reflects a public preference for fair politicians to make policy without bothering the citizen to become engaged. This is a position we find inconsistent with their own evidence, and which we will demonstrate to be inconsistent with the processes of institutional change in advanced industrial democracies.

We must also realize that actors in the democratic process adapt to changes in the political rules of the game, and these adaptations may undermine reforms or exchange one set of problems for another. Treschel and Sciarin (1998) suggest that the Swiss referendum process pushes elites into consensual decision-making that goes beyond the normal democratic tenets of majority rule. Similarly, in the midst of his current efforts to reform campaign finance laws in the United States, Sen. John McCain has openly acknowledged that if the reforms were passed they would have effect for a limited period until special interests adapted to the new system, and then a new round of reform would be needed. In short, because of the complexity of the democratic process, history teaches us to be cautious in making predictions about the long-term consequences of institutional reforms.

The following chapters assess the degree of institutional change that has actually occurred in the democratic institutions and processes of advanced industrial democracies. Are the initial examples of reform cited in the literature typical of a general pattern of institutional change, or is it their exceptionality that leads to their visibility in the literature? In addition, how have the three broad currents of democratic reform—the strengthening of representative democracy, the expansion of direct democracy, and the introduction of new forms of advocacy democracy—shaped this reform wave? To what extent has the rhetorical shift towards greater direct citizen governance been matched by change in practices or in outcomes?

In examining contemporary democratic institutional reforms our project focuses on three principles that tap the foundations of democracy, whether through representative, direct, or advocacy channels. Our analyses focus on three key principles of democratic politics.

1. *Access*. We first ask whether access to the political process has expanded over time. Access to decision-makers and participation in collective decisions is key to the democratic process; and the processes of representative democracy, direct democracy, and advocacy democracy can provide additional channels of access. Thus we examine whether the opportunities for citizen access have expanded within each domain, and whether citizen usage of these opportunities has increased.
2. *Transparency*. We are also concerned that citizens and other democratic participants have sufficient knowledge of the policy choices and the methods of policy-making. Better information about gov-

ernment policy, for example, empowers citizens regardless of which means of access they use. In addition, open government should increase the accountability of political elites as policy is made "in the sunshine" instead of behind closed doors.

3. *Accountability*. Finally, for democracy to be meaningful, public preferences should have a clear impact on policy outcomes. This is the essence of the democratic ideal. Many of the reforms we discuss are aimed at increasing the political accountability of elites, whether in party and parliamentary politics or in the administration of public policy.

These three principles are our initial yardsticks for measuring the effect of recent institutional reforms in changing the functioning of the democratic process. They enable us to assess whether contemporary democracies are moving towards the democratic ideal or experiencing a transformative set of reforms that are reshaping the nature of the democratic process.

* * *

Conclusion

Our project posits a tension between existing institutions and norms of democracy and developing public preferences for a more participatory democratic process. The democratization wave of the late twentieth century attempted to alter this balance—and our research determines the degree of this shift.

We do not anticipate that participatory reforms will erase parties or other established institutions of representative democracy. Rather, we ask whether the workings of the democratic process are broadening to include new institutional structures. If so, then it becomes important to investigate how the established political actors, especially the traditional actors of representative democracy, are responding to these new structures. Their responses will shape both the rate of institutional change and the exact trajectory of the trend.

In summary, the rise of citizen movements and existing evidence of institutional reform suggest that the pressures for democratic reform are real and significant. There is a potential for a significant transformation in the democratic process, but the breadth of these changes and their policy and institutional implications remain uncertain. This project assesses whether this potential for reform is truly being realized, and asks what the broader implications are for the nature and practice of democracy. In short, we want to know whether contemporary democracies have been transforming the representative institutions that were created nearly a century ago.

References

Almond, Gabriel and Verba, Sidney (1963). *The Civic Culture*. Princeton: Princeton University Press.

Altbach, Phillip and Laufer, Roberts (eds) (1972). *The New Pilgrims: Youth Protest in Transition*. New York: McKay.

Bang, Henrik (2001). *Governance, Governmentality and Democracy*. Manchester: University of Manchester Press.

Barber, Benjamin (1984). *Strong Democracy*. Berkeley: University of California Press.

Bentley, Michael (1987). *Politics Without Democracy*. Oxford: Basil Blackwell.

Berry, Jeffrey, Portney, Kent, and Thomson, Ken (1993). *The Rebirth of Urban Democracy*. Washington, DC: Brookings Institution Press.

Bille, Lars (2001). "Democratizing a Democratic Procedure: Myth or Reality?" *Party Politics,* 7: 363–80.

Blais, André (2000). *To Vote or Not to Vote: The Merits and Limits of Rational Choice Theory.* Pittsburgh: University of Pittsburgh Press.

Bobbio, Norberto (1987). *The Future of Democracy* (trans. Roger Griffen). Minneapolis: University of Minnesota Press.

Bowler, Shaun and Donovan, Todd (eds) (2001). *Demanding Choices: Opinion, Voting and Direct Democracy.* Ann Arbor: University of Michigan Press.

Bowler, Shaun, Donovan, Todd, and Tolbert, Caroline (eds) (1998). *Citizens as Legislators: Direct Democracy in the United States.* Columbus: Ohio State University Press.

Bruce, Andrew (1924). *The American Judge.* New York: Macmillan.

Butler, David and Ranney, Austin (eds.) (1994). *Referendums around the World: The Growing Use of Democracy?* Washington, DC: American Enterprise Institute.

Carey, John, Niemi, Richard, and Powell, Lynda (2000). *Term Limits in the State Legislatures.* Ann Arbor: University of Michigan Press.

Commission of the European Union (2001). *White Paper on Good Governance.* Brussels: Commission of the European Union.

Cree, Nathan (1892). *Direct Legislation by the People.* Chicago: A. C. McClurg & Company.

Croly, Herbert (1914). *Progressive Democracy.* New York: Macmillan.

Cronin, Thomas (1984). *Direct Democracy: The Politics of Initiative, Referendum and Recall.* Cambridge, MA: Harvard University Press.

Crozier, Michael, Huntington, Samuel, and Watanuki, Joji (1975). *The Crisis of Democracy.* New York: NYU Press.

Dahl, Robert (1989). *Democracy and Its Critics.* New Haven, CT: Yale University Press.

Dahrendorf, Ralf (2000). "Afterword," in Susan Pharr and Robert Putnam (eds), *Disaffected Democracies.* Princeton, NJ: Princeton University Press.

Dalton, Russell (2002). *Citizen Politics: Public Opinion and Political Parties in Advanced Industrial Democracies* (3rd edn). New York: Chatham House Publishers.

Dalton, Russell, Buerklin, Wilhelm, and Drummond, Andrew (2001). "Public Attitudes toward Direct Democracy." *Journal of Democracy,* 12: 141–53.

Dalton, Russell and Wattenberg, Martin (eds) (2000). *Parties without Partisans: Political Change in Advanced Industrial Democracies.* Oxford: Oxford University Press.

Elster, John (1998). *Deliberative Democracy.* New York: Cambridge University Press.

Farrell, David and Webb, Paul (2000). "Political Parties as Campaign Organizations," in Russell Dalton and Martin Wattenberg (eds), *Parties Without Partisans.* Oxford: Oxford University Press.

Fishkin, James S. (1995). *The Voice of the People: Public Opinion and Democracy.* New Haven, CT: Yale University Press.

Gallagher, Michael and Uleri, Pier Vincenzo (eds) (1996). *The Referendum Experience in Europe.* Basingstroke: Macmillan.

Goodnow, Frank (1900). *Politics and Administration.* New York: Macmillan.

Goodwyn, Lawrence (1976). *Democratic Promise: The Populist Movement in America.* New York: Oxford University Press.

Gray, Mark and Caul, Miki (2000). "Declining Voter Turnout in Advanced Industrial Democracies: 1950–1997." *Comparative Political Studies,* 33: 1091–122.

Habermas, Jürgen (1992a). *Faktizität und Geltung. Beiträge zur Diskurstheorie des Rechts und des demokratischen Rechtsstaates.* Frankfurt: Suhrkamp.

Habermas, Jürgen (1992b). "Drei Normative Modelle der Demokratie: Zum Begriff Deliberativer Politik," in Herfried Münkler (ed.), *Die Chancen der Freiheit.* Munich/Zurich: Piper.

Held, David (1996). *Models of Democracy* (2nd edn). Stanford: Stanford University Press.

Hibbing, John and Theiss-Morse, Elizabeth (2002). *Stealth Democracy: Americans' Beliefs about How Government Should Work*. New York: Cambridge University Press.

Hopkin, Jonathan (2001). "Bringing the Members Back In: Democratizing Candidate Selection in Britain and Spain." *Party Politics*, 7: 343–61.

Huntington, Samuel (1981). *American Politics: The Promise of Disharmony*. Cambridge: Harvard University Press.

——— (1993). *The Third Wave: Democratization in the Late Twentieth Century*. Norman: University of Oklahoma Press.

Inglehart, Ronald (1990). *Culture Shift*. Princeton, NJ: Princeton University Press.

——— (1997). *Modernization and Postmodernization: Cultural, Economic and Political Change in 43 Societies*. Princeton, NJ: Princeton University Press.

Ingram, Helen and Smith, Steven (1993). *Public Policy for Democracy*. Washington, DC: Brookings Institution.

Katz, Richard and Mair, Peter (1995). "Changing Models of Party Organization and Party Democracy: The Emergence of the Cartel Party." *Party Politics*, 1: 5–28.

Kornhauser, William (1959). *The Politics of Mass Society*. Glencoe, IL: Free Press.

Laycock, David (1990). *Populism and Democratic Thought in the Canadian Prairies*. Toronto: University of Toronto Press.

Lipset, Seymour Martin (1981). "The Revolt against Modernity," in P. Torsvik (ed.), *Mobilization, Center-Periphery Structures and Nation-building*. Bergen: Universitetsforlaget.

Lowell, Lawrence (1913). *Public Opinion and Popular Government*. New York: Longmans, Green and Company.

Luhmann, Niklas (1998). *Observations on Modernity*. Stanford: Stanford University Press.

Matthews, Forest David (1999). *Politics for People: Finding a Responsive Voice* (2nd edn). Urbana: University of Illinois Press.

McCrackan, W. D. (1893). "The Swiss Referendum: The Ideal Republican Government." *The Cosmopolitan*, 15: 329–33.

Meny, Yves and Surel, Yves (eds) (2002). *Democracies and the Populist Challenge*. New York: St. Martin's Press.

Michels, Robert (1958). *Political Parties*. Glencoe, IL: Free Press.

Morris, Dick (2000). *The New Prince*. New York: Renaissance Books.

Norris, Pippa (ed.) (1999). *Critical Citizens: Global Support for Democratic Governance*. Oxford: Oxford University Press.

——— (2002). *Democratic Phoenix: Reinventing Political Activism*. New York: Cambridge University Press.

Oberholtzer, Ellis (1900). *The Referendum in America*. New York: Charles Scribner's Sons.

OECD (Organization for Economic Cooperation and Development) (2000a). *Government of the Future*. Paris: OECD.

——— (2000b). *Regulatory Reform in Denmark*. Paris: OECD.

Pharr, Susan J. and Putnam, Robert D. (eds) (2000). *Disaffected Democracies: What's Troubling the Trilateral Countries?* Princeton: Princeton University Press.

Piven, Frances Fox and Cloward, Richard (1989). *Why Americans Don't Vote*. New York: Pantheon.

Putnam, Robert D. (2000). *Bowling Alone*. New York: Simon and Schuster.

Quagliariello, Gaetano (1996). *Politics without Parties*. Aldershot: Avebury.

Scarrow, Susan E. (1999). "Parties and the Expansion of Direct Democracy: Who Benefits?" *Party Politics*, 5: 341–62.

——— (2001). "Direct Democracy and Institutional Design: A Comparative Investigation." *Comparative Political Studies*, 34: 651–55.

———, Webb, Paul, and Farrell, David M. (2000). "From Social Integration to Electoral Contestation: The Changing Distribution of Power within Parties," in Russell J. Dalton and Martin P. Wattenberg (eds), *Parties Without Partisans*. New York: Oxford University Press.

Schattschneider, E. E. (1942). *Party Government.* New York: Rinehart.

Schiffers, Reinhard (1971). *Elemente direkter Demokratie im Weimarer Regierungssystem.* Düsseldorf: Droste Verlag.

Schumpeter, Joseph (1943). *Capitalism, Socialism and Democracy.* New York: Harper.

Shafer, Byron E. (1983). *Quiet Revolution: The Struggle for the Democratic Party and the Shaping of Post-reform Politics.* New York: Russell Sage Foundation.

Stone Sweet, Alec (2000). *Governing with Judges: Constitutional Politics in Europe.* New York: Oxford University Press.

Suksi, Markku (1993). *Bringing in the People: A Comparison of Constitutional Forms and Practices of the Referendum.* Dordrecht: Martinus Nijhoff.

Sullivan, J. W. (1892). *Direct Legislation by the Citizenship through the Initiative and Referendum.* New York: Twentieth Century Publishing Company.

Treschel, A. and Sciarini, Pascal (1998). "Direct Democracy in Switzerland: Do Elites Matter?" *European Journal of Political Research,* 33: 99–124.

Warren, Mark E. (2001). *Democracy and Association.* Princeton, NJ: Princeton University Press.

Wattenberg, Martin (2002). *Where Have All the Voters Gone?* Cambridge, MA: Harvard University Press.

Wuarin, Louis (1895). "Recent Political Experiments in the Swiss Democracy." *Annals of the American Academy of Political and Social Science,* 6: 361–80.

5.2

THE EXTREME RIGHT: DEFINING THE OBJECT AND ASSESSING THE CAUSES

Piero Ignazi

Piero Ignazi's work focuses on the widely noted phenomenon of the emergence of parties on the populist and extreme right. His work is one of a growing number of investigations into what some fear is a reemergence of the fascist right from the 1930s and 1940s that had such devastating consequences for the world. Ignazi speculates on the causes of the emergence of these parties and why they are stronger in some settings than in others. Students should consider whether Ignazi distinguishes the new wave of what some people have called the populist right (what others have called the radical right) from the fascist organizations that brought war to Europe. Are they a more extreme version of the mainstream right, or are they an essentially distinct category that appeals to a different segment of society and a different set of values? An unanswered question is whether the emergence of these parties is a permanent realignment of voter choice. In assessing the causes of the emergence of what Ignazi calls the extreme right, does he account for the variation in the strength and electoral success of these parties from country to country? Are they inspired by temporary changes in social and economic circumstances, or is their emergence likely to become a permanent part of the political landscape?

This chapter aims at surveying the current terminology of the "extreme/radical/populist right parties," stipulating criteria for the identification of such parties as a "party family" with its internal differentiations, and underlining a set of hypotheses on these parties' development with particular emphasis on the "political factors" and the general (Europe-wide) and particular (country-specific) timing.

The discussion will suggest that the term "extreme right" might be more plausible than others; the parties that meet the criteria of "anti-systemness" should be included in the extreme right parties family. Nevertheless, parties vary quite considerably along different lines, from solid ideological fascist imprinting to loosely anti-establishment-populist approach. As far as the rise of the extreme right parties is concerned, the neoconservative cultural mood of the eighties has provided the soil for the development of a discourse favorable to a more radical agenda. Such radicalization of the political conflict has produced both a shift to the right of "conservative-bourgeois" parties and a larger distance between parties in the political spectrum. Such changes in the party systems and in the pattern of competition is

---

Piero Ignazi, "The Extreme Right: Defining the Object and Assessing the Causes," in *Shadows Over Europe: The Development and Impact of the Extreme Right in Western Europe,* eds. M. Schain, A. Zolberg, and P. Hossay (New York: Palgrave Macmillan, 2002), chapter 2, 21–38.

matched with the diffusion of an "antipolitical" sentiment in the European mass public. Finally, the discussion will highlight how these general conditions (or preconditions) need a particular, country by country, structure of opportunity for the takeoff of an extreme right party.

Out of the Tower of Babel: Suggestions for a Definition

While it would seem redundant to devote some attention to a terminological question, the tower of Babel produced by an explosive growth of the literature in the field deems such an analysis necessary.

Radical right has an ambiguous connotation due to its original (and twofold) adoption. On one hand, this term was introduced by the famous, pioneering study by Daniel Bell, *The Radical Right* (1963). Two main difficulties arise from this and further studies. First, radical right refers to both the John Birch Society and the McCarthyism that are movements and not parties and that have been convincingly labeled as extreme conservative but not as "extreme right" (Kolkey 1983, 35ff). Although these movements are characterized by a strict moral traditionalism and an obsessive anti-communism, they cannot be considered as anti-system (Himmelstein 1990, 73ff). Second, the radical right is identified through individuals' personality traits (largely derived or influenced by the research of Adorno et al., *The Authoritarian Personality* [1950]) rather than through a set of values. Therefore, this definition is too ideographic and too loose to account for the right-wing political organizations, especially in contemporary Europe.

On the other hand, radical right has been used to designate those movements and groups that find their ideological imprinting in a counterrevolutionary anti-modern tradition of thought and that boast and even adopt violent means up to terrorist actions (Ferraresi 1996). Following this tradition, radical right would tap a very limited space of contemporary right wing extremism.

The use of the term New Right has raised even more confusion. New Right indicates the neoconservatist agenda, a cultural movement sustained by some think tanks and publishing enterprises that originated from and operate within the conservative political space. The French version of the term, *Nouvelle Droite*, is even more specific as it connotes a tiny group of brilliant intellectuals, based originally in France with Alain de Benoist at their head. The *Nouvelle Droite* is similar to the New Right for the reference to the cultural domain, but it does not share anything in terms of values: To summarize, the *Nouvelle Droite* is anti-liberal and anti-socialist, while the New Right is anti-socialist but pro-liberal.

A term that has found wide audience in the more recent literature is "populism." Hans-Georg Betz (1993) speaks of the "populist extreme right." Several authors have offered varying definitions of populism; most highlight the highly charismatic dependence on "common sense" and a rejection of existing political institutions (see Betz 1993, Taggart 1993, Pfahl-Traugher 1993, and Kitschelt 1995).

A wide range of properties, such as the organizational structure, leadership style, or electorate profile, have been suggested to characterize this kind of party. None of these, however, seems useful: no organizational structure nowadays pertains to a specific type of party; the classical typology by Duverger (1951), with the "militia" type linked to the fascist parties, no longer holds. No leadership style seems exclusive of the extreme right parties. No specific electoral profile connotes the extreme right electorate, because in the era of dealignment, class or denominational constituencies no longer hold and extreme right parties recruit their voters across class and religious lines.[1] In sum, the term "populist" faces the

1. The French FN, for example, demonstrates how its electorate is similar to the national mean (Mayer 1993, 1997, Perrineau 1997).

problem of diluting the concept in a series of variables or properties without assessing the "minimum set of proprieties" necessary to identify a populist party (a partial exception is provided by Kitschelt 1995).

Compared to these terms, "extreme right" has a series of advantages. First, it recalls the notion of extremeness in a political and ideological *space*. A more substantive element is particularly relevant in the German tradition of study on this field. The German term *extremismus* refers in fact to the anti-democratic, anti-liberal, and therefore anti-constitutional standings (Backes and Jesse 1993, Ueltzhoffer 1992, and Minkenberg, Chapter 11 in this volume): In other words, those issues and organizations that are "extreme" are at the same time "anti-system." It is precisely the anti-system connotation of the *extremismus* that gives the term "extreme right" more accuracy in identifying the phenomenon under scrutiny.

If we adopt this approach, it follows that the class of parties of the extreme right is ascertained through the double screening on ideology and location in the political spectrum. The first criterion revives the classical analysis by "*families spirituelles*" by Maurice Duverger; the second one states the usefulness of the left-right continuum as an approximate rule of thumb to differentiate the extreme right from the conservatives. The ideological criterion has higher priority because the "nature" of the party is provided by its identity; it serves to identify the party's political culture. The second criterion is less relevant as it works as a prerequisite. It assesses the "right extremeness" of the party: It ensures that the party is located close to the extreme right of the political spectrum, or at least closer than any other party. While this second criterion does not raise any problem of analysis, especially given its function of mere screening, the first one is quite problematic and needs a further discussion.

The Extreme Right Core Ideology

What do we mean then by the expression "extreme right"? In his classical study, René Rémond (1982) stressed that one of the three *courants* of the right is provided by counterrevolutionary thinking (Geingembre 1982), from Maistre and Bonnald up to Maurras. This tendency could be compared with the traditionalist and almost esoteric tradition represented by René Guenon and Julius Evola (Ferraresi 1996)—the same refusal of modernity. Both traditions of anti-democratic thought are nowadays followed by small groups, with no political relevance. The role of Julius Evola, however, goes far beyond this milieu as he has been reputed a master for generations of right-wingers.

Given the marginality of the counterrevolutionary reference, the extreme right ideology is basically informed by fascism. But having stated that, we know that fascism is an ideological labyrinth (von Beyme 1988). To reduce the complexity of the topic, we can focus on a "fascist minimum," those common traits that are "shared not only by the different political movements and ideologies which claim to be fascist, but also by those which reject the description yet nevertheless belong to the same family" (Sternhell 1987, 32).

Roger Griffin's analysis of fascism's "generic ideological core" (1993, 13) finds the "mythic core" of fascism in "a palingenetic form of populist ultranationalism" (Griffin 1993, 26). Fascist ideology points to a kind of resurgence or "rebirth" in order to create a new revolutionary order, a new society, and even a new man. This goal cannot be achieved except through a general, collective, unitary effort by the whole nation. And this aim is supported by the active participation of the masses, mobilized by partisan organizations. The idea of resurgence from a dark period; the emphasis of the nation as a collective, organic body; the projection into a glorious and beaming future; and the mass mobilization mainly through leaders' charismatic appeal all constitute the "ideal type of fascism."

Zeev Sternhell, in his masterful study on fascist ideology, has specified that fascist "political culture is communitarian, anti-individualist and anti-rationalist, and it is founded, first on the refusal of Enlightenment and of the French revolution heritage, and then, on the elaboration of a total overthrowing" (Sternhell 1987, 15). Belief in the authority of the State over the individual, and emphasis on natural community; distrust for the individual representation and parliamentary arrangements; limitations on personal and collective freedoms; collective identification in a great national destiny, against class or ethnic or religious divisions; hierarchical criteria for social organization—all these traits characterize fascist ideology.

More recently, Roger Eatwell has attempted to "move on" from these contributions and has suggested his own "minimum" definition of fascist ideology as "an ideology which strives to forge social rebirth based on a *holistic-national radical Third Way*" (Eatwell 1996, 313; italics in the original text). This synthetic definition regroups many crucial aspects of fascism: the hate of division and conflict, the emphasis on nationalism (while this is not so distinctive: Liberals and conservatives shared this attitude), the search for renewal or rebirth, the search for a different path between capitalism and socialism.

The final consequence of this analysis is that the extreme right is that political-ideological space where fascism is the key reference. However, attributing the intellectual or ideological tradition of the extreme right only to fascism (in its various streams) and to the counterrevolutionary sect is too narrow for the contemporary extreme right even if fascism is and has been a very powerful ideological reference in the political realm and by far the most powerful on the right-wing side.

The reference to fascism postulates the *sufficient* condition for membership of parties and movements in the extreme right family. The parties that explicitly or not recall fascism are part of the extreme right. But the reference to an elaborated and coherent set of ideas and beliefs (ideology in a "strong" meaning) is not the only way to define membership in a political family.

The Anti-Systemness Property

As stated above, ideology is a crucial element in our classification. However, its adoption in its "strong meaning" (Freedan 1996, 15) would limit the extreme right political family to neofascist parties. As we know (Ignazi, forthcoming), this kind of party is limited to few examples: the fringe that split from Alleanza Nazionale, the new Movimento Sociale–Fiamma Tricolore, the German NPD and DVU, the British BNP, and some other minor fringes. What about the other extreme right parties? How can such parties be detected? How can a "non-neofascist" party be included in the extreme right family?

Parties other than neofascists qualify for membership in the extreme right when their political culture stands against the fundamentals of the democratic system. The *necessary* condition for inclusion in the family of the extreme right is that right-wing parties radically oppose the system.

This raises the question of the degree and the mode of opposition: When does an opposition cease to be democratic and become antidemocratic? A tentative solution to this problem could be suggested by two classical references, Otto Kirchheimer and Giovanni Sartori. Kirchheimer identifies a typology of opposition (Kirchheimer 1966, 237): opposition of principle, in which "goal displacement is incompatible with the constitutional requirements of a given system"; and loyal opposition, which implies just a "goal differentiation." Sartori has introduced the concept of anti-system party: Such a party is characterized by an activity that undermines the legitimacy of the democratic regime and "a belief system that does not share the values of the political order within which it operates" (Sartori 1976, 133).

More recently, Gordon Smith has proposed a typology that combines "compatibility of aims and acceptability of behaviour" and has underlined the existence of a "grey zone of acceptability" according to different time and context. In other words, what is rated "incompatible with the system in one era may be accommodated in another" (Smith 1987, 63–64). Most of the extreme right parties (ERPs) belong to the category of non-compatibility of aims and acceptability of behavior. The refusal of violence, support for freedom, and practice of democratic representative institutions all represent the standard style of the ERPs.

Summing up, the extreme right parties should exhibit an "opposition of principle" through a well-constructed ideology or a rather loose "mentality," which undermines the constitutional rules of the democratic regime. Fascism, the extreme right ideology par excellence, is by any standard alien and extraneous to liberal-democratic systems. However, where such reference to this well-structured ideology does not exist, the presence of anti-system political attitudes and beliefs should be investigated. Many right-wing and most (non-fascist) parties share some common features that are clearly anti-system (for an empirical test, see Almond 1996).

As has been underlined, almost all ERPs do not openly advocate a non-democratic institutional setting; on the contrary, it is easy to find ritual homages to the democratic principles in their official statements and documents. Nevertheless, they undermine system legitimacy. While they do not share any nostalgia for the interwar fascist experiences and may even refuse any reference to fascism, they express anti-democratic values throughout their political discourse (Backes 1990, 3–4). As Annvi Gardberg rightly put in his thorough analysis, the political culture of the extreme right can be interpreted as a "subversive stream that is anti-egalitarian and anti-pluralist and that opposes the principle of democratic constitutional states" (Gardberg 1993, 32).

ERPs' opposition is inspired by a hatred of divisions and a search for harmony, an emphasis of natural community and a hostility towards foreigners. In addition, they express confidence in hierarchical structures and a distrust of democratic individual representation, a rejection of "unnatural" egalitarianism and excessive freedom, and a general uneasiness with modernity.

In sum, on the basis of the spatial, ideological, attitudinal criteria, we can offer a typology in which parties more on the right of the political spectrum are categorized according to the presence or absence of a fascist heritage and to the acceptance or refusal of the political system. In order to be included in the extreme right party family, the most right-wing parties should either fulfill the (ideological) fascist criterion, or exhibit a delegitimizing pattern with regard to the political system, through a series of issues, values, attitudes (rather than a structured and coherent ideology). If a party fits the ideological criteria as well as the systemic one, we can think of it as belonging to the old, traditional, neofascist type. If a party is not linked to fascism but has an anti-system profile, we can think of it as belonging to the new, postindustrial type.

[A discussion of two types of ERPs has been omitted.]

Hypothetical Causes of ERPs' Rise

. . . In an earlier work (Ignazi 1992), four hypotheses were set out to explain the resurgence of the extreme right (see also Ignazi 1989 for the French case): (1) the affirmation of neoconservatism; (2) the increasing radicalization and polarization of politics; (3) the breakthrough of new issues such as security and immigration; and (4) the growing system legitimacy deficit. Other analyses have suggested various sets of hypotheses (see Taggart 1995, Jackman and Volpert 1996). In the most ambitious work up to now, it has been proposed that "The NRR [New Radical Right] is the offspring of the postindustrialization of advanced capitalist economies, of changes within the patterns of competition within democratic party system and of political entrepreneurs finding new electoral 'market niches' they are able to exploit with racist, authoritarian and procapitalist slogans" (Kitschelt 1995, 43). Kitschelt's analysis takes into account both economic and value conflicts and rightly underlines the role of the political entrepreneurs and of the structure of opportunity for the development of the extreme right parties. The present work offers a different explanation of the rise of ERPs: On one side, we analyze the structure of opportunity along different dynamics and on the other we introduce the "crisis of confidence" in Western democracies as a crucial explanatory element.

A further minor point of dissent concerns the emphasis on the economic aspect and, more particularly, on the acceptance of pro-market positions by the ERPs. A pro-market leaning has been one of the distinctive features of most new ERPs. The hostility towards the logic of capitalist economy permeate the traditional ERPs (and this feature explains, among other things, their failure in the age of triumphant capitalism). It is exactly when Western countries recovered their economies (in the early-to-mid-1980s) and found their ideological pillar in the neoconservatism that the new ERPs emerged. However, it is not their acceptance of neoliberal economics that caused their breakthrough.

First, the new ERPs, as they were newly born, are "naturally" in tune with the modern society—that is, with the postindustrial effects of the late capitalist economy—and with the dominating neoliberal and neoconservative Zeitgeist. On the other hand, the loyalty to anti-capitalist positions engendered the weakness of the traditional neofascist parties.

The second element of caution is provided by the irrelevance of economic issues in the policies supported by the ERPs. The attention devoted to economic issues is minimal because of lack of "economic culture" by the leaders, the distance from the doors of government that favors a syndrome of excessive promises, and a lack of credibility even among the same party followers and voters.

My major divergence from Kitschelt's interpretation of the ERPs' rise, however, concerns the dynamic of competition within the party system. Kitschelt's hypothesis states, "*The convergence of SD [social democratic] and MC [moderate conservative] parties together with an extended period of government participation by the moderate conservatives thus creates the electoral opening for the authoritarian Right that induces voters to abandon their loyalty to established conservative parties*" (Kitschelt 1995, 17; italics in the original text). If this were true, moderate parties should have moved to the center *before* the growth of the ERPs, and the distance between the most rightist and leftist parties in the system should have decreased.

However, the "mainstream rightist parties" moved to the right before the ERPs' rise (generally speaking, around the early 1980s); only when the conservative parties regained a more centrist position did the ERPs arose. If this schema fits into each national case, one should control for the timing of radicalization, polarization, and the ERPs' rise.[2] The preceding years are those during which the radicalization and polarization should have occurred.

2. The timing is debatable in the Dutch case, whether one considers the CD success of the late eighties rather than the previous, more limited, appearance of the CP in 1984.

Radicalization

It is common wisdom that after the libertarianism and egalitarianism of the late sixties and early seventies, a turn toward the right occurred in the eighties. For the first time since World War II, as Daniel Bell pointed out (Bell 1980, 149–50), the left lost its hegemony in the cultural intellectual domain. Neoliberalism and neoconservatism made their breakthrough restating and partly remodeling the traditional liberal and conservative ideas and issues (Girvin 1988). This cultural trend captured many "bourgeois" parties in the early 1980s (see in particular Betz 1990 and Minkenberg 1992 for the German case and Ysmal 1984 and Taguieff 1985 for the French case). This new mood produced a shift to the right by the conservative parties in the eighties (Klingemann 1995, 190–93).

The radicalization experienced by most of the European conservative parties paved the way for more radical interpretations of the neoconservative agenda. It opened the political market of ideas to themes and issues that were previously kept out of politics, especially immigration and security. In other words, the boundaries of the political space were enlarged on the right-wing side. At the right-wing border of this "enlarged" space, the ERPs grew.

Therefore, the move back to the center of the mainstream right parties, especially when they reentered government, does not explain per se the rise of ERPs: One should take into account that the previous move to the right of the same mainstream right parties had altered and radicalized the political agenda by introducing and legitimizing new issues. While issues such as immigration and law and order had been only timidly announced by the conservative party, they were voiced with incomparable emphasis by the ERPs. Survey data from French polling institutes, for example, demonstrate quite clearly that French people have been concerned for many years with these questions (Ignazi 1989, 71–72, Perrineau 1997, 156–79). The sudden breakthrough of the Front National is linked with the unresponsiveness of traditional political parties to these issues that were particularly salient for a well-defined constituency. In the 1997 parliamentary election the FN voters rated the immigration and security issues respectively 45 and 30 percentage points above the national mean (Perrineau 1997, 178). And last but not least, these issues were not "material" issues; they should be regarded post- or non-material concerns.

Polarization

The rightward Zeitgeist of the 1980s is linked to the change in the pattern of competition of the party systems. Radicalization had produced a system polarization by raising the ideological temperature and by increasing the distance between the parties (Sartori 1976, 126). This process is clearly assessed by the data of party manifestos reported in a right-left scale. The distance between the most distant political families (communists and conservatives) in Europe increased in the 1980s from 2.30 to 2.86 (Klingemann 1995, 190). Moreover, if the green parties, which arose in the early eighties, were taken into account, the ideological distance would have further increased.[3]

In France the self-location on the left-right continuum of Rally pour la République (RPR) and Union de France (UDF) middle-level elites moved from 18 percent self-declaring center-right and right in 1978 to 72 percent in 1984 (Brechon et al. 1986, 131). In Denmark, "a great ideological distance" (Bille

3. Unfortunately, no cross-national longitudinal data are available. Appendix B in Laver and Schonfeld (1990) offers an exhaustive analysis.

1989, 52) occurred at the eve of the Progress Party rise in 1973. In the Netherlands in the early-to-mid-eighties the socialist party (PvDA) moved more to the left and the Christian party (CDA) more to the right (Tromp 1989, 96). In the early 1990s Germany also experienced heightened ideological temperature and increased distance between the parties (Betz 1990, Klingemann and Volkens 1992, 199).

In Austria, the rise of the greens and the shift to the right of the Austrian People's Party (Campbell 1991, 169) in the mid-eighties increased the ideological distance within the party system.[4] In Belgium the rise of the Greens (the strongest green party in Europe) and deepening of the ethnic cleavage, to which the Vlaams Blok refers, pulled apart the party system. On the other hand, Norway did not follow this path: In the years preceding the rise of the Progress Party, the system did not show any polarizing trend (Strøm and Leipart 1992, 105–106). In this case one can argue that the shift to the left of all the parties since the early 1960s (Strøm and Leipart 1992, 74) has left a vacuum for a radical right-wing entrepreneur. Finally, in the Italian case the preexisting status of a polarized system, with an already present extreme right party, remains constant until the late eighties or early nineties, even if the radicalization decreased considerably during the 1980s (Ignazi 1998).

In sum, polarization and radicalization, together with the politicization of new, salient and misconceived issues, seem to lie at the heart of the dynamic that fostered the ERPs' rise. Where radicalization and/or polarization decreased, such as in Italy, Spain, and Portugal (Morlino and Montero 1995), the old ERPs declined or were forced to change to survive as in the Italian case.

Crisis of Confidence

However, this values and system dynamic is not enough. A more general syndrome of postindustrial societies offers a more accurate explanation of ERPs' rise. This syndrome does not focus on the different relationships of production and the market, as suggested by Kitschelt (1995), Taggart (1995), and partly by Betz (1994) and Minkenberg (1992).

What further differentiates the present interpretation concerns the question of the "crisis of legitimacy" of Western societies. We are compelled to go down this road for two reasons. First, because historically fascism was also the outcome of such a crisis. Second, because the peculiar trait of the ERPs is not their exclusionist, nationalist, or xenophobic agenda, but their opposition to the legitimizing bases of the liberal-democratic systems.

Thus, if ERPs are "anti-system" in the above specified meaning, their development should be linked to a crisis of confidence in the democratic system itself, and the ERPs (both in their programs and declarations) should exhibit a very low confidence in the democratic system and values.

The thesis of a crisis of confidence has been circulating since the mid 1970s, when the Frankfurt school of criticism of capitalist and consumerist society—coupled with the 1968 student revolt and the emergence of the counterculture and the new social movements—on one side and the pending fiscal crisis of the State on the other side merged to bring into question the essence and the working of the democratic system. However, at a high level of abstraction, summarizing the outcome of the World Values Survey, Ken Newton stated that "relatively speaking the level of citizen satisfaction and dissatisfaction have remained fairly constant over the postwar period as a whole" (Newton 1994, 33). In other words, the variation over time of alienation does not show a rising trend.

4. In the Austrian case, however, the internal change within the FPO is a crucial explanatory factor: the takeover of Haider shifted the party dramatically to the right, moving it from 7.25 in 1985 to 8.27 in 1991 (Campbell 1991, 169).

But the level of confidence varies according to the different indicators. In fact, although there is a consensus for democracy per se as an ideal political system, across Western Europe, the satisfaction with the working of democracy has quite a lower percentage of support (a mean of 57 percent) with high oscillation across time and country (Fuchs, Guidorossi, and Svensson 1995, 349). Also the rates of approval for political institutions offers a less satisfactory picture: "less than half of the public in each nation expresses confidence in the national legislature, rating it eighth in the list of ten institutions" (Dalton 1996, 269).

This relatively optimistic picture changes, however, when satisfaction for democracy is controlled by the citizens' location on the right-left continuum: those [respondants] located at the extreme right are less supportive of democracy than those at the center and even the extreme left. This trend is particularly evident in Spain, Italy, Greece, and Portugal, which show a criss-cross of left-right positioning and support of democracy: moving from left to right the pro-system attitudes decline while the anti-system ones increase (Morlino and Montero 1995, 246–47). Also in Norway, Sweden, and the United States, "those who locate themselves on the ideological extremes tend to be most strongly alienated" and "those on the left are more trusting than citizens on the right" (Miller and Listhaug 1993, 185). The same goes for France, Germany, and Austria.

This pattern is even more clear when the voters of ERPs are taken into consideration. The MSI (Morlino and Montero 1995), Republikaner (Fuchs 1993, 262–63), and Front National (Mayer 1993) voters display a much higher level of dissatisfaction regarding democracy than the mean population. In 1989, 45 percent of the French who were "alienated" voted for the Front National; in Germany 24 percent would have voted Republikaner; in Italy 19 percent would vote for MSI. Compared to the national mean of alienated voters, the percentage of alienated voters is more than double for the MSI, three times for the Republikaner and four times for the FN voters (Ysmal 1991, 18–20). A similar pattern is discernible in the Austrian FPO whose voters the political system rated negatively much more than the population at large (47 percent against 28 percent), and they even preferred a dictatorship in spite of democracy (17 percent against 5 percent) (Betz 1994, 51).

The Norwegian and Danish progress parties follow a different pattern. The balance is slightly in favor of satisfaction (more for the Danish party than for the Norwegian one) while below the national mean (Klages and Neumiller 1993, 14–15). Other surveys show that the FRP voters have the higher level of dissatisfaction for the "political class" and the higher propensity for a "strong man" at the head of the state (Nielsen 1976, 149ff).

In sum, the hypothesis of a rise of ERPs as a consequence of a general crisis of democracy is to be rejected *as such*. The mass public has not shifted toward anti-system and anti-democratic attitudes. However, the limited quota of those who feel alienated regarding the democratic system is unevenly concentrated on the right pole and in the ERPs voters especially.

Notwithstanding this evidence, a fair amount of alienation in Western democracies does exist well beyond the ERPs electorate. It does not involve democracy per se or even the working of democracy. It does, however, tend to focus on political parties and politicians. This "anti-party sentiment" (Poguntke and Scarrow 1996) is clearly spreading in Western countries, where "there is a wide gap of confidence between the elites of the established parties and their electorate" (Deschouwer 1996, 276).[5] This loss of

5. As Russell Dalton (1996, 269) argues, "increasing public skepticism of political elites appears to be a common development in many advanced industrial democracies."

trust affects, to varying degrees, party systems throughout Europe (with the exception of the United Kingdom). In Germany a new word has been coined to express this sentiment—*Parteienverdrossenheit*, or disaffection with party (Scarrow 1996, 309ff). In Belgium, the Netherlands, and Austria, the consociational role of parties has come under attack; in France the loss of confidence dates back to the early 1980s (see above and Cayrol 1994) and has not been reversed; in Italy the absence of confidence in parties and politicians (and politics in general) represents an enduring element of national political culture (see the seminal Almond and Verba 1963, and more recently Morlino and Tarchi 1996). In Scandinavia, the emergence at different points in time of the ERPs (1973 in Denmark and Norway, 1991 in Sweden) has been related to "the fact that the electorate in Denmark, Norway and Sweden was influenced by feelings of distrust towards politicians" (Gooskens 1993, 17; see also Andersen and Bjorklund, this volume).

ERPs are anti-party because in their genetic code one finds the ideal of "harmonious unity" and the horror vacui of division: the national or local or ethnic community should be preserved against any sort of division. Pluralism is extraneous to the extreme right political culture, in which unity, strength, nation, State, ethnos, and *Volk* are the recurrent references. The individual never attains his or her own specificity: individual self-affirmation pertains to liberalism and therefore is totally alien to ERPs' political culture.[6] ERPs search for a national or subnational identity. They cannot conceive of a community where people are not "similar" to each other because difference would entail division. And as division is the essence of liberal democracy, their search for unity and identity leads them to conflict with the principles of the democratic system. This search does not come from "fascist" inspiration: it is the byproduct of a widely shared world-view in which the society must be a harmonious community. The natural targets of anti-pluralism are parties at the political level and foreigners at the social level.

The distrust vis-à-vis politicians and parties permeates the ERPs' political discourse. The French Front National leader, Jean-Marie Le Pen, used to address the four established French parties as the "gang of four," emphasizing the exclusion of the FN from that "club." The same goes for all the other leaders of the extreme parties from Haider to Dillen, from Glistrup to Lange and Hagen, from Ferret to Shonhuber, from Frey to Janmaat. (The MSI position on this point deviates somewhat from the trend: see Ignazi 1998.) The attitudes of the FN voters are in tune with such feelings: 58 percent, against a national mean of 36 percent, think that politicians do not care for people like the average voter (Perrineau 1997, 116–18). FPO voters pointed out that the most important motive for voting for Haider's party was precisely the extraneousness of that party to "the other parties scandals and privileges" (Riedelsperger 1992, 42; Schleder 1996). In Denmark the rise of the FRP has been associated with a "wave of distrust for the old parties, politicians and for 'the system,' " and the Glistrup party is seen as having "tried to undermine the legitimacy of the regime of the old parties" (Bille 1989, 49). The same goes for the other Scandinavian ERPs (Gooskens 1993). In the Netherlands the rise of the CP in 1983 to 1984 was attributed to a growing alienation and distrust of politics (Witte 1991). In Belgium and in the Netherlands the anti-party statements overflow from the party programs of the Vlaams Blok and of the CD and CP '86 (Swingendow 1995, Mudde 1996, 1998). All of this sketchy but consistent evidence supports the argument for a relationship between the diffusion of anti-party sentiment and the growth of the ERPs.

---

6. The relevance of the individual and of political liberalism in the Scandinavian progress parties is precisely one of the main puzzles regarding the inclusion of these parties into the ERPs family (see Harmel and Gibson 1995).

Conclusion

The rise of ERPs in the eighties is linked to the capacity to mobilize resources by political entrepreneurs, which exploited a favorable structure of opportunity at the political level (system polarization and radicalization) and at the cultural level (the rise of a neoconservative movement in the intellectual elite with its impact on the mass beliefs). The 1980s represent a watershed in the history of postwar extreme right politics. Up to that time it was represented only by the Italian MSI, the sole party to gain parliamentary representation with sizable percentages (around 5 percent) since 1948. Other parties had made some appearance but they neither obtained parliamentary seats at national level nor lasted for a long time. The German nationalist-nostalgic parties in the early fifties and the Austrian Verband der Unabhängigen (Independents' Union) are partial exceptions. Another deviant case is represented by the twin Scandinavian parties, the Danish and the Norwegian FRP, which made their breakthrough in the mid-1970s and which have traits that are sufficiently idiosyncratic that some scholars (Harmel and Gibson 1995) refuse to include them in the extreme right family.

In the mid-eighties the political landscape of the right-wing pole changed. The French FN emerged from a "decade of darkness and sarcasm," as Le Pen declared after the 1984 European elections, and became a prominent party in the French political system. In a few years, newly born parties such as the Belgian FN and the German Republikaners, or preexisting ones as the Belgian Vlaams Blok, the Dutch CD, and above all the Austrian FPÖ followed the French example. With national variants, all pointed to an appeal against the welfare state, democratic institutions, the establishment, and traditional parties and politicians.

The success of these new parties, contrary to the decline and even disappearance of the traditional ERPs, is linked to their different historical origin: they are the offspring of postindustrial society and they reflect demands and needs different from those that nurtured the neofascist parties. The postindustrial ERPs are the byproduct of a dissatisfaction with government policies on issues such as immigration and crime and, at a more profound level, an expression of uneasiness in a pluralistic, conflicted, multicultural, and perhaps globalizing society.

References

Almond, Gabriel A. 1996. "Political Science: The History of the Discipline." In *The New Handbook of Political Science*, eds. Robert Goodin and Hans-Dieter Klingemann, 50–96. Oxford: Oxford University Press.

Almond, Gabriel A. and Verba, Sidney, 1963. *The Civic Culture: Political Attitudes and Democracy in Five Nations*. Princeton: Princeton University Press.

Backes, Uwe, 1990. "Extremismus und Populismus von rechts." *Aus Politik und Zeitgeschichte. Beilage zur Wochenzeitung "Das Parlament,"* v. 46–47, no. 90.

——— and Eckhard Jesse, 1989. *Politischer Extremismus in der Bundesrepublik Deutschland*. Köln: Verlag Wissenschaft und Politik.

Bell, D., 1976. "The Extreme Right in France." In M. Kolkinsky and W. E. Paterson (eds.), *Social and Political Movements in Western Europe*. London: Croom Helm.

Betz, Hans-Georg, 1993. "The New Politics of Resentment: Radical Right-Wing Populist Parties in Western Europe." *Comparative Politics* v. 26: 413–27.

———, 1994. *Radical Right-Wing Populism in Western Europe*. New York: St. Martin's Press.

Bille, L., 1989. "Denmark: The Oscillating Party System." *West European Politics* v. 12: 42–58.

Dalton, Russell, 1996. *Citizen Politics*. Chatham, NJ: Chatham House.

Eatwell, Roger, 1996. "The Esoteric Ideology of the National Front in the 1980s." *The Failure of British Fascism.* Basingstroke: Macmillan.

Ferraresi, Franco, 1996. *Threats to Democracy: The Radical Right in Italy After the War.* Princeton: Princeton University Press.

Fuchs, Dieter, 1993. *A Metatheory of the Democratic Process.* Discussion Paper FS III 93-203. Wissenschaftszentrum Berlin für Sozialforschung.

Fuchs, Dieter, Giovanna Guidorossi, and Palle Svensson, 1995. "Support for the Democratic System." *Citizens and the State.* Oxford: Oxford University Press.

Gardberg, Annvi, 1993. *Against the Stranger, the Gangster and the Establishment: A Comparative Study of the Ideologies of the Swedish Ny Demokrati, the German Republikaner, the French Front National and the Belgian Vlaams Blok.* Helsinki: Swedish School of Social Science, University of Helsinki.

Girvin, Brian, 1988. *The Transformation of Contemporary Conservatism.* London: Sage.

Gooskens, M. P. J., 1993. *How Extreme Are the Extreme Right Parties in Scandinavia?* MA Thesis, Leiden: University of Leiden.

Griffin, Roger, 1991. *The Nature of Fascism.* New York: Routledge.

Harmel, A., and R. Gibson, 1995. "Right-Libertarian Parties and the 'New Values': A Re-examination." *Scandinavian Political Studies* v. 18, no. 2: 97–118.

———, 1992. "The Silent Counter-Revolution: Hypotheses on the Emergence of the Extreme Right-Wing Parties in Europe." *European Journal of Political Research* v. 22, no. 1–2 (July): 3–34.

Himmelstein, Jerome, 1990. *To the Right: The Transformation of American Conservatism.* Berkeley: University of California press.

Ignazi, Piero, 1989. *Il polo escluso: Profilo del Movimento Sociale Italiano.* Bologna: Il Mulino.

Jackman, R., and K. Volpert, 1996. "Conditions Favouring Parties of the Extreme Right in Western Europe." *British Journal of Political Science* v. 26: 501–21.

Kitschelt, Herbert, with Anthony J. McAnn, 1995. *The Radical Right in Western Europe: A Comparative Analysis.* Ann Arbor: University of Michigan.

Kirchheimer, Otto, 1966. "The Transformation of the Western European Party Systems." In M. Weiner and J. La-Palombara eds. *Political Parties and Political Development.* Princeton, N.J.: Princeton University Press.

Klages, E. P., and J. H. Neumiller, 1993. "Extremist Parties Within a New Politics Perspective." Paper presented at the APSA Annual Meeting, Washington, D.C.

Klingemann, Hans-Dieter, 1995. "Party Positions and Voter Orientations." In Hans-Dieter Klingemann and Dieter Fuchs, eds. *Citizens and the State.* Oxford: Oxford University Press, 183–205.

Kolkey, Jonathan Martin, 1983. *The New Right, 1960–1968: With Epilogue, 1969–1980.* Lanham, MD: University Press of America.

Laver, Michael, and Norman Schonfield, 1990. *Multiparty Government: The Politics of Coalition in Europe.* Oxford: Oxford University Press.

Mayer, Nonna, 1993. "The National Front Vote or the Fear Syndrome; Le Vote Front National Ou le Syndrome de la Peur." *Revue Internationale d'Action Communautaire* v. 30, no. 70 (autumn): 117–22.

Miller, H. A., and O. Listhaug, 1993. "Ideology and Political Alienation." *Scandinavian Political Studies* v. 16: 167–92.

Minkenberg, M., 1992. "The New Right in Germany: The Transformation of Conservatism and the Extreme Right." *European Journal of Political Research* v. 22, no. 1: 55–81.

Morlino, L. and J. R. Montero (1995). "Legitimacy and Democracy in Southern Europe." In *The Politics of Democratic Consolidation in Southern Europe* (N. Diamandouros, R. Gunther and H. J. Puhle, eds.). Baltimore: Johns Hopkins University Press.

Morlino, Leonardo and Marco Tarchi, 1996. "The Dissatisfied Society: The Roots of Political Change in Italy." *European Journal of Political Research* 30: 41–63.

Mudde, Cas, 1996. "The Paradox of the Anti-Party: Insights from the Extreme Right." *Party Politics* v. 2, no. 2 (April): 265–76.

———, 1998. "The Extreme Right Party Family." Ph.D. Thesis, Leiden University.

Newton, Kenneth, 1994. "Democratic Pathologies and Democratic Hypochrondia." *Disillusionment with Democracy: Political Parties, Participation and Non-participation in Democratic Institutions in Europe.* Strasbourg: Council of Europe Press, 26–42.

Perrineau, Pascal, 1997. *Le symptôme Le Pen.* Paris: Fayard.

Pfahl-Traugher, Armin, 1993. *Rechtsextremismus: Eine Kritische Bestandsaufnahme Nach der Wiedervereinigung.* Bonn: Bouvier.

Poguntke, T., and S. Scarrow (eds.), 1996. "The Politics of Anti-Party Sentiment." *European Journal of Political Research* (special issue).

Rémond, René, 1984. *Les Droites en France.* Paris: Aubier.

Riedelsperger, Max, 1992. "Heil Haider! The Revitalization of the Austrian Freedom Party Since 1986." *Politics and Society in Germany, Austria and Switzerland* v. 4, no. 3: 18–58.

Sartori, Giovanni, 1976. *Parties and Party Systems: A Framework for Analysis.* Cambridge: Cambridge University Press.

Schleder, A., 1996. "Anti-Political-Establishment Parties." *Party Politics* v. 2: 291–312.

Sternhell, Z., 1987. *Ni Droite ni Gauche. L'Ideologie Fasciste en France.* Paris: Editions Complexe.

Strøm, Kaare, and Jorn Y. Leipart, 1992. "Ideology, Strategy, and Party Competition in Postwar Norway." *European Journal of Political Research* v. 17: 263–88.

Swingendow, Marc, 1995. "Les nouveaux clivages dans la politique belgo-flamande." *Revue Française de Science Politique* v. 45: 775–90.

Taggart, Paul, 1993. "Muted Radicals: The Emerging 'New Populism' in West European Party Systems." Paper prepared for the annual meeting of the American Political Science Association Meeting, Washington, D.C.

———, 1995. "New Populist Parties in Western Europe." *West European Politics* v. 18, no. 1: 34–51.

von Beyme, Klaus, 1988. "Right-wing Extremism in Post-war Europe." *West European Politics* v. 11, no. 2 (April): 1–18.

Ysmal, Colette, 1984. "Le RPR et l'UDF Face Au Front National, Concurrence et Connivences." *Revue Politique et Parlementaire,* November–December.

———, 1991. "Les Cadres Du Front National: Les Habits Neufs de l'Extreme Droite." In O. Duhamel and J. Jaffre (eds.), *L'etat de l'Opinion 1991.* Paris: SOFRES Seuil: 181–97.

Chapter 6

DO ELECTORAL INSTITUTIONS MATTER?

Election systems have become an increasingly important object of study for political scientists. As a discipline, political science has become more focused on political behavior and its resulting outcomes, and given that electoral systems are perhaps a nation's most important political institution, they have received more attention from scholars as a result of this trend. In addition, a growing number of nations have replaced long-used electoral systems with entirely new sets of rules, such as New Zealand, which switched from a single-member district plurality system to a mixed member proportional system. Such changes have occurred in part because world leaders are paying increasing attention to what are known as issues of constitutional engineering, that is, the manner in which political institutions affect outcomes and, thus, the dynamics of a nation's politics. For example, by changing its electoral rules from single-member district plurality to PR, New Zealand changed from a two-party to a multiparty system. Political scientists have watched such developments and attempted to clarify what happens and why when electoral systems and processes are manipulated.

When political scientists use the phrase "electoral system," they are referring to a set of institutional features provided by law that formally define the manner in which elections are conducted in a country. These features include the number and size of election districts, the structure of the ballots through which citizens register their support for one or more candidates in elections, and the rules a nation uses for the translation of votes into legislative seats for both institutional (political parties) and individual actors seeking office.

The combination of electoral rules used by the nations of the world is nearly as varied as the actual number of nations conducting elections. Moreover, when it is said that electoral systems have enjoyed growing attention from political scientists, this means that scholars are looking more closely at how the various types of electoral systems have been used to conduct national elections throughout the world and contributed to the patterns witnessed in party systems. They can be combined to form institutional patterns that are either familiar and enjoy fairly wide use or are innovative and infrequently used for the conduct of national elections.

While the first systematic study of election systems can perhaps be traced to the work of nineteenth-century philosopher John Stuart Mill, who discussed various electoral rules as part of his philosophical study of representation, the study of election systems in contemporary political science began with the work of French political scientist Maurice Duverger in the 1950s and 1960s. Duverger was primarily interested in the organization and impact of modern political parties, but his study of their effect on the development of democratic politics led him to begin researching electoral systems. Specifically, Duverger observed that different types of election rules led to different patterns of party competition and, as a result, different configurations of party systems. He noted that single-member district systems with a plurality rule, like the one long used in the United Kingdom, tended to produce competition between two large parties, while those systems defined by larger district magnitudes and the use of some type of proportional representation formula, such as those used by most of the countries of continental Europe, tended to produce competition among several parties and, thus, multiparty systems.

This seminal finding attracted political scientists to the details of electoral systems, and the efforts of political scientists have since focused primarily on two aspects of these essential electoral institutions. The first concerns the specific components, like district magnitude and the rules used for converting votes into legislative seats, that give election systems their distinctive character and push party competition into certain patterns in the aggregate to form, for example, two-party or multiparty systems. The second important component is known as the allocation formula; these are the rules by which votes obtained by candidates and parties in elections are translated into legislative seats. Allocation formulas are a significant feature of election systems because they work in concert with district magnitudes to structure party competition and produce the aggregate patterns that define party systems.

There are two principal types of allocation formulas, plurality/majority and proportional representation, but there is a large amount of variation within each basic format. Plurality/majority formulas allocate legislative seats based on which candidates have the highest number of votes, whereas PR formulas employ a variety of mathematical procedures to ensure that each party's percentage of legislative seats is proportional to the percentage of votes it received. Moreover, the variation that exists within each type of allocation formula carries strong implications for the manner in which actors compete for support from a nation's electors, and the results of that the political competition will produce two- or multiparty systems. One final feature to consider is what is known as the threshold. This refers to a floor, or minimum percentage (or number) of votes, that a party (or candidate) must receive to be given the chance to obtain a legislative seat. Like the other features mentioned here, thresholds also have profound impact on party competition and the results that occur under electoral rules. For example, higher thresholds are an effective way to keep small, extreme parties from electing members to a country's legislature, helping to keep electoral politics more stable.

Given the diversity of electoral systems, classification can proceed along a number of lines. One way to classify these systems is by how they combine such features as district magnitudes and allocation formulas. This line of reasoning distinguishes between plurality/majority systems and PR systems and a more recent, but increasingly popular, electoral form known as mixed systems. There are different types of mixed systems, but all are similar in that they combine majority/plurality and PR rules in their electoral systems.

Another way to think about electoral systems is in terms of the aggregate tendencies that they produce. Since politics is about who emerges with power from an election, and because an election system structures the competition that occurs in such contests, it would be naïve to think that they are neutral with respect to political competition. In this way, election systems do have their negative features, the most notable of which concerns malapportionment, or the allocation of legislative seats in a way that is different from what is expected given a party or candidate's share of votes. This is an unfortunate feature of all election systems, but it is more notable in certain types, specifically, plurality systems that use single-member districts.

Another aspect of how political institutions matter concerns who can vote. Countries are different not only with respect to how they conduct their elections but also in terms of who is allowed to participate in them. This involves restrictions on the vote such as age, citizenship, and residency requirements, but it also concerns the manner in which different countries treat prisoners and those with mental disabilities. As the reading by Louis Massicotte, André Blais, and Antoine Yoshinaka in this section shows, most countries are pretty similar along these lines, but there is one voting rights area in which countries are quite different. There are approximately twenty countries in the world in which voting is compulsory—registered voters are required to turn out and cast ballots—but not all of these countries treat violators the same. Some, like Costa Rica and Portugal, have no legal repercussions if a voter does not turn out, whereas others, including Australia and Brazil, impose fines for this violation.

The readings in this section cover two different aspects of electoral institutions. Reading 6.1 by Rein Taagepera and Matthew Soberg Shugart discusses those institutions that govern how elections are structured and carried out in different countries and focuses on candidates and party elites. Reading 6.2 by Massicotte, Blais, and Yoshinaka, on the other hand, examines institutions governing voter qualifications and participation and, thus, is more concerned with the average citizen. Despite these differences of focus, both types of institutions are essential for understanding how elections are conducted and the results they are likely to produce.

6.1

WHY STUDY ELECTORAL SYSTEMS? AND GENERAL FEATURES OF ELECTORAL SYSTEMS

Rein Taagepera and Matthew Soberg Shugart

Rein Taagepera and Matthew Soberg Shugart are political scientists at the University of California, Irvine, and the University of California, San Diego, respectively. Each has written numerous articles on political institutions, but they may be best known for coauthoring *Seats and Votes,* the first scholarly text devoted entirely to the description and analysis of electoral rules. This work, from which the first reading in this chapter is drawn, introduced readers to the multiple ways that countries have dealt with the relationship between the votes cast in elections and the manner in which these are translated into legislative seats. Taagepera and Shugart show that the world's electoral systems come in various forms and that these differences typically reflect the social and political characteristics of the countries for which they were designed. This excerpt focuses on the significance of electoral systems and their component parts; the authors note that perhaps the most important component of any election system is its district magnitude (dm), that is, the average number of seats (or representatives) per election district, because it is the most notable feature that distinguishes one election system from another. It is also important for determining how party competition is structured in a country's political system. More specifically, electoral rules that involve higher dms are typically employed in segmented societies because they allow more political parties to place representatives in the legislature than do the British-style, single-member district plurality rules. In light of this, problems arise when electoral rules are used that do not match the social characteristics of the country.

Why Study Electoral Systems?

In 1970 Chile had three major candidates running for president. Socialist Salvador Allende narrowly surpassed a centrist and a rightist candidate and became president, although he received only 36.3 percent of the total vote. Allende's electoral platform committed him to carry out extensive social changes. However, his support base was too narrow, and his attempts to forge ahead with radical changes despite this drawback backfired badly. The centrists became alienated to the point where they acquiesced in a military coup. The outcome was a bloody dictatorship.

History could have been quite different if Chile had had different electoral rules. Chilean tradition demanded that the legislature confirm as president the candidate with the largest number of votes, al-

Rein Taagepera and Matthew Soberg Shugart, "Why Study Electoral Systems?" and "General Features of Electoral Systems," in *Seats and Votes* (New Haven, Conn.: Yale University Press, 1989), chapters 1 and 2, 1–6.

though Allende was the least desirable of the three candidates for more than half of the voters. In some other countries an absolute majority (that is, more than 50 percent of votes cast) is required for election. A majority can be achieved by having a second round of elections in which only the two candidates with the most votes participate. The outcome might be that the centrist candidate is eliminated, and the voters offered the choice between a rightist and a leftist. If most of the former supporters of the centrist candidate were to switch to the rightist, the latter could win, much to the dismay of many leftist voters. Instead of a second round, one can also have only one round of elections but ask voters for their second preferences. In this case, the centrist candidate would presumably be the second choice of both leftists and rightists, and the country would get a president at least semiacceptable to everybody.

The point here is not to argue that one of the possible methods or outcomes described above is better than the others. The point is that electoral rules matter: with the *same* distribution of votes, the presidency could go to the leftist, the centrist, or the rightist candidate, depending on the rules.

More broadly, electoral rules can make or break a party—or even a country—as will be seen in the next section. On the other hand, they are also easier to change than most other features of a political system and therefore offer a promising field for "political engineering" (although the ease of such change should not be overestimated)—a feature elaborated upon toward the end of this chapter. Finally, of all aspects of political science, the study of electoral systems is one of the most amenable to quantitative modeling, given that the input data (votes, seats, etc.) readily come in the form of numbers. As such, it is of broad theoretical interest even if no manipulation of existing systems is contemplated.

Electoral Rules Can Make or Break a Party—Or Even a Country

In 1929 the British Liberal party received 23.4 percent of the popular vote; but as that translated into less than 10 percent of the seats in Parliament because of the workings of the electoral rules, these votes for the previously powerful Liberals suddenly looked "wasted." This was part of the reason why in the next election only 7 percent of the voters chose the Liberals. This time they received almost no seats in Parliament. The Liberals had been one of the two major parties in Great Britain during the previous hundred years, but now they became a minor party for at least the next fifty.

In 1933 the Progressive party in Iceland received practically the same share of votes that destroyed the British Liberals: 23.9 percent. Far from being short-changed in terms of seats to the point of extermination, the Icelandic Progressives received 33.2 percent of the parliamentary seats, and they played a leading role in the country's political life. The country's electoral rules and the way in which district boundaries were drawn made the difference. So we see that same percentage of popular votes resulted in very different outcomes for the British Liberals and the Icelandic Progressives, in terms of parliamentary seats and political power.

These examples highlight some general facts about elections. Their outcomes do not depend only on popular votes but also on the rules used. Be it the single presidential seat or the many seats in the national or local assemblies, the seat allocation rules vary widely from country to country, and sometimes even within a country. It is a question of how the votes are compiled and how the seats are allocated. Some electoral rules work strongly in favor of the largest party or the two largest parties, so that third parties (like the British Liberals) are denied seats and tend to shrivel. Some other electoral rules give even the smallest parties a chance to obtain seats in proportion to their percentage of votes. This often enables so many parties to gain seats that any government must be based on a coalition (as is the case in Iceland).

Sometimes electoral rules that have worked reasonably well for a long time suddenly produce deadlock and civil strife (as in Chile). It has been argued that Hitler's ascendancy in Germany was helped by the existing electoral rules, which preserved a maddening profusion of parties and led to a widespread yearning for a single strong leader. The connection between electoral rules and Hitler's political success is debatable, but the very suggestion indicates that electoral rules might have serious consequences not only for a party but even for an entire country, its neighbors—and even the whole world. At the very least, such a suggestion shows the importance of understanding what effects electoral rules really do have, as well as what the prospects for changes in rules may be.

The way in which winners are determined and seats allocated does matter. Different countries use very different methods. Why don't nations simply pick the best way to allocate seats and stop playing games with electoral rules? Unfortunately there is no absolutely best way. It depends on what one wants to obtain. Some countries value proportional representation (PR), that is, seats allocated in proportion to votes obtained; but the resulting coalition governments may be unstable. Some countries value the governmental stability achieved by giving the largest party a comfortable majority so that it can rule alone even if it received less than 50 percent of the votes. However, the result may be gross underrepresentation of important minorities.

Some countries manage to have their cake and eat it too: for a long time Austria has had quite proportional representation and also stable one-party cabinets. Some others fare badly on both accounts, having neither PR nor stable government. In most cases such instability has nothing to do with electoral rules, but in some the electoral rules do play a role. Sometimes countries are not clear about how electoral rules work: they adopt certain rules in expectation of certain results, but the outcome is different. This is where a more systematic study of the electoral rules and their consequences can become especially important and useful.

The Most Easily Manipulable Feature of a Political System

Compared to other components of political systems, electoral systems are the easiest to manipulate with specific goals in view.[1] This does not mean that electoral rules are easy to change but only that the other components are usually even harder to change.

We have some idea of how to alter electoral rules so as to achieve goals such as more proportional representation, or exclusion of very small parties, or reinforcement of the single largest party. We cannot achieve all these contrary goals at once, but we can choose a combination. Once passed by the proper authorities (such as the legislative assembly), the rules can be implemented and the changes in outcomes should be measurable. If not satisfied, we can tinker further. In contrast, many other aspects of political systems cannot be changed by legislative decision (for example, people's political preferences); or it turns out that a decision cannot be implemented; or the outcome is the opposite of the one expected (for example, the U.S. Prohibition laws); or there is simply no way to determine whether the law has had any effect. In all these aspects electoral systems seem the easiest to handle.

However, countries are not free to shop among all the electoral systems practiced throughout the world. They are tied by local political conditions and traditions. Suppose a new country is formed, and the political elite happens to separate into a large number of parties. Then, to pass an electoral law, the

1. This is the point of view of Sartori's (1968) seminal article "Political Development and Political Engineering."

support of many such parties would be needed, some of them fairly small. The latter are not likely to support a law that would put them out of business by penalizing the small parties and giving a bonus to the larger ones. If, on the other hand, only one or two large parties form, they are not likely to establish a proportional representation system that would help small parties to gain a footing and the potential to whittle down the large parties' strength.

The same applies to later electoral reforms. Reforms usually require the approval of current assembly members. But these are by definition the very people whom the current electoral system has served well. Why should they want to change a system that got them elected? The British Liberals favor changes in the electoral rules because, as we have seen, the present system penalizes them. The two dominant parties who profit from the Liberal losses are quite happy with the system—and they have the parliamentary votes. One even suspects that if the Liberals ever were to become one of the two largest parties, they might quickly reconsider their interest in electoral reform.

Thus there is considerable inertia in electoral systems. Countries tend to stick to the electoral rules they happened to adopt around the time when the right to vote was extended to most adults (universal suffrage). The inertia often goes even deeper. A country that has three clearly distinct population groups—say, Catholics, Protestants, and Muslims—may develop three corresponding parties if religion is seen as the foremost political consideration. Under these circumstances it would be foolish for the country to adopt an electoral system that penalizes all but the largest party. The other two religious groups would be permanently underrepresented, and the country might risk unrest or even civil war.

Nonetheless, electoral reforms do occur. Major changes took place in France in 1958 and Northern Ireland in 1973. Fairly extensive changes occurred in Japan in 1982 (upper-house elections). Since 1960, electoral formulas have been altered in Austria and Sweden, and active discussion of electoral reform continues in many countries.

A Rosetta Stone?

Besides the "political engineering" aspect of the study of electoral systems, such study is of interest for its possible effects upon the development of quantitative studies in the broader field of political science. Compared to other political phenomena, electoral systems deal with fairly hard numerical data: number of votes, seats, electoral districts, and so on. Thus these studies are especially amenable to methods used in more established scientific disciplines. In this respect, studies of electoral systems might supply a Rosetta Stone for some other branches of political science. Votes might be to the quantitative development of political science what mass has been for physics and money for economics: a fairly measurable basic quantity. On the basis of more easily definable and measurable quantities (such as seats and votes), less easily definable notions, such as the number of parties, can be given precise operational meanings, as we shall see. Interaction of the number of parties with cabinet durability and the number of issue dimensions can, in turn, put these concepts on firmer measurable grounds. This process may eventually extend even further into related branches of political science.

* * *

General Features of Electoral Systems

Voting is a widespread practice in the modern world. Its supposed goal is to have "the people" express their will and choose their own leaders and representatives. It is a fairly new practice, though, in world history. Very few elections were being held two centuries ago, and even a hundred years ago very few people in very few places were entitled to participate. Nowadays most countries have some sort of elections, but the methods used and the outcomes obtained vary widely.

Elections with and without Choice

The distinction between choice and no choice is basic. In elections with choice, the voters are presented with several candidates or proposals to choose from. The scope of the choice varies. In some countries candidates may represent a wide range of opinions or ideologies: fascist, reactionary, conservative, liberal, socialist, communist. In other countries the choice may be limited to two middle-of-the-road candidates who carry different party labels but look very much the same, except in personality. In yet other countries (such as Tanzania) only one party is allowed, but within this common ideological framework several candidates may be nominated to compete with each other.

Even if the range of choice is wide, some of the candidates may have so much larger campaign funds or so much easier access to the state radio and television media that they have a definite advantage. But regardless of such inequities, some choice remains. If the voters are really fed up with the "fat cat" who spends millions on his campaign, they can find out who the other candidates are. If they are fed up with the venal party boss in the one-party but multicandidate elections, they can cast their votes for the young unknown candidate of the same party.

In elections without choice, voters are presented with one single candidate or issue, and they can vote either for or against. If people are voting on issues, as in plebiscites, the choiceless version is usual. One might, for instance, be given the chance to vote either for or against a proposal to change the constitution. Even if the choice is between monarchy and republic, it is essentially still a yes/no choice in most cases: a choice about whether to have a change or not. Giving more choices in a plebiscite would make the outcome very difficult to interpret, if no single outcome carried with more than 50 percent of the votes.

Some countries use the same yes/no approach in the election of representatives and leaders. For each seat or position, a single candidate is proposed by the ruling party or its front organizations. No competing candidates are allowed. This practice has been followed, for instance, in the Soviet Union, where casting an unmarked ballot is counted as a positive vote (see White 1985). In order to vote against, one has to cross out the single candidate's name. Few people do so, because it takes more effort, makes one conspicuous, and gives the voter little satisfaction: so you vote against someone, but whom are you voting *for*? Such choiceless elections are more in the nature of plebiscites than elections: one can only approve or disapprove of the ruling group, without any possibility of voicing support for a different group. In practice even disapproval is made difficult—and pointless, since the ruling group has the monopoly of counting (or miscounting) the votes. (In June 1987 the Soviet local elections for the first time involved some limited choice.)

Even formally multiparty systems do not always involve a choice for the individual voter. At times, as in Poland, the dominant party keeps a stable of docile secondary parties, for appearances' sake. In the few districts assigned to a secondary party, the dominant party will not field a candidate.

Perhaps one of the most creative ways in which an authoritarian regime remains in control while still allowing elections with choice is found in Taiwan. A 314-seat legislature with only 72 elected seats is justified by the ruling party's claim to be the government of all China. These 72 representatives are elected in constituencies in the areas under Taiwanese sovereignty. The remaining 242 seats are said to represent those areas "temporarily" under the control of the Communist party in Beijing. Since no elections can be held there, the government must appoint those legislators. Thus the ruling party is assured a huge majority, by the same justification which legitimizes its very existence in Taipei. (In 1988 a moderate increase in the number of elected seats was planned.)

. . . .Having some choice does not imply that such elections are necessarily free or fair (however one defines those somewhat nebulous terms). The ideological range may be limited; conceivably, only nonsocialist parties might be allowed to compete in some countries, and only socialist candidates might be allowed in some others. On a different level, the franchise (right to vote) may not extend to both sexes and to all social classes and racial groups (South Africa being a marked example). . . .

Voting Procedures

Ballot structure and the mechanics of voting. The ballot a voter receives may be very complex or very simple. The elections may involve only one level (say, the president) or many (the president, the upper- and lower-chamber representatives, the local council members, judges, etc.). In the latter case, the voter may have to choose only one of the many party symbols or names and hence automatically vote for all candidates of that party (for example, Venezuela), or he/she might be able to choose specific candidates at each level separately (for example, United States). Besides voting purely for a party list or purely for single candidates, intermediate and mixed ballots are also possible.

Regarding the mechanics of voting, we often talk as if the voter used the time-honored ballot printed on paper, checking off boxes of his/her choice. In actuality, the physical method may range from casting stones of different colors to pulling the levers or pushing the buttons of an electronic device. Voting method may make a difference psychologically, and also in terms of errors (pulling the wrong lever) and the real or imagined lack of confidentiality of voting.

Confidentiality is important. In some countries voters must go into an isolated booth, while in others marking one's ballot openly is accepted or even encouraged. (This practice becomes pronounced in choiceless elections where unmarked ballots are counted as positive votes.) In some countries the voter drops the ballot in a box, but in others he/she has to hand it to an official who drops it in the box in the voter's presence. The ballot itself may or may not carry a serial number. Suppose the voter is certain that the isolation booth is not being secretly observed, the voting machine is not bugged, the serial numbers are not used to track down the voter's identity, the officials have a neutral attitude, and no one cares to note whether one goes to the booth or not. In such a case all these details may seem unimportant. But if a country has a dominant party intent on staying in power, then any lapse of confidentiality may put pressure on the voters to vote for the dominant party. . . .

Categoric and ordinal ballot. Rae (1967) introduced the distinction between categoric and ordinal ballots. A vote is called categoric if the voter can vote for only one of the candidates (or parties) competing for the same post. A vote is called ordinal if the voter can rank the candidates (or parties). With an ordinal ballot, a voter can show that B is her first choice, but that if B cannot be elected, she would prefer C to A. In contrast, with a categoric ballot the voter may face a dilemma: if I vote for B, who seems unpopular, the outcome might be that A wins, and this would be the worst outcome for me; but if I vote for the more popular C, I will help C to win and reduce A's chances.

Consciously voting for a candidate (or party) that is not one's first choice is called "strategic," "sophisticated," or even "insincere" voting. In this context, the latter term does not imply anything dishonest, and insincere voting might well be the best rational strategy to avoid the possible worst outcome. However, this also means that a candidate whom most people actually prefer might receive very few votes if his popularity is underestimated by voters—a case of self-fulfilling prophecy. From this viewpoint, ordinal voting is a better way to determine people's real preferences. Nevertheless, categoric voting is much more widely used because it is simpler.

The distinction between categoric and ordinal ballots is not clear-cut: there is a continuum between two ideal types. A pure categoric ballot requires the voter to say, "I vote for this party over all others." A pure ordinal ballot allows the voter to rank-order as many candidates on the ballot as he desires, regardless of their party affiliation. Yet many systems allow voters to vote for more than one candidate or party for the same elective institution without being fully ordinal. Voters might be able to vote for both local and national representatives to the same legislative body (West Germany, Mexico, Guatemala, and Iceland). The existence of more than one vote makes these systems richer (not necessarily "better") in choice, and thus not truly categoric, yet certainly not ordinal. The degree of choice of an ordinal ballot is further approximated by systems that allow cumulative voting. In such a system the voter may cast more than one vote for a particular candidate, thus expressing a stronger choice for that candidate than for others but without specifically ranking candidates. Cumulative voting was formerly used for the Illinois state legislature in the United States.

Another electoral system in between the categoric and ordinal types is the approval vote. The voter may cast a vote for every candidate of whom he "approves" or, stated otherwise, may give an equally weighted vote to all but the least desirable candidate(s). The winner is the candidate with the most votes—the most widely "approved." Although this system has not yet been adopted for any major political office, it enjoys enthusiastic intellectual backing among some advocates of reform in U.S. presidential primaries.

Electoral districts and polling precincts. For the purposes of casting one's vote, voters are assigned to a specific precinct, in other words, the geographical subdivision where voters' rolls are kept to register voting and avoid double voting, and where the votes are later counted. The precinct may be further divided into polling station areas. In contrast, by electoral districts we mean the wider area over which the votes reported by precincts are gathered in order to determine which candidates have won.[2]

The term *district magnitude* denotes a very important factor: the number of seats distributed in a district. It can range from one to more than a hundred. The term *magnitude* is preferable to *size* because the latter may also refer to the number of voters in the district or even its geographical extent. . . . [T]he larger the district magnitude, the closer to proportional representation (PR) the seat distribution can come.

---

2. In some other writings, the meaning of districts and precincts may be different; it is up to the particular author to define the terms, and up to the reader to keep in mind in which of the various senses terms are used. For example, Nohlen (1984) uses *constituency* for what we call district, and *district* for what we call precinct.

Pathologies of Electoral Systems

Electoral fraud. Even if the proclaimed electoral rules are satisfactory, they are not always adhered to. The rules can be subverted in many ways, such as restricting nominations of candidates and campaigning, preventing people from voting, lack of confidentiality, and fraud in vote counting, the Philippines in February 1986 being an example of the last that received widespread attention. . . . Besides outright fraud, there are other ways to influence the electoral outcomes quite openly and legally and yet in a questionable manner. Malapportionment and "gerrymander" are among them.

Malapportionment and reapportionment. The previous discussion assumed that all districts have a number of seats proportional to the number of voters. This is not always the case. In countries with single-seat districts, some may have many more potential voters than others. What this means is that some voters' votes are more valuable than others, and thus the rule of "one person, one vote" is violated. Indeed, if there are three single-seat districts side by side, one of them with two thousand people entitled to vote and the two others with five hundred each, then the latter get the equivalent of two representatives per thousand people while the voters in the large district get only 0.5 representatives per thousand people. This is an example of malapportionment. District borders should be redrawn so as to have three districts of approximately one thousand potential voters each. Such an operation is called reapportionment or redistricting.

Even if one started out with equal-sized districts, people's migrations can eventually bring about inequalities. In particular, people tend to move from the countryside to the cities. Suppose that this happens in an initially rural country where the conservative Farmers' party is the predominant political force. The initially equal-sized districts may after a while look like those in our example above, with several underpopulated rural districts surrounding an overpopulated city district. The rural districts send to the assembly conservative representatives who predominate because of the large number of those districts. The cities, where most people now live, may elect mainly socialist representatives. The latter represent the majority of the people, but they are a minority in the assembly because of malapportionment. A reapportionment is overdue, but it would have to be decided by the conservative majority in the assembly—that is, by the very people who most stand to lose from a reapportionment. Hence they might try to delay it as long as possible.

In the United States considerable malapportionment developed before the Supreme Court decided to order reapportionment in the 1960s. Previously the Court had deemed that the matter was "political" and hence up to Congress.

Malapportionment can also arise when multi-seat districts are used, as in Iceland. The overrepresentation of the Icelandic Progressives mentioned in the previous chapter was due to their rural character. Despite several reapportionments, that overrepresentation tended to reappear as more and more people left the countryside.

With large-magnitude districts (that is, districts with more than ten seats), reapportionment does not require redrawing the traditional district borders. One can take a seat or two from one large district and reassign them to another. Because such changes rarely reverse the existing power relations in a typical PR electoral system, they tend to encounter less resistance than is the case in countries with one-seat districts.

Gerrymander. In the case of single-seat districts it also matters where the district borders are drawn, even when all districts have an equal number of potential voters. Consider the following situation, with eight equal-sized city quarters to be combined into four single-seat districts. The numbers shown are thousands of potential voters known to have Democratic and Republican preferences, respectively:

40–60	70–30	50–50	60–40
40–60	70–30	40–60	30–70

The total is an even 400:400, and one might expect each party to obtain two seats. However, if the Republicans can control the districting, they could join the areas vertically:

80–120	140–60	90–110	90–110

The Democrats would win overwhelmingly in the second district, but the Republicans would have a moderate but safe majority in the three others. If the Democrats are in control of the districting, they would prefer to join the areas horizontally:

110–90	110–90
110–90	70–130

Now the Republicans waste votes in an overkill in the lower right district, leaving the three other districts to the Democrats. A neutral reapportionment commission could combine the areas so that each party would predominate in two districts. There are three ways to obtain such a result in the case of this particular example, given the reasonable requirement that only areas adjacent to each other can be combined.

Which of the five possible district delineations is the best? There is no clear answer (see Niemi and Deegan 1978). But our simple example pales in face of the redistricting games actually played by the U.S. parties. The basic rule is always the same: pile all adversary votes in a few districts, leaving a moderate superiority for yourself in all the others. The game has received the name "gerrymander" ever since Governor Elbridge Gerry of Massachusetts managed in 1812 to concoct an outrageously elongated and twisted district that looked like a salamander and was called Gerry's Mander by his opponents. The game still continues. Some of the districts drawn in California in the 1980s looked even more distorted than Gerry's (see maps in Baker 1986).

The problem of gerrymander (and certain related abuses) is inherent in the system of one-seat districts. Changes in population make frequent reapportionment necessary if malapportionment is to be avoided, and there are no widely accepted simple rules on how to draw the district borders. The only consolation is that gerrymander sometimes backfires. If 11 percent of the usual Democratic voters should suddenly shift sides, then the three 110–90 victories in our example of Democratic gerrymander could turn into debacles, giving the Republicans all four seats, while more balanced districts would mostly preserve one seat for the Democrats.

In multi-seat districts gerrymander quickly becomes impractical as district magnitude increases. Another type of game, called "magnitude gerrymander" has at times been tried, for example, in Ireland. Regardless of the allocation rules used, low district magnitude tends to give a bonus to the party with the largest vote. Hence, in the regions where your party is strong, try to have as small districts as the law allows (say, three seats). In regions where your party is weaker and could fail to earn one seat out of three, try to have larger districts (say, five seats). The actual results of "magnitude gerrymander" have often been disappointing to its perpetrators. The game could be blocked by requiring all districts to have the same magnitude.

Potential and actual voters. In modern democracies all adults are, in principle, entitled to vote. Exceptions are made in various countries regarding illiterates, prisoners, military, and the mentally ill—for very different reasons. The age line used to be drawn somewhere above twenty, but it is now at eighteen in most countries.

Historically, the franchise (right to vote) was at first limited to older and wealthier males, preferably married and literate. In England, one of the pioneers of modern representative democracy, only as few as 4 percent of the adults could vote prior to 1830. The franchise was gradually broadened to include poorer and younger males, bachelors and illiterates included. By 1900 suffrage (another term for the right to vote) for all adult males was established in many Western countries, but almost all women remained disenfranchised. Nationwide universal suffrage including women was first introduced in New Zealand (1893). In Europe, Finland was the first (in 1906), and other countries soon followed suit. Only in Switzerland did voting remain a male privilege until 1971 (and in Liechtenstein until 1986). Newly independent or autonomous countries of this century usually adopted universal suffrage, if they practiced elections. Countries with elections without choice often pride themselves on being the most liberal regarding enfranchising the young. Given the validity of unmarked ballots and the absence of choice between competing candidates, the outcome would not be any different if they lowered the age limit even further.

Not all those entitled to vote bother registering. Voters' registration is almost automatic in some countries, along with the obligatory police registration regarding permanent or temporary residence. In some other countries, the procedure is more cumbersome and must be undertaken a long time before the elections, which means that people who have recently moved are temporarily disenfranchised. This is the case in many U.S. states.

Of those registered not all bother to vote, for various reasons. Participation rate among those entitled to vote is highest where voting is obligatory and the penalties for nonvoting are high. Choiceless elections in the Soviet Union typically report a 99 percent participation rate. When voting is obligatory but fines are moderate, as in Australia and the Netherlands (up to 1970), participation is typically 92 to 95 percent. In most developed countries with multichoice elections, participation varies from 70 to 90 percent, while in technologically underdeveloped countries the rate often drops to 60 or even 40 percent. In this respect the United States looks like an underdeveloped nation, and the reasons for low voting participation are much debated but unclear. Registration difficulties alone cannot account for the phenomenon. Overly frequent elections and a large number of elective positions may be factors. Let us merely note that one must distinguish between potential voters (those entitled to vote) and those who actually do vote.

Should districts be apportioned according to the total population (including children and others who cannot vote), or the population entitled to vote in principle, or those who have registered, or those who actually voted in the previous election? Under some circumstances it could make an appreciable difference. When the United States became independent, the southern states wanted congressional representation in proportion to the total population, including the slaves, who of course had no voting rights. The compromise was that slaves counted as half-persons for the purpose of allocating congressional seats to the states. (Women also lacked the franchise, but since they formed the same proportion of the population both in the South and the North, this did not cause any geographical imbalance.) Under conditions of universal suffrage, apportionment on the basis of adult population would not differ much from that based on the total population, and the latter tends to be used. Apportionment based on actual votes might be a strong incentive to increased participation in the United States, but it would go against the rule of "one person, one vote"—regardless of whether one makes use of one's vote.

References

Baker, G. E. 1986. "Whatever Happened to the Reapportionment Revolution in the United States?" In *Electoral Laws and Their Political Consequences,* edited by B. Grofman and A. Lijphart, 257–76. New York: Agathon Press.

Niemi, R. G., and J. Deegan, Jr. 1978. "A Theory of Political Districting." *American Political Science Review* 72: 1304–23.

Nohlen, D. 1984. *Elections and Electoral Systems.* Bonn: Friedrich-Ebert-Stiftung.

Rae, D. W. 1967 and 1971. *The Political Consequences of Electoral Laws.* New Haven: Yale University Press.

Sartori, G. 1968. "Political Development and Political Engineering." In *Public Policy,* vol. 17, edited by J. D. Montgomery and A. O. Hirschman. Cambridge: Cambridge University Press.

White, S. 1985. "Non-competitive Elections and National Politics: The USSR Supreme Soviet Elections of 1984." *Electoral Studies* 4: 215–29.

6.2

WHO HAS THE RIGHT TO VOTE?

Louis Massicotte, André Blais, and Antoine Yoshinaka

Electoral rules are fundamental to democratic politics because they set the tone in which political actors compete and seek support from potential voters. What the previous Taagepera and Shugart selection did not show is that electoral rules also determine who has the right to be a potential voter. This point is covered in this reading by Massicotte, Blais, and Yoshinaka. Louis Massicotte and André Blais are political scientists at the University of Montreal who have devoted their careers to studying the form and impact of various political institutions. In the reading included here, they team up with a younger formal theorist and political institutions specialist, Antoine Yoshinaka, to discuss how countries are different in terms of who is allowed to vote. As these authors show, democratic countries vary widely in terms of who can vote; depending on who possesses this right, political outcomes will vary. This reading then focuses on the impact that voters, not political elites, have on political outcomes. This piece is particularly interesting in its discussion of why certain countries have laws that make voting compulsory and how each deals with those who violate this law.

Universal suffrage is usually a basic criterion for an election to be deemed democratic. According to Dahl (1989, 233), one of the seven conditions for the existence of what he calls a polyarchy is that "practically all adults have the right to vote." Similarly, universal suffrage is the very first criterion listed by Butler, Penniman, and Ranney (1981, 3). Yet, as Katz (1997, 216) reminds us, "no country allows all adults to vote. . . . Although the basic trend over the last 200 years has been to remove one barrier after another, many restrictions remain."

Throughout the nineteenth and early twentieth centuries, the franchise was a lively issue. Whether women and less affluent citizens should be enfranchised was a hotly debated topic. In contrast, contemporary disqualifications affect smaller groups such as prison inmates, non-citizens, and mentally deficient persons. Still the issue of who should and should not have the right to vote is deeply perplexing.

Katz (1997, 216) identifies three major types of restrictions on the right to vote: "those based on community membership and having a personal stake in the election, those based on competence, and those based on autonomy." The distinction between competence and autonomy is fuzzy, as Katz (1997, 232)

Louis Massicotte, André Blais, and Antoine Yoshinaka, *Establishing the Rules of the Game* (Toronto: University of Toronto Press, 2004), 15–65.

himself acknowledges.[1] But the distinction between restrictions based on community and those based on competence is an important one.

Katz's first heading raises the question of whether only those who have formal citizenship should have the right to vote and whether they should have resided and should still be residing in the community in order to be qualified to vote. In the same vein, we would locate an issue not discussed by Katz—whether prisoners should have the right to vote—which raises the question of whether "imprisonment could still be looked on as the temporary exclusion of the individual from the community" (Report of the Royal Commission on the Electoral System 1986, 236).

Katz's second set of restrictions has to do with competence. This raises two sets of issues. First, at what age are people mature enough to be able to vote in a reasonable manner? Second, should people with mental disabilities have the right to vote, and/or should that right depend on the severity of the disability?

This chapter considers how democratic countries limit voting rights, and it examines compulsory voting. We look first at restrictions on the right to vote: those related to voting age, mental disabilities, citizenship, residence (district, country, abroad), and imprisonment. The chapter provides an overview of laws in place and of the debate about who should and who should not have the right to vote. We examine the general pattern of election laws. We describe the frequency and severity of the various restrictions. We look at whether a consensus exists among democratic countries about legitimate restrictions. We also identify particularly innovative kinds of legislation.

We consider, second, whether existing democracies perceive voting as a *right* or a *duty*. More precisely, we look at countries where voting is compulsory and sanctions for non-compliance.

Tables 1 and 2 present summary information on restrictions on the right to vote in the 63 countries. Tables 3 and 4 provide information on compulsory voting.

Restrictions on the Right to Vote

We first discuss competence-based restrictions on suffrage (age and mental disability), followed by restrictions based on community (citizenship, residence, and criminality).

Minimum Voting Age

The most common restriction based on competence is of course the voting age. Excluding non-adults from the franchise is commonly justified on the ground that only mature people can make reasoned choices and that, in view of the difficulty of measuring personal maturity, it is more useful to rely on age. Children and adolescents may lack the requisite knowledge and understanding and may be influenced by their parents. Supporters of a higher voting age believe that maturity increases over time; therefore the older, the better. Those who want to lower voting age argue that adolescents are better informed and more independent-minded than they used to be. They also point out that in other areas of life, teenagers are treated as adults: they may hold a job, they pay taxes, and, in some instances, they may be prosecuted in a court of law. They should therefore have the same rights as adults.

---

1. Autonomy is distinct from competence when it is defined in financial terms. But restrictions on the basis of financial dependence no longer prevail.

Yet there is a near-consensus within the democratic arena regarding the minimum voting age.[2] Fifty-nine of our countries (94 per cent) set the voting age at 18. Only Brazil has a lower threshold, at 16.[3] Japan and Taiwan set the voting age at 20. The highest minimum voting age that we find is 21, in Samoa. Every country has a single minimum voting age for all electors. This has not always been the case. Before 1995, the constitution of Bolivia made a distinction based on voters' marital status. Married citizens got the vote at 18, and all others at 21.[4] Since 1995, the minimum voting age in Bolivia has been 18 for all citizens.[5]

Two of the three countries with voting age higher than 18 are in Asia. The voting age is higher in a few other Asian countries not included in our analysis: South Korea (20), Malaysia (21), Maldives (21), Pakistan (21), and Singapore (21). Many Asian societies have a different conception of age—as testified by the greater prestige they bestow on the older generation—which leads them to believe that people achieve wisdom later in life and that there should be no hurry in allowing a person to vote. Whether in family life or in business, elders are revered and take more responsibility than their younger counterparts (Pye 1985).

Looking at Table 2, we find that established democracies are more likely to set the minimum voting age at 18. Indeed, while all established democracies set the voting age at 18, only 90 per cent of non-established ones do so.

Mental Disabilities

Depriving mentally deficient people of the right to vote is seemingly a self-evident solution. How can people make a reasonable choice when their very own sanity is in serious doubt? This lack of capacity and the impracticability of allowing patients in mental hospitals to vote are used to justify their disfranchisement (Robertson 1994, 289–92). Yet criteria for mental illness have varied across time and space, and while serious illness may warrant disqualification, lighter and occasional mental problems should not. However, it is nearly impossible to draw a line that is not arbitrary between "serious" and "non-serious" disabilities (Denoncourt 1991,120–1).

Only four countries—Canada, Ireland, Italy, and Sweden—do *not* restrict in any way the right to vote for mentally challenged persons. In Canada, this has been the case since a judicial decision rendered in 1988. Previously, mentally disabled persons did not have the vote. The remaining 58 countries all have some kind of restriction, usually on people adjudged incompetent or of unsound mind by a court of law.[6] In some cases, the simple fact of being a patient in a mental hospital is enough to warrant disfranchisement. Twelve countries, including Bulgaria, Chile, Estonia, Guyana, Jamaica, and the Netherlands, have disfranchisement for mental reasons entrenched in the constitution.

---

2. We find no countries with a maximum voting age.
3. Although this is outside the ambit of our inquiry, for municipal elections only, five German Länder now enfranchise citizens from the age of 16. In each case, candidates must be at least 18.
4. Katz 1997, 218–219, enumerates instances where similar distinctions based on marital status were found: Brazil (1824–89), Chile (1833–77), Colombia (1821–18 and 1853–86), Ecuador (1884–1946), Honduras (1894–1957), Mexico (1932–69), Peru (1860–1933), Portugal (1826–78), and Uruguay (1830–1918).
5. Britain's 1918 legislation enfranchised men at 21 and women at 30. This anomaly was removed in 1928. Such a double standard existed in Ireland between 1918 and 1923. In Finland between 1869 and 1906 farmers were enfranchised at 21 and town residents at 24.
6. In most countries the electoral law does not specify the details of disqualification based on mental deficiencies.

Table 2 shows a significant difference between more- and less-established democracies on this dimension. It is not that the former automatically allow all mentally deficient people to vote—very few countries do so. Only where democracy is strongly established does it seem to be possible to envisage ignoring serious mental deficiency as a cause for denying people the vote.

Citizenship Requirement

Requiring citizenship for voting purposes arguably helps to preserve the cohesiveness and boundaries of the national community. Before receiving the vote, one should be fully integrated in one's society. Recently arrived immigrants may be less familiar with issues and more vulnerable to manipulation. Some observers find it shocking that recent immigrants might in close contests prevent the majority of citizens of longer standing from getting what they want. Those who favour relaxation of the citizenship requirement for voting argue that it amounts to political discrimination, since it treats non-citizens as mere "subjects" of the state (Beaud 1992, 413).[7] Immigrants who pay taxes and obey the laws, should have a say on these taxes and laws. In John Stuart Mill's words (1972, 279), "it is a personal injustice to withhold from any one, unless for the prevention of greater evils, the ordinary privilege of having his voice reckoned in the disposal of affairs in which he has the same interest as other people."

We find that 48 countries (76 percent) restrict the right to vote to citizens. At the other end of the spectrum, four countries do not require voters to be citizens, but this does not automatically mean enfranchisement for everyone. Non-citizens must have been residing in Chile for at least five years to be granted the vote there. Malawi has a seven-year residence requirement. Uruguay requires fifteen years, coupled with "good conduct." In New Zealand, non-citizens must be permanent residents to vote.

The third possibility is to enfranchise non-citizens coming from specific countries only. We find eleven countries with such an arrangement. All but one (Portugal) share a common bond: they are former British colonies (plus the United Kingdom itself) and give the right to vote to current residents who are citizens of a Commonwealth country. "Commonwealth clauses" are found in Australia, Barbados, Belize, Guyana, Jamaica, St. Lucia, St. Vincent and the Grenadines, Trinidad and Tobago, and the United Kingdom[8]; Ireland extends the vote to British citizens only. Portugal grants the right to vote to citizens of the European Union ordinarily residing in the country and to Brazilian nationals, who have special "equal rights." [9]

While nearly all other countries limit the vote to citizens only (92 percent), only half of former British colonies do so (52 percent) (see Table 2). However, the "Commonwealth clause" enfranchises a rela-

---

7. Procedures for obtaining citizenship vary among countries, and it would be important to compare how demanding their requirements are. To our knowledge, no study of this kind exists on this topic, which is beyond the scope of the current volume.

8. In Australia, the franchise is extended to British subjects whose names were included on an electoral roll before 26 January 1984. The law does not extend the "Commonwealth clause" to more recent newcomers. Formerly, Canada also granted the right to vote to other British subjects; in 1970 it narrowed this right to those who were eligible to vote at the 1968 election, and the right lapsed in 1975. The experience of these two countries suggests that "Commonwealth clauses" might disappear in countries where they exist.

9. Furthermore, the Maastricht treaty sets rules for elections to the European Parliament and local elections. EU citizens residing in another EU country may vote at local and European elections in their country of residence. We also find countries that allow non-citizens to vote in local and regional elections. In Denmark, citizens of non–EU countries may vote in elections for county and municipal councils, if they have been residing in Denmark for three years prior to election day. In Ireland, non–EU citizens may vote in local elections only. In the Netherlands, non–Dutch nationals may vote in municipal and provincial elections, if they satisfy certain requirements. In Sweden, citizens of

tively small proportion of the electorate. If we exclude this exemption, the difference is no longer significant (only four countries let non-citizens vote, two of them former British colonies).

We find a statistically significant difference between established and non-established democracies (see Table 2). The former are less likely to restrict the right to vote to citizens. However, analogous to the difference between former British colonies and other countries, most of the erstwhile colonies are also established democracies. Once we factor this in, established democracies are no less likely than non-established to require citizenship.

In every country but two—Ireland and Taiwan—the citizenship requirement is the same for legislative and presidential elections. In Ireland, British citizens may vote only in legislative elections. For presidential elections, the electorate is composed of Irish citizens only. In Taiwan, to vote in presidential contests non-citizens need to have resided in the country for just four months, whereas only citizens may vote in legislative elections. In both countries, qualifications are less restrictive with respect to the more important national election.

Residence Requirements

Electoral District

The requirement that electors have been residing in their electoral district or constituency for some period prior to the election is defended on the ground that integration in a local community is essential for helping determine its future. Opponents claim that this can result in widespread disfranchisement of people who move frequently and that elections are national contests, not purely local ones.

Eighteen of our countries require a minimum period of residence in an electoral district. The duration varies from one month in Australia and New Zealand to six months in France, Mali, Panama, Papua New Guinea, and the Philippines. The median requirement in those countries is three months.[10] Although Britain has no such requirement, in order to vote for Westminster in Northern Ireland a person must have been residing there during the full three months prior to the qualifying date. Vanuatu is a unique case, with a three-month residence requirement for electors who wish to vote in an electoral district other than the one in which they were born. Barbados requires three months of residence in the electoral district only for those enfranchised under the "Commonwealth clause."

Table 2 shows the significant difference between former British colonies and other countries concerning residence requirement vis-à-vis electoral district. This might seem surprising, as the former colonies do not follow the example of the mother country. However, their electoral system may explain their higher propensity to require a minimum period of residence. Indeed, such residence requirements are rarer among countries using a system of proportional representation, or PR (7 percent), than in other countries (48 percent). And previous research has shown that former British colonies tend to adopt a first-past-the-post electoral system (Blais and Massicotte 1997). Furthermore, the average resi-

---

EU countries, Iceland, and Norway may vote in elections for county and municipal councils under the same conditions as Swedish nationals; citizens of other states may vote for county and municipal councils if on election day they have been registered residents of Sweden for three years uninterruptedly. In Venezuela, non-citizens who have been residing for at least 10 years in the country may vote in local elections.

10. The New Zealand Electoral Act specifies that those who do not meet the residence requirement retain the right to vote in the previous district of residence. The same rule applies in Australia and, presumably, in other countries.

dence requirement is shorter (2.7 months) there than in other countries with such a requirement (4.9 months).

Established and non-established democracies display no statistically significant difference in this matter. However, the former require on average shorter residence in the electoral district (2.6 months) than do non-established ones (4.3 months).

Country Residence

Requiring electors to have been residing in the country for some period prior to the election tends to be based on the belief that recent arrivals are not informed enough to cast a meaningful vote. Some observers counter that there is no reason to disfranchise people just because they happen to have been away in the recent past. These people have the same obligations; they should have the same rights.

How many of our democracies require a period of residence in the country? Eighteen do so (29 percent).[11] Minimum duration varies from three months in Germany to seven years in Malawi and St. Lucia. The median requirement is 12 months.[12]

In 12 countries, the requirement is not the same for all electors. For instance, in Belize, St. Lucia, St. Vincent and the Grenadines, and Trinidad and Tobago, the requirement applies only to "Commonwealth clause" electors. Costa Rica requires residence of one year for naturalized citizens; citizens by birth are exempted from this requirement. Chile imposes a five-year residence condition on non-citizens. In Samoa, there is a 12-month residence requirement only for those who are not citizens by birth or whose parents are not citizens. Uruguay stipulates that non-citizens must have resided in the country for at least 15 years, naturalized citizens for at least three years, and citizens by birth not at all.[13]

Table 2 shows that more former British colonies (55 percent) than other countries (15 percent) require a minimum period of residence in the country. However, in most former colonies, the minimum period of residence applies solely to Commonwealth citizens. Only 14 percent—the same proportion as in other countries—require a minimum period of residence for all citizens.

The difference between established and non-established democracies is not significant ($p < 0.12$). However, more established democracies (43 percent) than non-established ones (22 percent) require a minimum period of residence.

Citizens Residing Abroad

Demanding actual residence in the country for voting purposes was for long a standard and firm requirement of election laws. Canada relaxed this rule for soldiers, who had to serve abroad. It was felt unfair that military service should deprive them of a voice in the running of the country. This rationale led later to the extension of the same privilege to diplomats and other civil servants abroad. Many commentators argued that preserving the right to vote of civil and military servants abroad while disfranchising other citizens who happened to be abroad for study or travel, providing international assistance, and so on amounted to discrimination, especially where people are more likely to spend long periods

---

11. We consider only those cases that explicitly require residence in the country.
12. In Sweden, there is no minimum period of country residence required. However, one must have resided in the country at some point in order to have the right to vote.
13. We did not include Uruguay in the calculation of the median residence requirement, because it distinguishes three categories of electors.

Table 1 Restrictions on the Right to Vote

Country	Voting age	Disfranchisement of mentally deficient persons	Citizenship requirement	Minimum period of residence in the electoral district required
Argentina	18	Yes	Yes	NA
Australia	18	Yes	Yes or citizenship of another Commonwealth country before 1984	1 month
Bahamas	18	Yes	Yes	3 months
Bangladesh	18	Yes	Yes	No
Barbados	18	Yes or citizen of another commonwealth	Yes	3 months (Commonwealth Citizens only)
Belgium	18	Yes	Yes	No
Belize	18	Yes	Yes or citizen of another Commonwealth country	2 months
Benin	18	Yes	Yes	No
Bolivia	18	Yes	Yes	No
Brazil	16	Yes	Yes	No
Bulgaria	18	Yes	Yes	No
Canada	18	No	Yes	No
Cape Verde	18	Yes	Yes	No
Chile	18	Yes	Yes or residence for 5 years	No
Costa Rica	18	Yes	Yes	No
Cyprus	18	Yes	Yes	4 months
Czech Republic	18	Yes	Yes	No
Denmark	18	Yes	Yes	No
Ecuador	18	Yes	Yes	No
Estonia	18	Yes	Yes	No
France	18	Yes	Yes	6 months
Germany	18	Yes	Yes	No
Guyana	18	Yes	Yes or citizenship of another Commonwealth country	No
Hungary	18	Yes	Yes	No
India	18	Yes	Yes	No
Ireland	18	No	Yes or British citizenship	NA
Israel	18	NA	Yes	No
Italy	18	No	Yes	No
Jamaica	18	Yes	Yes or citizenship of another Commonwealth country	No
Japan	20	Yes	Yes	3 months
Latvia	18	Yes	Yes	No
Lithuania	18	Yes	Yes	No
Luxembourg	18	Yes	Yes	No
Madagascar	18	Yes	Yes	No
Malawi	18	Yes	Yes or residence for 7 years	No
Mali	18	Yes	Yes	6 months

Minimum period of residence in the country required	Disfranchisement of citizens residing abroad	Disfranchisement of prison inmates
No	No	Yes (sentence not available)
No	No, for 6 years (with the intention of returning to the country)	Yes, sentence of 5 years or more
No	Yes	Yes, any sentence
No	Yes	No
No	No, for 5 years	Yes, any sentence
No	No	Yes, sentence exceeding 4 months
1 year (Commonwealth citizens only)	Yes	Yes, sentence exceeding 1 year
	No	Yes, sentence of 3 months or more
No	Yes (No for presidential elections)	No
No	Yes (No for presidential elections)	Yes, any sentence
No	No	Yes, any sentence
No	No, for 5 years (with the intention of returning to the country)	Yes, sentence exceeding 2 years
No	No	Yes, any sentence
5 years (non-citizens only)	Yes	Yes, any sentence
1 year (naturalized citizens only)	No	NA
6 months	Yes	Yes, any sentence
No	No	No
No	No, for 12 years	No
No	Yes	Yes (sentence not available)
No	No	Yes, any sentence
No	No	Yes (certain offenses only)
3 months	No (in European countries) No for 10 years (in other countries)	No
1 year (Commonwealth citizens only)	Yes	No
No	Yes	Yes, any sentence
No	Yes	Yes, any sentence
NA	NA	No
No	Yes	NA
No	No	NA
1 year (Commonwealth citizens only)	Yes	Yes, sentence exceeding 6 months
No	NA	Yes (certain offenses only)
No	No	Yes, any sentence
No	No	No
No	No	Yes, any sentence
No	Yes	Yes, any sentence
7 years (non-citizens only)	Yes	No
No	No	Yes, sentence exceeding 1 month

(continued)

Table 1 **Restrictions on the Right to Vote** *(continued)*

Country	Voting age	Disfranchisement of mentally deficient persons	Citizenship requirement	Minimum period of residence in the electoral district required
Malta	18	Yes	Yes	No
Micronesia	18	Yes	Yes	3 months
Mongolia	18	Yes	Yes	No
Namibia	18	Yes	Yes	No
Netherlands	18	Yes	Yes	No
New Zealand	18	Yes	Yes or permanent residence	1 month
Panama	18	Yes	Yes	6 months
Papua New Guinea	18	Yes	Yes	6 months
Philippines	18	Yes	Yes	6 months
Poland	18	Yes	Yes	No
Portugal	18	Yes	Yes, or citizenship of EU member state, or Brazilian citizenship with equal rights status	No
Romania	18	Yes	Yes	No
St. Lucia	18	Yes	Yes or citizenship of another Commonwealth country	2 months
St. Vincent and the Grenadines	18	Yes	Yes or citizenship of another Commonwealth country	3 months
Samoa	21	Yes	Yes	No
Sao Tome and Principe	18	Yes	Yes	No
Slovakia	18	Yes	Yes	No
Slovenia	18	Yes	Yes	No
South Africa	18	Yes	Yes	No
Spain	18	Yes	Yes	No
Sweden	18	No	Yes	No
Taiwan	20	Yes	Yes	4 months
Trinidad and Tobago	18	Yes	Yes or citizenship of another Commonwealth country	2 months
United Kingdom	18	Yes*	Yes or citizenship of another Commonwealth country or of Ireland	No
Uruguay	18	Yes	Yes or residence for 15 years	No
Vanuatu	18	Yes	Yes	3 months (only for those voting in an electoral district other than the one in which they were born)
Venezuela	18	Yes	Yes	No

N/A=Not available.

* Under new legislation passed in 2000, patients resident in a mental hospital, whether voluntarily or detained as a result of mental health legislation, may now register to vote.

Minimum period of residence in the country required	Disfranchisement of citizens residing abroad	Disfranchisement of prison inmates
6 months (in the preceding 18 months)	No (as long as not more than 12 months outside the country in the preceding 18 months)	Yes, sentence exceeding 1 year
9 months	No	Yes, any sentence
No	Yes	Yes, any sentence
No	NA	No
No	No	Yes, sentence of 1 year or more (certain offenses only)
1 year	No, for 1 year (permanent residents) No, for 3 years (citizens)	Yes, sentence of 3 years or more
No	No	Yes, any sentence
No	Yes	Yes, sentence exceeding 9 months
1 year	No (with the intention of returning to the country)	Yes, sentence of 1 year or more
No	No	No
No	No (legislative elections only)	Yes, any sentence
No	No	No
7 years (Commonwealth citizens only)	No, for 3 years	Yes, any sentence
1 year (Commonwealth citizens only)	No, for 5 years	Yes, any sentence
1 year (only for those not citizens by birth or whose parents are not citizens)	No	Yes, any sentence
No	No	Yes (certain offenses only)
No	No	Yes (sentence not available)
No	No	No
No	NA	No
No	No	Yes (certain offenses only)
No	No	No
No	No	NA
1 year (Commonwealth citizens only)	Yes	Yes, sentence exceeding 1 year
No	No, for 20 years†	Yes, any sentence
3 years (naturalized citizens) or 15 years (non-citizens)	Yes	Yes, any sentence
No	No	No
No	No	Yes, any sentence

† Effective 2002, the qualifying period for overseas voters was reduced to 15 years.

Table 2 British Colonialism, Political Rights, and Restrictions on Right to Vote

	Voting age of 18	Disfranchisement of mentally deficient persons	Right to vote restricted to citizens only
British colonialism			
Former British	96% (n=23)	91% (n=22)	52%* (n=23)
Other countries	92% (n=39)	95% (n=39)	92% (n=39)
Political rights			
Established democracies	100%† (n=22)	82%† (n=22)	59%† (n=22)
Other countries	90% (n=41)	100% (n=40)	85% (n=41)
Total	94% (63 countries)	94% (62 countries)	76% (63 countries)

* Difference significant at 0.01 level (two-tailed *t*-test).
† Difference significant at 0.05 level (two-tailed *t*-test).

outside the country, which reasoning led Parliament in 1993 to provide voting mechanisms for these people as well.

In countries with high rates of emigration, maintaining the right to vote of expatriates may send a message to them that they are still part of the national community and will be welcome if they come back. Some observers insist that expatriates have less interest in the running of their country of origin, especially if they do not pay taxes there, or they point out the costs of such voting and the danger of fraud. Many feel that expatriates' right to vote in two different countries amounts to unacceptable privilege.

Do citizens residing abroad retain their right to vote in democratic countries? They do in a majority (40) of our countries. In 30, such as France, Mali, the Philippines, and Venezuela, they retain the right to vote indefinitely. In the remaining 10, they retain the right to vote for a period ranging from three to twenty years.[14] In New Zealand, citizens lose their right to vote three years after leaving the country, and permanent residents do so after only one year abroad. In Germany, citizens who live in a member state of the Council of Europe keep their vote indefinitely, while Germans living in any other country keep it for 10 years. In three countries, Australia, Canada, and the Philippines, citizens residing abroad must, on application for registration, state their intention of returning to the country in order not to be disfranchised. The latter condition was also in force in the United Kingdom from 1985 to 1989.

Three countries established different rules for different types of elections. In Bolivia and Brazil, citizens living abroad keep their right to vote in presidential elections only. In Portugal, they do so for legislative elections only.

14. When there were different time limits for different types of electors, we took into account the one that applied to the majority of the electorate.

Minimum period of residence in the electoral district required	Minimum period of residence in the country required	Disfranchisement of citizens residing abroad	Disfranchisement of prison inmates
50%† (n=22)	55%* (n=22)	55%† (n=20)	68% (n=22)
18% (n=38)	15% (n=39)	21% (n=38)	75% (n=36)
38% (n=21)	43% (n=21)	14%† (n=21)	80% (n=20)
25% (n=40)	22% (n=41)	42% (n=38)	69% (n=39)
30% (61 countries)	29% (62 countries)	32% (59 countries)	73% (59 countries)

The Netherlands constitutes an interesting case. Dutch citizens residing abroad have the right to vote, except for those residing in the Dutch Antilles or in Aruba and who have not been resident in the Netherlands for at least 10 years.

In some cases, however, the right to vote is more symbolic than real. We find ten countries where citizens residing abroad must return to the country in order to cast their vote on election day. This arrangement is found notably in Barbados, the Czech Republic, Italy, Malta, St. Lucia, and Slovakia. In Italy, while electors need to go back to the country to vote, the state tries to facilitate the exercise: state employees working abroad have up to three days to vote and have all their travel costs reimbursed by the state, while ordinary citizens residing abroad because of their work receive only train fare.

More than half of Britain's former colonies disfranchise citizens residing abroad; 21 percent of other countries do so. As with residence requirements, former British colonies are not in sync with the United Kingdom. However, it is only since 1985 that Britain has allowed its citizens residing abroad to vote. And many former British colonies are not known for massive emigration.

More established democracies are less inclined to disfranchise citizens residing abroad. The pattern is the same as with respect to mentally deficient persons. However, while there seems to be a clear norm among established democracies that citizens residing abroad should keep the right to vote, very few grant the same right to all mentally deficient persons.

Prison Inmates

The disfranchisement of prisoners stems from a belief that society is based on an implicit contract that obliges everyone to comply with the law. Those who break the law violate their pledge and are hence unworthy of participating in the democratic process: "only citizens have the right to vote, and it would not be reasonable to consider criminals as citizens" (Planinc 1987, 154). The possibility—however remote—that in a tight race the vote of people incarcerated could tip the balance is abhorrent to some. Allowing prison inmates to vote also raises practical problems, such as how and where they might vote. Enfranchising inmates is argued on various grounds. Some commentators believe that the contemporary penal regime aims ultimately at rehabilitation rather than at punishment and that preserving the voting rights of inmates facilitates their social reintegration. Some propose a distinction between those who serve short sentences and those incarcerated for serious crimes, and that only the latter should lose voting rights.

Are prisoners disfranchised in democratic countries for any prison sentence whatsoever? They are in 23 countries, such as Brazil, India, Portugal, the United Kingdom, and Venezuela. Yet 16 countries, such as Germany, Namibia, and Sweden, let all prisoners keep their voting rights.[15] Others remove the right to vote for sentences of specified length or longer, ranging from one month in Mali to five years in Australia. In France, Japan, Sao Tome and Principe, and Spain, only some prisoners lose their vote, depending on the nature of the crime.

In Belgium and the Philippines, disfranchisement extends beyond the prison sentence. Belgium disfranchises for life those imprisoned for five years or more, for 12 years those imprisoned for between three and five years, and for 6 years those imprisoned for between four months and three years. In the Philippines, disfranchisement of those imprisoned for a year or more expires five years after the completion of the sentence.[16]

Compulsory Voting

"The problem of the twentieth century," a British observer wrote in the 1920s, "has shown itself to be that of persuading the people to make use of the right for which they clamoured: to get them not only to vote in a responsible manner, but to get them to vote at all" (Robson 1923, 569). This issue became more salient during the 1990s, which saw electoral turnout declining in most democracies (Blais 2000). One radical solution is for the law to oblige electors to vote and even to make non-voters liable to some kind of sanction. Voting is then called "compulsory," whether there are sanctions or not, and normally occurs at levels substantially higher than those in other countries (Blais and Dobrzynska 1998; Franklin 1999; 2002).

The origins of compulsory voting have been traced back to the Swiss canton of St. Gallen in 1835 (Gosnell 1935). Belgium adopted that rule in 1893, and Australia in 1924. Some countries that formerly had compulsory voting, such as the Netherlands, Spain, and Czechoslovakia, dropped it later. Compulsory voting was advocated more frequently before the Second World War than it is today. Possibly the experience of the interwar period, when high-turnout Weimar Germany went totalitarian while lower-turnout Britain and the United States stayed democratic, led legislators to conclude that a high electoral turnout, while desirable in theory, was no guarantee for the survival of democracy.

This section looks at the cases for and against compulsory voting, at how widespread the practice is, and at what explains its existence.

---

15. In Canada, the electoral law removes the right to vote of prisoners sentenced to imprisonment for two years or more. This restriction was declared unconstitutional in 1996, and as a consequence prison inmates were allowed to vote in the 1997 federal election. The government launched an appeal, however, and won its case. Finally, in November 2002, the Supreme Court of Canada, by a 5-to-4 decision, decided that all prisoners should be enfranchised.
16. In the United States, 14 states impose permanent disfranchisement on their convicts (*Economist*, 24 Oct. 1998, 30).

The Cases for and against Compulsory Voting

Compulsory voting is premised on a view of voting as a civic duty, to be enforced by the state. Every member of the community should participate in the deliberations of the body politic. Low turnouts, it is alleged, hamper the legitimacy of elected officials by throwing doubt as to what the result would have been if every voter had gone to the polls. It is argued that compulsory voting yields collective, and ultimately individual, goods because it "permits citizens to be 'true citizens' in the Greenian sense (by enabling them to participate in the business of governing) but it also enables the state to be a 'true' one, that is, a state that actively works to prevent exclusion" (Hill 2002, 96). Less disinterested politicians may advocate compulsory voting as a way to improve the performance of parties that do well among sections of the electorate with traditionally low turnouts or more generally, as a way to spare all political parties from spending resources in order to bring electors to the polls (Jaensch 1995, 19–21).

Opponents of compulsory voting retort that voting is not a duty, but a right, and that people should be free to exercise or not to exercise that right. One scholar went as far as suggesting that compulsory voting is incompatible in principle with free elections, as "one of the democratic liberties is to decline to vote for any of the alternatives offered" (Mackenzie 1958, 131). In an era when politicians get little respect from the public (see Nevitte 1996), non-voting may be a legitimate way to express disillusionment with, or alienation from, standard party politics—a convenient warning signal to an out-of-touch political class. Some observers also point out the difficulty of enforcing such a rule in the face of massive non-compliance or the danger that electors dragged to the polls reluctantly may spoil their ballot or vote for extremist or marginal candidates. Finally, many feel, as a politician once disdainfully put it, that "the opinions of the negligent and apathetic section of the electors are not worth having" (quoted in Hughes 1966, 83).

Compulsory voting works to the advantage of parties supported by categories of people who would not vote otherwise. In Australia, there is evidence that Labor and Democrat supporters are overrepresented among those who would not turn out if voting was voluntary, while the Coalition parties (Liberal and National parties) have a huge lead among those who would have voted irrespective of compulsion (Jackman 1999).[17]

How Widespread Is Compulsory Voting?

On compulsory voting, countries fall into three groups: those where voting is compulsory and nonvoting is sanctioned by the law; those where voting is compulsory, but with no sanctions against nonvoters; and those where voting is not compulsory—or "voluntary voting."

The third group happens to include a strong majority of democracies: in 45 of our countries (71 percent), voting is not compulsory, and neither the constitution nor election law provides that it is one's "duty" to cast a ballot on election day. In the other 18 countries, voting is compulsory, with sanctions (11 countries) or without (7 countries). Table 3 lists these countries. Twelve of the 18 have written the obligation to vote in their constitution.[18]

---

17. See also Mike Steketee, "Voluntary Voting a Big Boost for Coalition," *Australian,* 8 Aug. 1996, 2. The article is based on a paper prepared by Malcolm Mackerras and Ian McAllister for the Australian Election Study.
18. They are Argentina, Belgium, Bolivia, Brazil, Chile, Costa Rica, Ecuador, Italy, Panama, Portugal, Uruguay, and Venezuela.

Table 3 Countries with Compulsory Voting

Countries	Applicable sanctions	Categories of electors exempted
Argentina	Fine No possibility of working in public service for three years following offence	Electors 70 and over Judges and their substitutes Electors living more than 500 km from the polling station Electors residing abroad Handicapped electors who are unable to vote and those attending to handicapped electors Certain categories of public servants
Australia	Fine Reprimand	None
Belgium	Fine Repeat offenders may be excluded from the electoral register for a period of 10 years, during which they may not receive any nomination, promotion, or distinction from a public authority.	Electors in custody
Bolivia	Fine	None
Brazil	Fine Repeat offenders excluded from electoral register Non-voters may not work in public service or receive passport	Electors 16–18 or 70 years and over Illiterate electors
Cape Verde	None (civic duty)	None
Chile	Fine	Electors unable to vote because of illness Electors abroad or located more than 200 km from the polling station
Costa Rica	None (civic duty)	None
Cyprus	Fine	Electors 70 and over and residing 50 miles or more from polling station
Ecuador	Fine	Electors over 75 Illiterate electors
Italy	None (civic duty)	None
Luxembourg	Fine	Electors residing in another commune Electors over 70 Electors with "reasonable motive"
Panama	None (civic duty)	None
Philippines	Fine Non-voter may not be candidate in following election Non-voter may not be appointed to public administration in following year	None
Portugal	None (civic duty)	None
Sao Tome and Principe	None (civic duty)	None
Uruguay	Fine Repeat offenders lose voting rights	None
Venezuela	None (civic duty)	None

The most stringent rule—compulsory voting backed by sanctions—is found in 11 countries (17 percent of democracies): Argentina, Australia, Belgium, Bolivia, Brazil, Chile, Cyprus, Ecuador, Luxembourg, the Philippines, and Uruguay. The nature of the penalties is specified by the law (they are listed by country in Table 3). In most cases, non-voting is sanctioned by a fine, which may be higher for repeat offenders. In some of these countries, non-voters may lose certain rights. For instance, in Argentina non-voters may not work in public administration for three years following the offence. In Brazil, those who do not vote in three consecutive elections are struck off the electoral register. In the Philippines, non-voters may not be candidates at the next election and may not be appointed to a position in public administration within the next year.

In a few of these countries, some groups of electors are excused if they do not vote. In Argentina, this is the case for electors aged 70 or more. In Brazil, voting is optional for electors aged between 16 and 18 years old or 70 and over. In Cyprus, those aged 70 and over are excused only if they reside at least 50 miles from the polling station (Table 3 lists the categories of electors exempted from compulsory voting).

Seven countries (Cape Verde, Costa Rica, Italy, Panama, Portugal, Sao Tome [and Principe], and Venezuela) make voting compulsory but impose no sanctions for non-voters. Hence legislators rely on voluntary adherence to the law to reach the desired outcome. For instance, in Italy, the notion of voting as a "civic duty" is entrenched in the constitution (section 48). Non-voters do not face any penalty per se. However, failure to vote is recorded on one's ID card for five years, and it is alleged that this may hurt chances of employment.

What Explains Compulsory Voting?

When grouping countries of both categories of compulsory voting together, we find that there are no major differences between established and non-established democracies (see Table 4). However, one finds significant differences between former British colonies, which tend not to oblige electors to vote, and other countries, 41 per cent of which have compulsory voting.

The list in Table 3 presents interesting patterns. Many countries with a Catholic majority require electors to vote.[19] Perhaps it is natural for Catholics to believe that citizens have moral obligations not only towards God and the church, but also towards the state. As a result, the act of voting may be portrayed as a criterion of good citizenship and communal life. A less disingenuous explanation is that historically the church has feared that political apathy might deny victory to church-supported parties and accordingly pressed for compulsory voting.

Every former Spanish and former Portuguese colony has some form of compulsory voting. Finding such similarity within a group of former colonies necessitates a look at the former colonial power. Indeed, Portugal currently has compulsory voting without sanctions. Two of its three former colonies in our sample—Cape Verde and Sao Tome—also do not penalize non-voters. However, Brazil does.

Voting was once compulsory in Spain. The electoral law of 1907 provided for compulsory voting and sanctions for non-voters, although enforcement was lax (Gosnell 1935). Furthermore, in continents such as North America, Africa, and Asia, where compulsory voting is the exception rather than the rule, former Spanish and Portuguese colonies are nevertheless inclined towards compulsory voting.[20]

19. These are countries where a majority of the population is Catholic, according to the *Encyclopaedia Universalis 1997*.
20. Countries that do not follow this pattern are Australia and Cyprus—two former British colonies located in Oceania and Asia, respectively—where voting is compulsory. Australia instituted compulsory voting because low turnouts (between 45 percent and 60 percent of votes) obliged parties to divert resources to take voters to the polls. Compul-

Table 4 British Colonialism, Political Rights, and Compulsory Voting

	Compulsory voting (irrespective of sanctions)
British colonialism	
Former British colonies	9%* (n=23)
Other countries	41% (n=39)
Political rights	
Established democracies	31% (n=22)
Other countries	27% (n=41)
Total	29% (63 countries)

* Difference significant at 0.01 level (two-tailed *t*-test).

In the 1920s, an observer noted that compulsory voting had been introduced in "countries of a great dissimilar character" (Robson 1923, 575). This still holds true today. Yet the chief finding of this chapter is that culture matters: while Anglo-Protestant countries, with the shining exception of Australia, do not have compulsory voting, most Hispanic Catholic countries do, even if, as in the Philippines, their democratic training took place under American rather than under Spanish colonial rule.

Conclusion

Of the seven potential restrictions to the right to vote examined in this chapter, only two have given rise to a near-consensus among democracies. An overwhelming majority have decided that the voting age should be 18 and that people with severe mental deficiency should not vote. Outside former British colonies, few countries grant the vote to non-citizens, and PR countries have no required minimum period of residence in the electoral district. There is wide divergence about disfranchisement of prison inmates, a country-residence requirement, and enfranchisement of citizens residing abroad.

This chapter on the franchise suggests that the most important issue concerning the right to vote in a democracy pertains to the residence requirement. The issues, especially of whether to allow citizens who reside abroad to vote, under what conditions, and for how long raise deep questions about the meaning of democracy in a world in which people are becoming increasingly mobile.

One of our objectives was to establish whether former British colonies have emulated the right-to-vote laws of the mother country, as they have done with respect to electoral systems. There is a clear

sory voting was also assumed to increase honesty in elections (for a full compendium of the arguments raised for and against compulsory voting in the Australian Parliament and state legislatures, see Hughes 1966, 81–3). As for Cyprus, the existence of compulsory voting may be explained by the influence of Greece, where voting is compulsory.

colonial heritage: about half of them have granted citizens of Commonwealth countries the right to vote. Partly because most of these erstwhile colonies have single-member constituencies, they are more likely to have electoral-district requirements. Most others do not allow citizens residing abroad to vote. In doing so, they follow what was British practice until 1985. How long will they wait before emulating the recent British law?

We have also looked at whether countries with secure political rights have fewer restrictions on the right to vote. The short answer is yes: they tend to be somewhat more inclusive, although the difference is relatively small.

On compulsory voting, most onetime British, Spanish, and Portuguese colonies follow their former rulers' lead. Even in continents with little compulsory voting, former Spanish and Portuguese colonies have adopted it. Does such a requirement enhance or hamper democracy? It is hard to say. Compulsory voting is rather uncommon in democracies, even well-established ones. Only one country (the Netherlands, in 1970) has changed its legislation (abolishing compulsory voting) in the recent past. Perhaps this is an issue that has remained dormant over the last few decades, but that may come back on the political agenda.[21]

References

Beaud, Olivier. 1992. "Le droit de vote des étrangers: l'apport de la jurisprudence constitutionnelle allemande à une théorie du droit de suffrage." *Revue française de droit administratif* 8: 409–24.

Blais, André. 2000. *To Vote or Not to Vote? The Merits and Limits of Rational Choice Theory.* Pittsburgh: University of Pittsburgh Press.

———, and Agnieszka Dobrzynska. 1998. "Turnout in Electoral Democracies." *European Journal of Political Research* 33: 239–62.

———, and Louis Massicotte. 1997. "Electoral Formulas: A Macroscopic Perspective." *European Journal of Political Research* 32: 107–29.

Butler, David E., Howard R. Penniman, and Austin Ranney. 1981. "Introduction: Democratic and Nondemocratic Election." In David Butler, Howard R. Penniman, and Austin Ranney, eds., *Democracy at the Polls: A Comparative Study of Competitive National Elections.* Washington, DC: American Enterprise Institute for Public Policy.

Dahl, Robert. 1989. *Democracy and its Critics.* New Haven, Conn.: Yale University Press.

Denoncourt, Yves. 1991. "Reflections on Criteria for Excluding Persons with Mental Disorders from the Right to Vote." In Michel Cassidy, ed., *Democratic Rights and Electoral Reform in Canada.* Vol. 10 of the Royal Commission on Electoral Reform and Party Financing. Toronto: Dundurn.

Franklin, Mark N. 1999. "Electoral Engineering and Cross-National Turnout Differences: What Role for Compulsory Voting?" *British Journal of Political Science* 29: 205–24.

———, 2002. "The Dynamics of Electoral Participation." In Lawrence LeDuc, Richard G. Niemi, and Pippa Norris, eds., *Comparing Democracies 2: New Challenges in the Study of Elections and Voting.* London: Sage.

Gosnell, Harold F. 1935. "Voting." In *The Encyclopaedia of the Social Sciences,* vol. 15. London: Macmillan & Co.

Hill, Lisa. 2002. "On the Reasonableness of Compelling Citizens to 'Vote': The Australian Case." *Political Studies* 50: 80–101.

Hughes, Colin A. 1966. "Compulsory Voting." *Politics* 1: 81–95.

21. For an interesting argument for compulsory voting, see Lijphart (1998) and Hill (2002).

Jackman, Simon. 1999. "Non-Compulsory Voting in Australia? What Surveys Can (and Can't) Tell Us." *Electoral Studies* 18: 29–48.

Jaensch, Dean. 1995. *Election! How and Why Australia Votes.* St Leonards: Allen & Unwin Pty Ltd.

Katz, Richard S. 1997. *Democracy and Elections.* Oxford: Oxford University Press.

Lijphart, Arend. 1998. "Unequal Participation: Democracy's Unresolved Dilemma." *American Political Science Review* 91: 1–14.

Mackenzie, W. J. M. 1958. *Free Elections.* London: George Allen & Unwin.

Nevitte, Neil. 1996. *The Decline of Deference: Canadian Value Change in Cross-National Perspective.* Peterborough, Ont.: Broadview Press.

Planinc, Zdravko. 1987. "Should Imprisoned Criminals Have a Constitutional Right to Vote?" *Canadian Journal of Law and Society* 2: 153–64.

Pye, Lucian W. 1985. *Asian Power and Politics: The Cultural Dimension of Authority.* Cambridge, Mass.: Belknap Press of Harvard University.

Report of the Royal Commission on the Electoral System. 1986. *Towards a Better Democracy.* New Zealand.

Robertson, Gerald B. 1994. *Mental Disability and the Law in Canada.* 2nd ed. Scarborough, Ont.: Carswell.

Robson, William A. 1923. "Compulsory Voting." *Political Science Quarterly* 38: 569–77.

Chapter 7

WHAT EXECUTIVE STYLE IS MOST FAVORABLE TO DEMOCRACY?

In the study of comparative politics today, many scholars examine the role of institutions on political outcomes. Peter Hall defines an institution as "the formal rules, compliance procedures, and standard operating practices that structure the relationship between individuals in various units of the polity and the economy." [1] Scholars have studied how political institutions, such as electoral systems or bureaucratic agencies, affect the workings of political systems in a variety of contexts.

From this central insight, scholars who analyze why democratic governments succeed or fail began to appreciate the role institutional design plays in these processes. James March and Johan Olsen state this position most succinctly by arguing that "political democracy depends not only on economic and social conditions but also on the design of political institutions." [2] Effectively designed institutions can encourage actors to follow democratic principles, as well as prevent unintended consequences that could endanger further democratization. Conversely, poorly designed institutions can prevent not only deeper consolidation, but also can prompt the return of nondemocratic government.

While political scientists have focused on a number of different institutions critical to successful democratization, including electoral systems and party systems, significant attention also has been paid to the choice of executive system: presidential or parliamentary. This research asks the provocative question: Which system, presidential or parliamentary, is more favorable for democratization?

Presidential systems have four specific attributes that differentiate them from other systems.[3] First, the chief executive is popularly elected. Second, the terms of office for both the executive and legislature are fixed. Consequently, neither branch can remove the other, as is often possible in parliamentary systems. Third, the chief executive forms and controls the government with little or no legislative interference. Finally, the constitution gives some independent legislative power to the president that encompasses a variety of powers from vetoes to executive decree powers.[4] As this definition spells out, the most important characteristic of a presidential system is the separate election and survival of the executive and legislative branches. The presidential system of the United States, for example, fits all of these criteria, as do systems in Brazil and Argentina.

In parliamentary systems, the legislature votes to form the government; and just as it can bring it into being, the legislature can also vote to replace it. Executives in parliamentary systems are often able to dissolve the legislature and call for new elections, unlike leaders in presidential systems. The United Kingdom, Germany, and Italy are classic examples of parliamentary systems.

So what do the detractors of presidential systems say? According to Juan Linz, presidential democracies suffer more frequently than parliamentary systems from periods during which the president and the legislature are unable to cooperate to make policy.[5] These periods of deadlock can undercut the performance of even the most established presidential systems, and in some cases, the executive-legislative impasses can be so detrimental that they undermine the support for democracy itself. The greater propensity for executive-legislative deadlock is the primary reason presidential democracies fail at a higher rate than parliamentary ones.[6] Certainly, political and factional differences, which lead to policy immobility, can and do occur in parliamentary systems; however, the rate at which presidential systems fail is higher than in parliamentary systems. So, are the sources of these impasses found within the institutional design of the system and not simply the reflection of diverse political interests? Does the system create incentives for both branches to avoid cooperation, which in turn weakens coalition building and prevents effective governance?

Some commentators point to the rigidity of presidential systems. Though the majority of such systems do feature impeachment procedures that allow for the removal of a president, these are often extremely cumbersome and focus on transgressions of a legal nature, not necessarily ones based on policy failures, which means that impeachment rarely serves as an effective means to remove an ineffective president. In contrast, if the executive no longer enjoys legislative support in a parliamentary system, the legislature can quickly remove that individual and elect a new one. The problem of rigidity can also occur as a result of a legislature's fixed term. Unlike many parliamentary systems, presidential systems do not usually allow presidents to dissolve intransigent legislatures—a presidential system saddled with a feckless legislature must wait until the next predetermined election to put a new elected body in place.

Critics of presidential systems also argue that they tend toward majoritarianism.[7] Since he or she won a nationwide election, a president may feel that he or she won a national mandate to rule; however, in the absence of a huge landslide, the president in actuality most likely only received support from a very small plurality of voters. Yet this plurality entitles the president to control the entire executive branch. In addition, presidential systems lack the beneficial effects that stem from the negotiation and compromise over the formation of the government that are found in parliamentary systems. Winners of a presidential election do not need to negotiate with the losers since they already maintain significant control over the formation of the executive branch. Similarly, the losers, unlikely to participate in the new executive body, have little reason to support the president.

The most intense problems of presidentialism stem from the very thing that defines it: the separate election and survival of the executive and legislative branches.[8] In parliamentary systems, legislative elections serve a dual purpose since they elect a legislature that in turn elects the executive. Furthermore, the government is ultimately dependent on the legislature for its survival. If it decides a change is necessary, the legislature can remove the government and elect a new one. A government in a parliamentary system, therefore, has a huge incentive to cooperate with the legislature to prevent dismissal.

This need only be contrasted with the incentives found in presidential systems to see how the institutional arrangement of the latter can encourage interbranch conflict. Since presidents and legislatures are elected independently and the legislature plays no role in the survival of the president, there are few incentives for the branches to cooperate. Legislators who are members of the president's political party will not threaten their party's control of the executive office, even if they'd prefer to vote against the president, and opposition legislators, who have no hope of gaining entrance into the executive inner circle, have even less incentive to vote for the president's policies. And since both the president and legislature have been elected in free and fair elections, each can claim correctly to speak on behalf of the population. This dual democratic legitimacy can further undermine cooperation between the branches, since each can claim a popular mandate to support its positions.

Differences in constituency base between presidents and legislators can considerably reinforce the problem of dual democratic legitimacy. Presidents are elected nationally. That is to say, the president tries to satisfy the desires of the entire the nation (or at least a large part of it), rather than a limited group of voters. Conversely, legislators usually represent geographically defined districts, and they must appease only the parochial interests of their constituents.[9] In the case of the United States, presidents often complain about pork-barrel projects that, for example, use federal government funds to build roads in a particular congressional district, because these projects are paid for by the whole nation but benefit only those in the narrow district. The difference in constituency base makes finding common ground difficult and fuels the conflicts that paralyze decision making.

One potential cure for presidential ills might be the adoption of aspects of parliamentarism within the presidential framework. Semipresidential systems, like that of France's Fifth Republic, might provide institutional solutions to such problems. In most semipresidential systems, the president is paired with a premier and a government dependent in some fashion on legislative support. Thus, instead of a single executive whose mandate only extends to the voters, semipresidential systems attempt to create an incentive for cooperation by linking a premier/government to the legislature and its support. This may mean that the premier and government need legislative approval or can be subject to a vote of no-confidence, as in semipresidential systems in Russia and France.

Recent scholarship has acknowledged that the effects of presidential systems are, perhaps, less detrimental for democracy than described above. Several recent single-country studies have cast doubt on whether presidential systems are especially prone to policy deadlocks.[10] The assertion that they fail more often than parliamentary systems has been openly questioned, based on a comparison of the number of failed presidential and parliamentary democracies in large-N studies. Matthew Soberg Shugart and John Carey found that presidential systems were not more likely to end in democratic failure than other system types were,[11] and Scott Mainwaring and Shugart argue that presidential systems are disproportionately found in Latin America and Africa, regions in which other obstacles to democracy proliferate and possibly obstruct the development of democracy as much as, or more than, the use of a presidential electoral system. They go on to note that parliamentary systems are concentrated in countries with a British colonial heritage, which increases the chances for a successful democracy as these states had an established example to emulate.[12] In addition, José Antonio Cheibub argued in a 2007 work that presidential systems are not prone to deadlock and low levels of cooperation.

Besides expressing doubts about the record of presidential systems, other scholars have begun to develop more nuanced critiques of their negative effects. Many presidential systems vary according to the powers allotted to chief executives by a state's constitution. Some presidents have extensive legislative powers, including the right to issue binding executive decrees or the right of legislative initiative in vital policy areas. Presidents may also enjoy sweeping emergency powers during periods of crisis. The presidential power over the government can also vary from system to system. The U.S. Constitution, for example, limits the Senate to an advise and consent role over certain executive appointments, whereas some semipresidential systems make the government completely dependent on the legislature. While the specific powers of presidents in different systems may vary, constitutions that give presidents greater legislative power and power over the cabinet were found to be more problematic for democracy than others.[13] *Strong* presidential systems, therefore, may pose the greatest threat to democracy, while presidential systems that limit the executive's range of powers tend to be more favorable to democracy.

The readings in this section highlight the issues found in the presidential system debate. Juan Linz provides his classical statement of the presidential critique in reading 7.1. It is an inherently institutional argument: the rules that govern presidential systems create incentives for individual behavior that may undermine successful democratization. Mainwaring and Shugart argue in reading 7.3 that the weak record of presidential systems is due, in part, to their presence in countries whose chances for survival are weakest.[14] Moreover, the most problematic systems are those in which the president maintains strong, independent power. Cheibub provides an alternative perspective in reading 7.2; through a rigorous analysis of the failures of presidential regimes, he finds that presidential systems fail at a higher rate due to the specific conditions within which they are formed.[15] He argues that presidential systems have been formed in contexts that are particularly inhospitable for the development of democracy. Overall, comparativists may accept the basic point that institutions are important explanatory factors; however, until we understand how they operate within more complex environments, this insight may not have moved us toward a better understanding of political outcomes.

Notes

1. Peter Hall, *Governing the Economy: The Politics of State Intervention in Britain and France* (New York: Oxford University Press, 1986).
2. James March and Johan Olsen, *Rediscovering Institutions* (New York: Free Press, 1989), 17.
3. Matthew Shugart and John Carey, *Presidents and Assemblies: Constitutional Design and Electoral Dynamics* (Cambridge: Cambridge University Press, 1992), 19.
4. This is the definition of a "pure" presidential system. Presidential systems, however, can vary along two major axes. First, the degree to which the president independently controls the government can vary from system to system. Second, presidential systems can differ in the level of separation between the government and the legislature. In semi-presidential systems, the president can dissolve the legislature, and the legislature can name and vote no confidence in the government.
5. Juan Linz, "Presidential or Parliamentary Democracy: Does It Make a Difference?" in *The Failure of Presidential Democracy,* eds. Juan Linz and Arturo Valenzuela (Baltimore: Johns Hopkins University Press, 1994), 6.
6. Stepan and Skach, for example, undertook a large N study and have found this to be true. Alfred Stepan and Cindy Skach, "Constitutional Frameworks and Democratic Consolidation: Parliamentarism and Presidentialism," *World Politics* 46 (October 1993): 34.
7. Arend Lijphart and Ronald Rogowski, "Separation of Powers and the Management of Political Cleavages," in *Political Institutions and Their Consequences,* ed. Kent Weaver and Bert Rockman (Washington, D.C.: Brookings Institution, 1991), 85.
8. Scott Mainwaring, "Presidentialism in Latin America: A Review Essay," *Latin American Research Review* 25 (1990): 160.
9. Ibid.
10. Argelina Cheibub Figueiredo and Fernando Limongi, "Presidential Power, Legislative Organization, and Party Behavior in Brazil," *Comparative Politics* 32, no. 2 (January 2000): 151–170.

11. Matthew Soberg Shugart and John Carey, *Presidents and Assemblies: Constitutional Design and Electoral Dynamics* (Cambridge: Cambridge University Press, 1992), 19.
12. Scott Mainwaring and Matthew Soberg Shugart, "Juan Linz, Presidentialism, and Democracy," *Comparative Politics* (July 1997): 460.
13. Shugart and Carey.
14. Mainwaring and Shugart.
15. José Antonio Cheibub, "What Makes Presidential Democracies Fragile?" in *Presidentialism, Parliamentarism, and Democracy* (Cambridge: Cambridge University Press, 2007, 136–164.

7.1

THE PERILS OF PRESIDENTIALISM

Juan J. Linz

Juan Linz, professor emeritus of political and social science at Yale University, has conducted extensive research on the politics of both authoritarian and democratizing regimes. In particular, his groundbreaking research has focused on the causes of democratic collapse. In this very accessible essay, Linz argues that the rules that govern presidential political systems provide too few incentives for interbranch cooperation, and for this reason undermine effective cooperation between the president and the legislature. As a result, presidential systems often feature significant interbranch gridlock that prevents the president and the legislature from agreeing on policy. This lack of cooperation ultimately can undermine support for democracy and lead to its collapse. While reading this essay, students should ask themselves what assumptions Linz is making about political leaders: Shouldn't they cooperate because it would be best for the country? Also, how well does the United States fit into Linz's description? While gridlock is often thought to be a problem in the country's political arena, the U.S. presidential system has functioned quite effectively for a number of years.

As more of the world's nations turn to democracy, interest in alternative constitutional forms and arrangements has expanded well beyond academic circles. In countries as dissimilar as Chile, South Korea, Brazil, Turkey, and Argentina, policymakers and constitutional experts have vigorously debated the relative merits of different types of democratic regimes. Some countries, like Sri Lanka, have switched from parliamentary to presidential constitutions. On the other hand, Latin Americans in particular have found themselves greatly impressed by the successful transition from authoritarianism to democracy that occurred in the 1970s in Spain, a transition to which the parliamentary form of government chosen by that country greatly contributed.

Nor is the Spanish case the only one in which parliamentarism has given evidence of its worth. Indeed, the vast majority of the stable democracies in the world today are parliamentary regimes, where executive power is generated by legislative majorities and depends on such majorities for survival.

By contrast, the only presidential democracy with a long history of constitutional continuity is the United States. The constitutions of Finland and France are hybrids rather than true presidential systems, and in the case of the French Fifth Republic, the jury is still out. Aside from the United States, only Chile

---

Juan J. Linz, "The Perils of Presidentialism," *Journal of Democracy* 1 (Winter 1990): 51–69.

has managed a century and a half of relatively undisturbed constitutional continuity under presidential government—but Chilean democracy broke down in the 1970s.

Parliamentary regimes, of course, can also be unstable, especially under conditions of bitter ethnic conflict, as recent African history attests. Yet the experiences of India and of some English-speaking countries in the Caribbean show that even in greatly divided societies, periodic parliamentary crises need not turn into full-blown regime crises and that the ousting of a prime minister and cabinet need not spell the end of democracy itself.

The burden of this essay is that the superior historical performance of parliamentary democracies is no accident. A careful comparison of parliamentarism as such with presidentialism as such leads to the conclusion that, on balance, the former is more conducive to stable democracy than the latter. This conclusion applies especially to nations with deep political cleavages and numerous political parties; for such countries, parliamentarism generally offers a better hope of preserving democracy.

Parliamentary vs. Presidential Systems

A parliamentary regime in the strict sense is one in which the only democratically legitimate institution is parliament; in such a regime, the government's authority is completely dependent upon parliamentary confidence. Although the growing personalization of party leadership in some parliamentary regimes has made prime ministers seem more and more like presidents, it remains true that barring dissolution of parliament and a call for new elections, premiers cannot appeal directly to the people over the heads of their representatives. Parliamentary systems may include presidents who are elected by direct popular vote, but they usually lack the ability to compete seriously for power with the prime minister.

In presidential systems an executive with considerable constitutional powers—generally including full control of the composition of the cabinet and administration—is directly elected by the people for a fixed term and is independent of parliamentary votes of confidence. He is not only the holder of executive power but also the symbolic head of state and can be removed between elections only by the drastic step of impeachment. In practice, as the history of the United States shows, presidential systems may be more or less dependent on the cooperation of the legislature; the balance between executive and legislative power in such systems can thus vary considerably.

Two things about presidential government stand out. The first is the president's strong claim to democratic, even plebiscitarian, legitimacy; the second is his fixed term in office. Both of these statements stand in need of qualification. Some presidents gain office with a smaller proportion of the popular vote than many premiers who head minority cabinets, although voters may see the latter as more weakly legitimated. To mention just one example, Salvador Allende's election as president of Chile in 1970—he had a 36.2-percent plurality obtained by a heterogeneous coalition—certainly put him in a position very different from that in which Adolfo Suárez of Spain found himself in 1979 when he became prime minister after receiving 35.1 percent of the vote. As we will see, Allende received a six-year mandate for controlling the government even with much less than a majority of the popular vote, while Suárez, with a plurality of roughly the same size, found it necessary to work with other parties to sustain a minority government. Following British political thinker Walter Bagehot, we might say that a presidential system endows the incumbent with both the "ceremonial" functions of a head of state and the "effective" functions of a chief executive, thus creating an aura, a self-image, and a set of popular expectations which are all quite different from those associated with a prime minister, no matter how popular he may be.

But what is most striking is that in a presidential system, the legislators, especially when they represent cohesive, disciplined parties that offer clear ideological and political alternatives, can also claim democratic legitimacy. This claim is thrown into high relief when a majority of the legislature represents a political option opposed to the one the president represents. Under such circumstances, who has the stronger claim to speak on behalf of the people: the president or the legislative majority that opposes his policies? Since both derive their power from the votes of the people in a free competition among well-defined alternatives, a conflict is always possible and at times may erupt dramatically. There is no democratic principle on the basis of which it can be resolved, and the mechanisms the constitution might provide are likely to prove too complicated and aridly legalistic to be of much force in the eyes of the electorate. It is therefore no accident that in some such situations in the past, the armed forces were often tempted to intervene as a mediating power. One might argue that the United States has successfully rendered such conflicts "normal" and thus defused them. To explain how American political institutions and practices have achieved this result would exceed the scope of this essay, but it is worth noting that the uniquely diffuse character of American political parties—which, ironically, exasperates many American political scientists and leads them to call for responsible, ideologically disciplined parties—has something to do with it. Unfortunately, the American case seems to be an exception; the development of modern political parties, particularly in socially and ideologically polarized countries, generally exacerbates, rather than moderates, conflicts between the legislative and the executive.

The second outstanding feature of presidential systems—the president's relatively fixed term in office—is also not without drawbacks. It breaks the political process into discontinuous, rigidly demarcated periods, leaving no room for the continuous readjustments that events may demand. The duration of the president's mandate becomes a crucial factor in the calculations of all political actors, a fact which (as we shall see) is fraught with important consequences. Consider, for instance, the provisions for succession in case of the president's death or incapacity: in some cases, the automatic successor may have been elected separately and may represent a political orientation different from the president's: in other cases, he may have been imposed by the president as his running mate without any consideration of his ability to exercise executive power or maintain popular support. Brazilian history provides us with examples of the first situation, while Maria Estela Martínez de Perón's succession of her husband in Argentina illustrates the second. It is a paradox of presidential government that while it leads to the personalization of power, its legal mechanisms may also lead, in the event of a sudden midterm succession, to the rise of someone whom the ordinary electoral process would never have made the chief of state.

Paradoxes of Presidentialism

Presidential constitutions paradoxically incorporate contradictory principles and assumptions. On the one hand, such systems set out to create a strong, stable executive with enough plebiscitarian legitimation to stand fast against the array of particular interests represented in the legislature. In the Rousseauian conception of democracy implied by the idea of "the people," for whom the president is supposed to speak, these interests lack legitimacy; so does the Anglo-American notion that democracy naturally involves a jostle—or even sometimes a melee—of interests. Interest group conflict then bids fair to manifest itself in areas other than the strictly political. On the other hand, presidential constitutions also reflect profound suspicion of the personalization of power: memories and fears of kings and caudillos do not dissipate easily. Foremost among the constitutional bulwarks against potentially arbitrary power is the prohibition on reelection. Other provisions like legislative advice-and-consent powers over presidential appointments, impeachment mechanisms, judicial independence, and institutions such as the Contraloría of Chile also reflect this suspicion. Indeed, political intervention by the armed forces acting as a *poder moderador* may even be seen in certain political cultures as a useful check on overweening executives. One could explore in depth the contradictions between the constitutional texts and political practices of Latin American presidential regimes; any student of the region's history could cite many examples.

It would be useful to explore the way in which the fundamental contradiction between the desire for a strong and stable executive and the latent suspicion of that same presidential power affects political decision making, the style of leadership, the political practices, and the rhetoric of both presidents and their opponents in presidential systems. It introduces a dimension of conflict that cannot be explained wholly by socioeconomic, political, or ideological circumstances. Even if one were to accept the debatable notion that Hispanic societies are inherently prone to *personalismo*, there can be little doubt that in some cases this tendency receives reinforcement from institutional arrangements.

Perhaps the best way to summarize the basic differences between presidential and parliamentary systems is to say that while parliamentarism imparts flexibility to the political process, presidentialism makes it rather rigid. Proponents of presidentialism might reply that this rigidity is an advantage, for it guards against the uncertainty and instability so characteristic of parliamentary politics. Under parliamentary government, after all, myriad actors—parties, their leaders, even rank-and-file legislators—may at any time between elections adopt basic changes, cause realignments, and, above all, make or break prime ministers. But while the need for authority and predictability would seem to favor presidentialism, there are unexpected developments—ranging from the death of the incumbent to serious errors in judgment committed under the pressure of unruly circumstances—that make presidential rule less predictable and often weaker than that of a prime minister. The latter can always seek to shore up his legitimacy and authority, either through a vote of confidence or the dissolution of parliament and the ensuing new elections. Moreover, a prime minister can be changed without necessarily creating a regime crisis.

Considerations of this sort loom especially large during periods of regime transition and consolidation, when the rigidities of a presidential constitution must seem inauspicious indeed compared to the prospect of adaptability that parliamentarism offers.

Zero-Sum Elections

The preceding discussion has focused principally on the institutional dimensions of the problem; the consideration of constitutional provisions—some written, some unwritten—has dominated the analysis. In addition, however, one must attend to the ways in which political competition is structured in systems of direct presidential elections; the styles of leadership in such systems; the relations between the president, the political elites, and society at large; and the ways in which power is exercised and conflicts are resolved. It is a fair assumption that institutional arrangements both directly and indirectly shape the entire political process, or "way of ruling." Once we have described the differences between parliamentary and presidential forms of government that result from their differing institutional arrangements, we shall be ready to ask which of the two forms offers the best prospect for creating, consolidating, and maintaining democracy.

Presidentialism is ineluctably problematic because it operates according to the rule of "winner-take-all"—an arrangement that tends to make democratic politics a zero-sum game, with all the potential for conflict such games portend. Although parliamentary elections can produce an absolute majority for a single party, they more often give representation to a number of parties. Power-sharing and coalition-forming are fairly common, and incumbents are accordingly attentive to the demands and interests of even the smaller parties. These parties in turn retain expectations of sharing in power and, therefore, of having a stake in the system as a whole. By contrast, the conviction that he possesses independent authority and a popular mandate is likely to imbue a president with a sense of power and mission, even if the plurality that elected him is a slender one. Given such assumptions about his standing and role, he will find the inevitable opposition to his policies far more irksome and demoralizing than would a prime minister, who knows himself to be but the spokesman for a temporary governing coalition rather than the voice of the nation or the tribune of the people.

Absent the support of an absolute and cohesive majority, a parliamentary system inevitably includes elements that become institutionalized in what has been called "consociational democracy." Presidential regimes may incorporate consociational elements as well, perhaps as part of the unwritten constitution. When democracy was reestablished under adverse circumstances in Venezuela and Colombia, for example, the written constitutions may have called for presidential government, but the leaders of the major parties quickly turned to consociational agreements to soften the harsh, winner-take-all implications of presidential elections.

The danger that zero-sum presidential elections pose is compounded by the rigidity of the president's fixed term in office. Winners and losers are sharply defined for the entire period of the presidential mandate. There is no hope for shifts in alliances, expansion of the government's base of support through national-unity or emergency grand coalitions, new elections in response to major new events, and so on. Instead, the losers must wait at least four or five years without any access to executive power and patronage. The zero-sum game in presidential regimes raises the stakes of presidential elections and inevitably exacerbates their attendant tension and polarization.

On the other hand, presidential elections do offer the indisputable advantage of allowing the people to choose their chief executive openly, directly, and for a predictable span rather than leaving that decision to the backstage maneuvering of the politicians. But this advantage can only be present if a clear mandate results. If there is no required minimum plurality and several candidates compete in a single round, the margin between the victor and the runner-up may be too thin to support any claim that a decisive plebiscite has taken place. To preclude this, electoral laws sometimes place a lower limit on the size of the winning plurality or create some mechanism for choosing among the candidates if none attains the minimum number of votes needed to win; such procedures need not necessarily award the office to the candidate with the most votes. More common are run-off provisions that set up a confrontation between the two major candidates, with possibilities for polarization that have already been mentioned. One of the possible consequences of two-candidate races in multiparty systems is that broad coalitions are likely to be formed (whether in run-offs or in preelection maneuvering) in which extremist parties gain undue influence. If significant numbers of voters identify strongly with such parties, one or more of them can plausibly claim to represent the decisive electoral bloc in a close contest and may make demands accordingly. Unless a strong candidate of the center rallies widespread support against the extremes, a presidential election can fragment and polarize the electorate.

In countries where the preponderance of voters is centrist, agrees on the exclusion of extremists and expects both rightist and leftist candidates to differ only within a larger, moderate consensus, the divisiveness latent in presidential competition is not a serious problem. With an overwhelmingly moderate electorate, anyone who makes alliances or takes positions that seem to incline him to the extremes is unlikely to win, as both Barry Goldwater and George McGovern discovered to their chagrin. But societies beset by grave social and economic problems, divided about recent authoritarian regimes that once enjoyed significant popular support, and in which well-disciplined extremist parties have considerable electoral appeal, do not fit the model presented by the United States. In a polarized society with a volatile electorate, no serious candidate in a single-round election can afford to ignore parties with which he would otherwise never collaborate.

A two-round election can avoid some of these problems, for the preliminary round shows the extremist parties the limits of their strength and allows the two major candidates to reckon just which alliances they must make to win. This reduces the degree of uncertainty and promotes more rational decisions on the part of both voters and candidates. In effect, the presidential system may thus reproduce something like the negotiations that "form a government" in parliamentary regimes. But the potential for polarization remains, as does the difficulty of isolating extremist factions that a significant portion of the voters and elites intensely dislike.

* * *

The Problem of Dual Legitimacy

Given his unavoidable institutional situation, a president bids fair to become the focus for whatever exaggerated expectations his supporters may harbor. They are prone to think that he has more power than he really has or should have and may sometimes be politically mobilized against any adversaries who bar his way. The interaction between a popular president and the crowd acclaiming him can generate fear among his opponents and a tense political climate. Something similar might be said about a president with a military background or close military ties—which are facilitated by the absence of the prominent defense minister one usually finds under cabinet government.

Ministers in parliamentary systems are situated quite differently from cabinet officers in presidential regimes. Especially in cases of coalition or minority governments, prime ministers are much closer to being on an equal footing with their fellow ministers than presidents will ever be with their cabinet appointees. (One must note, however, that there are certain trends which may lead to institutions like that of *Kanzlerdemokratie* in Germany, under which the premier is free to choose his cabinet without parliamentary approval of the individual ministers. Parliamentary systems with tightly disciplined parties and a prime minister who enjoys an absolute majority of legislative seats will tend to grow quite similar to presidential regimes. The tendency to personalize power in modern politics, thanks especially to the influence of television, has attenuated not only the independence of ministers but the degree of collegiality and collective responsibility in cabinet governments as well.)

A presidential cabinet is less likely than its parliamentary counterpart to contain strong and independent-minded members. The officers of a president's cabinet hold their posts purely at the sufferance of their chief; if dismissed, they are out of public life altogether. A premier's ministers, by contrast, are not his creatures but normally his parliamentary colleagues; they may go from the cabinet back to their seats in parliament and question the prime minister in party caucuses or during the ordinary course of parliamentary business just as freely as other members can. A president, moreover, can shield his cabinet members from criticism much more effectively than can a prime minister, whose cabinet members are regularly hauled before parliament to answer queries or even, in extreme cases, to face censure.

One need not delve into all the complexities of the relations between the executive and the legislature in various presidential regimes to see that all such systems are based on dual democratic legitimacy: no democratic principle exists to resolve disputes between the executive and the legislature about which of the two actually represents the will of the people. In practice, particularly in those developing countries where there are great regional inequalities in modernization, it is likely that the political and social outlook of the legislature will differ from that held by the president and his supporters. The territorial principle of representation, often reinforced by malapportionment or federal institutions like a nonproportional upper legislative chamber, tends to give greater legislative weight to small towns and rural areas. Circumstances like these can give the president grounds to question the democratic credentials of his legislative opponents. He may even charge that they represent nothing but local oligarchies and narrow, selfish clienteles. This may or may not be true, and it may or may not be worse to cast one's ballot under the tutelage of local notables, tribal chieftains, landowners, priests, or even bosses than under that of trade unions, neighborhood associations, or party machines. Whatever the case may be, modern urban elites will remain inclined to skepticism about the democratic bona fides of legislators from rural or provincial districts. In such a context, a president frustrated by legislative recalcitrance will be tempted to mobilize the people against the putative oligarchs and special interests, to claim for himself alone true democratic legitimacy as the tribune of the people, and to urge on his supporters in mass demonstrations against the opposition. It is also conceivable that in some countries the president might represent the more traditional or provincial electorates and could use their support against the more urban and modern sectors of society.

Even more ominously, in the absence of any principled method of distinguishing the true bearer of democratic legitimacy, the president may use ideological formulations to discredit his foes; institutional rivalry may thus assume the character of potentially explosive social and political strife. Institutional tensions that in some societies can be peacefully settled through negotiation or legal means may in other, less happy lands seek their resolution in the streets.

The Issue of Stability

Among the oft-cited advantages of presidentialism is its provision for the stability of the executive. This feature is said to furnish a welcome contrast to the tenuousness of many parliamentary governments, with their frequent cabinet crises and changes of prime minister, especially in the multiparty democracies of Western Europe. Certainly the spectacle of political instability presented by the Third and Fourth French Republics and, more recently, by Italy and Portugal has contributed to the low esteem in which many scholars—especially in Latin America—hold parliamentarism and their consequent preference for presidential government. But such invidious comparisons overlook the large degree of stability that actually characterizes parliamentary governments. The superficial volatility they sometimes exhibit obscures the continuity of parties in power, the enduring character of coalitions, and the way that party leaders and key ministers have of weathering cabinet crises without relinquishing their posts. In addition, the instability of presidential cabinets has been ignored by students of governmental stability. It is also insufficiently noted that parliamentary systems, precisely by virtue of their surface instability, often avoid deeper crises. A prime minister who becomes embroiled in scandal or loses the allegiance of his party or majority coalition and whose continuance in office might provoke grave turmoil can be much more easily removed than a corrupt or highly unpopular president. Unless partisan alignments make the formation of a democratically legitimate cabinet impossible, parliament should eventually be able to select a new prime minister who can form a new government. In some more serious cases, new elections may be called, although they often do not resolve the problem and can even, as in the case of Weimar Germany in the 1930s, compound it.

The government crises and ministerial changes of parliamentary regimes are of course excluded by the fixed term a president enjoys, but this great stability is bought at the price of similarly great rigidity. Flexibility in the face of constantly changing situations is not presidentialism's strong suit. Replacing a president who has lost the confidence of his party or the people is an extremely difficult proposition. Even when polarization has intensified to the point of violence and illegality, a stubborn incumbent may remain in office. By the time the cumbersome mechanisms provided to dislodge him in favor of a more able and conciliatory successor have done their work, it may be too late. Impeachment is a very uncertain and time-consuming process, especially compared with the simple parliamentary vote of no confidence. An embattled president can use his powers in such a way that his opponents might not be willing to wait until the end of his term to oust him, but there are no constitutional ways—save impeachment or resignation under pressure—to replace him. There are, moreover, risks attached even to these entirely legal methods; the incumbent's supporters may feel cheated by them and rally behind him, thus exacerbating the crisis. It is hard to imagine how the issue could be resolved purely by the political leaders, with no recourse or threat of recourse to the people or to nondemocratic institutions like the courts or—in the worst case—the military. The intense antagonisms underlying such crises cannot remain even partially concealed in the corridors and cloakrooms of the legislature. What in a parliamentary system would be a government crisis can become a full-blown regime crisis in a presidential system.

The same rigidity is apparent when an incumbent dies or suffers incapacitation while in office. In the latter case, there is a temptation to conceal the president's infirmity until the end of his term. In event of the president's death, resignation, impeachment, or incapacity, the presidential constitution very often assures an automatic and immediate succession with no interregnum or power vacuum. But the institution of vice-presidential succession, which has worked so well in the United States, may not function so smoothly elsewhere. Particularly at risk are countries whose constitutions, like the United States Constitution before the passage of the Twelfth Amendment in 1804, allow presidential tickets to be split so that the winning presidential candidate and the winning vice-presidential candidate may come from different parties. If the deceased or outgoing president and his legal successor are from different parties, those who supported the former incumbent might object that the successor does not represent their choice and lacks democratic legitimacy.

Today, of course, few constitutions would allow something like the United States' Jefferson-Burr election of 1800 to occur. Instead they require that presidential and vice-presidential candidates be nominated together, and forbid ticket-splitting in presidential balloting. But these formal measures can do nothing to control the criteria for nomination. There are undoubtedly cases where the vice-president has been nominated mainly to balance the ticket and therefore represents a discontinuity with the president. Instances where a weak vice-presidential candidate is deliberately picked by an incumbent jealous of his own power, or even where the incumbent chooses his own wife, are not unknown. Nothing about the presidential system guarantees that the country's voters or political leaders would have selected the vice-president to wield the powers they were willing to give to the former president. The continuity that the institution of automatic vice-presidential succession seems to ensure thus might prove more apparent than real. There remains the obvious possibility of a caretaker government that can fill in until new elections take place, preferably as soon as possible. Yet it hardly seems likely that the severe crisis which might have required the succession would also provide an auspicious moment for a new presidential election.

The Time Factor

Democracy is by definition a government pro tempore, a regime in which the electorate at regular intervals can hold its governors accountable and impose a change. The limited time that is allowed to elapse between elections is probably the greatest guarantee against overweening power and the last hope for those in the minority. Its drawback, however, is that it constrains a government's ability to make good on the promises it made in order to get elected If these promises were far-reaching, including major programs of social change, the majority may feel cheated of their realization by the limited term in office imposed on their chosen leader. On the other hand, the power of a president is at once so concentrated and so extensive that it seems unsafe not to check it by limiting the number of times any one president can be reelected. Such provisions can be frustrating, especially if the incumbent is highly ambitious; attempts to change the rule in the name of continuity have often appeared attractive.

Even if a president entertains no inordinate ambitions, his awareness of the time limits facing him and the program to which his name is tied cannot help but affect his political style. Anxiety about policy discontinuities and the character of possible successors encourages what Albert Hirschman has called "the wish of *vouloir conclure.*" This exaggerated sense of urgency on the part of the president may lead to ill-conceived policy initiatives, overly hasty stabs at implementation, unwarranted anger at the lawful opposition, and a host of other evils. A president who is desperate to build his Brasilia or implement his program of nationalization or land reform before he becomes ineligible for reelection is likely to spend money unwisely or risk polarizing the country for the sake of seeing his agenda become reality. A prime minister who can expect his party or governing coalition to win the next round of elections is relatively free from such pressures. Prime ministers have stayed in office over the course of several legislatures without rousing any fears of nascent dictatorship, for the possibility of changing the government without recourse to unconstitutional means always remained open.

The fixed term in office and the limit on reelection are institutions of unquestionable value in presidential constitutions, but they mean that the political system must produce a capable and popular leader every four years or so, and also that whatever "political capital" the outgoing president may have accumulated cannot endure beyond the end of his term.

All political leaders must worry about the ambitions of second-rank leaders, sometimes because of their jockeying for position in the order of succession and sometimes because of their intrigues. The fixed and definite date of succession that a presidential constitution sets can only exacerbate the incumbent's concerns on this score. Add to this the desire for continuity, and it requires no leap of logic to predict that the president will choose as his lieutenant and successor-apparent someone who is more likely to prove a yes-man than a leader in his own right.

The inevitable succession also creates a distinctive kind of tension between the ex-president and his successor. The new man may feel driven to assert his independence and distinguish himself from his predecessor, even though both might belong to the same party. The old president, for his part, having known the unique honor and sense of power that come with the office, will always find it hard to reconcile himself to being out of power for good, with no prospect of returning even if the new incumbent fails miserably. Parties and coalitions may publicly split because of such antagonisms and frustrations. They can also lead to intrigues, as when a still-prominent former president works behind the scenes to influence the next succession or to undercut the incumbent's policies or leadership of the party.

Of course similar problems can also emerge in parliamentary systems when a prominent leader finds himself out of office but eager to return. But parliamentary regimes can more easily mitigate such difficulties for a number of reasons. The acute need to preserve party unity, the deference accorded prominent party figures, and the new premier's keen awareness that he needs the help of his predecessor even if the latter does not sit on the government bench or the same side of the house—all these contribute to the maintenance of concord. Leaders of the same party may alternate as premiers; each knows that the other may be called upon to replace him at any time and that confrontations can be costly to both, so they share power. A similar logic applies to relations between leaders of competing parties or parliamentary coalitions.

The time constraints associated with presidentialism, combined with the zero-sum character of presidential elections, are likely to render such contests more dramatic and divisive than parliamentary elections. The political realignments that in a parliamentary system may take place between elections and within the halls of the legislature must occur publicly during election campaigns in presidential systems, where they are a necessary part of the process of building a winning coalition. Under presidentialism, time becomes an intensely important dimension of politics. The pace of politics is very different under a presidential, as opposed to a parliamentary, constitution. When presidential balloting is at hand, deals must be made not only publicly but decisively—for the winning side to renege on them before the next campaign would seem like a betrayal of the voters' trust. Compromises, however necessary, that might appear unprincipled, opportunistic, or ideologically unsound are much harder to make when they are to be scrutinized by the voters in an upcoming election. A presidential regime leaves much less room for tacit consensus-building, coalition-shifting, and the making of compromises which, though prudent, are hard to defend in public.

Consociational methods of compromise, negotiation, and power-sharing under presidential constitutions have played major roles in the return of democratic government to Colombia, Venezuela, and, more recently, Brazil. But these methods appeared as necessary antinomies—deviations from the rules of the system undertaken in order to limit the voters' choices to what has been termed, rather loosely and pejoratively, *democradura*. The restoration of democracy will no doubt continue to require consociational strategies such as the formation of grand coalitions and the making of many pacts; the drawback of presidentialism is that it rigidifies and formalizes them. They become binding for a fixed period, during which there is scant opportunity for revision or renegotiation. Moreover, as the Colombian case shows, such arrangements rob the electorate of some of its freedom of choice; parliamentary systems, like that of Spain with its *consenso*, make it much more likely that consociational agreements will be made only *after* the people have spoken.

Parliamentarism and Political Stability

This analysis of presidentialism's unpromising implications for democracy is not meant to imply that no presidential democracy can be stable; on the contrary, the world's most stable democracy—the

United States of America—has a presidential constitution. Nevertheless, one cannot help tentatively concluding that in many other societies the odds that presidentialism will help preserve democracy are far less favorable.

While it is true that parliamentarism provides a more flexible and adaptable institutional context for the establishment and consolidation of democracy, it does not follow that just any sort of parliamentary regime will do. Indeed, to complete the analysis one would need to reflect upon the best type of parliamentary constitution and its specific institutional features. Among these would be a prime-ministerial office combining power with responsibility, which would in turn require strong, well-disciplined political parties. Such features—there are of course many others we lack the space to discuss—would help foster responsible decision making and stable governments and would encourage genuine party competition without causing undue political fragmentation. In addition, every country has unique aspects that one must take into account—traditions of federalism, ethnic or cultural heterogeneity, and so on. Finally, it almost goes without saying that our analysis establishes only probabilities and tendencies, not determinisms. No one can guarantee that parliamentary systems will never experience grave crisis or even breakdown.

In the final analysis, all regimes, however wisely designed, must depend for their preservation upon the support of society at large—its major forces, groups, and institutions. They rely, therefore, on a public consensus which recognizes as legitimate authority only that power which is acquired through lawful and democratic means. They depend also on the ability of their leaders to govern, to inspire trust, to respect the limits of their power, and to reach an adequate degree of consensus. Although these qualities are most needed in a presidential system, it is precisely there that they are most difficult to achieve. Heavy reliance on the personal qualities of a political leader—on the virtue of a statesman, if you will—is a risky course, for one never knows if such a man can be found to fill the presidential office. But while no presidential constitution can guarantee a Washington, a Juárez, or a Lincoln, no parliamentary regime can guarantee an Adenauer or a Churchill either. Given such unavoidable uncertainty, the aim of this essay has been merely to help recover a debate on the role of alternative democratic institutions in building stable democratic polities.

7.2

WHAT MAKES PRESIDENTIAL DEMOCRACIES FRAGILE?

José Antonio Cheibub

José Antonio Cheibub is the Boeschenstein Scholar of Political Economy and Public Policy and associate professor of political science at the University of Illinois at Urbana-Champaign. His research has focused on democracy, democratization, political representation, and Latin American politics. In this chapter from his 2007 book *Presidentialism, Parliamentarism, and Democracy,* Cheibub attempts to explain why presidential systems are associated with failed democracies. Unlike Juan Linz, Cheibub does not find significant levels of noncooperation and gridlock between the branches in presidential systems; he posits instead that presidential democracies fail because of their contexts and not because of their institutional rules. He believes that presidential systems tend to occur in those countries that are transitioning to democracy following military dictatorships, and that it is the legacy of the dictatorship, not the presidential system, that causes the collapse of democracy in many presidential systems. While reading the chapter, students should ask themselves what the main source of disagreement between Cheibub and Linz is. Does Cheibub accurately discuss Linz's argument? How would Linz respond to Cheibub's arguments?

I have argued. . .that intrinsic features of presidentialism are not the reason why presidential democracies are more prone to breakdown. Little in the chain of reasoning that leads from separation of powers to the instability of presidential regimes can be supported either theoretically or empirically. Yet the fact remains that democracies tend to have shorter lives when they are presidential. Recall that, for the 1946–2002 period, the expected life of a presidential democracy was 24 years versus 58 for parliamentary ones. Why, then, are presidential democracies more likely to die?

In this chapter I argue that the difference in the survival rates of parliamentary and presidential democracies can be accounted for by the conditions under which these democracies have existed. However, these are not the conditions that have been identified by the extant literature. Thus, I first show that the usual suspects—level of economic development, size of the country, geographic location—are not sufficient to account for the differences in survival rates across democratic systems. Although some of these conditions do matter, they do not fully eliminate these differences. I then argue that some democracies emerge in countries where the probability of a democratic breakdown is high, regardless of the type of democracy that exists, and that presidential democracies have emerged more

---

José Antonio Cheibub, *Presidentialism, Parliamentarism, and Democracy* (New York: Cambridge University Press, 2007), chapter 6, 136–164.

frequently in such countries. Thus, the fragility of presidential democracies is a function not of presidentialism per se but of the fact that presidential democracies have existed in countries where the environment is inhospitable for any kind of democratic regime. Given that countries are mostly "stuck" with their broad constitutional framework, I conclude the chapter with a discussion of easier-to-implement, subconstitutional reforms aimed at improving, rather than abolishing, existing presidential democracies.

Income, Growth, Size, and Location

Parliamentarism is more frequent in wealthier countries, where democracy is much more likely, indeed certain, to survive (Przeworski et al. 2000). It is more frequent in countries that generate relatively high rates of economic growth (Alvarez 1997). Shugart and Mainwaring (1997), in turn, suggest that the difference in survival between the two types of regimes may involve location—presidential regimes tend to be located in Latin America and Africa, parliamentary regimes in Europe—and country size: parliamentary regimes tend to exist in small countries. These factors constitute the menu of exogenous conditions that have been invoked to explain why presidential democracies have shorter lives than parliamentary ones.

Such explanations are plausible and, as Table 1 indicates, have prima facie empirical validity. The average per capita income is 1.5 times higher in parliamentary democracies, and the average rate of economic growth is nearly 1.5 times higher under parliamentarism than under presidentialism. Parliamentary regimes are more frequent in small countries: about one quarter of them (against 8% of presidential democracies) are in countries that had 1980 populations of less than a million. And about 60% of presidential democracies are located in Latin America, whereas less than 1% of parliamentary ones—specifically, two years of mixed democracy in Brazil in 1961 and 1962—are in this region.

Even so, none of these factors is sufficient to account for the difference in survival rates across democratic regimes. Descriptive patterns are clear, as Table 2 shows. Although the probability that democracy would die falls steadily as per capita income increases under both parliamentarism and presidentialism, presidential democracies are more likely to die than parliamentary ones at all income levels. Short-term economic performance also matters, but it does not explain why presidential democracies die more frequently than parliamentary ones: the expected life of presidential democracies when the

Table 1 Characteristics of Parliamentary and Presidential Democracies

	Parliamentary[a]	Presidential
Per capital income (1995 PPP$)	6,764	4,467
Economic growth[b]	2.48%	1.59%
In small countries[c]	25.40%	8.49%
In Latin America[d]	0.09%	62.30%

[a] Includes mixed systems.
[b] Annual change in per capita income.
[c] Population less than 1 million in 1980.
[d] Nineteen Spanish- and Portuguese-speaking countries.

Table 2 **Transition Probabilities in Parliamentary and Presidential Democracies by Economic and Geographic Conditions**

	All	Parliamentary	Presidential
Per capita income (1985 PPP$)			
Less than 3,000	0.0453	0.0402	0.0517
Between 3,000 and 6,000	0.0153	0.0083	0.0311
More than 6,000	0.0009	0.0000	0.0059
Economic growth			
Positive	0.0127	0.0076	0.0264
Negative	0.0434	0.0331	0.0610
Country size (population)			
Small	0.0062	0.0053	0.0137
Large	0.0215	0.0137	0.0373
Location			
Latin America	0.0436	0.0000	0.0438
Outside of Latin America	0.0128	0.0116	0.0210

Note: Transition probabilities are defined as TJK_i/J, where TJK is the number of transitions away from democracy and J is the number of democracies.

economy is doing well is not much higher than that of parliamentary democracies when the economy is doing poorly. Although democracies in small countries do indeed have longer expected lives, presidential democracies die more frequently than parliamentary ones in small and large countries both.

* * *

Military–Presidential Nexus

. . .What kills democracies is not presidentialism but rather their military legacy. Since presidential democracies tend to follow military dictatorships more frequently than they follow civilian dictatorships, presidential democracies will die more frequently than parliamentary democracies. Thus there is a military–presidential nexus that accounts for the relatively high level of instability of presidential democracies.

* * *

. . .[P]residential democracies are more likely to follow military dictatorships, whereas parliamentary (and mixed) democracies are more likely to follow civilian dictatorships: two thirds of the observed presidential democracies—as opposed to less than a third of parliamentary (and mixed) democracies—follow dictatorships led by the military. The military–presidential nexus is the product of these two facts: that democracies following military dictatorships are more likely to become a dictatorship and that presidential democracies are more likely to follow military dictatorships. It is the concurrence of these facts that accounts for the higher overall regime instability of presidential democracies. Once the

Table 3 Regime Transition Matrix (country-years)

	Current regime							First-order transition probability
Past regime	Parl.	Mixed	Pres.	Civilian	Military	Royal	Total	
Parliamentary	1,780	1	0	4	17	1	1,803	0.0128
Mixed	1	445	1	1	4	0	452	0.0155
Presidential	0	2	870	5	27	0	904	0.0376
Civilian	11	10	15	2,214	62	2	2,314	0.0432
Military	11	9	40	46	1,450	0	1,556	0.0681
Royal	1	0	0	5	5	649	660	0.0167
Total	1,804	467	926	2,275	1,565	652	7,689	0.0365

current democracy's authoritarian legacy is held constant, presidential and parliamentary democracies that followed military dictatorships both face relatively short lifetimes: about 19 years for pure parliamentary and presidential democracies, 24 years if we add parliamentary and mixed democracies.

* * *

Note that it could be presidential institutions that generate the nexus between military dictatorships and presidentialism. In this case, and in accordance with the Linzian view, presidentialism would lead to frequent political deadlocks and subsequent military intervention aimed at resolving those deadlocks. In this story, the presidential institutions would generate a domestically strong and active military establishment, which would intervene in the political process and so lead to the breakdown of democracy. However, the military is the main agent of democratic breakdown, regardless of regime type. Table 3 portrays the regime transition matrix for the 1946–2002 period. The diagonal entries give the number of years during which each type of regime survived, while the off-diagonal entries count regime transitions. It turns out that when democracies collapse they most likely do so at the hands of the military, regardless of their constitutional framework: 27 out of 32 cases (85%) of breakdown of presidential democracies, and 21 out of 26 cases (81%) of breakdown of parliamentary and mixed democracies, occurred at the hands of the military. The military, it seems, does not discriminate between democracies it chooses to overthrow. Yet when the military departs from the government it generally leaves presidential regimes behind: 40 out of 60 (67% of) transitions to democracy away from military dictatorships led to a presidential democracy and 15 out of 36 (42% of) transitions to democracy away from civilian dictatorships led to a presidential democracy.

Since democracies are much more brittle when they succeed military dictatorships, and since military dictatorships are followed disproportionately often by presidential systems, presidential democracies have shorter lives. Hence, the reason for the instability of presidential democracies lies not in any intrinsic features of presidentialism but rather in the conditions under which they emerge—namely, the fact that presidential regimes tend to exist in countries that are also more likely to suffer from dictatorships led by the military.

Why a Military–Presidential Nexus?

What we know thus far is that military dictatorships tend to be followed by presidential systems and that democracies following military dictatorships have shorter lives, regardless of their institutional frameworks. Two stories, not necessarily rival, can be constructed to account for these patterns. In one the military-presidential nexus is causal; in the other it is purely coincidental, the product of historical accident. I shall argue here that the first story, while plausible, is not empirically accurate, whereas the second is compatible with empirical evidence.

The causal version of accounting for the military–presidential nexus runs as follows. The military has a preference for presidential institutions. Faced with the prospect of transition to democracy, the military prefers the hierarchical structure and concentration of authority in one national office over the explicitly partisan, contentious, and precarious existence of parliamentary governments, subject as they are to the whims of the current majority. Hence, the argument would go, when the military rules the dictatorship, transitions to democracy are more likely if civilians consent to presidential institutions. In turn, if the military has been in power, neither presidential nor parliamentary systems are able to subject it to civilian control and so reduce its role in politics. Under either system the military retains organizational autonomy and thus its capacity to intervene in politics. And once the military intervenes, neither democratic institutional system can dismantle its capacity to do so again; under this explanation, the military just happens to have an autonomous preference for presidentialism.

However, I do not believe it is historically correct to suppose that different democratic systems resulted from preferences of military dictators over the specific form of democratic government that succeeds them. For one thing, there is no reason for the military to prefer presidentialism on the grounds of preserving their capacity to return to power. Recall that the military is equally likely to overturn presidential and parliamentary democracies: one system is not any easier than the other for it to overthrow; [and democracies] that succeed dictatorships headed by the military are equally vulnerable to breakdown. This again suggests that the constitutional framework does not matter for the military's ability to suspend democracy.

Moreover, as far as I can tell, there have been few cases where the issue of regime type under democracy was on the agenda during the process of extricating the military from politics and eventual transition to democracy. Suberu and Diamond (2002) report that the military in Nigeria expressed a strong preference for presidential institutions prior to preparations for the 1979 constitution. Likewise, Than (2004) reports that one of the proposals of the military regime in Myanmar is the establishment of a presidential constitution, although this is not yet a case of transition to democracy and the military preference is not conditioned on a regime transition occurring. A case that is sometimes invoked as providing evidence of a military preference for presidentialism is Brazil, where the option of a mixed system (referred to as the "parliamentary" alternative) was seriously considered in 1986–1988, when a new constitution was being written. During this process the military allied itself with the side favoring the preservation of the presidential system (Elkins 2003). However, in 1986 the transition to democracy had already occurred (the first civilian president took office in March 1985), and there is no evidence that the form of government appeared anywhere as an item of negotiation or contention during the long period of liberalization that preceded the military's relinquishing of power in 1985.

Finally, if the nexus between military dictatorships and presidentialism were the product of the preference of incumbent dictators, then we should observe that military dictatorships always leave behind presidential democracies. But this is true only for Latin America, where all transitions to democracy away from a military dictatorship led to presidential democracies. In other areas of the world the military left behind both presidential and parliamentary institutions: of 34 transitions to democracy from a military dictatorship that took place outside of Latin America, 11 were to pure parliamentarism, 9 to mixed systems, and 14 to presidentialism.[1] Thus, whereas the story based on preferences of the military seems to fit the Latin American record, it does not fit transitions that occurred elsewhere. Even in Latin America, it is telling that the transitions occurring from civilian dictatorships also led to the establishment of presidential institutions.

Thus, it is improbable that democratic systems resulted from preferences of dictators over the form of democracies that succeed them. The nexus between the nature of the previous dictatorship and the institutional form of democracy, I argue, is purely accidental—that is, a product of the historical coincidence of two independent processes. The military–presidential nexus exists because the countries where militarism remained strong at the middle of the twentieth century were also countries that had adopted presidential institutions. Had these countries adopted parliamentary institutions, the level of instability of parliamentary democracies would be much higher than what is actually observed.

Given existing professional bias in favor of seeing important outcomes as the product of causal processes, it is rather unorthodox to invoke a historical coincidence when accounting for presidential instability. Yet I believe that this account is plausible—and closer to the truth than one that views the inherent features of presidentialism as causing the instability of presidential democracies.

There are four steps in the argument that the military–presidential nexus is the product of a historical coincidence.

1. Countries vary in their propensity toward military intervention. Militarism may be a function of social structure or a phenomenon that results from exogenous and conjunctural factors, but it is not likely to be a function of presidentialism itself.
2. Countries *adopt* their initial institutions for reasons that are unrelated to the ones that lead to the occurrence of military dictatorships; in other words, whether a country adopts a presidential or a parliamentary constitution has nothing to do with its propensity toward military intervention. This is particularly true for the relatively large number of Latin American countries that adopted presidential constitutions in the nineteenth century.
3. Countries *retain* the institutions under which they consolidated their existence as a nation-state. Institutions are, in general, sticky, and major institutions such as the form of government are even "stickier" than less encompassing ones.
4. Military intervention took place in many countries, but it persisted (at least until the 1980s) in countries that had adopted presidential institutions. This persistence had little to do with the fact that these countries were presidential and a lot to do with the onset of the Cold War and the military's role in "fighting" it.

1. The transitions to pure parliamentarism took place in Ghana, Greece (twice), Lesotho, Myanmar, Pakistan, Sudan, Thailand (twice), and Turkey (twice). The transitions to mixed democracies took place in the Central African Republic, the Congo, Haiti, Madagascar, Mali, Niger (twice), Poland, and Portugal.

The instability of presidential democracies is thus due to the fact that the countries that adopted and retained presidential institutions are those where the military endured after WWII, during the Cold War. Had the military also endured in countries with parliamentary institutions, the same instability that characterizes presidential democracies would also have characterized parliamentary ones. According to this argument, then, the intrinsic features of presidentialism are not the reason why presidential democracies tend to break down more frequently than parliamentary ones. The problem of presidential democracies is not that they are "institutionally flawed." Rather, the problem is that they tend to exist in societies where democracies of any type are likely to be unstable. Therefore, the problem of survival of presidential democracies is actually the problem of survival of democracies in general, regardless of their form of government.

In the remainder of this chapter I shall develop each of these points.

Military Intervention in Politics

Countries, as we know, are not equally likely to suffer from a dictatorship; moreover, among those that experience one, countries are not equally likely to experience a dictatorship led by the military. The reasons are many and probably not systematically known. There is a large but inconclusive early literature on the causes of military intervention in politics. One story points to the degree of social and economic inequality, which generates demands that cannot be accommodated without threatening the existing order. The military intervenes to repress these demands and guarantee the survival of the status quo. This line of argument can be traced to "sociological" explanations for the intervention of the military in politics. It can also be associated with more recent (and, for that matter, more sophisticated and less functionalist) arguments such as that developed by Engerman and Sokoloff (1997), who account for the difficulties of Latin American democracies in terms of the repressive nature of the institutions that were set up to organize colonial production (see Acemoglu, Johnson, and Robinson 2001, 2002). It is argued that these institutions generate high levels of inequality, which in turn generate the need for repression to organize economic production, thus perpetuating themselves. Other accounts have added a "supply" factor by considering the military's corporate interests and the emergence of ideologies that promote and justify military control over the political system (Stepan 1971, 1988; O'Donnell 1973).

An alternative view is that military intervention in politics happened at a certain historical conjuncture—but that once it happened it triggered other military interventions. Londregan and Poole (1990) were probably the first to establish that coups breed other coups, trapping countries in a cycle of instability and poverty. Along these lines, Przeworski (2004), building on findings reported in Przeworski et al. (2000), shows that all countries that have experienced more than one breakdown of democracy did so at the hands of the military; this suggests that one intervention by the military is likely to lead to subsequent interventions. As for the juncture at which the military became "activated," Figure 1 suggests that the interwar period—beginning in 1918 but with an inflection in 1930—is a good candidate: the proportion of authoritarian regimes led by the military increased from 6% in 1918 to 14% in 1920, to 21% in 1930, and to 31% in 1944. No other period in the twentieth century saw such a dramatic increase in the number of regimes led by the military.

The political activation of the military was not a specifically Latin American phenomenon. In 1917, only 25% of the dictatorships led by the military were located in Latin America. This number increased to 60% in 1921, but by 1926 it was down again to 33%; it increased again in 1930 to about 50%, where it remained until the end of WWII. The military dictatorships that emerged in Latin America in

Figure 1 Proportion of Dictatorships Led by the Military, 1900–2002

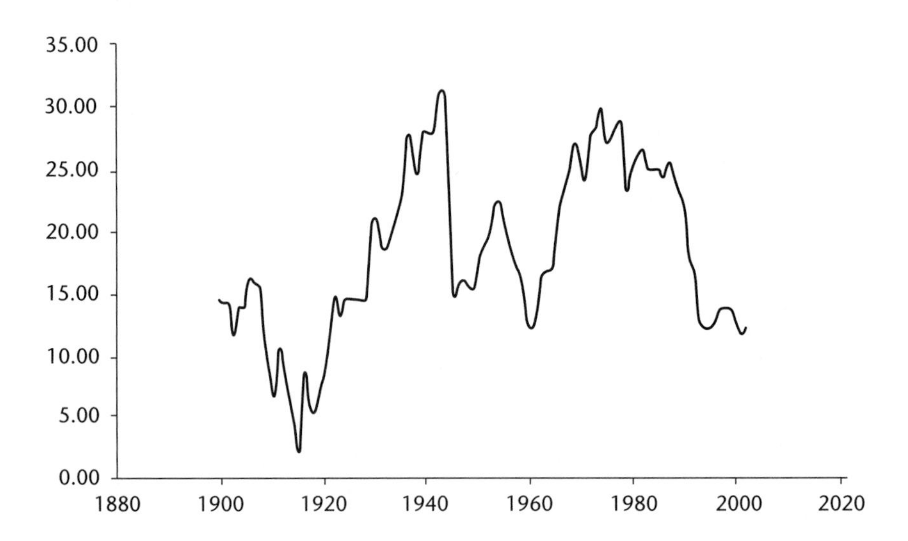

the first two decades of the twentieth century should not be seen as a mere continuation of the pattern of instability that characterized the region since independence. Przeworski and Curvale (2006) have shown that, by the third quarter of the nineteenth century, most Latin American countries had already put an end to the period of turmoil that followed independence. This means they were operating under a system of previously specified rules; in other words, they had stable political institutions.

Adoption of Initial Institutions

From the beginning of the nineteenth century to the breakup of the Soviet Union there have been five "waves" of independence in the world. The first, in Latin America, started in 1804 with Haiti's independence from France and lasted through the early 1820s; the second was due to the breakup of the Austro-Hungarian and Ottoman empires in the first two decades of the twentieth century; and the third came about with Africa's decolonization, which peaked in 1960 when seventeen new countries were created. The fourth wave occurred in the 1970s with the independence of small Caribbean countries; the last occurred with the breakup of the Soviet Union and Yugoslavia, leading to the emergence of nineteen new countries in Eastern and Central Europe and Central Asia.

There is probably no one set of factors that can account for the kind of constitutional framework that countries in each of these waves adopted. In nineteenth-century Latin America, after a considerable period of constitutional experimentation (Negretto and Aguilar-Rivera 2000; Gargarella 2004, 2005), all countries stabilized under presidential constitutions. European countries emerging out of the Austro-Hungarian and Ottoman empires adopted a variety of constitutions, but the majority had strong parliamentary elements. In Africa, some studies have suggested that the identity of the colonizer was central for shaping the constitution with which the new country started its life (Bernhard, Reenock, and Nordstrom 2004).

There might be factors that help explain why, given the availability of the choice, countries choose a presidential or a parliamentary constitution. Thus, it may be that the absence of a viable head of state (due to the occurrence of a revolution or an independence war) is associated with adoption of a presidential constitution, which provides for just such a head at the same time it constitutes the government. Likewise, it may be that the existence of a functioning legislature prior to independence, such as those that existed in India and in many African and Caribbean countries under British rule, is associated with adoption of a parliamentary system in which the government is accountable to the assembly. But the point is that countries adopt constitutions at the moment they come into being; and they do so for reasons that are, if not idiosyncratic, at least related to the specific historical moments in which they emerge.

Some may object to the idea that institutions are adopted for reasons independent of the propensity toward militarism. For instance, countries where inequality is high will experience conflict and instability, which may lead to both militarism (which helps contain the escalation of conflict) and presidentialism (which allegedly provides for relatively strong leadership). In this sense, the connection between presidentialism and militarism is not a historical accident but instead the consequence of a common cause: high levels of inequality.

In fact, this argument is often given to explain the adoption of presidentialism in the Latin American countries that became independent in the nineteenth century. The idea is that these countries were polarized and far from egalitarian, which led to the emergence of the military. At the same time, as institutions were being "designed," presidentialism appeared as the preferred choice because it provided "strong" government presumably capable of dealing with conflicts generated by the high level of inequality and high degree of instability inherent to those countries. Thus, presidentialism was adopted for the same reasons that militarism emerged—contrary to my claim that they were independent from one another.

Although plausible, this explanation is historically inaccurate and presumes the existence of a choice that was not available at the time Latin American countries were adopting their constitutional frameworks. When presidential constitutions were adopted in these countries in the nineteenth century, the choice was not between presidential and parliamentary forms of government—as it may be today and might have been, for instance, when African countries became independent in the 1960s. Rather, the choice was between monarchy (regimes in which the government is headed by a hereditary leader) and republic (regimes in which the government is headed by people who cannot make any claims of heredity). Parliamentarism—that is, a form of government in which the government is dependent on the confidence of a legislative majority—simply did not exist as an option at the time that the Americas, Latin and otherwise, were crafting their basic institutions. As Cox (1987) has shown in his book on the emergence of cabinet government in England, cabinet responsibility is something that did not emerge until the last decades of the nineteenth century.

At independence, Latin American countries were struggling with the same fundamental problem that leaders of the newly independent United States were struggling with after 1776: how to constitute authority in a context where the king is no longer ruler. As the early constitutional history of Latin American countries demonstrates, there was considerable experimentation before they all settled on a presidential constitutional form; all of the experiments involved some kind of monarchy, either elective or hereditary. It is telling that the one country (Brazil) in Latin America that did not depose the king kept a constitutional monarchy that might have evolved into a parliamentary democracy. It is also telling that, once the king was deposed (principally because of the monarchy's identification with slavery and the "republican agitation" that erupted in the 1870s; see Viotti da Costa 2000), the form of government adopted was presidential. Presidentialism, one can say, was the solution to a common problem faced by countries that emerged as such in the late eighteenth and nineteenth centuries: how to constitute national authority when the head of the government had been removed.

Institutional Inertia

Basic constitutional frameworks are difficult to change. The reasons are not hard to see: they structure the expectations of the actors operating under them and, in order to change the framework, actors must be willing to leap into the unknown. At the same time, constitutions serve as focal points: all of the transitions to democracy that took place in Argentina since the 1930s resulted in the re-adoption (without much discussion) of the 1853 constitution, which had ushered in probably the longest period of political stability in that country's history.

Indeed, democracies that have changed their form of government are rare. There are only three cases of such change in the world since 1946: Brazil in 1961 and 1963 and France in 1958. Changes are more frequent after an authoritarian interregnum but still are not common. Since the end of the nineteenth century there have been seventy cases of re-democratization in 49 countries; the constitutional framework of the new democracy was different in fifteen cases. Of these, eight involved changes to or from mixed democracies and a mere seven cases involved changes from a purely parliamentary to a presidential constitutional framework. No country that had a presidential constitution under democracy re-emerged under a parliamentary constitution.

In fact, basic constitutional frameworks tend to remain in place even as regimes change. The staying power of these institutions is simply overwhelming given the number of opportunities that have existed for them to be altered. Changes do occur, of course, but they are not very frequent. In the case of Latin America, where the first big wave of independence took place, all countries (with one exception) had presidential institutions by the time politics stabilized after independence; they kept these institutions in spite of the cycles of democracy and dictatorship that many experienced since then. Latin American dictators were usually called "presidents" and often governed with the "help" of independently elected legislatures. Brazil, which adopted presidentialism only with the first republican constitution in 1891, is the sole exception; but since then, presidentialism has survived six constitutions (1934, 1937, 1946, 1966, 1969, 1988) in spite of explicit and vigorous attempts by some actors to introduce parliamentary institutions.

The continuity in basic constitutional frameworks can also be seen in the continuity of titles adopted by rulers under democracy and dictatorship. It is striking that the countries with leaders who were ever called presidents and/or prime ministers continued to have leaders who were called presidents and/or prime ministers later in their histories. Presidents existed in 67.6% and prime ministers in 65.2% of the country-years between 1946 and 2002. Nearly 37% of these years featured both a prime minister and a president. All but three countries that were first observed with a president in 1946 (or at independence) had a president in 2002. Prime ministers seem to be more ephemeral, but only in appearance. By 2002, fifteen of the forty countries that had a prime minister in 1946 or at independence did not have one in 2002; in eleven of these fifteen, the prime minister office had been abolished and reinstated at least once, and there is nothing to suggest that it may not come back to life again. In only four cases

(Malawi in 1966, Nigeria in 1966. Seychelles in 1977, and Sudan in 1989) has the office of prime minister been abolished and the country gone on to live an extended period of time without such a figure. Thus even prime ministers, which under dictatorships seem to disappear more frequently than presidents, have staying power: once in place, they are likely to remain as part of the political landscape of a country.

Thus, "presidential" and "parliamentary" constitutions are resilient; once adopted, they provide the structure of offices and roles that actors will take for granted. When presidential democracies die, they most likely become dictatorships that are led by presidents. When parliamentary democracies die, prime ministers do not always disappear even if their powers do. The basic constitutional framework of countries tends to remain in place, regardless of whether or not government officials come to power through competitive elections.

Historical Coincidence

It is the coincidence of repeated military intervention in countries that had adopted presidential institutions that explains the pattern of unstable presidential democracies. The nexus between militarism and presidentialism is not the product of design or the outcome of a common cause. Rather, it simply reflects the fact that military dictatorships appeared, remained, and/or recurred—in other words, endured—in countries that had adopted presidential institutions.

Now refer back to Figure 1. The marked increase in the number of military dictatorships in the 1920s and 1930s is the result of democratic breakdowns in both Latin America and Europe. In 1938 the military ruled in dictatorships in Argentina, Bolivia, the Dominican Republic, El Salvador, Guatemala, Honduras, Nicaragua, Paraguay, Peru, and Venezuela. By this time, democracy had broken down in Austria, Bulgaria, Estonia, Finland, Germany, Greece, Italy, Latvia, Lithuania, Poland, Portugal (twice), Spain, and Yugoslavia. At the end of World War II, ten of nineteen Latin American countries were democratic. In the same year, most European countries that had not been formally or informally annexed by the Soviet Union in the course of the war were democratic (with the notable exceptions of Spain and Portugal). Not much changed with respect to political regimes in Europe until Portugal in 1975 and Spain in 1977 democratized. In Latin America, by 1970 all countries (with the exception of Colombia, Costa Rica, and Venezuela) were dictatorships, almost all of them led by the military.

Why, then, have postwar Austria, Germany, Italy, and Finland (and later Greece, Portugal, and Spain) become stable democracies, while not a single democracy that existed in 1946 survived in Latin America? Consider this assertion: Latin America continued to suffer from political instability because the dictatorships that were in place during World War II did not lose a war or, to put it in more general terms, were not discredited as a political force, as they were in Europe. There, the United States could not rely on authoritarian forces—discredited and defeated as they were during the war—to thwart the threat of communism. Hence the Cold War battles had to be waged through center-right democratic parties, such as the Christian Democrats in Germany and Italy. But in Latin America the right-wing military became the bulwark against the threat of communism, with the implication that it would step into the political arena whenever necessary. Obviously, the argument here is not that the military coups in Latin America were successful only, or even primarily, as instruments of U.S. intervention. I share what appears now to be the consensus view that military coups succeed only when they enjoy domestic civilian support. But if Latin American militaries had been discredited as the fascist forces in Europe were, these coups would not have been possible.

Thus, although parliamentary and presidential democracies are equally likely to die at the hands of the military, the military remained in a position to "kill" democratic regimes in an area of the world where, for reasons that should be traced to the constitutional experiments of the nineteenth century, presidential constitutions predominated. Where parliamentary institutions predominated, the military became discredited as a political force and its capacity to intervene in politics neutralized.[2] Dictators in Latin America found presidential institutions when they came to power, and this is what they left behind when they relinquished power. We can see, then, how a military–presidential nexus might have emerged from the coincidence of these historical processes.

The instability of presidential democracies is therefore a consequence of their following military dictatorships, which makes them inherently unstable. They follow military dictatorships, however, because of a set of historical circumstances that allowed the military to remain active and credible as a political force in a part of the world where presidential constitutions happened to be in place. Given the resilience of constitutional frameworks, presidential institutions in place when the military came into power would remain when the military relinquished power. If these institutions had been parliamentary then they would likewise have remained, and the puzzle with which this book started—that presidential democracies die more frequently than parliamentary ones—would not even have existed.

Observe that there is cause for optimism. There are economic and political reasons for us to believe that the spiral of instability has been broken in Latin America. In spite of the economic stagnation of Latin America in the past twenty years, many countries in the region (particularly those in the Southern Cone) now enjoy income levels at which threats to democracy are extremely rare. Even though they are relatively poor in comparison to Western Europe, right-wing Latin American elites have too much at risk economically to engage in yet another authoritarian adventure. But perhaps the more important reason is political. In Latin America, the military was disgraced both by its brutality and its indolence during the last wave of "bureaucratic–authoritarian" regimes. Given the absence of Cold War pressures, it seems that the prospects for a military return to power in the region are practically nonexistent.

Is the Military–Presidential Nexus About "Latin America"?

Much of the pattern we observe in connection with presidential democracies may stem from our historical tendency to observe presidentialism in Latin America, where we also observe enduring military dictatorships. Although not all presidential democracies are located in Latin America (the United States and some countries in Africa and Asia account for 37% of them), nearly all democracies in the region are presidential (excepting only the sixteen months of mixed institutions adopted in August 1961 in Brazil). However, the eighteen countries of Latin America do account disproportionately for the number of dictatorships that are led by military leaders. Although "only" 22.8% of the military dictatorships observed between 1946 and 1999 were in Latin America, during this period 49.8% of all regimes and 63% of the democracies in the region were preceded by a military dictatorship. Is there anything about Latin America, as distinct from presidentialism or militarism, that might account for the pattern of instability of presidential democracies?

2. It is interesting to note in this respect that the two European countries that did not directly involve their military in WWII (and hence survived the conflict unscathed) were Spain and Portugal, where dictatorship survived into the 1970s. The other country that experienced military dictatorship—Greece—also had a military force that was not damaged by WWII.

As we know, democracies that follow military dictatorships have shorter lives; and military dictatorships, in turn, have much shorter lives than civilian or monarchical ones. One should therefore expect that, once a country experiences a military dictatorship, a spiral of instability will characterize its subsequent history. Suppose a military regime overthrows a democracy; then, in view of the last two columns of Table 3 (which give first-order transition probabilities of the different regimes and their expected lives), we can expect this regime to last for fifteen years. Assume it is followed by presidentialism—which, given that it is preceded by a military dictatorship, is expected to last nineteen years—and that when this presidential democracy is in turn overthrown the result is a military regime that again lasts fifteen years. One would then expect to witness three regime transitions in about fifty years, more or less the period (1946–2002) covered by our data set of observed political regimes.

This cycle, as one will readily recognize, is reminiscent of the history of many Latin American countries. Indeed, not only is regime transition more frequent in Latin America than in other regions, but the average number of transitions in this region is close to what one would expect given the cycle just described. As Table 4 shows, although Latin America comprises fewer than 10% of the world's countries, 37% of transitions to and from democracy have occurred there. Between 1946 and 2002, the average number of transitions in Latin America was 2.9 versus 0.5 outside this region. This instability could be the product of some unobserved characteristics of Latin American countries that have nothing to do with militarism and presidentialism. How important, then, is "Latin America" in accounting for the survival of democracies?

[We can see] the impact of a dummy variable for Latin America (LA) on transitions to dictatorship while controlling for economic development level, presidentialism, and military legacy. [Neither] presidentialism nor this LA has an impact on the survival of democracies. It is the military legacy of presidential democracies in Latin America, not their form of government or their location, that makes them more brittle.

Figure 2 allows us to compare the relative effects of presidentialism and militarism at different levels of economic development. As is apparent from the figure, the real divide in terms of democratic breakdown occurs between those democracies that were preceded by military dictatorships and those that

Table 4 Regime Instability: Latin America and Elsewhere

Number of regime transitions	Number of countries	Latin America	Rest of the world
0	127	0	127
1	37	5	32
2	15	5	10
3	7	2	5
4	4	1	3
5	6	2	4
6	1	1	0
7	0	0	0
8	1	1	0
9	1	1	0
Total	199	18	181

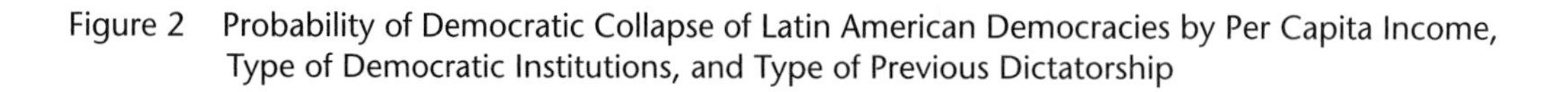
Figure 2 Probability of Democratic Collapse of Latin American Democracies by Per Capita Income, Type of Democratic Institutions, and Type of Previous Dictatorship

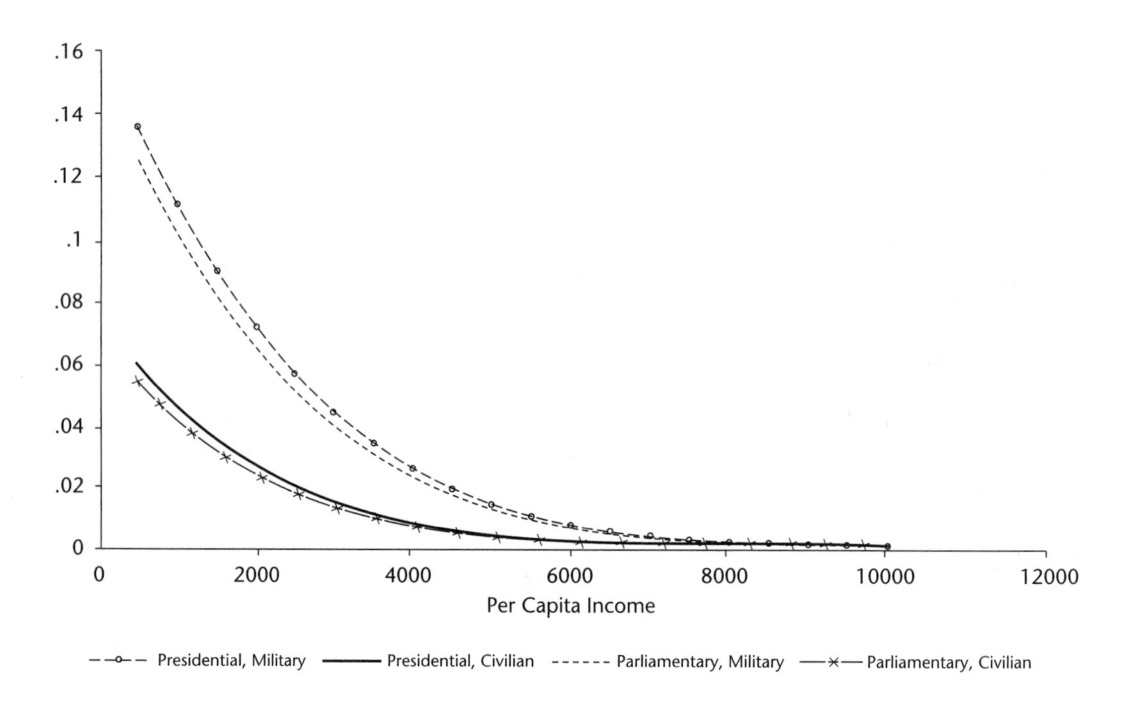

were preceded by civilian dictatorships. At every level of income per capita (at least up to about PPP$6,000) for which democracies are still likely to break down, democracies preceded by military dictatorship are much more likely to become a dictatorship. The effect of presidentialism is simply nonexistent. An almost identical picture would emerge were we to keep the form of government constant and vary the region of the world and the authoritarian legacy of the current democratic regime.

This, however, is not all. Although no dictatorships left behind parliamentary democracies in Latin America, some presidential democracies followed civilian dictatorships. If what causes regime instability is the legacy of military dictatorships and not some "Latin American" factor, then it must be true that, within the region, presidential democracies that followed military dictatorships were more brittle than those that followed civilian dictatorships. And the same pattern must be true for both presidential and parliamentary democracies outside of Latin America.

We already know that this last statement is true. Because no parliamentary democracy ever existed in Latin America, [there is a] probability that a non–Latin American parliamentary democracy will break down, conditioned on the type of dictatorship that preceded it. Recall that when the previous dictatorship was civilian, the expected life of the democracy was 89 years; and when the previous dictatorship was military, the expected life was only 20 years. A similar pattern, though not as dramatic, is true of presidential democracies outside of Latin America. Those that follow a civilian dictatorship tend to last for 37 years, whereas those that follow a military dictatorship tend to last for only 14 years. Finally, this is observed even among the presidential democracies within Latin America: those originating in civilian dictatorships are expected to live for 36 years, whereas those originating in military dictatorships are expected to live for 20 years. Clearly, the effect of military legacy seems to be weakened in Latin America, suggesting that there may exist other factors about the region that independently affect regime survival. Yet the effect of military legacy on the probability that a democracy will break down remains—regardless of whether the democracy is presidential or parliamentary and of whether it is in or outside of Latin America.

Thus, it is military intervention that mostly leads to instability in Latin America and, by extension, to instability of presidential democracies. We can therefore assert counterfactually that, had Latin America adopted parliamentary institutions in the aftermath of its independence, we would not be asking questions about the higher rates of regime instability of presidential democracies. The nexus between military dictatorships and presidential democracies is thus purely coincidental: military regimes are not more likely to overthrow presidential democracies than parliamentary ones, and military leaders are not more likely than other leaders to change the institutions they found. It just happened that military intervention occurred more frequently in the countries that adopted presidential institutions at independence, specifically in Latin America.

These systems were not established by "the military"; the very language is anachronistic. The military is a newcomer as an institution. As Rouquié (1994:236) observes, "there is no militarism in the strict sense of the term prior to the birth of standing armies and career officers," which did not happen in Latin America before the end of the nineteenth century, well after independence. It was only in the ten years following 1925, when the first military coups occurred in Ecuador and Chile, that the military stepped into politics as an organization. Argentina, Bolivia, Brazil, the Dominican Republic, Guyana, and Peru suffered military coups in 1930; the following year this was the fate of Ecuador and El Salvador, while Chile remained in the hands of ephemeral military juntas. From then on, a spiral of instability dominated the history of most Latin American countries. As a matter of fact, the notion that Latin America has been perennially and inherently unstable from the outset needs to be revisited. Many countries in the region experienced relatively long periods of routine (though not democratic) politics, including regular transfers of power, before they became chronically unstable. Thus, instability in Latin America is probably a more recent phenomenon whose causes still need to be identified.

In summary, the higher instability of presidential democracies—a fact noted by many analysts since Linz, and one that I do not dispute—is not due to any inherent defect of systems based on the separation of executive and legislative powers. Neither does this instability have much to do with the exogenous conditions that are often invoked to account for it: level of economic development, size of the country, and geographic location. Although location does matter for regime instability, and Latin America is by far the least stable region of the world, I hope to have made explicit the mechanism that underlies this relationship: the nexus between the military and presidentialism, the product of a combination of historical circumstances that (as I pointed out earlier) are no longer in place.

We may therefore conclude that the problem of presidential democracies is not that they are "institutionally flawed." Rather, the problem is that they tend to exist in societies where democracies of any type are likely to be unstable. Hence, fears arising from the choice of many new democracies for presidential institutions are unfounded. From a strictly institutional point of view, presidentialism can be as stable as parliamentarism. Given that constitutional frameworks are difficult to change, striving to replace them may be wasteful from a political point of view. It would be a misguided use of resources to attempt to change an institutional structure on the grounds of democratic stability when the source of instability has nothing to do with that structure. Hence, that countries with presidential institutions are "stuck" with them does not mean that they will experience regime instability in the future. It also does not mean that there is no room for improvement or that institutional reforms are pointless. There are actions that can be taken to help democracy survive that do not require altering hard-to-change institutional structures.

* * *

References

Acemoglu, Daron, Simon Johnson, and James A. Robinson. "The Colonial Origins of Comparative Development: An Empirical Investigation." *American Economic Review* 91, no. 5 (2001): 1369–1401.

———. "Reversal of Fortune: Geography and Institutions in the Making of the Modern World Income Distribution." *Quarterly Journal of Economics* 117, November (2002): 1231–94.

Alvarez, Michael. "Presidentialism and Parliamentarism: Which Works? Which Lasts?" Ph.D. dissertation, Department of Political Science, University of Chicago, 1997.

Bernhard, Michael, Christopher Reenock, and Timothy Nordstrom. "The Legacy of Western Overseas Colonialism on Democratic Survival." *International Studies Quarterly* 48, no. 1 (2004): 225–50.

Cox, Gary. *The Efficient Secret: The Cabinet and the Development of Political Parties in Victorian England.* Cambridge University Press, 1987.

Elkins, Zachary. "Designed by Diffusion: International Networks and the Spread of Democracy." Ph.D. dissertation, Department of Political Science, University of California, Berkeley, 2003.

Engerman, Stanley L., and Kenneth L. Sokoloff. "Factor Endowments, Institutions, and Differential Paths of Growth among New World Economies: A View from Economic Historians of the United States." In Stephen Haber (Ed.), *How Latin America Fell Behind,* pp. 260–304. Palo Alto, CA: Stanford University Press, 1997.

Gargarella, Roberto. "Towards a Typology of Latin American Constitutionalism, 1810–60." *Latin American Research Review* 39, no. 2 (2004): 141–53.

———. "The Constitution of Inequality: Constitutionalism in the Americas, 1776–1860." *International Journal of Constitutional Law* 3, no. 1 (2005): 1–23.

Londregan, John B., and Keith T. Poole. "Poverty, the Coup Trap, and the Seizure of Executive Power." *World Politics* 42 (1990): 151–83.

Negretto, Gabriel L., and Jose Antonio Aguilar-Rivera. "Rethinking the Legacy of the Liberal State in Latin America: The Cases of Argentina (1853–1916) and Mexico (1857–1910)." *Journal of Latin American Studies* 32 (2000): 361–97.

O'Donnell, Guillermo. *Modernization and Bureaucratic-Authoritarianism: Studies in South American Politics.* Berkeley: Institute of International Studies, University of California, 1973.

Przeworski, Adam. "Economic Development and Transitions to Democracy." Unpublished manuscript, Department of Politics, New York University, 2004.

Przeworski, Adam, Michael E. Alvarez, José Antonio Cheibub, and Fernando Limongi. *Democracy and Development: Political Institutions and Well-Being in the World, 1950–1990.* Cambridge University Press, 2000.

Przeworski, Adam, and Carolina Curvale. "Political Institutions and Economic Development in the Americas: The Long Run." Unpublished manuscript, Department of Politics, New York University, 2006.

Rouquié, Alain. "The Military in Latin American Politics Since 1930." In Leslie Bethell (Ed.), *Latin America Since 1930* (Cambridge History of Latin America, vol. 6). Cambridge University Press, 1994.

Shugart, Matthew Soberg, and Scott Mainwaring. "Presidentialism and Democracy in Latin America: Rethinking the Terms of the Debate." In Scott Mainwaring and Matthew Soberg Shugart (Eds.), *Presidentialism and Democracy in Latin America*, pp. 12–54. Cambridge University Press, 1997.

Stepan, Alfred. *Military in Politics: Changing Patterns in Brazil*. Princeton, NJ: Princeton University Press, 1971.

———. *Rethinking Military Politics: Brazil and the Southern Cone*. Princeton, NJ: Princeton University Press, 1988.

Suberu, Rotimi T., and Larry Diamond. "Institutional Design, Ethnic Conflict-Management and Democracy in Nigeria." In Andrew Reynolds (Ed.), *The Architecture of Democracy: Constitutional Design, Conflict Management, and Democracy*, pp. 400–28. Oxford University Press, 2002.

Than, Tin Maung Maung. "The Essential Tension: Democratization and the Unitary State in Myanmar (Burma)." *South East Asia Research* 12, no. 2 (2004): 187–212.

Viotti da Costa, Emilia. *The Brazilian Empire: Myths and Histories*. Chapel Hill: University of North Carolina Press, 2000.

7.3

JUAN LINZ, PRESIDENTIALISM, AND DEMOCRACY: A CRITICAL APPRAISAL

Scott Mainwaring and Matthew S. Shugart

Scott Mainwaring teaches political science and serves as director of the Helen Kellogg Institute for International Studies at the University of Notre Dame, and Matthew S. Shugart is a professor at the Graduate School of International Relations and Pacific Studies at the University of California, San Diego. Mainwaring has published extensively on democratization in Latin American countries, with a focus on democratic political institutions and political party systems, while Shugart's research has focused primarily on democratic political institutions in a number of different contexts. In this article, the authors reassess Juan Linz's arguments concerning presidential systems. While they agree with much of Linz's critique of presidentialism, they disagree with a number of points. According to Mainwaring and Shugart, presidential systems have failed not because of the composition of the systems themselves but because they have often been established in countries in which the propagation of democracy in any form would be difficult. They also believe that the legislative strength of presidents and the nature of political parties impact how presidential systems operate. Thus, to understand whether presidential systems undermine democracy, it is necessary to understand not only the powers of presidents, but also the context created by each country's political party system. With this in mind, students should carefully consider the relationship between institutional rules and the context of politics while reading this article. Specifically, how can the same institution, for example, presidentialism, operate differently in different contexts?

Since the 1960s Juan J. Linz has been one of the world's foremost contributors to our understanding of democracy, authoritarianism, and totalitarianism. Although many of his contributions have had a significant impact, few have been as far-reaching as his essay "Presidential or Parliamentary Democracy: Does It Make a Difference?," originally written in 1985. The essay argued that presidentialism is less likely than parliamentarism to sustain stable democratic regimes. It became a classic even in unpublished form. Among both policymakers and scholars it spawned a broad debate about the merits and especially the liabilities of presidential government. Now that the definitive version of the essay has appeared, we believe that a critical appraisal is timely. This task is especially important because Linz's arguments against presidentialism have gained widespread currency.

Scott Mainwaring and Matthew S. Shugart, "Juan Linz, Presidentialism, and Democracy: A Critical Appraisal," *Comparative Politics* 29, no. 4 (July 1997): 449–471.

This article critically assesses Linz's arguments about the perils of presidentialism. Although we agree with several of Linz's criticisms of presidentialism, we disagree that presidentialism is particularly oriented towards winner-takes-all results.[1] We argue that the superior record of parliamentary systems has rested partly on where parliamentary government has been implemented, and we claim that presidentialism has some advantages that partially offset its drawbacks. These advantages can be maximized by paying careful attention to differences among presidential systems. Other things being equal, presidentialism tends to function better where presidencies have weak legislative powers, parties are at least moderately disciplined, and party systems are not highly fragmented. Finally, we argue that switching from presidentialism to parliamentarism could exacerbate problems of governability in countries with undisciplined parties. Even if parliamentary government is more conducive to stable democracy, much rests on what kind of parliamentarism and presidentialism is implemented.[2]

By presidentialism we mean a regime in which, first, the president is always the chief executive and is elected by popular vote or, as in the U.S., by an electoral college with essentially no autonomy with respect to popular preferences and, second, the terms of office for the president and the assembly are fixed. Under pure presidentialism the president has the right to retain ministers of his or her choosing regardless of the composition of the congress.

* * *

A Critique of Linz's Argument

We agree with the main thrust of four of Linz's five basic criticisms of presidentialism. We concur that the issue of dual legitimacy is nettlesome in presidential systems, but we believe that his contrast between presidential and parliamentary systems is too stark. To a lesser degree than in presidential systems, conflicting claims to legitimacy also exist in parliamentary systems. Conflicts sometimes arise between the lower and upper houses of a bicameral legislature, each claiming to exercise legitimate power. If both houses have the power of confidence over the cabinet, the most likely outcome when the houses are controlled by different majorities is a compromise coalition cabinet. In this case dual legitimacy exists, not between executive and assembly, but between the two chambers of the assembly. This arrangement could be troublesome if the two chambers were controlled by opposed parties or blocs. In a few parliamentary systems, including Canada, Germany, and Japan, upper houses have significant powers over legislation but can not exercise a vote of no confidence against the government. In some the upper house can not be dissolved by the government. Then, there is a genuine dual legitimacy between the executive and part of the legislature. Thus, dual democratic legitimacy is not exclusively a problem of presidentialism, though it is more pronounced with it. A unicameral parliament would avoid the potential of dual legitimacy under parliamentarism, but it sacrifices the advantages of bicameralism, especially for large, federal, and plural countries.[3]

Another overlooked potential source of conflicting legitimacy in parliamentary republics is the role of the head of state, who is usually called "president" but tends to be elected by parliament. The constitutions of parliamentary republics usually give the president several powers that are—or may be, subject to constitutional interpretation—more than ceremonial. Examples include the president's exclusive discretion to dissolve parliament (Italy), the requirement of countersignatures of cabinet decrees (Italy), suspensory veto over legislation (Czech Republic, Slovakia), the power to decree new laws (Greece for some time after 1975), and appointments to high offices, sometimes (as in the Czech Republic and Slovakia) including ministries. Linz argues that the president in such systems "can play the role of adviser or arbiter by bringing party leaders together and facilitating the flow of information among them." He also notes that "no one in a presidential system is institutionally entitled to such a role." He is quite right that political systems often face moments when they need a "neutral" arbiter. However, for the position of head of state to be more than feckless it is necessary to make it "institutionally entitled" to other tasks as well. Linz correctly notes that, "if presidents in pure parliamentary republics were irrelevant, it would not make sense for politicians to put so much effort into electing their preferred candidate to the office." [4]

Paradoxically, the more authority the head of state is given, the greater is the potential for conflict, especially in newer democracies where roles have not yet been clearly defined by precedent. Hungary and especially Slovakia have had several constitutional crises involving the head of state, and in some Third World parliamentary republics such crises have at times been regime-threatening, as in Somalia (1961–68) and Pakistan. Politicians indeed care who holds the office, precisely because it has potential for applying brakes to the parliamentary majority. The office of the presidency may not be democratically legitimated via popular election, but it typically has a fixed term of office and a longer term than the parliament's. By praising the potential of the office in serving as arbiter, Linz implicitly acknowledges the Madisonian point that placing unchecked power in the hands of the assembly majority is not necessarily good. Again, the key is careful attention to the distribution of powers among the different political players who are involved in initiating or blocking policy.

We also agree that the rigidity of presidentialism, created by the fixed term of office, can be a liability, sometimes a serious one. With the fixed term it is difficult to get rid of unpopular or inept presidents without the system's breaking down, and it is constitutionally barred in many countries to reelect a good president. However, there is no reason why a presidential system must prohibit reelection. Provisions against reelection have been introduced primarily to reduce the president's incentives to abuse executive powers to secure reelection. Despite the potential for abuse, reelection can be permitted, and we believe it should be in countries where reliable institutions safeguard elections from egregious manipulation by incumbents.

Even if reelection is permitted, we are still left with the rigidity of fixed term lengths. One way of mitigating this problem is to shorten the presidential term so that if presidents lose support dramatically, they will not be in office for as long a time. Therefore, we believe that a four year term is usually preferable to the longer mandates that are common in Latin America.

The argument about the flexibility of replacing cabinets in parliamentary systems is two-edged. In a parliamentary system the prime minister's party can replace its leader or a coalition partner can withdraw its support and usher in a change of government short of the coup that might be the only way to remove a president who lacks support. We agree with Linz that cabinet instability need not lead to regime instability and can offer a safety valve. Yet crises in many failed parliamentary systems, including Somalia and Thailand, have come about precisely because of the difficulty of sustaining viable cabinets. Presidentialism raises the threshold for removing an executive; opponents must either wait out the term or else countenance undemocratic rule. There may be cases when this higher threshold for government change is desirable, as it could provide more predictability and stability to the policymaking process than the frequent dismantling and reconstructing of cabinets that afflict some parliamentary systems.

Theoretically, the problem of fixed terms could be remedied without adopting parliamentarism by permitting under certain conditions the calling of early elections. One way is to allow either the head of government or the assembly majority to demand early elections for both branches, as is the case under newly adopted Israeli rules. Such provisions represent a deviation from presidentialism, which is defined by its fixed terms. Nevertheless, as long as one branch can not dismiss the other without standing for reelection itself, the principle of separation of powers is still retained to an extent not present in any variant of parliamentarism.

We take issue with Linz's assertion that presidentialism induces more of a winner-takes-all approach to politics than does parliamentarism. As we see it, parliamentary systems do not afford an advantage on this point. The degree to which democracies promote winner-take-all rules depends mostly on the electoral and party system and on the federal or unitary nature of the system. Parliamentary systems with disciplined parties and a majority party offer the fewest checks on executive power, and hence promote a winner-takes-all approach more than presidential systems.[5] In Great Britain, for example, in the last two decades a party has often won a decisive majority of parliamentary seats despite winning well under 50 percent of the votes. Notwithstanding its lack of a decisive margin in popular votes, the party can control the entire executive and the legislature for a protracted period of time. It can even use its dissolution power strategically to renew its mandate for another five years by calling a new election before its current term ends.

Because of the combination of disciplined parties, single member plurality electoral districts, and the prime minister's ability to dissolve the parliament, Westminster systems provide a very weak legislative check on the premier. In principle, the MPs of the governing party control the cabinet, but in practice they usually support their own party's legislative initiatives regardless of the merits of particular proposals because their electoral fates are closely tied with that of the party leadership. As a norm, a disciplined majority party leaves the executive virtually unconstrained between elections.[6] Here, more than in any presidential system, the winner takes all. Given the majority of a single party in parliament, it is unlikely that a no confidence vote would prevail, so there is little or no opposition to check the government. Early elections occur not as a flexible mechanism to rid the country of an ineffective government, but at the discretion of a ruling majority using its dissolution power strategically to renew its mandate for another five years by calling a new election before its current term ends.[7]

Presidentialism is predicated upon a system of checks and balances. Such checks and balances usually inhibit winner-takes-all tendencies; indeed, they are designed precisely to limit the possibility that the winner would take all. If it loses the presidency, a party or coalition may still control congress, allowing it to block some presidential initiatives. If the president's own legislative powers are reactive only (a veto, but no decree powers), an opposition-controlled congress can be the prime mover in legislating, as it is in the United States and Costa Rica, the two longest standing presidential democracies. Controlling congress is not the biggest prize, and it usually does not enable a party or coalition to dictate policy, but it allows the party or coalition to establish parameters within which policy is made. It can be a big prize in its own right if the presidency has relatively weak legislative powers.

Moreover, compared to Westminster parliamentary systems, most presidential democracies offer greater prospects of dividing the cabinet among several parties. This practice, which is essentially unknown among the Westminster parliamentary democracies, is common in multiparty presidential systems. To get elected, presidents need to assemble a broad interparty coalition, either for the first round (if a plurality format obtains) or for the second (if a two round, absolute majority format obtains).

Generally, presidents allocate cabinet seats to parties other than their own in order to attract the support of these parties or, after elections, to reward them for such support. Dividing the cabinet in this manner allows losers in the presidential contest a piece of the pie. The norm in multiparty presidential systems is similar to that in multiparty parliamentary systems: a coalition governs, cabinet positions are divided among several parties, and the president typically must retain the support of these parties to govern effectively.

Thus, most parliamentary systems with single member district electoral systems have stronger winner-takes-all mechanisms than presidential systems. The combination of parliamentarism and a majority party specifically produces winner-takes-all results. This situation of extreme majoritarianism under parliamentarism is not uncommon; it is found throughout the Caribbean and some parts of the Third World. In fact, outside western Europe all parliamentary systems that have been continuously democratic from 1972 to 1994 have been based on the Westminster model (see Table 1). Thus, Linz is not right when he states that an absolute majority of seats for one party does not occur often in parliamentary systems.[8] In presidential systems with single member plurality districts, the party that does not win the presidency can control congress, thereby providing an important check on executive power.

Linz's fourth argument, that the style of presidential politics is less favorable to democracy than the style of parliamentary politics, rests in part on his view that presidentialism induces a winner-takes-all logic. We have already expressed our skepticism about this claim. We agree that the predominant style of politics differs somewhat between presidential and parliamentary systems, but we would place greater emphasis on differences of style that stem from constitutional design and the nature of the party system.

Finally, we agree with Linz that presidentialism is more conducive than parliamentarism to the election of a political outsider as head of government and that this process can entail serious problems. But in presidential democracies that have more institutionalized party systems the election of political outsiders is the exception. Costa Rica, Uruguay, Colombia, and Venezuela have not elected an outsider president in recent decades, unless one counts Rafael Caldera of Venezuela in his latest incarnation (1993). Argentina last elected an outsider president in 1945, when Perón had not yet built a party. In Chile political outsiders won the presidential campaigns of 1952 and 1958, but they were exceptions rather than the norm. The most notable recent cases of elections of political outsiders, Fernando Collor de Mello in Brazil (1989) and Alberto Fujimori in Peru (1990), owe much to the unraveling of the party systems in both countries and in Fujimori's case also to the majority run-off system that encouraged widespread party system fragmentation in the first round.

Assessing the Record of Presidentialism

Linz correctly states that most long established democracies have parliamentary systems. Presidentialism is poorly represented among long established democracies. This fact is apparent in Table 1, which lists countries that have a long, continuous democratic record according to the criteria of Freedom House.

Freedom House has been rating countries on a scale of 1 to 7 (with 1 being best) on political rights and civil rights since 1972. Table 1 lists all thirty-three countries that were continuously democratic from 1972 to 1994. We considered a country continuously democratic if it had an average score of 3 or better on political rights throughout this period.[9] Additionally, the scores for both political and civil rights needed to be 4 or better in every annual Freedom House survey for a country to be considered continuously democratic.

Table 1 Independent Countries That Were Continuously Democratic, 1972–1994

Inc. level	Pop. size	Parliamentary	Presidential	Other
Low/lower-middle	Micro			
	Small	Jamaica Mauritius	Costa Rica	
	Medium/large		Colombia Dominican Republic	
Upper-middle	Micro	Nauru Barbados Malta		
	Small	Botswana Trinidad and Tobago		
	Medium/large		Venezuela	
Upper	Micro	Luxembourg		Iceland
	Small	Ireland New Zealand Norway	Cyprus	
	Medium/large	Australia Belgium Canada Denmark Germany Israel Italy Japan Netherlands Sweden United Kingdom	United States	Austria Finland France Switzerland

Notes: All regimes in the "other" column are premier-presidential, except for Switzerland.
Countries that have become independent from Britain or a British Commonwealth state since 1945: Jamaica, Mauritius, Nauru, Barbados, Malta, Botswana, Trinidad and Tobago, Cyprus, Israel.

Of the thirty-three long established democracies, only six are presidential despite the prevalence of presidentialism in many parts of the globe. Twenty-two are parliamentary, and five fall into the "other" category. However, the superior record of parliamentarism is in part an artifact of where it has been implemented.

Table 1 provides information on three other issues that may play a role in a society's likelihood of sustaining democracy: income level, population size, and British colonial heritage. It is widely recognized that a relatively high income level is an important background condition for democracy.[10] In classifying countries by income levels, we followed the guidelines of the World Bank's *World Development Report 1993*: low is under \$635 per capita GNP; lower middle is \$636 to \$2,555; upper middle is

$2,556 to $7,910; and upper is above $7,911. We collapsed the bottom two categories. Table 2 summarizes the income categories of countries in Table 1.

Most of these long established democracies (twenty-eight of thirty-three) are in upper middle or upper income countries. But among the low to lower middle income countries there are actually more presidential (three) than parliamentary (two) systems. Fifteen of the parliamentary democracies are found in Europe or other high income countries such as Canada, Israel, and Japan. It is likely that these countries would have been democratic between 1972 and 1994 had they had presidential constitutions. So some of the success of parliamentary democracy is accidental: in part because of the evolution of constitutional monarchies into democracies, the region of the world that democratized and industrialized first is overwhelmingly populated with parliamentary systems.

Very small countries may have an advantage in democratic stability because they typically have relatively homogeneous populations in ethnic, religious, and linguistic terms, thereby attenuating potential sources of political conflict. We classified countries as micro (population under 500,000), small (500,000 to 5,000,000), and medium to large (over 5,000,000), using 1994 population data. Table 3 groups our thirty-three long established democracies by population size. Here, too, parliamentary systems enjoy an advantage. None of the five micronations with long established democracies has a presidential system.

The strong correlation between British colonial heritage and democracy has been widely recognized. Reasons for this association need not concern us here, but possibilities mentioned in the literature include the tendency to train civil servants, the governmental practices and institutions (which include but can not be reduced to parliamentarism) created by the British, and the lack of control of local landed elites over the colonial state.[11] Nine of the thirty-three long established democracies had British colonial experience. Among them, eight are parliamentary and one is presidential. Here, too, background conditions have been more favorable to parliamentary systems.

Table 2 Income Levels of Continuous Democracies, 1972–1994 (number of countries in each category)

Per Capita GNP in US $	Parliamentary	Presidential	Other
0–2,555	2	3	0
2,556–7,910	5	1	0
Over 7,911	15	2	5
Total	22	6	5

Table 3 Population Size of Continuous Democracies, 1972–1994 (number of countries in each category)

Population	Parliamentary	Presidential	Other
Under 500,000	4	0	1
500,000 to 5,000,000	7	2	0
Over 5,000,000	11	4	5
Total	22	6	5

Table 4 Independent Countries That Were Democratic for at Least Ten Years (But Less Than Twenty-Three) as of 1994

Inc. level	Pop. size	Parliamentary	Presidential	Other
Low/lower-middle	Micro	Belize (1981) Dominica (1978) Kiribati (1979) St. Lucia (1979) St. Vincent (1979) Solomons (1978) Tuvalu (1978) Vanuatu (1978)		
	Small	Papua New Guinea (1975)		
	Medium/large	India (1979)	Bolivia (1982) Brazil (1985) Ecuador (1979) El Salvador (1985) Honduras (1980)	
Middle	Micro	Antigua and Barbuda (1981) Grenada (1985) St. Kitts-Nevis (1983)		
	Small			
	Medium/large	Greece (1974)	Argentina (1983) Urugauy (1985)	Portugal[1] (1976)
Upper	Micro	Bahamas (1973)		
	Small			
	Medium/large	Spain (1977)		

Notes: Numbers in parenthese give the date when the transition to democracy took place or the date of independence for former colonies that were not independent as of 1972.
Countries that have become independent from Britain or a British Commonwealth state since 1945: Belize, Dominica, Kiribati, St. Lucia, St. Vincent, Solomons, Tuvalu, Vanuatu, Papua New Guinea, India, Antigua and Barbuda, Grenada, St. Kitts-Nevis, Bahamas.
[1] Portugal has a premier-presidential system.

It is not our purpose here to analyze the contributions of these factors to democracy; rather, we wanted to see if these factors correlated with regime type. If a background condition that is conducive to democracy is correlated with parliamentarism, then the superior record of parliamentarism may be more a product of the background condition than the regime type.

Table 4 shows twenty-four additional countries that had been continuously democratic by the same criteria used in Table 1, only for a shorter time period (at least ten years). Together, Tables 1 and 4 give us a complete look at contemporary democracies that have lasted at least ten years.

There are three striking facts about the additional countries in Table 4. First, they include a large number of microstates that became independent from Britain in the 1970s and 1980s, and all of them are parliamentary. All seven presidential democracies but only three of the sixteen parliamentary democracies are in medium to large countries (see Table 5). All sixteen of the democracies listed in Tables 1 and 4 with populations under one-half million (mostly island nations) are parliamentary, as are eight of ten democracies with populations between one-half and five million. In contrast, no presidential systems are in microstates, and many are in exceptionally large countries, such as Argentina, Brazil, and the United States.

Second, with Table 4 the number of presidential democracies increases substantially. Most are in the lower and lower middle income categories, and all are in Latin America. Table 6 summarizes the income status of the newer democracies listed in Table 4. Clearly, not all of parliamentarism's advantage stems from the advanced industrial states. Even in the lower to upper middle income categories, there are more parliamentary systems (twenty-one if we combine Tables 1 and 4, compared to eleven presidential systems). However, every one of the parliamentary democracies outside of the high income category is a former British colony. The only other democracies in these income categories are presidential, and all but Cyprus are in Latin America.

Thus, if the obstacles of lower income (or other factors not considered here) in Latin America continue to cause problems for the consolidation of democracy, the number of presidential breakdowns could be large once again in the future. More optimistically, if Latin American democracies achieve greater success in consolidating themselves this time around, the number of long established presidential democracies will grow substantially in the future.

Similarly, if British colonial heritage and small population size are conducive to democracy, parliamentarism has a built-in advantage simply because Britain colonized many small island territories. As a rule, British colonies had local self-government, always on the parliamentary model, before independence.[12] Further, if other aspects of Latin American societies (such as extreme inequality across classes or regions) are inimical to stable democracy, then presidentialism has a built-in disadvantage.

Table 5 Population Size of Continuous Democracies, 1985–1994 (number of countries in each category)

Population	Parliamentary	Presidential	Other
Under 500,000	12	0	0
500,000 to 5,000,000	1	0	0
Over 5,000,000	3	7	1
Total	16	7	1

Table 6 Income Levels of Continuous Democracies, 1985–1994 (number of countries in each category)

Per Capita GNP in US$	Parliamentary	Presidential	Other
0–2,555	12	0	0
2,556–7,910	4	5	1
Over 7,911	2	2	0
Total	16	7	1

In sum, presidentialism is more likely to be adopted in Latin America and in Africa than in other parts of the world, and these parts of the world have had more formidable obstacles to democracy regardless of the form of government. In contrast, parliamentarism has been the regime form of choice in most of Europe and in former British colonies (a large percentage of which are microstates), where conditions for democracy have generally been more favorable. Thus, the correlation between parliamentarism and democratic success is in part a product of where it has been implemented.

Advantages of Presidential Systems

Presidential systems afford some attractive features that can be maximized through careful attention to constitutional design. These advantages partially offset the liabilities of presidentialism.

Greater Choice for Voters

Competing claims to legitimacy are the flipside of one advantage. The direct election of the chief executive gives the voters two electoral choices instead of one—assuming unicameralism, for the sake of simplicity of argument. Having both executive and legislative elections gives voters a freer range of choices. Voters can support one party or candidate at the legislative level but another for the head of government.

Electoral Accountability and Identification

Presidentialism affords some advantages for accountability and identifiability. Electoral accountability describes the degree and means by which elected policymakers are electorally responsible to citizens, while identifiability refers to voters' ability to make an informed choice prior to elections based on their ability to assess the likely range of postelection governments.

The more straightforward the connection between the choices made by the electorate at the ballot box and the expectations to which policymakers are held can be made, the greater electoral accountability is. For maximizing direct accountability between voters and elected officials, presidentialism is superior to parliamentarism in multiparty contexts because the chief executive is directly chosen by popular vote. Presidents (if eligible for reelection) or their parties can be judged by voters in subsequent elections. Having both an executive and an assembly allows the presidential election to be structured so as to maximize accountability and the assembly election so as to permit broad representation.

One objection to presidentialism's claim to superior electoral accountability is that in most presidential systems presidents may not be reelected immediately, if at all. The electoral incentive for the president to remain responsive to voters is weakened in these countries, and electoral accountability suffers. Bans on reelection are deficiencies of most presidential systems, but not of presidentialism as a regime type. Direct accountability to the electorate exists in some presidential systems, and it is always possible under presidential government. If, as is often the case, the constitution bans immediate reelection but allows subsequent reelection, presidents who aspire to regain their office have a strong incentive to be responsive to voters and thereby face a mechanism of electoral accountability. Only if presidents can never be reelected and will become secondary (or non) players in national and party politics after their terms are incentives for accountability via popular election dramatically weakened. Even where immediate reelection is banned, voters can still directly hold the president's party accountable.

Under parliamentarism, with a deeply fragmented party system the lack of direct elections for the executive inevitably weakens electoral accountability, for a citizen can not be sure how to vote for or against a particular potential head of government. In multiparty parliamentary systems, even if a citizen has a clear notion of which parties should be held responsible for the shortcomings of a government, it is often not clear whether voting for a certain party will increase the likelihood of excluding a party from the governing coalition. Governments often change between elections, and even after an election parties that lose seats are frequently invited to join governing coalitions.

Strom used the term "identifiability" to denote the degree to which the possible alternative executive-controlling coalitions were discernible to voters before an election.[13] Identifiability is high when voters can assess the competitors for control of the executive and can make a straightforward logical connection between their preferred candidate or party and their optimal vote. Identifiability is low when voters can not predict easily what the effect of their vote will be in terms of the composition of the executive, either because postelection negotiations will determine the nature of the executive, as occurs in multiparty parliamentary systems, or because a large field of contenders for a single office makes it difficult to discern where a vote may be "wasted" and whether voting for a "lesser-of-evils" might be an optimal strategy.

Strom's indicator of "identifiability" runs from 0 to 1, with 1 indicating that in 100 percent of a given nation's post-World War II elections the resulting government was identifiable as a likely result of the election at the time voters went to the polls. The average of the sample of parliamentary nations in Western Europe from 1945 until 1987 is .39, that is, most of the time voters could not know for which government they were voting. Yet under a parliamentary regime voting for an MP or a party list is the only way voters can influence the choice of executive. In some parliamentary systems, such as Belgium (.10), Israel (.14), [a]nd Italy (.12), a voter could rarely predict the impact of a vote in parliamentary elections on the formation of the executive. The formation of the executive is the result of parliamentary negotiations among many participants. Therefore, it is virtually impossible for the voter, to foresee how best to support a particular executive.

In presidential systems with a plurality one round format, identifiability is likely to approach 1.00 in most cases because voters cast ballots for the executive and the number of significant competitors is likely to be small. Systems in which majority run-off is used to elect the president are different, as three or more candidates may be regarded prior to the first round as serious contenders. When plurality is used to elect the president and when congressional and presidential elections are held concurrently, the norm is for "serious" competition to be restricted to two candidates even when there is multiparty competition in congressional elections. Especially when the electoral method is not majority run-off, presidentialism tends to encourage coalition building before elections, thus clarifying the basic policy options being presented to voters in executive elections and simplifying the voting calculus.

Linz has responded to the argument that presidentialism engenders greater identifiability by arguing that voters in most parliamentary systems can indeed identify the likely prime ministers and cabinet ministers.[14] By the time individuals approach leadership status, they are well known to voters. While his rejoinder is valid on its face, Linz is using the term "identifiability" in a different manner from Strom or us. He is speaking of voters' ability to identify personnel rather than government teams, which, as we have noted, may not be at all identifiable.

Congressional Independence in Legislative Matters

Because representatives in a presidential system can act on legislation without worrying about immediate consequences for the survival of the government, issues can be considered on their merits rather than as matters of "confidence" in the leadership of the ruling party or coalition. In this specific sense, assembly members exercise independent judgment on legislative matters. Of course, this independence of the assembly from the executive can generate the problem of immobilism. This legislative independence is particularly problematic with highly fragmented multiparty systems, where presidents' parties typically are in the minority and legislative deadlock more easily ensues. However, where presidents enjoy substantial assembly support, congressional opposition to executive initiatives can promote consensus building and can avoid the passage of ill-considered legislation simply to prevent a crisis of confidence. The immobilism feared by presidentialism's detractors is the flip side of the checks and balances desired by the United States' founding fathers.

Congressional independence can encourage broad coalition building because even a majority president is not guaranteed the unreserved support of partisans in congress. In contrast, when a prime minister's party enjoys a majority, parliamentary systems exhibit highly majoritarian characteristics. Even a party with less than a majority of votes can rule almost unchecked if the electoral system "manufactures" a majority of seats for the party. The incentive not to jeopardize the survival of the government pressures members of parliament whose parties hold executive office not to buck cabinet directives. Thus, presidentialism is arguably better able than parliamentarism to combine the independence of legislators with an accountable and identifiable executive. If one desires the consensual and often painstaking task of coalition building to be undertaken on each major legislative initiative, rather than only on the formation of a government, then presidentialism has an advantage.

* * *

Switching from Presidential to Parliamentary Government: A Caution

Convinced that parliamentary systems are more likely to sustain stable democracy, Linz implicitly advocates switching to parliamentary government. We are less than sanguine about the results of shifting to parliamentary government in countries with undisciplined parties. Undisciplined parties create daunting problems in parliamentary systems.[15] In countries with undisciplined parties, switching to parliamentary government could exacerbate problems of governability and instability unless party and electoral legislation was simultaneously changed to promote greater discipline.

In parliamentary systems, the government depends on the ongoing confidence of the assembly. Where individual assembly members act as free agents, unfettered by party ties, the governmental majorities that were carefully crafted in postelection negotiations easily dissipate. Free to vote as they please, individual legislators abandon the government when it is politically expedient to do so. Under these conditions, the classic Achilles heel of some parliamentary systems, frequent cabinet changes, is likely to be a problem.

Linz counterargues that presidentialism has contributed to party weakness in some Latin American countries, so that switching to parliamentary government should strengthen parties by removing one of the causes of party weakness. Moreover, analysts might expect that the mechanism of confidence votes would itself promote party discipline, since remaining in office would hinge upon party discipline. We do not dismiss these claims, but in the short term switching to parliamentary government without effecting parallel changes to encourage greater party discipline could prove problematic.

Any switch to parliamentary government, therefore, would need to carefully design a panoply of institutions to increase the likelihood that it would function well. In presidential and parliamentary systems alike, institutional combinations are of paramount importance.[16]

Conclusion

While we greatly admire Linz's seminal contribution and agree with parts of it, we believe that he understated the importance of differences among constitutional and institutional designs within the broad category of presidential systems and in doing so overstated the extent to which presidentialism is inherently flawed, regardless of constitutional and institutional arrangements. Presidential systems can be designed to function more effectively than they usually have. We have argued that providing the president with limited legislative power, encouraging the formation of parties that are reasonably disciplined in the legislature, and preventing extreme fragmentation of the party system enhance the viability of presidentialism. Linz clearly recognizes that not any kind of parliamentarism will do. We make the same point about presidentialism.

Under some conditions the perils of presidentialism can be attenuated, a point that Linz underplays. It is important to pay attention to factors that can mitigate the problems of presidentialism because it may be politically more feasible to modify presidential systems than to switch to parliamentary government.

We have also argued that presidentialism, particularly if it is carefully designed, has some advantages over parliamentarism. In our view, Linz does not sufficiently consider this point. Moreover, on one key issue—the alleged winner-takes-all nature of presidentialism—we question Linz's argument. The sum effect of our arguments is to call more attention to institutional combinations and constitutional designs and to suggest that the advantages of parliamentarism may not be as pronounced as Linz argued. Nevertheless, we share the consensus that his pathbreaking article was one of the most important scholarly contributions of the past decade and deserves the ample attention among scholars and policymakers that it has already received.

Notes

We are grateful to Michael Coppedge, Steve Levitsky, Arend Lijphart, Timothy Scully, and two anonymous reviewers for helpful criticisms of earlier drafts of this article.

1. We follow Lijphart's understanding of a Westminster (British) style democracy. Arend Lijphart, *Democracies: Patterns of Majoritarian and Consensus Government in Twenty-One Countries* (New Haven: Yale University Press, 1984), esp. pp. 1–20. For our purposes, the most important features of a Westminster democracy are single party majority cabinets, disciplined parties, something approaching a two party system in the legislature, and plurality single member electoral districts.
2. See Adam Przeworski et al., "What Makes Democracies Endure?", *Journal of Democracy*, 7 (January 1996), 39–55.
3. Lijphart, ch. 6.
4. Linz, "Presidential or Parliamentary Democracy," pp. 47, 46.
5. Donald L. Horowitz, "Comparing Democratic Systems," *Journal of Democracy*, 1 (Fall 1990), 73–79; and George Tsebelis, "Decision Making in Political Systems: Veto Players in Presidentialism, Parliamentarism, Multicameralism and Multipartyism," *British Journal of Political Science*, 25 (1995), 289–325.
6. Assuming that the party remains united. If it does not, it may oust its leader and change the prime minister, as happened to Margaret Thatcher in Britain and Brian Mulroney in Canada. However, such intraparty leadership crises are the exception in majoritarian (Westminster) parliamentary systems.
7. A possible exception in Westminster systems is occasional minority government, which is more common than coalition government in such systems. Even then, the government is as likely to call early elections to attempt to convert its plurality into a majority as it is in response to a vote of no confidence.

8. Linz, "Presidential or Parliamentary Democracy," p. 15.
9. Using an average of 3 on both measures would have eliminated three countries (India and Colombia in Table 1 and Vanuatu in Table 3) that we consider basically democratic but that have had problems with protecting civil rights, partly because of a fight against violent groups.
10. Robert A. Dahl, *Polyarchy: Participation and Opposition* (New Haven: Yale University Press, 1973), pp. 62–80; Kenneth Bollen, "Political Democracy and the Timing of Development," *American Sociological Review*, 44 (August 1979), 572–87; Larry Diamond, "Economic Development and Democracy Reconsidered," in Gary Marks and Larry Diamond, eds., *Reexamining Democracy: Essays in Honor of Seymour Martin Lipset* (Newbury Park: SAGE, 1992), pp. 93–139; Seymour Martin Lipset et al., "A Comparative Analysis of the Social Requisites of Democracy," *International Social Science Journal*, 45 (May 1993), 155–75.
11. Larry Diamond, "Introduction: Persistence, Erosion, Breakdown, and Renewal," in Larry Diamond, Juan J. Linz, and Seymour Martin Lipset, eds., *Democracy in Developing Countries: Asia* (Boulder: Lynne Rienner, 1989); Myron Weiner, "Empirical Democratic Theory," in Myron Weiner and Ergun Özbudun, eds., *Competitive Elections in Developing Countries* (Washington, D.C.: American Enterprise Institute, 1987); Dietrich Rueschemeyer, Evelyne Huber Stephens, and John D. Stephens, *Capitalist Development and Democracy* (Chicago: University of Chicago Press, 1992).
12. Some British colonies later adopted presidential systems and did not become (or remain) democratic. However, in many cases democracy was ended (if it ever got underway) by a coup carried out by the prime minister and his associates. Not presidential democracies, but parliamentary proto-democracies broke down. Typical was the Seychelles. The failure of most of these countries to evolve back into democracy can not be attributed to presidentialism.
13. Kaare Strom, *Minority Government and Majority Rule* (Cambridge: Cambridge University Press, 1990).
14. Linz, "Presidential or Parliamentary Democracy," pp. 10–14.
15. Giovanni Sartori, "Neither Presidentialism nor Parliamentarism,"' in Linz and Valenzuela, eds., [*The Failure of Presidential Democracy* (Baltimore, MD: Johns Hopkins University Press, 1994), p. 115.]
16. James W. Ceaser, "In Defense of Separation of Powers," in Robert A. Goldwin and Art Kaufman, eds., *Separation of Powers: Does It Still Work?* (Washington, D.C.: American Enterprise Institute, 1986), pp. 168–93.

Chapter 8

WHAT IS THE IMPORTANCE OF THE NATION-STATE IN AN AGE OF GLOBALIZATION?

As discussed in chapter 1 of this volume, the postwar decades of the 1950s and 1960s witnessed a widely heralded "revolution" in political science, and especially in comparative politics, that transformed the field into an explanatory enterprise that conformed to the canons of scientific inquiry.[1] Before that revolution, what was being described were the constitutionally designated structures of government, in other words, the state. The societal context in which this state operated was consigned to the responsibilities of other social sciences such as sociology. Indeed, many leading departments in the field, including Harvard University's, eschewed any pretense at doing science and labeled themselves departments of government.

Yet political phenomena do not occur in a cultural vacuum, and the modern approach to political science encouraged a discovery of the social context in which states operate to the point that, as Theda Skocpol has noted, the state was relegated to the role of an arena in which interests and social groups competed to influence policy.[2] Thus, Western politics became associated with the concept of *pluralism,* a political process in which multiple elites and their interests compete to influence policy but no one interest gets everything it wants. In an extreme version of this perspective—group theory—policy was conceptualized not as the creation of an autonomous state, but rather as the impersonal outcome of this interaction of interests. From this perspective, the state is not independent; instead, it is reduced to the status of just another group.[3] The cascading relevance of emerging, less-developed countries also contributed to the growing tendency to look past the constitutionally designated state in the modern explanatory mode of political science. As younger scholars confronted countries in which the Western concept of the state or its essential counterparts simply did not exist, they forced a reorientation of the focus of political inquiry.

In a now classic essay, Gabriel Almond, borrowing heavily from sociological and anthropological theory, directed students of these less-developed countries to the functions that must be universally performed, including interest articulation and aggregation, political communication, and rulemaking, regardless of a country's political structures (or lack thereof).* This integration of formerly ignored social and cultural factors into political analysis constituted a widely acclaimed conceptual framework for the analysis of any country—developed or less-developed—known as functional analysis.

* Gabriel Almond, "A Developmental Approach to Political Systems," in *The Politics of the Developing Areas,* eds. G. Almond and James Coleman (Princeton, N.J.: Princeton University Press, 1960), 1–63.

The displacement of the traditional objects of political analysis, the institutions of the state, by indiscriminant borrowing of concepts (such as the functions in Almond's framework) from sociology and anthropology facilitated the increasingly popular analysis of less-developed and less-institutionalized nations. However, this sociological framework failed to produce rigorously testable propositions despite the best efforts of the leading scholars in comparative politics; the inherent flaws in the logic of functional analysis have been thoroughly discussed elsewhere.[4]

Another emerging trend in the field of comparative politics that contributed to a declining interest in the nation-state is a focus on globalization. This trend appears to have grown out of the almost self-evident fact that in this age of instant communication and world travel, national economies are not mutually isolated. Rather, they are part of what Immanuel Wallerstein calls "the capitalist world economy." [5] Samuel Huntington and others have identified this as the crisis of the state, or the inability of nation-states to address issues generated outside the realm of their governments. This state failure then leads to the dissatisfaction of a state's democratic public.[6] Readings 8.1 and 8.2 by Peter Evans and Dani Rodrik, respectively, address the question of the relevance of the state in an era of increasing globalization.

The assault on the relevance of the nation-state comes from two directions. On the one hand, the post–World War II era has witnessed the emergence of subcultural movements, or the refusal of culturally or ethnically defined groups to assimilate within the broader national culture. The goals of such groups may range from the desire for more authority and autonomy, as is the case with the Scottish nationalists in Britain, to actual secession from the nation-state, as is the case with the Basque separatists in Spain or the militant Québécois in Canada.

On the other hand, this same era has witnessed a growing awareness of international interdependence and the drive, especially among elites, to establish pan-national political institutions to replace the sovereign nation-state. Clearly, however, the state—with its legitimate status as policymaker and its monopoly on the legitimate use of force—has a far more autonomous status in the making and implementing of policy than has been suggested by the simplistic group theorists (who reject the state's independent role in making policy) and the cultural determinists (who argue that the state merely reflects the inputs from its society). As Eric Nordlinger has posited, the state is even more autonomous of public opinion than democratic theory would have allowed. And so scholars continue to disagree as to the extent to which globalization entails the diminution of the sovereignty and power of the nation-state. Evans's and Rodrik's essays in this chapter offer a skeptical examination of that proposition.

Notes

1. Roy Macridis, *The Study of Comparative Government* (New York: Random House, 1955). Harry Eckstein, "A Perspective on Comparative Politics, Past and Present," in *Comparative Politics: A Reader,* eds. Harry Eckstein and David Apter (New York: Free Press of Glencoe, 1963), 3–31; and Lawrence Mayer, *Redefining Comparative Politics* (Newbury Park, Calif.: SAGE Publications, Inc., 1989), 7–26.
2. Theda Skocpol, "Bringing the State Back In," *Items* 36, nos. 1 and 2 (June 1982).
3. Earl Latham, "The Group Basis of Politics: Notes for a Theory," in *Pressure Groups in American Politics,* ed. H. R. Mahoud (New York: Charles Scribner and Sons, 1967); and David Truman, *The Governmental Process* (New York: Knopf, 1951).
4. A. James Gregor, "Political Science and the Use of Functional Analysis," *American Political Science Review* 62, no. 2 (June 1968); Karl Hempel, "The Logic of Functional Analysis," in *Readings in the Philosophy of the So-*

cial Sciences, ed. May Brodbeck (New York: Macmillan, 1968); and Lawrence Mayer, *Comparative Political Inquiry* (Homewood, Ill.: Dorsey Press, 1972), 143–161.

5. Immanuel Wallerstein, *The Modern World System: Capitalist Agriculture and the Origins of the European World Economy in the Sixteenth Century* (New York: Academic Press, 1974).
6. Michel Crozier, Samuel Huntington, and Joji Watanuki, *The Crisis of Democracy* (New York: New York University Press, 1975).

8.1

THE ECLIPSE OF THE STATE? REFLECTIONS ON STATENESS IN AN ERA OF GLOBALIZATION

Peter B. Evans

Peter Evans, professor of sociology at the University of California, Berkeley, and a recognized authority on the modernization of third-world nations, is known as an outspoken skeptic in regard to explaining underdevelopment in terms of Western exploitation and expands this skepticism to the widely discussed cliché about the demise of the salience of the nation-state. This essay analyzes the now-popular assertion that globalization has rendered nation-states increasingly powerless to manage policymaking, their economies, and the unique interests of their publics. Evans asks the question, "What is the actual role of the state in this global economy?" Specifically, to what extent can a nation-state manage its own economic well-being independent of competing states in a world economic system? As with Dani Rodrik's selection (see reading 8.2), Evans finds that interactions between the global order and domestic policy are more complex than proponents of the more extreme views of globalization, which posit the virtual irrelevance of the nation-state, would have us believe. Both the functioning of the world economic system and the impact of civil society—the increasing importance of subnational levels of association—require an increasingly competent nation-state. Subsequently, Evans finds the reports of the supposed demise of the state exaggerated, raising questions about the actual role of the state. To what extent are states able to act independently of worldwide economic forces? Can one simply say that a state's options are circumscribed by international forces to a degree? Can students name any economic policies made independently of such pan-national forces?

J. P. Nettl's classic 1968 article on the state aimed to convince his fellow social scientists that "the thing exists and no amount of conceptual restructuring can dissolve it." [1] Analysis of the state was "not much in vogue," as Nettl put it, and he considered this an intellectual aberration. He was convinced that "stateness"—the institutional centrality of the state—varied in important ways among nations, and that political behavior and institutions could be understood only if the state were brought back into the center of political analysis. The three decades since have thoroughly vindicated Nettl. Issues of stateness regained and retained the kind of centrality that he argued they should have. The debate that he helped revive continues unabated.

Peter B. Evans, "The Eclipse of the State? Reflections on Stateness in an Era of Globalization," *World Politics* 50, no. 1 (October 1997): 62–87.

While Nettl has been vindicated, the form and content of his vindication are full of ironies. The spread of interest in the state to economics, a discipline almost completely ignored in Nettl's article,[2] has been central to the revival of debate. In part because of this disciplinary shift, the stakes are defined differently. For Nettl, the alternatives to "stateness" were systems of public authority in which other kinds of institutions (parties in Britain, the law and legal institutions in the United States) were salient. Current debates are less about the form of public institutions than about the extent to which private power can (or should) be checked by public authority. Reinvigorated political faith in the efficacy of markets combined with a rediscovery of civil society creates a charismatic set of substitutes for public institutions and a corresponding set of arguments for the "eclipse of the state."

Changing theoretical perspectives cannot be separated from real historical changes in the position of the state. In the brief decades since Nettl wrote, the demands on the state have burgeoned. In the OECD countries demographically driven increases in transfer payments have resulted in a doubling of government expenditures as a proportion of GDP. In developing countries the desire for more rapid economic development produced a similar expansion. Lagging development of political and administrative institutions resulted in an ominous "capacity gap." In some parts of the developing world, most dramatically Africa, real eclipses of the state, in the sense of full-blown institutional collapse, took place. Even where there was no threat of collapse, a worrisome erosion of public institutional capacity seemed to be under way. It was much harder to ignore the state in the 1990s than it was in the 1960s.

Perhaps most ironic, from the perspective of Nettl's analysis, is how changes in the international arena have affected "stateness." For Nettl, the state's role vis-à-vis the international system was "invariant," reinforcing stateness even when domestic institutions denied it.[3] Three decades later the international arena is viewed very differently. The collapse of the old bipolar world has diminished the power of statecentric political and military rivalries to dominate international relations. Simultaneously, the growth of opportunities for transnational economic gains has laid the foundation for a new series of arguments about why states are anachronisms. According to these arguments, the intensified development of economic transactions that cross national boundaries has undermined the power of the state, leaving it marginalized as an economic actor. The arena that Nettl saw as securing stateness is now seen as transcending the power of the nation-state.

Changes in the global ideological climate are as crucial as new flows of money and goods, and Nettl's analysis does anticipate a key aspect of those changes. For Nettl, England was the "stateless society *par excellence*" and "an American sociopolitical self-examination simply leaves no room for any valid notion of the state."[4] Thus, the relative neglect of the concept of the state during the twenty-five years preceding his article was a logical consequence of the "shift of the center of gravity of social science to the United States."[5] Today, the untrammeled hegemony of Anglo-American ideological premises is one of the most salient forces shaping the specific character of the current global economy, including the extent to which globalization is viewed as entailing the eclipse of the state.

In this environment pursuing Nettl's agenda requires a different starting point. Statelessness can no longer be treated simply as a feature of Anglo-American political culture. It must be dealt with as a dominant global ideology and potential institutional reality. Therefore, the question of whether the eclipse of the state is likely and, if so, what the consequences of such an institutional shift would be, takes precedence. The trick is to deal with the question of eclipse seriously without taking a positive answer for granted.

I will argue that while eclipse is a possibility, it is not a likely one. What the discourse of eclipse has done is to make responses to a genuine crisis of state capacity unrelentingly negative and defensive. The danger is not that states will end up as marginal institutions but that meaner, more repressive ways of organizing the state's role will be accepted as the only way of avoiding the collapse of public institutions. Preoccupation with eclipse cripples consideration of positive possibilities for working to increase states' capacity so that they can more effectively meet the new demands that confront them. The goal should be to work back toward something closer to Nettl's original agenda of comparing different kinds of "stateness" and their consequences, this time with more explicit attention to the effects of globalization.

I begin by looking at the impact of globalization on stateness and arguing that the structural logic of globalization and the recent history of the global economy can then be read as providing rationales for "high stateness" as well as "low stateness." That I will argue that the absence of a clear logic connecting economic globalization to low stateness makes the normative and ideological side of the global order a key determinant of how globalization affects stateness. I will then move from globalization to a discussion of current theoretical perspectives on stateness, arguing that these perspectives are both sources of insight into the nature of the contemporary global order and influential shapers of the political and ideological face of that order. Finally, I conclude with a discussion of what this analysis implies for future forms of stateness.

Globalization and the Role of the State

"Diminished," "defective," and "hollow" were typical adjectives applied to the contemporary state in a recent special issue of *Daedalus*.[6] Globalization is not the only reason for the perception that "state authority has leaked away, upwards, sidewards, and downwards" and in some matters "just evaporated," [7] but it is a central one. The effects of globalization flow through two interconnected but distinct channels. The increasing weight and changing character of transnational economic relations over the course of the last three decades have created a new, more constraining context for state action. The political effect of these structural changes has been channeled by the growing global hegemony of Anglo-American ideology.

The New Global Political Economy

Nettl's concluding assertion that "[t]here remains only the one constant—the invariant development of stateness for each national actor in the international field" has been inverted.[8] Now the presumed invariant is the international arena's negative effect on stateness. As wealth and power are increasingly generated by private transactions that take place across the borders of states rather than within them, it has become harder to sustain the image of states as the preeminent actors at the global level. No one questions that the traditional Waltzian logic of competing "national interests" continues to drive the "interstate system," [9] but the muted great power struggles of the post-bipolar world leave international relations increasingly contaminated and often overshadowed by the private logic of the global economy. Nettl likened the international arena to a "society" in which states were the "people," but in the current global order the unique political status of states must be balanced against the fact that the most economically empowered "citizens" of the international arena are transnational corporations (TNCs).[10]

The growing relative weight of transactions and organizational connections that cross national boundaries is the cornerstone of globalization. Exports and imports growing more than one and a half times faster than domestic transactions around the world and a doubling of the proportion of exports to GDP in the OECD countries are just the beginning. Foreign direct investment has been growing three times as fast as trade, and other sorts of transnational corporate connections (alliances, subcontracting, and so on) have probably been growing even faster.[11]

The impact of both trade and investment is magnified by the changing character of trade. Rather than being an exchange of goods between domestic productive systems, trade is increasingly a flow of goods within production networks that are organized globally rather than nationally.[12] Commodities are created through the integration of production processes performed in a multiplicity of national territories. Whether any given territory is included in global production networks or excluded from them depends on the decisions of private actors. States can try to make their territories attractive, but they cannot dictate the structure of global production networks.

In the classic realist world traditional military forms of statecraft were closely intertwined with possibilities for economic gain. Powerful economic actors were presumed to have an interest in the political and military capacities of "their" states, just as state managers had an interest in the capacities of "their" entrepreneurs. National economic prowess was the foundation of military (and therefore diplomatic) strength. Territorial expansion was a route to control over new productive assets. A world of global production networks makes the prospective economic gain from territorial conquest dubious, reducing the returns to realist statecraft. Access to capital and technology depends on strategic alliances with those who control global production networks, rather than on the control of any particular piece of territory. In a global economy where there is a surplus of labor, control over large amounts of territory and population can be more of a burden than an asset.

As long as private economic actors were dependent on the political environment provided by a particular state, it made sense for them to identify with the political successes and aspirations of that state. National aggrandizement held out the prospect of private profit; threats to sovereignty might also contain threats to profit. The operators of what Robert Reich calls "global webs" [13] have much less reason to identify with nationalist territorial ambitions and anxieties. From the perspective of these networks, the interstate system as a whole is an essential piece of economic infrastructure and conflicts among states are a source of disruption and uncertainty.

Underlying the transnational mobility of capital and the construction of global production networks is a radically globalized financial system, whose operation poses a fundamental challenge to public authority in the economic realm. There has always been footloose capital and states have often depended on the cooperation of international financiers, but the changes that have taken place in the last two decades are quite extraordinary. When Nettl was writing, the fixed exchange rate system was still in effect and most major industrialized countries continued to exercise controls over capital flows. By the end of the 1980s, by contrast, capital controls had been dismantled and the value of currencies was left more to markets than to states.[14] The effect of the new institutional framework was magnified by advances in communication and information systems.

Vincent Cable offers a succinct summary of the current disproportion between global financial markets and the economic leverage available to individual states: "Foreign exchange trading in the world's financial centers exceeds a trillion dollars a day. . .greater than the total stock of foreign exchange reserves held by all governments." [15] The result is what Fred Block has called "the dictatorship of international financial markets." Any state that engages in policies deemed "unwise" by private financial traders will be punished as the value of its currency declines and its access to capital shrinks.[16]

These processes of globalization certainly contribute to the perceived evaporation of state authority, but the connection is not as straightforward as it might first appear. The state is not eclipsed by the simple fact of its becoming more dependent on trade. Existing cross-national statistics suggest that greater reliance on trade is associated with an increased role for the state rather than a diminished one. Moreover, a look at the nations that have been most economically successful over the last thirty years suggests that high stateness may even be a competitive advantage in a globalized economy.

Twenty years ago David Cameron noticed that the statistical relationship in advanced industrial economies between openness (as measured by the share of trade in GDP) and the size of government was positive rather than negative.[17] The finding suggested a logic as plausible as that connecting globalization and eclipse. Higher trade shares increase a country's vulnerability to externally induced traumas; a larger public sector provides a protective counterweight. Peter Katzenstein's case studies of small European social democracies spelled out the institutional infrastructure underlying the operation of this logic.[18]

These relationships are not simply artifacts of what is now referred to as "the golden age of capitalism" (roughly 1950–73).[19] Recent analysis by Garrett, Kitschelt et al., and others shows how the configuration of public institutions continues to shape the impact of globalization.[20] Dani Rodrik has replicated and extended Cameron's statistical findings using contemporary data. Looking at data on OECD countries for the 1980s and the early 1990s, Rodrik found "a quite strong correlation among the OECD countries between government expenditures (as a share of GDP) and exposure to trade: countries that are more exposed to trade have bigger governments." [21] Furthermore, when he extends the analysis to more than one hundred countries, most of them developing, he not only finds "a striking positive relationship between size of government (in this case government consumption) and exposure to trade" but also finds that "the degree of openness during the early 1960's is a very good predictor of the *expansion* of government over the subsequent three decades." [22]

A look at contrasting regional growth trajectories over the past thirty years suggests that high stateness may do more than simply insulate domestic populations from external traumas. It may actually be a source of competitive advantage in a globalizing economy. The dizzying growth of transnationally organized production may have been the leading economic headline of the thirty years since Nettl wrote, but the major competing headline has been the spectacular growth of East Asian economies. Few would now dispute that the growth of East Asia over the past fifty years represents a historic shift in the economic hierarchy of nations, one that could eventually prove to be a regional shift comparable to the rise of Northwestern Europe 250 years earlier. If the globalization headline provides grist for the argument that the state is on the wane, the East Asia headline has very different implications for the evolution of stateness.

In the years since Nettl wrote, East Asian states—from Korea in the North to Singapore in the South with the People's Republic of China in the middle—have used various strategies in which the state played a central role to effect dramatic changes in Asia's position in the international division of labor. Obviously the role of the state varies across these cases, but no one would argue that they are stateless societies.[23] They offer a new variety of high stateness, quite different from Nettl's continental European model but perhaps more effective in economic terms.

East Asian successes force us to reexamine the idea that effective participation in a globalized economy is best achieved by restricting state involvement in economic affairs. They suggest that successful participation in global markets may be best achieved through more intense state involvement. Singapore is the most obvious case in point.[24] Singapore is not only a highly internationalized economy in terms of its extreme reliance on trade, but it is also exceptionally dependent for its local economic dynamism on foreign direct investment by transnational corporations. At the same time it is equally renowned for the capacity and power of its state bureaucracy.

This case, anomalous as it may be in terms of the conventional wisdom, underscores what should be logically obvious: small countries bargaining with large TNCs may do better if a competent, unified national agenda participates in the bargaining on the local side. There are many ways to make profits, some of them quite consistent with rising wages and high rates of local reinvestment. If a state can credibly promise an infrastructure consistent with such strategies, along with a predictable set of rules and competent rule makers with whom to dialogue, it is hardly surprising that there is no dearth of TNCs disposed to join the game.[25]

East Asia demonstrates the possibility of a positive connection between high stateness (albeit not Nettl's classic European variety) and success in a globalizing economy and puts historical meat on Cameron and Rodrik's regression results. If such a positive connection exists, then the currently pervasive belief that the institutional centrality of the state is incompatible with globalization must be explained in terms of the ideological face of the current global order.

Ideology and Interests in the Global Order

In any international regime, norms, formal rules, and shared assumptions are as important in shaping the role of the state as the flows of goods and capital. John Ruggie made the point impeccably fifteen years ago in his explication of how the global political economy of the golden age came to be characterized by "embedded liberalism." [26] Liberalism, in the sense of relatively unrestricted freedom for global capital, was "embedded" in a social compact that committed the advanced industrial states to insulating (at least partially) their citizens from the costs of such a system. Embedded liberalism was also an Anglo-American construction, but it was the product of an Anglo-American ideology significantly constrained by post-World War II fears that failure to protect domestic populations might reinitiate the political traumas of the preceding decades.

Like embedded liberalism, the current regime is a means of uniting the contradictory principals of national sovereignty (the keystone of the interstate system) and economic liberalism (which presumes that states will restrain their desire to exercise sovereignty over economic transactions that cross their borders). What is distinctive about the current regime is first of all the degree to which economic gain can be pursued independently of sovereignty and, second, the hegemony of a version of Anglo-American ideological precepts remarkably untrammeled by anxieties over potential political instability. Finally, unlike embedded liberalism, which was conceived of primarily as a regime for the industrialized West, the current normative regime is presumed to apply to rich and poor alike.

Whether active state involvement can increase the benefits that a country's citizens garner from the global economy becomes a moot point in an ideological climate that proscribes using territorial sovereignty to limit the discretion of private economic actors. In the current global order Anglo-American ideological prescriptions have been transcribed into formal rules of the game, to which individual states must commit themselves or risk becoming economic pariahs. GATT and the WTO are only the most obvious formal manifestations of the doctrine that as far as capital and goods are concerned the less individual states behave as economic actors, the better off the world will be.[27] Bilateral negotiations, at least those to which the United States is a party, convey the message even more aggressively.[28] The private representatives of international financial capital and, in the case of developing countries, international financial organizations like the IMF, impart the same tutelage.

The effect of global ideological consensus (sometimes aptly labeled the "Washington consensus") on individual states goes well beyond the constraints imposed by any structural logic of the international economy. The fact that becoming more actively engaged in trying to improve local economic conditions risks the opprobrium, not just of powerful private actors, but also of the global hegemon makes any state intervention a very risky proposition. An ideology that considers such action neither possible nor desirable does, however, at least release the local state from responsibility for whatever economic woes its citizenry may suffer at the hands of the global economy. Even richer states, with more highly developed institutional capacities for insulating their populations from economic uncertainty, are under the same pressure. They are more likely to resist and indeed have done so,[29] but given the asymmetries of international power, it is hard for any individual state to shift the balance.

The current order fits the ideological proclivities of both the only remaining superpower and the private firms that dominate the global economy. The question is whether it speaks effectively to their interests. If an economically stateless world could deliver in practice a global equilibrium that met the needs of TNCs, then eclipse might indeed be in the offing. In fact, transnational investors trying to integrate operations across a shifting variety of national contexts need competent, predictable public sector counterparts even more than do old-fashioned domestic investors who can concentrate their time and energy on building relations with a particular individual government apparatus.[30]

The same argument applies even more strongly to global financial capital. The "dictatorship of international finance" is really closer to a mutual hostage situation. The operation of the international financial system would descend quickly into chaos without responsible fiscal and monetary policies on the part of international actors. Financial markets can easily punish deviant states, but in the long run their returns depend on the existence of an interstate system in which the principal national economies are under the control of competent and "responsible" state actors. Those who sit astride the international financial system need capable regulators. The lightning speed at which transactions of great magnitude can be completed makes for great allocational efficiency in theory, but it also makes for great volatility in practice. "Rogue traders" are (as the name implies) supposed to be aberrations; yet the possibility of enormous returns from speculative activity makes the rogue role a continual temptation.[31] After a certain point, reducing the power of states to interfere increases collective exposure to risk more than it expands the possibilities for individual profits.

The fact that private transnational actors need competent, capable states more than their own ideology admits does not eliminate the possibility of eclipse. The calculations of even sophisticated managers are biased by their own worldviews. Bent on maximizing its room for maneuver, transnational capital could easily become an accomplice in the destruction of the infrastructure of public institutions on which its profits depend. Up to a point, constricting the ability of states to intervene in global markets may produce increased profits. By the time state capacity is so reduced that the unpredictability of the business environment becomes intolerable, even to major actors who have wide latitude in choosing where to do business, reconstructing public authority could be a long and painful process, even an impossible one.

The complicated interactions that connect the global order and domestic politics make miscalculation more likely. Accepting the prevailing global ideology constrains the ability of governments to protect ordinary citizens, especially those who bear the costs of shifts in the configuration of international production networks. Whether it is the Bolivian state cutting domestic expenditures for health and education in order to remain in conformity with the latest restructuring plan or the Clinton administration pushing through NAFTA in order to demonstrate its full faith in the free international movement of goods and capital, the perception of those who lack privileged positions vis-à-vis international markets is likely to be the same. The state is perceived, not as the ultimate representative of national interests, but instead as the instrument of dimly understood but somehow "foreign" interests.[32] Should transnational managers decide that it were in their interest to foster the reconstruction of state capacity, they would have to overcome accumulated political alienation, as well as reverse institutional atrophy.

If eclipse does occur, it will not be the inexorable result of any ironclad structural logic. The economic logic of globalization does not in itself dictate eclipse. While globalization does make it harder for states to exercise economic initiative, it also increases both the potential returns from effective state action and the costs of incompetence. Only when viewed through the peculiar prism of our current global ideological order does globalization logically entail movement toward statelessness. This global ideological order grows, in turn, as much out of the prejudices and ideologies of dominant global actors as out of any logic of interests. Given the degree to which political effects of global economic change are mediated by superimposed interpretative frames, contemporary theoretical perspectives on the state become consequential, not just for the insights they offer, but also because of their potential impact on policy.

New Perspectives on the State

Nettl helped spark a continuing, many-stranded debate on the nature and role of the state. Some of the strands consisted of efforts to demonstrate why variations in stateness must be a central element in political and economic analysis. They revitalized and refined pre-Nettl perspectives, like those of Weber, Hintze, and Gerschenkron, and added new arguments to them.[33] Other strands jibed better with the normative and ideological side of the emerging global order. The flourishing of neoclassical political economy and the renewed fascination with civil society are two of the best examples. The logic of each is quite independent of arguments about globalization, yet both resonated well with a global order built on Anglo-American visions of statelessness. These politically successful formulations must, however, be considered together with less public salient counterposing arguments that raise new reasons for the continuing importance of stateness. Once this is done, the weight of new perspectives on the state lies as much on the side of persistent stateness as on the side of eclipse.

New Economic Perspectives

Of the many strands of thinking on the state that have emerged in the thirty years since Nettl wrote, none has been more thoroughly incorporated into the public political debate than the "neoutilitarian" [34] version of neoclassical political economy. While this line of reasoning was quite independent of arguments for the historical inevitability of eclipse based on the supposed exigencies of globalization, it reinforced them, suggesting that eclipse might be not only inevitable but also desirable.

During the "golden age" most economists were willing to treat the state as a black box. Economics was a source of prescriptions for policies that would best promote economic growth, but it was not prominent as a tool for the institutional analysis of the state itself. As capitalist growth began to look more problematic in the mid-1970s, this changed. Ironically, the weak performance of market economies in the 1970s and 1980s in those countries where state involvement was least extensive (that is, Britain and the United States) was advanced as evidence of excessive public power over the economy.[35]

Concern with optimizing state policies continued but it was joined by efforts to analyze the institutional mechanisms that underlay "bad" policies (that is, those that did not jibe with economic prescriptions). Analysts of "rent seeking" conceptualized policy-making as an exchange: in return for political and material support, state bureaucrats produced rules that enabled private economic actors to reap unproductive rents.[36] States expanded, not because of increased demand for collective goods, but because of self-seeking bureaucrats. Rent seeking took what had been traditionally seen as aberrant, corrupt practices and transformed them into the core of the political economy of public institutions. In this framework approaches like Nettl's, in which the establishment and the maintenance of norms were preeminent among the state's outputs, did not make sense.

Reconceptualizing the state as a vehicle for rent seeking made it much easier to characterize state intervention as intrinsically pathological. Older arguments about the inefficiencies of bureaucracy and the impossibility of gathering sufficient information to make good policy were trumped by this reinvigorated neoclassical political economy. If the negative effects of state policies were a logical consequence of the nature of public institutions, then better information, more competent officials, and more knowledgeable advisers were not remedies. The only rational strategies for alleviating the problem were then either reducing the resources allocated by these perverse institutions to an absolute minimum or somehow "marketizing" the administrative structure itself, replacing reliance on norms of public service with the hard constraints of marketlike incentive systems.

Keynesian arguments in favor of state intervention were rejected as outmoded. Using taxes to channel some of society's collective output into public endeavors was equated with "the old practice of bleeding a patient with leeches in order to make the patient healthy." [37] The grudging acceptance of using the state as a means of ameliorating the lot of those disadvantaged by market outcomes, which had prevailed during the golden age, was supplanted by the firm conviction that as surely as private greed produced public good through the market, public welfare efforts only served to stunt the economic virtues of its recipients. Private economic power, constrained as little as possible by the distorting hand of public policy, was once again touted as the best protector of the public good, and the ideology of statelessness took on a harder, more aggressive edge.

Neoutilitarian models did provide an elegant way of explaining the corruption and venality that are undeniable facets of most public bureaucracies. As explanations of such pathologies, perspectives that focus on rent seeking are very useful. If, however, they crowd out all other interpretations of public behavior, leaving public authority a synonym for rent seeking and venality, they run the danger of becoming a self-fulfilling prophecy. To the extent that the prevalence of neoutilitarian views strips a career in public service of prestige and legitimates removing the resources public agencies need to deliver real services to constituents, rent seeking becomes indeed the only reasonable motivation for joining the public sector. Once norms and traditions of public service have been destroyed, reinstituting them on a piecemeal basis is an overwhelming task.

While neoclassical political economy was easily assimilated into policy analysis, other innovations, with more fundamental implications for economic theories of production and exchange, were harder to incorporate. The "new growth theory," which provided more elegant ways of formally endogenizing technological change and brought the idea of increasing returns back into the center of economic debates,[38] could easily be read as legitimating an expanded role for the state,[39] but was nonetheless extremely difficult to translate into policy prescriptions. Admitting the possibility of increasing returns also required accepting the fact that the evolution of markets and competition was often highly path dependent[40] and consequently characterized by multiple equilibria. This in turn made it harder to argue that unfettered markets could be counted on to automatically maximize efficiency (or welfare) but did not necessarily point to strategies that could improve on market outcomes.

The consequences of this vision of economic growth are magnified by the fact that an increasing number of products—from software to media images—are more ideas than things. Since the cost of reproducing an idea is essentially zero, returns increase indefinitely with the scope of the market. In an economy of "ideas" subject to increasing returns rather than "things" subject to decreasing ones, the distribution of income and profits is especially dependent on appropriability. The magnitude of returns to an idea does not flow from a logic of marginal production costs in a meaningful sense of the term, but it does depend on authoritative decisions, like the determination of the duration of copyright and patent protection and the intellectual property regime more generally.

As an economy produces more ideas, authoritative enforcement of property rights becomes both more difficult and more critical to profitability. In a global economy this requires an active, competent state that is able to secure the compliance of other states with its rules. In short, the most privileged economic actors in a global information economy (that is, global companies like Disney or Microsoft whose assets take the form of ideas) do not need weaker states; they need stronger ones, or at least states that are more sophisticated and active enforcers than the traditional "night watchman state."

The growing centrality of struggles over appropriability is evident from the global economic policies of the United States over the course of the last two decades. From "super 301s" to GATT negotiations to threatened cancellation of China's most-favored-nation status because of software piracy, the question of intellectual property rights has become a key facet of U.S. international economic policy. While other forms of regulation are in disrepute, this particular kind of policing is now treated as one of the cornerstones of economic civilization.

Intellectual property rights are a specific instance of a general point. In the complex exchange of novel intangibles, authoritative normative structures, which are provided in large measure by the state, become the keystones of efficient exchange. The new institutional economics, with its emphasis on the necessity of governance structures and the pervasive importance of institutional frameworks to any kind of economic transactions, further generalizes the argument that efficient markets can exist only in the context of effective and robust nonmarket institutions.[41]

Neoclassical political economy offers a good rationale for eclipse, but a broader look at the evolution of economic theorizing reinforces the conclusions that flowed from our earlier examination of globalization itself. Powerful transnational economic actors may have an interest in limiting the state's ability to constrain their own activities but they also depend on a capable state to protect their returns, especially those from intangible assets. In this optic, the persistence of the state's institutional centrality looks more likely than eclipse.

[A discussion of civil society and the state is omitted.]

The Future of Stateness

Newer political perspectives, like those in economics, contain as many arguments in favor of strengthening state capacities as in favor of eclipse. Analysis of these perspectives produces results that parallel those drawn from the analysis of globalization itself. Together, these arguments lead us to expect states to play a persistent role in the future of the global political economy, but such an outcome can hardly be taken for granted. Just because an information-oriented, globalized system of production would seem to depend even more than prior economies on the competent exercise of public authority does not mean that the institutional bases of such authority will survive. Just because the historical experience of those countries most successful at adapting to the modern globalized economy has been characterized by high levels of state involvement does not mean that their experience will be reflected in the institutional arrangements that prevail globally. Most obvious of all, a positive association between a more vibrant civil society and more capable state institutions will not prevent both from disappearing.

What then can be said about the future prospects of stateness in this era of globalization? One reasonable and optimistic hypothesis looks to the return of the ideological pendulum. In this view, the recent push to reduce the role of the state represented a natural reaction to the previous overreaching of politicians and state managers. The glaring capacity gap led to a period during which, in Dani Rodrik's words, "excessive optimism about what the state would be able to accomplish was replaced by excessive pessimism." Rodrik suggests further that, having now surmounted "excessive pessimism," we are "on the threshold of a serious reconsideration of the role of the state in development, one that will lead to an improved understanding of the role that governments can (and have to) play." [42]

This perspective makes sense. States took on more than they could handle during the period following World War II. Dealing with the capacity gap clearly required rethinking the state's role. Readjustment was necessary, and overzealousness in reducing the state's role, natural. The return of the pendulum need not sanction a return to the past, but it would legitimate new efforts to turn states into effective instruments for the achievement of collective goals. The question is whether the pendulum is likely to come to rest at a point that reflects dispassionate analysis of accumulated global experience with regard to the relative effectiveness of different forms and strategies of state action.

Nettl, however, brings a historical and ideological dimension to the story that makes the efficient middle seem harder to attain. His argument that "an American sociopolitical self-examination simply leaves no room for any valid notion of the state" suggests a hegemon unlikely to assess the proper position of the pendulum dispassionately.[43] To this must be added the problem that the nonstate actors most powerful in defining the global normative order are private corporate elites whose view of where the pendulum belongs is colored by their irreducible interest in protecting private managerial prerogatives. Generating a set of global norms that will encourage the search for ways to reduce demands on public institutions but also support the necessary enhancement of state capacity will require substantial ideological revisionism.

Grounds for expecting such a shift are scanty, but there are some. The shifting balance of economic dynamism in the interstate system is a possible source of revisionism. So far, the implications of East Asia's extraordinary economic success for the kind of stateness that is most effective in a globalized economy have found surprisingly little place in official discourse. Official (as opposed to academic) analysis has been remarkably obdurate in its suppression of the revisionist implications of East Asia's experience.[44] Nonetheless, the eventual assimilation of distinctively East Asian experiences of stateness into global discourse on the state seems inevitable.[45] Any movement in this direction would attenuate the current bias toward eclipse.

The increasing reluctance of the United States to shoulder, as hegemon, the burden of delivering what others perceive to be valuable global collective goods may also serve as an impetus for ideological change. Susan Strange, for example, argues that current asymmetries of interstate power have created a situation in which "the most powerful are able to block, even veto, any exercise of authority in global issues of the environment, of financial regulation, or of the universal provision of basic needs for food, shelter and health care." [46] She then presses further, saying that "the only way to remove the present hegemonic, do-nothing veto on better global governance is to build, bit by bit, a compelling opposition based on European-Japanese cooperation but embracing Latin Americans, Asians and Africans who share some of the same interests and concerns for the future." [47] However remote the prospects for this kind of collective action, Strange's argument does identify another potential impetus for ideological shift.[48]

These relatively implausible fonts of ideological change are likely to have consequences only insofar as they help to further undercut the already ambivalent relation of transnational business to any project of eclipse. Much as TNCs value the elimination of the ability of states to restrict their managerial prerogatives, they also recognize the benefits of dealing with robust and capable public interlocutors. They have an interest in keeping state managers on the defensive—something that escalating rhetoric on the inevitability and desirability of eclipse accomplishes nicely. But they also have an interest in avoiding the real institutional marginalization of the state. This above all else makes a return of the pendulum likely.

The main problem with a return-of-the-pendulum perspective is that it is easily conflated with a return to "embedded liberalism." Even if a return of the pendulum is more likely than eclipse, the threat of eclipse still shapes stateness. What the current global ideological environment does is to ensure that responses to a genuine crisis of capacity will be defensive. Strategies aimed at increasing state capacity in order to meet rising demand for collective goods and social protection look foolish in an ideological climate that resolutely denies the state's potential contribution to the general welfare. Beleaguered state managers and political leaders, bent on trying to preserve the state as an institution (and their own positions), may come up with some innovative organizational improvements and some salutary ways of reducing the scope of what states attempt, but their primary strategy is likely to be reneging on the old commitment to embedded liberalism. The problem of closing the capacity gap is redefined as a project of constructing a leaner, meaner kind of stateness.

In the most sinister version of this leaner, meaner stateness, politicians and state managers gain support for the state as an institution in return for restricting the state's role to activities essential for sustaining the profitability of transnational markets. The capacity to deliver services that the affluent can supply privately for themselves (for example, health and education) is sacrificed, while the more restricted institutional capacity necessary to deliver essential business services and security (domestic and global) is maintained. In turn, delivering security means devoting more resources to the repression of the more desperate and reckless among the excluded, both domestic and international.

Rescuing embedded liberalism would require a very different configuration of state-society relations and a correspondingly different kind of stateness, one founded on relations of mutual empowerment between state institutions and a broadly organized civil society of the kind suggested by Chazan and her colleagues.[49] Engaging the energy and imagination of citizens and communities in the coproduction of services is a way of enhancing the state's ability to deliver services without having to demand more scarce material resources from society. The increased social approbation that comes with more effective, responsive service then becomes an important intangible reward for those who work within the state. Since such a strategy simultaneously rewards the reinvigoration of civil society, thereby augmenting the reservoir of potential participants in coproduction, it is almost certainly subject to increasing returns. Like the returns to the development of bureaucratic forms of organization in an earlier era, the returns to more innovative forms of stateness based on state-society synergy could be prodigious.

Unfortunately, the movement toward eclipse has already made this kind of institutional development unlikely. The kind of capacity necessary to make the state a dependable partner in a strategy of state-society synergy is already in scarce supply. Civic groups are correspondingly less likely to be attracted to strategies of mutual empowerment that involve state agencies. Legitimate disillusionment with the state's capacity to deliver, exacerbated by the pervasive antistate discourse of the Anglo-American global order, has solidified into a domestic political climate that makes engaging the state as an ally seem far-fetched. Finally, and perhaps most important, private elites are likely to see a political threat in any form of state-society synergy that involves subordinate groups.

The political prospects of state-society synergy are slim, but they should not be discounted altogether. For beleaguered state managers or politicians disenchanted with leaner, meaner stateness, the political attractions of a strategy of state-society synergy are obvious. It promises a way out of the currently asphyxiating capacity gap. It also promises to generate a set of allies potentially much less ambivalent about the value of public institutions than are the business elites who constitute the principal political pillar of the leaner, meaner state. The logic is equally powerful from the point of view of civic organizations. Leaner, meaner will do little for them. They need capable state organizations to put their policy preferences into practice even more than TNCs need states to guarantee the global business climate. Leaner, meaner is still more likely, but the possibility that state apparatuses might forge new alliances with civic actors in the early decades of the new millennium is no less implausible than the alliances that were actually forged between labor organizations and the state during the early decades of the twentieth century.

Probing beneath the rhetoric of globalization and eclipse reveals a problematic quite consistent with Nettl's original admonitions. Projecting the institutional evaporation of the state provides little more illumination than ignoring it altogether. Preoccupation with eclipse distracts attention from serious ongoing shifts in the nature of stateness. It also inhibits exploration of more promising forms of stateness. Becoming mesmerized by the power of globalized production and exchange is equally counterproductive. Whether the future unfolds in the probable direction of a leaner, meaner state or embodies more unlikely elements of state-society synergy does not depend on the economic logic of globalization alone. It also depends on how people think about stateness.

Notes

1. Nettl, "The State as a Conceptual Variable," *World Politics* 20 (July 1968), 559.
2. Nettl was interdisciplinary—his footnotes refer to a wide range of sociologists, political scientists, and historians—but in 1968 he found references to economists or economic logic unnecessary in dealing with debates on the state.
3. Nettl (fn. 1) saw the international arena almost purely in realist terms, arguing that in the international arena the state was "the almost exclusive and acceptable locus of resource mobilization" (p. 563). In Nettl's view, "Here [in the international system] the state is the basic, irreducible unit, equivalent to the individual person in a society" (p. 563). Since the "international function is invariant," "even where the notion of the state is very weak, as in Britain and the United States, the effective extrasocietal or international role is not affected" (p. 564).
4. Nettl (fn. 1), 562, 561.
5. Ibid., 561.
6. *Daedalus* 24 (Spring 1995).
7. Susan Strange, "The Defective State," *Daedalus* 124 (Spring 1995), 56.
8. Nettl (fn. 1), 591.

9. Cf. Kenneth Waltz, *Theory of International Politics* (Reading, Mass.: Addison-Wesley, 1979).
10. Nettl's formulation is quoted in fn. 3.
11. Robert Wade, "Globalization and Its Limits: Reports of the Death of the National Economy Are Greatly Exaggerated," in Suzanne Berger and Ronald Dore, eds., *National Diversity and Global Capitalism* (Ithaca, N.Y.: Cornell University Press, 1996). Wade offers a compilation of other such statistics, along with a nicely skeptical and carefully balanced account of the ways in which such statistics may exaggerate globalization.
12. See Robert B. Reich, *The Work of Nations* (New York: Vintage Books, 1992); Gary Gereffi and Miguel Korzeniewicz, eds., *Commodity Chains and Global Capitalism* (Westport, Conn.: Praeger, 1994). For a comprehensive vision of the consequences of global networks for social organization, see Manuel Castells, *The Information Age: Economy, Society and Culture*, vol. 1, *The Rise of the Network Society* (Oxford: Blackwells, 1996).
13. Reich (fn. 12).
14. See Fred Block, *The Vampire State and Other Stories* (New York: New Press, 1996).
15. Cable, "The Diminished Nation-State: A Study in the Loss of Economic Power," *Daedalus* 124 (Spring 1995), 27.
16. Block (fn. 14). See also Geoffrey Garrett, "Capital Mobility, Trade and the Domestic Politics of Economic Policy," *International Organization* 49, no. 4 (1995). Garrett emphasizes the surprising extent to which European social democracies have been able to resist "the dictatorship of international financial markets," but he leaves no doubt that resistance imposes a growing price. For example, he concludes his study by saying: "[F]inancial markets have imposed significant interest rate premiums on the power of the left and organized labor; and these increased with the removal of barriers to cross-border capital flows. . . . In time, one might speculate that no government would be able to bear this burden" (p. 683).
17. Cameron, "The Expansion of the Public Economy: A Comparative Analysis," *American Political Science Review* 72, no. 4 (1978).
18. See Katzenstein, *Small States in World Markets: Industrial Policy in Europe* (Ithaca, N.Y.: Cornell University Press, 1985).
19. See Paul Bairoch and Richard Kozul-Wright, "Globalisation: Myths and Realities: Some Historical Reflections on Integration, Industrialisation and Growth in the World Economy" (Paper presented at the UNU/WIDER conference on "Transnational Corporations in the Developed, Developing and Transitional Economies: Changing Strategies and Policy Implications," Cambridge University, September 21–23, 1995).
20. Geoffrey Garrett's analysis (see fn. 16) of data from fifteen OECD countries over the period 1967–90, which included other measures of globalization, helps to further elucidate institutional connections between globalization and the expansion of government. He found that a "coincidence of strong leftist parties, capital mobility, strong trade unions, and high levels of trade led to greater government spending." For another analysis of the ways in which the consequences of globalization are mediated by national institutions, see Herbert Kitschelt et al., eds., *Continuity and Change in Contemporary Capitalism* (New York: Cambridge University Press, forthcoming).
21. Rodrik, "The Paradoxes of the Successful State" (Alfred Marshall Lecture, delivered during the European Economic Association meetings, Istanbul, August 22–24 [final version, September], 1996a), 31–32. See also idem, "Why Do More Open Economies Have Bigger Governments" (NBER Working Paper no. 5537, April 1996b).
22. Rodrik (fn. 21, 1996a), 32.
23. For a sampling of the now voluminous literature on the role of the state in the East Asian economic miracle, see Yilmaz Akyuz and Charles Gore, "The Investment-Profits Nexus in East Asian Industrialization" (Background paper prepared for the conference on "East Asian Development: Lessons for a New Global Environment," Kuala Lumpur, Malaysia, February 29 and March 1, 1996). See also the published version, *World Development* 24, no. 3 (1996); Alice Amsden, *Asia's Next Giant: South Korea and Late Industrialization* (New York: Oxford University Press, 1989); José Edgardo Campos and Hilton L. Root, *The Key to the Asian Miracle: Making Shared Growth Credible* (Washington, D.C.: Brookings Institution, 1996); Tun-jen Cheng, "The Politics of In-

dustrial Transformation: The Case of the East Asia NICs" (Ph.D. diss., University of California, Berkeley, 1987); Peter Evans, *Embedded Autonomy: States and Industrial Transformation* (Princeton: Princeton University Press, 1995); Stephan Haggard, *Pathways from the Periphery: The Politics of Growth in Newly Industrializing Countries* (Ithaca, N.Y.: Cornell University Press, 1990); Chalmers Johnson, *MITI and the Japanese Miracle: The Growth of Industrial Policy, 1925-1975* (Stanford, Calif.: Stanford University Press, 1982); Robert Wade, *Governing the Market: Economic Theory and the Role of Government in Taiwan's Industrialization* (Princeton: Princeton University Press, 1990); World Bank (IBRD), *The East Asian Miracle: Economic Growth and Public Policy* (*A World Bank Policy Research Report*) (New York: Oxford University Press, 1993).

24. On Singapore's internationalized strategy of development and the role of the state bureaucracy in this strategy, see Campos and Root (fn. 23); Cheng (fn. 23); Gillian Koh, "A Sociological Analysis of the Singapore Administrative Elite: The Bureaucracy in an Evolving Developmentalist State" (Ph.D. diss., University of Sheffield, England, 1995); Jonathan Quah, "The Public Bureaucracy and National Development in Singapore," in K. K. Tummala, ed., *Administrative Systems Abroad* (Washington, D.C.: University Press of America, 1982); idem, "The Rediscovery of the Market and Public Administration: Some Lessons from the Singapore Experience," *Australian Journal of Public Administration* 51, no. 3 (1993); Hilton L. Root, *Small Countries, Big Lessons: Governance and the Rise of East Asia* (Hong Kong: Oxford University Press, 1996).
25. See Peter Evans, "TNCs and Third World States: From the Old Internationalization to the New," in Richard Kozul-Wright and Robert Rowthorne, eds., *Transnational Corporations and the Global Economy* (London: MacMillan, forthcoming).
26. Ruggie, "International Regimes, Transactions and Change: Embedded Liberalism in the Postwar Economic Order," *International Organization* 36 (Spring 1982).
27. For a general discussion of changes in regulatory fashion since the golden age, see Ha-Joon Chang, "The Evolution of Perspectives on Regulation in the Postwar Era," Working Paper (Washington, D.C.: Economic Development Institute of the World Bank, 1995). For a discussion of the way in which the WTO constrains economically nationalist strategies such as industrial policy, see V. R. Panchamuki, "WTO and Industrial Policies," Study no. 7, UNCTAD Project on East Asian Development: Lessons for a New Global Environment (Geneva: United Nations, 1996).
28. See, for example, Peter Evans, "Declining Hegemony and Assertive Industrialization: U.S.Brazilian Conflict in the Computer Industry," *International Organization* 43 (Spring 1989).
29. Cf. Garrett (fn. 16); Kitschelt et al. (fn. 20).
30. For a general discussion of the extent to which firms rely on states to create and sustain markets, see Neil Fligstein, "Markets, Politics and Globalization" (Manuscript, Berkeley, 1996). See also idem, "Markets as Politics: A Political-Cultural Approach to Market Institutions," *American Sociological Review* 6 (August 1996).
31. See Block (fn. 14).
32. In the Third World there is, of course, a long-standing tradition of seeing the state in these terms, that is, as a "tool of imperialism." In the United States a lively folk tradition is rapidly developing along analogous lines. As nonsensical as fears of "black helicopters" and visions of the U.S. government as a pawn of the UN may be, this folk mythology does reflect an underlying sense that U.S. administrations are more responsive to transnational actors than to domestic pressure from below.
33. For a review of early efforts in this direction, see Peter Evans, Dietrich Reuschemeyer, and Theda Skocpol, eds., *Bringing the State Back In* (New York: Cambridge University Press, 1985), especially the initial essay by Skocpol.
34. See discussion in Evans (fn. 23), chap. 2.
35. Cf. Linda Weiss and John M. Hobson, *States and Economic Development: A Comparative Historical Analysis* (Cambridge, England: Polity Press, 1995).
36. See James M. Buchanan, Robert D. Tollison, and Gordon Tullock, eds., *Toward a Theory of Rent-Seeking Society* (College Station: Texas A&M University Press, 1980); David Collander, ed., *Neoclassical Political Econ-*

omy: An Analysis of Rent-Seeking and DUP Activities (Cambridge, Mass.: Ballinger, 1984); Anne O. Krueger, "The Political Economy of the Rent-Seeking Society," *American Economic Review* 64 (June 1974).

37. Speech by Senator Kyl in the Senate, January 20, 1995, quoted in Fred Block (fn. 14).
38. For a sophisticated but nontechnical exposition, see Paul Romer "The Origins of Endogenous Growth," *Journal of Economic Perspectives* 8 (Winter 1994).
39. For example, in the view of Garrett (fn. 16), "'New Growth' theory contends that active government involvement in the economy (for example, public spending on education, physical infrastructure, and research and development) may actually increase productivity and hence competitiveness by providing collective goods that are undersupplied by the market" (p. 658). Others, like Paul Krugman, would argue that government efforts to exploit the theoretical possibilities revealed by the new growth theory are likely to do more harm than good; see, for example, Krugman, *Peddling Prosperity: Economic Sense and Nonsense in the Age of Diminished Expectations* (New York: W. W. Norton, 1995). Nonetheless, even Krugman would not deny that new theoretical possibilities have been opened up.
40. See, for example, Brian W. Arthur, "Positive Feedbacks in the Economy," *Scientific American* (February 1990).
41. See, for example, Douglass C. North, *Institutions, Institutional Change and Economic Performance* (Cambridge: Cambridge University Press, 1990); and Oliver Williamson, *The Economic Institutions of Capitalism* (New York: Free Press, 1985).
42. Rodrik (fn. 21, 1996a), 2-3.
43. Nettl (fn. 1), 561.
44. See, for example, Robert Wade, "Japan, the World Bank and the Art of Paradigm Maintenance," *New Left Review* 217 (May-June 1996).
45. Some would argue that the East Asian experience already constitutes a competing model, at least for the developing countries of the region itself. See Barbara Stallings and Wolfgang Streeck, "Capitalisms in Conflict? The United States, Europe and Japan in the Post-Cold War World," in Stallings, ed., *Global Challenge, Regional Response: The New International Context of Development* (New York: Cambridge University Press, 1995).
46. Strange (fn. 7), 71.
47. Ibid.
48. Another potential source of normative change—also unlikely but still intriguing—is to be found in the networks of public organizations and officials that are part of the global order. John Meyer, in a classic article, presents a strong case for the collective power of public officials to shape global norms at the transnational level; see Meyer, "The World Polity and the Authority of the Nation-State," in Albert Bergesen, ed., *Studies in the Modern World System* (New York: Academic Press, 1980). Meyer's general model is unconvincing, especially in view of more recent changes in global ideology, but there are some very interesting, if modest, examples of transnational networks rooted in public institutions that have effected change in the global normative order. See, for example, Peter Haas, "Banning Chlorofluorocarbons: Epistemic Community Efforts to Protect Stratospheric Ozone," *International Organization* 46 (Winter 1992).
49. See Migdal, Kohli, and Shue (fn. 47), especially Kohli and Shue, "State Power and the Social Forces: On Political Contention and Accommodation in the Third World."

8.2

SENSE AND NONSENSE IN THE GLOBALIZATION DEBATE

Dani Rodrik

While some scholars believe that rapid transportation, instant communication, and the resulting globalization are sources of economic growth, others bemoan the perceived powerlessness of states to regulate their economies and the costs to certain interests or strata of populations. For example, some segments of organized labor fear free trade will mean the loss of their jobs to less-prosperous, lower-paying economies. Dani Rodrik, a professor at Harvard University's Kennedy School of Government and a prominent scholar known for his skepticism of globalization as well as author of *One Economics, Many Recipes: Globalization, Institutions, and Economic Growth,* analyzes these arguments and finds that while globalization in the form of international competition has indeed narrowed the choices available to policymakers at the nation-state level, national economies remain largely independent of one another, and the idea of a unified world market is an oversimplification. Rodrik is reacting to what he regards as an outpouring of overwrought claims that globalization has rendered the nation-state impotent and irrelevant. For this reading, students should understand the impact of globalization and its limits, as well as the trends in shifting policymaking to the pan-national level after a decade of focus on globalization.

Globalization, Thomas Friedman of the New York Times has observed, is "the next great foreign policy debate." Yet as the debate expands, it gets more confusing. Is globalization a source of economic growth and prosperity, as most economists and many in the policy community believe? Or is it a threat to social stability and the natural environment, as a curious mix of interests ranging from labor advocates to environmentalists—and including the unlikely trio of Ross Perot, George Soros, and Sir James Goldsmith—argue? Has globalization advanced so far that national governments are virtually powerless to regulate their economies and use their policy tools to further social ends? Is the shift of manufacturing activities to low-wage countries undermining global purchasing power, thus creating a glut in goods ranging from autos to aircraft? Or is globalization no more than a buzzword and its impact greatly exaggerated?

There are good reasons to be concerned about the quality of the globalization debate. What we are witnessing is more a dialogue of the deaf than a rational discussion. Those who favor international integration dismiss globalization's opponents as knee-jerk protectionists who do not understand the prin-

Dani Rodrik, "Sense and Nonsense in the Globalization Debate," *Foreign Policy* 107 (Summer 1997): 19–37.

ciple of comparative advantage and the complexities of trade laws and institutions. Globalization's critics, on the other hand, fault economists and trade specialists for their narrow, technocratic perspective. They argue that economists are too enamored with their fancy models and do not have a good handle on how the real world works. The result is that there is too much opponent bashing—and too little learning—on each side.

Both sides have valid complaints. Much of the popular discussion about globalization's effect on American wages, to pick one important example, ignores the considerable research that economists have undertaken. A reasonably informed reader of the nation's leading op-ed pages could be excused for not realizing that a substantial volume of literature on the relationship between trade and inequality exists, much of which contradicts the simplistic view that Americans or Europeans owe their deteriorating fortunes to low-wage competition from abroad. The mainstream academic view actually is that increased trade with developing countries may account for at most 20 percent of the reduction in the earnings of low-skilled American workers (relative to highly skilled workers) but not much more. One has to look elsewhere—to technological changes and deunionization, for example—to explain most of the increase in the wage gap between skilled and unskilled workers.

It is also true, however, that economists and proponents of trade have either neglected or pooh-poohed some of the broader complications associated with international economic integration. Consider the following questions: To what extent have capital mobility and the outsourcing of production increased the substitutability of domestic labor across national boundaries, thereby aggravating the economic insecurity confronting workers (in addition to exerting downward pressure on their wages)? Are the distributional implications of globalization—and certainly there are some—reconcilable with domestic concepts of distributive justice? Does trade with countries that have different norms and social institutions clash with and undermine long-standing domestic social bargains? To what extent does globalization undermine the ability of national governments to provide the public goods that their citizenries have come to expect, including social insurance against economic risks?

These are serious questions that underscore the potential of globally expanding markets to come into conflict with social stability, even as these markets provide benefits to exporters, investors, and consumers. Some of these questions have not yet been seriously scrutinized by economists. Others cannot be answered with economic and statistical analysis alone. But the full story of globalization cannot be told unless these broader issues are addressed as well.

The Limits of Globalization

Even with the revolution in transportation and communication and the substantial progress made in trade liberalization over the last three decades, national economies remain remarkably isolated from each other. This isolation has a critical implication, which has been repeatedly emphasized by economist Paul Krugman: Most governments in the advanced industrial world are not nearly as shackled by economic globalization as is commonly believed. They retain substantial autonomy in regulating their economies, in designing their social policies, and in maintaining institutions that differ from those of their trading partners.

The supposition that domestic economies are now submerged in a seamless, unified world market is belied by various pieces of evidence. Take the case of North America. Trade between Canada and the United States is among the freest in the world and is only minimally hampered by transport and communications costs. Yet a study by Canadian economist John McCallum has documented that trade between a Canadian province and a U.S. state (that is, international trade) is on average 20 times smaller than trade between two Canadian provinces (that is, [national] trade). Clearly, the U.S. and Canadian markets remain substantially delinked from each other. And if this is true of U.S.–Canadian trade, it must be all the more true of other bilateral trade relationships.

The evidence on the mobility of physical capital also contradicts current thought. Popular discussions take it for granted that capital is now entirely free to cross national borders in its search for the highest returns. As economists Martin Feldstein and Charles Horioka have pointed out, if this were true, the level of investment that is undertaken in France would depend only on the profitability of investment in France, and it would have no relationship to the available savings in France. Actually, however, this turns out to be false. Increased savings in one country translate into increased investments in that country almost one for one. Despite substantial crossborder money flows, different rates of return among countries persist and are not equalized by capital moving to higher-return economies.

One can easily multiply the examples. U.S. portfolios tend to be remarkably concentrated in U.S. stocks. The prices of apparently identical goods differ widely from one country to another despite the fact that the goods can be traded. In reality, national economies retain a considerable degree of isolation from each other, and national policymakers enjoy more autonomy than is assumed by most recent writings on the erosion of national sovereignty.

The limited nature of globalization can perhaps be better appreciated by placing it into historical context. By many measures, the world economy was more integrated at the height of the gold standard in the late 19th century than it is now. In the United States and Europe, trade volumes peaked before World War I and then collapsed during the interwar years. Trade surged again after 1950, but neither Europe nor the United States is significantly more open today (gauging by ratios of trade to national income) than it was under the gold standard. Japan actually exports less of its total production today than it did during the interwar period.

Globalization Matters

It would be a mistake to conclude from this evidence that globalization is irrelevant. Due to the increased importance of trade, the options available to national policymakers have narrowed appreciably over the last three decades. The oft-mentioned imperative of maintaining "international competitiveness" now looms much larger and imparts a definite bias to policymaking.

Consider labor market practices. As France, Germany, and other countries have shown, it is still possible to maintain labor market policies that increase the cost of labor. But globalization is raising the overall social cost of exercising this option. European nations can afford to have generous minimum wages and benefit levels if they choose to pay the costs. But the stakes—the resulting unemployment levels—have been raised by the increased international mobility of firms.

The consequences are apparent everywhere. In Japan, large corporations have started to dismantle the postwar practice of providing lifetime employment, one of Japan's most distinctive social institutions. In France and Germany, unions have been fighting government attempts to cut pension benefits. In South Korea, labor unions have taken to the streets to protest the government's relaxation of firing restrictions. Developing countries in Latin America are competing with each other in liberalizing trade, deregulating their economies, and privatizing public enterprises.

Ask business executives or government officials why these changes are necessary, and you will hear the same mantra repeated over and over again: "We need to remain (or become) competitive in a global economy." As some of these changes appear to violate long-standing social bargains in many countries, the widespread populist reaction to globalization is perhaps understandable.

The anxieties generated by globalization must be seen in the context of the demands placed on national governments, which have expanded radically since the late 19th century. At the height of the gold standard, governments were not yet expected to perform social-welfare functions on a large scale. Ensuring adequate levels of employment, establishing social safety nets, providing medical and social insurance, and caring for the poor were not parts of the government agenda. Such demands multiplied during the period following the Second World War. Indeed, a key component of the implicit postwar social bargain in the advanced industrial countries has been the provision of social insurance and safety nets at home (unemployment compensation, severance payments, and adjustment assistance, for example) in exchange for the adoption of freer trade policies.

This bargain is clearly eroding. Employers are less willing to provide the benefits of job security and stability, partly because of increased competition but also because their enhanced global mobility makes them less dependent on the goodwill of their local work force. Governments are less able to sustain social safety nets, because an important part of their tax base has become footloose because of the increased mobility of capital. Moreover, the ideological onslaught against the welfare state has paralyzed many governments and made them unable to respond to the domestic needs of a more integrated economy.

More Trade, More Government

The postwar period has witnessed two apparently contradictory trends: the growth of trade and the growth of government. Prior to the Second World War, government expenditures averaged around 20 percent of the gross domestic products (GDPs) of today's advanced industrialized countries. By the mid-1990s, that figure had more than doubled to 47 percent. The increased role of government is particularly striking in countries like the United States (from 9 to 34 percent), Sweden (from 10 to 69 percent), and the Netherlands (from 19 to 54 percent). The driving force behind the expansion of government during this period was the increase in social spending—and income transfers in particular.

It is not a coincidence that social spending increased alongside international trade. For example, the small, highly open European economies like Austria, the Netherlands, and Sweden have large governments in part as a result of their attempts to minimize the social impact of openness to the international economy. It is in the most open countries like Denmark, the Netherlands, and Sweden that spending on income transfers has expanded the most.

Indeed, there is a surprisingly strong association across countries between the degree of exposure to international trade and the importance of the government in the economy. [Figure 1] shows the relationship between trade and spending on social protection (including unemployment insurance, pensions, and family benefits) in 21 countries for which the Organization for Economic Cooperation and Development (OECD) publishes crossnationally comparable data. The [figure] reveals an unmistakably positive correlation between a nation's openness to trade and the amount of its spending on social programs. At one end of the distribution we have the United States and Japan, which have the lowest trade shares in GDP and some of the lowest shares of spending on social protection. At the other end, Luxembourg, Belgium, and the Netherlands have economies with high degrees of openness and large income transfers. This relationship is not confined to OECD economies: Developing nations also exhibit this pattern. Furthermore, the extent to which imports and exports were important in a country's economy in the early 1960s provided a good predictor of how big [its] government would become in the en-

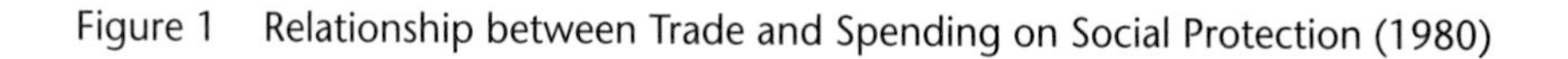

Figure 1 Relationship between Trade and Spending on Social Protection (1980)

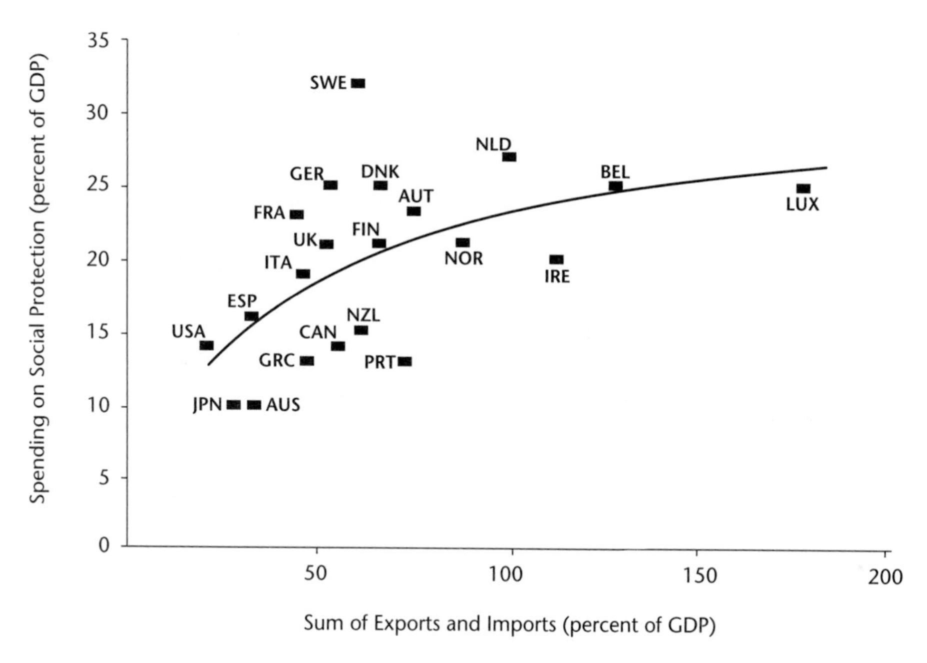

Source: Author

suing three decades, regardless of how developed it was. All the available evidence points to the same, unavoidable conclusion: The social welfare state has been the flip side of the open economy.

International economic integration thus poses a serious dilemma: Globalization increases the demand for social insurance while simultaneously constraining the ability of governments to respond effectively to that demand. Consequently, as globalization deepens, the social consensus required to keep domestic markets open to international trade erodes.

Since the early 1980s, tax rates on capital have tended to decrease in the leading industrial nations, while tax rates on labor have continued generally to increase. At the same time, social spending has stabilized in relation to national incomes. These outcomes reflect the tradeoffs facing governments in increasingly open economies: The demands for social programs are being balanced against the need to reduce the tax burden on capital, which has become more globally mobile.

By any standard, the postwar social bargain has served the world economy extremely well. Spurred by widespread trade liberalization, world trade has soared since the 1950s. This expansion did not cause major social dislocations and did not engender much opposition in the advanced industrial countries. Today, however, the process of international economic integration is taking place against a backdrop of retreating governments and diminished social obligations. Yet the need for social insurance for the vast majority of the population that lacks international mobility has not diminished. If anything, this need has grown.

The question, therefore, is how the tension between globalization and the pressure to mitigate risks can be eased. If the vital role that social insurance played in enabling the postwar expansion of trade is neglected and social safety nets are allowed to dwindle, the domestic consensus in favor of open markets will be eroded seriously, and protectionist pressures will soar.

The Global Trade in Social Values

In the markets for goods, services, labor, and capital, international trade creates arbitrage—the possibility of buying (or producing) in one place at one price and selling at a higher price elsewhere. Prices thus tend to converge in the long run, this convergence being the source of the gains from trade. But trade exerts pressure toward another kind of arbitrage as well: arbitrage in national norms and social institutions. This form of arbitrage results, indirectly, as the costs of maintaining divergent social arrangements go up. As a consequence, open trade can conflict with long-standing social contracts that protect certain activities from the relentlessness of the free market. This is a key tension generated by globalization.

As the technology for manufactured goods becomes standardized and diffused internationally, nations with different sets of values, norms, institutions, and collective preferences begin to compete head on in markets for similar goods. In the traditional approach to trade policy, this trend is of no consequence: Differences in national practices and social institutions are, in effect, treated just like any other differences that determine a country's comparative advantage (such as endowments of physical capital or skilled labor).

In practice, however, trade becomes contentious when it unleashes forces that undermine the social norms implicit in domestic practices. For example, not all residents of advanced industrial countries are comfortable with the weakening of domestic institutions through the forces of trade, such as when child labor in Honduras replaces workers in South Carolina or when cuts in pension benefits in France are called for in response to the requirements of the Treaty on European Union. This sense of unease is one way of interpreting the demands for "fair trade." Much of the discussion surrounding the new issues in trade policy—e.g., labor standards, the environment, competition policy, and corruption—can be cast in this light of procedural fairness.

Trade usually redistributes income among industries, regions, and individuals. Therefore, a principled defense of free trade cannot be constructed without addressing the question of the fairness and legitimacy of the practices that generate these distributional "costs." How comparative advantage is created matters. Low-wage foreign competition arising from an abundance of workers is different from competition that is created by foreign labor practices that violate norms at home. Low wages that result from demography or history are very different from low wages that result from government repression of unions.

From this perspective it is easier to understand why many people are often ill at ease with the consequences of international economic integration. Automatically branding all concerned groups as self-interested protectionists does not help much. This perspective also prepares us not to expect broad popular support for trade when trade involves exchanges that clash with (and erode) prevailing domestic social arrangements.

Consider labor rules, for example. Since the 1930s, U.S. laws have recognized that restrictions on "free contract" are legitimate to counteract the effects of unequal bargaining power. Consequently, the employment relationship in the United States (and elsewhere) is subject to a multitude of restrictions, such as those that regulate working hours, workplace safety, labor/management negotiations, and so forth. Many of these restrictions have been put in place to redress the asymmetry in bargaining power that would otherwise disadvantage workers vis-à-vis employers.

Globalization upsets this balance by creating a different sort of asymmetry: Employers can move abroad, but employees cannot. There is no substantive difference between American workers being driven from their jobs by their fellow domestic workers who agree to work 12-hour days, earn less than the minimum wage, or be fired if they join a union—all of which are illegal under U.S. law—and their being similarly disadvantaged by foreign workers doing the same. If society is unwilling to accept the former, why should it countenance the latter? Globalization generates an inequality in bargaining power that 60 years of labor legislation in the United States has tried to prevent. It is in effect eroding a social understanding that has long been settled.

Whether they derive from labor standards, environmental policy, or corruption, differences in domestic practices and institutions have become matters of international controversy. That is indeed the common theme that runs the gamut of the new issues on the agenda of the World Trade Organization (WTO). Conflicts arise both when these differences create trade—as in the cases of child labor or lax environmental policies—and when they reduce it—as industrial practices in Japan are alleged to do. As the New York Times editorialized on July 11, 1996, in connection with the Kodak-Fuji dispute on access to the photographic film market in Japan, "the Kodak case asks the WTO, in effect, to pass judgment on the way Japan does business."

The notions of "fair trade" and "leveling the playing field" that lie behind the pressures for putting these new issues on the trade agenda have been ridiculed by economists. But once it is recognized that trade has implications for domestic norms and social arrangements and that its legitimacy rests in part on its compatibility with these, such notions are not so outlandish. These sentiments are ways of addressing the concerns to which trade gives rise. Free trade among countries with different domestic practices requires an acceptance of either an erosion of domestic structures or the need for some degree of harmonization or convergence.

If this is the appropriate context in which demands for "fair trade" or "leveling the playing field" must be understood, it should also be clear that policymakers often take too many liberties in justifying their actions along such lines. Most of the pricing policies that pass as "unfair trade" in U.S. antidumping proceedings, for example, are standard business practice in the United States and other countries. While there may not be a sharp dividing line between what is fair and unfair in international trade, one clear sign that pure protectionism is at the root of a trade dispute is the prevalence of practices within the domestic economy that are identical or similar to those being protested in the international arena. Fairness cannot be eliminated from thinking about trade policy; but neither can it be invoked to justify trade restrictions when the practice in question does not conflict with domestic norms as revealed by actual practice.

* * *

Safety Nets, Not Trade Barriers

One need not be alarmed by globalization, but neither should one take a Panglossian view of it. Globalization greatly enhances the opportunities available to those who have the skills and mobility to flourish in world markets. It can help poor countries to escape poverty. It does not constrain national autonomy nearly as much as popular discussions assume. At the same time, globalization does exert downward pressure on the wages of underskilled workers in industrialized countries, exacerbate economic insecurity, call into question accepted social arrangements, and weaken social safety nets.

There are two dangers from complacency toward the social consequences of globalization. The first and more obvious one is the potential for a political backlash against trade. The candidacy of Patrick Buchanan in the 1996 Republican presidential primaries revealed that protectionism can be a rather easy sell at a time when broad segments of American society are experiencing anxieties related to globalization. The same can be said about the political influence of Vladimir Zhirinovsky in Russia or Jean-Marie Le Pen in France—influence that was achieved, at least in part, in response to the perceived effects of globalization. Economists may complain that protectionism is mere snake oil and argue that the ailments require altogether different medicine, but intellectual arguments will not win hearts and minds unless concrete solutions are offered. Trade protection, for all of its faults, has the benefit of concreteness.

Perhaps future Buchanans will ultimately be defeated, as Buchanan himself was, by the public's common sense. Even so, a second and perhaps more serious danger remains: The accumulation of globalization's side effects could lead to a new set of class divisions—between those who prosper in the globalized economy and those who do not; between those who share its values and those who would rather not; and between those who can diversify away its risks and those who cannot. This is not a pleasing prospect even for individuals on the winning side of the globalization divide: The deepening of social fissures harms us all.

National policymakers must not retreat behind protectionist walls. Protectionism would be of limited help, and it would create its own social tensions. Policymakers ought instead to complement the external strategy of liberalization with an internal strategy of compensation, training, and social insurance for those groups who are most at risk.

In the United States, President Bill Clinton's education initiatives represent a move in the right direction. However, the August 1996 welfare reform act could weaken social safety nets precisely at a time when globalization calls for the opposite. In Europe, as well, the pruning of the welfare state may exacerbate the strains of globalization.

Contrary to widespread belief, maintaining adequate safety nets for those at the bottom of the income distribution would not break the bank. Currently, old-age insurance is the most expensive income-transfer item for the advanced industrial countries. A reorientation of public resources away from pensions and toward labor-market and antipoverty programs would be a more appropriate way to address the challenges of globalization. This shift could be achieved while reducing overall public spending. Broad segments of the population in the industrial countries are understandably nervous about changing basic social-welfare arrangements. Therefore, political leadership will be required to render such changes palatable to these groups.

At the global level, the challenge is twofold. On the one hand, a set of rules that encourages greater harmonization of social and industrial policies on a voluntary basis is needed. Such harmonization could reduce tensions that arise from differing national practices. At the same time, flexibility sufficient to allow selective disengagement from multilateral disciplines needs to be built into the rules that govern international trade.

Currently, the WTO Agreement on Safeguards allows member states to impose temporary trade restrictions following an increase in imports—but only under a stringent set of conditions. One could imagine expanding the scope of the agreement to include a broader range of circumstances, reflecting concerns over labor standards, the environment, and even ethical norms in the importing country. The purpose of such an expanded "escape clause" mechanism would be to allow countries—under well-specified contingencies and subject to multilaterally approved procedures—greater breathing room to fulfill domestic requirements that conflict with free trade. If this flexibility could be achieved in exchange for a tightening of rules on antidumping, which have a highly corrosive effect on the world trading system, the benefits could be substantial.

Globalization is not occurring in a vacuum: It is part of a broader trend we may call marketization. Receding government, deregulation, and the shrinking of social obligations are the domestic counterparts of the intertwining of national economies. Globalization could not have advanced this far without these complementary forces at work. The broader challenge for the 21st century is to engineer a new balance between the market and society—one that will continue to unleash the creative energies of private entrepreneurship without eroding the social bases of cooperation.

* * *

Chapter 9

SHOULD THE NATION-STATE BE REPLACED BY LARGER POLITICAL UNITS?

Recently, there has been a trend to displace the state with supranational structures, such as the nascent European Union (EU); this trend has been enhanced by the widespread perception that the nation-state system—and the power politics that had dominated relations among those nation-states—produced a disastrous legacy of armed conflict that culminated in the world wars of the twentieth century. Multilateral approaches are seen by their advocates as recognition that the nation-state is an inadequate vehicle for coping with the increasingly multinational nature of today's issues.

While the limits of pan-national authority at the global level have been recognized in such provisions as the great power veto in the United Nations Security Council, among the European democracies the aim of pan-nationalists is clearly a federated Europe. A proposed federal constitution for the European Union was drawn up but rejected by France and the Netherlands in the only attempts at its ratification, as discussed in reading 9.3 by Kees Aarts and Henk van der Kolk. Meanwhile, although the countries of the EU adopted the euro as their common currency—effectively surrendering sovereign control over their monetary policy—Great Britain, Denmark, and Sweden remained outside the European Monetary System.

The proposed surrender of national sovereignty to the EU bureaucracy in Brussels has been primarily an elite-led movement that has generated passionate opposition among a significant portion of European publics on several grounds. This opposition is widely referred to as Euro-skepticism, a position typified by the Noel Malcolm selection (reading 9.1) in this chapter. The first complaint of Euro-skeptics concerns the real differences in interest that remain among the constituent member states, such as the conflicts generated by the attempt to impose a common agricultural policy which is strongly influenced by the French predilection toward protection of that country's small family farms or Norway's concerns for protecting its critical fishing industry in its coastal waters. Also, as Malcolm points out, the imposition of Germany's labor system, with its high level of benefits, on industries in other EU countries has had a devastating impact on the economies of these states.

A second set of concerns has to do with the question of whether it is even possible to create a viable political structure or state that is not more or less congruent with a well-established and legitimate nation. ("Nation" here refers to a culturally defined people who share some values, perhaps a sense of shared belonging, and a belief in a shared heritage.) In reading 15.1 in this volume, Edward Friedman argues that democracy can be crafted by political elites regardless of the cultural milieu; yet, the current attempt to build a viable Iraq has been rendered difficult by the apparent overriding of a national sense of identity by a stronger sense of religious and ethnic identity: Iraqis see themselves first and foremost as Shiite or Sunni Muslims or Kurds, not as Iraqis. The question for the incipient EU is whether the masses on the Continent see themselves first as Europeans or as French, British, Norwegian, and so on—countries each with a distinct sense of history, distinct geopolitical and economic interests, distinct religious traditions, and distinct languages. Are EU enthusiasts constructing a European state before the emergence of a European nation? Can such a state govern effectively over time and thereby create the sense of a European nation? Clearly, the analysis of the emerging European Union can yield valuable understanding of the limits to and possibilities of nation building.

A third set of concerns has to do with what Euro-skeptics call "the democratic deficit." This refers to the fact that democratically chosen nation-state governments are asked to surrender authority to a more remote set of institutions whose authority does not directly stem from competitive elections, as discussed by Alberta Sbragia, a University of Pittsburgh professor and EU enthusiast, in reading 9.2 in this chapter. The elected European Parliament is primarily an arena for discussion of EU matters; the actual decision making for the EU occurs behind closed doors in the Council of Ministers, a body whose members have been appointed, or in the vast bureaucracy of the European Commission. The agenda of the Council of Ministers is in the hands of the Committee of Permanent Representatives—appointed representatives of the member states who hold ambassadorial rank and meet weekly to prepare meetings of the Council of Ministers. The parliament must approve the budget, but this is usually a formality; the parliament has caused minor amending of the budget on just three occasions.

The efforts of Europeanists probably constitute the most significant challenge to the future of the sovereign nation-state, as that institution has defined the modern world for the past five hundred to six hundred years. Demands for multilateralism in the foreign policy of the last superpower, the United States, are another such challenge. The literature offered in this section indicates a great deal of uncertainty regarding the role of the traditional nation-state in international politics and in comparative political analysis.

9.1

THE CASE AGAINST "EUROPE"

Noel Malcolm

While a "global" perspective has been gaining strength among political elites in the Western world, a significant segment of Western society, especially the general public, is much more skeptical about compromising the sovereignty of the traditional nation-state to build a pan-European federalism. This skepticism was expressed by the surprising (to some) rejection of the proposed constitution for the European Union in popular referenda in the Netherlands and France in spring 2005. A pattern of growing international cooperation along functional lines, including the European Coal and Steel Community; Euratom; the European Economic Community; and the Single European Act, or Maastricht Treaty, culminated in the abortive attempt to integrate fifteen heretofore sovereign European nation-states into a political federation. The elite-driven attempt to federate Europe proved to be well beyond what the European public was ready to accept. In this selection, British writer and historian Noel Malcolm expresses the reasons for the popular resistance to the abandonment of existing nation-states as European elites tried to impose a European state before the development of a European nation or community. Malcolm cites reasons concerned with the persistence of distinct interests of the nation-states of Europe and in the perceived lack of democratic accountability for the remote EU leadership in Brussels. To what extent can the model of the uniting of thirteen then-sovereign American states into a successful federation be applied to the integration of the nations of Europe into a similar federation?

A Flawed Ideal

The case against "Europe" is not the same as a case against Europe. Quite the contrary. "Europe" is a project, a concept, a cause: the final goal that the European Community (EC) has been moving toward ever since its hesitant beginnings in the 1950s. It involves the creation of a united European state with its own constitution, government, parliament, currency, foreign policy, and army. Some of the machinery for this is already in place, and enough of the blueprints are in circulation for there to be little doubt about the overall design. Those who are in favor of Europe—that is, those who favor increasing the freedom and prosperity of all who live on the European continent—should view the creation of this hugely artificial political entity with a mixture of alarm and dismay.

Noel Malcolm, "The Case Against 'Europe'," *Foreign Affairs* 64, no. 2 (March/April 1995): 52–68.

The synthetic project of "Europe" has almost completely taken over the natural meaning of the word. In most European countries today, people talk simply about being "pro-Europe" or "anti-Europe"; anyone who questions more political integration can be dismissed as motivated by mere xenophobic hostility toward the rest of the continent. Other elements of the "European" political language reinforce this attitude. During the 1991-93 debate over the Maastricht treaty, for example, there was an almost hypnotic emphasis on clichés about transport. We were warned that we must not miss the boat or the bus, that we would be left standing on the platform when the European train went out, or that insufficient enthusiasm would cause us to suffer a bumpy ride in the rear wagon. All these images assumed a fixed itinerary and a preordained destination. Either you were for that destination, or you were against "Europe." The possibility that people might argue in favor of rival positive goals for Europe was thus eliminated from the consciousness of European politicians.

The concept of "Europe" is accompanied, in other words, by a doctrine of historical inevitability. This can take several different forms: a utopian belief in inevitable progress, a quasi-Marxist faith in the iron laws of history (again involving the withering away of the nation-state), or a kind of cartographic mysticism that intuits that certain large areas on the map are crying out to emerge as single geopolitical units. These beliefs have received some hard knocks from twentieth-century history. Inevitability is, indeed, a word most often heard on the lips of those who have to turn the world upside down to achieve the changes they desire.

On Little Cat Feet

The origins of the "European" political project can be traced back to a number of politicians, writers, and visionaries of the interwar period: people such as the half-Austrian, half-Japanese theorist Richard Coudenhove-Kalergi, former Italian Foreign Minister Carlo Sforza, and Jean Monnet, a French brandy salesman turned international bureaucrat. When their idea of a rationalized and unified Europe was first floated in the 1920s and 1930s, it sounded quite similar in spirit to the contemporaneous campaign to make Esperanto the world language. Who, at that stage, could confidently have declared that one of these schemes had the force of historical inevitability behind it and the other did not? Both had theoretical benefits to offer, although they were almost certainly outweighed by the practical difficulties of attaining them. It is not hard, surely, to imagine an alternative history of Europe after World War II in which the EC never came into existence and in which, therefore, the project of a united Europe would occupy a footnote almost as tiny as that devoted to the work of the International Esperanto League. Things seem inevitable only because people made them happen.

The impetus behind the "European" idea came from a handful of politicians in France and Germany who decided that a supranational enterprise might solve the problem of Franco-German rivalry, which they saw as the root cause of three great European wars since 1870. For this purpose alone, an arrangement involving just those two countries might have sufficed. But other factors coincidentally were at work, in particular the Cold War, which made the strengthening of Western Europe as a political bloc desirable, and the barely concealed resentment of French President Charles de Gaulle toward "les Anglo-Saxons," which made him look more favorably on the EC as an Anglo-Saxon-free area that could be politically dominated by France.

Even with these large-scale factors at work, however, it is doubtful whether the "European" project would have got off the ground without the ingenuity of a few individuals, notably Monnet and former French Foreign Minister Robert Schuman. The method they invented was what political theorists now call "functionalism." By meshing together the economies of participating countries bit by bit, they believed a point would eventually be reached where political unification would seem a natural expression of the way in which those countries were already interacting. As Schuman put it in 1950, "Europe will not be built all at once, or as a single whole: it will be built by concrete achievements which first create de facto solidarity."

And so the method has proceeded, from coal and steel (European Coal and Steel Community Treaty), through agriculture and commerce (Treaty of Rome), environmental regulation and research and development (Single European Act), to transport policy, training, immigration policy, and a whole battery of measures designed to bring about full economic and monetary union (the Maastricht treaty). Step by step with these developments has been the march toward political unification, with the growth of a European Court, the development of the European Parliament from a talking-shop of national appointees into a directly elected assembly with real legislative powers, the extension of majority voting at the Council of Ministers, and even the announcement, in the Maastricht treaty, of something called European citizenship, the rights and duties of which have yet to be defined. Almost every one of these political changes was justified at the time on practical grounds: just a slight adjustment to make things easier, or more effective, or to reflect new realities. The economic changes and the transfers of new areas of competence to EC institutions are likewise usually presented as mere practical adjustments. At the same time, many continental European politicians (such as German Chancellor Helmut Kohl and French President François Mitterrand) talk openly of the ultimate grand political goal: the creation of a federal European state.

There is a strange disjunction between these two types of "European" discourse, the practical and the ideal. But this is just a sign of functionalism successfully at work. The argument for "Europe" switches to and fro, from claims about practical benefits to expressions of political idealism and back again. If one disagrees with advocates of "Europe" about the practical advantages, they say, "Well, you may be right about this or that disadvantage, but surely it's a price worth paying for such a wonderful political ideal." And if one casts doubt on the political desirability of the ideal, they reply, "Never mind about that, just think of the economic advantages." The truth is that both arguments for "Europe" are fundamentally flawed.

Dunce Cap

The economic project embodied in the European Economic Community (EEC) was a true reflection of its origins in a piece of Franco-German bargaining. German industry was given the opportunity to flood other member states with its exports, thanks to a set of rules designed to eliminate artificial barriers to competition and trade within the "common market." France, on the other hand, was given an elaborate system of protection for its agriculture, the so-called Common Agricultural Policy (CAP).

The general aims of the CAP, as set out in Article 39 of the Treaty of Rome, included stable markets and "a fair standard of living for the agricultural community." On that slender basis, France established one of the most complex and expensive systems of agricultural protectionism in human history. It is based on high external tariffs, high export subsidies, and internal price support by means of intervention buying (the most costly system of price support yet invented, since it involves collecting and storing tens of millions of tons of excess produce). By the time this system was fully established in 1967, EEC farm prices had been driven up to 175 percent of world prices for beef, 185 percent for wheat, 400 percent for butter, and 440 percent for sugar. The annual cost of the CAP is now $45 billion and rising;

more than ten percent of this is believed to be paid to a myriad of scams. Thanks to this policy, a European family of four now pays more than $1,600 a year in additional food costs—a hidden tax greater than the poll tax that brought rioters out onto the streets of London.

Even the most hardened advocates of "Europe" are always a little embarrassed by the CAP. The massive corruption that flows from it—phantom exports picking up export subsidies, smuggled imports relabeled as EC products, nonexistent Italian olive groves receiving huge subsidies, and so on—is embarrassing enough, but it is the system itself that requires defense. Ten or twenty years ago, one used to hear its proponents arguing that at least there would be stocks of food available if Western Europe came under siege. That argument seemed thin then and sounds positively fatuous today. If pressed, they will insist that the CAP is gradually being reformed, pointing out that the beef mountains and wine lakes are getting smaller. These reforms, however, are achieved only by spending more money in such schemes as the infamous set-aside payments given to farmers as a reward for not growing anything. More commonly, though, the defenders of "Europe" will say that the CAP is just an unfortunate detail, that they are aware of its problems, and that one really should not use it to blacken "Europe's" name.

But the CAP is not just a detail. It is, by a huge margin, the largest single item of EC spending, taking up roughly 60 percent of the budget every year. It dominates the EC's external trade policy, distorting the world market and seriously undermining the ability of poorer countries elsewhere to export their own agricultural produce. It almost broke the Uruguay round of the General Agreement on Tariffs and Trade (GATT), thanks to the French government's irrational obsession with agricultural protectionism—irrational, that is, because agriculture accounts for only four percent of French GDP, and much of the other 96 percent would have benefited from lower world tariffs.

No account of the economic functioning of "Europe" can fail to begin with the CAP, and no study that examines it can fail to conclude that it is a colossal waste of money. Even the European Commission, which administers the scheme, has admitted that "farmers do not seem to have benefited from the increasing support which they have received." Enthusiasts for "Europe" often wax lyrical about European achievements such as the German highway system or the French railways—things that were built by national governments. Almost the only major achievement of the EC—the only thing it has constructed and operated itself—is the CAP. It is not an encouraging precedent.

Leveling the Playing Field

The CAP sets the tone for other areas of the EC's trading policy. Although it would be unfair to describe the EC as behaving like a "Fortress Europe" (so far), it is nevertheless true that "Europe" has evolved an elaborate system of tariffs and discriminatory trading agreements to protect its sensitive industries. Agriculture has the highest tariffs; ranging below it are such products as steel, textiles, clothing, and footwear (as Poland, Hungary, and the Czech Republic have discovered to their dismay—food, steel, textiles, clothing, and footwear being their own most important products). The EC has been at the forefront in developing so-called voluntary export restraints with countries such as Japan. In addition, "Europe" has shown extraordinary ingenuity in adapting the GATT's "antidumping" measures to block the flow of innumerable imports: electronic typewriters, hydraulic excavators, dot-matrix printers, audiocassettes, and halogen lights from Japan; compact disc players from Japan and Korea; small-screen color televisions from Korea, China, and Hong Kong, and so on.

A recent study of EC trade policy by L. A. Winters uses the phrase "managed liberalization" to describe the EC's foot-dragging progress toward freer trade. "Managed liberalization," notes Winters, "is a substitute for genuine liberalization, but a poor one, because it typically attenuates competition in precisely those sectors which are most in need of improved efficiency." Nor is this surprising, since the trade policy emerges from a system of political bargaining in which the governments of EC member states compete to protect their favorite industries. Massive state subsidies to flagship enterprises (French car manufacturers, Spanish steel mills, Belgian and Greek national airlines) are common practice. In addition, the officials at the European Commission in Brussels are strongly influenced by the French *dirigiste* tradition, which sees it as the role of the state to select and nurture special "champion" industries. This was the driving force behind the new powers granted to the EC in 1986 to "strengthen the scientific and technological basis of European industry." In practice, this means spending millions of taxpayers' dollars developing French microchips that will never compete with East Asian ones on the open market.

Inside the tariff wall, a kind of free trade area has indeed been created. Many obstacles to trade have been removed (though important barriers remain in the realm of services, as British insurance firms are still discovering when they try to break into the German market), and industry as a whole has benefited from this process of internal liberalization. However, the long-term effects may be more harmful than beneficial. In their attempt to create a level playing field for competition on equal terms within the EC, the administrators of "Europe" have leveled up, not down. They have tried to raise both the standards and the costs of industry throughout the community to the high levels practiced in Europe's foremost industrial country, Germany. When this process is complete, industrialists inside the EC may indeed sell goods to one another on equal terms, but their goods will all be uncompetitive on the world market.

This leveling up occurs in two areas. The first is the harmonization of standards. Brussels has issued a mass of regulations laying down the most minute specifications for industrial products and processes; the dominant influence on these has been the German Institute for Norms, which has the strictest standards in Europe. Harmonization is meant to simplify matters for producers, who now have only one standard within the EC instead of various national ones. But in many cases, as the task of matching product to standard becomes relatively simpler, it is also made absolutely more expensive. In addition, the EC has powers relating to environmental protection and health and safety at work, which are increasingly used to impose German-style costs on industries and services. The costs fall especially heavily on small enterprises, which have to pay disproportionately for monitoring equipment, inspection, and certification. This distorts the market in favor of large corporations, penalizing the small enterprises that are the seed corn of any growing economy.

The second way in which the playing field is leveled up to German standards is in the social costs of labor. German employers pay heavily for the privilege of giving people jobs: there are generous pension schemes to pay for health insurance, long holidays, maternity and paternity leave, and other forms of social insurance. As a consequence, labor costs are $25 per hour in the former West Germany (the highest in the world), as opposed to $17 in Japan, $16 in the United States, and $12 in the United Kingdom. German work practices mean that a machine in a German factory operates an average of only 53 hours a week, as opposed to 69 hours in France and 76 in Britain. And the average worker in Germany spends only 1,506 hours each year actually at work, as opposed to 1,635 hours in Britain, 1,847 in the United States, and 2,165 in Japan.

Over the last five years, the European Commission has proposed a whole range of measures to increase the rights of workers and limit their working hours. When measures in this so-called social action program could not gain the required unanimous support from member states (notably Britain), they were dressed up as health and safety matters, for which only a majority vote is required. Further costs on employers were imposed by a "social protocol" added to the Maastricht treaty. Although Britain was able to gain a special exemption from this agreement, it is likely that many of the new measures adopted under the protocol eventually will filter back to Britain through other parts of the "European" administrative machine.

Some of these measures are inspired, no doubt, by concern for the plight of the poorest workers in the community's southern member states. But the general aim of the policy is clearly to protect the high-labor-cost economies (above all, Germany) from competitors employing cheaper labor. In the short or medium term, this policy will damage the economies of the poorer countries, which will have artificially high labor costs imposed on them. In the long term, it will harm Germany, too, by reducing its incentive to adapt to worldwide competition. "Europe," whose share of world trade and relative rate of economic growth are already in decline, will enter the next century stumbling under the weight of its own costs like a woolly mammoth sinking into a melting tundra.

The final expression of this leveling-up syndrome is the plan for monetary union. As outlined in the Maastricht treaty, the idea is to create a Euro-deutsche mark, operated by a body closely modeled on the Bundesbank and situated in Frankfurt. Earlier moves in this direction were not encouraging: the European Exchange Rate Mechanism, which linked the currencies of member states to the deutsche mark, fell apart spectacularly in October 1992. In the process, the British government spent nearly $6 billion in a doomed attempt to prop up the pound, and Germany is thought to have spent roughly $14 billion in an equally futile effort to support the Italian lira. The artificially high interest rates that countries such as Britain had imposed to maintain their currency's parity with the deutsche mark severely intensified the 1989–93 recession; the human costs of the unnecessary indebtedness, bankruptcies, and unemployment cannot be calculated.

The Exchange Rate Mechanism was, as Professor Sir Alan Walters, an adviser to former British Prime Minister Margaret Thatcher, famously put it, "half-baked." Currencies were neither fully fixed nor freely floating but pegged to so-called fixed rates that could be changed. This provided the world markets, at times of pressure on any particular currency, with an irresistible one-way bet. That problem, of course, will not arise once the currencies of "Europe" are merged into a single Euro-mark—though the activities of the world currency markets in the days just before the conversion terms are announced will be a wonder to behold.

Once the Euro-mark is in place, a different set of problems will arise. Whatever the "economic convergence programs" dutifully embarked on by the governments of member states, this single currency will be covering a number of national economies with widely varying characteristics. Hitherto, changes in the values of their national currencies have been one of the essential ways in which the relative strengths and weaknesses of those countries were both expressed and adjusted. With that mechanism gone, other forms of expression will operate, such as the collapse of industries or the mass migration of labor.

The European Commission understands this problem and has a ready solution: massive transfers of money to the weaker economies of "Europe." The machinery to administer this huge program of subsidies is already in place, in the form of regional funds, "structural" funds, and "cohesion payments." All that is lacking so far is the actual money, for which purpose the outgoing president of the European Commission, Jacques Delors, recently proposed increasing the European budget by more than $150 billion over the next five years.

A model for the future of an economically unified Europe can be found in modern Italy, which united the prosperous, advanced provinces of the north with the Third World poverty of the south. After more than a century of political and economic union, huge disparities still remain between the two halves of Italy—despite (or indeed partly because of) all the subsidies that are poured into the south via institutions such as the Cassa del Mezzogiorno, the independent society established by the Italian government to help develop the south. As southern Italians have had the opportunity to discover, an economy based on subsidies unites the inefficiencies of state planning with almost limitless opportunities for graft and corruption. It is a sad irony that today, just as the leaders of "Europe" are preparing for unification, the politicians of Italy are seriously considering dismantling their country into two or three separate states.

Decaffeinated Politics

So much for the economic benefits of European unity. At this point the advocates of "Europe" usually shift to their other line of defense. This is not just a money-grubbing enterprise, they say, to be totted up in terms of profit and loss: "Europe" is a political ideal, a spiritual adventure, a new experiment in brotherhood and cooperation. Has it not made war in Europe unthinkable? Is it not the natural next step for mankind, at a time when the old idea of national sovereignty is evidently obsolete? Does it not show the way to the abolition of old-fashioned national feeling, with all its hostilities, prejudices, and resentments?

The answer to all these questions, unfortunately, is no. The argument that the EC is responsible for the lack of war in post-1945 Europe is hard to substantiate. A far more obvious reason is the Cold War, which obliged Western Europe to adopt a common defensive posture and a system of deterrence so effective that war between Western and Eastern Europe never happened. The fact that a group of West European countries were able to cooperate in the EC was more a symptom of the lack of belligerent tensions in postwar Western Europe than a cause. Liberal democracies had been established in most West European countries after 1945; even if the EEC had not existed, it is hard to imagine a scenario in which Germany would have wanted to invade France, or France drop nuclear bombs on Germany. Even if one concedes for the sake of argument that the EEC did ensure peace for the last generation or two, this cannot be used as a reason for closer integration, since the EEC had this supposed effect at a time when it was not a unified supranational entity but a group of cooperating nation-states.

The idea of "Europe" is founded, however, on the belief that the nation-state is obsolete. This is an article of faith against which rational arguments cannot prevail. It is no use pointing out that the most successful countries in the modern world—Japan, the United States, and indeed Germany itself—are nation-states. It matters little if one says that some of the most dynamic economies today belong to small states—South Korea, Taiwan, Singapore—that feel no need to submerge themselves in large multinational entities. And it is regarded as bad taste to point out that the multinational federations most recently in the news were the U.S.S.R. and the Federal Republic of Yugoslavia. They are merely the latest in a long list of multinational states that have collapsed in modern times, from the Austro-Hungarian Empire to the various postcolonial federations set up by the British in central Africa, east Africa, and the West Indies. Nigeria, for example, kept Biafra only by warfare and starvation; India needs armed force to retain Nagaland and Kashmir. "But Europe will not be like that," say the federalists. "We have traditions of mutual tolerance and civilized behavior." Yes, we have some such traditions; they are the traditions that have evolved within fairly stable nation-states. Whether they last indefinitely under the new conditions of multinational politics remains to be seen.

What will political life be like in the sort of European federation currently proposed in Brussels and Bonn? Some of the powers of national governments will be transferred upward to the European level, while others will move down to a "Europe of the regions" (Catalonia, Bavaria, Wales, etc.). The official vision of political life at the uppermost level is essentially that of Jean Monnet, the original inventor of the community: a technocrat's ideal, a world in which large-scale solutions are devised to large-scale problems by farsighted expert administrators. (The most common argument for abolishing nation-states is that problems nowadays are just too big for individual states to handle. In fact, there have always been issues that cross international borders, from postal services to drug enforcement to global trade. It cannot be the size of the problem that dictates that it must be dealt with by supranational authority rather than international cooperation, but some other reason that the advocates of European federation have yet to explain.)

This technocratic vision is of a decaffeinated political world, from which real politics has been carefully extracted. Things will surely turn out differently. Real politics will still operate at the European level. The one form it will not take, however, is that of federation-wide democratic politics. For that, we would need "Europe"-wide parties, operating across the whole federation in the way that the Republican and Democratic parties operate across the United States.

There are already some ghostly transnational groupings in the European Parliament: the Socialist Group, the European People's Party (the Christian Democrats), and so on. But these are just alliances formed at Strasbourg by members of the European Parliament elected on the tickets of their own national parties. No one can really envisage ordinary voters in, say, Denmark being inspired by the leader of their preferred Euro-party, who might make his or her speeches in Portuguese. The basic facts of linguistic, cultural, and geographic difference make it impossible to imagine federation-wide mass politics ever becoming the dominant form of political life in Europe. Instead, the pursuit of national interests by national politicians will continue at the highest "European" levels. Yet it will do so in a way subtly different from the way in which local representatives within a national political system press for the interests of their localities. Although a member of parliament for Yorkshire may push hard on Yorkshire's behalf, on all major issues the member votes according to what he or she thinks is in Britain's interest; the MP belongs to a national party that addresses those issues with national policies.

The art of "European" politics, on the other hand, will be to do nothing more than dress up national interests as if they were Europe-wide ones. With any particular nation paying only a small proportion of the European budget, each set of national politicians will seek to maximize those European spending projects that benefit their own country. The modus operandi of European politics, therefore (already visible in the Council of Ministers today), will be logrolling and back-scratching: you support my pet proposal, even though you think it is a bad one, and in return I shall back yours. This is a recipe not only for nonstop increases in spending, but also for radical incoherence in policymaking. And with politics at the highest level operating as a scramble for funds, it is hard to see how politicians at the lower level of Europe's "regions" can fail to replicate it: they will have fewer real governmental powers but more populist opportunities to woo their voters with spending.

This type of political life is accompanied by two grave dangers. In any system where democratic accountability is attenuated and the powers of politicians to make deals behind closed doors is strengthened, the likely consequence is a growth in political corruption. Corrupt practices are already common in the political life of several European countries: their exposure has led recently to the prosecution, flight into exile, or suicide of former prime ministers in Italy, Greece, and France. A federal Europe, far from correcting these vices, will offer them a wider field of action.

A more serious danger, however, lies in store for the political life of a federal "Europe": the revival of the politics of nationalist hostility and resentment. Aggressive nationalism is typically a syndrome of the dispossessed, of those who feel power has been taken from them. Foreigners are often the most convenient focus of such resentment, whatever the true causes of the powerlessness may be. But in a system where power really has been taken from national governments and transferred to European bodies in which, by definition, the majority vote will always lie in the hands of foreigners, such nationalist thinking will acquire an undeniable logic. Of course, if "Europe" moves ever onward and upward in an unprecedented increase in prosperity for all its citizens, the grounds for resentment may be slight; that is not, however, a scenario that anyone can take for granted.

In this respect, the whole "European" project furnishes a classic example of the fallacious belief that the way to remove hostility between groups, peoples, or states is to build new structures over their heads. Too often that method yields exactly the opposite result. The most commonly repeated version of this argument is that Germany needs to be "tied in" or "tied down" by a structure of European integration to prevent it from wandering off dangerously into the empty spaces of Mitteleuropa. If Germany really has different interests from the rest of "Europe," the way to deal with it, surely, is not to force it into an institutional straitjacket (which can only build up German resentment in the long run), but to devise ways of pursuing those interests that are compatible with the interests of its allies and partners. So far, Germany's involvement in "Europe" looks rather like the action of a jovial uncle at a children's party who, to show goodwill, allows his hands to be tied behind his back. It is not a posture that he will want to stay in for long, and his mood may change when he becomes aware of innumerable little fingers rifling through his pockets.

* * *

9.2

THE EU AND ITS "CONSTITUTION": PUBLIC OPINION, POLITICAL ELITES, AND THEIR INTERNATIONAL CONTEXT

Alberta Sbragia

The author of this piece, Alberta Sbragia, is director of the Center for West European Studies at the University of Pittsburgh and a strong proponent of European integration. Here, Sbragia focuses on the many useful tasks, such as the removal of barriers and regulations that impede trade across the Continent, that the European Union (EU) continues to perform despite the popular rejection of the proposed EU constitution by the French and Dutch voting publics. She argues that the political integration of Europe is such a valuable phenomenon that it will continue by other means (which she does not specify), but she fails to address the reasons for the constitution's rejection. And while she admits that the political integration of Europe is an elite-led process, she does not speculate on why the European publics are less than enamored with it. Students should ask whether she confronts any of the objections to the process posed by Noel Malcolm in his selection in this chapter. The political integration of Europe comes at a cost of giving up much of the power and symbolism that mobilized publics to support and sacrifice for love of country. Sbragia, however, is not especially fond of the traditions that heretofore defined the unique nations of Europe; hence, protection of the sovereign power of the nation-states of Europe is not a high priority for her.

The European Union is going about its regular business. It is putting forth proposals to keep the Doha Round alive, continuing to negotiate a major trade agreement with Mercosur in South America, keeping peace-keeping troops in Bosnia and Herzegovina, spending development aid in numerous poor countries, financially supporting the Palestine Authority while giving Israel preferential access to the EU market, investigating Microsoft's business practices, and battling over the reach and scope of an ambitious new legislative attempt to regulate the chemical industry. The EU Greenhouse Gas Emission Trading Scheme, the largest greenhouse emissions trading scheme in the world, is up and running. The European Central Bank is making monetary policy decisions while the euro makes up almost 20% of central banks' foreign currency holdings. The European Medicines Agency (EMEA) has called for suspending the sale of the children's vaccine Hexavac. The European Court of Justice, for its part, has recently declared illegal a high profile Italian law designed to prevent foreign takeover of Italian energy companies. And the commissioner for Health and Consumer Protection is playing a leading role in the EU's response to the threat of a pandemic of avian bird flu.

Alberta Sbragia, "The EU and its 'Constitution': Public Opinion, Political Elites and the International Context," *PS: Political Science and Politics* 39, no. 2 (April 2006): 237–241.

Meanwhile, EU citizens are enjoying the benefits of the EU in very direct ways—when they fly on a low cost airline, make a phone call which is far cheaper than it otherwise would have been, study abroad while receiving credit back at their home institution, cross national boundaries without passport or customs control, or use the euro in any one of the 12 EU member-states which have adopted it. Although the EU is often characterized as a regulatory rather than a welfare state (Majone 1996), it is responsible for many policy outputs which are generally popular.

The defeat of the EU Constitution[1] in French and Dutch referenda held in mid-2005 has not blocked the EU from carrying out its usual activities. Those are currently subject to the Treaty of Nice as well as the other treaties which have been ratified since 1958 and are still in force. Nor has it affected the kinds of benefits to which EU citizens have become accustomed. While there is angst and confusion about the future direction of the Union among political elites, it is important to note that the institutionalized machinery of governance which has evolved over nearly 50 years is in place and functioning. The fact that the Constitution's defeat did not alter the by now routine operations of policymaking highlights how embedded such policymaking is in the political life of an integrating Europe. The institutions of the European Union—the European Commission, the European Court of Justice, the European Parliament, the Council of Ministers, and the European Central Bank—are in place and doing the kind of substantive work they did before the Constitution was drafted.

Nonetheless, the Constitution's defeat is clearly an important moment in the history of European integration. For the first time, an agreement designed to further integration has been resoundingly defeated in two of the original six founding members of the European Union. Although supporters of the Constitution argue that the use of the referendum is an inappropriate mechanism for the approval of treaties, the referendum does enjoy a legitimacy which is difficult to negate. The impact of the "no" votes has been so great that many analysts argue the days of further integration in Europe are finished.

The medium to long-term impact of the Constitution's rejection, however, is far from clear. Even without the contingency endemic to international affairs, the Constitution's defeat very probably will have unanticipated consequences. And those consequences, in turn, may actually run counter to the predictions of those who argue that the future looks bleak for European integration.

Two basic arguments can be made regarding the implications for European integration of the Constitution's defeat. The first argues that the political context has changed so fundamentally that policymaking and the trajectory of further integration will be affected in irreversible ways. In that sense, the defeat is a strategic defeat for those who wish for Europe to move toward ever greater integration.

The second argues that, by contrast, this defeat will simply encourage Europe's political elites to continue the process of integration through means other than treaties put to a referendum. That process could include a new treaty focused on the institutional changes incorporated in the Constitution which would be submitted to parliamentary ratification only. More interestingly, however, it could also involve moving toward further integration by using the institutional instruments currently available under the Treaty of Nice—in spite of the fact that political elites supported the Constitution because they viewed those instruments as too weak to allow further integration. Both arguments can be justified.

1. The "Constitution" was actually a constitutional treaty rather than a constitution as traditionally understood. However, the political debate in most countries used the term "Constitution" rather than "constitutional treaty." and I therefore shall use the term "Constitution" as well.

The Constitution

The Constitution was clearly meant to drive integration forward. Although the "Constitution" was actually a constitutional treaty since it had to be ratified unanimously and could only be amended unanimously, it was viewed as the next major agreement which would lead both to more integration among the EU-25 and pave the way for further enlargement. It was written in a less intergovernmental fashion than had been previous treaties. Although national governments negotiating in an intergovernmental forum had the last word, national and (especially) European parliamentarians had an important role in shaping its content and direction.

The comparatively diverse group of participants in the Constitution-drafting process highlighted the Constitution's symbolic value. That symbolic value was in fact far greater than its actual substantive content would have warranted. And the question now stands—how much does its defeat matter?

Much of the EU Constitution was not new. It included "old" treaties which had been approved (at times in referenda in selected countries) and had been in effect for years. Those treaties will remain in effect. The defeat primarily affects proposed new institutional arrangements. Those included increasing the power of the European Parliament, establishing new voting weights for the various member-states, and strengthening the Union's external relations. It may, therefore, become more difficult, at the institutional level, to construct a more cohesive European Union in the global arena. Finally, enlargement will become more problematic, as the proposed institutional changes were designed to accommodate new members.

A Strategic Defeat?

There is no doubt that the defeats have re-framed the process of European integration in the minds of Europe's political class. There is currently a sense of indirection, of confusion, and of doubt as to where the grand project that the Six began with the Treaty of Paris in 1951 is going. The current climate is reminiscent of that which emerged after the Maastricht Treaty was approved by a margin of 1% in France in September 1992 and was only approved by the Danes in a second referendum in May 1993. At that time, too, the Commission was weakened, political elites were shaken, and the process of integration seemed much frailer than it had appeared only a few months earlier. The calls for full EU membership by the post-communist countries undergoing often difficult transitions to democracy added a kind of pressure which national leaders were at times reluctant to accept. Terms such as "a multi-speed Europe," "variable geometry," and a "Europe a la Carte" entered the political as well as academic discourse about future paths which European integration might follow (Stubb 1996).

Of course, the EU recovered in a spectacular fashion from the Maastricht crisis. Although a great deal was written at the time about the caution that elites would need to demonstrate given the French public's reluctance to whole-heartedly endorse the next stage of integration, the European Union in 2005 looks very different from its pre-Maastricht incarnation. It created the new institutions called for in the Treaty and continued to become more important as a global actor. The European Central Bank was established, the euro was accepted by 12 of the 15 members, and, on the international stage, the EU was critical to the establishment of an important new international institution—the International Criminal Court—as well as to the successful conclusion of the Uruguay Round. It even began developing a European Security and Defense Policy. Thus, the question arises of whether the long-term implications of the Constitution's defeat will be as transient as were those of the narrow margin of victory in France (and the necessity of holding a second referendum in Denmark) during the Maastricht process.

The difference between Maastricht and the Constitution lies in the clear and unequivocal distinction between approval (however slim the margin) and defeat. Maastricht became the treaty in force—with its commitment to a single currency and a more united European Union acting on the global stage. Furthermore, it was a much smaller EU that had to deal with the aftershocks of the Maastricht debate—the then EU-12 could more easily regroup than the current EU-25 (soon to be 27).

The consequences of defeat could in fact be far more damaging than the consequences of a razor-thin ratification. The political momentum which has traditionally been so important for the movement toward further integration could be absent, for political leaders would be unwilling to act against public opinion. The lack of a "permissive consensus" on the part of electorates could lead to a protracted stalemate, paralysis, and a gradual drift away from the kind of goals and aspirations which are traditionally associated with further integration. In particular, the attempt to create a stronger global presence would be stymied, and the move toward bringing ever more policy areas under the EU umbrella would be stopped or even reversed. The role of the so-called Community method—which involves a key policy-making role for the supranational European Commission, the European Parliament, and the European Court of Justice—would be at best frozen. And further enlargement—beyond the accession of Romania and Bulgaria—would become impossible.

In a worst case scenario, the lack of commitment by political leaders to the European Union would gradually infect the EU's institutions, for the latter's effectiveness is in fact anchored in the willingness of national institutions and elites to support the overall project of integration by supporting its supranational institutions.

The view that the defeat of the Constitution will sap the political momentum from the Union privileges the role of public opinion in the process of European integration. It implicitly argues that the hitherto elite-driven process of integration has been fundamentally transformed. The role of a majoritarian representative institution—the national parliament—in ratifying treaties which advance European integration would have been diminished by the expression of voters engaged in direct democracy through the referendum. In fact, given the role of party government and party discipline in national parliamentary systems, the role of political parties would have been diminished.

Since the major political parties in Europe (whether in government or in opposition) have supported treaty ratification since 1958 and supported the ratification of the Constitution, the view that European integration will stall privileges public opinion *vis à vis* the opinions of governmental and party elites. In brief, the key support for integration—elite consensus—would become less powerful as an effective driving force.

The role of public opinion in European integration over the past 50 years has been ambiguous. The scholarly literature has come to varied conclusions, and in general scholars of European integration have focused on the role of elites in driving integration forward. Yet it is fair to ask how such an elite-driven process could sustain itself over so many decades. The liberalization of markets in particular would have been expected to lead to more contentious politics directed specifically against the EU than has been evident (Imig and Tarrow 2001; Gabel 1998; Sbragia 2000). Perhaps the underlying assumption of those who assume that public opinion should be expected to play a central role in the integration process was most pungently expressed by Herbert Morrison, deputy prime minister of Britain at the time when the British Cabinet rejected the invitation to join the European Coal and Steel Community. As Morrison summed up the issue, "It's no good. We can't do it. The Durham miners would never wear it" (cited in Gilbert 2003, 42).

If public opinion were indeed to significantly slow the pace of integration or re-shape its nature in the post-Constitution phase, it would have entered the stage as a significant factor relatively late in the process of integration. Given that elections to the European Parliament have been viewed as "second order elections"—based far more on national issues and political cleavages as opposed to EU-wide political debate—and that elites have enjoyed a "permissive consensus" which they have used to deepen integration, the strengthening of the role of public opinion in determining the course of European integration would represent a major new phase in this project.

The EU: A Geo-Economic/Political Project?

Europe's political elites, however, may well continue the process of European integration, enlargement, and global integration *even if* key aspects of the Constitution are not ultimately resurrected in some fashion. This argument views the European Union as a key geo-economic/political project as well as a complex variant of a (con) or (semi) or (crypto) federation/federalism-constructing exercise (Sbragia 1993; Majone 2006).

It is quite possible that the EU's international dimension may well override the kinds of constraints imposed by public opinion. If the EU is viewed only or primarily as a domestic political system, the defeat of the Constitution would in fact be a strategic defeat. If the EU is also conceptualized as a geo-economic/political project, however, the defeat might well have unanticipated consequences which are far more conducive to further integration than might be evident in the short-term.

The beginning of the accession negotiations with Turkey in October in the face of widespread public hostility to Turkish membership symbolizes the determination of governments to carry out the promises they have already made to other international actors. Although governments opened the accession negotiations with Turkey after a good deal of conflict with each other and down-to-the-wire negotiations with the Austrian government (which wanted to leave open the possibility of a privileged partnership for Turkey rather than accession), what stands out is the fact that accession negotiations actually went forward as planned. A mere four months after the Constitution's defeat, the EU was not only back in business, but back in a very difficult kind of business. Although many analysts argue that Turkey will never actually join, the very fact of opening negotiations has triggered a process of long-term change within Turkey that makes the outcome less predictable than the skeptics admit.

In a similar vein, the active engagement of the EU in the Doha Round symbolizes the understanding by elites that Europe's economic well-being is nested within a larger—global—economic reality. Although French voters fear economic liberalization of the services sector, it is quite possible that at least some such liberalization will occur due to pressure from the Doha negotiations. The EU is enmeshed in a larger multilateral trading system, and the decisions made at that level affect it in ways which have not been well understood by either publics or political scientists.

I would argue that external challenges, although under-studied in the EU literature, have always been very significant in influencing the evolution of European integration.[2] The Soviet threat and the evolution of the GATT in the 1950s, the impact of de-colonization on states' commercial interests in the 1960s, the changes in economic competitiveness in the 1980s, and the perceived need for greater military and political power during the Balkan crises of the 1990s have all been influential in the process.

---

2. For a similar perspective on American politics, see Mayhew 2005.

The dynamics of European integration have been embedded in the larger international environment, and that environment cannot be ignored in explaining the extraordinary depth of European integration.

More specifically, the implementation of the customs union in goods was supported by the GATT negotiations in the Kennedy and Dillon rounds (Langhammer 2005). The Single European Act which brought the single market to the EU was motivated in great part by the sense that European firms were falling behind their Japanese and American counterparts (Sandholtz and Zysman 1989) while the Maastricht Treaty was shaped in significant ways by the fall of the Berlin Wall and the end of the division of Europe. The restructuring of the Common Agricultural Policy was partially driven by the Uruguay Round negotiations (Patterson 1997). The movement toward a European Security and Defense Policy was at least partially a response to pressure from Washington (Howorth 2005) as well as to Europe's failures in addressing the tragedy of the wars in the Balkans.

External economic and security pressures will continue to exert a deep influence. While some of the most immediate pressures have been addressed by extending membership to the EU-15's neighbors, the enlargement process cannot keep meeting that challenge indefinitely. The WTO, the rise of China, changes in American grand strategy, and new security threats on the periphery of the Union will unavoidably push the European project in new directions as elites attempt to deal with emerging situations in world politics.

Some of the most significant institutional changes that the Constitution would have made were in fact designed to help the EU address foreign policy challenges in a more cohesive and effective way. Ironically, public opinion across the EU seems to favor a more unified global posture on the part of Brussels (German Marshall Fund 2005). Europe does not exist in a vacuum, and both elites and publics are aware of that basic fact. A more cohesive Euro-level foreign policy may therefore emerge even in the absence of the institutional changes that the Constitution would have produced. It is very likely that elites can pull mass publics with them in the area of foreign policy. In fact, the effort to strengthen the Union as a global actor can serve to link elites and publics more firmly than have economic policies of liberalization and regulation.

Economic integration, inevitably involving economic liberalization, is not as intuitively attractive as is a "stronger Europe on the world stage." Whether such liberalization can be successfully presented to voters as necessary for the strengthening of the EU as a geo-economic project is unclear, but it is possible that the "twinning" of European economic and foreign policy integration would help make economic liberalization more appealing.

The argument that an elite-driven process of integration—which incorporates party, governmental, and many business elites as well as national parliamentarians—has suffered a disruption but neither a strategic change of direction nor a strategic defeat downplays the role of public opinion as expressed in the defeat of the Constitution. It assumes that elites will in fact be able to move toward further integration. External events will provide support for further integration—such as recent events in the area of energy have demonstrated.

One of the unanticipated consequences of the Constitution's defeat in France and the Netherlands may be that integration will proceed in new ways. Just as the defeat of the European Defence Community in 1954 led to the European Economic Community, so too the need to circumvent public opinion (or at least not consult it directly) may lead to new forms of integration. The American executive, for example, has developed a host of ways to deal with international affairs which essentially circumvent or limit the role of Congress. Executive agreements and "fast track authority" for trade agreements (now known as trade promotion authority) both have been designed to allow the executive to have more flexibility in international than domestic affairs.

Second, cohesion in the foreign policy arena may develop more quickly than it has heretofore. Integration in foreign policy has lagged integration in "domestic" affairs given the member-states' concern with sovereignty. However, elites' desire to continue the process of integration coupled with the need to matter in a world in which not only the U.S. but also such countries as China and India will be important actors may provide the impetus for moving forward in that area. The role that the EU has played since 1958 in the GATT/WTO provides a useful precedent.

The defeat of the Constitution ironically may lead national leaders to move forward, develop new mechanisms to forge agreements without creating a context in which referenda are called, and actually become far more cohesive in foreign policy than would have been expected. One of the motivating forces for the Constitution was the desire on the part of national elites that the European Union should become a more effective global actor. The defeat of the Constitution will not necessarily defeat that desire, and external pressures will continue to entice national leaders to follow that road. Geo-economics and geo-politics have always provided a rationale within domestic politics for the insulation of representative institutions from direct constituency pressures. It is very possible that they will provide the same kind of rationale for the European Union.

If the EU is in fact framed or presented by elites as a geo-economic and geo-political project which will maximize European influence on the world stage and thereby help it respond to external events, it is quite possible that mass publics will become more supportive and that integration will move relatively rapidly in the one area that has been most resistant to Europeanization—that of foreign policy. Furthermore "sensitive" domestic areas clearly subject to external influences, such as energy, will become Europeanized far more quickly than one would expect.

The lack of institutional efficiency which the Constitution was supposed to remedy will undoubtedly make this process messier and more convoluted than the Constitution's backers would have liked. That same inefficiency will, however, allow the new accession states to play a role more similar to that which the EU-15 have played and give them a chance to make their mark in the shaping of the EU-25. If external pressures do indeed allow political elites to move integration forward, convince public opinion that such integration is acceptable, and help integrate the new accession states politically rather than simply institutionally, the defeat of the Constitution may be viewed quite differently 20 years from now than it is at present.

References

Gabel, Matthew J. 1998. *Interest and Integration: Market Liberalization, Public Opinion, and European Union.* Ann Arbor: University of Michigan Press.

German Marshall Fund of the United States et al. 2005. *Transatlantic Trends: Key Findings 2005.* Washington, D.C.: German Marshall Fund of the United States.

Gilbert, Mark. 2003. *Surpassing Realism: The Politics of European Integration since 1945.* New York: Rowman and Littlefield.

Howorth, Jolyon. 2005. "Transatlantic Perspectives on European Security in the Coming Decade." *Yale Journal of International Affairs* (summer/fall): 8–22.

Imig, Doug, and Sidney Tarrow, eds. 2001. *Contentious Europeans: Protest and Politics in the New Europe.* Lanham, MD: Rowman and Littlefield.

Langhammer, Rolf J. 2005. "The EU Offer of Service Trade Liberalization in the Doha Round: Evidence of Not-Yet-Perfect Customs Union." *Journal of Common Market Studies* 51 (2): 311–325.

Majone, Giandomenico. 1996. *Regulating Europe*. New York: Routledge.

——. 2006. "The Common Sense of European Integration." Presented at the Princeton International Relations Faculty Colloquium. March 13.

Mayhew, David R. 2005. "Wars and American Politics." *Perspectives on Politics* 3 (September): 473–493.

Patterson, Lee Ann. 1997. "Agricultural Policy Reform in the European Community: A Three-Level Game Analysis." *International Organization* 51 (1): 135–165.

Sandholtz, Wayne, and John Zysman. 1989. "1992: Recasting the European Bargain." *World Politics* 42: 95–128.

Sbragia, Alberta. 1993. "The European Community: A Balancing Act." *Publius: The Journal of Federalism* 23 (summer): 23–38.

——. 2000. "Governance, the State, and the Market: What Is Going On?" *Governance* 13 (April): 243–250.

Stubb, Alexander C-G. 1996. "A Categorization of Differentiated Integration." *Journal of Common Market Studies* 13 (2): 283–295.

9.3

UNDERSTANDING THE DUTCH "NO": THE EURO, THE EAST, AND THE ELITE

Kees Aarts and Henk van der Kolk

The Dutch are considered among the most enthusiastic supporters of European integration, and so it came as something of a shock when the country's voting public decisively rejected the proposed ratification of a constitution for a federated Europe in 2005. This vote constituted a major setback in the movement to politically and economically unify Europe and vividly demonstrated that this movement was an elite-driven phenomenon. In this selection, Kees Aarts and Henk van der Kolk, two scholars from the Netherlands, demonstrate the size of the gap between the Dutch elite and the country's voting public by citing the difference between the voting results and the support for the EU constitution by the elites. Aarts and van der Kolk also discuss other reasons for the Dutch "no"—in particular, the threat that the inclusion of Eastern European countries in the EU would pose to Dutch power and Western culture. Students will want to think about the specific concerns the Dutch public has about the politically integrated EU and whether these concerns are justified. To what extent do considerations of national pride and patriotism make ordinary citizens reluctant to compromise the sovereignty of their nation-state, irrespective of whether their interests would be better served by membership in the EU?

The Dutch have been counted among the staunchest supporters of European integration ever since the parliamentary ratification of the European Community for Coal and Steel in late 1951. The major political parties—the Christian Democrats (CDA) and its forerunners, the Labor Party (PvdA), and the liberal parties VVD and D66—supported all important European treaties of the past decades. Only the smaller orthodox-Calvinist parties, some smaller left-wing parties, and, more recently, the List Pim Fortuyn (LPF) have opposed these treaties in parliament. This overwhelmingly large support in the Second Chamber of the Dutch parliament included the Treaty of Rome of 2004—the treaty establishing a constitution for Europe. One hundred twenty-eight out of 150 members of parliament favored the ratification of the European Constitution.

Support for European integration was not confined to the political elite. Trend data from the Eurobarometer surveys indicate that since the early 1970s the Dutch population was generally more enthusiastic about the European Union than the populations of the other five founding member states. According to these surveys, three out of every four Dutch citizens judged EU membership to be "a good

---

Kees Aarts and Henk van der Kolk, "Understanding the Dutch 'No': The Euro, the East and the Elite," *PS: Political Science and Politics* 39, no. 2 (April 2006): 243–246.

thing" in late 2004—more than the Germans (60%) or the French (56%). The same survey (Eurobarometer #62) finds that 73% of the Dutch supported *a* constitution for Europe.[1] And *after* the referendum a large majority of voters did express support for the EU.

Yet, at the same time many complained about the low awareness of Europe in the Netherlands. The observation in the Declaration of Laeken (2001) that "within the Union, the European institutions must be brought closer to its citizens" was especially true for the Dutch.[2] Attention to European affairs in the Dutch newspapers was infrequent. In many surveys the Dutch admitted to having only limited interest in news about the EU. The turnout in the 2004 elections for the European parliament was 39%—an increase after it had continuously declined from 58% in 1979, via 51% in 1984, 47% in 1989, 36% in 1994 to 30% in 1999—and was very low compared to local and national elections.

In this context, the result of the referendum on the European Constitution held in the Netherlands on June 1, 2005, came as a surprise. The referendum resulted in a 62-38% victory for the No-vote with an unexpectedly high turnout of 63%. How does this result fit in with the traditional image of the Dutch as champions of the European cause? And why did Dutch voters disagree so strongly with the overwhelming majority in the Dutch Parliament?

In this contribution we propose three partial answers to these questions. The first two pertain to the pace and the scope of the process of European integration. The pace of integration is perceived by many citizens to be too fast. The introduction of a common currency, the euro, in 12 member states in 1999–2002 was probably the most tangible result of this process so far, and it has become a preferred target for frustrated consumers. The current image of the EU is not that of an institution stimulating international trade for the open Dutch economy but rather that of an institution costing too much and threatening both our jobs and our social security.

This popular image of the EU is strengthened by its recent and prospective enlargement. In 2004, 10 new states were admitted to the EU, bringing the total number of members to 25. In late 2004, the Dutch presidency of the EU produced a clear time path for the start of membership negotiations with Turkey. Although the actual entry of Turkey will probably take at least another 10 years, the continuing eastbound expansion of the EU has met with growing popular discontent. The public perception of the expansion in 2004 and especially of the start of the negotiations with Turkey can be interpreted in at least three different but interrelated ways: a threat to the Dutch economy, a threat to Dutch (Western) culture, and a threat to Dutch power within the EU.

We show how these perceptions partially explain the popular attitude toward the EU. But why was there such a deep gap between the elite and the voters? We contend that this gap is not new, nor does it occur in the Netherlands only. The referendum instrument, which had never been used on the national scale in the Netherlands before, fully exposed this gap for the first time.

The data analyzed in this paper were collected in the 2005 Dutch Referendum Study.[3]

---

1. The corresponding figure for France at the time was 70%. The report with the Eurobarometer #62 survey's first results can be found at: http://europa.eu.int/comm/public_opinion/archives/eb/eb62/cb62first_en.pdf (accessed October 6, 2005).
2. See for the declaration of Laecken http://europa.eu.int/constitution/futurum/documents/offtext/doc151201_en.htm (accessed October 6, 2005).
3. The Dutch Referendum Study 2005 is a survey of a sample of the Dutch electorate. The survey consists of a pre- and post-referendum panel study. The pre-referendum study in turn consists of five independent weekly subsamples. The net response was 1,568 (pre-referendum) and 1,284 (post-referendum). The sample frame was formed by an existing

The Euro and the Vote

Enthusiasm for a common currency has always been much greater among the political elites than among the general public. A comparison of data from the 1994 European Election Study and a 1994 survey of Members of the European Parliament (MEPs) showed that most of the MEPs were strongly in favor of the introduction of the euro, whereas the public was much more hesitant.

The introduction of the euro in 2002, led by the then Dutch president of the European Central Bank, went smoothly. The budget requirements of the participating states (the Stability and Growth Pact), however, were a constant source of tension between the ministers of finance of the Euro Zone, with Dutch Minister Gerrit Zalm usually the most outspoken defender of a rigid budget discipline. The Dutch media reported extensively about these tensions and the Dutch position on the issues.

Meanwhile, many people became convinced that the introduction of the euro had led to a general increase in the prices of consumables—a conviction that was hardly affected by the government's frequent protests to the contrary.

The euro assumed a prominent role in the Dutch referendum campaign following a published interview (in April 2005) with one of the directors of the Dutch central bank, in which the director asserted that the Dutch guilder had been undervalued against the euro by 10% compared to the German mark. The euro continued to get extensive media attention during the last month of the campaign. The feeling that the Dutch had "sold" their guilder too cheaply was further fueled by the fact that the Netherlands had been one of the largest net contributors to the EU over the past two decades.

Table 1 Referendum Vote and Opinions on the Euro

	Agree (Completely)	% "No" in These Categories	Neither Agree nor Disagree	% "No" in This Category	Disagree (Completely)	% "No" in These Categories	n=
At the transition from the guilder to the euro, the Netherlands was put at a serious disadvantage	69.9	*73.4*	17.7	*36.8*	12.4	*29.5*	768
The introduction of the euro is favorable for the Dutch economy	26.6	*39.7*	20.2	*52.9*	53.2	*75.5*	767
As a result of the introduction of the euro, prices have gone up in the Netherlands	93.8	*63.9*	3.8	*27.6*	2.5	*21.1*	767
As a result of the introductionof the euro, it has become much easier to pay in other countries	96.2	*60.4*	2.7	*95.2*	1.0	*75.0*	766

Note: Data from 2005 Dutch Referendum Study. All questions were asked in the post-referendum wave of interviews. Data are weighted by socio-demographic characteristics and referendum outcome.

large household panel. The interviews were conducted by means of computer-assisted web-based interviewing (2/3) and computer-assisted telephone interviewing (1/3). The fieldwork was conducted by GfK Benelux. The data are currently being processed and documented. Details on the study and on its future availability can be obtained from the authors.

Table 2 Referendum Vote and Expectations of Further European Integration

	Certainly or Probably	% "No" in These Categories	Probably Not or Certainly Not	% "No" in These Categories	n=
Prosperity will increase	35.0	*36.8*	65.0	*74.4*	768
The wealthier member states will have to pay more	79.2	*61.7*	20.8	*60.6*	768

Note: Questions were asked in the pre-referendum wave of interviews. Data are weighted by socio-demographic characteristics and referendum outcome.

In our survey, we asked the respondents to what extent they agreed or disagreed with four statements about the euro. Table 1 shows both the frequency distributions for each statement as well as the percentage of "No" voters in each category.

At the time of the referendum, a large majority of Dutch voters was convinced that the Netherlands had been financially injured by the introduction of the euro. Although almost everyone believed that spending money in other countries had become much easier, a minority thought that the euro was good for the Dutch economy. Near unanimity existed about the statement that prices had gone up as a result of the conversion to the euro. The answers to these statements point to a clearly negative perception of the euro.

When we look at the reported referendum vote, it is strikingly clear that negative perceptions of the euro go together with large majorities for the "No" vote, whereas positive perceptions are associated with a majority for a "Yes" vote for the Constitution (see Table 1).

The negative attitude toward the euro reflects a lack of confidence that the EU will foster economic growth. The open Dutch economy depends to a large extent on foreign trade. The ability to foster economic growth had always been one of the strongest arguments for European integration and for the introduction of the euro. In our survey we also asked what people thought about the economic consequences of European integration (Table 2). A large majority was of the opinion that the EU will only cost money and does not produce its main goal: economic prosperity. In addition, our respondents expected that the wealthier member states would have to pay more. Both convictions were strongly related to the "No" vote.

The Expansion of the EU and the Vote

From 1973 until 1995, the expansion of the EU took place very gradually. In 1973, Britain, Denmark, and Ireland joined the six founders; in 1981, Greece joined, followed by Spain and Portugal in 1986 and by Sweden, Finland, and Austria in 1995. Nine new member states, all but one located in Western Europe, were thus gradually admitted over a period of 22 years. In 2004, 10 new members joined the EU in a single day, eight of which are located in Central and Eastern Europe. At the same time, the dragging talks with Turkey on the conditions for starting membership negotiations finally resulted in a clear time frame. A Turkish EU membership was no longer a pure theoretical possibility. The year 2004 can therefore be regarded as a turning point in the history of the EU when it comes to its geographical scope.

In the French referendum campaign, the legendary "Polish plumber" became a symbol for the negative side effects of the enlargement process: cheap labor from the newly admitted member states would

Table 3 Referendum Vote and Expectations of Further European Integration

	Certainly or Probably	% "No" in These Categories	Probably Not or Certainly Not	% "No" in These Categories	n=
The small member states will lose influence	83.3	*69.1*	16.7	*23.4*	768
Our language will be used less	55.6	*72.8*	44.4	*47.4*	766
Our national identity and culture will disappear	41.9	*88.2*	58.1	*42.2*	768
Jobs will be relocated to countries where production is cheaper	91.7	*64.6*	8.3	*26.6*	767

Note: Questions about expectations were asked in the pre-referendum wave of interviews. Data are weighted by socio-demographic characteristics and referendum outcome.

drive the expensive French craftsmen out of business. In the Netherlands, perhaps because the presence of Polish workers in market gardening is an accepted fact, the possible EU membership of Turkey assumed that role. In September 2004, Geert Wilders, an outspoken member of parliament for the VVD, left that party to found his own party precisely because he could not accept even the possibility that Turkey would join the EU. Wilders, the issue of the Turkish membership, and the enlargement issue more generally received extensive media coverage during the nine months preceding the referendum.

In his campaign, Wilders not only pointed to the threat of new reservoirs of cheap labor, but also to two other aspects of the EU's expansion: the threat to Dutch culture, especially when Turkey joined, and the declining voting power of the older member states. According to the European Constitution, the voting power of the member states would be more dependent on population size than before. When admitted, Turkey would be one of the largest and therefore most powerful member states. Thus, connecting the issue of Turkey's future admittance to the Constitution referendum proved quite simple.

In our survey, we asked the respondents before the referendum about the likelihood of several possible consequences of further European integration. Several of the consequences mentioned in the survey refer to side effects of the enlargement of the Union. Table 3 shows the response frequencies and their relationship with the "No" vote.

What are the most likely consequences of further integration according to Dutch voters in 2005? Basically these: jobs will be relocated to countries where production is cheaper than in the Netherlands and the small member states will lose influence. In addition, a large group of voters is of the opinion that Dutch language would be used less often and a large minority thinks Dutch culture would be threatened. The majority of the respondents who believe that these were the most likely consequences if the Constitution was adopted voted "No" in the referendum.

The Gap between Elite and Electorate on the European Issue

Finally, why did so many Dutch voters disagree with an overwhelming majority of the Dutch Parliament? All major political parties support further European integration: opposition occurs only at the orthodox Christian and extreme left ends of the political spectrum. Table 4 depicts, for each of the parties, its size in the Second Chamber of Parliament (number of seats), the average position of its voters

Table 4 Parties, Voters, and Their Attitude toward the European Constitution

Political Party	Party Type	Size (Seats in Parliament)	Mean Left-Right Position of Voters	Attitude of the Party toward the EU Constitution	Percentage of Voters Opposing the European Constitution
SGP	Orthodox protestant	2	8,3	Against	100%
List Pim Fortuyn	Populist, right wing	8	7,5	Against	86%
ChristenUnie	Orthodox protestant	3	6,7	Against	75%
VVD	Conservative liberal	28	7,3	In favor	48%
CDA	Christian democratic	44	6,9	In favor	49%
D66	Progressive liberal	6	5,8	In favor	37%
PvdA	Social democratic	42	4,7	In favor	63%
GreenLeft	Left wing ecological	8	4,7	In favor	53%
Socialist Party	Left wing	9	4,8	Against	88%

Note: Left-right was assessed by presenting an 11-point scale (0–10) in the pre-referendum interview. Data are weighted by socio-demographic characteristics and referendum outcome.

on a left-right scale, the party's position on the European Constitution, and the percentage of its voters who voted against the Constitution.

Left and right, or progressive and conservative, are the most important political labels used by both parties and voters in the Netherlands to summarize their positions on a large number of issues. These labels refer primarily to socio-economic issues such as the redistribution of income.[4] Government coalition parties also tend to cluster on the left-right dimension.[5] The present center-right government coalition is supported by VVD, CDA, and D66.

As in most other EU member states, voters' opinions about European integration are relatively unimportant for vote decision in elections for the national and the European Parliaments. For this reason, European Parliament elections are known as "second order" national elections: they are dominated by the national political arenas of the various member states (Reif and Schmitt 1980; van der Eijk, Franklin et al. 1996). Only recently, have issues pertaining to the speed and scope of European integration become more important in the voters' minds in, for example, Denmark and Britain. But with some exceptions, these issues have not yet translated into distinct party positions.

Table 4 confirms this general observation. Party choice in the 2003 election is only weakly related to voting behavior in the referendum on the European Constitution. Many voters of VVD, CDA, PVDA, D66, and GreenLeft (128 seats in parliament) voted against the Constitution, whereas their parties had supported and defended it.[6]

4. A second, less important dimension of political opinions is ethical or moral, and refers to issues such as abortion and euthanasia. It is strongly related to the religious beliefs of voters and their parties. In this article we ignore the dimension.
5. With the notable exception being the period from 1994–2002 when PVDA, VVD, and D66 formed a left-right coalition without the centrist CDA.
6. The Pearson correlation coefficient between the referendum vote (Yes/No) and the respondent's position on the left-right scale is –0.02. The position on the left-right scale is also uncorrelated (–0.00) with the respondent's position on a scale running from "European integration has already gone too far" to "European integration should go further."

The gap between parties and voters will probably not disappear after the referendum. Even after the lively referendum campaign, most of our respondents indicated that they were only "somewhat interested" in European affairs. Less than 4% thought they were "very interesting." The implication is that European issues will continue to play a secondary role at most in the national elections. As a consequence, new national elections will not radically alter the strong support for the EU in the Dutch Parliament. Political parties do not have incentives to adjust their position on this issue: it will not change their electoral prospects.

Conclusion and Discussion

Despite the unambiguous rejection of the European Constitution on June 1, many Dutch continue to support European integration, but the form it has assumed is disliked. The perceived costs are too high and the benefits too low. The euro is evaluated very negatively, and the common market is regarded as a threat rather than an opportunity. In addition, the prospective expansion of the EU deepens and broadens these perceptions among voters. It deepens them because the new member states are not seen as new markets to be explored, but as expensive reservoirs of cheap labor threatening Dutch jobs. It broadens the problems, because the power of the Netherlands in the EU will be further watered down, while at the same time Dutch, or Western, values are perceived to be in danger. But since these feelings have not yet affected voting behavior in national elections, the existing gap between a majority of the voters and a large majority of politicians will probably not disappear after the next national elections.

In June 2005, the government and the Second Chamber of Parliament announced a broad public debate about the future of Europe. But only a few months later, the political parties could not agree on the organization of this debate, and they eventually abandoned the idea. Most political parties now pledged to start a debate on the EU within their own ranks. This may eventually turn out to be one of the most important results of the referendum. The referendum itself was accompanied by heated, but short-lived media attention, and did not noticeably increase the public's interest in Europe and the EU. Although voters' awareness of the issues at stake increased during the campaign, many voters still had the feeling that they were not adequately informed.

The lack of political discussion in the Netherlands about the future of Europe cannot be remedied by a single campaign. Whether new debates within the political parties will lead to a change in the attitudes and opinions of politicians and/or voters is still unclear. Voters may eventually begin to appreciate the euro. They may even begin to appreciate the recent expansion of the EU. Politicians may adjust their traditional enthusiasm for European integration. Whatever happens, it will not deepen the gap between the electorate and the elite—we have probably just seen the bottom of it.

References

Aarts, Kees, and Henk van der Kolk. eds. 2005. *Nederlanders en Europa: Het referendum over de Europese grondwet.* Amsterdam: Bert Bakker.

Reif, Karlheinz, and Hermann Schmitt. 1980. "Nine Second-order National Elections: A Conceptual Framework for the Analysis of European Election Results." *European Journal of Political Research* 8: 3–44.

van der Eijk, Cees, Mark N. Franklin et al. 1996. *Choosing Europe? The European Electorate and National Politics in the Face of Union.* Ann Arbor: University of Michigan Press.

Chapter 10

DOES MODERNIZATION LEAD TO STABLE AND EFFECTIVE DEMOCRACY?

It is no accident that the conceptual and theoretical revolution in comparative politics in the post–World War II era that was documented in chapter 1 of this volume was accompanied by a shift from ethnocentric preoccupation with the major democracies of Western Europe to a focus on the emerging group of nations in Africa and Asia, including the Middle East, as well as the less-developed nations of Central and South America. These nation-states, many of which emerged from the postwar breakup of Europe's colonial empires, are frequently grouped under the label "less-developed countries," although the empirical content of the term "developed" is generally left imprecise. The nations listed in this category range from economically and institutionally primitive societies, such as Chad or Lesotho, to relatively complex and highly industrialized countries, such as Argentina or India—a range so great as to render the concept scientifically useless. Since these nations were not part of the Cold War and therefore not aligned with either the Western industrial bloc of democracies or the Soviet bloc of nations during that period, they were often referred to as "the Third World."

The emergence of the third-world bloc of nations presented conceptual challenges to the field of comparative political analysis that, as seen in earlier chapters of this book, was itself in a state of transition. Traditional units of analysis, that is, constitutionally designated structures of government and decision-making formats, were often inapplicable to nonindustrialized societies; in some of these countries, such structures only came into being in response to clear and present demands and were otherwise nearly invisible or geared to perform different functions. Therefore, scholars focusing on these third world, or less-developed, countries borrowed heavily and too often uncritically from sister social sciences oriented more toward society and less toward the invisible or elusive state. Concepts such as the functional requisites of society were co-opted from sociology without any apparent concern for definitional precision or empirical content.

The literature on these countries described a continuum running from undeveloped to developed: the "economic dimension" referred to the level of industrialization, a "social dimension" involved such questions as role specialization or division of labor, and the "political dimension" was often faced with a lack of consensus on the difference between a modern or less modern political system. The importance of the distinction between these dimensions of modernization was illustrated by Germany under the Nazi dictatorship: the country had the industrial might and technological know-how to conquer much of the Western World, but it relied on a political system based on the unrestrained will of one man, a very primitive political format. Not surprisingly, authors of the early literature on modernization tended to judge the level of development on each of these dimensions by the standard of Western, industrialized democracies. Moreover, this literature tended to assume an inevitable and linear movement always progressing in the same direction toward that ethnocentric standard. This literature comprises what is loosely called modernization theory, a theoretic framework that dominated the literature on the less-developed, or third world, nations in the 1950s and 1960s.

Modernization theory is based on the premise that social, structural, and cultural changes are interdependent factors that work together to drive political change. The theory further posits that this process of change is universal: all nations will ultimately undergo the same process, just at different speeds. A classic and oft-cited example of this perspective is Daniel Lerner's model of modernization. In Lerner's model, technological advances associated with economic development or industrialization necessitate urbanization. This urbanization breaks down traditional perspectives and broadens intellectual horizons, spreading literacy in the process. Literacy in turn increases media exposure. These developments encourage the growth of what Lerner calls a "participant society," a term that elliptically implies one with democratic values, which scholars like Lerner equate with modernity. Thus, his model may be represented as follows:

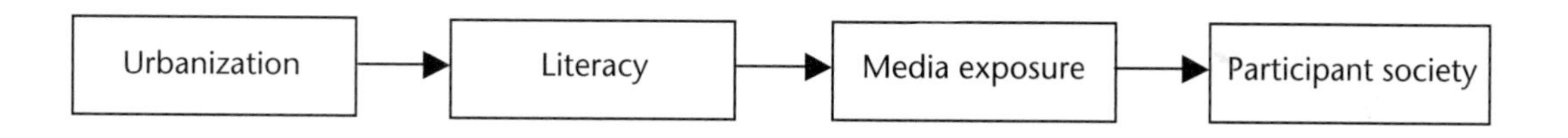

Other scholars have noted that the cultural changes associated with urbanization and industrialization—for example, secularization and tolerance of racial, religious, sexual, and ideological differences—may lead to a more participatory and responsive political system. While secularization has undoubtedly been occurring throughout much of the modern world, religiosity has intensified in many less-developed countries.

Modernization theory presumed that the mobilization of participation would necessarily lead political systems to adapt to the increased level of citizen demands by manifesting a greater capacity to respond. The theory focused on engineering change, especially in the direction of expanding participation and industrialization. Little concern was directed at values such as the stability and order of the relevant political formats under the apparent assumption that an economically prosperous social order would leave little incentive for assaults on the status quo. That assumption, that modernization would reduce the incidence of revolution and instability, was rudely shaken by reality: the experience of the postwar world was that revolution and political violence seemed to result from rapid socioeconomic change. Mancur Olson's article in this chapter (reading 10.1) addresses the reasons why the rapid changes associated with modernization not only do not inhibit political violence and instability but in fact render those phenomena more likely.

Samuel Huntington, in his classic article, "Political Development and Political Decay," [1] did not just accept Olson's destabilizing impact of modernization thesis, an implicit rejection of modernization theory's presumption of a linear phenomenon, but Huntington even offers an alternative strategy calculated to preserving political order. He suggests that rather than bringing about a one-directional process from tradition to modernity, rapid industrialization can result in the collapse of a political system's ability to process issues and maintain order, that is, to govern.

Huntington's emphasis on the maintenance of political order (rather than, say, a redistribution of material well-being or a mobilization of grievances) has earned him a reputation as being somewhat more conservative than many of his academic colleagues. His strategy is to delay mobilization until modernized and more capable institutions are developed to process the increased pressures generated by social mobilization. His criteria for modern and effective institutions: complexity, autonomy, and legitimacy, implicitly constitute the distinction between a modern and a less modern *political* system, as opposed to defining social modernization or industrialization. The question is whether his conceptualization of modern institutions lends itself to empirical inquiry.

Howard Wiarda, in reading 10.2, indicts modernization theory by cautioning those in the West that the Western model will not necessarily apply to many third world settings. Ronald Inglehart and Christian Welzel add their voices to the call for a reexamination of modernization theory by questioning the presumed linearity and the ethnocentrism of that theory. Their contribution to modernization theory is framed in the broader context of their theories of cultural change discussed in chapter 15.

Note

1. Samuel Huntington, "Political Development and Political Decay," *World Politics* 17 (March 1965): 386–430.

10.1

RAPID GROWTH AS A DESTABILIZING FORCE

Mancur Olson Jr.

The proposition that violence and instability are largely due to poverty and economic underdevelopment had almost reached the status of conventional wisdom in the years following World War II. Therefore, the leaders and many of the scholars in the West were dismayed when generous aid to encourage the rapid industrialization of less-developed countries seemed paradoxically to produce a greater incidence of instability and violence. Mancur Olson, a professor of economics at the University of Maryland, shows the logical process of how rapid economic growth and industrialization act to make instability and violence more likely by showing how modernization produces strata of a society that have an interest in destabilizing the modern social order and how industrialization worsens the standard of living for many people in the short run. The lesson here is to be cautious in stimulating rapid industrialization of less-developed countries. Given this, what are the implications of Olson's argument for U.S. foreign policy?

I

Many writers—some of them reputable scholars, others important public officials—have implicitly assumed or explicitly argued that economic growth leads toward political stability and perhaps even to peaceful democracy. They have argued that "economic development is one of the keys to stability and peace in the world";[1] that it is "conditions of want and instability on which communism breeds";[2] and that economic progress "serves as a bulwark against international communism." [3] A recent and justly famous book on revolution by Hannah Arendt ascribes the most violent forms of revolutionary extremism mainly to poverty.[4]

This view has had an influence on American foreign aid policy and more often than not foreign economic aid is regarded as "an investment in peace and orderly political evolution toward a democratic world." [5] In one of his presidential messages to Congress, for example, Eisenhower justified a request for foreign aid funds by saying that unless the underdeveloped nations "can hope for reasonable economic advance, the danger will be acute that their governments will be subverted by communism." [6] A committee of scholars, so distinguished that they nearly make up a *Who's Who* of American students of economic development, has prepared for the guidance of the Senate Foreign Relations Committee a report which later was published as a book on *The Emerging Nations*,[7] and which argues that the

Mancur Olson Jr., "Rapid Growth as a Destabilizing Force," *Journal of Economic History* 3, no. 4 (December 1963): 529–552.

United States should offer most of its economic aid to the countries in the "take-off" stage of economic development. The countries that are not yet ready for this stage of rapid development should get only modest amounts of aid, mainly in the form of technical assistance. This favoritism in the allocation of aid is justified on the grounds that a given amount of aid will bring about more growth if it is concentrated in the nations that are, in any case, in a stage of rapid development. This prescription for policy is justified, not on straightforward humanitarian grounds, but rather in the long term political interest of the United States, particularly in view of the cold war with the Soviet Union. While at least some of these students of economic development have denied that they accept a "crude materialist" explanation of the causes of political stability,[8] the obvious premise of their policy is that the rapid economic growth of selected underdeveloped countries is the "key to an effective foreign policy" for the United States in its cold war with the Soviet Union. Many communists have also shared the faith that poverty was the prelude to revolution: the poor, they argue, "have nothing to lose but their chains."

Several scholars, however, have suggested that the assumed connection between economic growth and political stability was much too simple, or that there was no such connection. But their denials of any positive relationship between economic growth and political stability have too often been mere *obiter dicta*. They have at least failed to convince many people. It is not, therefore, enough simply to deny that economic growth necessarily brings political stability. What is needed instead is a bold and sustained argument in the opposite direction. What is needed now is, not a cautious qualification of the argument that economic growth leads toward political stability, but rather a clear and decisive argument stating that rapid economic growth is a major force leading toward revolution and instability. Many of the reasons why rapid economic growth should lead to political instability have apparently never been discussed, at least in print; it is thus time that these reasons were stated and put together in an attempt to show that rapid economic growth is a profoundly destabilizing force.

II

Any adequate analysis of the relationship between economic growth and revolutionary political changes must consider the problem in terms of the individuals who bring revolutions about. Students of the sociology of revolution often argue that those people who participate in "mass movements" of the radical left or radical right—movements designed to bring about revolutionary rather than evolutionary change—tend to be distinguished by the relative absence of bonds that tie them to the established order. They tend to lack close attachments to any of the social subgroups that comprise a society—to extended families, for example, or to voluntary associations, professional groups, or social classes.

Thus some of these scholars have argued, not without evidence, that labor unions, which are often regarded as particularly likely sources of strength for communist revolutionaries, are in fact a force tending to reduce the chances for communist revolutions, mainly because they provide one more group connection that can hold the worker to the prevailing system. The social class, which Marx thought was the engine of revolutionary change, some sociologists regard instead as a stabilizing institution. Those who are *déclassé*, whose class ties are weakest, are most apt to support revolutionary changes, while those who are firmly caught up in a class are least likely to do so. Even those who are firmly caught up even in the lowest and least fortunate class are not normally in the revolutionary vanguard, for they are secure in their modest place in the social hierarchy. Those who are very poor, after meeting the exigencies of life, have in any case very little energy left for agitation for a better political system, even if they had much hope that real improvement was possible. "There is thus a conservatism of the destitute," says Eric Hoffer, "as profound as the conservatism of the privileged," [9] It is not those who are accustomed to poverty, but those whose place in the social order is changing, who resort to revolution.

III

The next thing is to ask how rapid economic growth might affect the number of individuals who are *déclassé*, or who have lost their identification with other social groups, and who are thus in circumstances conducive to revolutionary protest.

It is now generally understood that economic growth proceeds not so much through simple capital accumulation—through continuing the old methods of production with more capital—as it does through innovation and technical change. Economic growth—especially rapid economic growth—therefore involves vast changes in the methods of production. It involves vast changes in the importance of different industries, in the types of labor demanded, in the geographical configuration of production. It means vast changes in the ways and places in which people live and work. Above all, economic growth means vast changes in the distribution of income.

The fact that some gain a lot and others lose a lot, in a rapidly growing economy, means that the bonds of class and caste are weakened. Some rise above the circumstances of their birth and others fall behind. Both groups are normally *déclassé*. Their economic status keeps them from belonging wholly to the class or caste into which they were born and their social situation keeps them from belonging to the caste or class into which their income bracket should put them. Rapid economic growth therefore loosens the class and caste ties that help bind men to the social order.

But castes and social classes are not the only social groupings which rapid economic growth breaks down. Even the family group, and especially the clan or extended family, can be destroyed by the occupational and geographical mobility associated with economic growth. The replacement of subsistence agriculture and cottage industry, normally organized around the family, with factory production by workers hired individually, can weaken family ties. Similarly, modern business institutions are bound to weaken or even to destroy the tribe, the manor, the guild, and the rural village. The uprooted souls torn or enticed out of these groups by economic growth are naturally susceptible to the temptations of revolutionary agitation.

IV

When the focus is on the fact that rapid economic growth means rapid economic change, and that economic change entails social dislocation, it becomes clear that *both the gainers and the losers from economic growth can be destabilizing forces*. Both will be imperfectly adjusted to the existing order. This paper will argue, first, that economic growth increases the number of *nouveaux riches*, who may use their economic power to change the social and political order in their interest; and second, that economic growth may paradoxically also create a surprisingly large number of "*nouveaux pauvres*," who will be much more resentful of their poverty than those who have known nothing else.

The fact that there will be some who gain disproportionately from economic growth means that there will be a new distribution of economic power. But there will be an (almost Marxian) "contradiction" between this new distribution of economic power and the old distribution of social prestige and political power. Certain individuals are left in places in the economic order that are incompatible with their positions in the old social and political hierarchy. This means, not only that these people are in socially ambiguous situations that may leave them "alienated" from society; it means also that they have the resources with which they can ultimately change the social and political order in their own interest. The economic system, the social system, and the political system are obviously interdependent parts of a single society, and if one part changes quickly, there must also be instability in other parts of the society. The fact that the distribution of wealth will have both social and political effects is beyond dispute. In time, those groups who have gained the fruits of economic growth (or their children) will probably have built a new social and political order that is suited to the new distribution of economic power. But, especially if the economic growth is very rapid, the path to any new equilibrium may be highly unstable.

Something very like this seems to have happened in Europe as a result of the commercial and industrial revolutions. The growth of commerce and industry in early modern Europe created a larger and wealthier middle class; and as this middle class gained in numbers and in wealth, especially in relation to the landed aristocracy, it demanded, and it got, extra political power to match that wealth. These demands were obviously behind the middle class participation in the French Revolution, and were also fundamental to many of the other instances of political instability in the history of modern Europe. Liberalism and laissez-faire economic doctrine were also related to the newly achieved gains that the industrial revolution brought to Europe, and these ideas in turn tended further to destabilize the political environment.

The middle class in early modern and modern Europe was not the only group of gainers from economic growth that destabilized its environment. There are other types of gainers from economic growth who have also attempted to change the prevailing order. Urban areas, for example, normally grow disproportionately during periods of economic growth, and those who move from farm to city in pursuit of the more remunerative opportunities there are often also discontented gainers. The man who has been tempted away from his village, his manor, his tribe, or his extended family by the higher wages of burgeoning urban industry may well be a disaffected gainer from economic growth. He has been, albeit voluntarily, uprooted and is not apt soon to acquire comparable social connections in the city. He is, therefore, prone to join destabilizing mass movements. Those who leave rural areas for the higher wages or other gains that economic growth brings to the cities often display a nostalgia for the economically poorer, but socially more secure, life they left. The Chartists, for example, at one time proposed schemes that would give factory workers small agricultural estates. But after British workers had had some time to adjust to the urban, industrial order, this sort of scheme lost its popularity to programs designed to improve the conditions of urban industrial life. The degree of extremism of the different labor movements in the Scandinavian countries has also been related to the varying proportions of migrants from rural areas in the industrial work force, which in turn resulted from different rates of economic growth. The first and most gradual industrialization took place in Denmark, and there the rate at which migrants from rural areas were recruited into the urban work force was slow. In Sweden, and still more in Norway, industrialization and the absorption of rural migrants was later and faster, and the labor movements in turn revealed, especially in Norway, more disaffection and political extremism. The fact that the concentration of population in cities can sometimes make agitation cheaper and the spread of new ideas faster is also important, as is the fact that riots and revolts are often technically easier to organize in cities. Whenever an ideology, like Marxism, designed explicitly for the urban proletariat, is in the air, the growth of cities induced by economic expansion will be particularly conducive to revolt.

The movement from farm to city is moreover only one of the types of geographic mobility brought about by economic growth. Some industries and localities will expand rapidly with economic growth, and others, urban as well as rural, will decline. Individuals may move from city to city or from rural area to rural area in search of the gains from economic growth. These sorts of mobility can also lead to a frustrating severance of social ties. The radical elements in Jacksonian democracy, in Populism, in the unusually strong Socialist parties of some of the frontier states of the Great Plains, in the violent western mining unions, and in the Non-Partisan League, cannot be adequately explained by any hypothesis of economic decline or stagnation. The western areas near the frontier were growing rapidly when these destabilizing movements began, and they were often filled with people who had gained from this expansion. Perhaps in frontier areas, or in areas that have only recently been on the frontier, the social groupings that bind people to the social order have not had time to develop, and as a result there is a susceptibility to protests against established governments and inherited conventions. This factor may explain Turner's alleged "quasi-revolutionary" or rebellious frontier democracy, which has sometimes been ascribed to "self-reliant pioneer" and "labor safety valve" theories.

V

Just as the gainers can be a destabilizing force, so, of course, can the losers. Their position in the social order is changing too, and they are also imperfectly adjusted to the existing society.

Moreover, contrary to what is usually assumed, economic growth can significantly increase the number of losers. It can be associated with a decided increase in the number whose standard of living is falling. This may seem absurd at first glance, since economic growth by definition leads to an increase in average income—to a situation such that the gains of the gainers are more than sufficient to compensate for the losses of the losers. But when average income increases, the number who are getting poorer may nonetheless increase. The gains of a small percentage of large gainers may be so large that they may exceed the combined losses of a larger percentage of losers; median income might fall while average income rises. In other words, while average income is increasing, the income of the average man may be falling.

It is not only a logical possibility, but also at times a practical probability, that the number getting poorer will increase with rapid economic growth. This is because in periods of rapid economic growth there are often several forces that work toward a concentration of most of the gains in a relatively small number of hands and to a widespread diffusion of the losses. One of the forces that can work in this direction is the tendency for wages to be more sticky than prices. Thus, as demand increases with economic growth, businessmen may raise prices *pari-passu* with the increase in demand, but wages may rise much more slowly. The particular importance of this phenomenon during periods of inflation, which also seem to be correlated somewhat with economic growth, is of course familiar to every economic historian, because this same argument has been used to contend that inflation leads to a redistribution of income from wage earners to entrepreneurs.

Another force that leads toward inequality in the distribution of the fruits of rapid economic growth is the change of technology involved in economic growth. When one firm, or some group of firms, begins to use a new technique, a technique sufficiently superior to the old techniques to lead to rapid increases in productivity and efficiency, those firms with the old technology are apt to fail or at least to suffer falling profits. Unless the new technology is adopted by all firms in an industry at the same time, one would expect that the introduction or the arrival of this technology would increase the differences in profits or lead to the failure of some of the firms. When the factors of production—especially the labor—that the declining firms employ are considered, the problem becomes more important in human, and political, terms. The unskilled laborers or skilled craftsmen replaced by machines are apt to be a destabilizing force.

The increased productivity of the modern machinery and new techniques introduced in periods of rapid economic growth will no doubt in the long run increase the income of all classes. But those who suffer in the short run know that in the long run they will be dead and are all too apt to be susceptible to disruptive agitation. The British weavers who were left unemployed in the advance of the industrial revolution certainly lost a great deal in a period when the nation's total wealth and per capita income doubtless increased. The Luddite-type movements against new machinery that increased productivity illustrate the reactions against the unevenness of the short-run benefits of growth.

The fact that some groups in the population may in the short run lose from rapid economic growth is made all the worse by the fact that societies in the early stages of industrialization rarely have suitable institutions for mitigating the adversities that the losers in the process suffer. While traditional social institutions, like the tribe, the extended family, and the manor will often have appropriate ways of helping those among them who suffer adversities, and while mature industrial societies have developed welfare institutions, the society in an early stage of rapid industrialization will probably not have adequate institutions to care for those who suffer from the economic advance. Unemployment is not normally a serious problem for the preindustrial society. It could hardly have meaning in, say, a tribal society. The word "unemployment" is indeed a rather recent coinage. The unemployment, fictional or otherwise, that may result when a traditional society begins to industrialize and grow will therefore lead to serious losses for some parts of the society. And, since the problem is new, the society is not apt to deal with it successfully. The United States and Great Britain certainly had not yet developed systems for dealing with the unemployment that was becoming increasingly serious in their societies in the nineteenth century.

In short, rapid economic growth will bring about a situation where some lose part of their incomes, and others, because of the new problem of unemployment, lose *all* of their incomes. Thus a sense of grievance and insecurity may be a destabilizing force resulting from the fact that with economic growth, as with so many other things, there are both winners and losers.

In those cases where the number of gainers from economic growth exceeds the number of losers, there is apt to be a number of those who, while they have gained in absolute terms, have lost in relative terms; that is, they have come to have a lower position relative to the rest of the income earners in that society. Some of those whose gains from economic growth are rather modest may find that they have fallen in the economic scale because of the larger advances of some of the other gainers. There have been some studies that provide interesting indirect evidence about the reactions of people who are experiencing an absolute increase in income and a relative decline in their economic position. These studies, arising out of the controversies over the Keynesian consumption function, have suggested that families with a given level of income tend to spend a smaller percentage of that income when the others in that society have low incomes than they do when the others in that society have high incomes. A family's consumption, in short, is affected, not only by that family's level of income, but also by the level of incomes of the other people in that society. The evidence on this point Professor James S. Duesenberry has explained in terms of the "demonstration effect." The demonstration or evidence of higher consumption patterns in one's neighbors will increase one's desire for additional consumption, in the sense that it leads to saving a smaller proportion of income. From this in turn one can perhaps infer that, when a group's position in the economic hierarchy falls, there may be some dissatisfaction—dissatisfaction that would not necessarily be counteracted by an absolute increase in that group's level of income.

Therefore, quite apart from the fact that even the relative gainers may, as earlier parts of this paper argued, be destabilizing, and quite apart from the possibility that economic growth may increase the number of losers, there is still the further fact that, when the number of gainers from economic growth exceeds the number of losers, some of the gainers may have lost ground relative to the society in general and may display some degree of disaffection.[10]

* * *

VII

Since economic growth is associated, not only with capital accumulation, but also with the advance of education, skill, and technology, it will be connected in underdeveloped countries with an increasing knowledge of the possibilities of a better life, of new ideologies, and of new systems of government. It will be associated with a "revolution of rising expectations" that is apt to involve, above all, rising expectations about what the government should do. Economic growth, since it leads to higher incomes for some people who were previously at a lower standard, will itself stimulate and exacerbate these rising expectations. Thus it is possible that there may be something in the economic sphere corresponding to the tendency for the demands for reform to increase as soon as reform is begun. Alexis de Tocqueville made this point particularly clearly.

> It is not always by going from bad to worse that a society falls into revolution. It happens most often that a people, which has supported without complaint, as if they were not felt, the most oppressive laws, violently throws them off as soon as their weight is lightened. The social order destroyed by a revolution is almost always better than that which immediately preceded it, and experience shows that the most dangerous moment for a bad government is generally that in which it sets about reform. Only great genius can save a prince who undertakes to relieve his subjects after a long oppression. The evil, which was suffered patiently as inevitable, seems unendurable as soon as the idea of escaping from it is conceived. All the abuses then removed seem to throw into greater relief those which remain, so that their feeling is more painful. The evil, it is true, has become less, but sensibility to it has become more acute. Feudalism at the height of its power had not inspired Frenchmen with so much hatred as it did on the eve of its disappearing. The slightest acts of arbitrary power under Louis XVI seemed less easy to endure than all the despotism of Louis XIV.[11]

The awareness of racial injustice and the willingness to do something about it seem to be higher among American Negroes now than they have been for a long time. The discontent seems to have increased *after* the historic Supreme Court decision outlawing segregated schools and *after* a series of other steps in the direction of racial justice. (This discontent also appears to have been correlated with an economic improvement in the position of American Negroes.) Many other cases could be cited where reform nourishes revolt; but the relevant point here is that economic growth, like political reform, can awaken a people to the possibilities of further improvement and thereby generate additional discontent.

There is, however, at least one situation where economic growth need *not* be correlated with increased knowledge of new ideologies, new systems of government, and the like, or perhaps even with the possibilities of a better material life. That is in a modern totalitarian country, where the media of communication are controlled in such a way that they glorify the existing situation and keep out any ideas that would threaten the existing system. Modern totalitarian regimes of the Stalinist and Hitlerian kinds will also have other techniques for guaranteeing their own stability, most notably the practice of liquidating anyone who shows any lack of enthusiasm for the prevailing regime. There was rapid growth in the Soviet Union under Stalin's five-year plans; yet the nation was relatively stable, and for obvious reasons. Some other despotic regimes have been less thoroughgoing in their repression than Stalin or Hitler yet have nonetheless managed to control dissent fairly effectively. Japan before World War II would provide an example of this sort of situation.

Repression is not, of course, the only thing besides economic growth that can affect the degree of political instability. Clearly, charismatic leadership, religious controversy, ideological change, and probably other things as well, also have an independent influence on the degree of instability in any country. It would be absurd to attempt to explain political instability through economic growth alone. Indeed, a severe depression, or a sudden *decrease* in the level of income, could of course also be destabilizing—and for many of the same reasons that rapid economic growth itself can be destabilizing. A rapid economic decline, like rapid economic growth, will bring about important movements in the *relative* economic positions of people and will therefore set up contradictions between the structure of economic power and the distribution of social and political power. (Severe inflation of the German and Chinese types will have the same effect.) There is, accordingly, nothing inconsistent in saying that both rapid economic growth and rapid economic decline would tend toward political instability. It is economic stability—the absence of rapid economic growth or rapid economic decline—that should be regarded as conducive to social and political tranquility. But it would be absurd to suppose that economic stagnation would guarantee political stability. Since there are many factors in addition to rapid economic change that cause political instability, there can be political instability in a wide range of economic conditions.

This makes it extremely difficult to test the hypothesis that rapid economic growth is conducive to political instability. The hypothesis would not be proven even if every period of rapid economic growth were shown to be politically destabilizing, for the instability in these periods of rapid economic growth could be due to other factors that were operating at the same time. Similarly, the hypothesis that rapid economic growth is destabilizing would not be disproven if there were a negative relationship between rapid economic growth and political instability, for the extent of totalitarian repression or the presence of other stabilizing forces might keep the destabilizing tendencies of rapid economic growth from being manifest. If rapid economic change and political instability are positively or negatively correlated, all this will do is establish some tentative *presumption* that rapid economic growth is, or is not, destabilizing. A final judgment, if one could ever be made, would have to rest on detailed historical studies of a vast variety of cases. These historical studies would have to be so careful and so detailed that they looked, not only at the connection over time between economic and political change, but also at the complex of detailed economic, social, and political changes. They would have to identify both the gainers and the losers from rapid economic growth and all of the other factors affecting political stability, and then attempt to come to a judgment about the role of the economic changes. A massive set of historical studies of the kind needed, covering all historical periods and countries in which there has been rapid economic growth or political instability, is obviously out of the question in a brief paper, even if it were within my competence, which it is not. But it is nonetheless important that historians should start studying at least parts of the problem, however difficult, as soon as possible.

* * *

If there is indeed a connection between rapid economic growth and political instability, then those Western scholars who criticize the underdeveloped countries for attempting to provide some of the services of the modern welfare state may be a bit off the mark. It is no doubt true that the underdeveloped countries cannot afford modern welfare measures as well as the advanced nations can. But it is perhaps also true that they need these modern welfare institutions more than the advanced countries do. These welfare measures, though they might retard growth, could nonetheless be a profitable investment in social peace. They could ease the plight and alleviate the discontents of those who lose from economic growth.

Those who assume that, because certain welfare measures in underdeveloped countries might decrease the rate of growth, they are therefore undesirable, make the mistake that Karl Polanyi discussed in *The Great Transformation.* Polanyi was, in my opinion, quite correct in emphasizing that the relative merits of alternative economic policies had not been decided when it was shown that one led to a faster rate of growth than the others. The differing impacts of capitalistic and socialistic economic systems on the political and social life of a society also had to be considered. Polanyi felt that, while laissez-faire capitalism led to a high rate of growth, it imposed too great a burden of adjustment on society. His argument is indeed interesting; but to me he is quite wrong in identifying the social disorganization resulting from economic change with capitalism alone. Whatever the organization and control of the means of production, rapid economic growth must require painful adjustments. In few places has economic growth involved such painful adjustments as in the Soviet Union in Stalin's first five-year plan. And in the underdeveloped countries today, nationalized industries are often playing a major role in the struggle for economic growth. It would be hard to see how the nationalization of industry itself would reduce the disruption that economic growth causes. The person who leaves the tribe, the manor, the peasant village, or the extended family for the modern factory in the growing city will find that he is in an alien environment, no matter who runs the factory. If the factory is to be run in the interest of maximum production, under socialist or private management, it cannot fail to impose a new and burdensome discipline and a new style of life upon the recently recruited work force.

Thus the point is that rapid economic growth, whatever the nature of the economic system, must involve fast and deep changes in the ways that things are done, in the places that things are done, and in the distribution of power and prestige. Most people spend such a large proportion of their time working for a living and draw such a large part of their social status and political influence from their economic position that changes in the economic order must have great effects on other facets of life. This is especially true in underdeveloped societies, where the institutions that exist were developed in relatively static conditions and are not suited to making rapid adjustments. Therefore, until further research is done, the presumption must be that rapid economic growth, far from being the source of domestic tranquility it is sometimes supposed to be, is rather a disruptive and destabilizing force that leads to political instability. This does not mean that rapid economic growth is undesirable or that political instability is undesirable. It means, rather, that no one should promote the first without bracing to meet the second.

Notes

1. Grant S. McClellan, ed., *U.S. Foreign Aid* (The Reference Shelf, vol. 29, no. 5 [New York: The H. W. Wilson Company, 1957]), 90, taken for a speech by Eugene R. Black, made when he was President of the World Bank.
2. Ibid., p. 205, taken from a report by Richard Nixon to President Eisenhower.
3. Ibid., p. 140, taken from "Final Report of Eleventh American Assembly."
4. Hannah Arendt, *On Revolution* (New York: The Viking Press, 1963), pp. 15, 54–57, 61–63, 66–69, 74–76, 80–85, 87, 105–8, 135, 181, 224, 249.
5. McClellan, *Foreign Aid*, p. 122, taken from an article by Max F. Millikan.
6. Ibid., pp. 53–54, taken from a message to Congress of May 22, 1957. It is significant that all five of the quotations cited so far to illustrate the view that economic growth leads to political stability could be found in one anthology. The number of writers who have accepted this argument must be very large indeed.
7. Max Millikan and Donald Blackmer, eds., *The Emerging Nations* (Boston: Little, Brown, & Co., 1962), pp. 142–45; and Andrew Shonfield, *The Attack on World Poverty* (New York: Random House, 1960), pp. 3–14.
8. Max Millikan and W. W. Rostow, *A Proposal: Key to an Effective Foreign Policy* (New York: Harper & Brothers, 1957), pp. 19–23. See the criticism of this book in Edward C. Banfield's *American Foreign Aid Doctrines* (Washington, D.C.: American Enterprise Institute, 1963), especially p. 6.
9. Eric Hoffer, *The True Believer: Thoughts on the Nature of Mass Movements* (New York: The New American Library, 1951), p. 17 and passim. See also William Kornhauser, *The Politics of Mass Society* (Glencoe, Ill.: The Free Press, 1959), especially pp. 14–15; Seymour Martin Lipset, *Political Man: The Social Bases of Politics* (Garden City, N.Y.: Doubleday & Co., 1960).
10. The importance of this factor will be limited by the likelihood that most of the saving will come from the rich.
11. Alexis de Tocqueville, *L'Ancien Regime*, trans. M. W. Patterson (Oxford: Basil Blackwell, 1947), p. 186.

10.2

TOWARD A NON-ETHNOCENTRIC THEORY OF DEVELOPMENT

Howard J. Wiarda

Despite the widespread acceptance of modernization theory among Western scholars, Howard Wiarda argues that this Western model has been widely rejected by third-world leaders as inappropriate to their circumstances. Wiarda, who currently teaches at the University of Georgia and has served as an adviser to four presidents, is best known for his work on Latin America, but he also cites examples from Africa and the Islamic world in this essay. He posits that since culture affects political events, it should not be surprising that the Western model cannot be replicated in third-world settings, with their very different sets of values. Students should specify what these differences are and the impact they have had on the course of modernization. In addition, has Wiarda actually specified an alternative model of development appropriate to third-world settings?

[The Ayatullah] Khomeini has blown apart the comfortable myth that as the Third World industrializes, it will also adopt Western values.
Time (7 January 1980)

A revolution of far-reaching breadth and meaning is presently sweeping the Third World, and we in the West are only partially and incompletely aware of it. This revolution carries immense implications not only for the Third World and our relations with it but also, more generally, for the social sciences and the way we comprehend and come to grips with Third World change.

We are all aware of the new social and economic forces of modernization sweeping the Third World and perhaps to a somewhat lesser extent of the political and value changes also occurring, including anti-Americanism and anti-colonialism. What has received less attention is the way these changes are now finding parallel expression in a rejection of the basic developmental models and paradigms originating in the West, both Marxian and non-Marxian varieties, and a corresponding assertion of non-Western, nonethnocentric, and indigenous ones.[1]

The ongoing Iranian Revolution may not be typical, but it is illustrative. At the popular level, awareness of the profound changes occurring in Iran has been warped and obscured by events surrounding the revolution and the 1979 seizure of the hostages, by the discomfort those in the more pluralist societies of the West feel toward the Islamic fundamentalists' assertion that there is a single right way and

Howard J. Wiarda, *New Directions in Comparative Politics* (Boulder, Colo.: Westview Press, 1991), 131–153.

a wrong way to do everything, and by the general "ugliness" (at least as portrayed on our television screens) of some of the revolution's leaders. Even scholars and others more sympathetic to such fundamental transformations, in Iran and elsewhere, have tended to focus on the changes occurring in their one area or country of specialization and have not analyzed the more general phenomenon or placed it in a broader, global perspective.[2] Alternatively, they have preferred to see the Iranian Revolution and the coming to power of its ayatullah as an isolated event, readily subject to ridicule and agreed-upon moral outrage and therefore not representing a serious challenge to established Western values and social science understandings.

The proposition argued here, however, is that the rejection of the Western (that is, North-West European and U.S.) model of development, in its several varieties, is now widespread throughout the Third World and that there are many new and exciting efforts on the part of intellectuals and political elites throughout these areas to assert new, indigenous models of development. Furthermore, these efforts represent serious and fundamental challenges to many cherished social science assumptions and understandings and even to the presumption of a universal social science of development. Scholars disregard such changes at the risk of both perpetuating Western malcomprehension of the Third World areas and retaining a social science of development that is parochial and ethnocentric rather than accurate and comprehensive.[3]

The Iranian Revolution, with its assertion of Islamic fundamentalism and of a distinctively Islamic social science (or model) of development, is in fact but one illustration of a far more general Third World phenomenon. There are common themes in the reexaminations presently under way by many Third World leaders: of Indian caste associations and their potential role in modernization; of African tribalism, not as a traditional institution that is necessarily dysfunctional and therefore to be discarded but as a base upon which to build new kinds of societies; of Latin American organicism, corporatism, populism, and new forms of bureaucratic-authoritarianism or of democracy; of family and interpersonal solidarities in Japan; of the overlaps of Confucian and Maoist conceptions in China. The common themes in these areas include hostility toward and often a sense of the inappropriateness of the Western developmental models in non-Western or only partially Western areas, the nationalistic and often quite original assertion of local and indigenous ones, and the questioning of some basic notions regarding the universality of the social sciences. Third World scholars and political leaders believe there are not just one or two (First and Second World) paths to development, but many diverse ones, and that the dichotomy drawn between traditional and modern is false for societies where the blending and fusion of these is more likely than the necessary or automatic replacement of the former by the latter.[4]

These themes are controversial and provocative, and not all the dimensions and issues can be dealt with here. Rather, my purpose is to present the critique Third World areas are now directing at the Western and, we often presume, "universal" developmental model; to examine the alternatives they themselves are now in the process of formulating; to assess the problems and difficulties in these alternative formulations; and to offer some conclusions regarding the issue of particularism versus universalism in the social sciences.

The Third World Critique of the Western Developmental Model

In all frankness, much of our self-inflicted disaster has its intellectual roots in our social sciences faculties.
West Indian economist Courtney N. Blackman, in "Science, Development, and Being Ourselves," *Caribbean Studies Newsletter* (Winter 1980)

The Third World critique of the Western model and pattern of development as inappropriate and irrelevant, or partially so, to its circumstances and conditions is widespread and growing. There has long been a powerful strain of anti-Westernism (as well as anticolonialism) among Third World intellectuals, but now that sentiment is stronger and well-nigh universal. The recent trends differ from earlier critiques of Western modernization theory in that the attacks have become far more pervasive; they are shared more generally by Third World society as a whole; they have taken on global rather than simply area- or country-specific connotations; and the criticisms are no longer solely negative but are now accompanied by an assertion of other, alternative, often indigenous approaches. Moreover the debate is no longer just a scholarly dispute between competing social science development models; rather, it has powerful policy implications as well.

One should not overstate the case. As yet, the critiques one reads are frequently as inchoate and uncertain as the concept of the Third World itself. They tend to be incomplete, fragmented, and unsystematic; long on rhetoric but short on reality; and are often as nationalistic and parochial as the Western theories they seek to replace. Yet one cannot but be impressed by the growing strength of these critiques, their increasing acceptance by Third World leaders, and the dawning realization of common themes, criticisms, and problems encountered with the Western model across diverse continents, nations, and cultural traditions.

The criticism centers, to begin with, on the bias and ethnocentrism perceived in the Western model, which makes it inapplicable to societies with quite different traditions, histories, societies, and cultural patterns.[5] For societies cast in quite different traditions from the Judeo-Christian one, lacking the sociopolitical precepts of Greece, Rome, and the Bible, without the same experiences of feudalism and capitalism, the Western model has only limited relevance.[6] Western political theory is faulted for its almost entirely European focus and its complete lack of attention to other intellectual traditions; political sociology in Emile Durkheim, Auguste Comte, Max Weber, or Talcott Parsons is shown to be based almost exclusively on the European transition from "agraria" to "industria" and its accompanying sociopolitical effects, which have proved somewhat less than universal;[7] and political economy, in both its Marxist and non-Marxist variants, is criticized for the exclusively European and hence less-than-universal origins of its major precepts: philosophical constructs derived (especially in Marx) from Germany, a conception of sociopolitical change derived chiefly from the French tradition, and an understanding of industrialization and its effects stemming chiefly from the English experience. Even our celebrated "liberal arts education" (basically Western European) has come in for criticism as constituting not an experience of universal relevance but merely the first area of studies program.[8] These criticisms of the narrowness and parochialism of our major social science traditions and concepts, as grounded essentially on the singular experience of Western Europe and without appreciation of or applicability to the rest of the world, are both sweeping and, with proper qualification, persuasive.

Third World intellectuals have begun to argue secondly that the timing, sequence, and stages of development in the West may not necessarily be replicable in their own areas. Again, this argument is not new, but its sophisticated expression by so many Third World leaders is. For example, Western political sociology generally asserts, based on the European experience, that bureaucratization and urbanization accompanied and were products of industrialization; in Latin America and elsewhere, however, many Third World scholars are arguing that the phenomena of preindustrial urbanization and bureaucratization requires different kinds of analyses.[9] With regard to timing, it seems obvious that countries developing and modernizing in the late twentieth century should face different kinds of problems than those that developed in the nineteenth; because their developmental response must necessarily be different, there seems to be no necessary reason the former should merely palely and retardedly repeat the experience of the latter.[10] In terms of stages, the European experience suggests that capitalism must necessarily replace feudalism; in much of the Third World, however, feudalism in accord with the classic French case seems never to have existed,[11] capitalism exists in forms (populist, patrimonialist, etatist) that hardly existed in the West, and rather than capitalism definitely *replacing* feudalism, it seems more likely that the two will continue to exist side by side. The timing, sequences, and stages of development in most Third World nations are sufficiently different, indeed, that virtually all Western precepts require fundamental reinterpretation when applied there: the so-called demographic transition, the role of the emerging middle classes, military behavior and professionalization, the role of peasants and workers, the presumption of greater pluralism as societies develop, notions of differentiation and rationalization.[12]

Not only are the timing, sequences, and stages of Third World development likely to be quite different, but the international context is entirely altered as well. In the nineteenth century, Great Britain, Japan, and the United States were able to develop relatively autonomously; for today's Third World nations, that is no longer possible. To cite only a handful of many possible illustrations, these nations often become pawns in Cold War struggles over which they have no control; they are absolutely dependent on outside capital, technology, and markets for their products;[13] and they are part of an international community and of a web of international military, diplomatic, political, commercial, cultural, communications, and other ties from which they cannot divorce themselves. Many are entirely dependent for their continued development on external energy sources, making them victims of skyrocketing prices that have wreaked havoc with their national economies. In these and other ways it seems clear the international context of development is entirely different from that of a century to a century and a half ago.

A fourth area of difference perceived by leaders from the Third World relates to the role of traditional institutions. Western political sociology largely assumes that such traditional institutions as tribes, castes, clans, patrimonialist authority, and historic corporate units must either yield (the liberal tradition) under the impact of modernization or be overwhelmed (the revolutionary tradition) by it. Nevertheless, we have learned that in much of the Third World so-called traditional institutions have, first of all, proved remarkably resilient, persistent, and long-lasting; rather than fading or being crushed under the impact of change, they have instead proved flexible, accommodative, and adaptive, bending to the currents of modernization without necessarily being replaced by them.[14] Second, these traditional institutions have often served as filters of the modernization process, accepting what was useful and what they themselves could absorb in modernity while rejecting the rest. Third, we have learned that such traditional institutions as India's caste associations, African tribalism, and Latin American corporatism can often be transformed into agents of modernization, bridging some wrenching transitions and even serving as the base for new and more revered forms of indigenous development.[15] Indeed one of the more interesting illustrations of this process is the way a new generation of African leaders, rather than rejecting tribalism as traditional and to be discarded, as the *geist* of Western political sociology would have them do, are now reexamining tribalism's persistent presence as an indigenous, realistic, and perhaps viable base on which to construct a new kind of authentic African society.[16]

Fifth, Third World intellectuals are beginning to argue that the Eurocentrism of the major development models has skewed, biased, and distorted their own and the outside world's understanding of Third World societies, making them into something of a laughingstock, the butt of cruel, ethnic, and sometimes racial gibes. For example, the Western bias led scholars from the West and sometimes those from the Third World to overemphasize such presumably modernizing institutions as trade unions and political parties; yet in many Third World countries these institutions may not count for very much, and their absence or weakness often caused these societies to be labeled underdeveloped or dysfunctional. At the same time, institutions that Western political sociology has proclaimed traditional and hence fated to disappear, such as patronage networks, clan groups, religious institutions and movements, and extended families, have been woefully understudied. This has made for immense gaps in Western knowledge of these societies, and some fundamental misinterpretations have resulted.[17]

Meanwhile, these nations actually do modernize and develop in their own terms if not always in ours—that is, through coups and barracks revolts that sometimes contribute to an expanding circulation of elites, through larger patronage and spoils systems now transferred to the national level, through assistance from abroad that is often employed not entirely inappropriately in ways other than those intended, and through elaborated corporate group, family, clan, or tribal networks. Yet the actual dynamics of change and modernization in these nations have often been made the stuff of opéra bouffe in *New York Times* headlines or *New Yorker* cartoons or have led to appalled, holier-than-thou attitudes among Westerners who would still like to remake the Third World in accordance with Judeo-Christian morality and Anglo-American legal and political precepts. As scholars and researchers, our excessive attention to some institutions that our ofttimes wishful sociology would elevate to a higher plane than they deserve, the neglect of others, and our ethnocentrism and general ignorance as to how Third World societies do in fact develop has perpetuated our woeful misunderstanding.[18] It is indeed ironic that for a long time Third World intellectuals bought, or were sold, the same essentially Western categories as the westernizers themselves had internalized, and that their understanding of their own societies therefore was often no greater than our own. That condition is now changing very rapidly.[19]

The Western development perspective has recently been subjected to an additional criticism: that it is part of the Western ideological and intellectual offensive to keep the Third World within the Western orbit.[20] In perhaps the most widespread criticism of the Western development model current in the Third World, Western modernization and development theory is seen as still another "imperialist" Cold War strategy aimed at tying Third World nations into a Western and liberal (that is, U.S.) development pattern, of keeping them within the U.S. sphere of influence, and of denying them the possibility of alternative developmental patterns. Of course, not all who fashioned the early and influential development literature had such manifest Cold War or "New Mandarin" goals in mind. Some clearly did,[21] but among other U.S. scholars the development literature was popular chiefly because it corresponded to cherished notions about the United States (that it is a liberal, democratic, pluralist, socially just, and modern nation) and to the belief that the developing nations could emulate the West if they worked hard and recast themselves in accord with the U.S. or Western model. This strategy was remarkably successful from the late 1950s, when the first development literature began to appear, until the early 1970s. Since that time, however, the development literature has been increasingly tarred with the imperialist brush and discredited throughout the Third World. A whole new generation of young Third World leaders and intellectuals no longer accepts the Western developmentalist concepts and perspectives and is searching for possible alternatives.[22]

Finally, and perhaps most harmful in terms of the long-term development of the Third World, is the damage that has been inflicted on Third World institutions because of the Western biases. "Development" is no mere intellectual construct, nor is it benignly neutral. There are consequences, often negative, in following a Western-oriented development strategy. This goes beyond the kind of damage inflicted on countries such as the Dominican Republic by Cold War rivalries and U.S. interventionism (1965), or by agencies like the International Monetary Fund, whose financial advice to Third World nations has often been unenlightened. Even more serious is the role "development" has had in undermining such viable traditional institutions as extended family networks, patronage ties, clan and tribal loyalties, corporate group linkages, churches and religious movements, historic authority relations, and the like. By eroding and often eliminating these traditional institutions before modern ones could be created, development helped destroy some of the only agencies in many Third World nations that might have enabled them to make a genuine transition to real modernity. The destruction, in the name of modernization, of these kinds of traditional institutions throughout the Third World may well be one of the most important legacies of developmentalism, and it will powerfully affect future relations between the Third World and the First. By our patronizing, ethnocentric efforts to promote development among the less-developed countries, we in the West may have inadvertently denied them the possibility of real development while at the same time erasing the very indigenous and at one time viable institutions they are now attempting, perhaps futilely and too late, to resurrect.[23]

* * *

The Assertion of Indigenous Third World Development Models

The problem with us Africans is that we've not been educated to appreciate our art and culture. So many of us have been influenced by the British system of education. I went through this system here not knowing enough about my own country. It was almost as if what we natives did wasn't important enough to be studied. I knew all about British history and British art, but about Ghana and Africa nothing.

Ghanaian art historian and intellectual Nana Apt, quoted in *New York Times*, 13 September 1980, p. 16

The purpose of this section is to provide an overview of the new development models emerging from the Third World. Space constraints rule out any detailed treatment here; this survey will provide only a hint of the new ideas, concepts, and theories.[24] Nevertheless, even this brief discussion should suffice to convey some of the main themes from each of the major areas, to show their common currents, and to begin to analyze the larger patterns. More detailed treatment is reserved for a planned book-length study.[25]

In his influential work *Beyond Marxism: Towards an Alternative Perspective*, Indian political theorist Vrajenda Raj Mehta argues that neither liberal democracy nor communism are appropriate frameworks for Indian development. He attributes their inadequacy to their unidimensional views of man and society. The liberal-democratic view that man is a consumer of utilities and producer of goods serves to legitimize a selfish, atomistic, egoistic society. Communism, he says, reduces all human dimensions to one, the economic, and transforms all human activity into one, state activity, which erodes all choice and destroys life's diversities.[26]

Mehta further argues for a multidimensional conception of man and society incorporating (1) the objective, external, rational; (2) the subjective, internal, intuitive; (3) the ethical, normative, harmonious; and (4) the spiritual and fiduciary. For the development of man's multidimensional personality, society must be structured as an "oceanic circle," an integral-pluralist system of wholes within wholes. The four social wholes of Mehta's well-organized society consist of "those devoted to the pursuit of knowledge, those who run the administration and protect the community from external aggression, those who manage the exchange of services of goods, and those who attend to manual and elementary tasks" (p. 54). Mehta claims that such an integralist-pluralist order will overcome the atomistic limitations of liberal democracy and the economic and bureaucratic collectivism of communism. The logic of "developing wholes" means that each sector of society must have autonomy or *swaraj* within an overall system of harmony and oceanic circles. Emphasizing both the autonomy of the several societal sectors and their integration within a larger whole, Mehta calls this essentially Indian-organic-corporatist system "integral pluralism." "Integral pluralism insists that the development of society has to be the development of the whole society. The whole is not one, but itself consists of various wholes, of economics and politics, ethics and religion, as also of different types of individuals. The relationship of each of them to each other is in the nature of oceanic circles" (p. 60).

Particularly interesting for our purposes are Mehta's attempts to ground his theory in the reality of Indian culture, history, and civilization. "Each national community," he says, "has its own law of development, its own way to fulfill itself." "The broken mosaic of Indian society," he goes on, "cannot be recreated in the image of the West—India must find its own strategy of development and nation-building suited to its own peculiar conditions" (p. 92). Instead of being dazzled by the national progress of the West and futilely trying to emulate its development model, India should define its goals and choose its means "separately in terms of its own resources and the role it wants to play on the world scene." Rejecting the thesis of a single and universal pattern of development, Mehta advocates an indigenous process of change attuned to the needs of individual societies: "A welcome process of social change in all societies is a process towards increasing self-awareness in terms of certain normatively defined goals in each case, and that the direction of the process and the definition of ends is largely defined by the society's own distinct history and way of life" (p. 104).

Mehta's theory of integral pluralism is a bold and erudite exposition of a model of indigenous development for India. Although he draws some of his ideas from the West, the specific sources of inspiration for his model are Indian: the Vedic seers, the *Mahabharata*, Rabindranath Tagore, and Gandhi. In contemporary India the model derives particular support from nationalists and from those who advocate the Gandhian model of development, which emphasizes a decentralized economy based on small industries, a reorientation of production in terms of criteria besides prosperity only, a possible decentralized defense industry, and hence a particularly Indian route to development.

* * *

The new and often parallel currents stirring the Islamic world have received far more popular attention than have those in India. There can be no doubt that a major religious revival is sweeping the world of Islam,[27] but Western understanding of the forces at work has been obscured, biased and retarded by events in Iran and by general Western hostility. It is relatively easy in the Iranian case to express appalled indignation at the summary trials and executions, the brutal treatment of the U.S. hostages and the sometimes wild fulminations of an aging ayatullah; but by so doing students may miss some of the deeper, permanent, and more important aspects of the changes under way.[28]

Two major features of the Islamic revival command special attention here. Both also occur in the Indian case. One is the criticism of the Western models, either liberal or communist, as inappropriate and undesirable in the Islamic context. The widespread sentiment in favor of rejecting Western values and the Western developmental model has been obscured in the popular media by their focusing only on the sometimes ludicrous comments of Iran's religious leaders that the Western model is sinful and satanic. This makes it easy to satirize and dismiss what is, in fact, a widespread and serious criticism that, coming from other Islamic mouths and pens—in, for instance, Saudi Arabia and Pakistan—is quite realistic and telling. The Islamic argument is that the excessive individualism of the liberal model and the excessive statism of the communist one are both inappropriate in the Islamic context: They violate its customs and traditions by importing a system without strong indigenous roots, and they are positively damaging to the Islamic world's own preferred values and institutions.[29]

The second aspect, complementary to the first, is the effort by the Iranians and others, once the Western influences were excised or repudiated, to reconstruct society and polity on the bases of indigenous Islamic concepts and institutions. Once more, what is in fact a serious process has frequently been ridiculed in the media, where only the comic-opera and most brutal aspects have received attention. But surely the efforts to reforge the links between state and society that had been largely destroyed by the shah, to lay stress on the family, the local community, a corporate group life and solidarity, and on a leader who provides both direction and moral values—in contrast to the alienation and mass society that are among the more visible results of the Western pattern of development—are serious and therefore must command our attention. Important too are the efforts at religious revival and the attempts to reconstruct law, society, and behavior in accordance with religious and moral principles, to rejoin politics and ethics in ways that in the West have been abandoned since Machiavelli. Rather than reject such developments out of hand—which further postpones understanding of them—Westerners must begin to take Islamic society on its own terms, not from the point of view of automatic rejection or a haughty sense of superiority, but with empathy and understanding. Among the more fascinating products of this Islamic revival are both a set of new, indigenous institutions and a distinctive Islamic social science of development to go with it.[30]

In Africa the institution around which the discussion revolves is tribalism. Tribalism is one of those traditional institutions, like India's caste associations or Islamic fundamentalism, that was supposed to decline or disappear as modernization went forward. The belief that tribalism was destined for the dustbins of history was so deeply ingrained that African leaders themselves often felt ashamed of their own background and origins. Tribalism was repressed and denied and the nation-state or the single-party mass-mobilizing system was elevated to an artificial importance.[31] When tribalism refused to die, it was rebaptized under the rubric of ethnicity and ethnic conflict, which somehow made it seem more modern.

There are still Westerners and Africans alike who deny the existence of tribalism or seek to stamp it out, but among other Africans there is a new and refreshing realism about tribalism, even some interesting—albeit not as yet overly successful—efforts to reconstruct African society using tribalism as a base. These include new variations on the federal principle, new forms of consociationalism, a corporately based communalism in Tanzania, or the African authenticity of Zaire. Whatever the precise name and form, these newer approaches to tribalism are both more realistic and more interesting than the past denial of or wishful thinking about it.

At a minimum, the tribe often gives people what little they have in rural Africa: a patch of land for their huts and maize, leadership, order, and coherence. The tribe often has its own police force, which offers a measure of security. In some countries without effective national welfare or social security, tribal authority and tradition help provide for the old and sick. Tribal ties and solidarities in the cities also help provide jobs, patronage, and positions within the army or bureaucracy. Parties and interest associations are often organized along tribal lines. In the absence of strong states and national political structures, the tribe may be an effective intermediary association providing services and brokering relations between the individual, family, or clan and the national government. Tribalism may weaken over time, but it surely will not disappear, and there is a growing and realistic recognition on the part of African leaders that tribalism is part of Africa. Many will find this new realism refreshing and see the effort to refashion African polities and social structures in accordance with its own indigenous traditions exciting and innovative.[32]

The case of Latin America is somewhat different since it is an area that we think of as already Western.[33] Properly qualified (taking into account Latin America's large indigenous populations, the periodic efforts to resurrect and glorify its Indian past, and the efforts of nations such as Mexico to ground their nationalism in part upon their mestizo heritage—the new "cosmic race"), this assertion is valid. One must also remember, however, that Latin America is an offshoot or historical fragment of a special time and place in the West, Iberia circa 1500,[34] whose own conformity to the Western model has been and in many ways still is somewhat less than total.[35] With this in mind, Latin America may be looked on as something of a mixed case, Western and Third World at the same time.

In various writings I have wrestled with the issue of where and in what ways Latin America conforms to the Western pattern and where it diverges.[36] In the context of this discussion, however, what is striking are the remarkable parallels between the newer currents in Latin America and in other Third World areas. First, there is a growing nationalistic rejection of the U.S. favored route to development, a rejection that has even stronger historical roots than in other Third World areas and that found expression as early as the nineteenth century in fears and hostility toward the "colossus of the north" and in widespread acceptance of the arguments of José E. Rodó, who contrasted the spiritualism, Catholicism, personalism, and humanism of Latin America (Ariel) with the crassness, materialism, secularism, pragmatism, and utilitarianism of the United States (Caliban).[37]

The reverse side of this coin is the effort to identify what is distinctive in Latin America's own past and present and to determine whether these characteristics can be used to erect a separate Latin American political sociology of development. Such a formulation would emphasize Latin America's persistent corporatism and organic statism, its neomercantilist and state-capitalist economic structures, its personalism and kinship patterns, its Catholicism and the institutions and behavioral patterns of Catholic political culture, its patrimonialism and unabashed patriarchalism, its patron-client networks now extended to the national political level, its distinctive patterns and arenas of state-society relations, and its historical relations of dependency (particularly in recent times) vis-à-vis the United States.[38] There are, as we shall see in the next section, problems with these formulations, not the least of which is that not all Latin Americans accept them or wish to accept them, still preferring to see themselves in terms of and to cast their lot with the Western model. Nevertheless, the parallels with other Third World areas are striking, and the attempts by Latin Americans to fashion their own indigenous model and social science of development deserve our attention.

Analogous developments in other areas also merit serious study, though only passing mention can be made of them here. In China, for example, the combination of Marxist and Confucian elements in Mao's thought provided not only a new and fascinating synthesis but also some of the key ingredients in the distinctively Chinese model of development.[39] Japan has achieved phenomenal economic growth rates by borrowing, copying, or synthesizing the technology and organizational models of the West and adapting these to historic and preferred Japanese forms, structures, and ways of doing things.[40] In Poland and elsewhere in Eastern Europe, Marxism is being adapted to local institutions such as Catholicism and nationalism. In the Soviet Union there is of course a Marxist socialist state, but no one would disagree it is also a *Russian* Marxist state (however ambiguous and open to disagreement may be its precise meaning).[41] Finally, in Western Europe itself, which originally inspired the Western model, there is both a new questioning of what the Western model consists of and whether even the nations of Western Europe conform to it, as well as a rethinking of whether that Western model is in fact applicable to the rest of the world.[42]

These various national and regional traditions need to be examined in greater detail and the arguments more fully amplified. What seems clear even from this brief survey, however, is that there is a growing rejection of the Western model as irrelevant and inappropriate in areas and nations where the traditions and institutions are quite different and that there exists a growing search for indigenous national institutions and models, based on local traditions instead of those imported from or imposed by the West. These trends seem now to transcend national and cultural boundaries.

Problem Areas and Dilemmas

The notion of a bright new world made up of young emerging nations is a fairy tale.
V. S. Naipaul, *Among the Believers*

The idea of a native, indigenous model and social science of development, reflecting and deeply rooted in local practices and institutions rather than imported and surface ones, is enormously attractive. Social scientists need to analyze this rather than merely celebrate it, however, and when that is done numerous problems arise.

First, the search for indigenous models of development may prove to be more romantic and nostalgic than realistic.[43] In some areas and nations (several of the Central American countries, for example), indigenous institutions may well prove weak or nonexistent, incapable of serving as the base for national development. They may, as with the Western model, reflect the preferences of intellectuals rather than those of the general population—or they may reflect a nostalgic longing for a past that cannot be revived. Such indigenous institutions may have been destroyed in whole or in part by the colonial powers or discredited by the earlier generation of Western-oriented local elites. There may be no institutional foundation of indigenous institutions and practices on which to build and hence, for many Third World nations, no light at the end of the development tunnel. The Western model has not worked well, but an indigenous one will not work either if it reflects the politics of romance and nostalgia rather than the politics of reality.[44]

Second, there are class, partisan, and other biases often implicit in a political strategy that seeks to fashion a model of development based upon indigenous institutions. Such a strategy could serve to defend the status quo or to restore the status quo ante, both nationally and internationally. It could justify an existing class, caste, leadership group, or clan remaining in power. It may be manipulated for partisan or personal advantage. For example, in Francisco Franco's efforts to restore and maintain traditional Spanish institutions and practices, it was clear that only his rather narrow and particular interpretation of what that special tradition was would be allowed and that other currents and possibilities within that tradition would be suppressed.[45]

Third, the actual practice of regimes that have followed an indigenous development strategy has not produced very many successes. Even on its own terms, it is hard to call the Iranian Revolution, so far, a success. The Mexican Revolution that was once trumpeted as providing an indigenous third way is acknowledged to have sold out, run its course, or died.[46] There has been a lot of talk about African authenticity in recent years, but in countries such as Togo or Zaire the application of the concept has served mainly to shore up corrupt and despotic regimes. Even in Tanzania, which has been widely cited as an example of a serious attempt to build an original African development model, there are immense difficulties accompanying this experiment and a notable lack of enthusiasm on the part of both the peasants who are presumably its prime beneficiaries and the government officials charged with implementing it.[47]

Fourth, in the present world, indigenous developmental models may no longer be possible. The time when a nation could maintain itself in isolation and develop on its own terms may well have passed. All of the Third World is now affected by what Lucian Pye once called the "world culture"—not only styles in dress and music (largely Western) but in social and political systems as well.[48] Third World countries are also caught up in what Immanuel Wallerstein called the "world system"—factors such as trade patterns, economic dependency relationships, world market prices, oil requirements, and so on, which have major effects on them but over which they have no control.[49] Additionally, whether one speaks of Afghanistan, El Salvador, or numerous other Third World nations, Cold War and other international political conflicts make them pawns in the global arena and often profoundly affect their internal development as well. All these conditions make it virtually impossible that the outside world would not impinge on any effort at indigenous development, if not destroying it then certainly requiring compromise in numerous areas.[50]

Fifth, not all indigenous elites and intellectuals wish to follow a native path. For them, traditional and indigenous institutions are not necessarily symbols of pride and nationalism. They may see them as signs of backwardness and underdevelopment, or have mixed feelings that breed confusion, irresolution, and lack of direction. By no means are all African leaders convinced that tribalism can become a new basis of political organization; hence in Kenya and elsewhere concerted efforts are under way not to build it up but to snuff tribalism out. Indian intellectuals, especially from the lower castes, are not yet ready to accept arguments concerning the modernizing role the castes may play. Not all Iranian intellectuals accept the virtues of a theocratic state led by the ayatullah or, even if they are believers in Islamic fundamentalism, agree on what precise institutional form that should take.

Latin America is an especially interesting area in this regard, for while most of its intellectuals share varying degrees of antipathy to the United States model and the U.S.-favored development route and want to have a hand in fashioning a nationalistic and Latin American one, they are also terribly uncomfortable with the implications of that position. That new route would imply acceptance of a political system built in some degree upon the principles of corporatism, hierarchy, authoritarianism, and organic-statism—none of which are popular or fashionable in the more democratic nations and salons of the modern world, into which Latin America and its intellectuals, historically plagued by a sense of inferiority and backwardness, also wish to be accepted. Hence they have ambivalent feelings regarding indigenous models and prefer theories of dependency or international stratification that conveniently and more comfortably place the blame on external instead of internal forces.[51]

Sixth and finally, emphasis must be placed on the sheer diversity of Third World nations and areas and hence the immense difficulties of achieving a consensus on any development strategy, indigenous or otherwise. At some levels of analysis, Latin America (and Iberia) may be thought of as part of a single culture area, but it must also be kept in mind that Paraguay is quite different from Argentina, Brazil and Peru from Chile, Nicaragua from Mexico—and all are at different levels of development. Hence different strategies and models of modernization, even if they could be conceptualized within certain common parameters, would have to be designed for each country of the area.[52] In the Islamic world the same qualifications would have to be introduced; it obviously also makes a major difference if we are talking of the Sunni, Shiite, or other traditions and combinations of them.[53] A similar case exists in Africa: Some observers feel that Islam is the only organized cultural and ideological force capable of offering a coherent and continent-wide alternative to the heretofore dominant Western model. This point of view, however, ignores the still-strong Christian and Western influences, the fact that only a small minority of African states are essentially Muslim (that is, at least 75 percent Islamic), the continuing influence of traditional beliefs, and in some parts of Africa, the lack of a strong cultural identity of any sort. All of these factors would have to be taken into account in creating an indigenous model, or models, of development. Nor should one underestimate the sheer confusion, uncertainty, and chaos surrounding these issues in many Third World nations. In the Third World as a whole and in its component geographic regions and distinct cultural areas, there is too much diversity to be subsumed under any single theory or set of concepts.

Conclusion: Toward a Nonethnocentric Theory of Development

The aspiration for something different, better, more truly indigenous than Western systems of development and yet as socially and materially effective is palpable everywhere. "Our own way" is the persistent theme; but it is far more often advanced as a creed than as a plan.
Flora Lewis, *New York Times*, 31 December 1979

In numerous areas, the West and the Western model of development intimately associated with its earlier progress seem to be in decline. Western Europe suffers from various malaises of uncertain and often obscure origins; the economies of the Western nations have experienced severe recessions; U.S. institutions have not always worked well in recent years; NATO and the Western Alliance are in disarray; and the global system of U.S. hegemony and dominance is being challenged. With this Spenglerian "Decline of the West" [54] has come a new questioning of and challenge to the development model that was a part of the nearly 500-year-long Western era of domination. It is not just the model itself that is now being challenged, however, but the larger, preeminently Western, and for that reason parochial and ethnocentric, philosophical and intellectual tradition that went with it. What many Westerners assumed to be a universal set of norms and processes by which societies developed and modernized—with the West as presumed leader and model—has now been demonstrated to be parochial and ethnocentric.

With the decline of Western hegemony and the pretension to universalism of the intellectual constructs that are part and parcel of it, and concomitant with the rise and new assertiveness of various non-Western and Third World areas, have come demands for local, indigenous models of development. The critique of the Western model as particularistic, parochial, Eurocentric, considerably less than universal, and hopelessly biased, as not only perpetuating misunderstanding regarding these areas but also wreaking downright harm upon them, seems devastating, persuasive, and perhaps unchallengeable. The question is no longer whether the Western model applies or whether it is salvageable but what is the precise nature of the models that have risen to take its place and whether these new models are functional and viable for the Third World areas from which they are emerging.

These issues would seem to represent the next great frontier in the social sciences.[55] Shorn of its romantic and nostalgic aspects, unfettered by the class or partisan biases that sometimes surround it, incorporating both national currents and international ones, taking account of practical realities and not just intellectual constructs, cognizant of both the mixed sentiments of local elites and the diversities of the societies studied—or at least recognizing these when they do occur—the notion of a nonethnocentric theory of development is now on the front burner. The study of such local, indigenous, native cultural traditions and models, Samuel P. Huntington has said, may well be the wave of the future for the social sciences.[56]

Scholars need now for the first time to begin to take non-Western areas and their ofttimes peculiar institutions seriously, in their own context and traditions rather than from the slanted perspective of the Western social sciences. They need to reexamine virtually all of the Western social science notions of development. A serious mistake made by Western scholars, for example, is to assume that as people become modernized and educated, they also become westernized. In much of the Middle East, for instance, urbanization and the growth of a literate middle class are prime causes in the growth of interest in Islam. The examples could easily be multiplied. Scholars should see local indigenous institutions not necessarily as dysfunctional or doomed but frequently as viable and necessary, as filters and winnowers of the modernization process, as agencies of transition between traditional and modern, and as a means for reconciling and blending the global with the indigenous, the nationalist with the international. This undertaking implies both greater empathy on our part and greater modesty in terms of the claims made for the universalism of the Western examples.

The implications of coming to grips with indigenous institutions and nonethnocentric theories and concepts of development are enormous.[57] Three major areas of impact may be noted here. The first has to do with the Third World and non-Western nations themselves: their efforts to overcome historical inferiority complexes, their reconceived possibilities for development, the newfound importance of their traditional institutions, the rediscovery of many complex routes to development, their new sense of pride and accomplishment and so on. It will take some time before the Third World is able to articulate and mold these diverse concepts into realistic development models, and the translation of concepts like authenticity into concrete political institutions, educational policies, and health programs is liable to take even longer. Nevertheless, we cannot doubt the reality or growth of such new interpretations, perspectives, and syntheses—as between Marxism and an indigenous development tradition, for example, or in the form of a homegrown type of democracy, or as an updated and modernized Islam.

Second, the arguments presented here have immense implications for the social sciences. Not only must we reexamine a host of essentially Western social science assumptions but we must also be prepared to accept an Islamic social science of development, an African social science of development, a Latin American social science of development—and to strike some new balances between what is particular in the development process and what does in fact conform to more universal patterns. In exploring such indigenous models, scholars will need to fashion a dynamic theory of change as well as examine a variety of normative orientations. . . .[58]

* * *

Notes

1. P. T. Bauer, *Dissent on Development* (Cambridge, MA: Harvard University Press, 1976); David E. Schmitt, ed., *Dynamics of the Third World* (Cambridge, MA: Winthrop, 1974); Frank Tachau, ed., *The Developing Nations: What Path to Modernization?* (New York: Dodd, Mead, 1972); W. A. Beling and G. O. Totten, eds., *The Developing Nations: Quest for a Model* (New York: Van Nostrand, 1970); Robert E. Gamer, *The Developing Nations* (Boston: Allyn and Bacon, 1976); Lyman Tower Sargent, *Contemporary Political Ideologies* (Homewood, IL: Dorsey, 1981); Paul E. Sigmund, ed., *The Ideologies of the Developing Nations* (New York: Praeger, 1972); and John Kenneth Galbraith, *The Voice of the Poor* (Cambridge, MA: Harvard University Press, 1982).
2. For example, Edward Said, *Orientalism* (New York: Pantheon, 1978); Howard J. Wiarda, ed., *Politics and Social Change in Latin America: The Distinct Tradition*, 2d ed. rev. (Amherst: University of Massachusetts Press, 1982).
3. These arguments are expanded in Howard J. Wiarda, "The Ethnocentrism of the Social Sciences: Implications for Research and Policy," *Review of Politics* 42 (April 1981):163–97.
4. For some parallel arguments see Reinhard Bendix, "Tradition and Modernity Reconsidered," *Comparative Studies in Society and History* 9 (April 1967):292–346, reprinted in his *Embattled Reason* (New York: Oxford University Press, 1970); also Joseph R. Gusfield, "Tradition and Modernity: Misplaced Polarities in the Study of Social Change," *American Journal of Sociology* 72 (January 1967): 351–62.
5. This and other criticisms will not be new to many students of political development. What is new is the widespread articulation of such views within the Third World. Moreover, this critique of the Western model needs to be presented as a prelude to the discussion of indigenous models that follows. For some earlier critiques of the Western development model see Wiarda, "Ethnocentrism"; Bendix, "Tradition and Modernity"; Dean C. Tipps, "Modernization Theory and the Comparative Studies of Society: A Critical Perspective," *Comparative Studies of Society and History* 15 (March 1973): 199–226; and C. D. Hah and J. Schneider, "A Critique of Current Theories of Political Development and Modernization," *Social Research* 35 (Spring 1968): 130–58. See also the statements on the different meanings of democracy by Costa Rican President Luis Alberto Monge and Nigerian President Alhaji Shehu Shagari at the Conference on Free Elections, Department of State, Washington, DC, 4–6 November 1982; also R. William Liddle, "Comparative Political Science and the Third World," mimeographed (Columbus: Ohio State University, Department of Political Science).
6. An excellent treatment of these themes is Claudio Veliz, *The Centralist Tradition in Latin America* (Princeton, NJ: Princeton University Press, 1980); also Clifford Geertz, *Negara: The Theatre State in Nineteenth Century Bali* (Princeton, NJ: Princeton University Press, 1980), in which he shows that the culture and the theater are the substance, not just superstructure.
7. Especially relevant is the general critique of the Western sociological bias in T. O. Wilkinson's "Family Structure and Industrialization in Japan," *American Sociological Review* 27 (October 1962):678–82; also Alberto Guerreiro Ramos, "Modernization: Toward a Possibility Model," in *Developing Nations*, ed. Beling and Totten, pp. 21–59; and Gusfield, "Tradition and Modernity."
8. William P. Glade, "Problems of Research in Latin American Studies," in *New Directions in Language and Area Studies* (Milwaukee: University of Wisconsin at Milwaukee for the Consortium of Latin American Studies Programs, 1979), pp. 81–101.
9. Veliz, *The Centralist Tradition.*
10. For a general statement, Leonard S. Binder et al., eds., *Crises and Sequences in Political Development* (Princeton, NJ: Princeton University Press, 1971).
11. See the classic statement by Marc Bloch, *Feudal Society* (Chicago: University of Chicago Press, 1961).
12. Daniel Bell, *The Coming of Post-Industrial Society* (New York: Basic Books, 1973). On 26 May 1981, in a personal conversation, Professor Bell asserted that by a quite different route he had also "come to similar conclusions regarding the inadequacies of many social science concepts since they derive almost exclusively from a par-

ticular Western tradition." Much of the new social science literature emanating from Latin America since the 1960s makes many of the same arguments.

13. The dependency literature is extensive; among the best statements is Fernando Henrique Cardoso and Enzo Faletto, *Dependency and Development in Latin America* (Berkeley: University of California Press, 1978).
14. For a general discussion, S. N. Eisenstadt, "Post-Traditional Societies and the Continuity and Reconstruction of Tradition," *Daedalus* 102 (Winter 1973): 1–27; and also by Eisenstadt, *Modernization: Protest and Change* (Englewood Cliffs, NJ: Prentice-Hall, 1966).
15. Lloyd I. Rudolph and Susanne Hoeber Rudolph, *The Modernity of Tradition* (Chicago: University of Chicago Press, 1967).
16. The case of Tanzania is especially interesting in this regard.
17. The arguments are detailed in Wiarda, "Ethnocentrism."
18. A more complete discussion with regard to one region is in Howard J. Wiarda, ed., *The Continuing Struggle for Democracy in Latin America* (Boulder, CO: Westview Press, 1980).
19. G. A. D. Soares, "Latin American Studies in the United States," *Latin American Research Review* 11 (1976); and Howard J. Wiarda, "Latin American Intellectuals and the 'Myth' of Underdevelopment" (Presentation made at the Seventh National Meeting of the Latin American Studies Association, Houston, 2–5 November 1977), in Wiarda, *Corporatism and National Development in Latin America* (Boulder, CO: Westview Press, 1981), pp. 236–38.
20. Susanne J. Bodenheimer, *The Ideology of Developmentalism: The American Paradigm-Surrogate for Latin American Studies* (Beverly Hills, CA: Sage Publications, 1971); Teresa Hayter, *Aid as Imperialism* (Baltimore, MD: Penguin, 1971); Ronald H. Chilcote, *Theories of Comparative Politics: The Search for a Paradigm* (Boulder, CO: Westview Press, 1981); Hah and Schneider, "Critique."
21. In our Harvard faculty Seminar, several of whose members were part of the original and highly influential SSRC Committee on Comparative Politics, it was striking to note in the occasional Seminar remarks by these members how strongly the anticommunist ideology of that time pervaded the SSRC Committee's assumptions. One of our Seminar members, himself part of the original SSRC Committee, flatly stated that the purpose of this group was to formulate a noncommunist theory of change and thus to provide a non-Marxist alternative for the developing nations.
22. Selig S. Harrison, *The Widening Gulf: Asian Nationalism and American Policy* (New York: Free Press, 1978). My critique of the development paradigm is contained in "Is Latin America Democratic and Does It Want to Be? The Crisis and Quest of Democracy in the Hemisphere," in Wiarda, *The Continuing Struggle*, pp. 3–24.
23. Samuel P. Huntington, *Political Order in Changing Societies* (New Haven, CT: Yale University Press, 1968); and Wiarda, "Ethnocentrism."
24. See also Sigmund, *Ideologies*. Especially striking are the differences between the old and new editions of this study, and the differences in Sigmund's own thinking as contained in his introductions.
25. Tentatively entitled *Third World Conceptions of Development*, also growing out of the Harvard seminar on "New Directions in Comparative Politics."
26. Vrajenda Raj Mehta, *Beyond Marxism: Towards an Alternative Perspective* (New Delhi: Manohar Publications, 1978), p. 12. I am grateful to my colleague Thomas Pantham for bringing this work and the debate that swirls about it to my attention. Subsequent page references to Mehta will be in parentheses in the text. A parallel volume from Latin America is José Arico, *Marx e a America Latina* (Rio de Janeiro: Paz e Terra, 1982).
27. G. H. Jansen, *Militant Islam* (New York: Harper and Row, 1980), as well as the special series by Sir Willie Morris in the *Christian Science Monitor*, August-September 1980, and that by Flora Lewis in *New York Times*, December 1979.
28. An especially good statement is by Harvard anthropologist Mary Catherine Bateson, "Iran's Misunderstood Revolution," *New York Times*, 20 February 1979, p. 14.

29. Jansen, *Militant Islam*; Said, *Orientalism*; Barry Rubin, *Paved with Good Intentions* (New York: Oxford University Press, 1980); Shahrough Akhavi, *Religion and Politics in Contemporary Iran* (Albany: State University of New York Press, 1980); Ali Masalehdan, "Values and Political Development in Iran" (Ph.D. diss., University of Massachusetts at Amherst, 1981); and Michael Fischer, *Iran: From Religious Dispute to Revolution* (Cambridge, MA: Harvard University Press, 1980). See also the discussion led by Fischer on "Iran: Is It an Example of Populist Neo-Traditionalism?" Joint Seminar on Political Development (JOSPOD), Cambridge, MA, Minutes of the Meeting of 15 October 1980.
30. Anwar Syed, *Pakistan: Islam, Politics and National Solidarity* (New York: Praeger, 1982). The implications of Syed's discussion are considerably broader than the case he discusses. See also Inayatullah, *Transfer of Western Development Model to Asia and Its Impact* (Kuala Lumpur: Asian Center for Development Administration, 1975).
31. David Apter, *Ghana in Transition* (New York: Atheneum, 1967); and Ruth Schachter Morgenthau, "Single Party Systems in West Africa," *American Political Science Review* 55 (June 1961) have both helped to popularize (and, to a degree, romanticize) the notion of the viability of African single party systems. Henry L. Bretton, *Power and Politics in Africa* (Chicago: Aldine, 1973) helped to explode those myths.
32. My understanding of these currents in Africa has been enriched by various exchanges with and the seminar presentations of Africanist Naomi Chazan, a colleague in both Jerusalem and Cambridge; and by the writings of Swiss sociologist Pierre Pradervand, *Family Planning Programmes in Africa* (Paris: Organization for Economic Cooperation and Development, 1970) and "Africa—The Fragile Giant," a series of articles in the *Christian Science Monitor*, December 1980. See also Crawford Young, *The Politics of Cultural Pluralism* (Madison: University of Wisconsin Press, 1976).
33. For a partial and inconclusive exchange on this theme see the comments of Susan Bourque, Samuel P. Huntington, Merilee Grindle, Brian Smith, and me in a JOSPOD seminar on "Neo-Traditionalism in Latin America," in Minutes of the Meeting of 19 November 1980.
34. Louis Hartz et al., *The Founding of New Societies* (New York: Harcourt, Brace, 1964).
35. Howard J. Wiarda, "Spain and Portugal," in *Western European Party Systems*, ed. Peter Merkl (New York: Free Press, 1980), pp. 298–328; and Wiarda, "Does Europe Still Stop at the Pyrenees, or Does Latin America Begin There? Iberia, Latin America, and the Second Enlargement of the European Community," in *The Impact of an Enlarged European Community on Latin America*, ed. Georges D. Landau and G. Harvey Summ (forthcoming); also published under the same title as Occasional Paper no. 2 (Washington: American Enterprise Institute for Public Policy Research, January 1982).
36. Wiarda, *Politics and Social Change; Corporatism and Development; The Continuing Struggle*; and "Toward a Framework for the Study of Political Change in the Iberic-Latin Tradition: The Corporative Model," *World Politics* 25 (January 1973): 206–35.
37. José E. Rodó, *Ariel* (Montevideo: Dornaleche y Reyes, 1900); an English translation by F. J. Stimson was published under the same title (Boston: Houghton Mifflin, 1922).
38. Among others, Veliz, *The Centralist Tradition;* Glen Dealy, *The Public Man: An Interpretation of Latin America and Other Catholic Countries* (Amherst: University of Massachusetts Press, 1977); Leopoldo Zea, *The Latin American Mind* (Norman: University of Oklahoma Press, 1963); Octavio Paz, *The Labyrinth of Solitude* (New York: Grove Press, 1961); Richard M. Morse, "The Heritage of Latin America," in Hartz, *The Founding.*
39. H. G. Creel, *Chinese Thought: From Confucius to Mao Tse-tung* (Chicago: University of Chicago Press, 1963); Stuart H. Schram, *The Political Thought of Mao Tse-tung* (New York: Praeger, 1976).
40. T. O. Wilkinson, *The Urbanization of Japanese Labor* (Amherst: University of Massachusetts Press, 1965); Ezra F. Vogel, *Japan as No. 1* (Cambridge: Harvard University Press, 1979); and Peter Berger, "Secularity—West and East" (Paper presented at the American Enterprise Institute Public Policy Week, Washington, DC, 6–9 December 1982).

41. For example, Stanley Rothman and George W. Breslauer, *Soviet Politics and Society* (St. Paul, MN: West, 1978); Archie Brown and Jack Gray, eds., *Political Culture and Political Change in Communist States* (New York: Holmes and Meier, 1978); Jerry F. Hough and Merle Fainsod, *How the Soviet Union Is Governed* (Cambridge, MA: Harvard University Press, 1979).
42. See, for instance, Raymond Grew, ed., *Crises of Political Development in Europe and the United States* (Princeton, NJ: Princeton University Press, 1978); and Charles Tilly, ed., *The Formation of Nation States in Western Europe* (Princeton, NJ: Princeton University Press, 1975).
43. This is one of the criticisms leveled in Pantham, "Integral Pluralism?" against Mehta's *Beyond Marxism*.
44. Pradervand, "Africa."
45. Pantham, "Integral Pluralism" and "Political Culture, Political Structure, and Underdevelopment in India," *Indian Journal of Political Science* 41 (September 1980): 432–56; also Wiarda, *Corporatism and National Development*.
46. Susan Eckstein, *The Poverty of Revolution: The State and the Urban Poor in Mexico* (Princeton, NJ: Princeton University Press, 1977); Kenneth F. Johnson, *Mexican Democracy: A Critical View* (Boston: Allyn and Bacon, 1971); Octavio Paz, *The Other Mexico* (New York: Grove Press, 1972).
47. Pradervand, "Africa."
48. Lucian Pye, *Aspects of Political Development* (Boston: Little, Brown, 1966).
49. Immanuel Wallerstein, *The Modern World-System* (New York: Academic Press, 1976).
50. Unless of course a nation is willing to withdraw entirely and consciously into isolation, but as Cambodia illustrates, that strategy may not work very well either.
51. These issues are addressed in the introduction to the Portuguese language version of Wiarda, *Corporatism and National Development*, published as *O modelo corporativo na América Latina e a Latinoamericanizaçã dos Estados Unidos* (Rio de Janeiro: Ed. Vozes, 1983). For an example of such ambivalence see Norbert Lechner, ed., *Estado y política en América Latina* (Mexico City: Siglo Veintiuno Editores, 1981); also Carlos Franco, *Del Marxismo Eurocentrico al Marxismo Latino-americano* (Lima: Centro de Estudios para el Desarrollo y la Participacion, 1981).
52. For a country-by-country analysis combined with a common set of theoretical concepts see Howard J. Wiarda and Harvey F. Kline, *Latin American Politics and Development*, 2d ed. (Boulder, CO: Westview Press, 1985).
53. Masalehdan, *Values and Political Development in Iran*.
54. Oswald Spengler, *The Decline of the West* (New York: Knopf, 1932); and much recent literature.
55. See the research agenda set forth in Howard J. Wiarda, ed., *Third World Conceptions of Development*, forthcoming. See also Chapter 1 in this book.
56. In a personal conversation with the author, December 1979.
57. The research perspectives suggested here and the implications of these as set forth in the concluding paragraphs are explored in greater detail in Wiarda, "Ethnocentrism"; *Politics and Social Change; The Continuing Struggle for Democracy*; and *Corporatism and National Development*.
58. I have attempted to formulate such a theory in "Toward a Framework for the Study of Political Change in the Iberic-Latin Tradition," and in *Corporatism and National Development*.

Chapter 11

IS DEPENDENCY THEORY AN EXPLANATION OR AN IDEOLOGY?

The substantial gap between the prosperity levels of countries in the advanced industrial world and that of less-developed countries (LDCs) has alarmed many of the scholars whose research concentrates on these LDCs and regard that gap as unjust. The quest for a remedy to this perceived injustice produced a vigorous debate on the causes of this inequality. While some scholars regard the underdevelopment and poverty of third world countries as simply a matter of their being at an earlier stage of the modernization process—a situation that will be remedied with time—other scholars identify specific causes of underdevelopment that presumably could be modified by intentional policy decisions.

Scholars on the political left tend to place the blame for underdevelopment on the need for the capitalist nations of the West to exploit third world countries, thereby preventing them from what would otherwise be their inevitable modernization. These scholars argue from a Marxist-Leninist perspective that Western countries must exploit the LDCs and keep them in a state of political and economic dependency to prevent the otherwise inevitable collapse of capitalism. In making this argument about the supposed evil effects of capitalism, these scholars shift the blame for underdevelopment from the LDCs to the capitalist West. Susanne Jonas's article (reading 11.1) exemplifies this perspective, known as dependency theory.

Dependency theory was quite popular in the 1970s and 1980s; however, in recent decades it has fallen into disfavor among scholars who are not on the far left. Charles Doran's article (reading 11.2) in this chapter typifies this response to dependency theory among more conservative scholars who stress alternative explanations for underdevelopment among LDCs, such as cultural and demographic factors, including a rigid ideologism or rapid population growth. Doran and others claim that such alternative explanations better fit the facts than does dependency theory.

Dependency theorists do identify some truths. Clearly, there has been exploitation of the Third World by the capitalist West. However, an explanation of such a complex phenomenon that relies solely on one factor is almost certainly a considerable simplification of a reality that differs from one case to the next. Since some of the most underdeveloped societies, such as Liberia and Ethiopia, have had relatively little contact with the West and hence can hardly blame their status on exploitation, some claim the dependency theory fails as an explanation but rather serves the role of a political and ideological agenda. Doran claims that other factors internal to the less-developed systems constitute better explanations.

11.1

DEPENDENCY AND IMPERIALISM: THE ROOTS OF LATIN AMERICAN UNDERDEVELOPMENT

Susanne Jonas (Bodenheimer)

Susanne Jonas's essay epitomizes the argument among those who subscribe to V. I. Lenin's theory that the capitalist West avoided its otherwise inevitable collapse by engineering underdevelopment in third world countries and that underdevelopment is simply a product of exploitation by the Western capitalist system. Jonas, who actively published moral indictments of Western capitalism in the 1970s, argues that the West both creates and perpetuates underdevelopment by:

1. utilizing the non-Western countries as captive markets to absorb the otherwise inevitable Western overproduction;
2. fostering an economic structure limited to extractive enterprises, such as mining indigenous resources of use to the West; and
3. sponsoring and financing indigenous elites to keep the native populations in line with Western needs.

In Jonas's view, the more that the West is involved economically with the less-developed world—as with the Alliance for Progress aid to Latin America—the more underdevelopment and dependency is created. Her argument assumes the Marxist-Leninist analysis of capitalism, a closed thought system not susceptible to the testability criterion discussed in chapter 1. Students should ask whether she addresses alternative explanations of underdevelopment and whether her theory fits the pattern of development in the real world.

Nine years ago any critic of the Alliance for Progress was dismissed as a cynic, a malicious troublemaker, or worse yet, a Communist. Today such criticism has become so respectable in Washington that disillusioned liberals like Senator Frank Church and corporate hardliners such as Nelson Rockefeller openly acknowledge the bankruptcy of the Alliance policy.

Quite aside from their evaluations, there is far more eloquent testimony to the failure of the Alliance to achieve its stated objective of peaceful social and economic revolution in Latin America:[1]

Susanne Jonas (Bodenheimer), "Dependency and Imperialism: The Roots of Latin American Under-Development," in *Readings in U.S. Imperialism,* ed. K. Fann and D. Hodges (Boston: Porter Sargent, 1971): 155–182.

- annual average growth rates during the 1960's were lower than those of the previous decade, and fell far short of the target (2.5 per cent per capita) established in 1961;
- social problems such as urban poverty, unemployment, and inequality of income distribution have been aggravated rather than resolved: e.g., while average per capita income is $410, the lower half of the population receives an average of $120, and the top 5 per cent of the population receives $2600; U.N. agencies estimate present equivalent unemployment to be about 25 per cent of the labor force;
- the serious agrarian and tax reforms envisioned in 1961 have not been made: e.g., in no country other than Venezuela and Paraguay was more than 10 per cent of the rural population resettled through agrarian reform;
- given the declining value of Latin American exports, and the rising prices of goods imported by the region, Latin America faces an increasingly serious balance of payments crisis and a "virtual commercial deficit" in the coming decade.

These examples indicate the magnitude of Latin America's development problems, and the failure of the Alliance to cope with them in terms of its own rhetoric and *stated* goals.

* * *

Rather than listing and criticizing, point-by-point, the various theories devised by American social scientists to explain Latin underdevelopment (as I have done elsewhere),[2] I shall focus here upon the principal distortion underlying all of these theories: the failure—perhaps the refusal—to examine Latin America in terms of its relationship to the advanced industrial nations, particularly the U.S. Most American social scientists have evaded this task either by: 1) treating Latin countries as self-contained units, whose economic, social, or political systems can be analyzed in themselves; or 2) arguing (or assuming) that Latin American development has been stimulated by the region's contact with the advanced industrial nations.[3] The first type of analysis ignores the position of Latin America in an international environment dominated by the developed nations. The second, which maintains or assumes that there has been a net inflow of capital and technology from the developed nations into Latin America (through foreign investment and aid) and that the region has benefitted from that inflow, flies directly in the face of the facts.[4]

It has been shown in a number of studies that foreign investment by the U.S. and other industrial nations in under-developed areas has resulted in a net outflow of capital from the underdeveloped to the developed nations, a decapitalization of the former. In a number of Latin countries and for the region as a whole, the input from foreign private investment has been far exceeded by the outflow of profit remittances abroad. (According to U.S. Department of Commerce figures, the outflow from Latin America was $7.5 billion greater than inflow from 1950 to 1965.) This drain through foreign investment is aggravated by the clear deterioration of the terms of trade for the Latin nations and of their position in world trade. (Between 1950 and 1968 Latin America's share of world trade shrank from 11 per cent to 5.1 per cent.) Foreign aid has become continually more "tied" to conditions imposed by creditor nations to meet their own balance of payments difficulties or to accommodate private business interests. Service (interest and amortization) payments of the foreign debt, as well as the flow of profits abroad, continue to mount in Latin nations, and consume an ever-increasing share of export earnings (now more than 35 per cent for the region as a whole). By the mid-1960's the total paid by Latin countries in debt service payments exceeded the amount of new loans, and at the end of the decade the external debt had doubled since 1960.

Recognition of the distortions in existing theories leads directly to the starting-point for a critical analysis of Latin underdevelopment; *that Latin America is today, and has been since the sixteenth century, part of an international system dominated by the now-developed nations, and that Latin underdevelopment is the outcome of a particular series of relationships to that international system.*

The Dependency Model

The basic premises of the dependency model, as first elaborated by a group of Latin American social scientists,[5] differ sharply from those of American social science development theories. "Dependency" is conceived as a "conditioning situation," i.e. one which "determines the limits and possibilities for human action and conduct"—in this case, for development in Latin America. We shall accept the definition of dependency as:

> a situation in which the economy of a certain group of countries is conditioned by the development and expansion of another economy, to which their own [economy] is subjected. . .an historical condition which shapes a certain structure of the world economy such that it favors some countries to the detriment of others, and limits the development possibilities of the [subordinate] economies. . .[6]

What does this mean? That Latin America has fulfilled certain definite functions in the "world economy" or world market, and the domestic development of Latin America has been limited or conditioned by the needs of the dominant economies within that world market. To be sure, no nation has ever developed entirely outside the context of the world market. The distinguishing feature of dependent (as contrasted with interdependent) development is that growth in the dependent nations occurs as a reflex of the expansion of the dominant nations, and is geared toward the needs of the dominant economies—i.e., foreign rather than national needs. In the dependent countries imported factors of production (e.g., capital and technology) have become the central determinants of economic development and socio-political life. And while the world market served as an instrument of expansion in European and American development, it restricts autonomous development in the dependent nations. Dependency means, then, that the alternatives open to the dependent nation are defined and limited by its integration into and functions within the world market.

At this point, we must clarify the concrete meanings of the "world market" and the "international system." By itself, the world market encompasses all flows of goods and services among nations outside the Communist trade bloc—all capital transfers (including foreign aid and overseas investment) and all commodity exchanges. But the world market is the core of a broader "international system." This international system includes not only a network of economic (market) relations, but also the entire complex of political, military, social, and cultural international relations organized by and around that market (e.g., the Monroe Doctrine, the Organization of American States, "Free World" defense treaties and organizations, and media and communications networks). The international system is the static expression and outcome of a dynamic historical process; the transnational or global expansion of capitalism.

By focusing on the international system, the dependency model proceeds from a basic concrete fact of Latin American history: that since the Spanish conquest—that is, since its existence as Latin American rather than indigenous Indian society—Latin America has played a certain role in the political economy of one or another dominant capitalist nation (Spain and Portugal in the colonial and early post-independence period, England during most of the nineteenth century, and the U.S. since the beginning of the twentieth century). Thus, unlike *un*developed societies (those few which have *no* market relations with the industrialized nations), the *under*developed Latin economics have always been shaped by the global expansion and consolidation of the capitalist system, and by their own incorporation into that system. In this sense, Latin societies "brought into existence with their birth" their relation to the international system, and hence their relations of dependency.

Although the particular function of Latin America in the international system has varied, the development of that region has been shaped since the Spanish conquest by a general structural characteristic of capitalist expansion: its unevenness. "Unevenness" means that some nations or regions have developed more rapidly than—often at the expense of—others. For Latin America this has entailed increasing relative poverty, as the gap in income and growth rates between the industrial nations and Latin America is constantly widening. (Since 1957, for example, the growth rate of per capita income in Latin America has been less than 1.5 per cent a year, as contrasted with nearly 2.5 per cent in the U.S. and 4 per cent in Europe.[7]) Similar disparities have marked the uneven development of various regions within Latin America.

This unevenness has been manifested through an "international division of labor"; while Western Europe and the U.S. industrialized, Latin America remained for centuries an exporter of primary raw materials and agricultural products. Even the faltering steps toward industrialization more recently have not altered the fundamentally complementary character of the Latin economies: the industrial sectors remain dependent on imports (of capital goods) and, as a result of the increasing foreign control over these sectors, growth is still governed largely by the needs of foreign economies. The international division of labor has persisted (the 1969 *Rockefeller Report* even calls for making it "more efficient"); only its form has changed. This complementarity is not incidental but essential to the underdevelopment of the Latin economics. As is widely recognized, the periods of relative growth and development in Latin America (e.g., industrialization in the 1930's) have occurred during the phases of relative contraction in the world market (during periods of international war or depression), when the region's ties to that market and to the dominant nations have been weakest. Politically as well, Latin American development has been limited by the fact that policy decisions about resource allocation and all aspects of national development are conditioned and limited by the interests of the developed societies.

From the foregoing, it becomes clear that underdevelopment in Latin America is structurally linked to development in the dominant nations. European and American development and Latin underdevelopment are not two isolated phenomena, but rather two outcomes of the same historical process: the global expansion of capitalism.

Insofar as Latin American development has been limited since the sixteenth century by fulfilling one or another function in the international system, the *fact* of dependency has been a constant. But the *forms* of dependency, in particular countries at particular historical moments, have varied according to the specific characteristics of the international system at that time and the specific functions of the Latin country within the system.

Characteristics of the international system:

- the prevalent form of capitalism (mercantile or industrial, corporate or financial);
- the principal needs of the dominant nation(s) in the international system (agricultural commodities, minerals, cheap labor, commodity markets, capital markets, etc.);

- the degree of concentration of capital in the dominant nation(s) (competitive or monopolistic capitalism);
- the degree of concentration internationally (one hegemonic power or rival powers and, if one hegemonic power, which nation [Spain, England, or the U.S.]);
- the typical form of world trade (mercantilism, "free trade," or protectionism).

Characteristics of the Latin country within the international system:

- function primarily as a supplier of raw materials or agricultural products, as a market for manufactured goods, as a supplier of certain manufactured commodities, as an arena for direct foreign investment, or any combination of the preceding;
- the degree of relative autonomy (periods of international war or depression *vs.* "normal" periods of capitalist expansion);
- the degree of foreign control in the principal economic sectors;
- the nature of political ties to the dominant power(s) (colonial or nominal independence).

The specific forms of dependency in Latin America in any given historical period are shaped by the characteristics of the international system and of Latin America's function within it. Latin America was first integrated into the international system in its mercantile phase, under Spanish dominance, and served primarily as a provider of raw materials and agricultural commodities. Thus dependency during the colonial period and during much of the nineteenth century was manifested primarily through the development of export-import "enclaves." The conditions which shape Latin dependency today are quite distinct. The international system today is characterized by: advanced industrial capitalism (corporate integrated with financial capital); the dominant nations' need for raw materials and, more important, for commodity and capital markets; monopolistic concentration of capital; American hegemony (*vis-à-vis* Latin America); and increasing international integration of capital. Trade within the international system is increasingly protectionist (tariffs or quotas imposed by the dominant nations) and is increasingly incorporated within the structure of the multinational corporations. Latin America's function within the system is shifting from a supplier of raw materials and agricultural commodities to an arena where certain phases of industrial production are carried out—but still under the auspices of foreign corporations.[8] The degree of foreign control in the principal economic sectors is increasing, and Latin America's integration into the orbit of the dominant capitalist nations is becoming more complete, despite nominal political independence.

These characteristics of the international system and of Latin America's function within it impose definite limitations on the possibilities for Latin development. Nevertheless, it would be an oversimplification to say that the international system causes underdevelopment directly; it does so *indirectly*, by generating and reinforcing within Latin America an *infrastructure of dependency.* What is the infrastructure (internal structures) of dependency? The international system affects development in Latin America by means of certain institutions, social classes, and processes (industrial structure, socioeconomic elites, urbanization, and so on). These aspects of Latin society become part of the infrastructure of dependency when they function or occur in a manner that responds to the interests or needs of the dominant powers in the international system, rather than to national interests or needs. It is through the infrastructure of dependency that the international system becomes operative within Latin

America. And it is through the infrastructure of dependency that the legacy of Latin America's integration into the international system is transmitted and perpetuated within Latin America, thereby limiting the possibilities for development.

Let us take two examples of the infrastructure of dependency. *(a)* Industrialization in the broadest sense implies far more than the construction of new factories and the production or processing of commodities. In most Latin nations the industrial sectors lie at the heart of the entire national economy. In addition the quality of industrialization is integrally related to, among other things, political decision-making, social structure, and urbanization. Industrialization is not by nature dependent; it becomes so when the industrial structure is integrated into and complementary to the needs of foreign economies. Some specific characteristics of dependent industrialization are: 1) increasing foreign control over the most dynamic and strategic industrial sectors through direct ownership and control over production, control of marketing and distribution, or control of patents and licenses (in many sectors foreign corporations have been buying out formerly national industries); 2) increasing competitive advantages for (often monopolistic) foreign enterprises over local firms, particularly in industries of scale; 3) as a result of foreign ownership, outflow of capital (profits) abroad; 4) despite some production for the internal market, adaptation of the entire economic structure to the needs of the buyers of Latin exports in the dominant nations; 5) introduction of advanced, capital intensive foreign technology, without regard to size or composition of the local labor market, and consequent aggravation of unemployment (which in turn results in restriction of the domestic market): in several countries (e.g. Chile, Colombia, Peru) employment in manufacturing industry actually declined as a percentage of total employment between 1925 and 1960; 6) also as a result of foreign control over technology, its restriction to those sectors in which foreign capital has a direct interest; 7) lack of a domestic capital goods industry in most countries, and consequently an increased rather than reduced dependence on imports and rigidities in the composition of imports. In short, dependent industrialization has aggravated rather than resolved such basic problems as balance of payments deficits, unemployment, income disparities, and an insufficient domestic market.

(*b*) Intersecting the process of dependent industrialization is another, equally fundamental, dimension of dependency: the creation and/or reinforcement of clientele social classes. Clientele classes are those which have a vested interest in the existing international system. These classes carry out certain functions on behalf of foreign interests; in return they enjoy a privileged and increasingly dominant and hegemonic position within their own societies, based largely on economic, political, or military support from abroad. In this sense the clientele classes come to play in Latin America today the role historically performed by the *comprador* bourgeoisie (export-import mercantile elites, whose strength, interests, and very existence were derived from their function in the world market). Like their behavior, the ideologies of these classes reflect their dual position as junior partners of metropolitan interests, yet dominant elites within their own societies. The clearest example of clientele classes today are those elements of the Latin industrial bourgeoisie which "expand and thrive within the orbit of foreign capital... [whether as] wholesalers...or as suppliers of local materials to foreign enterprises or as caterers to various other needs of foreign firms and their staffs. . . ." [9]

The state bureaucracy and other sectors of the middle class—for example, the technical, managerial, professional or intellectual elites—become clientele when their interests, actions, and privileged positions are derived from their ties to foreign interests. Particularly with the expanded role of the state in the national economy, the state bureaucracy (including the military in many countries) has been viewed by some as the key to national autonomy. Nevertheless, when the primary function of the state is to stimulate private enterprise, when the private sector is largely controlled by foreign interests, and when the state bureaucracy itself relies on material and ideological support from abroad (as in Brazil today), the "autonomy" of the state bureaucracy must be illusory.

The alliances and conflicts of clientele classes with other domestic classes are shaped to a considerable extent by their previous and present alliances with foreign interests. Thus, for example, no less important than the alliances or conflicts of a São Paulo industrialist with the Brazilian proletariat of coffee-growing interests are his economic and ideological alignments with Wall Street bankers or foreign industrial interests; indeed the former are often shaped by the latter. The existence of these clientele classes in the dependent nation, whose interests correspond to those of the dominant classes in the dominant nations, is the kingpin and the *sine qua non* of dependency.

From the preceding discussion, it may be seen that dependency does not simply mean external domination, unilaterally superimposed from abroad and unilaterally producing "internal consequences." The internal dynamics of dependency are as much a function of *penetration* as of domination. It is in this way that dependency in Latin America differs from that of a formal colony: while the chains binding the latter to the mother country are overt and direct (administrative control), those of the former are subtler and are internal to the nation—and for that reason are much more difficult to break. In this sense, the infrastructure of dependency may be seen as the functional equivalent of a formal colonial apparatus—the principal difference being, perhaps, that since all classes and structures in Latin society have to a greater or lesser degree internalized and institutionalized the legacy of dependency, that legacy is much more difficult to overcome.

From this analysis follow certain political implications. Even if the U.S. and every other dominant capitalist nation were to suddenly disappear. Latin American dependency would not be immediately ruptured. And thus, by implication, Latin nations cannot break the chains of dependency merely by severing (or attempting to sever) their ties to the international system. A total rupturing of dependency as an internal condition of underdevelopment requires simultaneously—and indeed as a precondition for lasting autonomy or independence from the international system a profound transformation, an anti-capitalist, socialist transformation, of their own socio-economic order.

Thus, as experience has demonstrated, the various efforts to build "bourgeois nationalist" or "national capitalist" or, more recently, "state capitalist" solutions must fail in the end because the social classes on whom such solutions are based (the bourgeoisie) are themselves limited by their role in the international system. They may advocate a foreign policy "independent" of the U.S. (as in Brazil during the early 1960's); or they may successfully expropriate foreign holdings in some sectors, as has been done in Peru and as may be increasingly the case in other countries. But so long as they follow the capitalist road of development, they will continue to depend upon foreign investment, and thus will eventually have to make their compromises with and cater to foreign interests. And regardless of their intentions to implement far-reaching domestic reforms, they will be limited in practice by the legacy of dependency as institutionalized, within their own class interests and alliances, within the existing industrial base, and so on. To break out of dependency means, then, to break out of the capitalist order whose expression in Latin America is dependency.

The Predecessors of the Dependency Model

The dependency model was not the first attempt to relate Latin American underdevelopment to the region's function in the world market. Why, then, was this model in some sense "necessary?" In order to understand both the continuities and the differences of the dependency model with respect to its predecessors, we shall deal briefly with two previous "international system" analyses of Latin underdevelopment: the classical model of the U.N. Economic Commission for Latin America (CEPAL) and that of André Gunder Frank.

The starting-point of the CEPAL analysis[10] is Latin America's "peripheral" status *vis-à-vis* the advanced industrial "centers," as manifested primarily in the region's historical evolution as an exporter of primary commodities. Until the 1930's, when some Latin nations began to industrialize, their economies (and the economy of the region as a whole) typified *desarrollo hacia afuera* (externally-oriented development), geared to the needs of the then-industrializing nations which dominated the world market, rather than to the needs of their national markets. This historical condition finds its contemporary expression in the unfavorable position of the "peripheral" nations in world trade, stemming from the low income elasticity of demand for Latin American exports and the high income elasticity of demand for the industrial imports into those countries. As a means of overcoming Latin America's inherent disadvantage in the world market and excessive dependence upon one or a few primary exports, and as a means of stimulating internally rather than externally-oriented development, the CEPAL solution has been import-substituting industrialization. Import-substitution was expected to lessen dependence on foreign trade, transfer the "centers of decision-making" to Latin America, and expand production for the internal market. The rise of a national industrial bourgeoisie would weaken the traditional oligarchies (mainly landed and import-export interests). And, if coupled with an agrarian reform, import-substitution could lead to income redistribution and incorporation of the lower classes into the national economy. Since industrialization required far more capital than was currently available from domestic sources, foreign investment and foreign aid on terms favorable to Latin America were seen as necessary and desirable.

Although the CEPAL thesis (which has been grossly over-simplified here) was fruitful when first put forth, in that it linked Latin American underdevelopment to the international economic system, it is limited in several respects. First, its explanation of why Latin America has been at such a disadvantage in the world market relies too heavily on the nature of traditional Latin exports, and pays insufficient attention to the conscious policies and the specific needs of the developed nations. As has been seen above, it is no natural accident that the Latin countries have remained, until recently, exporters of primary products and importers of manufactured goods. Second, CEPAL's class analysis places the entire responsibility for retarded industrialization upon "traditional" or "feudal" oligarchies within Latin America. But the characterization of Latin society as having been "pre-capitalist" or "feudal" or dominated by feudal oligarchies is misleading, since Latin American society and modes of production since the sixteenth century have been mercantile, that is, geared toward exporting to an international capitalist market. In addition the CEPAL theorists assumed that an indigenous industrial bourgeoisie would be developmentalist, progressive, and nationalistic—a premise which clearly requires reexamination, in view of the actual behavior of that bourgeoisie.

Third, and perhaps most important, the CEPAL analysis has been partially invalidated by facts: specifically, the increasing dependence upon the international system of those countries which have been import-substituting for more than 30 years (e.g., Chile, Argentina, Brazil), and the stagnation plaguing those nations in recent years, which is a symptom of the exhaustion of import-substitution possibilities. To mention only three examples: since beginning to industrialize, Latin America has become more dependent than ever upon certain critical imports (heavy capital goods for industrial facilities); foreign ownership and control of industry have increased, thus contradicting the expectation that decision-making would be transferred to Latin America; and growth rates for the entire region and for some of the most industrialized nations were lower during the 1960's than during the 1945-60 period. In short, the CEPAL diagnosis took insufficient account of the built-in limitations of the import-substitution solution, arising from Latin America's historical dependency.

Faced with the by now obvious bankruptcy of import-substitution during the 1960's, CEPAL has avoided a thorough reappraisal of its analysis by discovering yet another panacea: regional economic integration. But, in the absence of a transformation of the national economic structures, this panacea (supported by U.S. and international aid agencies as well as CEPAL) promises to be no more viable than import-substitution: first, because, unless accompanied by strict regulations on foreign investment, economic integration will benefit foreign rather than local firms, the former having the capital and advanced technology to support regional enterprises which are beyond the capacity of local firms; second, because the increased scale and advanced technology of regional enterprises aggravate national development problems such as unemployment unless these negative effects are counteracted through deliberate policies; third, because regional integration of markets removes the pressure for drastic social reforms which would normally be created by industries of scale requiring large markets. Instead of enlarging the consumer base within each country by improving the economic status of the majority of the population, it is possible to combine middle and upper class consumer bases of several nations (as is currently happening in Central America). These factors do not imply the invalidity of the *idea* of integration, but rather the illusory nature of integration under present conditions as a substitute for basic structural changes.

Fourth, on the grounds that capital shortage has been one of the main obstacles to industrialization, CEPAL recommends increased foreign investment and aid. But this recommendation flies in the face of considerable evidence that foreign investment and aid have served as channels for the outflow of capital from Latin America rather than the inflow. Thus the CEPAL analysis calls for the intensification rather than the rupturing of ties to the dominant world powers—and (unintentionally) for the intensification of dependency.

In short, the CEPAL model provides at best a partial explanation of Latin underdevelopment; it confronts the symptoms rather than the basic causes. Perhaps this is more understandable in the light of its socio-economic roots. The CEPAL strategy is the expression of a Latin bourgeoisie trying to be national, but confined by the contradictions of the national capitalist "solution" to dependency, and forced, in the end, to call for additional foreign capital as a requisite for development. The inadequacy of the CEPAL model represents the failure of a particular social class, with particular interests, to offer a long-range alternative to Latin America.[11]

The second "international system" analysis, which goes considerably beyond the classical CEPAL model, is André Gunder Frank's Marxist model of relations between "metropolitan" and "satellite" nations. Frank traces the underdevelopment of Latin America and all the manifestations of that underdevelopment to the global expansion of capitalism and its penetration of the non-Western nations: "Underdevelopment [in Latin America] was and still is generated by the very same historical process which also generated economic development [in the U.S. and Europe]: the development of capitalism itself." [12] This process has resulted in a hierarchical chain of metropolis-satellite relations, in which each metropolis appropriates the economic surplus generated in its satellites, and "each of the satellites. . .serves as an instrument to suck capital or economic surplus out of its own satellites, and to channel part of this surplus to the world metropolis of which all are satellites." Within Latin America power has always rested with the subordinate metropolises, particularly the bourgeoisie, intimately tied to foreign interests, yet dominant at home.

Frank addresses the major weaknesses of the CEPAL model. He provides a causal explanation for Latin America's unfavorable position in the world market, specifying clearly the role of the dominant classes in the developed societies as well as of the local metropolises (dominant classes and regions) in the Latin nations. He refutes the myth that Latin America is currently emerging from a feudal social order, which must be destroyed by the triumph of the national bourgeoisie over the feudal oligarchy. He suggests why industrialization, import-substituting or otherwise, will not rupture the cycle of underdevelopment and dependency unless the existing structure of metropolis-satellite relations, both domestic and international, is overthrown. Thus he projects no hopes as to the "positive contribution" which might be made by foreign investment and aid; these are, in Frank's model, instruments for the extraction of capital from Latin America, rather than for its infusion into the region.

There remain, however, several problems in Frank's analysis. For our purposes it is necessary to mention only the most relevant one. It is just because his theory is so sweeping and "elegant" (in the sense of reducing complex phenomena to one basic set of principles and relationships) that it tends to be one-dimensional. Although the extraction of economic surplus may be the basis for all metropolis-satellite relations, both international and internal, it is not the only important dimension of those relations or of Latin dependency. The concept of dependency calls attention to many other aspects of Latin America's relation to the international system which cannot be reduced to the extraction of economic surplus. It is for this reason (among others) that the dependency theorists did not simply adopt Frank's model as it stood, but developed a somewhat different version of the same basic thesis: that Latin underdevelopment and dependency are an expression and a consequence of the global expansion of capitalism. Thus the dependency model has incorporated the important theoretical contributions of its predecessors, while attempting to avoid their problems and limitations.

The Limits of the Dependency Model and Its Integration With a Theory of Imperialism

Insofar as the international system lies at the heart of dependency, that system must be understood in its entirety—not only at its point of impact on Latin America, but also at its origins in the dominant nations. It is at this point that we reach the limits of the dependency model. While providing the basis for an analysis of the impact of capitalist expansion and the functioning of the international system in Latin America, by itself it is not very explicit about the reasons for the expansion of capitalism or the roots of the international system in the dominant nations (for our purposes, the U.S.). Furthermore, (although a certain conception is implicit within the writings of a number of the dependency theorists) it does not make explicit the relation between the state and private capital in the American political economy. Private capital remains the driving force in the international system; nevertheless, the state or public sector of the dominant nations plays an important role in relations with Latin America and even in the operations of private capital. It is in terms of the relation between the state and private capital in the dominant nations that we may understand why the international system perpetuates underdevelopment in Latin America—and ultimately why policies such as the Alliance for Progess cannot resolve the underdevelopment problem.

In attempting to fill the "gap" left by the dependency model, we may choose from among several alternative theories which presume to explain U.S. relations with Latin America. For our purposes these theories may be classified in three groups: international relations theories, non-Marxist theories of imperialism, and Marxist theories of imperialism. After suggesting the insufficiencies of the first two bodies of theory for the specific problem at hand, I shall indicate why the third provides an appropriate complement to the dependency model.

In most conventional international relations theories[13] the international context is depicted as an arena in which independent (though not necessarily equal) players bargain about competing or conflicting national interests, and in which war occasionally erupts when the bargaining process breaks down. In the case of U.S. relations with Latin America this model is inappropriate. It assumes that Latin American nations are separate units, led by autonomous decision-makers. It implicitly or explicitly postulates a clear dichotomy between internal and international structures, thus ignoring the reality of Latin American dependency. In addition, international relations theories tend to deal with "policy choices," the implication being that Latin governments, acting autonomously, could make alternative decisions. In fact, so long as they remain within the international capitalist system, the range of alternatives open to these governments is limited to changing certain minor aspects of their relation to the dominant nations (for example, gaining trade concessions, more economic or military aid). This restricted range of options is, in fact, a principal feature of Latin American dependency. Moreover, the autonomy of Latin American decision-makers is not to be taken for granted; while they may go through the motions of deciding policy, the substance of their decisions often reflects foreign interests more nearly than national interests.

From the standpoint of the U.S. as well, international relations theories tend to obscure the essentials of U.S.-Latin American relations. They generally treat those relations in terms of policies and policy choices, which presumably could have been or could be changed by more "enlightened" policy-makers. (Thus, for example, the Alliance for Progress and, thirty years earlier, the Good Neighbor Policy were seen as real departures from previous U.S. policies.) To be sure, American strategies and policies toward Latin America *do* change; but these changes represent variations of a less flexible underlying relationship between the U.S. and Latin America, rather than alterations in the basic relationship. The exclusive focus on U.S. policy also precludes attention to the institutions and social groups within the U.S. socio-economic system which shape these policies. Given the dichotomy between domestic and international politics, foreign policy is seen as part of the state (public) apparatus, is assumed to reflect the "public interest," and hence is seldom examined in terms of dominant private interests within the U.S. By obscuring the essential relationship between public policy and private interests, international relations theories must devise *ad hoc* explanations—or excuses—for the failure of policies such as the Alliance for Progress; their own assumptions preclude a real understanding of its roots, and thus of its consequences.

The basic assumption of most international relations theories, that there exists at least a minimal autonomy and freedom of action for all nations as actors in the international arena, is challenged by all theories of imperialism. The notion of an imperialistic relation between two or more nations implies (regardless of the particular theory of imperialism) a decisive inequality between those nations, an exploitative relationship (that is, one which serves the interests of the dominant nation at the expense of the subordinate nation), and the crippling of the latter's autonomy. The subordinate nation becomes, to one degree or another, the object of the needs and interests of certain groups in the dominant nation. Beyond the very general notion of imperialism as exploitative, however, Marxist theories differ sharply from most non-Marxist theories in analyzing the nature and causes of imperialism.

Given the great diversity of non-Marxist theories of imperialism, these remarks must be limited to those tendencies which have direct bearing on Latin American dependency.[14] First, there is a tendency to associate imperialism with expansionism (territorial expansion or protracted political domination) and/or the military aggression and intervention generally accompanying such expansion. By associating imperialism with a phenomenon that has characterized international political relations since the beginning of time, this conception is so broad as to deprive the term "imperialism" of any specific meaning. Nor does it contribute toward an explanation of dependency in Latin America: for dependency is not created by occasional military interventions or even gunboat diplomacy (which historically involved prolonged occupation and/or overt political control by the U.S. or other hegemonic powers). Rather, dependency has been a chronic condition of Latin development, maintained by the day-to-day and for the most part peaceful relations between Latin America and the dominant nations. The very identification of imperialism with physical or direct coercion projects an oversimplified image of overt domination, and almost automatically excludes from examination the subtler mechanisms through which dependency has been internalized and perpetuated in Latin America.

Second, non-Marxist theories tend to dissociate imperialism from the economic system (for our purposes, capitalism) in the dominant country. Thus they may resort to ideological-political-military explanations (such as the obsessive anti-Communism of American leaders, the doctrine of the "American responsibility" held by the "national security bureaucracy," independent of economic interests, and the needs of the defense establishment). Or they may argue that imperialism is "unprofitable" or "irrational" in a capitalist society, basically a "vestige" of "atavism" surviving from a pre-capitalist era. By conceptualizing imperialism too narrowly in terms of the actions of the state, or implicitly distinguishing *a priori* the interests of the state ("national security") from those of the dominant socio-economic classes, these theories do not consider imperialism to be systemically related to capitalism. But if imperialism is dissociated from capitalism, then it must be regarded as little more than a policy; in this respect the logical conclusions of many non-Marxist theories of imperialism almost converge with those of international relations theory. And if imperialism is dissociated from the global expansion of capitalism on the international level, the concept loses its potential as an explanation of dependency in Latin America.

In contrast to the above, a Marxist theory of imperialism[15] addresses itself directly to the economic basis (as well as the political-military aspects) of American policies and to the causes of dependency and underdevelopment in Latin America. For our purposes the adoption of a Marxist framework implies an integral relation between the actions of the U.S. government abroad and the structure of the American socio-economic system; it analyzes U.S. relations with Latin America as one aspect of American capitalism. In this sense American imperialism is not "irrational" or "accidental," but rather is a necessary extension of capitalism. It is not a fleeting policy, but *a stage in the development of capitalism as a world system.* Moreover, while recognizing the importance, necessity and inevitability of military or coercive actions abroad, a Marxist analysis understands these not as the essence of imperialism, but rather as the ultimate recourse, when the subtler mechanisms of imperialism are insufficient to contain a threat to the existing international system. This analysis is appropriate to a specific feature of contemporary U.S. relations with Latin America: namely, the attempt to avoid and to obviate the need for overt military intervention or direct political control wherever possible. To accept a theory of economic imperialism as a general hypothesis does not imply the necessary reduction of every *specific* political or military action by the state to pure economic motives; there are occasions (such as the Cuban missile crisis) when "security" considerations are decisive. This theory insists, however, that isolated military or political actions be understood in their over-all context, which is the preservation of capitalism as an economic order.

To introduce the model of contemporary imperialism, we begin with a skeletal description of the main units of contemporary capitalism and imperialism. This sketch is based on a particular Marxist model which takes *monopoly capital* as the defining feature of the U.S. political economy today:

> Today the typical unit in the capitalist world is not the small firm producing a negligible fraction of a homogeneous output for an anonymous market, but a large-scale enterprise producing a significant share of the output of an industry or even several industries, and able to control its prices, the volume of its production, and the type and amounts of its investments. The typical economic unit, in other words, has the attributes which were once thought to be possessed only by monopolies.[16]

The outstanding features of these economic units are, briefly: 1) increasing concentration of capital and resources under the control of fewer units, through the traditional forms: horizontal integration (increasing concentration of control over the production of a commodity or class of commodities) and vertical integration (increasing concentration of control over all phases of the production process, from the supply of raw materials to the marketing and distribution of the commodity to consumers); 2) a growing tendency toward conglomeration or diversification—that is, the control by a smaller number of corporations over production in various different and often unrelated sectors, thus augmenting the corporation's strength, and simultaneously minimizing the risks of production or marketing, in any one sector; 3), increasing "internationalization" or "multinationalization" of the operation (*not* the ownership or control) of capital. Multinational corporations are: plants that purchase inputs from one branch of a corporation located in the same or a different country and sell outputs to another branch of the same corporation located elsewhere. . .[They] are able to mobilize, transform, and dispose of capital on a regional or even world-wide scale—in effect constituting themselves as extra-territorial bodies[17]—in short, the (non-Communist) world has replaced the nation as the arena for their operations in both production and marketing; 4) the progressive shift from rivalry among the capitalist powers (such as prevailed, for example, during the heyday of colonialism, from 1870 to 1914) toward closer integration of the capitalist world, and inability of the secondary capitalist powers thus far to offer a serious challenge to American hegemony. (This is especially the case *vis-à-vis* Latin America.)

These characteristics of contemporary capitalism give rise to certain generally shared interests of the multinational corporations with respect to their overseas operations.[18] First, there arises a need to control all aspects of the production process, including the sources of supply and processing of raw materials, as well as the markets or outlets for commodities. Second, as the scale, monopolistic concentration, conglomeration, and internationalization of private capital increase, the dependence upon immediate profit returns from overseas investments is reduced. The emphasis shifts toward long-range planning, maximum security and avoidance of risk, and preservation of a favorable climate (ideological, political, and social as well as economic) for the *perpetuation* of corporate operations and for long-range profits—a concern frequently expressed by U.S. businessmen themselves.[19] To insure against sudden changes in the "rules of the game," controls over the political situation in Latin America—generally informal and indirect—must be tightened. And in the international environment there is need of an apparatus to guarantee not only the rationalization of international capital flows and monetary transactions, but also maximum political stability. "Hemispheric security" comes to mean protection not against interference by non-hemispheric powers or even "International Communism," but rather against the threat of truly independent regimes of any type in Latin America.

Third, corporate capitalists acquire an interest in a limited measure of "development" in Latin America. A moderate redistribution of income in Latin America provides a larger market for U.S. exports, as well as a safeguard against potential political instability. A relatively healthy Latin economy improves the climate for investment and trade. In this sense modern imperialism has an element of "welfare imperialism." Under these conditions, however, Latin development responds primarily to the needs of the foreign corporations, rather than national needs; it is, in short, fragmented, dependent, and ultimately illusory development. Fourth (and partly as a response to the failure to achieve real income redistribution or expansion of the domestic market in Latin countries), there is an interest in regional integration of markets. As *Fortune* (June, 1967) points out, the advantages of integration are that it not only eliminates tariff barriers, but it also provides "the chance to move to the broader, more competitive, and potentially more profitable task of supplying a market big enough to be economic on its own terms. . ."

Finally, the nature of private corporate operations overseas is such that they require protection by the (imperialist) state. Thus the multinational corporation has an increasing stake in consolidating its influence over "public" or (U.S.) government decisions, that is, over the apparatus of the state. This implies not only a strong influence over government foreign policies, but also the active participation of the state in international economic relationships which serve their interests. As the interests of the state come to overlap with those of the multinational corporations, "the state enlists more and more private capital in its crusade to maintain world capitalism intact," and there arises a "partnership" between public and private capital.[20] For our purposes, the significance of this partnership is that the state performs certain services which are essential to the overseas operations of the multinational corporations.

To take only a few examples of the ways in which state agencies service U.S. corporate interests abroad: the CIA, the State Department, and the Pentagon exercise numerous forms of political pressure, provide training for local military "civic action" and counter-insurgency programs, military assistance, and ultimate direct protection of U.S. investors—and in extreme cases of noncooperation by Latin governments, they have played decisive roles in overthrowing those governments. The in-country U.S. embassies provide crucial information to the corporations, represent their interests to the local governments, and influence local government policies. The U.S. Treasury Department exerts pressures for tariffs and quotas on imports from Latin America which are competitive with U.S. goods, and so on.

Foreign aid agencies perform a variety of services for the corporations:[21] they socialize the indirect operating costs of the multinational corporations (transferring those costs from the corporations to the American—ultimately the Latin American—taxpayers); they create advantages for U.S. firms over existing or potential local competitors; and they facilitate long-range planning and minimize the risks of foreign investment for the corporations, principally by stabilizing the local investment climate. In addition to these services for specific corporations, foreign aid fulfills more general functions for the preservation of U.S. capitalism (e.g., keeping Latin America in the capitalist orbit and gaining cooperation of Latin governments by offering loans as rewards or threatening to withhold aid; and providing markets for and in effect subsidizing U.S. exports through such mechanisms as "tied aid").

This analysis is not to imply that the state *never* acts independently of, or even in direct opposition to, private corporate interests in particular situations. Indeed there have been potable instances. Moreover, the state is sometimes faced with conflicting interests among the multinational corporations. In short, the state (and even the corporations themselves) are sometimes forced to sacrifice specific interests in order to serve the "higher interest"—the preservation of the capitalist system as a whole. In this sense the overriding task of the modern capitalist state is the stabilization and rationalization of world capitalism and imperialism as a socio-economic order.

We may now draw together the two parts of the analysis. By itself the dependency model provides a view "from below." It traces Latin American underdevelopment to that region's function in the world market and international system, which is governed by the interests of the dominant nations. The theory of imperialism provides a view "from above"—an explanation of the specific nature of the international system and its roots in the dominant nations. Through it the principal force which has conditioned Latin development—the global expansion of capitalism, which is the engine of the international system—is personified. For the theory of imperialism specifies *whose* particular needs or interests in the dominant nations—that is, those of the corporate and financial capitalists—are served by the international system. And on the basis of the ties between the state and private interests in the dominant nations, the theory offers an account of U.S. relations with Latin America, thus converging with the dependency model. Dependency and imperialism are, thus, two names for one and the same system.

* * *

Notes

1. The following figures are taken from: U.N. Economic Commission for Latin America (CEPAL), *El Segundo Decento de las Naciones Unidas para el Desarrollo: Aspectos Básicos de la Estrategia del Desarrollo de América Latina* (Lima, CEPAL, April 14-23, 1969); Keith Griffin, *Underdevelopment in Spanish America* (London, Allen and Unwin, 1969); U.N. figures cited by André Gunder Frank, "The Underdevelopment Policy of the United Nations in Latin America," *NACLA Newsletter*, Dec. 1969; Simon Hanson, "The Alliance for Progress: The Sixth Year," *Inter-American Economic Affairs*, Winter, 1968; CEPAL, *Los Déficit Virtuales de Comercio y de Ahorro Interno y la Desocupación Estructural de América Latina* (Santiago, CEPAL).
2. "The Ideology of Developmentalism: American Political Science's Paradigm Surrogate for Latin American Studies," *Berkeley Journal of Sociology*, 1970.
3. The first approach is exemplified in the work of structural functionalists such as Gabriel Almond; the second argument, that foreign investment and aid stimulate development, is made in W. W. Rostow, *The Stages of Economic Growth* (London, Cambridge Univ. Press, 1962), pp. 142-3; Rostow and Max Millikan, *A Proposal* (N. Y., Harper & Bros., 1957), p. 56; Claude McMillan and Richard Gonzales, *International Enterprise in a Developing Economy* (Lansing, Mich., 1964); selections by Frederic Bonham and others in Gerald Meier, ed., *Leading Issues in Development Economics* (N.Y., Oxford Univ. Press, 1964), pp. 131 ff.
4. These figures are taken from: Frank, "Sociology of Development and Underdevelopment of Sociology," *Catalyst*, Summer, 1967, pp. 46-9; Frank, *Capitalism and Underdevelopment in Latin America* (N.Y., Monthly Review Press, 1967); Keith Griffin and Ricardo French-Davis, "El Capital Extranjero y el Desarrollo," *Revista Económica*, 1964, pp. 16-22; Luis Vitale, "Latin America: Feudal or Capitalist?", James Petras and Maurice Zeitlin, eds., *Latin America: Reform or Revolution*? (Greenwich, Conn., Fawcett, 1968); Maurice Halperin, "Growth and Crisis in the Latin American Economy," in Petras and Zeitlin, eds., *op. cit.*; Griffin, *op. cit.*, pp. 144-5; CEPAL, *Estudio Económico de América Latina* (annual) (Santiago, CEPAL); U.N. Dept. of Economic and Social Affairs, *Foreign Capital in Latin America* (N.Y., U.N., 1955). p. 15; Harry Magdoff, "Economic Aspects of U.S. Imperialism," *Monthly Review*, Nov., 1966; U.S. Department of Commerce data (*Balance of Pay-*

ments Statistical Supplement, Survey of Current Business); CEPAL, *El Segundo Decenio*, p. 9; Miguel Wionczek, "El Endeudamiento Público Externo y la Inversión Privada Extranjera en América Latina," presented to Consejo Latinoamericano de Ciencias Sociales, Lima, Oct. 1968, p. 6 (mimeo).

5. The principal ones are: Theotonio Dos Santos, Fernando Cardoso, Enzo Faletto, Aníbal Quijano, Osvaldo Sunkel, José Luis Reyna, Edelberto Torres, Tomas Vasconi, Marcos Kaplan, Pablo González-Casanova, and Dale Johnson.

   The specific impetus for the dependency theorists was their increasing dissatisfaction with an earlier Latin American model, that of the U.N. Economic Commission for Latin America (CEPAL), and particularly its failure to explain the economic stagnation and aggravation of social problems in Latin America during the 1960's. (See below.) They also incorporated some of the principal theoretical contributions of André Gunder Frank's analysis of underdevelopment. Although my account of the dependency model is taken largely from the work of these Latin Americans, they should not be held responsible for those elements (e.g. the infrastructure of dependency) which I have added here.
6. Dos Santos, "Crisis de la Teoría del Desarollo y las Relaciones de Dependencia en América Latina," reprint from *Boletin de CESO*, Oct.-Nov. 1968, pp. 26, 29.
7. Griffin, *op. cit.*, pp. 62, 265.
8. According to CEPAL, *External Financing in Latin America* (N.Y., U.N., 1965), p. 215, the proportion of U.S. private investment directed toward the industrial sector in Latin America has risen from 35 per cent in 1951 to 60 per cent in 1962.
9. Paul Baran, *The Political Economy of Growth* (New York, Monthly Review Press, 1957), pp. 194-5.
10. For a good example of the classical CEPAL model, see Raúl Prebisch, *Toward a Dynamic Development Policy for Latin America* (N.Y., U.N., 1963). Good critiques of the classical CEPAL assumptions and analysis have been presented by A. G. Frank, "Latin America: A Decrepit Capitalist Castle with a Feudal-Seeming Facade," *Monthly Review*, Dec., 1963, and "The Underdevelopment Policy. . ."; Dos Santos, "Crisis de la Teoria. . ." and "Dependencia Económica. . ."; Vitale, *op. cit.*; Sergio Bagú, "La Economía de la Sociedad Colonial," *Pensamiento Crítico*, April, 1969.
11. The irony is that much of the empirical evidence which contradicts (and is used to refute) the classical CEPAL analysis and strategy comes from the very thorough annual and periodic studies made by CEPAL itself.
12. A. G. Frank, "The Development of Underdevelopment," *Monthly Review*, September, 1966; see also *Capitalism and Underdevelopment* and other works cited above.
13. Examples of international relations theory may be found in several selections in Stanley Hoffmann, ed., *Contemporary Theory in International Relations* (Englewood Cliffs, N.J. Prentice-Hall, 1960), e.g., Frederick Dunn, "The Scope of International Relations."
14. The main theorists discussed here are: Joseph Schumpeter, *Imperialism, Social Classes* (N.Y., Meridian, 1955); John Strachey, *The End of Empire* (N.Y., Praeger, 1964); Richard Barnet, *Intervention and Revolution* (N.Y., World Publishing Co., 1968); Juan Bosch, *Pentagonism, A Substitute for Imperialism* (N.Y., Grove Press, 1968). Franz Schurmann, "On Imperialism" (mimeo, 1967); Bernard Semmel, *Imperialism and Social Reform* (Garden City, N.Y., Anchor, 1968). A notable non-Marxist exception to the following discussion is J. A. Hobson, *Imperialism* (Ann Arbor, Univ. of Michigan Press, 1965).
15. The theory presented here is Marxist in the sense of remaining within the Marxist tradition even though Marx himself left little in the way of an explicit *theory* of imperialism. This does not necessarily imply blanket acceptance of the works of Lenin, Luxemburg, or any other individual Marxist. Even among Marxists there is considerable controversy as to the specific nature of modern imperialism. See: V. I. Lenin, *Imperialism, The Highest Stage of Capitalism* (Peking Foreign Languages Press, 1965); Rosa Luxemburg, *The Accumulation of Capital* (N. Y. Monthly Review Press, 1964); Victor Perlo, *The Empire of High Finance* (N.Y., International Publishers, 1956); Heather Dean, "Scarce Resources" (Ann Arbor, Radical Education Project); Michael Barrat-Brown, *After Imperialism* (London, Heinemann, 1963); Baran, *op. cit.* Moreover, many of the classical Marx-

ist writings on imperialism are specific to a particular historical era (e.g., the late nineteenth and early twentieth centuries).

16. Paul Baran and Paul Sweezy, *Monopoly Capital* (N.Y., Monthly Review Press, 1966), p. 6. Other works based on the monopoly capital model include: James O'Connor, "The Meaning of Economic Imperialism," "Notes on the Multinational Corporation" (elsewhere in this volume), and other writings; Harry Magdoff, *The Age of Imperialism"* (N.Y., Monthly Review Press, 1969) and "Economic Aspects of U.S. Imperialism"; David Horowitz, *Empire and Revolution* (N.Y., Random House, 1969).

    The emphasis given here to the monopolistic corporations is not meant to detract from the importance of the institutions of financial capital (particularly banks) not to underestimate the extent to which corporate and financial capital have been integrated. In a sense the entire dispute about financial *vs.* corporate capital is distorted. Lenin himself defined "financial capital" as "the concentration of production, the monopolies arising therefrom, the merging or coalescence of the banks with industry" (*Imperialism,* p. 52).
17. O'Connor. "The International Corporations and Economic Underdevelopment," *Science and Society,* Spring, 1970, pp. 45-6.
18. The following account of generally shared interests of the multinational corporations should not be taken to imply the absence of conflicting interests between individual corporations (or even within one conglomerate), indeed such conflicts exist and remain important. But given the essentially monopolistic (rather than competitive) nature of contemporary capitalism, particular interests are often superseded by the overriding common interests of corporate capital.
19. A recent article in *Fortune* (Juan Cameron, "Threatening Weather in South America," Oct., 1969) stated: "[U.S. investors in Latin America] find the rules that govern foreign investment constantly changing, almost always in what, from the American investor's point of view, is an undesirable direction. Day-to-day operations are becoming more and more difficult, and planning for the future uncertain and sometimes futile . . ." This concern is also frequently expressed by organizations representing U.S. business, such as the Council for Latin America.
20. O'Connor, "The Meaning of Economic Imperialism"; see also Raymond Mikesell, ed., *U.S. Government and Private Investment Abroad* (Eugene, Ore., Univ. of Oregon Press, 1962).
21. For more details on the functions of aid (whose importance to American corporations overseas has been repeatedly confirmed by U.S. corporate and aid officials), see: John Montgomery, *The Politics of Foreign Aid* (N.Y., Praeger, 1962), Mikesell, ed., *op. cit.;* Mikesell, *Public International Lending for Development* (N.Y., Random House, 1966); Hamza Alavi, "Imperialism, Old and New," *Socialist Register*, 1964; William Caspary, "American Economic Imperialism" (Ann Arbor, Radical Education Project); and even Congressional testimony and reports such as "New Directions for the 1970's: Toward a Strategy of Inter-American Development," Subcommittee on Inter-American Affairs of the House Committee on Foreign Affairs (Washington, Government Printing Office, 1969).

11.2

STRUCTURING THE CONCEPTS OF DEPENDENCY REVERSAL

Charles F. Doran

In response to Susanne Jonas's (see reading 11.1) position that underdevelopment, defined in terms of low economic growth and productivity, is solely a product of exploitation by the capitalist West, Charles Doran takes note of such internal barriers to development as exponential population growth, illiteracy, and low rates of savings and investment; these barriers constitute an entirely plausible alternative explanation for underdevelopment. An expert on international relations who teaches at Johns Hopkins University, Doran argues that three conflicting goals of development must be kept in balance in order for a nation-state to undergo development: economic growth, equality, and system autonomy. What his analysis leaves unresolved is the question of the relative impact of the external and internal barriers to development.

While the situation of dependencia received a good deal of scholarly attention in the 1970s, the idea of dependency reversal as an equally researchable and integral process of development has only recently attracted much discussion.[1]

Dependency Reversal and the Goals of Development

What are the chief concerns expressed by the dependencia outlook, concerns that lie at the heart of its developmental critique? In order to address the question of goals in dependencia terms, it is necessary to step outside this framework for a moment to consider the question of goals in the larger sense of modernization and economic development.[2] Among the generalized goals of the developing polity, three objectives are prominent: economic growth, greater income equality, and increased political independence. Different social systems will weigh each of these differently. Political ideology, cultural tradition, the peculiarities of the historical interval, and internal societal conditions all will affect the priorities given to these goals. But each Third World polity shares an affinity for each goal according to the polity's own internally generated hierarchy of preferences.

From the broader strategic perspective, however, comes the question: Can a single strategy of development and modernization achieve all three of these goals equally well? Or are the strategic paths to these objectives essentially independent of each other in terms of the values and resources necessary to achieve the objectives? A government may not be able to maximize progress on all three dimensions si-

Charles F. Doran, "Structuring the Concept of Dependency Reversal," in *North/South Relations: Studies of Dependency Reversal*, ed. Charles F. Doran, George Modelski, and Cal Clark (New York: Praeger, 1983), 1–27.

multaneously. Indeed if each goal is located on a separate strategic dimension in the statistical sense, the paths to the achievement of these goals may be essentially uncorrelated.

The liberal trade and investment model, for example, may tend to accentuate growth, but at the cost of reduced political autonomy and income equality.[3] Similarly, the Marxist path to development may achieve greater income equality but at considerable cost in terms of growth because of the inefficiencies involved in central planning, and in terms of political autonomy (if the Cuban case is relevant) because of aid, trade, and ideological dependence.[4] In fact the greater recent inclusion of market decision making into the economies of China, Yugoslavia, and Hungary is designed to accelerate growth even at the cost of some income inequality, foreign trade, and financial dependence.

Finally, a country may opt for substantially increased political autonomy through a nationalist/populist strategy, isolating itself from the rest of the international system in trade and investment terms. Such a strategy may maximize foreign policy flexibility and nationalist goals, but it is likely to undermine growth and interfere with the developmental processes necessary to sustain and increase income equality.

. . .Theoretically, of course, a single strategy could optimize a developmental path among these objectives such that progress is achieved equally on all of them. But the temptation for those who implement policy is not to follow the dictates of balanced growth and development but rather to slip off the optimal path toward one or another of the three dimensions, thus forfeiting progress along the other two.

The problem for the theory of dependency reversal is to avoid this dilemma by devising a strategy that copes with excessive income inequality and political dependence while not sacrificing economic growth. Rapid economic growth is necessary to reduce the internal effects of external trade and investment dependence and to facilitate greater equalization of income, both across individuals and sectors, without raising domestic political tensions to an unacceptable level. Thus the theory of dependency reversal is a prisoner of certain constraints imposed by the dialectic of development. The synthesis emerging out of the dependency reversal process is a reaction against unidimensional strategy that has proven unsatisfactory. . . . [U]nidimensional strategy alone is not likely to achieve balanced growth and development.

. . .Although a number of analysts have noted the difficulty of summarizing the dependencia notion,[5] I accept as a working definition of dependencia the following:

> The distinguishing feature of dependent (as contrasted with interdependent) development is that growth in the dependent nations occurs as a reflex of the expansion of the dominant economies. . . .[6]
>
> In the realization of policies of accumulation and development, though the bureaucratic framework may be in the hands of a technocratic-bureaucracy or a corporative military (together or separately), the nature of the dominant state relationship develops through the strengthening of the alliance between the local entrepreneurial sector, associated with the multinational foreign enterprises, and the state productive sector.[7]

The key elements of dependencia thought, however, are that relations with a core state or states create a *context* of distortions within the economy of the peripheral actor;[8] these distortions in turn are responsible for restrictions on growth and desirable development.[9] Direct private foreign investment, external assistance and loans, and trade, are thought to be the key means by which the peripheral economy is dominated and penetrated.[10] Principal distortions arising from such penetration involve takeovers of local firms; failure to use the correct level of capital intensiveness; absorption of the most talented local entrepreneurs; acceleration of the "brain drain"; dessication of local capital markets; marginalization of workers; reorientation of production toward the needs of the world market rather than of the local economy; unfavorable alteration of local purchasing preferences; and worsened income inequality between individuals and between industrial sectors. Finally, the psychology of the inability [to] achieve, and to become self-reliant, is perhaps the most damaging facet of dependency. Part of the criticism voiced by dependendistas is directed at the *impact* of perceived foreign control on the dependent economy of the peripheral actor, part seems directed at the *fact* of perceived foreign control itself.[11]

Dynamics of Dependency Reversal

Like dependencia, dependency reversal is a composite of variables and processes that *condition* economic development in the dependent polity. Neither dependencia nor dependency reversal are causal in the strict and narrow sense of the term. Each creates a framework that influences outcomes but is not solely determinative of those outcomes. Each is more than a catalyst of the development process, but less than a mono-causal explanation.

Similarly, dependencia and dependency reversal are elements of a dynamic, historical process of interaction; they are part of a dialectic in which a new synthesis is slowly emerging in the developing world at a higher level of material achievement and political self-expression. If, in this dynamic process, dependencia is the thesis, dependency reversal is the antithesis; at a subsequent stage of economic development a new synthesis will emerge between these two processes, both within the developing polity, and within the international system. In language less Hegelian or Marxist, a new equilibrium will emerge at a subsequent phase of modernization and development between dependencia and dependency reversal. It is this "higher stage" of development (changing equilibrium) that the theorist must explore in order to assess the significance of dependency reversal at present as an explanatory concept.

To use the language of modern social science, where is the dependent variable in all of this? The dependent variable, or "that which is to be explained," is of course *stagnation and lack of economic progress*.[12] What is preventing reasonable rates of growth and economic development in certain countries on the periphery of the global trading system? This is the thesis question of the dependencia literature. The variable that must be accounted for, or "explained," is stagnation and lack of sufficiently broad or rapid economic development. Much confusion has risen in attempts to operationalize dependencia because the literature has often treated the target variable, or that which is to be explained, in an obscure or implicit way.

Any encompassing expression of overall development involving the notion of dependency reversal must recognize that, in addition to the force of dependencia, *per se*, another set of indigenous impediments to development already exist within the peripheral actor. The way to visualize their existence is to think of the developing polity for a moment as totally isolated from the rest of the international system. Nothing impinges upon the polity from the outside. Trade, foreign investment, and aid all are considered exogenous in this exercise, not just in terms of origin, but in terms of process as well. The internal impediments to progress are thus evident: low per capita income, high rates of population growth, illiteracy, poor public health, low rates of saving and investment, and low labor productivity and employment. These in effect are the "givens" of the internal development situation in each peripheral country. They vary from country to counry in magnitude and in the way each variable relates to the others domestically. Yet together they comprise the set of internal impediments to economic development and growth that public policy must overcome.

It is in this context that the contribution of the dependencia literature becomes most clear. In contrast to the assumptions of liberal writers, the dependencia theorists hold that the impact of external capital flows on the developing polity is to constrain development, not accelerate it. Improperly incorporated into the development process, trade, aid, and foreign investment can become an additional constraint on industrialization and the improvement in welfare, not a panacea as most liberal theorists have supposed. Distortions in the economy and society that result from some types of external interaction and transaction may in fact undermine balanced, equitable, and rapid economic progress.

Dependencia thus appears to reinforce the effect of the prior existing internal impediments to development and growth. In a strict technical sense, dependencia does not cause underdevelopment. But it creates a social and political context in which distortions occur that serve to slow down and to further restrict growth and development. Summarized most briefly, the effect of dependencia on economic growth and development is two-fold: externally, oligopoly controls and international trade specialization limit the opportunity of the polity to expand and to diversify its production; internally, social inequality and class differences limit the opportunity of the citizens of the peripheral state to participate in the development process and to benefit fully from its rewards.

So far we have identified three broad clusters of variables: (1) stagnation and lack of proper economic development, (2) indigenous impediments to development, and (3) the elements of dependencia. The last cluster of variables relevant to this perspective regarding the overall development process are the elements of dependency reversal. The balance of this section on dynamics explores in theoretical terms the nature and significance of the dependency reversal idea.

Dependency reversal has two primary effects. First, it tends to counter stagnation and lack of economic development directly. As we explain more fully in the next section on mechanisms, dependency reversal operates upon economic stagnation and developmental distortion directly by changing the structure of power between the core state and other actors within the international system and by urbanization and altering per capita incomes internal to the peripheral state. Dependency reversal removes some of the obstacles to enhanced economic growth and development by providing some capital in a useful and productive form.

Second, dependency reversal operates indirectly through dependencia. By countering some of the effects of dependencia, dependency reversal also lightens the burden of economic stagnation and distortion. Externally by diversifying trade among partners, by strengthening the bargaining power of leading Third World actors such as Saudi Arabia, and by penetrating new industrial sectors such as textiles, shipping, and the semimanufactures, dependency reversal cuts at the roots of the dependencia syndrome. Internally, the political reaction to dependencia creates new political and class alliances hostile to exploitation, destroys the base of monopoly capital, and generates governmental reforms that eliminate some of the societal distortions for which dependencia has been responsible. Thus by countering dependencia, dependency reversal eventually has a positive impact on the elimination of economic stagnation and the lack of real growth. In contrast to the former effects that operate directly on the developmental process, this latter set of effects of dependency reversal are of a second order sort. Let us now turn to a more detailed discussion of each of these sets of effects of the dependency reversal process.

First Order Dependency Reversal Effects

In the history of the modern state system no country has remained at the apex of the system permanently.[13] While the French presence was dominant in the early eighteenth century, British predominance was greatest about at the time of the Napoleonic Wars and the Congress of Vienna (1815). Despite an effervescence of British colonial activity late in the nineteenth century, British trade and commercial primacy was already seriously in decline by mid-nineteenth century. By the mid-twentieth century, in the aftermath of World War II, only one actor, the United States, remained at the apex of power, although as decades passed this position was increasingly shared with the Soviet Union.

Dependency reversal is thus built into the structure of the international system. Those actors at the top of the systemic hierarchy lose their preeminence. An extreme case is that of the Spanish-Austrian Hapsburg complex, the most powerful actor on the early modern stage (1580–1640), but an entity that faced defeat on the ocean in 1588, and on land in 1639, but that was still represented in European councils as one of the five leading actors after 1867 in the form of Austria-Hungary. In reality decline preceded final dismemberment at the Treaty of Versailles. Some of the actors with sufficient latent capability, and adequate territorial and population size rise to challenge the leading states in the system. Figure 1 depicts this relationship for Great Britain and the United States, indexing the capability of each state against eight other actors in the system.[14] The striking feature of these findings is the fact that as Britain lost power, the United States gained power, almost in inverse fashion. British trade and commercial dominance no more thwarted the rise of U.S. power, however, than U.S. dominance at mid-twentieth century has prevented the emergence of the present major contenders for regional and global influence. The forces of dependencia and dependency reversal were undoubtedly at work in all of these cases, but the outcome did not invariably favor dependencia.

What underlies the type of dependency reversal that operates directly on the inertia characterizing premodern economic development? At least three considerations seem to undermine the perpetuation of systemic dominance.[15] First, growth in power (of which GNP is a critical component) is limited *in a relative sense* by the size of a nation's territory and initial capital and natural resource endowments. Only a few trade-oriented states such as Hong Kong and Japan appear to challenge this finding. Second, in the early growth phase institutional factors may encourage saving, investment, and efficiency, but these same factors may later inhibit growth if rigidity and overcentralization occur. Third, diffusion of power away from the core may take place in later phases of development, for example, through external migration. Thus dependency reversal may occur because of considerations internal to the core state as well as external to it.

* * *

Dependency reversal also operates directly on the inertia of development through a second mechanism, the terms of trade. An intellectual precursor of dependencia theory, and still an element of dependencia, is the deteriorating terms of trade idea popularized by Raol Prebisch and supported empirically by the study, *Industrialization and Foreign Trade* (Geneva, 1945), and the United Nations publication *Relative Prices of Exports and Imports of Under-developed Countries* (New York, 1949). According to these studies a long-term decline in the prices of primary goods in relation to industrial goods accounts for much of the external dependence of the Third World on the advanced industrial countries. To the extent that this argument is empirically valid, the deteriorating terms of trade notion epitomizes the type of external dependence that imprisons the peripheral actor in a net of trade relations from which the core actors are able to extract disproportionate benefits. Conversely, because of the importance of world trade—both on the import and export sides—to many Third World countries, an improving terms of trade situation would constitute a form of dependency reversal.

Figure 1 Relative Power of Great Britain and the United States (1815–1975)

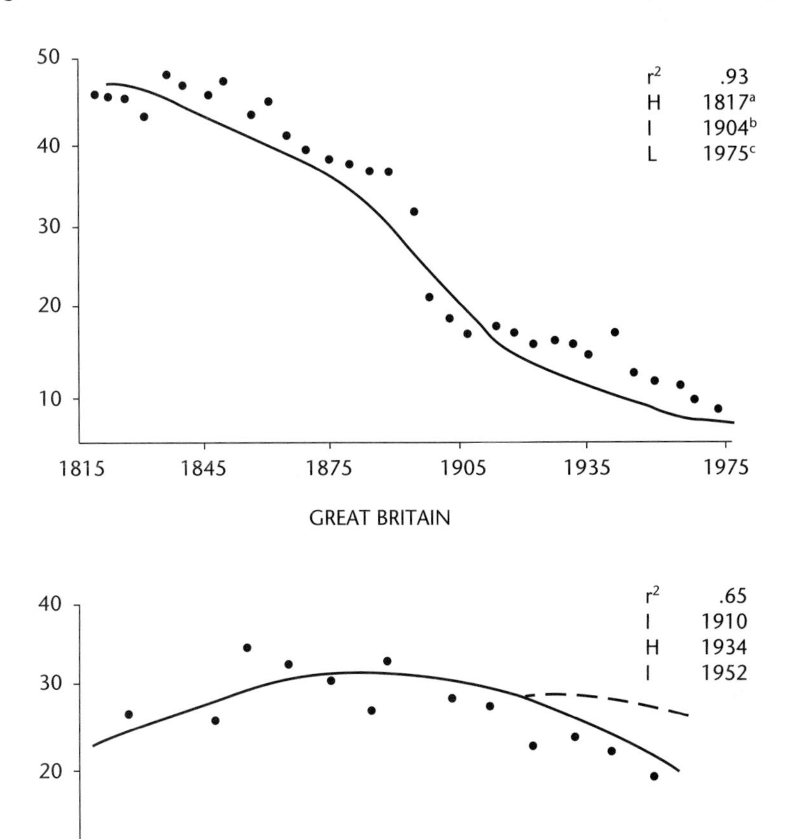

New data using updated GNP figures.
[a]H—Year of high point
[b]I—Year of inflection point
[c]L—Year of low point

Source: Charles F. Doran and Wes Parsons, "War and the Cycle of Relative Power," *American Political Science Review* 74 (1980): 947–65, for operationalization and data source.

Current empirical evidence now suggests that no secular deterioration in the terms of trade of raw materials versus manufactures seems to have occurred in the twentieth century.[16] Indeed the opposite is the case. An improvement in the relative prices of raw materials exports from the developing countries took place, but this improvement was masked by a massive fall in transport costs. Between 1954 and 1962, a serious decline did occur, serious enough to wipe out virtually all of the benefits of real total aid flows into the poorer regions.[17] This decline in the terms of trade was the result of several factors: (1) an increase in the supply of primary products; (2) more effective assimilation of the gains from increased productivity by advanced industrial countries; and (3) the effect of new synthetics and raw material substitutes. But the decline was altered after 1962 in a number of agricultural and commodity areas; the price revolution in petroleum after 1973 was only the most spectacular of these advances.

* * *

Internal to the peripheral actors, the processes of dependency reversal also operate on economic stagnation. The two principal sources of such reversal involve the incremental long-term impact of urbanization on population growth on the one hand, and the forces that underlie a substantial increase in agricultural productivity on the other.[18] Where these two complex sets of processes operate simultaneously, dependency reversal has a large potential for success.

If low and unequal per capita incomes are the principal deficit that marks underdevelopment, rapid population growth because of reduced child mortality, increased longevity, and a high, sustained birth rate is a principal source of economic stagnation. What is sometimes overlooked is that when the core states of the present system industrialized, the rate of population growth was a fraction of what it is today. The present high annual population growth rate between 2.6 and 2.8 percent is exceeded only by the rate of urbanization.[19]

While the many reported correlations between urbanization and development probably suffer from spuriousness, the correlation between urbanization and the eventual decline in population growth does not. Of course three-fifths of the Third World's labor force still works on the land. Despite the contingent problems of unemployment and highly visible human degradation (rural life styles tend to conceal these patterns) often associated with a too rapid migration into the cities, the overall process of urbanization does serve to reduce population growth by changing mores concerning idealized family size, knowledge concerning birth control, and eventually, the overall birth rate itself. Hence, in the long-term sense, urbanization is an important element of dependency reversal influencing the origins of economic stagnation directly.

The other major domestic source of directly inducing dependency reversal is increasing agricultural productivity.[20] Unfortunately, in many parts of the Third World agricultural productivity has declined rather than increased, although the physical availability of land in Latin America has helped offset this trend there. The basic problem is that the introduction of mechanization, new techniques of cultivation, and new, sometimes less disease resistant varieties of seed have not offset the population explosion; two times as many people produce approximately the same amount of food today as at the beginning of the twentieth century.

But where agricultural productivity increases, dependency reversal can occur. Savings rates in the Third World are not the problem. The presence of low incomes and failure to invest in industrial and commercial ventures are problems. But with high agricultural incomes and a more effective mechanism for private or public investment, the already acceptable savings rate will create funds necessary to industrialize for purposes of import substitution or for export. Increasing agricultural productivity is perhaps the key to industrialization efforts. But the direct effect of dependency reversal on develomental inertia must be combined with indirect (second order) effects as well so as to obtain a fuller impact, especially where dependency itself is pronounced.

Second Order Dependency Reversal Effects

These effects are second order because they cause a reduction in stagnation and the lack of economic development only secondarily *through the elements of dependencia.* The route to the impact on developmental inertia is a secondary route; but the impact on dependencia is necessarily prior and therefore primary. In other words, dependency reversal operates on developmental inertia here by negating dependencia. Again these effects may be either internal to the peripheral actor or external to it, that is between it and the core state in the international systemic sense.

At least five commonly understood types of external dependency reversal are likely to be present in most developmental settings. They are in constant tension with the forces of dependencia, establishing a kind of equilibrium that over time may be unstable in either direction, or relatively stable. The processes of dependency reversal here include (1) trade internalization, (2) trade diversification, (3) commodity diversification, (4) regulation of the transnational firm, and (5) expropriation. The former three processes involve trade policy, the latter two involve matters for commercial policy to decide.

In examining the trade variables the following operationalization on dependency seems appropriate:[21]

External Trade Dependence =
Volume of Foreign Trade/GDP (Concentration of Export Commodities +
Concentration among Trading Partners)

The functional relationship between the two concentration variables must be additive for if the value of either were zero the other could still exist as a positive coefficient. Theoretically, concentration among trading partners, for example, could be so low (equal distribution) that for all practical purposes it was nonexistent. But at the same time, concentration among export commodities might be very high if a country was virtually a one-commodity mineral or agricultural exporter. Unlike the functional relationship between the concentration variables, however, the relationship between these variables and the volume of foreign trade variable is multiplicative. If the level of foreign trade relative to gross domestic product (GDP) were to go to zero the concentration indexes would also disappear. The relationship between volume of trade and the concentration indexes cannot be additive.

* * *

But how likely are these reversal effects to occur in practical terms? Over long time periods the relative volume of trade can change decidely. In general the larger the size of the internal economy, the less important foreign trade. Thus poor countries with a potentially large domestic market are far more likely to achieve dependency reversal than countries with a small market. But as countries industrialize, foreign trade becomes less important initially as the movement to achieve import substitution occurs. Once this initial effort to replace imports by local production has spent itself, the international market once again becomes critical for the developmental effort. Thus if dependency reversal in an overall sense is to be successful in later stages of development, an increasing volume of trade to GDP ratio must be offset by corresponding declines in trading partner concentration and export concentration.

Of all these variables, commodity concentration may be the most important and the most difficult to change in the short term. High commodity concentration epitomizes the dependencia dilemma. Natural factors such as the physical availability of a mineral or the presence of certain soil and climatic combinations facilitate certain types of production, usually for export. But other aspects of "comparative advantage" are purely contrived by historical circumstance and may keep a producer entrapped for decades in an area of output where expansion is minimal and spillovers into other areas of employment and technological development are nonexistent. Such costs—infrastructure, manpower training, traditional market ties, and unimaginative management—all may contribute to high commodity concentration of an undesirable sort. Dependency reversal is nonetheless often possible.

Empirical findings, for example, support the criticism that plantation agriculture seldom contributes much to improved agricultural productivity.[22] Similarly in some Less Developed Countries (LDCs) plantation agriculture is principally responsible for a high foreign trade to GDP ratio on the export side because of the need to sell a commodity like sugar or coffee abroad and on the import side because other food products and manufactured goods must be imported. Thus a shift toward import substitution in the primary foods sector may possess the benefit of reducing external trade dependence on all three principal indexes and of increasing agricultural productivity as well.

One of the considerations that is responsible for preventing a greater amount of dependency reversal on the commodity concentration index and often on the trading partner concentration index as well, is the system of concatenated tariff structures among the advanced industrial countries that protects finished goods most and raw materials least.[23] Such structures prevent dependency reversal from proceeding more rapidly by discouraging the diversification of trading partners and the migration of finished processing and semiprocessing industries to countries exporting raw materials. Transforming the tariff structures of the advanced industrial countries could be one of the most import instruments favoring dependency reversal on the trade account.

Dependency reversal involving trading partner concentration is of dubious value if diversification is purchased at the cost of lower rates of economic development.[24] Diversification among a larger number of trading partners, for example, is scarcely helpful if these new trading partners buy more raw materials and fewer finished goods than the core state did initially. But with this caveat trade diversification may be an important component of dependency reversal. For small states this form of dependency reversal may be most readily obtainable within a regional common market. Over the few years that the Central American Common Market was in existence, for example, its impact on helping to reduce trading partner concentration was quite remarkable.[25]

* * *

While the Cuban case has been much analyzed, it is nonetheless quite instructive. The advent of the centrally planned economy and integration within the Communist trade system may have improved the welfare of the Cuban people although at some cost in terms of individual political freedom.[26]... But two consequences in the context of trade dependence are striking. The identity of dominant trading partners has been changed more sharply than the concentration. Commodity concentration has not been altered as much by the Cuban Revolution as many observers anticipated. Moreover the foreign trade to GDP ratio is still very much a prisoner of the small size of the Cuban economy, absence of economies of scale, and need to rely on the global market for goods that cannot be produced at reasonable cost in the home market. Thus the foreign trade to GDP ratio is much less a function of regime ideology or cultural preference and much more a function of market size.

Governments can sharply reduce trade dependence by forcibly isolating themselves much as the Soviet Union and China did for a time during the consolidation of their revolutions and as Albania and Burma appear to be doing today. But what is interesting about each of these exercises is the governments either shifted away from this autarkic focus once they became sufficiently self-confident politically, or they retained the autarkic focus but at the cost of much visible economic growth or development. The pull of the global trading market is neither capitalist, as Andre Gunder Frank recently argues,[27] nor socialist; one ideological sphere is not assimilating or dominating the other. The principal actors within each sphere are attempting to manage their own economic problems without becoming subjected to unacceptable trade dependence while at the same time benefiting as much as possible from world trading relationships. Autarky is scarcely a reasonable goal for dependency reversal involving trade matters; not even the largest countries have pursued it with much success. On the other hand, extreme trade dependence of various sorts can create "enclaves" of comparatively unproductive trade out of which the peripheral polity must seek to break.[28] But the focus of such a strategy may be as much internal to the polity as external.

The other set of dependency reversal mechanisms that operate directly on dependency, and are externally focused, involve commerce. Much of the dependencia literature concludes that economic development and the transnational corporation are incompatible.[29] If private foreign investment provides very few benefits to the peripheral polity yet foreign firms continue to invest, a convenient conclusion is that the firms are there by the grace of a conspiracy between the management of the firms and the ruling elites within the polities. The elites may benefit from the arrangement, according to this hypothesis, but the polity as a whole does not. Through manipulation and coercion, moreover, the elites remain in power in defiance of the public interest, obtaining the support of the foreign firm and core state government wherever possible. The principal assumptions here are as follows:

1. Private foreign investment provides virtually no growth or developmental benefits to the recipient polity.
2. The managers of the firm and the ruling elite collude.
3. The ruling elites extract benefits from the firm that are not passed along to the polity as a whole.
4. The ruling elites are able to remain in power over long periods through the use of force and manipulation in defiance of societal changes and the public interest.

Without attempting to probe intensively the validity or lack of validity of these assumptions, what can be said regarding dependency reversal in the commercial in area? If (1) is true, but (2) and (3) are not, the government of a host polity may employ dependency reversal to throw out foreign investment that is unproductive. Between 1960 and 1975 more than 500 such expropriations took place, ranging from limited individual takeovers to massive liquidation of the private sector such as occurred in Algeria, Cuba, and Ethiopia. The fact of expropriation does not prove the validity of (1), nor does it demonstrate the invalidity of (2) and (3) in all cases. But the reality of expropriation does suggest that whatever benefits national elites may receive from firms, and however much collusion may occur, the bond between firm and elite is far from impervious to alteration. Dependencia and dependency reversal are in uneasy equilibrium in many Third World countries and the foreign firm is held accountable. Expropriation is a very common form of dependency reversal on a global scale.

....The problem has always been, however, that the lack of institutionalization and the widespread presence of corruption in some host countries has undermined the capacity of host governments to regulate. Instead of regulating multinational firms, these governments have been driven to expropriate. Expropriation has eliminated the possibility of using the foreign firm in an optional sense for developmental purposes. But empirical data on expropriation behavior by industry suggests that, over time, expropriation tends to follow a logistic curve and that in the 1980s a number of industries find themselves at the top of this curve.[30] In other words the rate of expropriation has fallen off decisively. One of the explanations for this finding is that as host governments become more sophisticated about dealing with transnational firms, they need to rely upon expropriation less....

Elite dissociation, the second form of dependency reversal operating directly on dependencia, is a process evident in even the most monolithic of societies. It is the tendency of branches of a governing elite to adopt nationalist outlooks that place the government in opposition to foreign linkages, whether commercial or primarily security oriented.[31] This is the kind of dissociation that made possible the nationalization of the oil industry in Mexico during the 1930s, for example, and that continues to mark the Mexican outlook toward foreign investment today. It is also the kind of dissociation that enables political opposition groups to take control of the government, either through electoral or extra-electoral means, because a populist stance against affiliation with foreign firms, or governments is popular with powerful elite groups. It significantly qualifies the dependencia claim that collusion between domestic elites and foreign governments is a constant and universal norm. Rather, elite dissociation and collusion are in perpetual tension. Political careers are made as easily on the basis of elite dissociation, because of the popularity of the stance, as on the basis of collusion. Elite dissociation does not require that a full theory of pluralism be operative within the society, or that opposition parties in a formal sense exist. Elite dissociation is an internal political phenomenon that emerges out of reaction to real or perceived external domination. If the possibility of elite dissociation is not considered, the realities of expropriation, corporate regulation, and rejection of core state political initiatives become very difficult to explain in an orthodox dependencia framework. This framework must be modified to account for the actual diverse pressures occurring within the elites of most Third World countries.

In sum, the above has been an attempt to outline a number of the underlying variables by which dependency reversal influences the developmental process within and external to the peripheral actor. Dependency reversal affects the inertia and stagnation of economic development directly. Dependency reversal also affects dependencia and through this interaction eventually influences the developmental process. Thus dependency reversal takes two paths simultaneously. In the language of social science, dependency reversal creates sets of "first order" and "second order" effects that must be kept analytically separate. The full significance of this distinction becomes clearer in the graphical representation of the model.

Mechanisms of Dependency Reversal and Dependencia

A model composed of at least four "state" variables provides a parsimonious representation of the mechanisms of dependency reversal and dependencia. The variable to be explained is stagnation and lack of economic development. In shorthand terms, this is the *inertia* within the Third World development context.[32] Causally prior are the indigenous impediments to development such as illiteracy, poor public health, high rates of population growth and unemployment, and low and unequal per capita incomes. Again in shorthand terms, these are the *deficits* within the developmental setting. Both the deficits and the inertia vary substantially from state to state, region to region, and across time. Between the deficits and the inertia of development, however, are the two key, complex mechanisms, *dependencia* on the one hand and *dependency reversal* on the other.

For purposes of clarity, Figure 2 indicates only the most important causal linkages and directions of flow. The indigenous impediments to development contribute centrally to stagnation and lack of economic progress. The more serious these deficits, the more difficult is the task of getting the development process moving. Countries, for example, in the Sahael region of sub-Saharan Africa face obstacles to development that are simply of a far greater magnitude than those in Latin America where per capita incomes are so much higher and where worker productivity is two or more times greater. The deficits are themselves then causally related to lack of adequate developmental progress.

Indigenous impediments or deficits are also related to the elements of dependencia. Dependencia is far more a problem for the Dominican Republic than it is for Hong Kong. The impact of commodity and trading partner concentration on the economy of the peripheral actor is far more troublesome for a country with a lower per capita income and a very fragile economy than such concentration is for a country higher on the developmental ladder. Indeed once a country enters the circle of the advanced industrial actors, dependencia loses much of its meaning and is displaced by interdependence.[33] As the

Figure 2 Simple Recursive Model Involving Dependency Reversal (Emphasis of Primary Linkages)

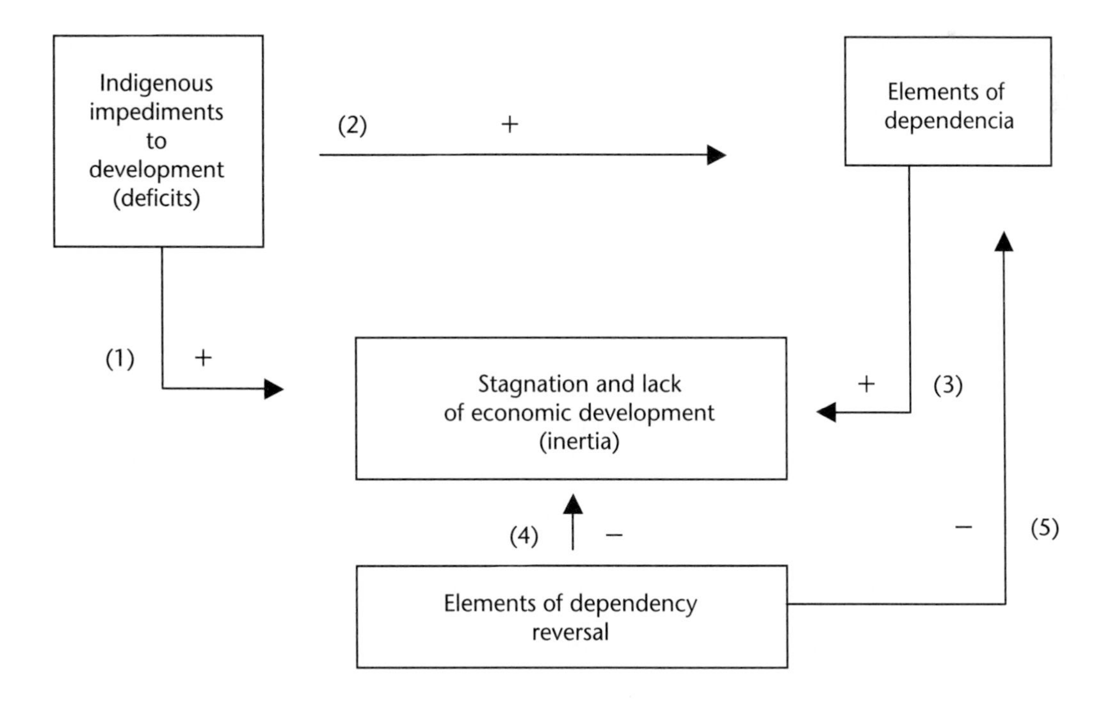

Source: Compiled by the author.

declining U.S. share of world trade and total world output indicates, interdependence and greater economic equality is quite evident among the advanced industrial countries themselves. But among the poorest of countries with the narrowest industrial bases and the largest foreign trade to GDP ratios, the deficits of development reinforce the elements of dependencia directly.

Path (3) in Figure 2 is the central linkage in the whole dependencia thesis. Operationalized elsewhere, the elements of dependencia are not repeated here.[34] Nor is the direction of causal flow much contested. At issue, however, perhaps is whether path (3) or path (1) is the more dominant. Is dependencia more of an explanator of developmental inertia than the deficits of the developmental process? This is a theoretical question about which debate continues without convincing empirical evidence on either side. But what is clear is that one cannot speak of the effects of dependencia on growth and development without taking the deficits of the developmental process into account. Even in an historical sense the indigenous impediments to development provide a base or a starting point for analysis. Dependencia involving "the new dependency" was temporally subsequent to the reality of poverty and illiteracy. This does not mean that dependencia by logical or historical imperative is less a causal variable than the deficits themselves; such a question regarding importance is for empirical analysis to answer. But what the framework stresses is that even if dependencia had not come into existence, economic development would not be smooth or automatic.

Paths (4) and (5) comprise the bulk of the theoretical discussion in this chapter examining the impact of dependency reversal on inertia directly in the former instance and indirectly through dependencia in the latter case. The sign of the association in each case is negative, indicating that dependency reversal tends to offset the other flows. Additional theoretical issues concerning the impact of dependencia and dependency reversal on the overall growth and development process characterize linkages (4) and (5).

At least four paradigms of the growth and development situation, as revealed in Figure 3, accentuate the presence of these linkages. Figure 3 shows [the] relationship between differing degrees of dependencia and differing levels of development. Two of the paradigms (A and B) emphasize conclusions that are quite familiar. Paradigm A represents the situation in which strong effects of dependencia create the familiar condition of economic stagnation. Referring to Figure 2, Path (2) and especially Path (3) are dominant, corresponding to the situation in which large initial deficits stimulate dependencia; dependencia in turn has a very constraining effect on economic growth and development.

The other familiar situation is depicted by Paradigm B in which weak dependencia leads to an outcome in which some growth and development is possible. In terms of Figure 2, Paradigm B is illustrated by a condition in which Path (3) shows rather minimal association with developmental inertia and where the effects of the deficits are probably insignificant as well. In other words since dependencia is not much of a problem, growth and development within the polity are allowed to proceed in a normal fashion.

But Paradigms C and D result in other than the conventional theoretical outcomes. Nonetheless, they correspond to real world situtations that have been too little examined by the dependencia literature. In Paradigm C, a condition of weak dependencia results in a situation where relatively little growth and development can occur. How can such a situation arise? The answer of course is that no single factor explains all the variance in a dependent variable. Single factor explanations in history have seldom been satisfactory. So with dependencia, the influence of other variables can, under certain circumstances, confound the impact of a benign political environment. Referring to Figure 2 again, the absence of effects from Paths (2) and (3) is still not sufficient to get the development process moving if Path (1) is itself

Figure 3 Matrix of Dependencia/Development Outcomes

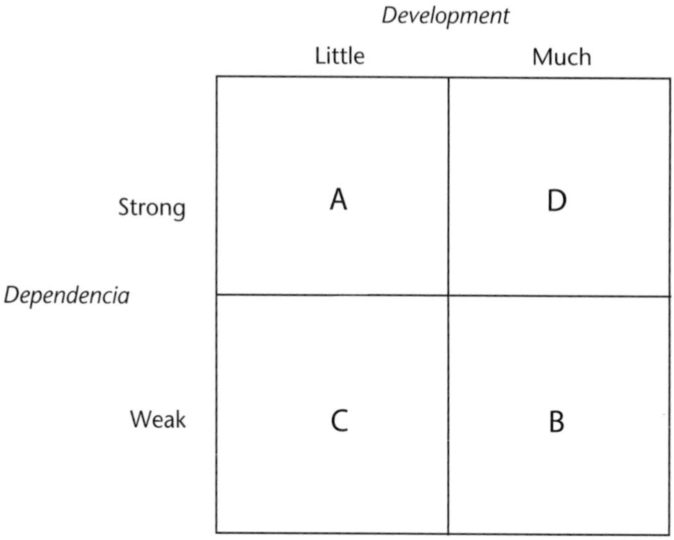

Dependencia	*Development*: Little	*Development*: Much
Strong	A	D
Weak	C	B

(A) Strong Dependencia Little Development
Paths 2 and 3 dominant

(B) Weak Dependencia Much Development
Paths 3 and 1 minimal

(C) Weak Dependencia Little Development
Path 1 dominant, Paths 2 and 3 minimal

(D) Strong Dependencia Much Development
Paths 4 and 5 dominant (Path 1 minimal)

Source: Compiled by the author.

too dominant. In other words, where the indigenous impediments to development are overwhelming, even the absence of dependencia may not be sufficient to promote significant industrialization. In circumstances where deficits are enormous, negligible negative external impacts may make very little difference to the eventual outcome. Paradigm C has a number of contemporary real world analogues. Elimination of dependencia will of itself not always result in positive economic prospects.

The other rather surprising outcome is depicted by Paradigm D, in which the strong effect of dependencia somehow is nonetheless insufficient to prevent economic growth and development from occurring. The explanation for this outcome, seldom explored in the dependencia literature, is that the effect of dependency reversal on dependencia [Path (5)] and the direct effect of dependency reversal on the stagnation and lack of economic development variable are together able to offset the strong presence of dependencia in the system. Thus in politics where economic size, regime commitment, or governmental regulatory capacity is sufficient to compensate for the presence of a high degree of dependencia, economic progress is possible even in an external systemic environment that is not particularly conducive to developmental change. A rather weak association between the indigenous impediments to development and developmental inertia [Path (1)] is helpful to this end as well.

Thus, essentially four developmental paradigms are possible in the model so far described. Critical to the articulation of this model, and to its societal equivalent, is the relationship of dependency reversal to dependencia. The actual number of polities corresponding to each of the development paradigms is a matter for empirical research to ascertain. What this theoretical analysis emphasizes is that a simple correlation between dependencia and development is probably inadequate to reveal the true variety of outcomes observable in the present Third World system.[35]

But the greater richness of analysis attempted in this model enables the analyst to account for situations in which growth and development seem to occur in spite of the presence of dependencia, and conversely, situations wherein the relative absence of dependencia little economic progress is in evidence. While a more complicated model might incorporate additional elements of economic and political reality, the four variable model articulated here appears fundamental. Where parsimony is a virtue in theory construction and model building, such a four variable conception of the development process encompasses perhaps some of the most critical variations and the most crucial functional relationships. Each variable is itself indexed by a variety of subelements that act together on the overall economic and political system. But, at a high level of abstraction, the four variable conception of the developmental context outlined here logically prefaces fuller elaboration.

In short, dependencia and dependency reversal in many Third World countries are two ongoing processes that form a changing equilibrium and create a far larger variety of outcomes than many dependendistas have so far recognized. Acknowledgment of the role that dependency reversal plays complicates analysis, but not needlessly so, and creates a more positive intellectual climate for discussion and policy implementation. Dependencia appeared to remove virtually all options from the hands of local decision makers within the peripheral polity; dependency reversal puts options back into the hands of these decisions makers. The developing polity is not a mere pawn of the international environment.

On the one hand, the simple notion that the market economy is at the root of the dependency problem and that therefore by getting rid of the market form through Marxist revolution all dependency problems will be resolved, is also questioned by this theoretical discussion. Just as models incorporating dependency reversal indicate that the reality of dependency is much more complicated than at first asserted, so the routes to the resolution of the dependency dilemma are more manifold, yet selective, than was first anticipated.

Notes

1. While dependency theorists hold out the possibility that opposition to dependency may occur both internal and external to the peripheral polity, thus undermining the foundations of dependency, they spend little time outlining the nature of this opposition or examining the implication for dependency theory. See for example, Fernando Henrique Cardoso and Enzo Faletto, *Dependency and Development in Latin America*, trans, by Marjory Mattingly Urquidi (Berkeley: University of California Press, 1979), p. xi; Andre Gunder Frank, *Crisis: In*

the World Economy (New York: Holmes and Meier, 1980), pp. 18-19; Osvaldo Sunkel, "Big Business and 'Dependencia': A Latin American View," *Foreign Affairs* (April 1972): 530.

Via a number of papers, at a series of conferences, a small group of scholars has discussed for some time the presence and theoretical implications of dependency reversal. My own first attempt to understand the dynamic in the context of OPEC was initially presented at a panel organized and chaired by Raymond Duvall at the 1977 meeting of the American Political Science Association in Washington, D.C., and was later published as "OPEC Structure and Cohesion: Exploring the Determinants of Cartel Policy," *Journal of Politics* 42 (1980): 82–101. See also "Modeling United States/Latin American Cooperation and Conflict: Dependencia Arguments," W. Ladd Hollist and Thomas H. Johnson; and "Conflict and Coercion in Dependent States," Steven Jackson, Bruce Russett, Duncan Snidal, and David Sylvan, each of which was presented on the same panel.

At a subsequent panel, which I organized and George Modelski chaired, at the 1979 Convention of the International Studies Association in Toronto, Ontario, additional papers were presented: Caleb Clark and Donna Bahry, "Dependency in the Soviet Bloc: A Reversal of the Economic-Political Nexus"; Charles F. Doran, "Canada and the Politics of Dependency Reversal"; Steven J. Kobrin, "Political-Economic Factors Underlying the Propensity to Expropriate Foreign Enterprise"; Steve Ropp, "The New Panama Canal Treaties: Politics of Dependency Reversal"; all of which are summarized in the presentation by Keith Orton and George Modelski, later published as "National Attributes and Systemic Processes," *Mondes En Developpement* 2 (1979): 379–95. Cal Clark and Ronald T. Libby presented two further papers, respectively, "The Process of Dependence and Dependency Reversal" and "A Typology of Dependent Economic Structures, Social Formation, and the State in the World Capitalist System" at the 1980 Convention (Los Angeles) of the International Studies Association.

2. Arthur M. Okun, *Equality and Efficiency: The Big Trade-Off* (Washington, D.C.: The Brookings Institution, 1975); William R. Cline, ed., *Policy Alternatives for a New International Economic Order* (New York: Praeger, 1979); G. M. Meier, *International Trade and Development* (New York: Harper and Row, 1963), especially chaps. 2 and 3.
3. J. E. Meade, *Efficiency, Equality and the Ownership of Property* (Cambridge: Harvard University Press, 1965); Lester Thurow, "Toward a Definition of Economic Justice," *Public Interest*, no. 31 (Spring 1973): 60–65.
4. Jodish N. Bhagwati, "Economics and World Order from the 1970s to 1990s: The Key Issues," in *Economics and World Order: From the 1970s to the 1990s*, ed. Jodish N. Bhagwati (New York: The Free Press, 1972), p. 20.
5. These concerns are highlighted in Robert A. Packenham, "The New Utopianism: Political Development Ideas in the Dependency Literature" (paper delivered at the American Political Science Association, New York, 1978); André Tiano, "Hindrances to Dependency Studies" (Unpublished Paper, University of Montpellier I, 1981), pp. 13–15.
6. Susanne Bodenheimer, "Dependency and Imperialism: The Roots of Latin American Underdevelopment," in *Readings in U.S. Imperialism*, eds. K. T. Fann and Donald C. Hodges (Boston: Porter Sargent, 1971), p. 158.
7. Cardoso and Faletto, op. cit., p. 210.
8. This point is made very effectively in Raymond D. Duvall, "Dependence and Dependencia Theory: Notes Toward Precision of Concept and Argument." *Dependence and Dependency in the Global System, International Organization* 32 (Winter 1978): 51–78.
9. Raymond Duvall, Steven Jackson, Bruce Russett, Duncan Snidal, and David Sylvan, "A Formal Model of 'Dependencia' Theory: Structure and Measurement" (revised version of paper presented at World Congress of the International Political Science Association, Edinburgh, August, 1976); see also Christopher Chase-Dunn, "The Effects of International Economic Dependence on Development and Inequality: A Cross-National Study," *American Sociological Review* 40 (December 1975); Lynn K. Mytelka, "Technological Dependence in the Andean Group," and Patrick J. McGowan and Dale L. Smith, "Economic Dependency in Black Africa: An Analysis of Competing Theories," *International Organization*, op. cit. (Winter 1978): pp. 101–40 and 179–236; Neil R. Richardson, *Foreign Policy and Economic Dependency* (Austin: University of Texas, 1978).

10. Cardoso and Faletto, op. cit., Preface to English Edition.
11. Thomas E. Weisskopf, "Capitalism, Underdevelopment and the Future of the Poor Countries," in Bhagwati, op. cit., pp. 43–78.
12. The word dependent here is not to be confused with dependencia usage; nor is the search for a dependent variable to deny the awareness that in a truly interactive social system of nonrecursive relationships a number of variables may appear both dependent and independent. Note here the helpful discussion of "dependent development" by James A. Caporaso in "Dependency Theory: Continuities and Discontinuities in Development Studies," *International Organization*, 34 (1980): 605–28. Cardoso and Faletto assert that "development" in the dependency sense does not mean the "achievement of a more egalitarian or more just society" because "these are not consequences expected from capitalist development." In other words, stagnation and lack of development, or lack of improved income equality, is what these authors expect from dependence and dependency.
13. Charles F. Doran, *The Politics of Assimilation: Hegemony and Its Aftermath* (Baltimore: Johns Hopkins University Press, 1971); Charles F. Doran and Wes Parsons, "War and the Cycle of Relative Power," *American Political Science Reviews* 74 (December 1980): 947–65.
14. This index of capability is a compound index using nonmonetary indicators. It attempts to avoid problems of noncomparability due to exchange rate deficiencies, inflation, and qualitative technological changes. The indicators involved are (1) iron and steel production, (2) population size, (3) size of armed forces, (4) energy use (coal production), and (5) urbanization. These indicators together constitute the two principal dimensions of capability, namely *size* (1), (2), and (3) and *development* (4) and (5). For a discussion of capability applied in a single actor context, see Peyton Lyon and Brian Tomlin, *Canada as an International Actor* (Toronto: Macmillan of Canada, 1979).
15. Doran and Parson, op cit., p. 949.
16. R. Prebisch, "Commercial Policy in Underdeveloped Countries," *American Economic Review* 49, Proceedings (May 1959); Paul Bairoch, *The Economic Development of the Third World Since 1900* (Berkeley: University of California Press, 1977), pp. 111–34.
17. Ibid., pp. 127–28.
18. W. Arthur Lewis, *The Evolution of the International Economic Order* (Princeton: Princeton University Press, 1978).
19. L. Henry and R. Pressot, "Perspectives de population dans les pays sous-développés," in *Tiers-Monds, sous-développement et développement* (Paris, 1956), pp. 189–213.
20. Paul Bairoch, "Agriculture and the Industrial Revolution," in *The Fontana Economic History of Europe* (London: Collins, 1969); Lewis, op. cit., pp. 36–37.
21. For a contrasting operationalization of relative trade dependence, commodity concentration, and trade partner concentration, see Duvall, Jackson, Russett, Snidal and Sylvan, op. cit., pp. 19–23. Trade vulnerability according to this operationalization is "simply a composite" of the three variables treated multiplicatively. For the reasons stated in the text, I believe the relationship must include both additive and multiplicative components.
22. Bairoch, *Economic Development*, p. 195.
23. I. F. Pearce, "The Optimal Tariff," *International Trade* (New York: W.W. Norton, 1970), pp. 179–87; H. G. Johnson, "The Cost of Protection and the Scientific Tariff," *Journal of Political Economy* (August 1960).
24. Canada's announcement of a "Third Option" in foreign policy diversifying trade away from the primary U.S. market has confronted some of these difficulties. The Canadian objective is both to maximize the rate of economic development and to advance the cause of political and trade independence through diversification. But the principal alternate trade partners, Japan and Germany, buy fewer Canadian manufactured goods and more raw materials relative to the total volume of trade than the United States. This means that trade diversification is purchased at the cost of less industrialization.
25. Jeffrey B. Nugent, *Economic Integration in Central America: Empirical Investigations* (Baltimore: Johns Hopkins University Press, 1974), p. 10.

26. Despite a felicitous riposte to the critics of dependencia, Richard Fagan fails to emphasize one cost of the Cuban Revolution, personal political freedom, a point perhaps too obvious to mention, but a point certainly not lost on the Cuban people themselves. See Richard R. Fagan, "A Funny Thing Happened on the Way to the Market: Thoughts on Extending Dependency Ideas," *International Organization* 32 (Winter 1978): 287–300.
27. Andre Gunder Frank, op. cit., pp. 315–19.
28. Note the qualifications observed in Vincent A. Mahler, "Britain, the European Community, and the Developing Commonwealth: Dependence, Interdependence, and the Political Economy of Sugar," *International Organization* 35 (Summer 1981): 467–92; Tony Smith, "The Underdevelopment of Development Literature: The Case of Dependency Theory," *World Politics* 31 (January 1979): 247–88; John W. Sloan, "Dependency Theory and Latin American Development: Another Key Fails to Open the Door," *Inter-American Economic Affairs* 31 (Winter 1977): 21–40.
29. For example, see Stephen Hymer, "The Multinational Corporation and the Law of Uneven Development," in *Economics and World Order*, ed. Jodish N. Bhagwati, pp. 113–35; for a counterview see J. S. Nye and Seymour J. Rubin, "The Longer Range Political Role of the Multinational Corporation," in *Global Companies: The Political Economy of World Business*, ed. George Ball (Englewood Cliffs: Prentice-Hall, 1975), pp. 122–56.
30. Charles F. Doran, "Expropriation Behavior Follows the Logic of the Logistic: An Empirical Test by Industry" (forthcoming article).
31. T. B. Bottomore, *Elites and Society* (London: Penguin Books, 1973); Georges Friedmann, *Problèmes d'Amérique Latine* (Paris: Gallimard, 1959).
32. Volker Bornschier argues in "Dependent Reproduction in the World System: A Study on the Incidence of 'Dependency Reversal,' " that in a phase of economic downturn, the impact of "The monopolistic system of MNCs" is to constrain economic growth. James Lee Ray notes the problem of lagging economic growth in Cuba and the dependence on Soviet aid, "The Cuban Path to Dependency Reversal" (Papers prepared for Conference on Dependency Reversal, Las Cruces, New Mexico, 1981.) This inertia in the growth process as well as the development process appears to be a crucial element of the "dependent variable" associated with dependencia.
33. To illustrate the disagreement among Marxist writers over whether dependence can become interdependence contrast the views of Arghiri Emmanuel, *Unequal Exchange* (New York: Monthly Review Press, 1972); and Samir Amin, *Imperialism and Unequal Development* (New York: Monthly Review Press, 1977). My own conclusion is that interdependence occurs horizontally but not vertically within the structure of the international system and that as one moves toward the upper power strata the degree of interdependence increases. But at the very top of the present bi-polar system interdependence falls off abruptly.
34. See Duvall, Jackson, et al., op. cit.
35. By disaggregating the empirical analysis one loses degrees of freedom statistically and runs the risk of alienating those who prefer "holistic" treatments; on the other hand, one also increases the probability of finding undiluted variance in both the dependency reversal and dependencia variables, thus making the strongest possible empirical case for this form of theoretical argumentation.

Chapter 12

WHICH APPROACH, MACRO OR MICRO, BEST EXPLAINS POLITICAL VIOLENCE?

In the aftermath of the French Revolution and in the post–World War II era, a mass mobilization of populations unleashed intense demands and expectations regarding a more equitable distribution of material well-being and social and political rights among these publics. The institutions and processes of still-modernizing states were fragile and emergent and frequently unable to accommodate these demands; for this reason, the modern world has been beset with frequent cases of violence and coerced regime change imposed on overwhelmed political systems unable to meet needs and expectations.[1]

Social revolutions involve fundamental change in the stratification system of the old society and mobilization of a substantial part of the mass public in effecting that change.[2] Furthermore, such revolutions involve fundamental transformation of the rules of the political game and fundamental change in the bases of legitimacy.[3] Of course, not all politically motivated violence is a social revolution, as the authors of the selections offered in this chapter make clear. Such politically motivated violence as mob violence may have a goal of protest or policy change that falls far short of seeking the replacement of a regime. An example of such violence might be the racially based riots and arson that plagued several inner cities in the United States during the late 1960s.

While these episodes of violence, coerced regime change, and social revolutions were unleashed in the pursuit of some vision of social justice, their actual results were frequently something entirely different. Whatever the shortcomings of the challenged regime, the functions of government, including the maintenance of some degree of order, must be performed. So it's not surprising to see that mass-revolutionary upheavals tend to be terminated by a reestablishment of strong authority, the so-called Thermidorean reactions, to use the analogy of the French Revolution of 1789 that resulted in the reign of Napoleon Bonaparte.[4] Similarly, the Soviet upheaval of 1917, with its ideal of populist communes, ended with the Stalinist dictatorship; Mexico's independence struggle ended in 1821 under the direction of authoritarian conservative Gen. Agustín de Iturbide; and the peasant-driven revolution in China ended in 1949 in the dictatorship of Mao Tse Tung. This pattern could be discerned in most social revolutions.

Coups d'état, another form of political violence, involve the coerced displacement of the ruling elite by an alternative elite without the involvement of the general populace. Unlike social revolutions, such coups do not seek the restructuring of the stratification system or the political order. In Nigeria, for example, existing heads of state were ousted by a small group of mid-level officers and the troops under their command (what is called a military junta) in 1985 and 1993, and such coups have been all-too-frequent occurrences in Latin America.

In reading 12.1 in this chapter, Ted Gurr utilizes a three-fold categorization of politically relevant violence, which he labels "civil strife": turmoil, conspiracy, and internal war that respectively refer to mob violence or riots, coups or terrorism, and social revolution. Terrorism, a subjectively defined form of politically motivated violence that has come into prominence in recent years, has become a normatively charged term. That is, proponents and advocates believe that if their cause is just, the actions they carry out are not terrorism. Yet, terrorism does have a widely accepted analytical conceptualization that defines it not by the rightness of the cause but by the defenselessness of the targets so as to create an aura of anxiety throughout the target society even among nonvictims. It refers to random violence against civilians and other noncombatants; the softness of the targets makes terrorism a useful tool of the weak against the strong. Clearly, what Gurr's piece shows is that political violence is not a simple phenomenon with a single cause. The theoretical question that scholars of comparative politics still debate is whether social revolution is a more intense, more widespread, longer-lasting version of mob violence or coups d'état, or if it is a distinct phenomenon with distinct causes that call for distinct remedies.

Scholars have attempted to delineate patterns in and causes of social revolutions, producing works such as Crane Brinton's classic opus, *The Anatomy of Revolution;* Harry Eckstein's piece, "On the Etiology of Internal Wars"; Theda Skocpol's several works on social revolutions (an example of which is offered in this chapter), and Mark Hagopian's *Regimes, Movements and Ideologies.* These works delineate patterns in social revolutions and the milieu in which they occur by focusing on the macro factors that affect the likelihood of revolution.

On the flip side is a literature that purports to explain violence by focusing on psychological causes. This approach is exemplified by the works of Ivo and Rosalind Feierabend, Betty Nesvold, Ted Gurr, and Douglas Hibbs.[5] These works apply an adaptation of the widely accepted theory in social psychology that the propensity to resort to violence is driven by the mental state of frustration. Early work by the Feierabends and Nesvold conceptualized frustration as a ratio between wants and satisfactions (that is, what one gets). Want formation is inferred from such measurable data as literacy rates and media exposure, whereas want satisfaction is inferred from such data as caloric intake per capita or number of physicians per ten thousand people. This inferred measure of frustration was found to significantly correlate over a range of nations with a weighted index of violence, including various incidents ranging from protest behavior to social revolution. Yet these findings have been criticized on the basis of the validity of the inferred measures and the ecological fallacy of inferring individual-level relationships from aggregate data.

Gurr takes this theoretic perspective a step further by conceptualizing his causal factor, "relative deprivation," as the ratio between what people think they deserve and what they expect to get. This idea implicitly brings the concept of justice into the equation. In *The Anatomy of Revolution,* Brinton argued that revolutions cannot occur without a sense of justice denied, a proposition that might well apply to other forms of political violence. His work, published in the early 1950s, drew its conclusions impressionistically, without reference to systematic data, as opposed to the rigorously quantitative work of Gurr. Gurr, however, moves away from the psychological explanation in the latter part of his article and finds more explanatory power in such structural factors as the existence of institutions like radical parties with the inclination and capacity to mobilize discontent in violent action. By tying the likelihood of revolution or political violence to the rapid mobilization of a population and the rapid increase in either demands or a sense of justice denied, this literature by Gurr and others suggests that modernization of an agrarian or less-industrialized society makes political violence, including revolution, more likely. This point was driven home in Mancur Olson's article in chapter 10 (reading 10.1).

Rather than focusing on the supposed causes of social revolutions, the article by Skocpol (reproduced here as reading 12.2) is concerned with the outcomes of social revolutions, specifically, their centralized and enhanced capacities for mobilization and war-making. However, in her important work on social revolutions, she is concerned with such macro-level factors as the stratification system and the role of class instead of focusing on individual psychological causes.[6]

Moving away from the Marxian analysis of revolution, with its focus on the preeminent role of the urban proletariat, Skocpol and others note the recurring role of the peasantry in social revolutions of both the far left and the far right. Peasants, for example, constituted a significant portion of the mass base for the radical phase of the French Revolution of 1789 and also a major part of the mass base for the counterrevolution of 1793 in the Vendee. Hagopian sees peasants as constituting one of what he calls "the crisis strata," [7] classes whose role in the socioeconomic order have been rendered useless by modernization and which therefore no longer perceive themselves as having a stake in the well-being of that order. These strata include peasants or owners of small family farms, clerks and the lower middle class, and intellectuals, groups alienated from the existing order and easily mobilized by social movements based on irrational antagonisms to the modern world. These strata were mobilized against the Jews by the Nazis in 1920s Germany as the source of German troubles. The grievance of these strata is really modernization itself; hence, the alienation of these groups cannot be ameliorated by negotiation.

A condition of modernization is secularization, or the breakdown of the salience of traditional religions. Some conservative thinkers, such as Joseph de Maistre, argued that the Enlightenment-era weakening of faith also weakened the sense of purpose and values that contributed to an acceptance of one's station in life. A premodern sense of faith, with its focus on such otherworldly values as salvation, can thus weaken the demand for worldly satisfactions. Clearly, religion was one of the bases of legitimacy in most of the traditional monarchies of Europe, whose rulers often claimed they ruled by "divine right." When the legitimacy of the existing political order and the distribution of material well-being are weakened, violent action against that order becomes an acceptable or even attractive option.

Another aspect of modernization rendered possible by the spread of education and literacy is the emergence of the intellectuals, individuals whose principal function in life is the formulation, manipulation, and dissemination of ideas. (These do not have to be good ideas, and intellectuals are not necessarily intelligent.) Intellectuals may articulate a legitimating of the existing regime and its rules, what Gaetano Mosca called "the political formula"; however, given that the task of intellectuals is the critical examination of ideas, they frequently become critics of the existing order, a phenomenon that Brinton called "the desertion of the intellectuals." In that capacity, they play a key rule in mobilizing whatever psychological discontent may exist into protest behaviors. Writers and philosophers such as Rousseau, Voltaire, and Condorcet clearly played this role in eighteenth-century France, leading to the Revolution of 1789.

It is important to recognize the distinction that Eckstein made between preconditions and precipitants of violence.[8] The former refers to the psychological, cultural, economic, or structural conditions that render the outbreak of violence or revolution more likely in a given setting, what is frequently identified as the causes of revolution and violence. The latter refers to the idiosyncratic phenomenon or event that actually ignites the conflagration. For example, the shooting of Austrian archduke Franz Ferdinand in Sarajevo is not identified as a cause of World War I, but did set it into motion. Of course, the inability to generalize about the idiosyncratic precipitants makes it impossible to predict any given event of violent or revolutionary behavior.

Samuel Huntington's essay on "The Clash of Civilizations" (reading 12.3) constitutes the initial statement of an idea that was expanded into a much-discussed book of the same name. Huntington argues that at the broad level of human organization, civilizations are defined by those values and ideas inherently incompatible with those of other civilizations. In particular, he argues that almost all of the clashes between civilizations in recent decades have been between an inherently expansionist Islamic civilization and Western Christendom, which, he argues, is insufficiently mobilized to defend itself against this assault. Students should ask themselves if Huntington is accurate in characterizing civilizations as monolithic entities largely free from serious internal conflict.

Notes

1. The idea of legitimate institutions as a bulwark against the violence and revolution that accompanies modernity is classically associated with Samuel Huntington in his *Political Order in Changing Societies* (New Haven: Yale University Press, 1968), chapter 1, and "Political Development and Political Decay," *World Politics* 17, no. 3 (April 1965): 386–430.
2. This is one of several possible conceptualizations of social revolution and is to a large extent drawn from Mark Hagopian, *The Phenomenon of Revolution* (New York: Dodd Mead, 1974). The idea of mobilization, the rapidly increased recruitment into the political process of previously apathetic or ignorant strata as central to the concept of revolution, is drawn from Huntington, *Political Order in Changing Societies,* chapter 1.
3. S. N. Eisenstadt, "Frameworks of the Great Revolutions: Culture, Social Structure, History and Human Agency," *International Social Science Journal* 133 (August 1992): 385–401.
4. The discerning of this pattern in major social revolutions may be found in Crane Brinton's classic, *The Anatomy of Revolution* (Englewood Cliffs, N.J.: Prentice Hall, 1952).
5. For example, Ivo Feierabend and Rosalind Feierabend, "Systemic Conditions of Political Aggression: An Application of Frustration Aggression Theory," *Journal of Conflict Resolution* 10, no. 3 (September 1966): 249–271. Douglas, Hibbs, *Mass Political Violence: A Cross National Analysis* (New York: John Wiley, 1973). Cf. James Davies, "Toward a Theory of Revolution," *American Sociological Review* 27 (February 1962).
6. Theda Skocpol, *States and Social Revolutions: A Comparative Analysis of France, Russia, and China* (Cambridge: Cambridge University Press, 1979), and Skopol, *Social Revolutions in the Modern World* (Cambridge: Cambridge University Press, 1994).
7. Mark Hagopian, *Regimes, Movements and Ideologies* (New York: Longman, 1984), 25–30.
8. Harry Eckstein, "On the Etiology of Internal War," in *Anger, Violence and Politics,* ed. Ivo Feierabend, Rosalind Feierabend, and Ted Gurr (Englewood Cliffs, N.J.: Prentice Hall, 1972), 13.

12.1

A CAUSAL MODEL OF CIVIL STRIFE: A COMPARATIVE ANALYSIS USING NEW INDICES

Ted R. Gurr

Ted Gurr, professor of politics and government at the University of Maryland and one of the leading authorities on the causes of political violence, continues the tradition of Rosalind and Ivo Feierabend and Betty Nesvold of using aggregate data to seek a psychological explanation of the political violence known as "civil strife." Rather than the Feierabend and Nesvold focus on the relationship between want formation and want satisfaction, however, Gurr instead adopts the psychological variable of "relative deprivation," which he defines as the relationship between the values to which people believe they are entitled and the values they expect to get. Given that this idea implicitly brings the concept of justice into the equation, Gurr adds the perception of justice denied. He creatively posits an impressive array of inferred measures of both his independent and dependent variables, but the question of validity can always be raised about the use of such indirect aggregate measures of an individual psychological concept. Students should ask whether indirect indicators, such as inflation or economic growth rates, actually predict the psychological concepts in his model. Gurr goes beyond the earlier work on political violence in testing for the impact of several intervening variables, including "structural facilitation" (institutions to mobilize discontent into action that turn out to have a greater impact on the level of civil strife than does the original psychological factor); hence, his ultimate causal model contains both micro and macro factors that make for a more complex and complete explanation.

I. Theoretical Considerations

The basic theoretical proposition is that a psychological variable, relative deprivation, is the basic precondition for civil strife of any kind, and that the more widespread and intense deprivation is among members of a population, the greater is the magnitude of strife in one or another form. Relative deprivation is defined as actors' perceptions of discrepancy between their value expectations (the goods and conditions of the life to which they believe they are justifiably entitled) and their value capabilities (the amounts of those goods and conditions that they think they are able to get and keep). The underlying causal mechanism is derived from psychological theory and evidence to the effect that one innate response to perceived deprivation is discontent or anger, and that anger is a motivating state for which

Ted R. Gurr, "A Causal Model of Civil Strife: A Comparative Analysis Using New Indices," *American Political Science Review* 62, no. 4 (December 1968): 1104–1124.

aggression is an inherently satisfying response. The term relative deprivation is used below to denote the perceived discrepancy; [the term] discontent [is used] to denote the motivating state which is the postulated response to it. The relationship between discontent and participation in strife is however mediated by a number of intervening social conditions. The initial theoretical model stipulated three such societal variables that are explored here, namely coercive potential, institutionalization, and social facilitation.[1] Results of a previous attempt to operationalize some of these variables and relate them to strife suggested that a fourth variable whose effects should be controlled is the legitimacy of the political regime in which strife occurs.[2]

The initial model, sketched in simplified form in Figure 1, specified no hierarchical or causal interactions among the mediating variables. Each was assumed to have an independent effect on the fundamental relationship between deprivation and strife. The theoretical arguments with reference to each variable are briefly stated here.

Great importance is attributed in psychological theory and equally, in theoretical and empirical studies of revolutionary behavior, to the inhibiting effects of punishment or coercion, actual or threatened, on the outcome of deprivation. The relationship is not necessarily a linear one whereby increasing levels of coercion are associated with declining levels of violence. Psychological evidence suggests that if an aggressive response to deprivation is thwarted by fear of punishment, this interference is itself a deprivation and increases the instigation to aggression. Comparative studies of civil strife suggest a curvi-

Figure 1

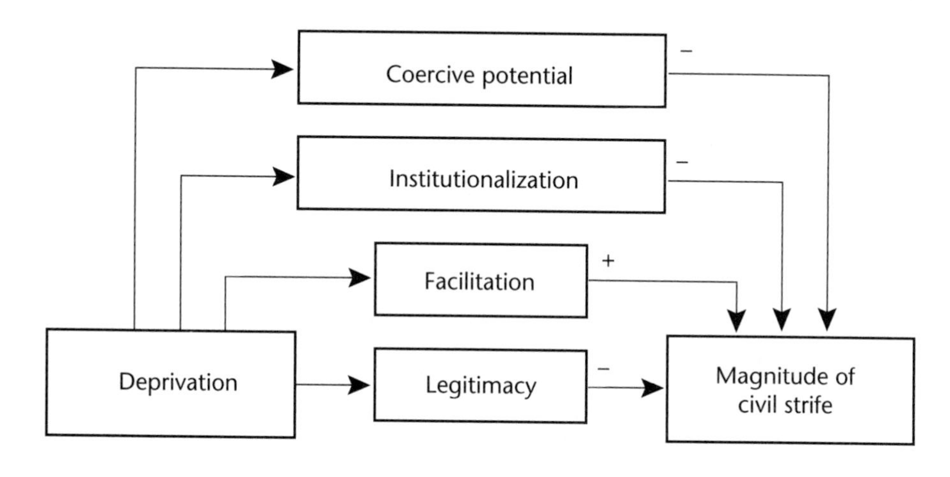

1. Coercive potential is labelled "retribution" in [Ted Gurr, "Psychological Factors in Civil Violence," *World Politics*, 20 (January 1968), 245–278]. The theoretical model also stipulates a set of variables that determines the intensity of deprivation. In the research reported in the present article, deprivation was operationalized directly rather than by reference to its component variables. The causal mechanism of the theory is the frustration-aggression relationship, which the author has attempted to modify and apply to collective strife in the light of recent empirical and theoretical work, e.g., Leonard Berkowitz, *Aggression: A Social Psychological Analysis* (New York: McGraw-Hill, 1962), and Aubrey J. Yates, *Frustration and Conflict* (New York: Wiley, 1962).
2. Ted Gurr with Charles Ruttenberg, *The Conditions of Civil Violence: First Tests of a Causal Model* (Princeton: Center of International Studies, Princeton University, Research Monograph No. 28, April 1967).

linear relationship whereby medium levels of coercion, indexed for example by military participation ratios or ratings of regime repressiveness, are associated with the highest magnitudes of strife. Only very high levels of coercion appear to limit effectively the extent of strife.[3] No systematic comparative study has examined whether the curvilinear relationship also holds for levels of coercion actually applied. Comparative studies have, however, emphasized the importance of the loyalty of coercive forces to the regime as a factor of equal or greater importance than the size of those forces in deterring strife, and this relationship is almost certainly linear, i.e., the greater the loyalty of coercive forces, the more effective they are, *ceteris paribus*, in deterring strife.[4] Two measures of coercion are used in this study: *coercive force size*, which is hypothesized to vary curvilinearly with levels of strife, and coercive force size weighted for the degree of loyalty of coercive forces to the regime, referred to throughout as *coercive potential*, which is expected to have a linear relationship with strife.

The second intervening variable is *institutionalization*, i.e., the extent to which societal structures beyond the primary level are broad in scope, command substantial resources and/or personnel, and are stable and persisting. Representative of the diverse arguments about the role of associational structures in minimizing strife are Huntington on the necessity of political institutionalization for political stability, Kornhauser on the need for structures intervening between mass and elite to minimize mass movements, and a variety of authors on the long-range tendencies of labor organizations to minimize violent economically-based conflict.[5] Two underlying psychological processes are likely to affect the intensity of and responses to discontent. One is that the existence of such structures increases men's value opportunities, i.e., their repertory of alternative ways to attain value satisfaction. A complementary function is that of displacement: labor unions, political parties, and a range of other associations may provide the discontented with routinized and typically non-violent means for expressing their discontents.[6] The proposed relationship is linear: the greater the institutionalization, the lower the magnitude of strife is likely to be.

Given the existence of widespread discontent in a population, a great number of social and environmental conditions may be present that facilitate the outbreak and persistence of strife. They may be categorized according to their inferred psychological effects, for example, according to whether they facilitate interaction among the discontented, or provide the discontented with a sense that violent responses to deprivation are justified, or give them the means to make such responses with maximum effect, or shelter them from retribution.[7] Two aspects of facilitation are treated separately in this study: *past levels of civil strife* and *social and structural facilitation* per se. The theoretical basis for the first of these variables is that populations in which strife is chronic tend to develop, by an interaction process, a set

---

3. See Douglas Bwy, "Governmental Instability in Latin America: The Preliminary Test of a Causal Model of the Impulse to 'Extra-Legal' Change," paper read at the American Psychological Association Annual Convention, New York, September 2–6, 1966; Jennifer Walton, "Correlates of Coerciveness and Permissiveness of National Political Systems: A Cross-National Study," (M.A. thesis, San Diego State College, 1965); Gurr and Ruttenberg, *The Conditions of Civil Violence . . .*, 81–84.
4. See, for example, Chalmers Johnson, *Revolution and the Social System* (Stanford: The Hoover Institute on War, Revolution and Peace, 1964), pp. 14-22.
5. Samuel Huntington, "Political Development and Political Decay," *World Politics*, 17 (April, 1965), 386-430; William Kornhauser, *The Politics of Mass Society* (New York: The Free Press, 1959); and Arthur M. Ross and George W. Hartman, *Changing Patterns of Industrial Conflict* (New York: Wiley, 1960) among others.
6. Gurr, "Psychological Factors. . ."
7. *Ibid.*

of beliefs justfying violent responses to deprivation; the French tradition of urban "revolution" is a striking example. Social and structural facilitation (referred to below as "facilitation") comprises aspects of organizational and environmental facilitation of strife, and the provision of external assistance. The operational hypotheses are that the greater the levels of past strife, and of social and structural facilitation, the greater is the magnitude of strife.

Two considerations suggested the incorporation of the fourth intervening variable examined in this study, *legitimacy of the regime*. A study of strife for the years 1961–1963 identified a number of nations that had less strife than might be expected on the basis of characteristics they shared with more strife-ridden polities.[8] One apparent common denominator among them was a high degree of popular support for the regime. This appeared consistent with Merelman's recently proposed learning-theory rationale for legitimacy, to the effect that people comply with directives of the regime in order to gain both the symbolic rewards of governmental action and the actual rewards with which government first associated itself, an argument that applies equally well to acceptance of deprivation and is compatible with experimental findings, in work on the frustration-aggression relationship, that people are less aggressive when they perceive frustration to be reasonable or justifiable.[9] The proposed relationship of legitimacy as an intervening variable is linear: the greater is regime legitimacy at a given level of deprivation, the less the magnitude of consequent strife.

II. Operational Measures

The universe of analysis chosen for evaluating the model comprised 114 distinct national and colonial political entities, each of which had a population of one million or more in 1962.[10] Data on civil strife were collected for 1961 through 1965. Cross-sectional multiple and partial correlation techniques were used. The use of product-moment correlation coefficients was justified on grounds of their necessity for multiple regression, although not all the indicators formally meet the order-of-measurement requirements of the techniques used.

Because of the very considerable difficulties of operationalizing a number of the variables, and the fact that most of the indicators constructed are new, this article gives relatively close attention to the data collection and scaling procedures.

With the exception of magnitude of strife and its components, the underlying variables examined in this study are unmeasured and must be inferred from indicators. In most instances they are in fact unmeasureable by aggregate data, since they relate in the instance of deprivation-induced discontent to a state of mind, and in the case of the intervening variables to conditions that have their effect only insofar as the discontented perceive them, and moreover perceive them as relevant to their response to deprivation. Following Blalock's recommendation that "when dealing with unmeasured variables it will usually be advisable to make use of more than one indicator for each underlying variable," each of the summary measures used in this study is derived by combining two to seven indicators of the underly-

8. Gurr and Ruttenberg. *The Conditions of Civil Violence . . .*, 100–106.
9. Richard M. Merelman, "Learning and Legitimacy," *The American Political Science Review*, 60 (September 1966); see also the work of Pastore and of Kregarman and Worchel, reviewed in Berkowitz, *op. cit., passim.*
10. Five polities meeting these criteria were excluded: Laos on grounds that at no time in the 1960's did it have even the forms of a unified regime, and Albania, Mongolia, North Korea, and North Vietnam for lack of sufficient reliable data. The universe nonetheless includes polities with more than 98 percent of the world's population.

ing variable. This procedure has not only the advantage Blalock attributes to it, namely of minimizing the effects of confounding variables, but also facilitates incorporation of various empirically-discrete conditions that have theoretically-identical effects.[11]

Magnitude of Civil Strife

The dependent variable of the theoretical model is magnitude of civil strife. Civil strife is defined as all collective, nongovernmental attacks on persons or property that occur within the boundaries of an autonomous or colonial political unit. By "nongovernmental" is meant acts by subjects and citizens who are not employees or agents of the regime, as well as acts of such employees or agents contrary to role norms, such as mutinies and coups d'état. Operationally the definition is qualified by the inclusion of symbolic demonstrative attacks on political persons or policies, e.g., political demonstrations, and by the exclusion of turmoil and internal war events in which less than 100 persons take part.

A three-fold typology of civil strife is also employed, based on an empirical typology of civil strife events identified by Rummel, Tanter, and others in a series of factor analyses. The general categories, and representative subcategories, are:

1. *Turmoil:* relatively spontaneous, unstructured mass strife, including demonstrations, political strikes, riots, political clashes, and localized rebellions.
2. *Conspiracy:* intensively organized, relatively small-scale civil strife, including political assassinations, small-scale terrorism, small-scale guerrilla wars, coups, mutinies, and plots and purges, the last two on grounds that they are evidence of planned strive.
3. *Internal war:* large-scale, organized, focused civil strife, almost always accompanied by extensive violence, including large-scale revolts.[12]

Various measures of the relative extent of civil strife have been used in recent literature, among them counts by country of number of strife events of various types, factor scores derived from such typologies, number of deaths from violent strife, man-days of participation in strife, and scaling procedures that take account of both number of events and their severity.[13] One can infer from frustration-aggres-

---

11. Hubert M. Blalock, Jr., *Causal Inferences in Nonexperimental Research* (Chapel Hill: University of North Carolina Press, 1964), pp. 166–167, italicized in original.

12. In each of a number of analyses by Rummel and others a set of "domestic conflict" measures was factor analyzed. Turmoil, indexed by riots and demonstrations, is found to be a distinct dimension in all the analyses; two other factors, labelled by Rummel "revolution" and "subversion," are in some cases separate and in others combined. Principal components of the "revolution" dimension are coups, palace revolutions, plots, and purges; the category is labelled here conspiracy. Guerrilla war and terrorism are major components of the "subversion" dimension, here labelled internal war. See Rudolph J. Rummel, "A Field Theory of Social Action with Application to Conflict within Nations," *Yearbook of the Society for General Systems Research*, X (1965), 189–195; and Raymond Tanter, "Dimensions of Conflict Behavior Within Nations, 1955–1960: Turmoil and Internal War," *Peace Research Society Papers*, III (1965), 159–183. The subcategories used here are adapted, with their operational definitions, from Rummel, "Dimensions of Conflict Behavior Within and Between Nations," *Yearbook of the Society for General Systems Research*, VIII (1963), 25–26.

13. See, for example, Rummel, *op. cit.*; Tanter, *op. cit.*; Bruce M. Russett, "Inequality and Instability: The Relation of Land Tenure to Politics," *World Polities*, 16 (April 1964), 442–454; Charles Tilly and James Rule, *Measuring Political Upheaval* (Princeton: Center of International Studies, Princeton University, 1965); and Ivo K. and Rosalind L. Feierabend, "Aggressive Behaviors within Polities, 1948–1962: A Cross-National Study," *Journal of Conflict Resolution*, 10 (September 1966), 249–271.

sion theory that no single measure of magnitude of aggression, individual or collective, is likely to be sufficient. It is likely that high levels of discontent may be expressed either in intense, short-lived violence or in more protracted but less severe strife. Moreover, the proportion of a collectivity that participates in civil strife ought to vary with the modal intensity of discontent: mild discontent will motivate few to participate, whereas rage is likely to galvanize large segments of a collectivity into action.

Three aspects of civil strife thus ought to be taken into account in specifying its magnitude:

1. *Pervasiveness:* the extent of participation by the affected population, operationally defined for this study as the sum of the estimated number of participants in all acts of strife as a proportion of the total population of each polity, expressed in terms of participants per 100,000 population.
2. *Duration:* the persistence of strife, indexed here by the sum of the spans of time of all strife events in each polity, whatever the relative scale of the events, expressed in days.
3. *Intensity:* the human cost of strife, indexed here by the total estimated casualties, dead and injured, in all strife events in each polity as a proportion of the total population, expressed as casualties per 10,000,000 population.

* * *

Measures of Deprivation

A very large number of conditions are likely to impose some degree of relative deprivation on some proportion of a nation's citizens. Similarly, all men are likely to be discontented about some of their conditions of life at some point in time. On the basis of prior theoretical and empirical work, however, it was possible to construct, and subsequently to combine, a set of cross-nationally comparable indices of conditions that by inference cause pervasive and intense types of deprivation, relying in part on aggregate data and in part on indices constructed by coding narrative and historical material. In the initial stages of data collection a large number of measures were constructed, some of them representing short-term and some persisting conditions, some of each relating to economic, political, and sociocultural deprivation. Whenever possible, separate measures were included of the intensity of inferred deprivation and of its pervasiveness, i.e., of the proportion of population presumably affected, plus a third measure combining the two elements. A correlation matrix for 48 such measures and a variety of strife measures was generated, and 13 representative deprivation measures selected for combination.[14] The general rationale for the two general types of measure, short-term and persisting deprivation, and the measures finally selected, are summarized [in the list below].

1. *Economic discrimination* is defined as systematic exclusion of social groups from higher economic value positions on ascriptive bases. For each polity the proportion of population so discriminated against, if any, was specified to the nearest .05, and the intensity of deprivation coded on a four-point scale (see below). The proportion and the intensity score were multiplied to obtain a polity score.

14. The 48 deprivation measures, with only one statistically significant exception, were positively associated with strife, most of them at a relatively low level. The thirteen were selected with regard to their representativeness, relatively high correlations with the dependent variables, and low intercorrelations.

2. *Political discrimination* is similarly defined in terms of systematic limitation in form, norm, or practice of social groups' opportunities to participate in political activities or to attain elite positions on the basis of ascribed characteristics. Proportionality and intensity scores were determined and combined in the same manner as economic discrimination scores. The "intensity" scales were defined as follows:

Intensity Score	*Economic Discrimination*	*Political Discrimination*
1	Most higher economic value positions, *or* some specific classes of economic activity, are closed to the group.	Some significant political elite positions are closed to the group, *or* some participatory activities (party membership, voting, etc.).
2	Most higher and some medium economic value positions are closed, *or* many specific classes of economic activity.	Most or all political elite positions are closed *or* most participatory activities, *or* some of both.
3	Most higher and most medium economic value positions are closed.	Most or all political elite positions and some participatory activities are closed.
4	Almost all higher, medium, and some lower economic value positions are closed.	Most or all political elite positions and most or all participatory activities are closed.

3. *Potential separatism* was indexed by multiplying the proportional size of historically-separatist regional or ethnic groups by a four-point intensity measure.[15] The intensity of separatist deprivation was scored as follows:

Intensity Score	*Type of Inferred Separatism*
1	The separatist region or group was incorporated in the polity by its own request or mutual agreement.
2	The separatist region or group was assigned to the polity by international agreement or by fiat of a former colonial or governing power, except when (3) or (4) below holds.
3	The separatist region or group was forcibly assimilated into the polity prior to the twentieth century, *or* was forcibly conquered by a former colonial power prior to the twentieth century.
4	The separatist region or group was forcibly assimilated into the polity during the twentieth century, *or* was forcibly reassimilated in the twentieth century after a period of autonomy due to rebellion or other circumstance.

15. Coding judgments for both discrimination indices and for separatism were made on the basis of country studies. The proportionality measures are versions of indices reported in Ted Gurr, *New Error-Compensated Measures for Comparing Nations* (Princeton: Center of International Studies, Princeton University, 1966), 67–90.

4. *Dependence on private foreign capital*, indexed by negative net factor payments abroad as a percentage of Gross Domestic Product in the late 1950's, is assumed to be a chronic source of dissatisfaction in an era characterized by economic nationalism. The greater the proportion of national product that accrues to foreign suppliers of goods or capital, the greater the inferred intensity of deprivation; the extent of such deprivation was assumed equal to the proportion of population engaged in the monetary economy. The polity score is the extent score × the intensity score.[16]
5. *Religious cleavages* are a chronic source of deprivation-inducing conflict. The scale for intensity of religious cleavage takes account both of number of organized religious groups with two percent or more of total population (the major Christian and Muslim subdivisions are counted as separate groups) and of the duration of their coexistence, the greater that duration the less the inferred intensity. The extent measure is the proportion of the population belonging to any organized religious group. The polity score is the product of the two scores.
6. *Lack of educational opportunity* was indexed, in proportionality terms only, by subtracting primary plus secondary school enrollment ratios ca. 1960 from 100. Education is so widely regarded as an essential first step for individual socioeconomic advancement that one can infer deprivation among the uneducated, and among the parents of children who cannot attend school if not yet among the children themselves.

Persisting Deprivation

In the very long run men's expectations about the goods and conditions of life to which they are entitled tend to adjust to what they are capable of attaining. In the shorter span, however, some groups may persistently demand and expect values, such as greater economic opportunity, political autonomy, or freedom of religious expression, that their societies will not or cannot provide. Six indicators of persisting deprivation were combined to obtain a single long-run deprivation measure.

These six measures all had distributions approaching normality, and correlations with several strife measures ranging from .09 to .27. To combine them they were weighted to bring their means into approximate correspondence, and each polity's scores added and then averaged to circumvent the missing data problem.

Short-Term Deprivation

Any sharp increase in peoples' expectations that is unaccompanied by the perception of an increase in value capabilities, or any abrupt limitation on what they have or can hope to obtain, constitute relative deprivation. We inferred that short-term, relative declines in system economic and political performance were likely to be perceived as increased deprivation for substantial numbers of people. Indices were devised of five kinds of short-term economic deprivation and two of political deprivation.

* * *

16. A crude measure of the proportion of each polity's population engaged in the monetary economy, to the nearest .10, was constructed for the purpose of weighting this and some other measures. The measure was based primarily on labor census data.

Measures of the Mediating Variables

Coercive Potential and Size of Coercive Forces

A composite index was constructed to take into account four aspects of the regime's apparent potential for controlling strife. Two of the component indices represent the manpower resources available to the regime, namely military and internal security forces participation ratios, i.e., military personnel per 10,000 adults ca. 1960 (n = 112), and internal security forces per 10,000 adults (n = 102). The two distributions were normalized and their means brought into correspondence by rescaling them using 10-interval geometric progressions. The other two component indices deal respectively with the degree of *past loyalty of coercive forces to the regime*, and the extent of *illicit coercive-force participation in strife in the 1960–65 period*.

The rationale for the five-point coercive-force loyalty scale, below, is that the more recently coercive forces had attacked the regime, the less efficacious they would be perceived to be by those who might initiate strife—and the more likely they might be to do so again themselves. Countries were scored on the basis of information from a variety of historical sources.

Loyalty Score	*Regime States and Military Attempts to Seize Control of the Regime*
5	As of 1960 the polity or its metropolitan power had been autonomous for 25 years or more and had experienced no military intervention since 1910.
4	As of 1960 the polity or its metropolitan power had been autonomous for 5 to 24 years and had experienced no military intervention during that period; *or* had been autonomous for a longer period but experienced military intervention between 1910 and 1934.
3	The polity last experienced military intervention between 1935 and 1950, inclusive.
2	The polity last experienced military intervention between 1951 and 1957, inclusive.
1	The polity last experienced military intervention between 1958 and 1960, inclusive.

For 28 polities that became independent after 1957 no "loyalty" score was assigned unless the military or police did in fact intervene between independence and the end of 1960. For purposes of calculating the summary score, below, a military loyalty score for these polities was derived from the "legitimacy" score.

Insofar as the military or police themselves illicitly initiated strife in the 1961–65 period, they lost all deterrent effect. To quantify the extent of such involvement, all military or police participation in strife was determined from the data bank of 1100 events and for each polity a "coercive forces strife participation" score calculated, by weighting each involvement in a mutiny or a turmoil event as one and each involvement in any other event (typically coups and civil wars) as two, and summing for each country.

All four of the "coercive potential" measures were correlated in the predicted direction with several preliminary measures of strife levels. The participation ratios had low but consistently negative correlations with strife; the "loyalty" and "strife participation" indices had correlations of the order of –40 and +40 with strife respectively.[17] The composite "coercive potential" score was calculated by the following formula:

17. These are product-moment correlation coefficients, the strife measures including measures of duration, pervasiveness, intensity, and total magnitude of strife for 1961–65. The last two strife measures are defined differently from those employed in the present analysis, but are derived from the same 1100-event data bank.

$$\text{Coercive potential} = 10 \cdot \sqrt{\frac{L[2(HiR) + 1(loR)]}{1 + P}}$$

where: L = "loyalty" score;
HiR = the higher of the scaled military and security forces participation ratios;[18]
loR = the lower of the participation ratios; and
P = "coercive forces strife participation" score.

The effect of the formula is to give the highest coercive potential scores to countries with large coercive forces characterized by both historical and concurrent loyalty to the regime. The more recently and extensively such forces have been involved in strife, however, the lower their coercive potential score.

A second coercion measure was included in the final analysis to permit a further test of the curvilinearity hypothesis. The measure used is the expression in brackets in the coercive potential formula above, i.e., a weighted measure of the relative sizes of military and internal security forces (*coercive force size*).

Institutionalization

Indices of institutional strength and stability which I found in previous analyses to be negatively associated with strife are the *ratio of labor union membership to nonagricultural employment, central government budgeted expenditure as a percentage of Gross Domestic Product*, ca. *1962*, and the *stability of the political party system*.[19] A ten-interval geometric progression was used to normalize the first of these indices, the second was multiplied by 100 and rounded to the nearest 10. To index characteristics of party systems two scales were used, one relating to the number of parties, the other to party system stability per se:

No. of parties score	*Characteristics*
0	no parties, or all parties illegal or ineffective
1	one or several parties, membership sharply restricted on ascriptive bases (typically along ethnic lines) to less than 20 percent of the population
2	one party with no formal or substantial informal restrictions on membership
3	one party dominant
4	two-party (reasonable expectation of party rotation)
5	multi-party

18. If one or the other ratio was missing, it was assumed equal to the known ratio. Internal security force ratios for 94 polities are reported in Gurr, *New Error-Compensated Measures for Comparing Nations*, 111–126.

19. The first two indices are reported in *ibid.*, 33–66, 91–110. Correlations among all three and strife measures are reported in Gurr and Ruttenberg, *The Conditions of Civil Violence, passim*. The party characteristics are recoded from Arthur S. Banks and Robert B. Textor, *A Cross-Polity Survey* (Cambridge: M.I.T. Press, 1963), raw characteristics 41 and 43.

Party system stability score	*Party System Characteristics*
0	no parties, or membership restricted on ascriptive bases to less than 20 percent of population
1	unstable
2	all parties relatively new (founded after 1945), long-range stability not yet ascertainable
3	moderately stable
4	stable

Scores on these two scales were combined on an 8-point scale using party stability as the primary indicator of institutionalization but giving highest scores at each stability level to systems with larger numbers of party structures.

The summary institutionalization measure was constructed using this formula:

Institutionalization = 3(hiI) + 2(midI) + loI,

where: hiI = the highest of the three institutionalization scores, etc.

This procedure gives greatest weight to the most institutionalized sector of society on the assumption that high institutionalization in one sector compensates for lower levels in others. The highest scores are attained by the Eastern European Communist states while the scores of the Western European democracies are slightly lower. The lowest-scoring polities are Ethiopia, Haiti, Nepal, and Yemen.

Facilitation

Two aspects of facilitation were indexed separately: *past levels of civil strife* and *"social and structural facilitation"* per se. The "past levels of strife" measure was derived from the Eckstein data on frequency of internal wars of various types in the period 1946–59; although its reliability is only moderate it covers a longer period and a larger number of polities than other available data.[20] Data were collected for those of the 114 polities not included in the Eckstein tabulation, using the same procedure, a *New York Times Index* count, and recollected for a few others. Weights were assigned to events in various categories, e.g., riots = 1, coups = 5, and a summary score for each polity calculated. The distribution was normalized with a log (X + 1) transformation.

The terrain and transportation network of a county constitute a basic structural limitation on the capabilities of insurgents for maintaining a durable insurrection. A complex "inaccessibility" index was constructed taking account of the extent of transportation networks related to area, population density, and the extent of waste, forest, and mountainous terrain; the highest inaccessibility scores were received by polities like Bolivia, Sudan, and Yemen, which have limited transportation networks and large portions of rugged terrain.[21]

20. Harry Eckstein, "Internal War: The Problem of Anticipation," in Ithiel de Sola Pool *et al., Social Science Research and National Security* (Washington, D.C.: Smithsonian Institution, March 5, 1963).

21. Inaccessibility appears to be an almost but-not-quite necessary condition for protracted internal wars. With one exception all such internal wars in the post-1945 period occurred in polities with high or very high scores on this index; the exception, a notable one, is Cuba.

A crucial "social" variable that facilitates strife is the extent to which the discontented can and do organize for collective action. The relative strength of Communist Party organizations was used as a partial index, taking into account both the number of party members per 10,000 population and the status of the party. Unfortunately no comparable data could be obtained for extremist parties of the right. Party-membership ratios were rescaled to an 11-point scale based on a geometric progression of 2. The party status scale, below, is based on the premise that illegal parties are more facilitative of strife because their membership is likely, because of the exigencies of repression, to be more dedicated, better organized, and committed to the more violent forms of conflict. Factionalized parties are assumed to be more facilitative because they offer more numerous organizational foci for action.

Score	*Communist party status and characteristics*
0	In power *or* nonexistent.
1	Out of power; no serious factionalization or multiple organization; party permitted to participate in electoral activities.
2	Out of power; multiple factions or organizations; party permitted to participate in electoral activities.
3	Out of power; party excluded from electoral activities but other party activities tolerated.
4	Out of power; no serious factionalization or multiple organization; party illegal and/or actively suppressed.
5	Out of power; multiple factions or organizations; party illegal and/or actively suppressed.

The score for each polity is the scaled membership ratio times the party status score.

The third measure of facilitation is the extent of external support for initiators of strife in the 1961–65 period. Each strife event in the 1100-event data bank was coded for the degree of support for initiators (if any) and for the number of nations supporting the initiators in any of these ways. The scale points for "degree of support" are provision of arms and supplies (= 1), refuge (= 2), facilities and training (= 3), military advisors and mercenaries (= 4), and large (1,000 +) military units (= 5). The event support score is the "degree" score times the "number of nations" score, these scores then being summed for all events for each polity to obtain a polity score. This measure alone has a relatively high correlation with strife level measures, ranging from .3 to .4; its two extreme outliers, South Vietnam and the Congo, are also among the three extreme outliers on the total magnitude of strife distribution.

The three social and structural facilitation measures were weighted to bring their means into approximate correspondence, several missing-data items estimated, and the weighted measures added to obtain the composite index.

Legitimacy

The legitimacy of a regime can be defined behaviorally in terms of popular compliance, and psychologically by reference to the extent to which its directives are regarded by its citizens as properly made and worthy of obedience. In lieu of evidence on compliance or allegiance necessary to operationalize the concept directly, I combined one indicator of an inferred cause of legitimacy, the circumstances under which the regime attained its present form, with an indicator of an inferred effect, the durability of the regime. The "character" of the regime was scored on a seven-point scale:

Character Score	*Origins of national political institutions*
7	Institutions are wholly or primarily accretive and autochthonous; reformations, if any, had indigenous roots (although limited foreign elements may have been assimilated into indigenous institutions).
6	Institutions are a mixture of substantial autochthonous and foreign elements, e.g., polities with externally-derived parliamentary and/or bureaucratic systems grafted to a traditional monarchy.
5	Institutions are primarily foreign in origin, were deliberately chosen by indigenous leaders, and have been adapted over time to indigenous political conditions. (By adaptation is meant either the modification of regime institutions themselves or development of intermediate institutions to incorporate politically the bulk of the population.)
4	Institutions are primarily foreign in origin, have been adapted over time to indigenous political conditions, but were inculcated under the tutelage of a foreign power rather than chosen by indigenous leaders of their own volition.
3	Institutions are primarily foreign in origin, were deliberately chosen by indigenous leaders, but have *not* been adapted over time to indigenous political conditions.
2	Institutions are primarily foreign in origin, were inculcated under the tutelage of a foreign power, and have not been adapted to indigenous political conditions.
1	Institutions are imposed by, and maintained under threat of sanctions by, foreign powers (including polities under colonial rule as of 1965).

A similar scale, based on the number of generations the regime had persisted as of 1960 without substantial, abrupt reformation, was constructed for durability:

Durability Score	*Last major reformation of institutions before 1960*
7	More than eight generations before 1960 (before 1800).
6	Four to eight generations (1801–1880).
5	Two to four generations (1881–1920).
4	One to two generations (1921–1940).
3	One-half to one generation (1941–1950).
2	One-quarter to one-half generation (1951–1955).
1	Institutions originated between 1956 and 1960, or were in 1960 in the process of transition.

Examples of coding decisions about "major reformations" are that France experienced such a change in 1957; that most French tropical African polities date their basic institutional structures from the 1946 reforms, not the year of formal independence; that the Canadian regime dates from 1867, when dominion status was attained; and that many Latin American regimes, despite performance of musical chairs at the executive level, attained their basic institutional structures at various (historically specified and coded) points in the mid- or late nineteenth century.

The summary legitimacy index was constructed by summing and rescaling the "character" and "durability" scores.[22]

III. Results of Correlation and Regression Analysis

The results of four multiple regression analyses are discussed in this paper, one of them in detail. The dependent variables in the four analyses are, respectively, total magnitude of civil strife, magnitude of conspiracy, magnitude of internal war, and magnitude of turmoil. The correlations between the ten summary independent variables and these four strife measures are given in Table 1. The independent variables all correlate with the dependent variables in the predicted direction, with the exception of coer-

Table 1 Correlates of Civil Strife[a]

Variable[b]	1	2	3	4	5	6	7	8	9	10	11	12	13	14
1. Economic deprivation (+)		48	83	−02	−17	−16	−36	−09	26	32	34	31	25	44
2. Political deprivation (+)			88	08	−18	03	−37	−20	33	27	44	18	30	38
3. Short-term deprivation (+)[c]				04	−20	−07	−42	−17	34	34	46	28	32	48
4. Persisting deprivation (+)					−04	−21	−14	−37	−04	17	29	26	27	36
5. Legitimacy (−)						25	48	02	−05	−15	−29	−23	−29	−37
6. Coercive force size (±)							53	27	31	04	−23	−11	−01	−14
7. Coercive potential (−)								41	−14	−37	−44	−39	−35	−51
8. Institutionalization (−)									−19	−40	−35	−23	−26	−33
9. Past strife levels (+)										41	24	16	30	30
10. Facilitation (+)											42	57	30	67
11. Magnitude of conspiracy												30	32	59
12. Magnitude of internal war													17	79
13. Magnitude of turnoil														61
14. Total magnitude of strife														

[a] Product moment correlation coefficients, multiplied by 100. Underlined r's are significant, for $n = 114$, at the .01 level. Correlations between 18 and 23, inclusive, are significant at the .05 level.

[b] The proposed relationships between the independent variables, nos. 1 to 10, and the strife measures are shown in parentheses, the ± for coercive force size signifying a proposed curvilinear relationship. Examination of the r's between the independent and dependent variables, in the box, shows that all are in the predicted direction with the anticipated exception of coercive force size, and that all but one are significant at the .05 level.

[c] Short-term deprivation is the sum of scores on the short-term economic and short-term political deprivation measures. The separate short-term deprivation measures were used in the regression analyses reported below; the summary measure was used in the causal inference analysis.

---

22. The following rescaling was used, the sum of the "durability" and "character" scores being given on the upper line, the final legitimacy score on the lower:

Sum:	3,4	5	6	7	8	9	10	11	12	13,14
Legitimacy:	0	1	2	3	4	5	6	7	8	9

cive force size. The r's for the remaining nine independent variables are significant at the .01 level except for four correlates of internal war, three of which are significant at the .05 level.

The hypothetical curvilinear relationship between coercive force size and total magnitude of strife (TMCS) is examined graphically in Figures 2 and 3, each of which is a smoothed curve of deciles of the independent variable plotted against TMCS. Figure 2, based on all 114 polities, suggests an apparent tendency, among countries with relatively small forces, for strife to increase with the size of those forces, and also a slight increase in TMCS at very high levels of coercive forces.[23] It is quite likely that countries with protracted political violence expand their coercive forces to meet it. It also seems likely that armies in countries facing foreign threats cause less dissatisfaction—by their presence or actions—than armies in states not significantly involved in international conflict. Both factors might contaminate the proposed curvilinear relationship, so countries with either or both characteristics were removed and the relationship plotted for the remaining 69 countries; the results, in Figure 3, show curvilinearity even more distinctly. Figure 4 indicates that the measure of coercive force potential, in which size is weighted for military loyalty to the regime, is essentially linear, as predicted. The latter measure is used in the multiple regression analyses, below.[24]

Eight of the ten independent variables (excluding coercive force size and short-term deprivation, the sum of the two specific short-term deprivation measures) are included in the multiple regression analy-

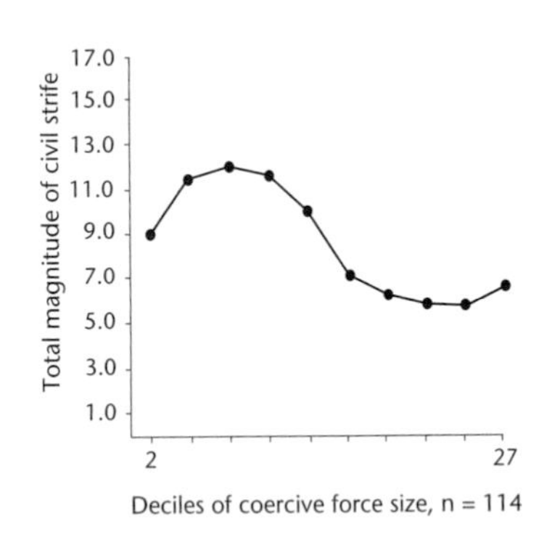

Figure 2 Magnitude of civil strife and coercive force size, 114 polities.

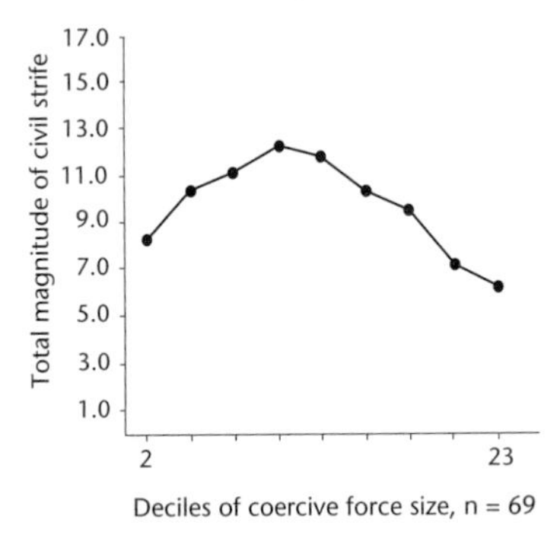

Figure 3 Magnitude of civil strife and coercive force size, 69 low-conflict polities.

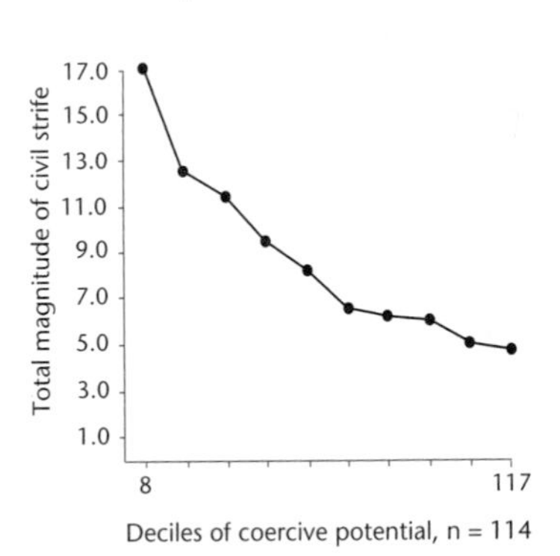

Figure 4 Magnitude of civil strife and coercive potential.

23. The S-shape of this relationship is considerably more pronounced when coercive force size is related to total magnitude of turmoil; see Ted Gurr, "Urban Disorder: Perspectives from the Comparative Study of Civil Strife," *American Behavioral Scientist*, 10 (March-April 1968).

24. Note: The vertical axes in Figures 2, 3 and 4 give the average magnitude of civil strife scores for deciles of countries with coercive forces of increasing size (Figures 2 and 3) and for deciles of countries with increasingly large coercive forces relative to their loyalty. The range of TMCS scores for the 114 polities is 0.0 to 48.7, their mean 9.0, and their standard deviation 7.7. Units on the horizontal axes represent numbers of cases, not proportional increases in force size/loyalty; the figures represent the scores of the extreme cases. Eleven rather than ten groupings of cases were used in computations for Figures 2 and 4; the curves of all three figures were smoothed by averaging successive pairs of decile scores.

ses summarized in Table 2. The variables yield considerable and significant multiple correlation coefficients (R), including a high R of .806 for total magnitude of strife ($R^2 = .650$); a moderately high R for conspiracy of .630 ($R^2 = .397$); a similar R for internal war of .648 ($R^2 = .420$); and a somewhat lower

Table 2 Partial Correlations and Standard Weight[a]

	Independent Variables								
Dependent Variables	Econ. dep.	Pol. dep.	Per. dep.	Coerce.	Instit.	Past CS	SS facil.	Legit.	R, R^2
Total magnitude of strife:									
Simple r's	44	38	36	−51	−33	30	67	−37	
Partial r's	24	(09)	39	−17	(07)	(04)	55	−26	R = .806
Constant	−3.11								
Weights	.177	.066	.271	−.140	.056	.024	.481	−.184	$R^2 = .650$
Magnitude of conspiracy:									
Simple r's	34	44	29	−44	−35	24	42	−29	
Partial r's	(10)	24	22	(−11)	(−09)	(03)	19	(−15)	R = .630
Constant	1.10								
Weights	.094	.238	.194	−.120	−.088	.026	.181	−.135	$R^2 = .397$
Magnitude of internal war:									
Simple r's	31	18	26	−39	−23	16	57	−23	
Partial r's	(14)	(−08)	22	−17	(11)	(−07)	48	(−07)	R = .648
Constant	−3.66								
Weights	.128	−.073	.186	−.179	.102	−.066	.513	−.063	R^2 .420
Magnitude of turmoil:									
Simple r's	25	30	27	−35	−26	30	30	−29	
Partial r's	(07)	(08)	23	(−09)	(−05)	21	(04)	−19	R = .533
Constant	1.37								
Weights	.072	.085	.223	−.102	−.056	.205	.043	−.192	$R^2 = .284$

[a] Simple correlations from Table 1 are repeated here to facilitate comparisons. Partial correlations in parentheses have standard beta weights that are significant at less than the .05 level, using the one-tailed *t* test with n = 114. Since this analysis is concerned with what is, effectively, the entire universe of polities, all the correlations are in one sense "significant," but those in parentheses are of substantially less consequence than the others. The weights are reported to facilitate comparisons of the relative importance of the independent variables; because of the use of a variety of scaling and combination procedures for both independent and dependent variables, the weights do not permit direct interpretations, for example, of the effect of a one-unit decrease in intensity of economic discrimination on extent of turmoil.

---

25. Significant computational errors in internal war and TMCS scores of several countries were identified and corrected after completion of the analyses reported here. Robert van den Helm of Princeton University has analyzed the corrected data, using the combined short-term deprivation measure in lieu of the two separate measures, with these multiple regression results: for TMCS, $R^2 = .638$; conspiracy, $R^2 = .391$; internal war, $R^2 = .472$; and turmoil, $R^2 = .284$. The significant increase in the degree of explanation for internal war is the result of increased correlations between magnitude of internal war and short-term deprivation (from .28 in Table 1 to .34); facilitation (from .57 to .61); and legitimacy (from −.23 to −.26). The r between magnitudes of turmoil and internal war increases from .17 to .23, the r between TMCS and internal war from .79 to .86. No other results of the analyses reported here are significantly affected by the reanalysis. The actual TMCS scores shown in Table 3 are corrected ones.

R for turmoil of .533 (R^2 = .284).[25] There are several possible explanations for the finding that total magnitude of strife is accounted for nearly twice as well as the several forms of strife. One technical factor is that all the class-of-strife measures have greater distributional irregularities than does TMCS, hence TMCS should be somewhat better explained. It is also possible that the categorization employed has less empirical merit than other work has suggested, i.e., that conspiracy, internal war, and turmoil are not sharply distinct forms of civil strife. To qualify this possibility, the correlation matrix in Table 1 suggests that the forms of strife are only weakly related in magnitude—the highest r among the three is .32—but it may still be that they are more strongly related in likelihood, and hence that the universe of strife is more homogenous than the typology suggests. The least-predicted class of strife—turmoil—might be better accounted for if turmoil events in the context of internal wars, e.g., riots and localized rebellions in such polities as the Congo and South Vietnam, were categorized as aspects of the internal wars in these countries rather than turmoil per se. The most likely substantive interpretation of the relatively low predictability of turmoil, however, is that much turmoil is a response to a variety of locally-incident deprivations and social conditions of a sort not represented in the indices used in this study.

The multiple regression equation for total magnitude of strife was used to calculate predicted magnitude of strife scores. Only ten polities have predicted scores that differ from their actual scores by more than one standard deviation (7.70 units of TMCS). These polities, and three others that have discrepancies approaching one standard deviation, are listed in Table 3.

In five of the thirteen polities—the Congo, Indonesia, Zambia, Rwanda, and Yemen—there is probably systematic error from data-estimation procedures. All of these countries had intense but inadequately-reported civil violence for which only rough and quite possibly exaggerated estimates of deaths were available. When estimates of "wounded" were added to deaths estimates, using a ratio of about twelve to one based on better-reported but smaller-scale events (see above), the result was almost cer-

Table 3 Polities with Least-Predicted Total Magnitude of Civil Strife[a]

Polity	Predicted TMCS	Actual TMCS[b]	Residual
Congo-Kinshasa	31.6	48.7	+17.1
Rwanda	12.7	28.2	+15.5
Yemen	9.4	23.6	+14.2
Indonesia	23.8	33.7	+9.9
Dominican Republic	12.1	21.9	+9.8
Italy	3.1	12.3	+9.2
Belgium	2.4	10.5	+8.1
Zambia	8.1	15.5	+7.4
Israel	6.9	14.0	+7.1
Argentina	20.5	13.2	−7.3
Ecuador	18.6	10.1	−8.5
Volta	9.3	0.0	−9.3
Paraguay	17.2	5.0	−12.2

[a] See text. A negative residual indicates that a polity had less strife than would be predicted on the basis of the characteristics it shares with other polities; a positive residual indicates more than predicted strife.
[b] Corrected scores. See footnote 25.

tainly a gross inflation of actual casualties, and hence inflation of TMCS scores. The high actual TMCS score for Israel is the result of a questionable coding judgment about the extent and duration of extremist Orthodox religious conflict. More substantive questions are raised by some of the countries. Paraguay, Argentina, Ecuador, and Volta all could be argued to have had an unrealized potential for strife: in fact both Argentina and Ecuador experienced coups in the mid-1960's that according to their initiators were preventive or protective in nature, and early in 1966 the government of Volta succumbed to rioting followed by a coup. In the Dominican Republic, the Congo, and Rwanda the unexpectedly high levels of violence followed the collapse of rigid, authoritarian regimes; one can infer a time-lag effect from the deprivation incurred under the old regimes. These are special explanations rather than general ones however. The lack of apparent substantive similarities among the thirteen poorly-predicted polities suggests that the analysis has included measures of most if not all the general determinants of magnitudes of civil strife.

IV. A Revised Causal Model

One striking result of the regression analyses is that the partial correlations of several of the variables tend to disappear when the other variables are introduced (see Table 2). The short-term deprivation measures consistently decline in consequence, in most instances falling below the .05 level of significance. Institutionalization is in all analyses controlled for by the other variables. One or the other of the two facilitation variables declines to zero in each analysis, "past levels of strife" vanishing in three of the four. Coercive potential and legitimacy also decline in their relation to strife rather sharply. The only variable that is consistently unaffected by the introduction of the control variables specified by the model is persisting deprivation. A preliminary analysis of the behavior of first- and second-order partials suggests what causal interactions and sequences may be involved in these results. The causal path analysis is concerned principally with the sources of the total magnitude of strife, examining the causal sequences of the specific forms of strife only when they appear to deviate from that of all strife.

A basic supposition for the evaluation of causal models is that, if X_1 is an indirect cause of X_3 whose effects are mediated by an intervening variable X_2, then if X_2's effects are controlled the resulting partial correlation between X_1 and X_3 should be approximately zero. Similarly, if several intervening variables are specified, controlling for all of them or for the last in a causal chain should, if the causal model is not to be falsified, result in a partial correlation not significantly different from zero.[26]

The initial model of the causes of civil strife (Figure 1) postulated that all the mediating variables intervened separately and simultaneously between deprivation and strife. The results indicate that this supposition is only partly correct: none of the mediating variables appear to affect the relationship between *persisting deprivation* and strife, i.e., there is a certain inevitability about the association between such deprivation and strife. Persisting deprivation is moreover equally potent as a source of conspiracy, internal war, and turmoil. With the partial and weak exception of institutionalization, no patterns of

26. These and other fundamental arguments about causal inference are well summarized in Blalock, *Causal Inferences . . .*, Chapters 2 and 3. A partial correlation coefficient can be most easily regarded as the correlation between X and Z after the portions of X and Z that are accounted for by Y are removed, or held constant. The results discussed below are based on the use of only one of a variety of related causal inference techniques and are open to further, more refined analysis and interpretation. For other applicable approaches see, for example, Hayward R. Alker, Jr., *Mathematics and Politics* (New York: Macmillan, 1965), Chapters 5 and 6.

societal arrangements nor coercive potential that are included in the model have any consistent effect on its impact.

The effects of short-term deprivation on strife are substantially different—and, it should be added, uncorrelated with persisting deprivation. The intervening variables do tend to control for shortterm deprivation's effects. To determine which one or ones exercise primary control, first-order partials were calculated for the several postulated intervening variables, with these results.

1. The simple r between short-term deprivation and strife = .48[27]
2. The partial r between short-term deprivation and strife is: when the control variable is:

The partial r between short-term deprivation and strife is:	when the control variable is:
.46	Institutionalization
.45	Legitimacy
.42	Past strife
.36	Facilitation
.34	Coercive potential

Only the last two constitute a significant reduction, and moreover when they are combined, the second-order partial, $r_dS \cdot _{fc}$, = .27, i.e., *coercive potential* and *facilitation* are the only consequential intervening variables affecting the outcome of short-term deprivation. Short-term deprivation taken alone accounts for $(.48)^2 = .23$ of the magnitude of strife; controlling for coercive potential and facilitation reduces the proportion of strife directly accounted for to $(.27)^2 = .07$, a relatively small but still significant amount.

The same controlling effects of coercive potential and facilitation on short-term deprivation occur among the three generic forms of strife. It is worth noting that when the mediating variables are controlled, short-term economic deprivation still accounts directly for a portion of strife, internal war in particular, while political deprivation contributes significantly to conspiracy. These relationships may reflect contamination of the independent and dependent variables because of their partial temporal overlap. Some short-term economic deprivation in the early 1960's may be attributable to protracted internal wars, and successful conspirators may impose politically-depriving policies once they are in power. The relationship between short-term deprivation of both types and the magnitude of turmoil, however, is effectively mediated or controlled by characteristics of the society and its response to strife.

The relationships among the mediating variables remain to be examined. Institutionalization has no significant relation to any measure of strife when the other variables are controlled, and in the case of magnitude of total strife and of internal war a weak *positive* relationship emerges, i.e., there is a slight though not statistically significant tendency for high institutionalization to be associated with higher levels of strife. A computation of partials between institutionalization and the other three mediating variables indicates that institutionalization has a preceding or causal relationship both to coercive potential and to the facilitation variables, as shown in the revised model in Figure 3. Polities with high levels of institutionalization tend to have high coercive potential and to have few of the conditions that facilitate strife.

---

27. To simplify evaluation of the effects of the control variables, the summary short-term deprivation variable was employed rather than its economic and political components separately.

Legitimacy apparently has a causal relationship with strife independent either of deprivation or the other intervening variables. About half of the initial correlation between legitimacy and strife is accounted for by the apparent causal relation between legitimacy and coercive potential, i.e., legitimate regimes tend to have large and, most importantly, loyal military and police establishments. Separately from this, however, high legitimacy is significantly associated with low levels of strife, a finding consistent with the postulate that political legitimacy itself is a desired value, one whose absence constitutes a deprivation that incites men to take violent action against their regimes. The relationship is relatively strongest for total magnitude of strife, less so for turmoil and conspiracy, and inconsequential for internal war.

Coercive potential appears in several respects to be a crucial variable in the revised causal model: it is evidently attributable in part to both levels of institutionalization and of legitimacy, and has a major mediating effect on short-term deprivation. Nonetheless, when all variables are controlled (see Table 2), the partial *r* between coercive potential and strife is sharply reduced, in two instances below the .05 level of significance. This is in part due to the effects of legitimacy, which is causally linked to both strife and coercive potential.[28] The other major intervening variable is facilitation

(r_{cs} = -.52;
$r_{cs \cdot f}$ = -.40,

where: c = coercive potential,
s = strife, and
f = social and structural facilitation),

i.e., whether or not facilitative conditions exist for civil strife is partly dependent upon the coercive potential of the regime, and thus indirectly dependent upon legitimacy as well. (The relationship is evidently between coercive potential on the one hand and the "Communist party status" and the "external support for initiators" components of facilitation on the other; coercive potential cannot have any consequential effects on "physical inaccessibility.")

This completes the revision of the causal model with the exception of the second component of facilitation, *past strife levels.* This variable has a consistently lower relationship with strife than other variables, with the exception of the turmoil analysis. Moreover its partial correlation is reduced to zero in these analyses, with the same exception, the sole significant controlling variable being *social and structural facilitation.* Among the causes of turmoil, however, social and structural facilitation is controlled for by several variables—principally past strife, coercive potential, and institutionalization—whereas past strife remains significant when other effects are partialled out. Both findings support the theoretical argument that suggested the "past strife" measure: a history of chronic strife apparently re-

28. Analysis of the correlation coefficients does not indicate definitively that legitimacy contributes to coercive potential rather than vice versa; nor would it be impossible to argue, on the basis of the partial r's alone, that short-term deprivation is a weak intervening variable between coercive potential and facilitation, on the one hand, and strife on the other. It is the plausibility of the theoretical arguments, in each case, that gives deciding force to the interpretation proposed. For a comparable argument see Hugh Donald Forbes and Edward R. Tufte, "A Note of Caution in Causal Modelling," *American Political Science Review*, LXII (December 1968), 1258–64.

flects, and contributes to, attitudes that directly facilitate future turmoil, and indirectly acts to facilitate general levels of strife.

The revised model, with proportional weights inserted, is sketched in Figure 5. The most proximate and potent variable is social and structural facilitation, which accounts for nearly half the explained variance. The deprivation variables account directly for over one-third the magnitude of strife, legitimacy and institutionalization for one-eighth. But these proportions refer only to direct effects, and in the case of both coercive potential and facilitation part of the direct effect, i.e., the illicit participation of the military in strife and the provision of foreign support for initiators, can be determined only from the characteristics of strife itself.[29] The more remote causes of strife, namely deprivation, institutionalization, legitimacy, and prior strife, are the more fundamental and persisting ones. Some additional regression analyses provide some comparisons. Four of the independent variables relate to inferred states of mind: the two short-term deprivation measures, persisting deprivation, and legitimacy. The R based on these variables is .65, compared with .81 when the remaining four variables are added. The R based on the three deprivation variables alone is .60. These analyses show that all "states-of-mind" conditions contribute significantly to magnitude of strife, but that long-term deprivation has a partial controlling effect on political deprivation. The inference is that short-term political deprivation, as indexed in this study, is most likely to lead to strife if it summates with conditions of persisting deprivation.

We can also ask, and answer, the question, To what extent do the remaining four mediating conditions alone account for magnitude of strife? The variables coercive potential, facilitation, institutionalization, and past strife give a multiple R of .73, with almost all the explained variance accounted for by the first two variables. This result should provide aid and comfort to those concerned with "levels of analysis" problems: research of this sort can focus on aggregative, societal characteristics—which the mediating variables represent—and the (inferred) psychological level can be ignored with relatively little loss of statistical explanatory power. Why these variables are strongly operative and others, like levels of development and type of political system, are relatively weak still needs answering; the answer may be to treat psychological variables as unoperationalized assumptions, or to replace them with variables whose rationale is strictly in terms of effects of social structure or processes on stability.

A further problem is identification of the set of variables that provides the most parsimonious account of magnitude of civil strife. As one approach to the answer, Figure 5 implies that three variables can be eliminated: coercive potential, institutionalization, and past strife, all of which have no consequential direct effects on TMCS. The remaining five variables—the "state of mind" variables and facilitation—give an R of .80 and R^2 of .64, results almost identical to those obtained when all eight variables are included.[30] Four of the five variables included contribute substantially to the regression equation; as expected, the effects of short-term deprivation, political deprivation in particular, are partially controlled. One important observation is that *social and structural facilitation*, though it is sub-

29. Tanter has examined time-lag effects between a number of measures of foreign economic and military assistance for the regime and magnitude of civil violence in 1961–63 for Latin American nations and finds generally weak relationships. The only consequential positive relationship, an indirect one, is between levels of U.S. military assistance and subsequent strife. Raymond Tanter, "Toward A Theory of Conflict Behavior in Latin America." (Paper read to the International Political Science Association, Brussels, September, 1967).

30. In a reanalysis using corrected data (see footnote 24), four variables—the combined short-term deprivation measure, persisting deprivation, legitimacy, and facilitation—give an R^2 of .629.

Figure 5 Revised causal model of the determinants of magnitude of civil strife. The proportion at the top of each cell is the simple r^2 between the variable and civil strife, i.e., the proportion of strife accounted for by each variable separately. The pecentages are the proportion of explained variance accounted for by each variable when the effects of all others are controlled, determined by squaring each partial r, summing the squares and expressing each as a percentage of the sum. The explained variance, R^2, is .65.

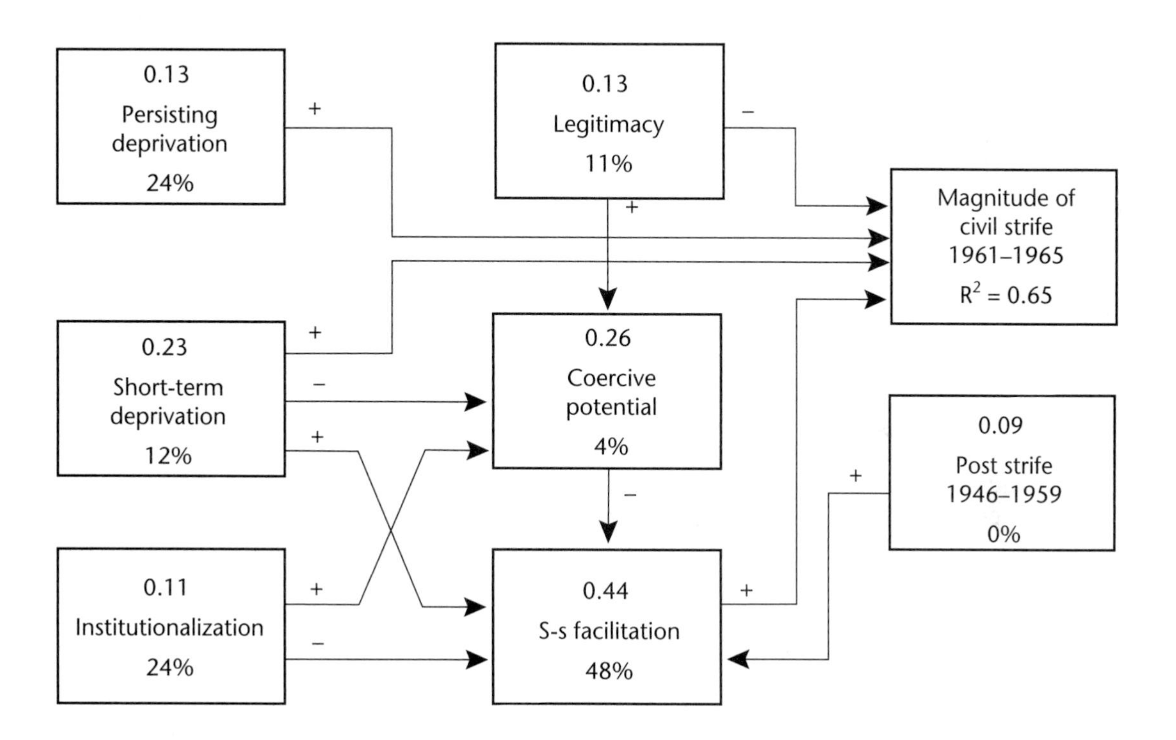

stantially the strongest explanatory variable,[31] has here, as in Figure 5, only a moderate direct controlling effect on short-term deprivation. One interpretation is that some of the effects of facilitation on TMCS are independent of deprivation. Two of its three component measures, Communist Party status and external support for initiators, have in common a "tactical" element, i.e., one can infer that underlying them are calculations about gains to be achieved through the employment of strife. This tactical element is not wholly independent of deprivation, inasmuch as three of the four correlations between facilitation and deprivation measures are significant, ranging from .17 to .34 (see Table 1). The basic proposition of this study, that relative deprivation is a necessary precondition for strife, is not chal-

31. The partial r's for these five variables are: economic deprivation, .27; political deprivation, .13; persisting deprivation, .39; legitimacy .36; facilitation. .61.

lenged by these observations. They do, however, suggest that tactical motives for civil strife are of sufficient importance that they deserve separate operational attention comparable to the conceptual attention given them by conflict theorists.[32]

A number of additional causal inference analyses can be made which might lead to modifications of these conclusions, and of the causal model in Figure 5. Other articles will report the results of causal analyses of various subsets of the universe of polities, and of the causal sequences that can be identified for the several forms of strife.[33]

* * *

32. For example Kenneth E. Boulding, *Conflict and Defense: A General Theory* (New York: Harper and Row, 1962); Lewis Coser, *The Functions of Social Conflict* (New York: The Free Press, 1956); and Thomas C. Schelling, *The Strategy of Conflict* (Cambridge, Mass.: Harvard University Press, 1960).

33. See Gurr, "Urban Disorder," for a causal inference analysis of the sources of turmoil. The turmoil model differs principally in that "past strife levels" has the primary mediating role that facilitation has in the TMCS model.

12.2

SOCIAL REVOLUTIONS AND MASS MILITARY MOBILIZATION

Theda Skocpol

In contrast to the research by Ted Gurr (see reading 12.1) and others, which used sophisticated quantitative analysis of a few variables in a large number of cases, Theda Skocpol analyzes a larger number of factors in a few cases—a selected number of actual social revolutions (as opposed to Gurr's broader concept of violence in general) and the social and historical contexts in which they occurred. Skocpol, a sociologist and political scientist at Harvard University, discerns patterns in these otherwise unique events and classifies the great social revolutions into two categories: those that transformed imperial-monarchical states, such as the French Revolution of 1789, and those that occurred in colonial or postcolonial societies, such as the many revolutions for independence, including the Vietnamese struggle against the French in the 1950s. Although these social revolutions generally failed to achieve anything resembling modern democracies, they proved successful at mobilizing their populations for military purposes.

"The changes in the state order which a revolution produces are no less important than the changes in the social order." [1] Franz Borkenau's insight, published in 1937, has become the central theme of more recent comparative studies. "A complete revolution," writes Samuel P. Huntington in *Political Order in Changing Societies*, "involves. . .the creation and institutionalization of a new political order," into which an "explosion" of popular participation in national affairs is channeled.[2] Similarly, in my *States and Social Revolutions: A Comparative Analysis of France, Russia, and China*, I argue that in "each New Regime, there was much greater popular incorporation into the state-run affairs of the nation. And the new state organizations forged during the Revolutions were more centralized and rationalized than those of the Old Regime." [3]

Huntington has developed his arguments about revolutionary accomplishments in critical dialogue with liberal-minded modernization theorists, while I have developed mine in critical dialogue with Marxian class analysts. Modernization theorists and Marxians both analyze revolutionary transformations primarily in relation to long-term socioeconomic change. These scholars also highlight the contributions of certain revolutions to liberalism or to democratic socialism—that is, to "democracy" understood *in opposition to* authoritarian state power.

Theda Skocpol, "Social Revolutions and Mass Military Mobilization," *World Politics* 40, no. 2 (January 1988): 147–168.

The classical Marxist vision on revolutionary accomplishments was unblinkingly optimistic. According to this view, "bourgeois revolutions" clear away obstacles to capitalist economic development and lay the basis for historically progressive but socially limited forms of liberal democracy. "Proletarian revolutions," in turn, create the conditions for classless economies and for universal social and political democracy, accompanied by the progressive "withering away of the state." The first modern social revolution to be accomplished in the name of Marxism, the Russian Revolution of 1917, obviously belied this vision, however, for it established a communist dictatorship that ruled in the name of the proletariat while actually exploiting workers for purposes of crash industrialization, and imposing a brutal "internal colonialism" on the peasant majority.[4]

Reacting to the Stalinist denouement of the Russian Revolution, liberal-minded theorists operating within the broad framework of modernization theory have offered their own view of the accomplishments of revolutions. Theorists as disparate as S. N. Eisenstadt and Michael Walzer agree that the only salutary revolutions have been the mildest ones—the least violent and the least suddenly transformative of preexisting social and political relations.[5] In contrast to such supposedly liberal revolutions as the French and the English, the more severe and thoroughgoing revolutions boomeranged to produce totalitarian dictatorships—more penetrating authoritarian regimes—rather than democratization as these modernization theorists understand it.

Modernization theorists, moreover, tend to view the political aspects of the revolutions as inefficient and probably temporary aberrations in the course of socioeconomic development. An ideologically committed vanguard may rise to central-state power—and perhaps stay there—through the mobilization and manipulation of grass roots political organizations such as militias, workplace councils, or neighborhood surveillance committees. From the perspective of modernization theorists, however, this kind of revolutionary political mobilization—known either as "the terror" or as totalitarianism, depending on whether it is a phase or an institutionalized outcome in any given revolution—is both morally reprehensible and technically inefficient for dealing with the practical tasks that modern governments must face.

Converging on what might be called a realist perspective, analysts like Huntington and myself have reached different conclusions about the political accomplishments of revolutions. In the realist view, a special sort of democratization—understood not as an extension of political liberalism or the realization of democratic socialism, but as an enhancement of popular involvement in national political life—*accompanies* the revolutionary strengthening of centralized national states directed by authoritarian executives or political parties.

Briefly put, this happens because during revolutionary interregnums competition among elites for coercive and authoritative control spurs certain leadership groups to mobilize previously politically excluded popular forces by means of both material and ideological incentives. Popular participation is especially sought in the forging of organizations that can be used to subdue less "radical" contenders. New state organizations—armies, administrations, committees of surveillance, and so forth—are at once authoritarian and unprecedentedly mass-mobilizing. In some revolutions, especially those involving prolonged guerrilla wars, this process works itself out prior to the formal seizure of national-state power; in others, especially those in which inter-elite struggles are fought out in urban street battles, it tends to occur during and after that seizure. Either way, the logic of state-building through which social revolutions are successfully accomplished promotes both authoritarianism and popular mobilization.

In the realist view, moreover, the strengthened political and state orders that emerge from social-revolutionary transformations may perform some kinds of tasks very effectively—certainly more effectively than did the old regimes they displaced. But which tasks? Perhaps because we have argued with the modernization and Marxian theorists, Huntington and I tend to explore the accomplishments of revolutionary regimes in such areas as maintaining political order during the course of socioeconomic transformation, enforcing individual or collective property rights, and promoting state-led industrialization. Yet I would argue that the task which revolutionized regimes in the modern world have performed best is the mobilization of citizen support across class lines for protracted international warfare.

There is a straightforward reason why this should be true: the types of organizations formed and the political ties forged between revolutionary vanguards and supporters (in the course of defeating other elites and consolidating the new regime's state controls) can readily be converted to the tasks of mobilizing resources, including dedicated officers and soldiers, for international warfare. Guerrilla armies and their support systems are an obvious case in point. So are urban militias and committees of surveillance, which seem to have served as splendid agencies for military recruitment from the French Revolution to the Iranian. Moreover, if revolutionary leaders can find ways to link a war against foreigners to domestic power struggles, they may be able to tap into broad nationalist feelings—as well as exploit class and political divisions—in order to motivate supporters to fight and die on behalf of the new regime. Talented members of families that supported the old regime can often be recruited to the revolutionary-nationalist cause, along with enthusiasts from among those who had previously been excluded from national politics.

Whether we in the liberal-democratic West like to acknowledge it or not, the authoritarian regimes brought to power through revolutionary transformations—from the French Revolution of the late 18th century to the Iranian Revolution of the present—have been democratizing in the mass-mobilizing sense. The best evidence of this has been the enhanced ability of such revolutionized regimes to conduct humanly costly wars with a special fusion of popular zeal, meritocratic professionalism, and central coordination. Whatever the capacities of revolutionary regimes to cope with tasks of economic development (and the historical record suggests that those capacities are questionable), they seem to excel at motivating their populations to make supreme sacrifices for the nation in war. That is no mean accomplishment in view of the fact that the prerevolutionary polities in question excluded most of the people from symbolic or practical participation in national politics.

In the remainder of this brief essay, I will illustrate the plausibility of these arguments by surveying two groups of social revolutions in modern world history. First, I will examine the classic social revolutions that transformed the imperial-monarchical states of Bourbon France, Romanov Russia, and Manchu China, probing their accomplishments in relation to the expectations of the liberal, Marxian, and realist perspectives just outlined. Then I will discuss a number of the nation-building social revolutions that have transformed postcolonial and neocolonial countries in the 20th century. I shall pay special attention to the ways in which the geopolitical contexts of particular revolutions have facilitated or discouraged the channeling of popular political participation into defensive and aggressive wars. Whether "communist" or not, I argue, revolutionary elites have been able to build the strongest states in those countries whose geopolitical circumstances allowed or required the emerging new regimes to become engaged in protracted and labor-intensive international warfare.

Can one make rigorous statements about the geopolitical circumstances that affect revolutions in progress, and that are in turn affected by them? Revolutionary outbreaks do seem to make wars more likely because domestic conflicts tend to spill over to involve foreign partners, and because revolutions create perceived threats and opportunities for other states. Beyond this, however, no glib generalizations are possible; for example, more sweeping revolutions do not automatically generate greater wars or stronger efforts at foreign intervention. As we are about to see, the geopolitical contexts of social revolutions in the modern world have varied greatly; so have the intersections of domestic state-building struggles with international threats or conflicts. At this point in the development of knowledge about these matters, the best way to proceed is through exploratory analyses and comparisons of a wide range of historical cases.

Social Revolutions and War-Making in France, Russia, and China

The word "revolution" did not take on its modern connotation of a fundamental sociopolitical change accompanied by violent upheavals from below until the French Revolution of the late 18th century.[6] This etymological fact appropriately signals the reality that the French Revolution (unlike the English, Dutch, and American) was a *social* revolution, in which class-based revolts from below, especially peasant revolts against landlords, propelled sudden transformations in the class structure along with permanently centralizing changes in the structures of state power. In *States and Social Revolutions*, I group the French Revolution for comparative analysis with the Russian Revolution from 1917 to the 1930s and with the Chinese Revolution from 1911 to the 1960s. The French Revolution, I argue, was neither primarily "bourgeois" in the Marxist sense nor "liberal" in the modernization sense. Nor was the Russian Revolution "proletarian" in the Marxist sense. Rather, the French, Russian, and Chinese revolutions, despite important variations, displayed striking similarities of context, cause, process, and outcomes.

All three classic social revolutions occurred in large, previously independent, predominantly agrarian monarchical states that found themselves pressured militarily by economically more developed competitors on the international scene. Social revolutions were sufficiently caused when (a) the centralized, semi-bureaucratic administrative and military organizations of the old regimes disintegrated due to combinations of international pressures and disputes between monarchs and landed commercial upper classes, and (b) widespread peasant revolts took place against landlords. After more or less protracted struggles by political forces trying to consolidate new state organizations, all three revolutions resulted in more centralized and mass-mobilizing national states, more powerful in relation to all domestic social groups, and also more powerful then the prerevolutionary regimes had been in relation to foreign competitors. In particular, all three social revolutions markedly raised their nations' capacities to wage humanly costly wars.[7]

The differences in the outcomes and accomplishments of the French, Russian, and Chinese revolutions are not well explained by referring, as a Marxist analyst would do, to the greater role of bourgeois class forces in the French case or to the unique contributions of proletarian revolts to the urban struggles of 1917 in Russia. Nor can one explain the different outcomes, as the modernization theorists do, by suggesting that the milder, less violent, and less thoroughgoing the revolutionary conflicts and changes, and the briefer the rule of an ideological vanguard, the more efficient and liberal-democratic the revolutionary outcome. None of these revolutions had a liberal-democratic outcome, and none of them resulted in a socialist democracy. Instead, the differences in the essentially mass-mobilizing and authoritarian outcomes and accomplishments of the French, Russian, and Chinese revolutions are in large part attributable to the international geopolitical contexts in which the conflicts of these revolutions played themselves out. They are also attributable to the political relationships established, during and immediately after the revolutionary interregnums, between state-building leaderships and rebellious lower classes. One feature that these three social revolutions have in common is that all of them enhanced national capacities to wage humanly costly foreign wars.

The French Revolution has typically been characterized as a modernizing liberal-democratic revolution or as a bourgeois, capitalist revolution. In terms of economics, it is difficult if not impossible to show that the French Revolution was necessary for the "economic modernization" or "capitalist development" of France: the absolutist old regime had been facilitating commercialization and petty industry just as much as postrevolutionary regimes did.[8] Politically, moreover, analysts tend to forget that the end result of the French Revolution was not any form of liberalism, but Napoleon's nationalist dictatorship, which left the enduring legacy of a highly centralized and bureaucratic French state with a recurrent tendency to seek national glory through military exploits.

The political phases of the French Revolution from 1789 through 1800 certainly included attempts to institutionalize civil liberties and electoral democracy, as well as the important legalization of undivided private property rights for peasants and bourgeois alike. Moreover, the fact that the French Revolution created a private-propertied society rather than a party-state that aspired to manage the national economy directly left open space for the eventual emergence of liberal-democratic political arrangements in France. At the time of the Revolution itself, however, democratization was more emphatically and enduringly furthered through "careers open to talent" in the military officer corps, through mass military conscription, and through the more efficient pressing of the state's fiscal demands on all citizens.

From a European continental perspective, the most striking and consequential accomplishment of the French Revolution was its ability to launch highly mobile armies of motivated citizen-soldiers, coordinated with enhanced deployment of artillery forces. The Jacobins from 1792 to 1794 began the process of amalgamating political commissioners and *sans-culotte* militias with the remnants of the royal standing armies.[9] Even though they did not find a way to stabilize their "Republic of Virtue," the Montagnard Jacobins fended off the most pressing domestic and international counterrevolutionary threats. Yet their fall was not the end of military mass-mobilization in France. Napoleon consolidated a conservative bureaucratic regime and came to terms with private property holders (including the peasant smallholders) and with the Church (including the local priests so influential with the peasantry). Then he expanded the process of French military mobilization, deploying citizen armies of an unprecedented size and a capacity for rapid maneuver.[10] The enhanced popular political participation and the messianic sense of French nationalism and democratic mission unleashed by the Revolution were thus directed outward. Before their eventual exhaustion in the unconquerable vastness of Russia, French citizen armies redrew the political map of modern Europe in irreversible ways and inspired the emergence of other European nationalisms in response.

Russia and China both experienced thoroughgoing social revolutionary transformations that resulted in the rule of communist-directed party-states. These social revolutions occurred under Leninist party leaderships in the modern industrial era, when the model of a state-managed economy was available; and both occurred in countries more hard-pressed geopolitically than late 18th-cetury France had been. The authoritarian and mass-mobilizing energies of the immediate postrevolutionary regimes, both in Soviet Russia and Communist China, were mainly directed not to *imperial* military conquests as in France, but to the promotion of national economic development, which was deemed to be the key to national independence in a world dominated by major industrial powers. Even so, in due course both of the new regimes demonstrated greatly enhanced capacities (compared to the prerevolutionary era) for successfully waging international war.

From the modernization perspective, the Russian and the Chinese revolutions were tyrannical and antidemocratic: they were more violent and transformative than the French Revolution, and ideological vanguards stayed in power both in Russia and in China. (By contrast, the Montagnard perpetrators of the Terror fell from power in France.) The Soviet regime, however, through the Stalinist "revolution from above," became more coercive and inegalitarian than did the Chinese Communist regime after 1949. Modernization theory cannot explain the contrasts between the Russian and Chinese new regimes. The civil war interregnum of the Chinese Revolution, stretching from 1911 to 1949, was much more protracted than the brief Russian revolutionary civil war of 1917-1921; and in practice, the Soviet regime probably built directly upon more structures and policies from Russia's tsarist past than the Chinese Communist regime did on China's Confucian-imperial past. Nor do the contrasting revolutionary outcomes make sense from a Marxian perspective: the Russian Revolution was politically based on the urban industrial proletariat, and thus should have resulted in practices closer to socialist ideals than the peasant-based Chinese Revolution.

The somewhat less murderous and less authoritarian features of the Chinese Communist state after 1949—at least from the point of view of local peasant communities—can be attributed to the guerrilla mode by which the Chinese Communist Party came to power. The party could not achieve national state power directly in the cities; instead, it found itself faced with the necessity of waging rural guerrilla warfare against both the Japanese invaders and its Kuomintang competitors for domestic political control. Nationalist appeals helped the Chinese communists in the early 1940s to attract educated middle-class citizens to their cause. Attention to the pressing material and self-defense needs of the peasantry in North China also allowed the communists to gain sufficient access to the villages to reorganize poor and middle-class peasants into associations that would support the Red Armies economically and militarily.[11]

After 1949, the Chinese communists were able, by building upon their preexisting political relations with much of the peasantry, to carry out agricultural collectivization with less brutality than the Bolsheviks.[12] Simultaneously, the relatively favorable geopolitical context of postrevolutionary China, situated in a world of nuclear superpower balance between the Soviet Union and the United States, allowed the Chinese communists to place less emphasis upon creating a heavy industrial capacity for mechanized military forces than they might otherwise have done. Their limited resources sufficed, however, to establish an independent Chinese nuclear capacity, symbol of major-power status in the post-World War II era.[13]

Communist China was able to pursue economic development policies that stressed light industries and rural development as well as some heavy industries. Meanwhile, the party could also infuse peasant-based, guerrilla-style military practices inherited from the revolutionary civil war into standing forces that could intervene effectively in the Korean War and make limited forays against India and Vietnam. As Jonathan Adelman has argued, performance of the People's Liberation Army in the Korean War battles of 1950–51 was "simply outstanding" compared to the "disastrous" Kuomintang military performance against the Japanese in the 1930s and 1940s.[14] The Revolution, Adelman concludes, had "created a whole new Chinese army." [15]

By contrast, the Soviet regime consolidated under Stalin's auspices took a much more brutal stance toward the peasant majority. Essentially, it substituted an autocratic dictatorship for a mass-mobilizing revolutionary regime. The Bolsheviks originally claimed state power in 1917 through political and very limited military maneuverings in the cities and towns of Russia, and they initially abstained from efforts at nationalist military mobilization. Most of the Russian populace acquiesced in their rule simply because of the exhaustion brought by Imperial Russia's defeat in World War I. The Russian revolutionary civil war of 1917 to 1921 was won by the deployment of urban guards and conventionally structured standing armies. Peasants were involved only as reluctantly coerced conscripts.[16] The one major foreign adventure of the fledgling Bolshevik regime, the invasion of Poland in 1920, ended in military defeat. In fact, the new Russian regime was fortunate that World War I had defeated or exhausted its major foreign opponents. For new-born Soviet Russia did not conform to the pattern of most other social revolutions: its central authorities were not in a good position to channel mass political participation into international warfare. Instead, they turned toward deepening internal warfare—against the peasantry and among-elites.

After 1921, the Bolshevik regime lacked organized political ties to the peasant villages, which had made their own autonomous local revolutions against landlords in 1917 and 1918. Stalin rose to power in the 1920s and 1930s by convincing many cadres in the Soviet party-state that Russian "socialism" would have to be built "in one country" that was isolated and threatened economically and militarily by Western industrial powers. The crash program of heavy industrialization was alleged to be necessary not only to build Marxian socialism, but also to prepare Russia for land-based military warfare. The peasantry became a domestic obstacle to Stalinist policies when it refused to provide economic surpluses at exploitative rates. Stalin's subsequent bureaucratic and terroristic drive to force peasant communities into centrally controlled agricultural collectives succeeded only at a terrible cost in human lives and agricultural productivity; the political reverberations in urban and official Russia helped to spur his purges of the Soviet elite in the 1930s. Stalinist consolidation of the new regime was thus initially a product of conflicts between an urban-based party-state and the peasantry, played out in a geopolitically threatening environment—though *not* in an environment in which direct national mobilization for international war was either necessary or possible.[17]

It is significant that Stalinism evolved into a *popular* mass-mobilizing regime as a result of the travails of World War II.[18] When the invading Nazis conducted themselves with great brutality against the Slav populations they conquered, Stalinist Russia finally had to mobilize for a total international war. Despite the setbacks of the first few months, the Soviet Union met the military challenges of World War II much more effectively than tsarist Russia had met the exigencies of World War I.[19] The Soviet people and armed forces fought back with considerable efficiency and amazing zeal in the face of terrible casualties. For the first time since 1917, Soviet rulers were able to use Russian nationalism to bolster their leadership. Stalin did not hesitate to revive many symbols of Russian national identity from prerevolutionary times, and he also restored prerogatives of rank and expertise in the military.[20] It is therefore not surprising that, when World War II ended in victory for the U.S.S.R. and the Allies, the Soviet rulers' domestic legitimacy—as well as the country's global great-power status—had been enhanced significantly.

Social Revolutions in Dependent Countries: Geopolitical Contexts and the Possibilities for Militarization

In the classic social revolutions of France, Russia, and China, long-established monarchical states were transformed into mass-mobilizing national regimes; most other social revolutions in the modern era, however, have occurred in smaller, dependent countries.[21] In some, such as Vietnam and the Portuguese colonies of Africa, which had been colonized by foreign imperial powers, social-revolutionary transformations were part of the process of national liberation from colonialism. In others, such as Cuba, Mexico, Iran, and Nicaragua, neopatrimonial dictatorships were caught in webs of great-power rivalries within the capitalist world economy and the global geopolitical system. Social revolutions in these countries have forged stronger states that are markedly more nationalist and mass-incorporating than the previous regimes and other countries in their respective regions. Still, the new regimes have remained minor powers on the world scene.

With the exception of the Iranian Revolution of 1977–1979, which was primarily carried out through urban demonstrations and strikes, all third-world social revolutions have depended on at least a modicum of peasant support for their success. In most instances, both peasants and city dwellers were mobilized for guerrilla warfare by nationalist revolutionary elites; only in the Mexican and Bolivian revolutions were peasant communities able to rebel on their own as did the French and Russian peasant communities.[22] Most third-world social revolutions have been played out as military struggles among leaderships contending to create or redefine the missions of national states. And these revolutions have happened in settings so penetrated by foreign influences—economic, military, and cultural—that social-revolutionary transformations have been as much about the definition of autonomous identities on the international scene as they have been about the forging of new political ties between indigenous revolutionaries and their mass constituents.

Consequently, the various international contexts in which third-world revolutions have occurred become crucial in conditioning the new regimes that have emerged from them. One basic aspect of the international situation is the relationship between a country undergoing revolution and the great powers, whatever they may be in a given phase of world history. Military, economic, and cultural aspects of such relations all need to be considered in our analysis. The regional context of each revolution also matters: What have been the possibilities for military conflicts with immediate neighbors? Have revolutionized third-world nations faced invasions by third-world neighbors, or have they been able to invade their neighbors without automatically involving great powers in the conflict? As I will illustrate in the remainder of this section, attention to international contexts can help us to explain at least as much about the structures and orientations of social-revolutionary new regimes in the third world as analyses of their class basis or propositions about the inherent logic of modernization and the violence and disruptiveness of various revolutions.

Social Revolutions in the Shadow of a Great Power

A great power can use actual or threatenend military intervention to prevent revolutionary transformations near its borders, as the Soviet Union has done in postwar Eastern Europe and as the United States used to do in Central America. Short of that, major political transformations of any kind that proceed in a great power's sphere of military dominance are invariably profoundly influenced by possibilities for rebellion or accommodation. Throughout the 20th century, social revolutions in Central and Latin America, if they happened at all, have been affected by the actions and inactions of the United States as the hegemonic power in the hemisphere. These revolutions have also been affected by the global power balances of their day. The cases of Mexico, Cuba, Bolivia, and the still-unfolding revolution in Nicaragua suggest a number of ways in which the great powers have influenced the shape of the new regimes that emerged from social-revolutionary interregnums.

In one sense, the most "benign" example of U.S. influence is demonstrated in relation to Mexico: the social revolution there was originally allowed to proceed, and was eventually consolidated into a regime that is a unique hybrid between a Western-style electoral democracy and a single-party authoritarian regime.[23] Still, we should note that unlike most other social-revolutionary regimes in the modern world, that of Mexico has never been able to engage in mass mobilization for international warfare. Nationalist self-assertion has been restricted to state-led economic development, particularly in periods such as the 1930s and 1940s, when the United States was distracted by larger domestic or world crises. Popular political participation has been managed by a corporatist, patronage-oriented party-state that preserves order in economically inefficient ways.

Originally, the anti-imperialist thrust of the Mexican Revolution was directed primarily against the European powers that were heavily involved in the economic and military affairs of the prerevolutionary regime of Porfirio Díaz; yet relations with the United States increasingly figured in successive phases of the revolution.[24] The Mexican Revolution could not have broken out at all in 1910–1911 had not the northern forces opposed to Porfirio Díaz been able to move back and forth across the U.S. border, counting on tacit American support in an era when the European great powers were the prime targets of Mexican nationalists. In addition, if the United States had been able and willing to launch sustained antirevolutionary interventions, the Revolution could not have continued after the defeats of Francisco Madero and General Victoriano Huerta made it potentially socially radical. Some scattered U.S. interventions were launched, but they were so minor that their only consequence was to provoke Mexican resentment. World War I and the presidency of Woodrow Wilson brought these American counterrevolutionary efforts to an end and gave the Mexicans space to begin the process of consolidating a new regime under populist and nationalist auspices. During the 1930s and World War II, U.S. abstention from unusual levels of meddling in Mexican affairs was again important in allowing Lazaro Cárdenas to complete construction of a populist, single-party "democracy" with sufficient nationalist clout to expropriate U.S. oil companies.[25]

Due to the basic geopolitical context, there was never any question of a new regime devoted to mass mobilization for military purposes at any point during the Mexican Revolution. Full-scale war with the United States would obviously have been fatal to any revolutionary leadership, and attempts to export revolution to the south would probably have provoked the ire of the northern colossus. Given some breathing space by the United States, Mexican revolutionary nationalists chose instead to ritualize mass mobilization into the subordinate incorporation of peasant communes and workers' unions into the ruling Institutional Revolutionary Party. They produced what is perhaps the most nonmartial nationalist regime ever to emerge from a social-revolutionary transformation in the modern world. They also produced a patronage-oriented party-state that has become steadily more economically inefficient over the years, requiring a constant flow of graft to buy off elite factions and to coopt popular leaders.[26]

The other major social revolution right on America's doorstep, the Cuban Revolution of 1959, culminated in a new regime remarkably adept at mobilizing human resources for military adventures across the globe. The failure of the United States to prevent or overthrow Fidel Castro's triumph over the Batista dictatorship helped to account for this outcome. But the global superpower rivalry of the United States and the Soviet Union was also a crucial ingredient, for Soviet willingness to protect and bankroll the new regime gave Cuban "anti-imperialists" a leverage against the United States that would have been unimaginable to the earlier Mexican revolutionaries.

Once established in power, Castro could assert Cuban national autonomy against the overwhelming U.S. economic and cultural presence. Having done so, he could then protect his rule from U.S.-sponsored overthrow only by allying himself domestically with the Cuban Communist Party and internationally with the Soviet Union. Subsequently, Cuba has become economically and militarily so dependent on Moscow that it finds itself serving Soviet interests throughout the third world.[27] Cubans are trained and mobilized for foreign service both as military advisors and as educated civilian technicians, which is a way in which Castro can partially repay the Soviets. In addition, it is an opportunity for a small, dependent revolutionary nation to create enhanced mobility for trained citizens.[28] It also allows Cuba to exert considerable military and ideological influence on the world scene—an amazing feat for such a tiny country located only ninety miles from a hostile superpower.

The weakest and poorest southern neighbors of the United States to experience social revolutions have been Bolivia in 1952–1964 and Nicaragua since 1979. These two cases demonstrate opposite effects of U.S. determination to counter radical change in contexts where the Soviet Union could not or would not do as much as it did for Castro's Cuba.

* * *

In Nicaragua as in Cuba, U.S. authorities initially acquiesced in the overthrow of a corrupt and domestically weakened patrimonial dictator even though he had originally been installed under U.S. sponsorship. Then, again as in Cuba, a dialectic got underway between a revolutionary radicalization couched in anti-American rhetoric and increasing efforts by U.S. authorities to roll back or overthrow the revolution.[29] American counterrevolutionary efforts became more determined and sustained after Ronald Reagan was elected President in 1980. At first, they seemed to make some headway when economic shortages and domestic unrest in the face of an unpopular military draft tended to undercut the Sandinistas' legitimacy as leaders of a popular guerrilla movement against the Somoza regime. Because of domestic political constraints, however, the United States has been unable to invade Sandinista Nicaragua, having to rely instead on economic pressures and the financing of Nicaraguan counterrevolutionary fighters; but the latter have proved to be neither militarily efficient nor politically adept.

* * *

Militarized Third-World Revolutions under Communism and Islam

Far removed from the areas of the New World that are close to the United States, the Vietnamese and Iranian revolutions are two instances in which great-power rivalries, along with geographical distance, have made it possible for revolutionary regimes to take a stand against "American imperialism" without being overthrown by U.S. military intervention. What is more, Vietnam and Iran in the mid-20th century, like France in the late 18th, are examples of the awesome power of social-revolutionary regimes to wage humanly costly wars and to transform regional political patterns and international balances of power. Both revolutions demonstrate this, even though one is a "communist" revolution and the other "Islamic" and thus militantly anticommunist.

Analysts of agrarian class struggles have stressed that the Vietnamese Revolution was grounded in peasant support in both the northern and southern parts of the country.[30] But attempts to explain the overall logic of this revolution in terms of the social conditions of either the northern or the southern peasantry have inevitably missed the other main ingredient in the revolution's success. From the French colonial period on, educated Vietnamese found the Communist Party of Vietnam and the various movements associated with it to be the most effective and persistent instruments of resistance to foreign domination—first by the French colonialists, then by the Japanese occupiers during World War II, then by the returning French, and finally by the United States. The Vietnamese communists were their country's most uncompromising nationalists; they were willing, when conditions required or allowed, to wage guerrilla warfare through peasant mobilization.[31] By contrast, foreign occupiers and their Vietnamese collaborators worked from the cities outward, especially in the south, which had been the center of French colonial control.

Geopolitically, the Vietnamese communists benefited from the distance the French and American forces had to traverse to confront them, from the availability of sanctuaries in Laos and Cambodia, and (after the partial victory in the north) from their ability to receive supplies through China from both China and the Soviet Union. Had the United States been able or willing to use nuclear weapons in the Southeast Asian theatre, or had the Soviet Union and China not temporarily cooperated to help the Vietnamese, it seems doubtful that the Vietnamese Revolution could have reunified the country, notwithstanding the extraordinary willingness of northern and many southern Vietnamese to die fighting the U.S. forces.

Since the defeat of the United States in southern Vietnam, the Hanoi regime has faced difficult economic conditions; it seems to tackle such problems with much less efficiency and zeal than it tackled the anti-imperialist wars from the 1940s to the 1970s. As the unquestionably dominant military power in its region, the Vietnamese state has invaded and occupied Cambodia and engaged in occasional battles with a now-hostile China. Vietnam continues to rely on Soviet help to counterbalance U.S. hostility and the armed power of China. But, what is perhaps more important now that Vietnam is indeed "the Prussia of Southeast Asia," the Vietnamese communists still find it possible to legitimate their leadership through never-ending mobilization of their people for national military efforts. The Chinese threat, Cambodian resistance, and American opposition to the normalization of Vietnam's gains have provided just the kind of internationally threatening context that the Vietnamese communists, after so many years of warfare, find most congenial to their domestic political style.

The militant Shi'a clerics of Iran, who seem to be so different from the Vietnamese communists, are another mass-mobilizing and state-building revolutionary elite that has been helped immensely by a facilitating geopolitical context and protracted international warfare.[32] The Iranian Revolution is still in progress, and it is therefore too early to characterize its outcome in any definitive way. Nevertheless, the process of this remarkable upheaval has already dramatized the appropriateness of viewing contemporary social revolutions as promoting ideologically reconstructed national identities involving the sudden incorporation of formerly excluded popular groups into state-directed projects. Moreover, this revolution shows that mass mobilization for war, aggressive as well as defensive, is an especially congenial state-directed project for revolutionary leaders.

From both Marxian and modernization perspectives, the Iranian Revolution, especially the consolidation of state power by the Ayatollah Khomeini and the Islamic Republican Party since the overthrow of the Shah in 1979, has been a puzzle. Marxist analysts have been reluctant to call this a "social revolution" because class conflicts and transformations of economic property rights have not defined the main terms of struggle or the patterns of sociopolitical change. Modernization theorists, meanwhile, have been surprised at the capacity of the untrained and traditionist Islamic clerics to consolidate their rule; these theorists expected that, after a brief "terror," such noncommunist and ideologically fanatical leaders would give way to technically trained bureaucrats if not to liberal-democratic politicians.

In fact, from 1979 through 1982, the Islamic Republican Party in Iran systematically reconstructed state organizations to embody direct controls by Shi'a clerics. Step by step, all other leading political forces—liberal Westernizers, the Mujhahedeen, the Tudeh Party, and technocrats and professional military officers loyal to Aholhassan Bani-Sadr—were eliminated from what had once been the all-encompassing revolutionary alliance. The party did this by deploying and combining the classic ingredients for successful revolutionary state building.

For one thing, the Islamic Republican clerics shared a commitment to a political ideology that gave them unlimited warrant to rule exclusively in the name of all the Shi'a believers. Khomeini had developed a militant-traditionalist reading of Shi'a beliefs, calling on the clerics themselves to govern in place of secular Iranian rulers corrupted by Western cultural imperialism. The Islamic Republican Constitution for Iran officially enshrined such clerical supervision over all affairs of state; concrete political organizations, including the Islamic Republican Party that dominated the Majlis (parliament), also embodied this orientation.

Moreover, the Islamic Republican clerics and their devout nonclerical associates did not hesitate to organize, mobilize, and manipulate mass popular support, including the unemployed as well as workers and lower-middle-class people in Teheran and other cities. Islamic judges supervised neighborhood surveillance bodies; Islamic militants organized revolutionary guards for police and military duties; and consumer rations and welfare benefits for the needy were dispensed through neighborhood mosques. Iranians never before involved in national political life became directly energized through such organization; those with doubts were subjected to peer controls as well as to elite supervision. With these means of mass-based power at their disposal, the Islamic Republican Party had little trouble eliminating liberal and leftist competitors from public political life.

Right after the Shah's overthrow, ideologically committed Islamic cadres, backed by mass organizations, reconstructed major public institutions in Iranian national life. Not only special committees of revolutionary justice, but also traditionally educated clerical judges took over the criminal and civil legal system, reorienting it to procedural and substantive norms in line with their understanding of the Koran. The next targets were Western-oriented cultural institutions, particularly schools and universities. These were first closed and then purged, turned into bastions of Islamic education and revolutionary propaganda. Civil state bureaucracies were similarly purged and transformed; and so, in due course, were the remnants of the Shah's military forces, particularly the army.

The kinds of transformations I have just summarized took place not automatically but through hard-fought political, bureaucratic, and street struggles that pitted other elites—alternative would-be consolidators of the Iranian Revolution—against the militant clerics and their supporters. As these struggles within Iran unfolded, the emerging clerical authoritarianism repeatedly benefited from international conditions and happenings that allowed them to deploy their ideological and organizational resources to maximum advantage.

Overall, the version of the Iranian Revolution that the clerics sought to institutionalize has been virulently anti-Western, and defined especially in opposition to "U.S. imperialism." Opposition to Soviet imperialism has also been a consistent theme. Fortunately for the clerics, the fiscal basis of the Iranian state after as well as before the revolution lies in the export of oil, for which an international market has continued to exist.[33] A geopolitical given is coterminous with this economic given: neither the Soviet Union nor the United States has been in a position to intervene militarily against the Iranian Revolution, in part because Iran lies between their two spheres of direct control. It is also fortunate for Iran's radical clerics that the United States has acted in ways that were symbolically provocative while not being materially or militarily powerful enough to control events in Iran. The admission of the deposed Shah to the United States, the subsequent seizure of the American embassy by pro-Khomeini youths, and the ensuing unsuccessful efforts of the U.S. authorities to free the American hostages, all created an excellent political matrix within Iran for the clerics to discredit as pro-American a whole series of their secular competitors for state power.

* * *

In the end, the Iranian Revolution will probably settle down into some sort of Islamic-nationalist authoritarianism that coexists, however uneasily, with its neighbors. The Iranian armies are unlikely to overrun the Middle East the way the French revolutionary armies temporarily overran much of continental Europe. Iran is still a third-world nation; on the global scene, it faces superpowers who can inhibit its wildest aspirations. Nevertheless, Iran's military accomplishments have already disproved the expectation of modernization theorists that a regime run by anti-Western Shi'a clerics would not be viable in the contemporary world. By consolidating and reconstructing state power through ideologically coordinated mass mobilization, and by directing popular zeal against a faraway superpower and channeling it into a war against a less populous neighboring state, the Islamic Republicans of Iran have proven once again that social revolutions are less about class struggles or "modernization" than about state building and the forging of newly assertive national identities in a modern world that remains culturally pluralistic even as it inexorably becomes economically more interdependent.

Conclusion

If, as Franz Borkenau argued, students of revolutions must attend to "changes in the state order," much remains to be understood about the kinds of political transformation that revolutions have accomplished and the activities to which their enhanced state capacities have been directed with varying degrees of success. In this essay, which is suggestive rather than conclusive, I have speculated that many social-revolutionary regimes have excelled at channeling enhanced popular participation into protracted international warfare. Because of the ways revolutionary leaders mobilize popular support in the course of struggles for state power, the emerging regimes can tackle mobilization for war better than any other task, including the promotion of national economic development. The full realization of this revolutionary potential for building strong states depends on threatening but not overwhelming geopolitical circumstances.

* * *

Notes

1. Borkenau, "State and Revolution in the Paris Commune, the Russian Revolution, and the Spanish Civil War," *Sociological Review* 29 (January 1937), 41–75, at 41.

2. Huntington, *Political Order in Changing Societies* (New Haven: Yale University Press, 1968), 266. Chapter 5 in its entirety is also relevant.
3. See Theda Skocpol, *States and Social Revolutions: A Comparative Analysis of France, Russia, and China* (New York and Cambridge: Cambridge University Press, 1979), 161.
4. This characterization comes from Alvin Gouldner, "Stalinism: A Study of Internal Colonialism," in *Political Power and Social Theory* (research annual edited by Maurice Zeitlin) 1 (1980) (Greenwich, CT: JAI Press), 209–59.
5. Eisenstadt, *Revolution and the Transformation of Societies* (New York: Free Press, 1978); Walzer, "A Theory of Revolution," *Marxist Perspectives*, No. 5 (Spring 1979), 30–44.
6. Karl Griewank, "The Emergence of the Concept of Revolution," in Bruce Mazlish, Arthur D. Kaledin, and David B. Ralston, eds., *Revolution: A Reader* (New York: Macmillan, 1971), 13–17.
7. Thorough elaboration and documentation of this conclusion appears in Jonathan R. Adelman, *Revolution, Armies, and War: A Political History* (Boulder, CO: Lynne Rienner Publishers, 1985), chaps. 3–11.
8. For fuller discussion and references, see Skocpol (fn. 3), 174–77.
9. S. F. Scott, "The Regeneration of the Line Army During the French Revolution," *Journal of Modern History* 42 (September 1970), 307–30.
10. Adelman (fn. 7), chap. 3; Theodore Ropp, *War in the Modern World*, rev. ed. (New York: Collier Books, 1962), chap. 4; Alfred Vagts, *A History of Militarism*, rev. ed. (New York: Free Press, 1959), chap. 4; John Ellis, *Armies in Revolution* (New York: Oxford University Press, 1974), chap. 4.
11. Mark Selden, *The Yenan Way in Revolutionary China* (Cambridge: Harvard University Press, 1971): Ellis (fn. 10), chap. 4.
12. Thomas P. Bernstein, "Leadership and Mass Mobilisation in the Soviet and Chinese Collectivisation Campaigns of 1929–30 and 1955–56: A Comparison," *China Quarterly* 31 (July–September 1967), 1–47. Bernstein characterizes Chinese collectivization techniques as "persuasive" in contrast to the more "coercive" Soviet practices. Subsequent to collectivization, however, the Chinese "Great Leap Forward" did devolve into considerable coercion by cadres against peasants.
13. Franz Schurmann, *The Logic of World Power* (New York: Pantheon, 1974), part II.
14. Adelman (fn. 7), 139.
15. *Ibid.*, 144.
16. Ellis (fn. 10), chap. 5.
17. Background for this analysis of Stalin's "revolution from above" comes especially from Bernstein (fn. 12); Stephen F. Cohen, *Bukharin and the Bolshevik Revolution* (New York: Knopf, 1973); and Moshe Lewin, *Russian Peasants and Soviet Power*, trans. Irene Nove (Evanston: Northwestern University Press, 1968).
18. An insightful discussion of the different phases of nationalist mobilization in Russia and China appears in William G. Rosenberg and Marilyn Young, *Transforming Russia and China: Revolutionary Struggle in the Twentieth Century* (New York: Oxford University Press, 1982).
19. Adelman (fn. 7), chaps. 4–7.
20. Alf Edeen, "The Civil Service: Its Composition and Status," in Cyril E. Black, ed., *The Transformation of Russian Society* (Cambridge: Harvard University Press, 1960), 274–91; see esp, 286–87.
21. For useful overviews, see Eric R. Wolf, *Peasant Wars of the Twentieth Century* (New York: Harper & Row, 1969), chaps. 1, 4–6; John Dunn, *Modern Revolutions* (Cambridge: Cambridge University Press, 1972), chaps. 2, 4–8.
22. Alternative modes of peasant involvement in social revolutions are analyzed in Theda Skocpol, "What Makes Peasants Revolutionary?" *Comparative Politics* 14 (April 1982), 351–75.
23. Huntington (fn. 2), 315–24, discusses the postrevolutionary Mexican regime. See also Nora Hamilton, *The Limits of State Autonomy: Post-Revolutionary Mexico* (Princeton: Princeton University Press, 1982), and Roger D. Hansen, *The Politics of Mexican Development* (Baltimore: The Johns Hopkins University Press, 1971).

24. On the Mexican Revolution and its relations with foreign states, see Wolf (fn. 21), chap. 1; Dunn (fn. 21), chap. 2; Friedrich Katz, *The Secret War in Mexico: Europe, the United States, and the Mexican Revolution* (Chicago: University of Chicago Press, 1981); Walter Goldfrank, "World System, State Structure, and the Onset of the Mexican Revolution," *Politics and Society* 5 (No. 4, 1975), 417–39; and John Womack, Jr., *Zapata and the Mexican Revolution* (New York: Alfred A. Knopf, 1969).
25. Hamilton (fn. 23), chaps. 4–7.
26. Hansen (fn. 23); Susan Eckstein, *The Poverty of Revolution: The State and the Urban Poor in Mexico* (Princeton: Princeton University Press, 1977).
27. Kosmos Tsokhas, "The Political Economy of Cuban Dependence on the Soviet Union," *Theory and Society* 9 (March 1980), 319–62.
28. Susan Eckstein, "Structural and Ideological Bases of Cuba's Overseas Programs," *Politics and Society* 11 (No. 1) 1982, 95–121.
29. My account of Nicaragua draws upon Walter LaFeber, *Inevitable Revolutions: The United States in Central America* (New York: W. W. Norton, 1983); Shirley Christian, *Nicaragua: Revolution in the Family* (New York: Vintage Books, 1986); and Lawrence Shaeter, "Nicaraguan-United States Bilateral Relations: The Problems within Revolution and Reconstruction" (Senior honors thesis, University of Chicago, 1984).
30. See, for instance, Wolf (fn. 21), chap. 4. For a discussion of alternative perspectives on the Vietnamese peasantry, see Skocpol (fn. 22).
31. Dunn (fn. 21), chap. 5; Huynh Kim Khanh, *Vietnamese Communism, 1925–1945* (Ithaca. NY: Cornell University Press, 1982); John T. McAlister, Jr., *Vietnam: The Origins of Revolution* (New York; Knopf, 1969).
32. The following discussion draws on Theda Skocpol, "Rentier State and Shi'a Islam in the Iranian Revolution," *Theory and Society* 11 (No. 3, 1982), 265–84. It also relies heavily on R. K. Ramazani, *Revolutionary Iran: Challenge and Response in the Middle East* (Baltimore: The Johns Hopkins University Press, 1986), and Shaul Bakhash, *The Reign of the Ayatollahs: Iran and the Islamic Revolution* (New York: Basic Books), 1984.
33. Ramzani (fn. 33), chaps. 13–14; Shaul Bakhash, *The Politics of Oil and Revolution in Iran* (Washington, DC: Staff Paper, The Brookings Institution, 1982); and "Oil Revenue Lifts Iranian Economy," *The New York Times*, Friday, July 9, 1982, pp. D1, D4.

12.3

THE CLASH OF CIVILIZATIONS?

Samuel P. Huntington

This controversial essay by Samuel Huntington, who gained prominence as a scholar in the 1960s and advised presidents Lyndon B. Johnson and Jimmy Carter before taking on his current role as a professor at Harvard University, was expanded into a book of the same name in 1996. In this essay, Huntington proposes that culturally defined civilizations will to a large extent displace nation-states as the primary basis of conflict. As part of the renaissance of culture, religion will play an increasingly important role in the less modern parts of the world, creating a sharp contrast to the diminishing salience of religiosity in the West. Although not developed in this essay, in the book Huntington raises the question of whether the West, with its weaker commitment to religious heritage, will be able to withstand the assault of other intensely and devoutly religious states. Especially threatening in this regard is the ongoing clash between the Muslim civilization and other major civilizations that Huntington presciently claims will be the basis of "fault-line" conflict for the foreseeable future. He further sees an ongoing struggle with non-Western civilizations (especially militant Islamist civilizations) that resist the imposition of such Western values as gender equality, the separation of religion and state, and democracy. Students should consider whether Huntington is mistaken in characterizing Islam as a monolithic entity with nearly all of its members militantly hostile to the West and its values.

I. The Next Pattern of Conflict

World politics is entering a new phase, and intellectuals have not hesitated to proliferate visions of what it will be—the end of history, the return of traditional rivalries between nation states, and the decline of the nation state from the conflicting pulls of tribalism and globalism, among others. Each of these visions catches aspects of the emerging reality. Yet they all miss a crucial, indeed a central, aspect of what global politics is likely to be in the coming years.

It is my hypothesis that the fundamental source of conflict in this new world will not be primarily ideological or primarily economic. The great divisions among humankind and the dominating source of conflict will be cultural. Nation states will remain the most powerful actors in world affairs, but the

---

Samuel P. Huntington, "The Clash of Civilizations?" *Foreign Affairs* 72, no. 3 (Summer 1993): 22–49.

principal conflicts of global politics will occur between nations and groups of different civilizations. The clash of civilizations will be the battle lines of the future.

Conflict between civilizations will be the latest phase of the evolution of conflict in the modern world. For a century and a half after the emergence of the modern international system of the Peace of Westphalia, the conflicts of the Western world were largely among princes—emperors, absolute monarchs and constitutional monarchs attempting to expand their bureaucracies, their armies, their mercantilist economic strength and, most important, the territory they ruled. In the process they created nation states, and beginning with the French Revolution the principal lines of conflict were between nations rather than princes. In 1793, as R. R. Palmer put it, "The wars of kings were over; the wars of peoples had begun." This nineteenth-century pattern lasted until the end of World War I. Then, as a result of the Russian Revolution and the reaction against it, the conflict of nations yielded to the conflict of ideologies, first among communism, fascism–Nazism and liberal democracy, and then between communism and liberal democracy. During the Cold War, this latter conflict became embodied in the struggle between the two superpowers, neither of which was a nation state in the classical European sense and each of which defined its identity in terms of ideology.

These conflicts between princes, nation states and ideologies were primarily conflicts within Western civilization, "Western civil wars," as William Lind has labeled them. This was as true of the Cold War as it was of the world wars and the earlier wars of the seventeenth, eighteenth and nineteenth centuries. With the end of the Cold War, international politics moves out of its Western phase, and its center-piece becomes the interaction between the West and non-Western civilizations and among non-Western civilizations. In the politics of civilizations, the people and governments of non-Western civilizations no longer remain the objects of history as targets of Western colonialism but join the West as movers and shapers of history.

II. The Nature of Civilizations

During the cold war the world was divided into the First, Second and Third Worlds. Those divisions are no longer relevant. It is far more meaningful now to group countries not in terms of their political or economic systems or in terms of their level of economic development but rather in terms of their culture and civilization.

What do we mean when we talk of a civilization? A civilization is a cultural entity. Villages, regions, ethnic groups, nationalities, religious groups, all have distinct cultures at different levels of cultural heterogeneity. The culture of a village in southern Italy may be different from that of a village in northern Italy, but both will share in a common Italian culture that distinguishes them from German villages. European communities, in turn, will share cultural features that distinguish them from Arab or Chinese communities. Arabs, Chinese and Westerners, however, are not part of any broader cultural entity. They constitute civilizations. A civilization is thus the highest cultural grouping of people and the broadest level of cultural identity people have short of that which distinguishes humans from other species. It is defined both by common objective elements, such as language, history, religion, customs, institutions, and by the subjective self-identification of people. People have levels of identity: a resident of Rome may define himself with varying degrees of intensity as a Roman, an Italian, a Catholic, a Christian, a European, a Westerner. The civilization to which he belongs is the broadest level of identification with which he intensely identifies. People can and do redefine their identities and, as a result, the composition and boundaries of civilizations change.

Civilizations may involve a large number of people, as with China ("a civilization pretending to be a state," as Lucian Pye put it), or a very small number of people, such as the Anglophone Caribbean. A civilization may include several nation states, as is the case with Western, Latin American and Arab civilizations, or only one, as is the case with Japanese civilization. Civilizations obviously blend and overlap, and may include subcivilizations. Western civilization has two major variants, European and North American, and Islam has its Arab, Turkic and Malay subdivisions. Civilizations are nonetheless meaningful entities, and while the lines between them are seldom sharp, they are real. Civilizations are dynamic; they rise and fall; they divide and merge. And, as any student of history knows, civilizations disappear and are buried in the sands of time.

Westerners tend to think of nation states as the principal actors in global affairs. They have been that, however, for only a few centuries. The broader reaches of human history have been the history of civilizations. In *A Study of History,* Arnold Toynbee identified 21 major civilizations; only six of them exist in the contemporary world.

III. Why Civilizations Will Clash

Civilization identity will be increasingly important in the future, and the world will be shaped in large measure by the interactions among seven or eight major civilizations. These include Western, Confucian, Japanese, Islamic, Hindu, Slavic-Orthodox, Latin American and possibly African civilization. The most important conflicts of the future will occur along the cultural fault lines separating these civilizations from one another.

Why will this be the case?

First, differences among civilizations are not only real; they are basic. Civilizations are differentiated from each other by history, language, culture, tradition and, most important, religion. The people of different civilizations have different views on the relations between God and man, the individual and the group, the citizen and the state, parents and children, husband and wife, as well as differing views of the relative importance of rights and responsibilities, liberty and authority, equality and hierarchy. These differences are the product of centuries. They will not soon disappear. They are far more fundamental than differences among political ideologies and political regimes. Differences do not necessarily mean conflict, and conflict does not necessarily mean violence. Over the centuries, however, differences among civilizations have generated the most prolonged and the most violent conflicts.

Second, the world is becoming a smaller place. The interactions between peoples of different civilizations are increasing; these increasing interactions intensify civilization consciousness and awareness of differences between civilizations and commonalities within civilizations. North African immigration to France generates hostility among Frenchmen and at the same time increased receptivity to immigration by "good" European Catholic Poles. Americans react far more negatively to Japanese investment than to larger investments from Canada and European countries. Similarly, as Donald Horowitz has pointed out, "An Ibo may be. . .an Owerri Ibo or an Onitsha Ibo in what was the Eastern region of Nigeria. In Lagos, he is simply an Ibo. In London, he is a Nigerian. In New York, he is an African." The interactions among peoples of different civilizations enhance the civilization-consciousness of people that, in turn, invigorates differences and animosities stretching or thought to stretch back deep into history.

Third, the processes of economic modernization and social change throughout the world are separating people from longstanding local identities. They also weaken the nation state as a source of identity. In much of the world religion has moved in to fill this gap, often in the form of movements that are labeled "fundamentalist." Such movements are found in Western Christianity, Judaism, Buddhism and Hinduism, as well as in Islam. In most countries and most religions the people active in fundamentalist movements are young, college-educated, middle-class technicians, professionals and business persons. The "unsecularization of the world," George Weigel has remarked, "is one of the dominant social factors of life in the late twentieth century." The revival of religion, "la revanche de Dieu," as Gilles Kepel labeled it, provides a basis for identity and commitment that transcends national boundaries and unites civilizations.

Fourth, the growth of civilization-consciousness is enhanced by the dual role of the West. On the one hand, the West is at a peak of power. At the same time, however, and perhaps as a result, a return to the roots phenomenon is occurring among non-Western civilizations. Increasingly one hears references to trends toward a turning inward and "Asianization" in Japan, the end of the Nehru legacy and the "Hinduization" of India, the failure of Western ideas of socialism and nationalism and hence "re-Islamization" of the Middle East, and now a debate over Westernization versus Russianization in Boris Yeltsin's country. A West at the peak of its power confronts non-Wests that increasingly have the desire, the will and the resources to shape the world in non-Western ways.

In the past, the elites of non-Western societies were usually the people who were most involved with the West, had been educated at Oxford, the Sorbonne or Sandhurst, and had absorbed Western attitudes and values. At the same time, the populace in non-Western countries often remained deeply imbued with the indigenous culture. Now, however, these relationships are being reversed. A de-Westernization and indigenization of elites is occurring in many non-Western countries at the same time that Western, usually American, cultures, styles and habits become more popular among the mass of the people.

Fifth, cultural characteristics and differences are less mutable and hence less easily compromised and resolved than political and economic ones. In the former Soviet Union, communists can become democrats, the rich can become poor and the poor rich, but Russians cannot become Estonians and Azeris cannot become Armenians. In class and ideological conflicts, the key question was "Which side are you on?" and people could and did choose sides and change sides. In conflicts between civilizations, the question is "What are you?" That is a given that cannot be changed. And as we know, from Bosnia to the Caucasus to the Sudan, the wrong answer to that question can mean a bullet in the head. Even more than ethnicity, religion discriminates sharply and exclusively among people. A person can be half-French and half-Arab and simultaneously even a citizen of two countries. It is more difficult to be half-Catholic and half-Muslim.

Finally, economic regionalism is increasing. The proportions of total trade that are intraregional rose between 1980 and 1989 from 51 percent to 59 percent in Europe, 33 percent to 37 percent in East Asia, and 32 percent to 36 percent in North America. The importance of regional economic blocs is likely to continue to increase in the future. On the one hand, successful economic regionalism will reinforce civilization-consciousness. On the other hand, economic regionalism may succeed only when it is rooted in a common civilization. The European Community rests on the shared foundation of European culture and Western Christianity. . .

Common culture, in contrast, is clearly facilitating the rapid expansion of the economic relations between the People's Republic of China and Hong Kong, Taiwan, Singapore and the overseas Chinese communities in other Asian countries. With the Cold War over, cultural commonalities increasingly overcome ideological differences, and mainland China and Taiwan move closer together. If cultural commonality is a prerequisite for economic integration, the principal East Asian economic bloc of the future is likely to be centered on China. This bloc is, in fact, already coming into existence. As Murray Weidenbaum has observed,

> Despite the current Japanese dominance of the region, the Chinese-based economy of Asia is rapidly emerging as a new epicenter for industry, commerce and finance. . .[1]

Culture and religion also form the basis of the Economic Cooperation Organization, which brings together ten non-Arab Muslim countries: Iran, Pakistan, Turkey, Azerbaijan, Kazakhstan, Kyrgyzstan, Turkmenistan, Tadjikistan, Uzbekistan and Afghanistan. One impetus to the revival and expansion of this organization, founded originally in the 1960s by Turkey, Pakistan and Iran, is the realization by the leaders of several of these countries that they had no chance of admission to the European Community. . .

As people define their identity in ethnic and religious terms, they are likely to see an "us" versus "them" relation existing between themselves and people of different ethnicity or religion. The end of ideologically defined states in Eastern Europe and the former Soviet Union permits traditional ethnic identities and animosities to come to the fore. Differences in culture and religion create differences over policy issues, ranging from human rights to immigration to trade and commerce to the environment. Geographical propinquity gives rise to conflicting territorial claims from Bosnia to Mindanao. Most important, the efforts of the West to promote its values of democracy and liberalism to universal values, to maintain its military predominance and to advance its economic interests engender countering responses from other civilizations. Decreasingly able to mobilize support and form coalitions on the basis of ideology, governments and groups will increasingly attempt to mobilize support by appealing to common religion and civilization identity.

The clash of civilizations thus occurs at two levels. At the micro-level, adjacent groups along the fault lines between civilizations struggle, often violently, over the control of territory and each other. At the macro-level, states from different civilizations compete for relative military and economic power, struggle over the control of international institutions and third parties, and competitively promote their particular political and religious values.

IV. The Fault Lines Between Civilizations

The fault lines between civilizations are replacing the political and ideological boundaries of the Cold War as the flash points for crisis and bloodshed. The Cold War began when the Iron Curtain divided Europe politically and ideologically. The Cold War ended with the end of the Iron Curtain. As the ideological division of Europe has disappeared, the cultural division of Europe between Western Christianity, on the one hand, and Orthodox Christianity and Islam, on the other, has reemerged. The most significant dividing line in Europe, as William Wallace has suggested, may well be the eastern boundary of Western Christianity in the year 1500. This line runs along what are now the boundaries between Finland and Russia and between the Baltic states and Russia, cuts through Belarus and Ukraine separating the more Catholic western Ukraine from Orthodox eastern Ukraine, swings westward separating Transylvania from the rest of Romania, and then goes through Yugoslavia almost exactly along the line now separating Croatia and Slovenia from the rest of Yugoslavia. In the Balkans this line, of course, coincides with the historic boundary between the Hapsburg and Ottoman empires. The peoples to the north and west of this line are Protestant or Catholic; they shared the common experiences of European history—feudalism, the Renaissance, the Reformation, the Enlightenment, the French Revolution, the Industrial Revolution; they are generally economically better off than the peoples to the east; and they may now look forward to increasing involvement in a common European economy and to the consolidation of democratic political systems. The peoples to the east and south of this line are Orthodox or Muslim; they historically belonged to the Ottoman or Tsarist empires and were only lightly touched by the shaping events in the rest of Europe; they are generally less advanced economically; they seem much less likely to develop stable democratic political systems. The Velvet Curtain of culture has replaced the Iron Curtain of ideology as the most significant dividing line in Europe. As the events in Yugoslavia show, it is not only a line of difference; it is also at times a line of bloody conflict.

Conflict along the fault line between Western and Islamic civilizations has been going on for 1,300 years. After the founding of Islam, the Arab and Moorish surge west and north only ended at Tours in 732. From the eleventh to the thirteenth century the Crusaders attempted with temporary success to bring Christianity and Christian rule to the Holy Land. From the fourteenth to the seventeenth century, the Ottoman Turks reversed the balance, extended their sway over the Middle East and the Balkans, captured Constantinople, and twice laid siege to Vienna. In the nineteenth and early twentieth centuries a[s] Ottoman power declined Britain, France, and Italy established Western control over most of North Africa and the Middle East.

After World War II, the West, in turn, began to retreat; the colonial empires disappeared; first Arab nationalism and then Islamic fundamentalism manifested themselves; the West became heavily dependent on the Persian Gulf countries for its energy; the oil-rich Muslim countries became money-rich and, when they wished to, weapons-rich. Several wars occurred between Arabs and Israel (created by the West). France fought a bloody and ruthless war in Algeria for most of the 1950s; British and French forces invaded Egypt in 1956; American forces returned to Lebanon, attacked Libya, and engaged in various military encounters with Iran; Arab and Islamic terrorists, supported by at least three Middle Eastern governments, employed the weapon of the weak and bombed Western planes and installations and seized Western hostages. This warfare between Arabs and the West culminated in 1990, when the United States sent a massive army to the Persian Gulf to defend some Arab countries against aggression by another. In its aftermath NATO planning is increasingly directed to potential threats and instability along its "southern tier."

This centuries-old military interaction between the West and Islam is unlikely to decline. It could become more virulent. The Gulf War left some Arabs feeling proud that Saddam Hussein had attacked Israel and stood up to the West. It also left many feeling humiliated and resentful of the West's military presence in the Persian Gulf, the West's overwhelming military dominance, and their apparent inability to shape their own destiny. Many Arab countries, in addition to the oil exporters, are reaching levels of economic and social development where autocratic forms of government become inappropriate and efforts to introduce democracy become stronger. Some openings in Arab political systems have already occurred. The principal beneficiaries of these openings have been Islamist movements. In the Arab world, in short, Western democracy strengthens anti-Western political forces. This may be a passing phenomenon, but it surely complicates relations between Islamic countries and the West.

Those relations are also complicated by demography. The spectacular population growth in Arab countries, particularly in North Africa, has led to increased migration to Western Europe. The movement within Western Europe toward minimizing internal boundaries has sharpened political sensitivities with respect to this development. In Italy, France and Germany, racism is increasingly open, and political reactions and violence against Arab and Turkish migrants have become more intense and more widespread since 1990.

On both sides the interaction between Islam and the West is seen as a clash of civilizations. The West's "next confrontation," observes M. J. Akbar, an Indian Muslim author, "is definitely going to come from the Muslim world. It is in the sweep of the Islamic nations from the Meghreb to Pakistan that the struggle for a new world order will begin." Bernard Lewis comes to a regular conclusion:

> We are facing a need and a movement far transcending the level of issues and policies and the governments that pursue them. This is no less than a clash of civilizations—the perhaps irrational but surely historic reaction of an ancient rival against our Judeo-Christian heritage, our secular present, and the worldwide expansion of both.[2]

Historically, the other great antagonistic interaction of Arab Islamic civilization has been with the pagan, animist, and now increasingly Christian black peoples to the south. In the past, this antagonism was epitomized in the image of Arab slave dealers and black slaves. It has been reflected in the on-going civil war in the Sudan between Arabs and blacks, the fighting in Chad between Libyan-supported insurgents and the government, the tensions between Orthodox Christians and Muslims in the Horn of Africa, and the political conflicts, recurring riots and communal violence between Muslims and Christians in Nigeria. The modernization of Africa and the spread of Christianity in Nigeria. . .are likely to enhance the probability of violence along this fault line. . .

On the northern border of Islam, conflict has increasingly erupted between Orthodox and Muslim peoples, including the carnage of Bosnia and Sarajevo, the simmering violence between Serb and Albanian, the tenuous relation between Bulgarians and their Turkish minority, the violence between Ossetians and Ingush, the unremitting slaughter of each other by Armenians and Azeris, the tense relations between Russians and Muslims in Central Asia, and the deployment of Russian troops to protect Russian interests in the Caucasus and Central Asia. Religion reinforces the revival of ethnic identities and restimulates Russian fears about the security of their southern borders. This concern is well captured by Archie Roosevelt:

> Much of Russian history concerns the struggle between Slavs and the Turkish peoples on their borders, which dates back to the foundation of the Russian state more than a thousand years ago. In the Slavs' millennium-long confrontation with their eastern neighbors lies the key to an understanding not only of Russian history, but Russian character. . .[3]

The conflict of civilizations is deeply rooted elsewhere in Asia. The historic clash between Muslim and Hindu in the subcontinent manifests itself now not only in the rivalry between Pakistan and India but also in intensifying religious strife within India between increasingly militant Hindu groups and India's substantial Muslim minority. The destruction of the Ayodhya mosque in December 1992 brought to the fore the issue of whether India will remain a secular democratic state or become a Hindu one. In East Asia, China has outstanding territorial disputes with most of its neighbors. It has pursued a ruthless policy toward the Buddhist people of Tibet, and it is pursuing an increasingly ruthless policy toward its Turkic-Muslim minority. With the Cold War over, the underlying differences between China and the United States have reasserted themselves in areas such as human rights, trade and weapons proliferation. These differences are unlikely to moderate. A "new cold war," Deng Xaioping reportedly asserted in 1991, is under way between China and America.

The same phrase has been applied to the increasingly difficult relations between Japan and the United States. Here cultural difference exacerbates economic conflict. People on each side allege racism on the other, but at least on the American side the antipathies are not racial but cultural. The basic values, attitudes, behavioral patterns of the two societies could hardly be more different. The economic issues between the United States and Europe are no less serious than those between the United States and Japan, but they do not have the same political salience and emotional intensity because the differences between American culture and European culture are so much less than those between American civilization and Japanese civilization.

The interactions between civilizations vary greatly in the extent to which they are likely to be characterized by violence. Economic competition clearly predominates between the American and European subcivilizations of the West and between both of them and Japan. On the Eurasian continent, however, the proliferation of ethnic conflict, epitomized at the extreme in "ethnic cleansing," has not been totally random. It has been most frequent and most violent between groups belonging to different civilizations. In Eurasia the great historic fault lines between civilizations are once more aflame. This is particularly true along the boundaries of the crescent-shaped Islamic bloc of nations from the bulge of Africa to central Asia. Violence also occurs between Muslims, on the one hand, and Orthodox Serbs in the Balkans, Jews in Israel, Hindus in India, Buddhists in Burma and Catholics in the Philippines. Islam has bloody borders.

V. Civilization Rallying

The kin-country syndrome groups or states belonging to one civilization that become involved in war with people from a different civilization naturally try to rally support from other members of their own civilization. As the post-Cold War world evolves, civilization commonality, what H. D. S. Greenway has termed the "kin-country" syndrome, is replacing political ideology and traditional balance of power considerations as the principal basis for cooperation and coalitions. It can be seen gradually emerging in the post-Cold War conflicts in the Persian Gulf, the Caucasus and Bosnia. None of these was a full-scale war between civilizations, but each involved some elements of civilization rallying, which seemed to become more important as the conflict continued and which may provide a foretaste of the future.

First, in the Gulf War one Arab state invaded another and then fought a coalition of Arab, Western and other states. While only a few Muslim governments overtly supported Saddam Hussein, many Arab elites privately cheered him on, and he was highly popular among large sections of the Arab publics. Islamic fundamentalist movements universally supported Iraq rather than the Western-backed governments of Kuwait and Saudi Arabia. Forswearing Arab nationalism, Saddam Hussein explicitly invoked an Islamic appeal. He and his supporters attempted to define the war as a war between civilizations. "It is not the world against Iraq," as Safar Al-Hawali, dean of Islamic Studies at the Umm Al-Qura University in Mecca, put it in a widely circulated tape. "It is the West against Islam." Ignoring the rivalry between Iran and Iraq, the chief Iranian religious leader, Ayatollah Ali Khamenei, called for a holy war against the West: "The struggle against American aggression, greed, plans and policies will be counted as a jahad, and anybody who is killed on that path is a martyr." "This is a war," King Hussein of Jordan argued, "against all Arabs and all Muslims and not against Iraq alone."

The rallying of substantial sections of Arab elites and publics behind Saddam Hussein called those Arab governments in the anti-Iraq coalition to moderate their activities and temper their public statements. Arab governments opposed or distanced themselves from subsequent Western efforts to apply pressure on Iraq, including enforcement of a no-fly zone in the summer of 1992 and the bombing of Iraq in January 1993. The Western-Soviet-Turkish-Arab anti-Iraq coalition of 1990 had by 1993 become a coalition of almost only the West and Kuwait against Iraq.

Muslims contrasted Western actions against Iraq with the West's failure to protect Bosnians against Serbs and to impose sanctions on Israel for violating U.N. resolutions. The West, they allege, was using a double standard. A world of clashing civilizations, however, is inevitably a world of double standards: people apply one standard to their kin-countries and a different standard to others.

* * *

[W]ith respect to the fighting in the former Yugoslavia, Western publics manifested sympathy and support for the Bosnian Muslims and the horrors they suffered at the hands of the Serbs. Relatively little concern was expressed, however, over Croatian attacks on Muslims and participation in the dismemberment of Bosnia-Herzegovina. In the early stages of the Yugoslav breakup, Germany, in an unusual display of diplomatic initiative and muscle, induced the other 11 members of the European Community to follow its lead in recognizing Slovenia and Croatia. As a result of the pope's determination to provide strong backing to the two Catholic countries, the Vatican extended recognition even before the Community did. The United States followed the European lead. Thus the leading actors in Western civilization rallied behind its coreligionists. Subsequently Croatia was reported to be receiving substantial quantities of arms from Central European and other Western countries. Boris Yeltsin's government, on the other hand, attempted to pursue a middle course that would be sympathetic to the Orthodox Serbs but not alienate Russia from the West. Russian conservative and nationalist groups, however, including many legislators, attacked the government for not being more forthcoming in its support for the Serbs. By early 1993 several hundred Russians apparently were serving with the Serbian forces, and reports circulated of Russian arms being supplied to Serbia.

Islamic governments and groups, on the other hand, castigated the West for not coming to the defense of the Bosnians. Iranian leaders urged Muslims from all countries to provide help to Bosnia; in violation of the U.N. arms embargo, Iran supplied weapons and men for the Bosnians; Iranian-supported Lebanese groups sent guerrillas to train and organize the Bosnian forces.

In 1993 up to 4,000 Muslims from over two dozen Islamic countries were reported to be fighting in Bosnia. The governments of Saudi Arabia and other countries felt under increasing pressure from fundamentalist groups in their own societies to provide more vigorous support for the Bosnians. By the end of 1992, Saudi Arabia had reportedly supplied substantial funding for weapons and supplies for the Bosnians, which significantly increased their military capabilities vis-à-vis the Serbs.

In the 1930s the Spanish Civil War provoked intervention from countries that politically were fascist, communist and democratic. In the 1990s the Yugoslav conflict is provoking intervention from countries that are Muslim, Orthodox and Western Christian. The parallel has not gone unnoticed. "The war in Bosnia-Herzegovina has become the emotional equivalent of the fight against fascism in the Spanish Civil War," one Saudi editor observed. "Those who died there are regarded as martyrs who tried to save their fellow Muslims."

Conflicts and violence will also occur between states and groups within the same civilization. Such conflicts, however, are likely to be less intense and less likely to expand than conflicts between civilizations. Common membership in a civilization reduces the probability of violence in situations where it might otherwise occur. In 1991 and 1992 many people were alarmed by the possibility of violent conflict between Russia and Ukraine over territory, particularly Crimea, the Black Sea fleet, nuclear weapons and economic issues. If civilization is what counts, however, the likelihood of violence between Ukrainians and Russians should be low. They are two Slavic, primarily Orthodox peoples who have had close relationships with each other for centuries. As of early 1993, despite all the reasons for conflict, the leaders of the two countries were effectively negotiating and defusing the issues between the two countries. While there has been serious fighting between Muslims and Christians elsewhere in the former Soviet Union and much tension and some fighting between Western and Orthodox Christians in the Baltic states, there has been virtually no violence between Russians and Ukrainians.

Civilization rallying to date has been limited, but it has been growing, and it clearly has the potential to spread much further. As the conflicts in the Persian Gulf, the Caucasus and Bosnia continued, the positions of nations and the cleavages between them increasingly were along civilizational lines. Populist politicians, religious leaders and the media have found it a potential means of arousing mass support and of pressuring hesitant governments. In the coming years, the local conflicts most likely to escalate into major wars will be those, as in Bosnia and the Caucasus, along the fault lines between civilizations. The next world war, if there is one, will be a war between civilizations.

VI. The West versus the Rest

The West is now at an extraordinary peak of power in relation to other civilizations. Its superpower opponent has disappeared from the map. Military conflict among Western states is unthinkable, and Western military power is unrivaled. Apart from Japan, the West faces no economic challenge. It dominates international economic institutions. Global political and security issues are effectively settled by a directorate of the United States, Britain and France, world economic issues by a directorate of the United States, Germany and Japan, all of which maintain extraordinarily close relations with each other to the exclusion of lesser and largely non-Western countries. Decisions made at the U.N. Security Council or in the International Monetary Fund that reflect the interests of the West are presented to the world as reflecting the desires of the world community. The very phrase "the world community" has become the euphemistic collective noun (replacing "the Free World") to give global legitimacy to actions reflecting the interests of the United States and other Western powers.[4] Through the IMF and other international economic institutions, the West promotes its economic interests and imposes on other nations the economic policies it thinks appropriate. In any poll of non-Western peoples, the IMF undoubtedly would win the support of finance ministers and a few others, but get an overwhelmingly unfavorable rating from just about everyone else, who would agree with Georgy Arbatov's characterization of IMF officials as "neo-Bolsheviks who love expropriating other people's money, imposing undemocratic and alien rules of economic and political conduct and stifling economic freedom."

Western domination of the U.N. Security Council and its decisions, tempered only by occasional abstention by China, produced U.N. legitimation of the West's use of force to drive Iraq out of Kuwait and its elimination of Iraq's sophisticated weapons and capacity to produce such weapons. It also produced the quite unprecedented action by the United States, Britain and France in getting the Security Council to demand that Libya hand over the Pan Am 103 bombing suspects and then to impose sanctions when Libya refused. After defeating the largest Arab army, the West did not hesitate to throw its weight around in the Arab world. The West in effect is using international institutions, military power and economic resources to run the world in ways that will maintain Western predominance, protect Western interests and promote Western political and economic values.

That at least is the way in which non-Westerners see the new world, and there is a significant element of truth in their view. Differences in power and struggles for military, economic and institutional power are thus one source of conflict between the West and other civilizations. Differences in culture, that is basic values and beliefs, are a second source of conflict. V. S. Naipaul has argued that Western civilization is the "universal civilization" that "fits all men." At a superficial level much of Western culture has indeed permeated the rest of the world. At a more basic level, however, Western concepts differ fundamentally from those prevalent in other civilizations. Western ideas of individualism, liberalism, constitutionalism, human rights, equality, liberty, the rule of law, democracy, free markets, the separation of church and state, often have little resonance in Islamic, Confucian, Japanese, Hindu, Buddhist or Orthodox cultures. Western efforts to propagate each ideas produce instead a reaction against "human rights imperialism" and a reaffirmation of indigenous values, as can be seen in the support for religious fundamentalism by the younger generation in non-Western cultures. The very notion that there could be a "universal civilization" is a Western idea, directly at odds with the particularism of most Asian societies and their emphasis on what distinguishes one people from another. Indeed, the author of a review of 100 comparative studies of values in different societies concluded that "the values that are most important in the West are least important worldwide." [5] In the political realm, of course, these differences are most manifest in the efforts of the United States and other Western powers to induce other peoples to adopt Western ideas concerning democracy and human rights. Modern democratic government originated in the West. . .

The central axis of world politics in the future is likely to be, in Kishore Mahbubani's phrase, the conflict between "the West and the Rest" and the responses of non-Western civilizations to Western power and values.[6] Those responses generally take one or a combination of three forms. At one extreme, non-Western states can, like Burma and North Korea, attempt to pursue a course of isolation, to insulate their societies from penetration or "corruption" by the West, and, in effect, to opt out of participation in the Western-dominated global community. The costs of this course, however, are high, and few states have pursued it exclusively. A second alternative, the equivalent of "band-wagoning" in international relations theory, is to attempt to join the West and accept its values and institutions. The third alternative is to attempt to "balance" the West by developing economic and military power and cooperating with other non-Western societies against the West, while preserving indigenous values and institutions; in short, to modernize but not to Westernize.

VII. The Torn Countries

In the future, as people differentiate themselves by civilization, countries with large numbers of people of different civilizations, such as the Soviet Union and Yugoslavia, are candidates for dismemberment. Some other countries have a fair degree of cultural homogeneity but are divided over whether their society belongs to one civilization or another. These are torn countries. Their leaders typically wish to pursue a bandwagoning strategy and to make their countries members of the West, but the history, culture and traditions of their countries are non-Western. The most obvious and prototypical torn country is Turkey. The late twentieth-century leaders of Turkey have followed in the Attaturk tradition and defined Turkey as a modern, secular, Western nation state. They allied Turkey with the West in NATO and in the Gulf War; they applied for membership in the European Community. At the same time, however, elements in Turkish society have supported an Islamic revival and have argued that Turkey is basically a Middle Eastern Muslim society. In addition, while the elite of Turkey has defined Turkey as a Western society, the elite of the West refuses to accept Turkey as such. Turkey will not become a member of the European Community, and the real reason, as President Özal said, "is that we are Muslim and they are Christian and they don't say that." Having rejected Mecca, and then being rejected by Brussels, where does Turkey look? Tashkent may be the answer. The end of the Soviet Union gives Turkey the opportunity to become the leader of a revived Turkic civilization involving seven countries from the borders of Greece to those of China. Encouraged by the West, Turkey is making strenuous efforts to carve out this new identity for itself.

During the past decade Mexico has assumed a position somewhat similar to that of Turkey. Just as Turkey abandoned its historic opposition to Europe and attempted to join Europe, Mexico has stopped defining itself by its opposition to the United States and is instead attempting to imitate the United States and to join it in the North American Free Trade Area. Mexican leaders are engaged in the great task of redefining Mexican identity and have introduced fundamental economic reforms that eventually will lead to fundamental political change. In 1991 a top adviser to President Carlos Salinas de Gortari described at length to me all the changes the Salinas government was making. When he finished, I remarked: "That's most impressive. It seems to me that basically you want to change Mexico from a Latin American country into a North American country." He looked at me with surprise and exclaimed: "Exactly! That's precisely what we are trying to do, but of course we could never say so publicly." As his remark indicates, in Mexico as in Turkey, significant elements in society resist the redefinition of their country's identity. In Turkey, European-oriented leaders have to make gestures to Islam (Ozal's pilgrimage to Mecca); so also Mexico's North American-oriented leaders have to make gestures to those who hold Mexico to be a Latin American country (Salinas' Ibero-American Guadalajara summit).

Historically Turkey has been the most profoundly torn country. For the United States, Mexico is the most immediate torn country. Globally the most important torn country is Russia. The question of whether Russia is part of the West or the leader of the Slavic-Orthodox civilization has been a recurring one in Russian history. That issue was obscured by the communist victory in Russia, which imported a Western ideology, adapted it to Russian conditions and then challenged the West in the name of that ideology. The dominance of communism shut off the historic debate over Westernization versus Russification. With communism discredited Russians once again face that question.

President Yeltsin is adopting Western principles and goals and seeking to make Russia a "normal" country and a part of the West. Yet both the Russian elite and the Russian public are divided on this issue. Among the more moderate dissenters, Sergei Stankevich argues that Russia should reject the "Atlanticist" course, which would lead it "to become European, to become a part of the world economy in rapid and organized fashion, to become the eighth member of the Seven, and to particular emphasis on Germany and the United States as the two dominant members of the Atlantic alliance." While also rejecting an exclusively Eurasian policy, Stankevich nonetheless argues that Russia should give priority to the protection of Russians in other countries, emphasize its Turkic and Muslim connections, and promote "an appreciable redistribution of our resources, our options, our ties, and our interests in favor of Asia, of the eastern direction." People of this persuasion criticize Yeltsin for subordinating Russia's interests to those of the West, for reducing Russian military strength, for failing to support traditional friends such as Serbia, and for pushing economic and political reform in ways injurious to the Russian people. Indicative of this trend is the new popularity of the ideas of Petr Savitsky, who in the 1920s argued that Russia was a unique Eurasian civilization.[7] More extreme dissidents voice much more blatantly nationalist, anti-Western and anti-Semitic views, and urge Russia to redevelop its military strength and to establish closer ties with China and Muslim countries. The people of Russia are as divided as the elite. An opinion survey in European Russia in the spring of 1992 revealed that 40 percent of the public had positive attitudes toward the West and 36 percent had negative attitudes. As it has been for much of its history, Russia in the early 1990s is truly a torn country.

To redefine its civilization identity, a torn country must meet three requirements. First, its political and economic elite has to be generally supportive of and enthusiastic about the move. Second, its public has to be willing to acquiesce in the redefinition. Third, the dominant groups in the recipient civilization have to be willing to embrace the convert. All three requirements in large part exist with respect to Mexico. The first two in large part exist with respect to Turkey. It is not clear that any of them exist with respect to Russia's joining the West. The conflict between liberal democracy and Marxism-Leninism was between ideologies which, despite their major differences, ostensibly shared ultimate goals of freedom, equality and prosperity. A traditional, authoritarian, nationalist Russia could have quite different goals. A Western democrat could carry on an intellectual debate with a Soviet Marxist. It would be virtually impossible for him to do that with a Russian traditionalist. If, as the Russians stop behaving like Marxists, they reject liberal democracy and begin behaving like Russians but not like Westerners, the relations between Russia and the West could again become distant and conflictual.[8]

[section VIII omitted]

IX. Implications for the West

This article does not argue that civilization identities will replace all other identities, that nation states will disappear, that each civilization will become a single coherent political entity, that groups within a civilization will not conflict with and even fight each other. This paper does set forth the hypotheses that differences between civilizations are real and important; civilization-consciousness is increasing; conflict between civilizations will supplant ideological and other forms of conflict as the dominant global form of conflict; international relations, historically a game played out within Western civilization, will increasingly be de-Westernized and become a game in which non-Western civilizations are actors and not simply objects; successful political, security and economic international institutions are more likely to develop within civilizations than across civilizations; conflicts between groups in different civilizations will be more frequent, more sustained and more violent than conflicts between groups in the same civilization; violent conflicts between groups in different civilizations are the most likely and most dangerous source of escalation that could lead to global wars; the paramount axis of world politics will be the relations between "the West and the Rest"; the elites in some torn non-Western countries will try to make their countries part of the West, but in most cases face major obstacles to accomplishing this; a central focus of conflict for the immediate future will be between the West and several Islamic-Confucian states.

This is not to advocate the desirability of conflicts between civilizations. It is to set forth descriptive hypotheses as to what the future may be like. If these are plausible hypotheses, however, it is necessary to consider their implications for Western policy. These implications should be divided between short-term advantage and long-term accommodation. In the short term it is clearly in the interest of the West to promote greater cooperation and unity within its own civilization, particularly between its European and North American components; to incorporate into the West societies in Eastern Europe and Latin America whose cultures are close to those of the West; to promote and maintain cooperative relations with Russia and Japan; to prevent escalation of local inter-civilization conflicts into major inter-civilization wars; to limit the expansion of the military strength of Confucian and Islamic states; to moderate the reduction of counter military capabilities and maintain military superiority in East and Southwest Asia; to exploit differences and conflicts among Confucian and Islamic states; to support in other civilizations groups sympathetic to Western values and interests; to strengthen international institutions that reflect and legitimate Western interests and values and to promote the involvement of non-Western states in those institutions.

In the longer term other measures would be called for. Western civilization is both Western and modern. Non-Western civilizations have attempted to become modern without becoming Western. To date only Japan has fully succeeded in this quest. Non-Western civilization will continue to attempt to acquire the wealth, technology, skills, machines and weapons that are part of being modern. They will also attempt to reconcile this modernity with their traditional culture and values. Their economic and military strength relative to the West will increase. Hence the West will increasingly have to accommodate these non-Western modern civilizations whose power approaches that of the West but whose values and interests differ significantly from those of the West. This will require the West to maintain the economic and military power necessary to protect its interests in relation to these civilizations. It will also, however, require the West to develop a more profound understanding of the basic religious and philosophical assumptions underlying other civilizations and the ways in which people in those civilizations see their interests. It will require an effort to identify elements of commonality between Western and other civilizations. For the relevant future, there will be no universal civilization, but instead a world of different civilizations, each of which will have to learn to coexist with the others.

Notes

1. Murray Weidenbaum, *Greater China: The Next Economic Superpower?*, St. Louis: Washington University Center for the Study of American Business, Contemporary Issues, Series 57, February 1993, pp. 2–3.
2. Bernard Lewis, "The Roots of Muslim Rage," *The Atlantic Monthly,* vol. 266, September 1990, p. 60; *Time,* June 15 1992, pp. 24–28.
3. Archie Roosevelt, *For Lust of Knowing,* Boston: Little, Brown, 1988, pp. 332–333.
4. Almost invariably Western leaders claim they are acting on behalf of "the world community." One minor lapse occurred during the run-up to the Gulf War. In an interview on "Good Morning America," Dec. 21, 1990, British Prime Minister John Major referred to the actions "the West" was taking against Saddam Hussein. He quickly corrected himself and subsequently referred to "the world community." He was, however, right when he erred.
5. Harry C. Triandis, *The New York Times,* Dec. 25, 1990, p. 41, and "Cross-Cultural Studies of Individualism and Collectivism," Nebraska Symposium on Motivation, vol. 37, 1989, pp. 41–133.
6. Kishore Mahbubani, "The West and the Rest," *The National Interest,* Summer 1992, pp. 3–13.
7. Sergei Stankevich, "Russia in Search of Itself," *The National Interest,* Summer 1992, pp. 47–51; Daniel Schneider, "A Russian Movement Rejects Western Tilt," *Christian Science Monitor,* Feb. 5, 1993, pp. 5–7.

8. Owen Harries has pointed out that Australia is trying (unwisely in his view) to become a torn country in reverse. Although it has been a full member not only of the West but also of the ABCA military and intelligence core of the West, its current leaders are in effect proposing that it defect from the West, redefine itself as an Asian country and cultivate close ties with its neighbors. Australia's future, they argue, is with the dynamic economies of East Asia. But, as I have suggested, close economic cooperation normally requires a common cultural base. In addition, none of the three conditions necessary for a torn country to join another civilization is likely to exist in Australia's case.

Chapter 13

WHAT CAUSES TRANSITIONS TO DEMOCRACY?

Where does democracy come from? Given that it is considered by most to be the best type of government, political scientists have long debated its origins, and while this debate is wide-ranging, the majority of the research can be divided into two schools of thought. One emphasizes the structure of society, in particular its social classes; the other focuses on the conditions under which political leaders select democracy over other forms of government.

The structuralist school of thought, perhaps best typified by the work of American political sociologist Barrington Moore in the 1960s, argues that the origins of democracies lie in the social structure of societies.[1] For a democracy to develop, a country must have the correct balance of social forces or class structure, and central to most of these visions of democracy is the development of the middle, or bourgeois, class. Moore states this requirement for a democratic transition in his now-famous quote, "No bourgeois, no democracy." [2] An active middle class is thought to not only demand democracy, but to contain the resources to support it. The bourgeoisie sees democracy as a political system that empowers it at the expense of other groups, such as the state or the landed aristocrats. Others have added to this line of thought by noting the importance of labor movements in democratic transition, arguing that in some cases only labor is truly interested in the further liberalization of the political system that leads to democracy.[3] Nonetheless, all scholars from the structuralist school of thought agree that democracy is created in a society in which the balance of social classes is appropriate.

This raises the inevitable question: Where does the appropriate social structure come from? The answer is capitalist economic development. The creation of a capitalist economic system propels the creation of the two classes most likely to support democracy: the middle class and labor. Moreover, capitalist development destroys classes that are often inimical to democracy, such as the landed aristocracy. This insight formed the basis of the development of modernization theory in the1950s and 1960s that was used as the basis for theories of economic and political development in the developing world; these countries were told that the key to becoming a democracy was to create a capitalist economy.

While structuralism persists in modern comparative politics, it has increasingly come under attack. The most influential early criticism of the structuralist school came in Dankwart Rustow's 1970 article, "Transitions to Democracy," in which he makes one critical point:

> No two existing democracies have gone through a struggle between the very same forces over the same issues with the same institutional outcomes. Hence, it seems unlikely that any future democracy will follow in the precise footsteps of any of its predecessors.[4]

Thus, critics of the structuralist approach question whether or not capitalist economic development creates the appropriate class structure for a democracy, given the wide variation in historical experiences that have led to democracy in different countries. In a more recent work criticizing the structuralist camp, Przeworski and Limongi point out through their empirical analysis of capitalist development that while increases in national wealth are correlated with democratization at low levels, this correlation tops out. Once above a certain level, the correlation ends.[5] This variation leads critics of the structuralist approach to a different cause for democracy: the rational decision of key political actors.

Dubbed the "transitions" school, critics of the stucturalist approach prefer to focus on the specific actions of actors in the political system. Rustow states, that the development of democracy is "[a] deliberate decision by political leaders to accept the existence of diversity and institutionalize some aspect of democracy." [6] The denizens of the transitions school, therefore, see the development of democracy as a decision made by political leaders when they themselves see a benefit in accepting democratic institutions and rules.[7] For the transitions school, democracy can develop in almost any context, irrespective of the level of development or the type of political culture in a society. Instead, transition scholars focus on explaining why elites are willing to share control over the political system.

Critics of the transitions school point out that it reveals very little about the specific conditions under which actors may find democracy rational.[8] For example, while it makes sense that the elites who control the military may find it in their interest to support democracy, the transitions perspective does not explain much about the actual conditions that may cause them to do this. If military elites decide that a democracy will best protect them from the growing power of a militant labor movement, then one cannot help but think that maybe the rise of that labor group, spurred by capitalist economic development, "caused" the military elites to accept democracy. This scenario seems to move toward a structural explanation.

The readings in this section cover the vital aspects of the debate over the causes of democratization. Rustow begins the process of the development of the transitions school in reading 13.2, whereas in reading 13.1 Kitschelt provides a thoughtful and thorough analysis of the two different schools of thought that dominate the study of democratic transitions.

Notes

1. Herbert Kitschelt "Political Regime Change: Structure and Process Driven Explanations," *American Political Science Review* 86, no. 4 (1992): 1028–1034.
2. Barrington Moore, *The Social Origin of Dictatorship and Democracy* (Boston: Beacon Press, 1966), 148.
3. Eva Bellin, "Contingent Democrats: Industrialists, Labor, and Democratization in Late-Developing Countries," *World Politics* 52, no. 2 (2000): 175–205; and Dietrich Rueschemeyer, Evelyn Huber Stephens, and John Stephens, *Capitalist Development and Democracy* (Chicago: University of Chicago Press, 1992).
4. Dankwart Rustow, "Transitions to Democracy," *Comparative Politics* 2, no. 3 (1970): 333–363.

5. Adam Przeworski and Fernando Limongi, "Modernization: Theories and Facts," *World Politics* 42, no. 2 (January 1997): 155–183.
6. Rustow, "Transitions," 356.
7. Przeworski and Limongi (1997); Kitschelt (1992); and Adam Przeworski, *Democracy and the Market; Political and Economic Reforms in Eastern Europe and Latin America* (New York: Cambridge University Press, 1991).
8. Kitschelt, "Political Regime Change."

13.1

POLITICAL REGIME CHANGE: STRUCTURE AND PROCESS-DRIVEN EXPLANATIONS

Herbert Kitschelt

Herbert Kitschelt is the George V. Allen Professor of International Relations in the department of political science at Duke University. He specializes in research that focuses on political parties, public policy, political economy, and social theory, and much of his recent work has focused on political party development in postcommunist countries. In his essay, Kitschelt compares and contrasts the two major approaches to democratization—the structural approach and the process approach. The structural approach focuses on how social structural factors like class cause democracy, whereas the process approach focuses on how decisions by individual political actors cause democracy. While reading this essay, students should ask themselves whether there are, in fact, significant differences between these two schools of thought. Some differences students should ponder include the unity of analysis, the role of individuals in determining political outcomes, the relationship between wealth and democracy, and the timing of democratization.

Political regimes may be defined as the rules and basic political resource allocations according to which actors exercise authority by imposing and enforcing collective decisions on a bounded constituency. Over the past decades, profound political regime transformations in southern Europe, Latin America, East Asia, Eastern Europe, and perhaps now even Africa have revived political scientists' concern with the breakdown and replacement of political governance structures. The main theoretical division within this field is drawn between those who seek more "structural" and "configurational" explanations, on the one side, and those who focus on the process of change itself—the sequence of events and the strategic moves of the actors.

The differences between the two camps encompass theory, methodology, and research design. Structure-oriented scholars typically assume that historical actors face extremely narrow choice sets *or* that their rational choices are clearly constrained by the distribution of resource endowments and their exogenous interest to maximize income and/or power, in light of which they calculate optimal strategies. Process-oriented scholars, in contrast, are primarily interested in the actors' manipulation of their own and their adversaries' cognitive and normative frames. Such change may eventually bring about political regime changes that were neither anticipated nor desired by any of the participants at the beginning of the process.

Herbert Kitschelt, "Political Regime Change: Structure and Process-Driven Explanations," *American Political Science Review* 86, no. 4 (December 1992): 1028–1034.

In other words, the main division in the field of studies on regime transformation is *not* one between historical and political institutionalists, on the one hand, and economic institutionalists with rational choice models, on the other. These two currents represent only strands within the structuralist camp. At most, the two differ on the nature of actors' interests (self- or other-regarding) and the relationship between interests and structural constraints (exogenous or endogenous). What is at stake between structure- and process-oriented studies of political regime change is a more fundamental division concerning the *concept of choice in political action itself.* For structuralists, choices represent calculations in light of given preferences and institutional constraints.[1] For process-oriented scholars, choices are caught up in a continuous redefinition of actors' perceptions of preferences and constraints.[2]

I shall focus the debate within the structuralist camp and between structuralists and process-oriented approaches on the question whether Barrington Moore's seminal hypotheses about regime trajectories in *The Social Origins of Dictatorship and Democracy* (1966) can still be considered valid. In a nutshell, Moore argues that the deconcentration of political power and economic power before the advent of industrialization (precipitated by a commercialization of land, a rising bourgeoisie, and a fragmentation of state power) was beneficial to democratization. At least four of the five structuralist and process-oriented approaches I shall examine address these hypotheses directly or indirectly.

Structure- and process-oriented approaches also differ on methodological and design-related questions. Structuralists prefer systematic macroquantitative or conceptually disciplined qualitative comparison, with countries as units of analysis. As the books by Huntington, Luebbert, and Rueschemeyer, Stephens and Stephens testify, followers of the comparative case study methodology have also ventured to increase the number of cases they compare and thus to lend more credibility to their main theoretical contentions.[3] In contrast to structural approaches, the process-oriented literature revolves around descriptive diachronic reconstructions of individual cases of regime transition with very little systematic comparison across a wider universe of countries. Whatever comparison is brought in remains on the illustrative and impressionistic level. I know of no single process-oriented study that supplies a systematic comparative analysis of regime transitions for a large number of instances.[4]

I wish to argue that structuralist and process-oriented analyses do not directly compete with each other but focus on different objects of explanation with different research methods and comparative designs. Taken as absolutes, structuralist approaches tend to explain "too much," whereas process approaches explain "too little." Structuralist approaches are good at accounting for the general causes of

---

1. For examples, Ronald Rogowski's *Commerce and Coalitions* (1989) is an avowedly rational-choice–based account; yet it considers itself to provide a generalization of Gerschenkron's and Moore's comparative-historical class-based structuralism. Conversely, Theda Skocpol's *States and Revolutions* (1979) is explicitly based on structuralist premises yet implicitly assumes rational actors who maximize wealth or power and are not driven by more illusive ideas.
2. Sometimes contributors to studies of regime transformation misunderstand their own accomplishments. In this sense, Adam Przeworski in *Democracy and the Market* (1991) wishes to offer a rational-choice–based explanation of regime change yet really falls back onto a historical institutionalism plus a process-oriented reconstruction of actors' changing cognitive frames.
3. Rogowski's book (see n. 1) is the other major example of this more comprehensive comparative approach.
4. Probably closest to the systematic and encompassing comparison of transition processes I am looking for are Terry Karl's articles, especially "Dilemmas of Democratization in Latin America" (*Comparative Politics* [1990]) and (with Philippe Schmitter) "Modes of Transition in Latin America, Southern and Eastern Europe" (*International Social Science Journal,* May 1991). In these and other examples, however, the conceptualization of the main independent variable, modes of regime transition, is not sufficiently refined.

regime breakdown and the consolidation of new regimes. Process approaches may explain the timing of breakdown and transition as well as the specific trial-and-error process of searching for a new viable regime. Structuralists have little to say about timing and transitions; nor have process-oriented studies succeeded in predicting regime consolidation. As far as the probability of democratic consolidations is concerned, a modified version of Moore's arguments still appears to have considerable plausibility.

Structuralist Approaches

Gregory Luebbert concludes his study of regime change in the interwar period with an unabashed structuralist proclamation: "One of the cardinal lessons of the story I have told is that leadership and meaningful choice played no role in the outcomes" (p. 306). Drawing upon a wide range of cases essentially covering the entirety of Europe, including the Balkan states, Luebbert claims that it is class cleavages and class alliances articulated on the level of group and party mobilization that determined whether regimes became fascist, liberal democratic, or social democratic in the interwar period. In a nutshell, the strength of liberal democratic free-market-oriented parties before and after World War I is key. Such parties were furthered before World War I by the absence of religious, ethnic, or regional cross-class cleavages that could have divided nonsocialist voters. Dominant liberal parties were able to enter alliances with the emerging labor parties against entrenched conservative and antidemocratic elites and thus weakened and coopted the labor movement in a democratized capitalist order (Britain, France, Switzerland). Whereas strong liberalism with weak labor movements persevered during the interwar decades of economic crisis, divided bourgeois parties and strong labor mobilization before and after World War I led to fascist regimes where the peasantry threw in its lot with the reaction (esp. Germany, Italy, Austria, and, to a lesser extent, Spain) and to social democracy where the peasantry entered red–green coalitions (Scandinavia). In eastern and southern Europe, mass political mobilization, particularly that of the working class, had not proceeded far enough to yield anything beyond an authoritarian dictatorship, regardless of whether fascism, liberalism, or social democracy are considered (pp. 258–66).

Whereas Barrington Moore saw large landholders and labor-repressive agriculture as a key force promoting fascism in the twentieth century, Luebbert maintains that by the 1920s, the German Junkers no longer played a critical economic role and that the landed elite did not control the votes of rural laborers anyway (p. 309). Luebbert's argument, however, fails to recognize that an application of Moore's thesis to twentieth-century regimes must necessarily emphasize the imprints past class dominance had left on the political organization of the state and on the mobilization of the peasantry. In fact, where feudal and absolutist regimes based on large landowners had disappeared early, fascism had no basis for success because either the state organization (military, bureaucracy, judiciary) was inimical to a new authoritarianism or a class of family farmers had an independent political voice that usually favored democratization, or both.

The critical cases undermining Luebbert's arguments are Belgium and the Netherlands, included among the countries he classifies as without hegemonic liberalism before World War I; yet contrary to his theoretical expectations, they did not produce fascism in the interwar period. Both countries are, however, characterized by the early demise of feudalism, the dominance of family farms, and a large market-based middle class.

Luebbert's argument that late industrialization has nothing to do with the failure of liberalism (pp. 59–62) also rests on weak foundations. Timing may not be as important as the character of late industrialization in critical countries in order to account for regime outcomes. Late industrialization is often associated with an initially state-led process of industrialization yielding a highly "organized" capitalism with a bourgeoisie closely intertwined with an antidemocratic state apparatus. If there were no offsetting conditions, such as an independent liberal-democratic peasantry (Sweden), this pattern of industrialization favored authoritarianism (Germany, Japan). Again, this interpretation explains why Belgium and the Netherlands escaped authoritarianism in spite of cross cleavages dividing liberal parties. Both countries experienced a gradual and relatively spontaneous, decentralized process of industrialization.

Although Luebbert is a structuralist, he is forced to admit the contingency of political choice in at least one critical instance. He argues that whether or not farmers allied with the Left or with fascism essentially depended on the socialists' choice to mobilize farm workers. If socialists engaged in that strategy, they tended to unite midsized farmers and large landholders against the Left and thus prepared the way for a fascist coalition, whereas in other instances red–green alliances were feasible (pp. 277–95).[5] In the spirit of Luebbert's structuralism, however, it must be noted that countries where peasants coalesced with fascism had a different legacy of agricultural property rights than countries where they did not. Conversely, if historical patterns of landholding and their political consequences did not matter, political choice on the part of socialist party leaders is clearly critical in accounting for interwar regime outcomes. Luebbert cannot have it both ways, that is, both deny the political consequences of rural political economy and provide a structuralist account of interwar regime outcomes.

Overall, Luebbert's account convincingly demonstrates that structures matter, but he may push this point too far. For example, the *timing* of the anti-democratic relapse in Germany, Italy, or Spain could hardly be accounted for by his model. Moreover, structuralism yields no deterministic, but a probabilistic, prediction. Even if all the structural constraints were right, would there have been a rise of the German Nazi party to power in 1933 had it not been for the Depression and the unique form of elite politics ushered in by the provisions of the Weimar constitution?

Luebbert's historical account yields rather pessimistic conclusions for the future of democratization in the late twentieth century. Liberalism and democracy were compatible only before the working class acquired the capacity to mobilize and disrupt the operation of free markets early in this century. Liberal–Labor alliances, modeled on pre-World War I Britain or France, between the urban middle class and the working class are thus extremely unlikely (p. 315). At the same time, a rural middle class was critical in the past and does not appear to be present in most countries still facing the possibility of democratization. Luebbert also does not hold out much hope for a "tutelary," restrained democratization under elite control because it will only compound the problems of democratic stabilization (p. 313). Under these circumstances, he envisions instability as the only "stable" outcome, "a cycle of establishment of democracy and its collapse, military intervention, and withdrawal" (p. 315).

---

5. I am setting aside here the question whether it is still adequate in light of recent historical research to refer to the rise of Scandinavian social democracy as a "red-green" coalition of workers and farmers against the bourgeoisie. As Swenson's research makes clear, there emerged, if anything, a sectoral coalition in which parts of Labor and business cooperated with agriculture against Labor and business in other sectors. See Peter Swenson's "Bringing Capital Back In" (*World Politics* 43[1991]).

Luebbert's book is an impressive achievement in its comparative scope and its unrelenting, tenacious defense of a clear analytical thesis; yet it ultimately leaves too many empirical anomalies unaddressed, maybe because Luebbert did not take Barrington Moore seriously enough. In contrast, Rueschemeyer, Stephens and Stephens's *Capitalist Development and Democracy*, though analytically more complex and less tightly knit, incorporates more aspects of Moore's thinking and arrives at more plausible and valid explanations of an even wider range of cases than Luebbert considered. The authors' objective is to synthesize two hitherto antagonistic traditions in research on regime change and apply the synthesis to regime change in today's advanced industrial countries (Western Europe and British settler democracies), Latin America, and the Caribbean. Macroquantitative studies have consistently found that economic development furthers democracy. Comparative historical analyses in the political economy tradition from Weber to Moore, however, have emphasized class relations and political institutions. Rueschemeyer and his coauthors argue that comparative historical political economy provides the *mechanisms* that explain why, when, and how economic development translates into democracy. Moreover, political economy can explain the cases that remain "outliers" in macroquantitative analysis.

Greater explanatory specificity in accounts of regime transformation requires examination of three sets of variables. First, class interests and class alliances matter, but in ways that modify Barrington Moore's master thesis. Consistent with Moore, Rueschemeyer, Stephens and Stephens show that labor-intensive and labor-repressive agriculture under the direction of large landowners is inimical to democracy. They also demonstrate that in the late nineteenth and early twentieth century the political effects of long-term political hegemony of landowners on state structures (military, bureaucracy, judiciary) may be as important for political regime forms as the direct impact of agricultural property rights.

Contrary to Moore's thesis, Rueschemeyer, Stephens and Stephens argue that the bourgeoisie is generally inimical to democracy. The true source of persistent democratic drives is working-class mobilization, which, in combination with middle-class support, can bring about a political constellation favorable to democracy. The authors qualify their emphasis on the working class in several respects. When turning to Latin America, they note that the middle class is critical in bringing about full democratization (pp. 167, 181, 216–7). Even for advanced industrial societies, however, the subordinate role of the middle classes may be questioned. If the working class is mostly for democracy, it is really the middle class—a concept the authors define as "urban professionals, state employees and employees in the private sector, artisans and craftsmen, and small entrepreneurs, sometimes joined by small and medium farmers" (p. 185)—whose variable position determines regime outcomes. A good part of Rueschemeyer, Stephens and Stephens's middle class may be covered by Moore's concept of bourgeoisie, thus reducing the gap between the two accounts. Going beyond simple structural accounts of stratification, Rueschemeyer, Stephens and Stephens emphasize that class formation is an organizational process, rather than a political-economic configuration of property rights. But they might have further developed this insight in systematic comparisons of working-class, "middle"-class, and bourgeois-class formation to highlight their position vis-à-vis Moore.

The other two sets of variables explicitly theorized in Rueschemeyer, Stephens and Stephens's explanatory framework are state structures and transnational power structures. In general, the more resources state elites control independently of socioeconomic classes and the more they represent a hierarchically integrated and ideologically united state apparatus, the more likely it is that authoritarian regimes will take hold. The precise nature of state influence depends on the countervailing force of independent voluntary associations ("civil society") and the nature of the dominant class from which the state is autonomous. Also, transnational power structures have highly contingent effects. In general, dependency in the periphery of the world system involves mechanisms unfavorable to democracy (foreign direct investment, capital-intensive and sectorally constrained industrialization, or labor-repressive and labor-intensive agriculture). But the authors also show that British colonialism and its legacies in state structures also had indirect effects that kept the "British" Caribbean, with few exceptions, democratic in the post-World War II era, whereas the "hispanic" Caribbean under U.S. influence experienced some of the most repressive and exploitative dictatorships of that era. In addition, other international factors, such as war, the Cold War, and alliance systems, have significant but varied effects on regime change.

Whereas these three sets of variables (particularly class structures and alliances) tend to account for democratization in advanced industrial countries very well and also cover the four cases of authoritarian breakdown (Italy, Germany, Austria, and Spain [pp. 99–121]), the discussion of Latin America and of the Caribbean requires a further set of variables, namely, the institutionalization of political parties. The authors discover that only where parties are institutionalized as lasting competitive organizational alternatives (whether based on clientelistic linkages or programmatic differences) do democracies survive for any length of time. It is somewhat unfortunate that the systemic role played by parties is not emphasized also for Western democratization. Characteristically, in Germany, Italy, and Spain the nonsocialist parties did not solidify around firm party organizations in the interwar period and were easily swept away by fascism. Austria is the exception, but here a full-fledged fascism was imposed only through Germany's annexation of the country. The importance of parties in twentieth-century political regime change would have allowed the authors to marry Moore's and Luebbert's central insights in a more encompassing framework.

The authors touch upon the role of ideology in regime change briefly but postulate that it is "linked to structural and organizational realities" (p. 50). In particular, this applies to religion. While the authors maintain that religious organization is more important than church doctrines (p. 275), the two elements are usually so highly intertwined that it is not clear in which direction the causal arrow runs. Moreover, lacking a close analysis of countries beyond the reach of Christian doctrines and church organizations, it is hard to determine how important either aspect of religion is for political regimes.[6]

Given the complexity of the variables Rueschemeyer, Stephens and Stephens take into account, what is the analytical bite of their study? What events and trajectories of regime change does it rule out? The discussion of the Latin American cases (preceded by a 12-page summary of the main argument), in particular, is so complex that it is not entirely clear in the end what has been achieved in terms of explanatory parsimony. Rueschemeyer, Stephens and Stephens do wish to argue against a facile modernization theory associating industrialization with democracy; yet at the same time, they embrace it as a partial explanation. They emphasize the role of the working class but do not get around the role of the middle class. The discussion of state structures and transnational relations leaves so many options and contingencies open that just about anything appears to be possible. One wishes the authors would have explored some less complex structural explanations, such as Ronald Rogowski's elegant and provocative account of political cleavages and regime alternatives in *Commerce and Coalitions* (1989) to show that a complex approach still combines the virtues of greater empirical verisimilitude and of discrimination between predicted, possible, and impossible pathways of regime transition.

---

6. To explore the influence of religion, see especially the broad comparative neo-Weberian account in John Hall's *Powers and Liberties* (1985).

At times, one has the impression that Rueschemeyer, Stephens and Stephens try to convert every contingency into a structural historical determinacy in order to exorcize the role of a process-oriented account of regime change. Particularly in Latin America, where it is often hard to say whether regimes ever "consolidated," this standard may be driving the structuralist approach too far. Rueschemeyer, Stephens and Stephens argue against the "presentism" of process-oriented explanations of democratic regime transitions (p. 35); but they do not confront these explanations with their own findings. The complexity of their account is rooted in the ambition to explain regime trajectories exhaustively and represent complex configurations and sequences of causation. In light of the result documented in their book, however, more than a few readers may conclude that the isolation of individual mechanisms affecting political regimes and the selective consideration of contingencies to account for outliers promises to provide a more manageable structuralist research strategy than explanatory holism. Nevertheless, Rueschemeyer, Stephens and Stephens have produced a splendid book that will definitely further theorizing on political regime change.

In the spirit of Moore, there is one very important hard-and-fast message that consistently comes across in Rueschemeyer, Stephens and Stephens's study: countries with labor-intensive and labor-repressive agricultures will not become stable democracies. This message also influences their concluding speculations about the future of democracy. In Taiwan and South Korea, the absence of a landlord class and rapid industrialization combined with the strength of autonomous states yields moderately favorable prospects for democracy. The decline of agriculture has also brightened hopes in Latin America; but the weakness of working-class organization, state and military autonomy, dependence on foreign capital, and the lack of strong parties cast dark shadows over the future of democracy on that continent. In Eastern Europe, finally, the *nomenklatura* may constitute the functional equivalent of a landlord class and the large autonomous state apparatuses within weak civil societies also do not bode well for democracy. Even in the early 1990s, structuralists like Luebbert or Rueschemeyer, Stephens and Stephens arrive at muted-to-pessimistic conclusions about the future spread of democratization.

Process-Oriented Approaches

Whereas structuralists hold actors' preferences constant and focus on changing institutional constraints, process-oriented studies of regime transformation emphasize the contingency of all parameters of choice. In this regard, Paul Brooker's *The Faces of Fraternalism* represents an analysis at the crossroads between the two perspectives. It is emphatically rooted in Durkheimian sociology in its emphasis on the changing role of a comprehensive collective conscience/consciousness for societal integration and regime stability. Yet Brooker is careful to explain in the first three chapters of his study that efforts to revive a communitarian spirit by "fraternal" political regimes in Germany, Italy, and Japan in the first half of the twentieth century cannot be explained in social-structural terms. Fraternal appeals did not initially inspire a mass following; nor did it necessarily come to the fore before, or even soon after, national socialism, fascism, and its Japanese military variant came to power. Thus, contrary to Durkheim, fraternalism does not grow out of a segmental division of labor with mechanical solidarity but somehow emerges in advanced, functionally differentiated societies with organic solidarity, something that would appear to be an anachronism to Durkheim. For this reason, Brooker offers a quasi-rational explanation of fraternalism in twentieth-century politics. In order to consolidate domestic regime entrenchment and to mobilize psychological resources for their external imperialist plans, totalitarian regimes decided to engage in fraternalist appeals and mass organizations (p. 74). Over more than two hundred pages, Brooker then provides a detailed account of the organizations and mechanisms each of the three regimes employed to instill fraternalism in the population. The concluding assessment argues that fraternalism was carried furthest in Japan yet remained more or less unsuccessful in Germany and Italy. In the most successful case, however, structural conditions for fraternalism were most conducive.

Brooker warns his readers on the first page of the preface that "most political scientists and sociologists will view the book as conceptually lightweight" (v); and this, indeed, is the book's major problem. Its conceptual apparatus and explanatory thrust could have been strengthened by engaging in a variety of related or competing theoretical approaches to fascism and to the rise of segmental or "pillarized" mass parties and reactionary social movements in order to explore why these, but few other, countries were vulnerable to the lures of a totalitarian order appealing to a new spirit of particularist (racist, nationalist) community. In terms of comparative design, Brooker samples on the dependent variable. Fraternalist regimes would appear in a much starker light if they were contrasted to regimes that failed to become fraternalist when faced with similar decision problems and political crises. Why is it that fraternalist appeals struck a resonant cord within elites primarily in Germany, Italy, and Japan but not in most other industrial countries? Brooker does not answer this question. In the end, Brooker provides an instructive description of the internal institutions of totalitarian rule in the three countries but little more. The book's greatest weakness, in fact, may be that it does not discuss alternative structuralist comparative accounts of regime change, such as the strand of analysis to which Barrington Moore had contributed.

Guiseppe Di Palma's *To Craft Democracies* has rather different ambitions and is firmly rooted in the "proceduralist" view of democratic regime change. Not structural conditions but human actions achieve democratic consolidation. At the center of Di Palma's concerns is the process of "democratic crafting" involving "negotiated agreements" between challengers of the old order and incumbent elites that move common perceptions of self-interest toward accepting democracy as the best possible regime form under given conditions. The establishment of democracy, unlike that of other systems, does not legislate a particular distribution of resources among social groups, but institutes uncertainties over outcomes as Adam Przeworski (1991) argued in *Democracy and the Market.* For this reason, Di Palma believes that the game between authoritarian elites and challengers can be more easily converted into a positive sum game, provided that the right steps in the process of regime transition are undertaken. Authoritarian elites must be assured of "coexistence" and fair play. For this reason, the transition should be engineered through negotiated agreements (pacts) that focus on rules of decision making, rather than outcomes. Demonstration effects and the diffusion of successful examples from abroad may be important in precipitating such steps. Careful crafting can exploit the elites' internal divisions on strategy and their sense of uncertainty about their own interests. Di Palma demonstrates these strategies of *garantismo* with an analytical reconstruction of the Italian and Spanish experience and contrasts it to the Portuguese case, where democratization almost failed.

Di Palma then discusses a number of tactical devices that facilitate the transition process. In addition to pacts, a speedy timetable of electoral reform and balanced concessions among all participating forces pave the road to democracy. Over time, the rules that are instituted generate their own support, once actors devise their strategies around the new opportunity structures. For this reason, "legitimacy," as a normative belief in the correctness of the system of rules, is certainly not a precondition of democracy. Institutional habituation of actors' strategies to democratic procedures is the overriding goal of democratic crafting.

While not denying that tactical moves on the part of democratic challengers and skilled techniques of converting games into positive-sum payoff structures facilitate a transition to democracy, we must ask how far such processes carry us in explaining democratic consolidation? Much of his attack on structuralism targets a vague modernization-theoretic version that stresses democratic values and elite attitudes yet not the more hard-nosed comparative studies in the tradition of Moore and others that focus on property rights, class relations, and state institutions. After Di Palma raises some rather strong claims for procedural analysis in the opening chapters of his book, he takes much of them back in chapter 8 where he begins to compare, in a rather impressionistic and unsystematic manner, the structural conduciveness of different regions and countries to democratic crafting. Such crafting, taken by itself, is insufficient to explain democratic prospects in particular cases: "Even when we favored explanations that focus on the transition and its strategies, these in turn have begged for their own explanations—often of a deeper historical and structural nature" (p. 156). The final chapter of the book also raises the importance of international system configurations and concedes that hegemonic powers play a critical role in regime change.

In the end, Di Palma's book provides several interesting insights into transition techniques that may make a difference in countries characterized by roughly similar structural conduciveness to democratization. These observations, however, could be analytically sharpened. For examples, Di Palma's study puts a great deal of emphasis on pacts and agreements between incumbent and challenging elites yet never engages in a specific analysis of the different scope, bindingness, timing, and longevity of pacts in the transition process. More importantly, the book does not deliver a specification of the structural circumstances that may give significance to different techniques of crafting for the ultimate outcome. Di Palma delivers a timely reminder that economic, political, and cultural determinants are not everything when we try to understand regime change but does not present a sufficiently crisp and precise analysis, corroborated through systematic comparison, to advance the emerging field of "transitology" in significant respects. Whereas structural approaches explain too much, Di Palma's "transitology" explains too little. For this reason, Di Palma's optimism requires a more robust theoretical base.

Combining Structural and Procedural Accounts of Democratization

Samuel Huntington, in *The Third Wave*, lays out a broad, eclectic canvass that encompasses structural and procedural arguments. He also considers the most comprehensive universe of cases and treats them in a more rigorous comparative analysis than does Di Palma; but he is less systematic than Luebbert or Rueschemeyer, Stephens and Stephens in tracing the impact of different sets of variables on regime patterns. Huntington resists efforts to pigeon-hole his account as "nomothetic" or "ideographic" from the very beginning (p. xiii). Democracies are complex phenomena, and they are caused by many forces' contributing to historical "waves" of democratization. In contrast to the first two waves following on the heels of the two world wars in the twentieth century, the third wave of democratization beginning with the 1974 Portuguese revolution appears not to be triggered by international political events but by a variety of domestic forces. It is important to note that 23 of the 39 countries democratizing since 1974 had at least one previous democratic experience, whereas most countries that had never been democratic stayed authoritarian until 1990 (p. 44). This association reestablishes a linkage to externally induced democratization in previous waves.

Overall, Huntington sees five causes of the third wave—at least three of them structural but one unambiguously procedural. First, authoritarian regimes are unable to dissociate the regime's economic effectiveness from the legitimacy of rulers or the legitimacy of rulers from legitimacy of rules of governance. Hence, the oil shocks and the economic dislocations and structural transformation of the world economy in the 1970s and 1980s precipitated the downfall of many dictatorships. With the decline of communism, "outside of Africa and a few countries elsewhere, democracy had come to be seen as the only legitimate and viable alternative to authoritarian regimes of any type" (p. 58). Second, Huntington stresses the importance of economic development but sees it as neither a necessary nor a sufficient condition. Going beyond older modernization approaches, he argues that the source and distribution of wealth are important. Hence, the oil-rich, state-centered regimes did not become democratic; but countries that generate a broad-based urban middle class through a wide diversification of a growing industrial economy did. Huntington's analysis is here quite close to Rueschemeyer, Stephens and Stephens's main hypothesis and certainly consistent with the overall gist of Moore's earlier analysis. Third, however, Huntington emphasizes the independent effect of religious doctrine and religious change. Reversing Weber's causal chain, he notes the rise of Christianity—particularly an individualist and socially activist Christianity—in democratizing countries that has forced Catholicism to withdraw support from the political status quo. Fourth, beyond these structural changes, new transnational politics effected by the United States, the Soviet Union, the European Community, and the Vatican improved the atmosphere for democratic change in the 1980s. Finally, the democratic wave began to feed on itself. Demonstration effects and snowballing reinforced opposition efforts to bring about democracy in countries where structural conditions were even mildly conducive to regime change.

Huntington shows that the mode of transition interacts with the nature of incumbent political regimes (p. 133); thus, he goes significantly beyond the structuralism/proceduralism divide. Elite-initiated or elite-negotiated transitions are most typical in bureaucratic one-party or military regimes, whereas personal "sultanistic" dictatorships hold out less promise for change and often require the wholesale replacement of the ruling elite. For each of the patterns of transition, Huntington provides detailed descriptions of actors' moves and tops off each analysis with a set of lessons actors might draw. For example, reformers should always participate in elections, because even rigged elections, monitored by foreign observers, weaken an authoritarian regime. In any case, rulers usually miscalculate their chances in open elections, except in cases where there is only a small urban middle class (p. 179).

Huntington finally discusses various aspects of democratic stabilization, such as how to decide on the prosecution of authoritarian elites and how to deal with the military. The most interesting segment deals with the prospects of democratization of countries that have made initial steps in the third wave of democratization (pp. 270–79). Based on their previous democratic experiences, economic development, location in the international system, and duration of democratization effort in the third wave, Huntington is least optimistic about Mongolia, Sudan, Pakistan, Nicaragua, Romania, Bulgaria, Nigeria, and El Salvador.[7] He remains especially pessimistic about democratic prospects in regions of the world that have not entered democratization, especially homegrown Marxist–Leninist regimes linked to nationalist appeals, sub-Saharan Africa, Islamic countries, and certain areas of East Asia. Huntington

7. I have added up rankings of the countries on each of Huntington's four criteria and singled out countries with the four lowest rankings. At the top of democratic promise are Spain, Greece, Portugal, Turkey, Uruguay, Chile, Ecuador, Czechoslovakia, Hungary, Bolivia, Brazil, Peru, Philippines, and South Korea.

makes a special point to highlight the antidemocratic implications of Confucian and Islamic religious doctrines, a factor not considered by any of the other studies.[8]

Huntington's analysis is impressive in scope; but at times he is compelled to trade sophistication in conceptualizing critical variables for breadth of comparison. Rueschemeyer, Stephens, and Stephens's account of economic development, class structure, and democratization tends to go in the opposite direction. Clearly, Huntington's book does not provide as detailed an analysis of political institutions and regime structures preceding democratization (pp. 110–21). Huntington's global reach, however, has its own virtues; it encompasses structure and process and, due to its global reach, is able to say more on such contentious issues as the role of religion for political regime transformation.

Overall, the two studies from which most can be learned for the further analysis of regime change are Huntington's and Rueschemeyer, Stephens, and Stephens's. Luebbert's study is a close runner-up. All of these analyses in one way or another feature the importance of Barrington Moore's insights and of the tradition on which Moore built. All of them also refrain from extreme optimism or pessimism about the future avenue of global democratization. Huntington and Rueschemeyer, Stephens, and Stephens lead us to hypothesize that in the Middle East or sub-Saharan Africa, but also in some of the postcommunist successor regimes, chances for democratic consolidation are poor. Conversely, there are a number of countries and regions of the world that give reason for hope to those who welcome democracy.

Against the backdrop of these studies, what future avenues may be open for analyzing political regime change? Luebbert and Rueschemeyer, Stephens, and Stephens have probably pushed the case-oriented systematic historical–comparative approach as far as it can productively go. Conversely, Huntington offers a broad, variable-oriented comparison, which still remains bivariate in its consideration of causal elements. In the future, multivariate analysis or Boolean algebra, as proposed by Charles Ragin (*The Comparative Method* [1987]) may help us to develop a more formal representation of casual complexity in pathways of regime transition. At the same time, it is desirable to spell out more clearly the precise mechanisms that make each causal force relevant if we are to see sharper analysis of regime transitions.

References

The Faces of Fraternalism: Nazi Germany, Fascist Italy, and Imperial Japan. By Paul Brooker. New York: Oxford University Press, 1991.

To Craft Democracies: An Essay on Democratic Transitions. By Guiseppe Di Palma. Berkeley: University of California Press, 1990.

The Third Wave: Democratization in the Late Twentieth Century. By Samuel P. Huntington. Norman: University of Oklahoma Press, 1991.

Liberalism, Facism, or Social Democracy: Social Classes and the Political Origins of Regimes in Interwar Europe. By Gregory M. Luebbert. New York: Oxford University Press, 1991.

Capitalist Development and Democracy. By Dietrich Rueschemeyer, Evelyne Huber Stephens, and John D. Stephens. Chicago: University of Chicago Press, 1992.

---

8. According to Huntington, even formal democracies in predominantly Confucian countries are characterized by the absence of government turnover (p. 304).

13.2

TRANSITIONS TO DEMOCRACY: TOWARD A DYNAMIC MODEL

Dankwart A. Rustow

Dankwart Rustow was professor of political science and sociology at the City University of New York's Graduate Center after serving on the faculties at both Princeton University and Columbia University. The essay presented here is his most famous contribution to political science and one of the most significant publications in the literature on democratization. In this essay, Rustow was one of the first scholars to question the fundamental modernization concept that capitalist economic development inexorably led to democracy. For him, the "transition" to democracy was not simply the result of economic factors, but also depended on other political factors that led political actors to select democracy over other alternatives. His work led directly to the development of what Herbert Kitschelt, in reading 13.1, refers to as the process school. Students should focus on the fundamental question at issue here: Is economic development necessary for democracy? They also should ponder how well Rustow answers this question. Students should ask themselves whether Rustow's basic argument can be accepted while still retaining the belief that economic development is key to democracy.

I

What conditions make democracy possible and what conditions make it thrive? Thinkers from Locke to Tocqueville and A. D. Lindsay have given many answers. Democracy, we are told, is rooted in man's innate capacity for self-government or in the Christian ethical or the Teutonic legal tradition. Its birthplace was the field at Putney where Cromwell's angry young privates debated their officers, or the more sedate House at Westminster, or the rock at Plymouth, or the forest cantons above Lake Lucerne, or the fevered brain of Jean Jacques Rousseau. Its natural champions are sturdy yeomen, or industrious merchants, or a prosperous middle class. It must be combined with strong local government, with a two-party system, with a vigorous tradition of civil rights, or with a multitude of private associations.

Recent writings of American sociologists and political scientists favor three types of explanation. One of these, proposed by Seymour Martin Lipset, Philips Cutright, and others, connects stable democracy with certain economic and social background conditions, such as high per capita income, widespread literacy, and prevalent urban residence. A second type of explanation dwells on the need for certain be-

Dankwart A. Rustow, "Transitions to Democracy: Toward a Dynamic Model," *Comparative Politics* 2 (April 1970): 337–363.

liefs or psychological attitudes among the citizens. A long line of authors from Walter Bagehot to Ernest Barker has stressed the need for consensus as the basis of democracy—either in the form of a common belief in certain fundamentals or of procedural consensus on the rules of the game, which Barker calls "the Agreement to Differ." Among civic attitudes required for the successful working of a democratic system, Daniel Lerner has proposed a capacity for empathy and a willingness to participate. To Gabriel Almond and Sidney Verba, on the other hand, the ideal "civic culture" of a democracy suggests not only such participant but also other traditional or parochial attitudes.[1]

A third type of explanation looks at certain features of social and political structure. In contrast to the prevailing consensus theory, authors such as Carl J. Friedrich, E. E. Schattschneider, Bernard Crick, Ralf Dahrendorf, and Arend Lijphart have insisted that conflict and reconciliation are essential to democracy.[2] Starting with a similar assumption, David B. Truman has attributed the vitality of American institutions to the citizens' "multiple membership in potential groups"—a relationship which Lipset has called one of "crosscutting politically relevant associations."[3] Robert A. Dahl and Herbert McClosky, among others, have argued that democratic stability requires a commitment to democratic values or rules, not among the electorate at large but among the professional politicians—each of these presumably linked to the other through effective ties of political organization.[4] Harry Eckstein, finally, has proposed a rather subtle theory of "congruence": to make democracy stable, the structures of authority throughout society, such as family, church, business, and trade unions, must prove the more democratic the more directly they impinge on processes of government.[5]

Some of these hypotheses are compatible with each other, though they may also be held independently—for example, those about prosperity, literacy, and consensus. Others—such as those about consensus and conflict—are contradictory unless carefully restricted or reconciled. Precisely such a synthesis has been the import of a large body of writing. Dahl, for instance, has proposed that in polyarchy (or "minorities rule," the closest real-life approximation to democracy) the policies of successive governments tend to fall within a broad range of majority consensus.[6] Indeed, after an intense preoccupation with consensus in the World War II years, it is now widely accepted that democracy is indeed a process of "accommodation" involving a combination of "division and cohesion" and of "conflict and consent"—to quote the key terms from a number of recent book titles.[7]

The scholarly debate thus continues, and answers diverge. Yet there are two notable points of agreement. Nearly all the authors ask the same sort of question and support their answers with the same sort of evidence. The question is not how a democratic system comes into existence. Rather it is how a democracy, assumed to be already in existence, can best preserve or enhance its health and stability. The evidence adduced generally consists of contemporary information, whether in the form of comparative statistics, interviews, surveys, or other types of data. This remains true even of authors who spend considerable time discussing the historical background of the phenomena that concern them—Almond and Verba of the civic culture, Eckstein of congruence among Norwegian social structures, and Dahl of the ruling minorities of New Haven and of oppositions in Western countries.[8] Their key propositions are couched in the present tense.

There may be a third feature of similarity underlying the current American literature of democracy. All scientific inquiry starts with the conscious or unconscious perception of a puzzle.[9] What has puzzled the more influential authors evidently has been the contrast between the relatively smooth functioning of democracy in the English-speaking and Scandinavian countries and the recurrent crises and final collapse of democracy in the French Third and Fourth Republics and in the Weimar Republic of Germany.

This curiosity is of course wholly legitimate. The growing literature and the increasingly subtle theorizing on the bases of democracy indicate how fruitful it has been. The initial curiosity leads logically enough to the functional, as opposed to the genetic, question. And that question, in turn, is most readily answered by an examination of contemporary data about functioning democracies—perhaps with badly functioning democracies and nondemocracies thrown in for contrast. The functional curiosity also comes naturally to scholars of a country that took its crucial steps toward democracy as far back as the days of Thomas Jefferson and Andrew Jackson. It accords, moreover, with some of the characteristic trends in American social science in the last generation or two—with the interest in systematic equilibria, in quantitative correlations, and in survey data engendered by the researcher's own questions. Above all, it accords with a deep-seated prejudice against causality. As Herbert A. Simon has strikingly put it, "...we are wary, in the social sciences, of asymmetrical relations. They remind us of pre-Humeian and pre-Newtonian notions of causality. By whip and sword we have been converted to the doctrine that there is no causation, only functional interrelation, and that functional relations are perfectly symmetrical. We may even have taken over, as a very persuasive analogy, the proposition 'for every action, there is an equal and opposite reaction.' "[10]

Students of developing regions, such as the Middle East, Southern Asia, tropical Africa, or Latin America, naturally enough have a somewhat different curiosity about democracy. The contrast that is likely to puzzle them is that between mature democracies, such as the United States, Britain, or Sweden today, and countries that are struggling on the verge of democracy, such as Ceylon, Lebanon, Turkey, Peru, or Venezuela. This will lead them to the genetic question of how a democracy comes into being in the first place.[11] The question is (or at least was, until the Russian invasion of Czechoslovakia in 1968) of almost equal interest in Eastern Europe. The genesis of democracy, thus, has not only considerable intrinsic interest for most of the world; it has greater pragmatic relevance than further panegyrics about the virtues of Anglo-American democracy or laments over the fatal illnesses of democracy in Weimar or in several of the French Republics.

In the following sections of this article I should like to examine some of the methodological problems involved in the shift from functional to genetic inquiry and then proceed to outline one possible model of the transition to democracy.

II

* * *

The best known attempts to apply a single world-wide perspective to democracy, whether nascent or mature, are the statistical correlations compiled by Lipset and by Cutright.[12] But Lipset's article well illustrates the difficulty of applying the functional perspective to the genetic question. Strictly interpreted, his data bear only on function. His statistical findings all take the form of correlations at a given single point in time. In the 1950s his "stable democracies" generally had substantially higher per capita incomes and literacy rates than did his "unstable democracies," or his unstable and stable authoritarianisms. Now, correlation evidently is not the same as causation—it provides at best a clue to some sort of causal connection without indicating its direction. Lipset's data leave it entirely open, for example, whether affluent and literate citizens make the better democrats; whether democracies provide superior schools and a more bracing climate for economic growth; whether there is some sort of reciprocal connection so that a given increase in affluence or literacy and in democracy will produce a corresponding increment in the other; or whether there is some further set of factors, such as the industrial economy perhaps, that causes both democracy *and* affluence and literacy. A corresponding objection can be urged against the findings of Almond, Verba, and others that are based mainly on contemporary opinion or attitude surveys. Only further investigation could show whether such attitudes as "civic culture," an eagerness to participate, a consensus on fundamentals, or an agreement on procedures are cause or effect of democracy, or both, or neither.

* * *

Any genetic theory of democracy would do well to assume a two-way flow of causality, or some form of circular interaction, between politics on the one hand and economic and social conditions on the other. Wherever social or economic background conditions enter the theory, it must seek to specify the mechanisms, presumably in part political, by which these penetrate to the democratic foreground. The political scientist, moreover, is entitled to his rights within the general division of labor and may wish to concentrate on some of the political factors without denying the significance of the social or economic ones. With Truman, Dahl, and others, I would tend to see the patterns of conflict and of recurrent or changing alignments as one of the central features of any political system. With Apter, I would consider choice as one of the central concerns of the political process.[13]

What goes for economics and sociology goes for psychology as well. Here, too, the relationship with politics is one of interaction and interdependence, so that political phenomena may have psychological consequences as well as vice versa. In explaining the origins of democracy we need not assume—as does much of the current survey research literature—that beliefs unilaterally influence actions. Rather, we may recognize with Leon Festinger and other social psychologists of the "cognitive dissonance" school that there are reciprocal influences between beliefs and actions.[14] Many of the current theories about democracy seem to imply that to promote democracy you must first foster democrats—perhaps by preachment, propaganda, education, or perhaps as an automatic byproduct of growing prosperity. Instead, we should allow for the possibility that circumstances may force, trick, lure, or cajole non-democrats into democratic behavior and that their beliefs may adjust in due course by some process of rationalization or adaptation.

* * *

III

The methodological argument I have been advancing may be condensed into a number of succinct propositions.

1. The factors that keep a democracy stable may not be the ones that brought it into existence: explanations of democracy must distinguish between function and genesis.
2. Correlation is not the same as causation: a genetic theory must concentrate on the latter.
3. Not all causal links run from social and economic to political factors.
4. Not all causal links run from beliefs and attitudes to actions.
5. The genesis of democracy need not be geographically uniform: there may be many roads to democracy.

6. The genesis of democracy need not be temporally uniform: different factors may become crucial during successive phases.
7. The genesis of democracy need not be socially uniform: even in the same place and time the attitudes that promote it may not be the same for politicians and for common citizens.

My refrain, like Sportin' Life's, has been, "It ain't necessarily so." Each proposition pleads for the lifting of some conventional restriction, for the dropping of some simplifying assumption made in the previous literature, for the introduction of complicating, diversifying factors. If the argument were to conclude on this sceptical note, it would set the researcher completely adrift and make the task of constructing a theory of democratic genesis well-nigh unmanageable.

Fortunately, the genetic perspective requires or makes possible a number of new restrictions that more than compensate for the loss of the seven others. We may continue the listing of summary propositions before elaborating this second part of the methodological argument.

8. Empirical data in support of a genetic theory must cover, for any given country, a time period from just before until just after the advent of democracy.
9. To examine the logic of transformation *within* political systems, we may leave aside countries where a major impetus came from abroad.
10. A model or ideal type of the transition may be derived from a close examination of two or three empirical cases and tested by application to the rest.

That diachronic data, covering more than a single point in time, are essential to any genetic theory should be obvious. Such a theory, moreover, must be based on cases where the process is substantially complete. Although control data on nondemocracies and on abortive and incipient cases may become important at a later stage of theorizing, it is more convenient to start out by studying a phenomenon where it actually has come into existence. The "advent" of democracy must not, of course, be understood as occurring in a single year. Since the emergence of new social groups and the formation of new habits are involved, one generation is probably the minimum period of transition. In countries that had no earlier models to emulate, the transition is likely to have come even more slowly. In Britain, for example, it may be argued that it began before 1640 and was not accomplished until 1918. For an initial set of hypotheses, however, it may be best to turn to countries where the process occurred relatively rapidly.

* * *

To speak of "major impulses from outside" or transitions "mainly within the system" acknowledges that foreign influences are almost always present. Throughout history, warfare has been a major democratizing force, because it has made necessary the marshalling of additional human resources.[15] Democratic ideas, moreover, have proved infectious whether in the days of Rousseau or of John F. Kennedy. And the violent overthrow of one oligarchy (e.g., France in 1830, Germany in 1918) has often frightened another into peaceful surrender (e.g., Britain in 1832, Sweden in 1918). From such ever present international influences we may distinguish situations where people arriving from abroad took an active part in the internal political process of democratization. A theory of democratic origins, that is to say, should leave aside at the beginning those countries where military occupation played a major role (postwar Germany and Japan), where democratic institutions or attitudes were brought along by immigrants (Australia and New Zealand), or where in these and other ways immigration played a major role (Canada, the United States, and Israel).

* * *

The model I should like to sketch in the next few pages is based in large part on my studies of Sweden, a Western country that made the transition to democracy in the period from 1890 to 1920, and of Turkey, a Westernizing country where that process began about 1945 and is still underway. The choice of these two is accidental—except in terms of an autobiographical account for which this is not the occasion. I am now in the early stages of a study that will seek to refine the same set of hypotheses in the light of materials from a slightly larger and less arbitrary selection of countries.

IV

A. Background Condition

The model starts with a single background condition—national unity. This implies nothing mysterious about *Blut und Boden* or daily pledges of allegiance, about personal identity in the psychoanalyst's sense, or about a grand political purpose pursued by the citizenry as a whole. It simply means that the vast majority of citizens in a democracy-to-be must have no doubt or mental reservations as to which political community they belong to. This excludes situations of latent secession, as in the late Habsburg and Ottoman Empires or in many African states today, and, conversely, situations of serious aspirations for merger as in many Arab states. Democracy is a system of rule by temporary majorities. In order that rulers and policies may freely change, the boundaries must endure, the composition of the citizenry be continuous. As Ivor Jennings phrased it tersely, "the people cannot decide until somebody decides who are the people." [16]

National unity is listed as a background condition in the sense that it must precede all the other phases of democratization but that otherwise its timing is irrelevant. It may have been achieved in prehistoric times, as in Japan or Sweden; or it may have preceded the other phases by centuries, as in France, or by decades, as in Turkey.

Nor does it matter by what means national unity has been established. The geographic situation may be such that no serious alternative has ever arisen—Japan once again being the best example. Or a sense of nationality may be the product of a sudden intensification of social communication in a new idiom developed for the purpose. On the other hand, it may be the legacy of some dynastic or administrative process of unification. The various hypotheses proposed by Deutsch clearly become relevant here.[17]

I have argued elsewhere that in an age of modernization men are unlikely to feel a preponderant sense of loyalty except to a political community large enough to achieve some considerable degree of modernity in its social and economic life.[18] This sort of hypothesis must be examined as part of a theory of nationhood, not of one of democratic development. What matters in the present context is only the result.

I hesitate to call this result a consensus, for at least two reasons. First, national unity, as Deutsch argues, is the product less of shared attitudes and opinions than of responsiveness and complementarity. Second, "consensus" connotes consciously held opinion and deliberate agreement. The background condition, however, is best fulfilled when national unity is accepted unthinkingly, is silently taken for granted. Any vocal consensus about national unity, in fact, should make us wary. Most of the rhetoric of nationalism has poured from the lips of people who felt least secure in their sense of national identity—Germans and Italians in the past century and Arabs and Africans in the present, never Englishmen, Swedes, or Japanese.

To single out national unity as the sole background condition implies that no minimal level of economic development or social differentiation is necessary as a prerequisite to democracy. These social and economic factors enter the model only indirectly as one of several alternative bases for national unity or for entrenched conflict (see B below). Those social and economic indicators that authors are fond of citing as "background conditions" seem somewhat implausible at any rate. There are always nondemocracies that rank suspiciously high, such as Kuwait, Nazi Germany, Cuba, or Congo-Kinshasa. Conversely, the United States in 1820, France in 1870, and Sweden in 1890 would have been sure to fail one or another of the proposed tests of urbanization or per capita income —not to speak of newspaper copies in circulation, or doctors, movies, and telephones available to each one thousand inhabitants.

The model thus deliberately leaves open the possibility of democracies (properly so called) in premodern, prenationalist times and at low levels of economic development. To find a meaningful definition of democracy that would cover modern parliamentary systems along with medieval forest cantons, ancient city states (the ones where slavery and metics were absent), and some of the pre-Columbian Indians may prove difficult. It is not a task that forms part of the present project; still, I should not like to foreclose the attempt.

B. Preparatory Phase

I hypothesize that, against this single background condition, the dynamic process of democratization itself is set off by a prolonged and inconclusive political struggle. To give it those qualities, the protagonists must represent well-entrenched forces (typically social classes), and the issues must have profound meaning to them. Such a struggle is likely to begin as the result of the emergence of a new elite that arouses a depressed and previously leaderless social group into concerted action. Yet the particular social composition of the contending forces, both leaders and followers, and the specific nature of the issues will vary widely from one country to the next and in the same country from period to period.

In Sweden at the turn of the century, it was a struggle first of farmers and then of an urban lower-middle and working class against a conservative alliance of bureaucrats, large landowners, and industrialists; and the issues were tariffs, taxation, military service, and suffrage. In Turkey in the last twenty years it has mainly been a contest of countryside versus city, more precisely of large and middling-size farmers (supported by most of the peasant electorate) against the heirs of the Kemalist bureaucratic-military establishment; the central issue has been industrialization versus agricultural development. In both these examples, economic factors have been of prime importance, yet the direction of causality has varied. In Sweden, it was a period of intense economic development that created new political tensions; at one crucial point, rising wages enabled the Stockholm workers to overcome the existing tax barrier for the franchise. In Turkey, conversely, the demand for rural development was the consequence, not the cause, of beginning democratization.[19]

There may be situations where economic factors have played a much lesser role. In India and in the Philippines the prolonged contest between nationalist forces and an imperial bureaucracy over the issue of self-government may have served the same preparatory function as did class conflict elsewhere. In Lebanon the continuing struggle is mainly between denominational groups and the stakes are mainly government offices. Although political struggles of this sort naturally have their economic dimensions, only a doctrinaire economic determinist would derive colonialism or religious divisions from solely economic causes.

James Bryce found in his classic comparative study that, "One road only has in the past led into democracy, viz., the wish to be rid of tangible evils." [20] Democracy was not the original or primary aim; it was sought as a means to some other end or it came as a fortuitous byproduct of the struggle. But, since the tangible evils that befall human societies are legion, Bryce's single road dissolves into many separate paths. No two existing democracies have gone through a struggle between the very same forces over the same issues and with the same institutional outcome. Hence, it seems unlikely that any future democracy will follow in the precise footsteps of any of its predecessors. As Albert Hirschman has warned in his discussion of economic development, the search for ever more numerous preconditions or prerequisites may end up by proving conclusively that development always will be impossible—and always has been.[21]

More positively, Hirschman and other economists have argued that a country can best launch into a phase of growth not by slavishly imitating the example of nations already industrialized, but rather by making the most of its particular natural and human resources and by fitting these accurately into the international division of labor.[22] Similarly, a country is likely to attain democracy not by copying the constitutional laws or parliamentary practices of some previous democracy, but rather by honestly facing up to its particular conflicts and by devising or adapting effective procedures for their accommodation.

The serious and prolonged nature of the struggle is likely to force the protagonists to rally around two banners. Hence polarization, rather than pluralism, is the hallmark of this preparatory phase. Yet there are limitations implicit in the requirement of national unity—which, of course, must not only preexist but also continue. If the division is on sharply regional lines, secession rather than democracy is likely to result. Even among contestants geographically interspersed there must be some sense of community or some even balance of forces that makes wholesale expulsion or genocide impossible. The Turks are beginning to develop a set of democratic practices among themselves, but fifty years ago they did not deal democratically with Armenians or Greeks. Crosscutting cleavages have their place in this preparatory phase as a possible means of strengthening or preserving that sense of community.

Dahl notes wistfully that "one perennial problem of opposition is that there is either too much or too little." [23] The first two elements of the model between them will ensure that there is the right amount. But struggle and national unity cannot simply be averaged out, since they cannot be measured along the same scale. Strong doses of both must be combined, just as it may be possible to combine sharp polarization with crosscutting cleavages. Furthermore, as Mary Parker Follett, Lewis A. Coser, and others have insisted, certain types of conflict in themselves constitute creative processes of integration.[24] What infant democracy requires is not a lukewarm struggle but a hot family feud.

This delicate combination implies, of course, that many things can go wrong during the preparatory phase. The fight may go on and on till the protagonists weary and the issues fade away without the emergence of any democratic solution along the way. Or one group may find a way of crushing the opponents after all. In these and other ways an apparent evolution toward democracy may be deflected, and at no time more easily than during the preparatory phase.

C. Decision Phase

Robert Dahl has written that, "Legal party opposition. . .is a recent and unplanned invention."[25] This accords with Bryce's emphasis on the redress of specific grievances as democracy's vehicle and with the assumption here that the transition to democracy is a complex process stretching over many decades. But it does not rule out suffrage or freedom of opposition as conscious goals in the preparatory struggle. Nor does it suggest that a country ever becomes a democracy in a fit of absentmindedness. On the contrary, what concludes the preparatory phase is a deliberate decision on the part of political leaders to accept the existence of diversity in unity and, to that end, to institutionalize some crucial aspect of democratic procedure. Such was the decision in 1907, which I have called the "Great Compromise" of Swedish politics, to adopt universal suffrage combined with proportional representation.[26] Instead of a single decision there may be several. In Britain, as is well-known, the principle of limited government was laid down in the compromise of 1688, cabinet government evolved in the eighteenth century, and suffrage reform was launched as late as 1832. Even in Sweden, the dramatic change of 1907 was followed by the further suffrage reform of 1918 which also confirmed the principle of cabinet government.

Whether democracy is purchased wholesale as in Sweden in 1907 or on the installment plan as in Britain, it is acquired by a process of conscious decision at least on the part of the top political leadership. Politicians are specialists in power, and a fundamental power shift such as that from oligarchy to democracy will not escape their notice.

Decision means choice, and while the choice of democracy does not arise until the background and preparatory conditions are in hand, it is a genuine choice and does not flow automatically from those two conditions. The history of Lebanon illustrates the possibilities of benevolent autocracy or of foreign rule as alternative solutions to entrenched struggles within a political community.[27] And of course a decision in favor of democracy, or some crucial ingredient of it, may be proposed and rejected—thus leading to a continuation of the preparatory phase or to some sort of abortive outcome.

The decision in favor of democracy results from the interplay of a number of forces. Since precise terms must be negotiated and heavy risks with regard to the future taken, a small circle of leaders is likely to play a disproportionate role. Among the negotiating groups and their leaders may be the protagonists of the preparatory struggle. Other participants may include groups that split off from one or the other side or new arrivals on the political stage. In Sweden these new and intermediate groups played a crucial role. Conservatives and Radicals (led by industrialists on one side and intellectuals on the other) had sharpened and crystallized the issues throughout the 1890s. Then came a period of stalemate when discipline in all the recently formed parliamentary parties broke down—a sort of randomization process in which many compromises, combinations, and permutations were devised and explored. The formula that carried the day in 1907 included crucial contributions from a moderately conservative bishop and a moderately liberal farmer, neither of whom played a very prominent role in politics before or after this decision phase.

Just as there can be different types of sponsors and different contents of the decision, so the motives from which it is proposed and accepted will vary from case to case. The forces of conservatism may yield from fear that continued resistance may lose them even more ground in the end. (Such thoughts were on the minds of British Whigs in 1832 and of Swedish conservatives in 1907.) Or they may belatedly wish to live up to principles long proclaimed; such was the Turkish transition to a multiparty system announced by President Inönü in 1945. The radicals may accept the compromise as a first installment, confident that time is on their side and that future installments are bound to follow. Both conservatives and radicals may feel exhausted from a long struggle or fearful of a civil war. This consideration is likely to loom large if they have been through such a war in recent memory. As Barrington Moore has aptly proposed, the English civil war was a crucial "contribution of early violence to later gradualism." [28] In short, democracy, like any collective human action, is likely to stem from a large variety of mixed motives.

The decision phase may well be considered an act of deliberate, explicit consensus. But, once again, this somewhat nebulous term should be carefully considered and perhaps replaced with less ambiguous synonyms. First of all, as Bryce suggests, the democratic content of the decision may be incidental to other substantive issues. Second, in so far as it is a genuine compromise it will seem second-best to all major parties involved—it certainly will not represent any agreement on fundamentals. Third, even on procedures there are likely to be continuing differences of preference. Universal suffrage with proportional representation, the content of the Swedish compromise of 1907, was about equally distasteful to the conservatives (who would rather have continued the old plutocratic voting system) and to the liberals and socialists (who wanted majority rule undiluted by proportional representation). What matters at the decision stage is not what values the leaders hold dear in the abstract, but what concrete steps they are willing to take. Fourth, the agreement worked out by the leaders is far from universal. It must be transmitted to the professional politicians and to the citizenry at large. These are two aspects of the final, or habituation, phase of the model.

D. Habituation Phase

A distasteful decision, once made, is likely to seem more palatable as one is forced to live with it. Everyday experience can supply concrete illustrations of this probability for each of us. Festinger's theory of "cognitive dissonance" supplies a technical explanation and experimental support.[29] Democracy, moreover, is by definition a competitive process, and this competition gives an edge to those who can rationalize their commitment to it, and an even greater edge to those who sincerely believe in it. The transformation of the Swedish Conservative Party from 1918 to 1936 vividly illustrates the point. After two decades those leaders who had grudgingly put up with democracy or pragmatically accepted it retired or died and were replaced by others who sincerely believed in it. Similarly, in Turkey there is a remarkable change from the leadership of Ismet Inönü, who promoted democracy out of a sense of duty, and Adnan Menderes, who saw in it an unprecedented vehicle for his ambition, to younger leaders in each of their parties who understand democracy more fully and embrace it more wholeheartedly. In short, the very process of democracy institutes a double process of Darwinian selectivity in favor of convinced democrats: one among parties in general elections and the other among politicians vying for leadership within these parties.

But politics consists not only of competition for office. It is, above all, a process for resolving conflicts within human groups—whether these arise from the clash of interests or from uncertainty about the future. A new political regime is a novel prescription for taking joint chances on the unknown. With its basic practice of multilateral debate, democracy in particular involves a process of trial and error, a joint learning experience. The first grand compromise that establishes democracy, if it proves at all viable, is in itself a proof of the efficacy of the principle of conciliation and accommodation. The first success, therefore, may encourage contending political forces and their leaders to submit other major questions to resolution by democratic procedures.

In Sweden, for instance, there had been a general political stalemate in the last third of the nineteenth century over the prime issues of the day—the taxation and conscription systems inherited from the sixteenth century. But in the two decades after 1918, when democracy was fully adopted by the Swedes, a whole host of thorny questions was wittingly or unwittingly resolved. The Social Democrats surrendered their earlier pacifism, anticlericalism, and republicanism, as well as the demand for nationalization of industry (although they found it hard to admit this last point). The conservatives, once staunchly nationalist, endorsed Swedish participation in international organizations. Above all, conservatives and liberals fully accepted government intervention in the economy and the social welfare state.

Of course, the spiral that in Sweden went upward to greater and greater successes for the democratic process may also go downward. A conspicuous failure to resolve some urgent political question will damage the prospects of democracy; if such a failure comes early in the habituation phase, it may prove fatal.

Surveying the evolution of political debate and conflict in the Western democracies over the last century, it is striking to observe the difference between social and economic issues, which democracies handled with comparative ease, and issues of community, which have proved far more troublesome.[30] With the advantage of a century's hindsight, it is easy to see that Marx's estimate was wrong at crucial points. In nationality he saw a cloak for bourgeois class interests. He denounced religion as the opiate of the masses. In economics, by contrast, he foresaw very real and increasingly bitter struggles that would end by bringing bourgeois democracy crashing down. But in fact democracy has proved most effective in resolving political questions where the major divisions have been social and economic, as in Britain, Australia, New Zealand, and the Scandinavian countries. It has been the fight among religious, national, and racial groups, instead, that has proved most tenacious and has caused recurrent bitterness, as in Belgium, Holland, Canada, and the United States.

The reasons are not hard to find. On the socioeconomic front Marxism itself became a sufficient force in Europe to serve to some extent as a self-disconfirming prophecy. But beyond this there is a fundamental difference in the nature of the issues. On matters of economic policy and social expenditures you can always split the difference. In an expanding economy, you can even have it both ways: the contest for higher wages, profits, consumer savings, and social welfare payments can be turned into a positive-sum game. But there is no middle position between Flemish and French as official languages, or between Calvinism, Catholicism, and secularism as principles of education. The best you can get here is an "inclusive compromise"[31]—a log-rolling deal whereby some government offices speak French and some Flemish, or some children are taught according to Aquinas, some, Calvin, and some, Voltaire. Such a solution may partly depoliticize the question. Yet it also entrenches the differences instead of removing them, and accordingly it may convert political conflict into a form of trench warfare.

The difficulty that democracy finds in resolving issues of community emphasizes the importance of national unity as the background condition of the democratization process. The hardest struggles in a democracy are those against the birth defects of the political community.

The transition to democracy, it was suggested earlier, may require some common attitudes and some distinct attitudes on the part of the politician and of the common citizen. The distinction is already apparent during the decision phase when the leaders search for compromise while their followers wearily uphold the banners of the old struggle. It becomes even more readily apparent during the habituation phase, when three sorts of process are at work. First, both politicians and citizens learn from the successful resolution of some issues to place their faith in the new rules and to apply them to new issues. Their trust will grow more quickly if, in the early decades of the new regime, a wide variety of political tendencies can participate in the conduct of affairs, either by joining various coalitions or by taking turns as government and opposition. Second, as we just saw, experience with democratic techniques and competitive recruitment will confirm the politicians in their democratic practices and beliefs. Third, the population at large will become firmly fitted into the new structure by the forging of effective links of party organization that connect the politicians in the capital with the mass electorate throughout the country.

These party organizations may be a direct continuation of those that were active during the preparatory, or conflict, phase of democratization, and a suffrage extension at the time of the democratic "decision" may now have given them a free field. It is possible, on the other hand, that no parties with a broad popular base emerged during the conflict phase and that the suffrage extension was very limited. Even under such conditions of partial democratization of the political structure, a competitive dynamic that completes the process may have been set off. The parliamentary parties will seek support from constituency organizations to insure a steady supply of members for their group in future parliaments. Now this and now that political group may see a chance to steal a march on its opponents by enlarging the electorate or by removing other obstacles to majority control. This, roughly, would seem to have been the nature of British developments between 1832 and 1918. Complete democratization, of course, is the only logical stopping point for such a dynamic.

V

The model here presented makes three broad assertions. First, it says that certain ingredients are indispensable to the genesis of democracy. For one thing, there must be a sense of national unity. For another, there must be entrenched and serious conflict. For a third, there must be a conscious adoption of democratic rules. And, finally, both politicians and electorate must be habituated to these rules.

Secondly, the model asserts that these ingredients must be assembled one at a time. Each task has its own logic and each has its natural protagonists—a network of administrators or a group of nationalist literati for the task of unification, a mass movement of the lower class, perhaps led by upper class dissidents, for the task of preparatory struggle, a small circle of political leaders skilled at negotiation and compromise for the formulation of democratic rules, and a variety of organization men and their organizations for the task of habituation. The model thus abandons the quest for "functional requisites" of democracy; for such a quest heaps all these tasks together and thus makes the total job of democratization quite unmanageable. The argument here is analogous to that which has been made by Hirschman and others against the theory of balanced economic growth. These economists do not deny that the transition from a primitive subsistence economy to a mature industrial society involves changes on all fronts—in working skills, in capital formation, in the distribution system, in consumption habits, in the monetary system, and so forth. But they insist that any country that attempted all these tasks at once would in practice find itself totally paralysed—that the stablest balance is that of stagnation. Hence the economic developer's problem, in their view, becomes one of finding backward and forward "linkages," that is, of devising a manageable sequence of tasks.

Thirdly, the model does suggest one such sequence from national unity as background, through struggle, compromise, and habituation, to democracy. The cogency of this sequence is brought home by a deviant development in Turkey in the years after 1945. The Turkish commitment to democracy was made in the absence of prior overt conflict between major social groups or their leading elites. In 1950 there was the first change of government as the result of a new electoral majority, but in the next decade there was a drift back into authoritarian practices on the part of this newly elected party, and in 1960–1961 the democratic experiment was interrupted by a military coup. These developments are not unconnected: Turkey paid the price in 1960 for having received its first democratic regime as a free gift from the hands of a dictator. But after 1961 there was a further evolution in the more appropriate sequence. The crisis of 1960-1961 had made social and political conflict far more acceptable, and a full range of social and economic issues was debated for the first time. The conflict that shaped up was between the military on one side and the spokesmen of the agrarian majority on the other—and the compromise between these two allowed the resumption of the democratic experiment on a more secure basis by 1965.

* * *

Notes

1. Ernest Barker, *Reflections on Government* (Oxford, 1942), p. 63; Daniel Lerner et al., *The Passing of Traditional Society* (Glencoe, 1958), pp. 49ff., 60ff.; Gabriel Almond and Sidney Verba, *The Civic Culture* (Princeton, 1963).
2. Carl J. Friedrich, *The New Belief in the Common Man* (Boston, 1942); E. E. Schattschneider, *The Semi-Sovereign People* (New York, 1960); Bernard Crick, *In Defence of Politics*, rev. ed. (Penguin Books, 1964); Ralf Dahrendorf, *Class and Class Conflict in Industrial Society* (Stanford, 1959); Arend Lijphart, *The Politics of Accommodation* (Berkeley and Los Angeles, 1968).
3. David B. Truman, *The Governmental Process* (New York, 1951), p. 514; S. M. Lipset, *Political Man* (New York, 1960), pp. 88ff. Already A. Lawrence Lowell had spoken of the need for a party alignment where "the line of division is vertical," cutting across the horizontal division of classes. *Government and Parties in Continental Europe* (Boston, 1896), vol. 2, pp. 65ff.
4. Robert A. Dahl, *Who Governs?* (New Haven, 1961); Herbert McClosky, "Consensus and Ideology in American Politics," *American Political Science Review*, LVIII (June 1964); James W. Prothro and Charles M. Grigg, "Fundamental Principles of Democracy: Bases of Agreement and Disagreement," *Journal of Politics*, XXII (May 1960).
5. Harry Eckstein, *The Theory of Stable Democracy* (Princeton, 1961) and *Division and Cohesion in a Democracy* (Princeton, 1965).
6. Robert A. Dahl, *A Preface to Democratic Theory* (Chicago, 1956).
7. Lijphart; Eckstein; Dahl, *Pluralist Democracy in the United States: Conflict and Consent* (Chicago, 1967).
8. Almond and Verba; Eckstein; Dahl, *Who Governs?* and ed. *Political Oppositions in Western Democracies* (New Haven, 1966).
9. See Thomas Kuhn, *The Structure of Scientific Revolutions* (Chicago, 1962).
10. Herbert A. Simon, *Models of Man: Social and Rational* (New York, 1957), p. 65.
11. For a general discussion of the question of democracy in the context of recent modernizing countries, see Rustow, *A World of Nations: Problems of Political Modernization* (Washington, 1967), Ch. 7, which states some of the present argument in summary form.
12. Seymour Martin Lipset, "Some Social Requisites of Democracy: Economic Development and Political Legitimacy," *American Political Science Review*, LIII (March 1959); idem, *Political Man*; Philips Cutright, "National Political Development: Measurement and Analysis," *American Sociological Review*, XXVIII (April 1963).

13. David E. Apter, *The Politics of Modernization* (Chicago, 1965).
14. Leon Festinger, *A Theory of Cognitive Dissonance* (Stanford, 1957).
15. See, e.g., Bertrand de Jouvenel, *On Power* (New York, 1948).
16. W. Ivor Jennings, *The Approach to Self-Government* (Cambridge, 1956), p. 56.
17. Deutsch, *Nationalism and Social Communication*; Deutsch et al., *Political Community and the North Atlantic Area.*
18. Rustow, *A World of Nations*, pp. 30ff. and *International Encyclopedia of the Social Sciences*, s.v. "Nation."
19. For developments in Sweden see Rustow, *The Politics of Compromise: A Study of Parties and Cabinet Government in Sweden* (Princeton, 1955), Chs. 1-3, and Douglas A. Verney, *Parliamentary Reform in Sweden, 1866-1921* (Oxford, 1957). On Turkey see Ward and Rustow and the following essays by Rustow: "Politics and Islam in Turkey," in R. N. Frye, ed. *Islam and the West* (The Hague, 1957), pp. 69-107; "Turkey: The Tradition of Modernity," in Lucian W. Pye and Verba, eds. *Political Culture and Political Development* (Princeton, 1965), pp. 171-198; "The Development of Parties in Turkey," in Joseph LaPalombara and Myron Weiner, eds. *Political Parties and Political Development* (Princeton, 1966), pp. 107-133; and "Politics and Development Policy," in F. C. Shorter, ed. *Four Studies in the Economic Development of Turkey* (London, 1967), pp. 5-31.
20. James Bryce, *Modern Democracies* (London, 1921), vol. 2, p. 602.
21. Albert O. Hirschman, *Journeys Toward Progress* (New York, 1963), pp. 6ff.
22. Ibid., and Hirschman, *The Strategy of Economic Development* (New Haven, 1958), and Hirschman, "Obstacles to Development: A Classification and a Quasi-Vanishing Act," *Economic Development and Cultural Change*, XIII (July 1965), 385-393.
23. Dahl et al., *Political Oppositions in Western Democracies*, p. 397.
24. Mary Parker Follett, *The New State* (New York, 1918), and *Creative Experience* (New York, 1924); Lewis A. Coser, *The Function of Social Conflict* (Glencoe, 1956), p. 121 and passim. A widespread contrary position has recently been restated by Edward Shils, who writes in reference to Lebanon: "Civility will not be strengthened by crisis. It can only grow slowly and in a calm atmosphere. The growth of civility is a necessary condition for Lebanon's development . . . into a genuinely democratic system" (in Binder et al., *Politics in Lebanon*, p. 10). I find it hard to think of situations where there have been any notable advances in either civility or democracy except as the result of crisis.
25. Dahl et al., *Political Oppositions in Western Democracies*, p. xi.
26. Rustow, *The Politics of Compromise*, p. 69.
27. Binder, ed. *Politics in Lebanon.*
28. Barrington Moore, Jr., *Social Origins of Dictatorship and Democracy* (Boston, 1966), p. 3.
29. Festinger, *A Theory of Cognitive Dissonance.*
30. The contrast emerges implicitly from the country studies in Dahl, ed. *Political Oppositions in Western Democracies.*
31. Rustow, *Politics of Compromise*, p. 231.

Chapter 14

CAN DEMOCRATIC TRANSITION BE CONSOLIDATED?

Simply "transitioning" to democracy does not in and of itself mean that democracy will last. Some countries may have a successful democratic transition only to slide back into authoritarianism in the future. Consequently, comparativists must understand not only the factors that led to a transition, but also those factors that create what political scientists call a "democratic consolidation"—in other words, a democracy that is secure and sustained.

The issue of what causes a democratic consolidation is complicated, given that knowing exactly what a consolidated democracy is remains a contentious topic. Some scholars state that a consolidated democracy is one in which "democracy is the only game in town." Juan Linz and Alfred Stepan argue that a consolidated democracy is one in which no major groups want to overthrow it, the people want to keep it (even in times of crisis), and democratic rules have been institutionalized.[1] Inevitably, discussions of democratic consolidation lead to disagreement over the formal prerequisites, but they all end with the general agreement that such things exist and can be seen, even if it is difficult to describe them.

The question of what causes a consolidated democracy is fluid as well. While a variety of definitions of consolidation exists, most emphasize the belief that at the very least it rests on the acceptance of democratic rules by elites and the population. Certainly, the formal rules of democracy matter. A democracy cannot be consolidated if its institutions, for example, do not guarantee free and fair elections. Yet most definitions begin with the assumption that consolidated democracies are those in which social groups accept the legitimacy of the institutions.

The question then becomes: From where does this legitimacy come? Here scholars often return to the ideas concerning democratic transitions; for example, Adam Przeworski focuses on the conditions under which actors will see democracy as rational.[2] That is to say, democratic consolidation comes about through the actions of actors in the political system who undertake a cost-benefit calculation that shows that their interests are best served by maintaining the democratic system. Other scholars point to consolidation stemming from an appropriate political culture or the habituation of democratic rules. For political culture explanations, many link the development of a democratic political culture to the development of a capitalist economy and the rise of the middle class. Thus, debates over the causes of democratic consolidation often mirror those over democratic transitions.

The readings in this section are designed to cover vital aspects of these debates. Guillermo O'Donnell (reading 14.1) and Juan Linz and Alfred Stepan (reading 14.2) directly take on the issues of democratic consolidation and discuss the strengths and weaknesses of various approaches.

Notes

1. Juan Linz and Alfred Stepan, "Toward Consolidated Democracies," *Journal of Democracy* 7, no. 2 (1996): 14–33.
2. Adam Przeworski, *Democracy and the Market: Political and Economic Reforms in Eastern Europe and Latin America* (New York: Cambridge University Press, 1991), 2–4.

14.1

ILLUSIONS ABOUT CONSOLIDATION

Guillermo A. O'Donnell

Guillermo O'Donnell is Helen Kellogg Professor of Government and Senior Fellow of the Kellogg Institute for International Studies at the University of Notre Dame. O'Donnell has undertaken revolutionary research on Latin America that focuses on authoritarianism, democratic transitions, and democratic consolidations. In this intriguing article, he uses Latin American countries as his backdrop while attempting to define democratic consolidation. Yet he does not do so simply to help us know one when we see one, but also to highlight the conceptual difficulties associated with this concept. In fact, his article reveals incredible differences between types of democratic regimes that raise questions about the concept of democratic consolidation as a whole. Read in conjunction with Juan Linz and Alfred Stepan's piece (see reading 14.2), students should be able to compare and contrast the different conceptions of consolidation produced in each piece, and they should ask themselves if the authors agree on what democratic consolidation is. Finally, students should reflect on these definitions of democratic consolidation to determine whether they meet their ideas about democracy.

Democracies used to be few in number, and most were located in the northwestern quarter of the world. Over the last two decades, however, many countries have rid themselves of authoritarian regimes. There are many variations among these countries. Some of them have reverted to new brands of authoritarianism (even if from time to time they hold elections), while others have clearly embraced democracy. Still others seem to inhabit a gray area; they bear a family resemblance to the old established democracies, but either lack or only precariously possess some of their key attributes. The bulk of the contemporary scholarly literature tells us that these "incomplete" democracies are failing to become consolidated, or institutionalized.

This poses two tasks. One is to establish a cutoff point that separates all democracies from all non-democracies. This point's location depends on the questions we ask, and so is always arbitrary. Many definitions of democracy have been offered.[1] The one that I find particularly useful is Robert Dahl's concept of "polyarchy." Once a reasonably well-delimited set of democracies is obtained, the second task is to examine the criteria that a given stream of the literature uses for comparing cases within this set.

Guillermo A. O'Donnell, *Consolidating the Third Wave Democracies,* ed. Larry Diamond, et al. (Baltimore: Johns Hopkins University Press, 1997), 40–57.

If the criteria are found wanting, the next step is to propose alternative concepts for these comparisons. This is what I attempt here, albeit in preliminary and schematic fashion.

Contemporary Latin America is my empirical referent, although my discussion probably also applies to various newly democratized countries in other parts of the world. The main argument is that, contrary to what most of current scholarship holds, the problem with many new polyarchies is not that they lack institutionalization. Rather, the way in which political scientists usually conceptualize some institutions prevents us from recognizing that these polyarchies actually have two extremely important institutions. One is highly formalized, but intermittent: elections. The other is informal, permanent, and pervasive: particularism (or clientelism, broadly defined). An important fact is that, in contrast to previous periods of authoritarian rule, particularism now exists in uneasy tension with the formal rules and institutions of what I call the "full institutional package" of polyarchy. These arguments open up a series of issues that in future publications I will analyze with the detail and nuance they deserve. My purpose at present is to furnish some elements of what I believe are needed revisions in the conceptual and comparative agenda for the study of all existing polyarchies, especially those that are *informally institutionalized*.[2]

Polyarchy, as defined by Dahl, has seven attributes: 1) elected officials; 2) free and fair elections; 3) inclusive suffrage; 4) the right to run for office; 5) freedom of expression; 6) alternative information; and 7) associational autonomy.[3] Attributes 1 to 4 tell us that a basic aspect of polyarchy is that elections are inclusive, fair, and competitive. Attributes 5 to 7 refer to political and social freedoms that are minimally necessary not only during but also between elections as a condition for elections to be fair and competitive. According to these criteria, some countries of Latin America currently are not polyarchies: the Dominican Republic, Haiti, and Mexico have recently held elections, but these were marred by serious irregularities before, during, and after the voting.

Other attributes need to be added to Dahl's list. One is that elected (and some appointed) officials should not be arbitrarily terminated before the end of their constitutionally mandated terms (Peru's Alberto Fujimori and Russia's Boris Yeltsin may have been elected in fair elections, but they abolished polyarchy when they forcefully closed their countries' congresses and fired their supreme courts). A second addition is that the elected authorities should not be subject to severe constraints, vetoes, or exclusion from certain policy domains by other, nonelected actors, especially the armed forces.[4] In this sense, Guatemala and Paraguay, as well as probably El Salvador and Honduras, do not qualify as polyarchies.[5] Chile is an odd case, where restrictions of this sort are part of a constitution inherited from the authoritarian regime. But Chile clearly meets Dahl's seven criteria of polyarchy. Peru is another doubtful case, since the 1995 presidential elections were not untarnished, and the armed forces retain tutelary powers over various policy areas. Third, there should be an uncontested national territory that clearly defines the voting population.[6] Finally, an appropriate definition of polyarchy should also include an intertemporal dimension: the generalized expectation that a fair electoral process and its surrounding freedoms will continue into an indefinite future.

These criteria leave us with the three polyarchies—Colombia, Costa Rica, and Venezuela—whose origins date from before the wave of democratization that began in the mid-1970s, and with nine others that resulted from this wave: Argentina, Bolivia, Brazil, Ecuador, Nicaragua, Panama, Uruguay and, with the caveats noted, Chile and Peru. Only in the oldest Latin American polyarchy (Costa Rica) and in two cases of redemocratization (Chile and Uruguay) do the executive branch, congress, parties, and the judiciary function in a manner that is reasonably close to their formal institutional rules, making them effective institutional knots in the flow of political power and policy. Colombia and Venezuela used to function like this, but do so no longer. These two countries, jointly with Argentina, Bolivia, Brazil, Ecuador, Nicaragua, Panama, and Peru—a set that includes a large majority of the Latin American population and GNP—function in ways that current democratic theory has ill prepared us to understand.

We must go back to the definition of polyarchy. This definition, precise in regard to elections (attributes 1 to 4) and rather generic about contextual freedoms (attributes 5 to 7), is mute with respect to institutional features such as parliamentarism or presidentialism, centralism or federalism, majoritarianism or consensualism, and the presence or absence of a written constitution and judicial review. Also, the definition of polyarchy is silent about important but elusive themes such as if, how, and to what degree governments are responsive or accountable to citizens between elections, and the degree to which the rule of law extends over the country's geographic and social terrain.[7] These silences are appropriate: the definition of polyarchy, let us recall, establishes a crucial cutoff point—one that separates cases where there exist inclusive, fair, and competitive elections and basic accompanying freedoms from all others, including not only unabashed authoritarian regimes but also countries that hold elections but lack some of the characteristics that jointly define polyarchy.

Among polyarchies, however, there are many variations. These differences are empirical, but they can also be normatively evaluated, and their likely effect on the survival prospects of each polyarchy may eventually be assessed. These are important issues that merit some conceptual clarification.

By definition, all the Latin American cases that I have labeled polyarchies are such because of a simple but crucial fact: elections are institutionalized. By an institution I mean a regularized pattern of interaction that is known, practiced, and accepted (if not necessarily approved) by actors who expect to continue interacting under the rules sanctioned and backed by that pattern.[8] Institutions are typically taken for granted, in their existence and continuity, by the actors who interact with and through them. Institutions are "there," usually unquestioned regulators of expectations and behavior. Sometimes, institutions become complex organizations: they are supposed to operate under highly formalized and explicit rules, and materialize in buildings, rituals, and officials. These are the institutions on which both "prebehavioral" and most of contemporary neo-institutionalist political science focus. An unusual characteristic of elections *qua* institutions is that they are highly formalized by detailed and explicit rules, but function intermittently and do not always have a permanent organizational embodiment.

In all polyarchies, old and new, elections are institutionalized, both in themselves and in the reasonable[9] effectiveness of the surrounding conditions of freedom of expression, access to alternative information, and associational autonomy. Leaders and voters take for granted that in the future inclusive, fair, and competitive elections will take place as legally scheduled, voters will be properly registered and free from physical coercion, and their votes will be counted fairly. It is also taken for granted that the winners will take office, and will not have their terms arbitrarily terminated. Furthermore, for this electoral process to exist, freedom of opinion and of association (including the freedom to form political parties) and an uncensored media must also exist. Countries where elections do not have these characteristics do not qualify as polyarchies.[10]

* * *

Theories of "Consolidation"

When elections and their surrounding freedoms are institutionalized, it might be said that polyarchy (or political democracy) is "consolidated," i.e., likely to endure. This, jointly with the proviso of absence of veto powers over elected authorities, is the influential definition of "democratic consolidation" offered by Juan J. Linz, who calls it a state of affairs "in which none of the major political actors, parties, or organized interests, forces, or institutions consider that there is any alternative to democratic processes to gain power, and. . .no political institution or group has a claim to veto the action of democratically elected decision makers. . . . To put it simply, democracy must be seen as the 'only game in town.' " [11] This minimalist definition has important advantages. Still, I see little analytical gain in attaching the term "consolidated" to something that will probably though not certainly endure—"democracy" and "consolidation" are terms too polysemic to make a good pair.

Other authors offer more expanded definitions of democratic consolidation, many of them centered on the achievement of a high degree of "institutionalization." [12] Usually these definitions do not see elections as an institution.[13] They focus on complex organizations, basically the executive, parties, congress, and sometimes the judiciary. Many valuable studies have been conducted from this point of view. By the very logic of their assessment of many new polyarchies as noninstitutionalized, however, these studies presuppose, as their comparative yardstick, a generic and somewhat idealized view of the old polyarchies. The meaning of such a yardstick perplexes me: often it is unclear whether it is something like an average of characteristics observed within the set of old polyarchies, or an ideal type generated from some of these characteristics, or a generalization to the whole set of the characteristics of some of its members, or a normative statement of preferred traits. Furthermore, this mode of reasoning carries a strong teleological flavor. Cases that have not "arrived" at full institutionalization, or that do not seem to be moving in this direction, are seen as stunted, frozen, protractedly unconsolidated, and the like. Such a view presupposes that there are, or should be, factors working in favor of increased consolidation or institutionalization, but that countervailing "obstacles" stymie a process of change that otherwise would operate unfettered.[14] That some of these polyarchies have been in a state of "protracted unconsolidation" [15] for some 20 years suggests that there is something extremely odd about this kind of thinking.

* * *

There is no theory that would tell us why and how the new polyarchies that have institutionalized elections will "complete" their institutional set, or otherwise become "consolidated." All we can say at present is that, as long as elections are institutionalized, polyarchies are likely to endure. We can add the hypothesis that this likelihood is greater for polyarchies that are formally institutionalized. But this proposition is not terribly interesting unless we take into account other factors that most likely have strong independent effects on the survival chances of polyarchies.[16] Consequently, calling some polyarchies "consolidated" or "highly institutionalized" may be no more than saying that they are institutionalized in ways that one expects and of which one approves. Without a theory of how and why this may happen, it is at best premature to expect that newer polyarchies will or should become "consolidated" or "highly institutionalized." In any event, such a theory can only be elaborated on the basis of a positive description of the main traits of the pertinent cases.

The Importance of Informal Rules

Polyarchy is the happy result of centuries-long processes, mostly in countries in the global Northwest. In spite of many variations among these countries, polyarchy is embodied in an institutional package: a set of rules and institutions (many of them complex organizations) that is explicitly formalized in constitutions and auxiliary legislation. Rules are supposed to guide how individuals in institutions, and individuals interacting with institutions, behave. The extent to which behavior and expectations hew to or deviate from formal rules is difficult to gauge empirically. But when the fit is reasonably close, formal rules simplify our task; they are good predictors of behavior and expectations. In this case, one may conclude that all or most of the formal rules and institutions of polyarchy are fully, or close to fully, institutionalized.[17] When the fit is loose or practically nonexistent, we are confronted with the double task of describing actual behavior and discovering the (usually informal) rules that behavior and expectations do follow. Actors are as rational in these settings as in highly formalized ones, but the contours of their rationality cannot be traced without knowing the actual rules, and the common knowledge of these rules, that they follow. One may define this situation negatively, emphasizing the lack of fit between formal rules and observed behavior. As anthropologists have long known, however, this is no substitute for studying the actual rules that are being followed; nor does it authorize the assumption that somehow there is a tendency toward increasing compliance with formal rules. This is especially true when informal rules are widely shared and deeply rooted; in this case, it may be said that these rules (rather than the formal ones) are highly institutionalized.[18]

To some extent this also happens in the old polyarchies. The various laments, from all parts of the ideological spectrum, about the decay of democracy in these countries are largely a consequence of the visible and apparently increasing gap between formal rules and the behavior of all sorts of political actors. But the gap is even larger in many new polyarchies, where the formal rules about how political institutions are supposed to work are often poor guides to what actually happens.

Many new polyarchies do not lack institutionalization, but a fixation on highly formalized and complex organizations prevents us from seeing an extremely influential, informal, and sometimes concealed institution: clientelism and, more generally, particularism. For brevity's sake, I will put details and nuances aside[19] and use these terms to refer broadly to various sorts of nonuniversalistic relationships, ranging from hierarchical particularistic exchanges, patronage, nepotism, and favors to actions that, under the formal rules of the institutional package of polyarchy, would be considered corrupt.[20]

Particularism—like its counterparts, neopatrimonial[21] and delegative conceptions and practices of rule—is antagonistic to one of the main aspects of the full institutional package of polyarchy: the behavioral, legal, and normative distinction between a public and a private sphere. This distinction is an important aspect of the formal institutionalization of polyarchy. Individuals performing roles in political and state institutions are supposed to be guided not by particularistic motives but by universalistic orientations to some version of the public good. The boundaries between the public and the private are often blurred in the old polyarchies, but the very notion of the boundary is broadly accepted and, often, vigorously asserted when it seems breached by public officials acting from particularistic motives. Where particularism is pervasive, this notion is weaker, less widely held, and seldom enforced.

But polyarchy matters, even in the institutional spheres that, against their formal rules, are dominated by particularism. In congress, the judiciary, and some actions of the executive, rituals and discourses are performed as if the formal rules were the main guides of behavior. The consequences are twofold. On one side, by paying tribute to the formal rules, these rituals and discourses encourage demands that these rules be truly followed and that public-oriented governmental behavior prevail. On the other side, the blatant hypocrisy of many of these rituals and discourses breeds cynicism about the institutions of polyarchy, their incumbents, and "politicians" in general. As long as this second consequence is highly visible, particularism is taken for granted, and practiced as the main way of gaining and wielding political power. In such polyarchies, particularism is an important part of the regime.[22] Polyarchies are regimes, but not all polyarchies are the same kind of regime.

Here we see the ambiguity of the assertion made by Juan J. Linz, Adam Przeworski,[23] and others who argue that consolidation occurs when democracy becomes "the only game in town." It is clear that these authors are referring to the formal rules of polyarchy. More generally, even though they may not refer to "institutionalization," authors who limit themselves to the term "consolidation" also assert, more or less implicitly, the same close fit between formal rules and actual behavior.[24] For example, Przeworski argues that democratic consolidation occurs "when no one can imagine acting outside the democratic institutions." But this does not preclude the possibility that the games played "inside" the democratic institutions are different from the ones dictated by their formal rules. Przeworski also states: "To put it somewhat more technically, democracy is consolidated when compliance—acting within the institutional framework—constitutes the equilibrium of the decentralized strategies of all the relevant forces."[25] Clearly, Przeworski is assuming that there is only one equilibrium, the one generated by a close fit between formal rules and behavior. Yet however inferior they may be in terms of performances and outcomes that we value, the situations that I am describing may constitute an equilibrium, too.[26]

A Theoretical Limbo

If the main criterion for democratic consolidation or institutionalization is more or less explicitly a reasonably close fit between formal rules and actual behavior, then what of countries such as Italy, Japan, and India? These are long-enduring polyarchies where, by all indications, various forms of particularism are rampant. Yet these cases do not appear problematic in the literature I am discussing. That they are listed as "consolidated" (or, at least, not listed as "unconsolidated") suggests the strength—and the inconsistency—of this view. It attaches the label "consolidated" to cases that clearly do not fit its arguments but that have endured for a significantly longer period than the new polyarchies have so far. This is a typical paradigmatic anomaly. It deals with these cases by relegating them to a theoretical limbo,[27] as if, because they are somehow considered to be "consolidated," the big gaps between their formal rules and behavior were irrelevant. This is a pity, because variations that are theoretically and empirically important for the study of the whole set of existing polyarchies are thereby obscured.

Another confusing issue is raised by the requirement of "legitimacy" that some definitions of consolidation add. Who must accept formal democratic rules, and how deep must this acceptance run? Here, the literature oscillates between holding that only certain leaders need adhere to democratic principles and arguing that most of the country's people should be democrats, and between requiring normative acceptance of these principles and resting content with a mere perception that there is no feasible alternative to democracy. The scope of this adherence is also problematic: Is it enough that it refers to the formal institutions of the regime, or should it extend to other areas, such as a broadly shared democratic political culture?

Given these conceptual quandaries, it is not surprising that it is impossible clearly to specify when a democracy has become "consolidated." To illustrate this point, consider the "tests" of democratic consolidation that Gunther, Diamandouros, and Puhle propose. These tests supposedly help them to differentiate the consolidated Southern European cases from the unconsolidated Latin American, as well as East European and Asian, ones. The indicators that "may constitute evidence that a regime is consolidated" are: 1) "alternation in power between former rivals";[28] 2) "continued widespread support and stability during times of extreme economic hardship"; 3) "successful defeat and punishment of a handful of strategically placed rebels"; 4) "regime stability in the face of a radical restructuring of the party system"; and 5) "the absence of a politically significant antisystem party or social movement" (pp. 12–13).

* * *

Polyarchies, Particularism, and Accountability

It almost goes without saying that all actual cases exhibit various combinations of universalism and particularism across various relevant dimensions. This observation, however, should not lead to the Procrustean solution of lumping all cases together; differences in the degree to which each case approximates either pole may justify their separate classification and analysis. Of course, one may for various reasons prefer a political process that adheres quite closely to the formal rules of the full institutional package of polyarchy. Yet there exist polyarchies—some of them as old as Italy, India, and Japan, or in Latin America, Colombia, and Venezuela—that endure even though they do not function as their formal rules dictate. To understand these cases we need to know what games are really being played, and under what rules.

* * *

That some polyarchies are informally institutionalized has important consequences. Here I want to stress one that is closely related to the blurring of the boundary between the private and the public spheres: accountability, a crucial aspect of formally institutionalized polyarchy, is seriously hindered. To be sure, the institutionalization of elections means that retrospective electoral accountability exists, and a reasonably free press and various active segments of society see to it that some egregiously unlawful acts of government are exposed (if seldom punished). Polyarchy, even if not formally institutionalized, marks a huge improvement over authoritarian regimes of all kinds. What is largely lacking, however, is another dimension of accountability, which I call "horizontal." By this I mean the controls that state agencies are supposed to exercise over other state agencies. All formally institutionalized polyarchies include various agencies endowed with legally defined authority to sanction unlawful or otherwise inappropriate actions by other state agents. This is an often-overlooked expression of the rule of law in one of the areas where it is hardest to implant, i.e., over state agents, especially high-ranking officials. The basic idea is that formal institutions have well-defined, legally established boundaries that delimit the proper exercise of their authority, and that there are state agencies empowered to control and redress trespasses of these boundaries by any official or agency. These boundaries are closely related to the private-public boundary, in that those who perform public roles are supposed to follow universalistic and public-oriented rules, rather than their own particular interests. Even though its actual functioning is far from perfect, this network of boundaries and accountabilities is an important part of the formal institutionalization of the full package of polyarchy.[29]

By contrast, little horizontal accountability exists in most new polyarchies. Furthermore, in many of them the executive makes strenuous, and often successful, efforts to erode whatever horizontal accountability does exist. The combination of institutionalized elections, particularism as a dominant political institution, and a big gap between the formal rules and the way most political institutions actually work makes for a strong affinity with delegative, not representative, notions of political authority. By this I mean a caesaristic, plebiscitarian executive that once elected sees itself as empowered to govern the country as it deems fit. Reinforced by the urgencies of severe socioeconomic crises and consonant with old *volkisch*, nonindividualistic conceptions of politics, delegative practices strive headlong against formal political institutionalization; congress, the judiciary, and various state agencies of control are seen as hindrances placed in the way of the proper discharge of the tasks that the voters have delegated to the executive. The executive's efforts to weaken these institutions, invade their legal authority, and lower their prestige are a logical corollary of this view.[30] On the other hand, as Max Weber warned, institutions deprived of real power and responsibility tend to act in ways that seem to confirm the reasons adduced for this deprivation. In the cases that concern us here, particularism becomes even more rampant in congress and parties, courts ostensively fail to administer justice, and agencies of control are eliminated or reduced to passivity. This context encourages the further erosion of legally established authority, renders the boundary between public and private even more tenuous, and creates enormous temptations for corruption.

In this sea of particularism and blurred boundaries, why does the universalistic process of fair and competitive elections survive? Governments willing to tamper with laws are hardly solid guarantors of the integrity of electoral processes. Part of the answer, at least with respect to elections to top national positions, is close international attention and wide reporting abroad of electoral irregularities. Fair elections are the main, if not the only, characteristic that certifies countries as democratic before other governments and international opinion. Nowadays this certification has important advantages for countries and for those who govern them. Within the country, elections are a moment when something similar to horizontal accountability operates: parties other than the one in government are present at the polling places, sharing an interest in preventing fraud. Elections create a sharp focus on political matters and on the symbols and rituals that surround the act of voting. At this moment, the citizens' sense of basic fairness manifests itself with special intensity. Violations are likely to be immediately reported. Faced with the protests that might ensue and their repercussions in the international media, and considering the further damage that would come from trying to impose obviously tainted results, most governments are willing to run the risks inherent in fair and competitive elections.

Pervasive particularism, delegative rule, and weak horizontal accountability have at least two serious drawbacks. The first is that the generalized lack of control enables old authoritarian practices to reassert themselves.[31] The second is that, in countries that inaugurated polyarchy under conditions of sharp and increasing inequality, the making and implementation of policy becomes further biased in favor of highly organized and economically powerful interests.

In the countries that occupy us here, the more properly political, *democratic* freedoms are effective: uncoerced voting; freedom of opinion, movement, and association; and others already listed. But for large sections of the population, basic *liberal* freedoms are denied or recurrently trampled. The rights of battered women to sue their husbands and of peasants to obtain a fair trial against their landlords, the inviolability of domiciles in poor neighborhoods, and in general the right of the poor and various minorities to decent treatment and fair access to public agencies and courts are often denied. The effectiveness of the whole ensemble of rights, democratic and liberal, makes for full civil and political citizenship. In many of the new polyarchies, individuals are citizens only in relation to the one institution that functions in a manner close to what its formal rules prescribe—elections. As for full citizenship, only the members of a privileged minority enjoy it.[32] Formally institutionalized polyarchies exhibit various mixes of democracy, liberalism, and republicanism (understood as a view that concurs with liberalism in tracing a clear public-private distinction, but that adds an ennobling and personally demanding conception of participation in the public sphere). Informally institutionalized polyarchies are democratic, in the sense just defined; when they add, as they often do, the plebiscitarian component of delegative rule, they are also strongly majoritarian. But their liberal and republican components are extremely weak.

Freeing Ourselves from Some Illusions

I have rapidly covered complicated terrain.[33] Lest there be any misunderstanding, let me insist that I, too, prefer situations that get close to real observance of the formal rules of polyarchy, a citizenry that firmly approves democratic procedures and values, fair application of the law in all social and geographical locations, and low inequality. Precisely because of this preference, I have argued for the need to improve our conceptual tools in the complex task of studying and comparing the whole set of existing polyarchies. It is through a nonteleological and, indeed, nonethnocentric, positive analysis of the main traits of these polyarchies that we scholars can contribute to their much-needed improvement. This is especially true of the polyarchies that are institutionalized in ways we dislike and often overlook, even if they do not—and some of them may never—closely resemble the "consolidated democracies" of the Northwest.

For this purpose, we must begin by freeing ourselves from some illusions. As an author who has committed most of the mistakes I criticize here, I suspect that we students of democratization are still swayed by the mood of the times that many countries have more or less recently passed through. We believe that democracy, even in the rather modest guise of polyarchy, is vastly preferable to the assortment of authoritarian regimes that it has replaced. We shared in the joy when those regimes gave way, and some of us participated in these historic events. These were moments of huge enthusiasm and hope. Multitudes demanded democracy, and international opinion supported them. The demand for democracy had many meanings, but in all cases it had a powerful common denominator: "Never Again!"[34] Whatever confused, utopian, or limited ideas anyone held concerning democracy, it was clear that it meant getting rid of the despots once and for all. Democracy, even if—or perhaps precisely because—it had so many different meanings attached to it, was the central mobilizing demand that had to be achieved and preserved forever. Somehow, it was felt, this democracy would soon come to resemble the sort of democracy found in admired countries of the Northwest—admired for their long-enduring regimes and for their wealth, and because both things seemed to go together. As in these countries, after the transition democracy was to be stabilized, or consolidated; the Northwest was seen as the endpoint of a trajectory that would be largely traversed by getting rid of the authoritarian rulers. This illusion was extremely useful during the hard and uncertain times of the transition. Its residue is still strong enough to make democracy and consolidation powerful, and consequently pragmatically valid, terms of political discourse.[35] Their analytical cogency is another matter.

On the other hand, because the values that inspired the demands for democracy are as important as ever, the present text is an effort toward opening more disciplined avenues for the study of a topic—and a concern—I share with most of the authors that I have discussed: the quality, in some cases rather dismal, of the social life that is interwoven with the workings of various types of polyarchy. How this quality might be improved depends in part on how realistically we understand the past and present situation of each case.

Notes

For their comments on an earlier version of this text, I am grateful to Michael Coppedge, Gabriela Ippolito-O'Donnell, Scott Mainwaring, Sebastián Mazzuca, Peter Moody, Gerardo Munck, and Adam Przeworski.

1. Reflecting the lack of clearly established criteria in the literature, David Collier and Steven Levitsky have inventoried and interestingly discussed the more than one hundred qualifiers that have been attached to the term "democracy." Many such qualifiers are intended to indicate that the respective cases are in some sense lacking the full attributes of democracy as defined by each author. See Collier and Levitsky, "Democracy 'With Adjectives': Finding Conceptual Order in Recent Comparative Research" (unpubl. ms., University of California–Berkeley, Political Science Department, 1995).
2. I have tried unsuccessfully to find terms appropriate to what the literature refers to as highly versus noninstitutionalized (or poorly institutionalized), or as consolidated versus unconsolidated democracies, with most of the old polyarchies belonging to the first terms of these pairs, and most of the new ones to the second. For reasons that will be clear below, I have opted for labeling the first group "formally institutionalized" and the second "informally institutionalized," but not without misgivings: in the first set of countries, many things happen outside formally prescribed institutional rules, while the second set includes one highly formalized institution, elections.
3. This list is from Robert Dahl, *Democracy and Its Critics* (New Haven: Yale University Press, 1989), 221; the reader may want to examine further details of these attributes, discussed by Dahl in this book.
4. See, especially, J. Samuel Valenzuela, "Democratic Consolidation in Post-Transitional Settings: Notion, Process, and Facilitating Conditions," in Scott Mainwaring, Guillermo O'Donnell, and J. Samuel Valenzuela, eds., *Issues in Democratic Consolidation: The New South American Democracies in Comparative Perspective* (Notre Dame: University of Notre Dame Press, 1992), 57–104; and Philippe C. Schmitter and Terry Lynn Karl, "What Democracy Is . . . and Is Not," *Journal of Democracy* 2 (Summer 1991): 75–88.
5. See Terry Lynn Karl, "The Hybrid Regimes of Central America," *Journal of Democracy* 6 (July 1995): 73–86; and "Imposing Consent? Electoralism vs. Democratization in El Salvador," in Paul Drake and Eduardo Silva, eds., *Elections and Democratization in Latin America, 1980–85* (San Diego: Center for Iberian and Latin American Studies, 1986), 9–36.
6. See, especially, Juan J. Linz and Alfred Stepan, *Problems of Democratic Transition and Consolidation: Southern Europe, South America, and Postcommunist Europe* (Baltimore: Johns Hopkins University Press, forthcoming); and Philippe Schmitter, "Dangers and Dilemmas of Democracy," *Journal of Democracy* 5 (April 1994): 57–74.
7. For a useful listing of these institutional variations, see Schmitter and Karl, "What Democracy Is . . . and Is Not."
8. For a more-detailed discussion of institutions, see my "Delegative Democracy," *Journal of Democracy* 5 (January 1994): 56–69.
9. The term "reasonable" is admittedly ambiguous. Nowhere are these freedoms completely uncurtailed, if by nothing else than the political consequences of social inequality. By "reasonable" I mean that there are neither de jure prohibitions on these freedoms nor systematic and usually successful efforts by the government or private actors to annul them.

10. On the other hand, elections can be made more authentically competitive by, say, measures that diminish the advantages of incumbents or of economically powerful parties. These are, of course, important issues. But the point I want to make at the moment is that these differences obtain among countries that already qualify as polyarchies.
11. Juan J. Linz, "Transitions to Democracy," *Washington Quarterly* 13 (1990): 156. The assertion about "the only game in town" entails some ambiguities that I discuss below.
12. Even though most definitions of democratic consolidation are centered around "institutionalization" (whether explicitly or implicitly, by asserting acceptance or approval of democratic institutions and their formal rules), they offer a wide variety of additional criteria. My own count in a recent review of the literature is twelve; see Doh Chull Shin, "On the Third Wave of Democratization: A Synthesis and Evaluation of Recent Theory and Research," *World Politics* 47 (October 1994): 135–70.
13. Even though he does not use this language, an exception is the definition of democratic consolidation offered by J. Samuel Valenzuela, which is centered in what I call here the institutionalization of elections and the absence of veto powers; see his "Democratic Consolidation in Post-Transitional Settings," 69.
14. It is high time for self-criticism. The term "stunted" I used jointly with Scott Mainwaring and J. Samuel Valenzuela in the introduction to our *Issues in Democratic Consolidation*, 11. Furthermore, in my chapter in the same volume (pp. 17–56), I offer a nonminimalist definition of democratic consolidation, and propose the concept of a "second transition," from a democratically elected government to a consolidated democratic regime. These concepts partake of the teleology I criticize here. This teleological view is homologous to the one used by many modernization studies in the 1950s and 1960s; it was abundantly, but evidently not decisively, criticized at the time. For a critique of the concept of "democratic consolidation" that is convergent with mine, see Ben Ross Schneider, "Democratic Consolidations: Some Broad Comparisons and Sweeping Arguments," *Latin American Research Review* 30 (1995): 215–34; Schneider concludes by warning against "the fallacy of excessive universalism" (p. 231).
15. Philippe C. Schmitter with Terry Lynn Karl, "The Conceptual Travels of Transitologists and Consolidologists: How Far to the East Should They Attempt to Go?" *Slavic Review* 63 (Spring 1994): 173–85.
16. Adam Przeworski and his collaborators found that higher economic development and a parliamentary regime increase the average survival rate of polyarchies. These are important findings, but the authors have not tested the impacts of socioeconomic inequality and of the kind of informal institutionalization that I discuss below. Pending further research, it is impossible to assess the causal direction and weight of all these variables. I suspect that high socioeconomic inequality has a close relationship with informal institutionalization. But we do not know if either or both, directly or indirectly, affect the chances of survival of polyarchy, or if they might cancel the effect of economic development that Przeworski et al. found. See Adam Przeworski and Fernando Limongi, "Modernization: Theories and Facts" (Working Paper No. 4, Chicago Center for Democracy, University of Chicago, November 1994); and Adam Przeworski, Michael Alvarez, José Antonio Cheibub, and Fernando Limongi, "What Makes Democracies Endure?" *Journal of Democracy* 7 (January 1996): 39–55.
17. A topic that does not concern me here is the extent to which formal rules are institutionalized across various old polyarchies and, within them, across various issue areas, though the variations seem quite important on both counts.
18. The lore of many countries is filled with jokes about the naive foreigner or the native sucker who gets in trouble by following the formal rules of a given situation. I have explored some of these issues with reference to Brazil and Argentina in "Democracia en la Argentina: Micro y Macro" (Working Paper No. 2, Notre Dame, Kellogg Institute, 1983); "Y a mí qué me importa? Notas Sobre Sociabilidad y Política en Argentina y Brasil" (Working Paper No. 9, Notre Dame, Kellogg Institute, 1984); and "Micro-Escenas de la Privatización de lo Público en Brasil" (Working Paper No. 21, with commentaries by Roberto DaMatta and J. Samuel Valenzuela, Notre Dame, Kellogg Institute, 1989).

19. For the purposes of the generic argument presented in this essay, and not without hesitation because of its vagueness, from now on I will use the term "particularism" to refer to these phenomena. On the contemporary relevance of clientelism, see Luis Roniger and Ayse Gunes-Ayata, eds., *Democracy, Clientelism, and Civil Society* (Boulder, Co.: Lynne Rienner, 1994). For studies focused on Latin America that are germane to my argument, see especially Roberto DaMatta, *A Case e a Rua: Espaco, Cidadania, Mulher e Morte no Brasil* (São Paulo: Editora Brasiliense, 1985); Jonathan Fox, "The Difficult Transition from Clientelism to Citizenship," *World Politics* 46 (January 1994): 151–84; Francis Hagopian, "The Compromised Transition: The Political Class in the Brazilian Transition," in Mainwaring et al., *Issues in Democratic Consolidation*, 243–93; and Scott Mainwaring, "Brazilian Party Underdevelopment in Comparative Perspective," *Political Science Quarterly* 107 (Winter 1992–93): 677–707. These and other studies show that particularism and its concomitants are not ignored by good field researchers. But, attesting to the paradigmatic force of the prevalent views on democratization, in this literature the rich data and findings emerging from such case studies are not conceptually processed as an intrinsic part of the *problématique* of democratization, or are seen as just "obstacles" interposed in the way of its presumed direction of change.
20. Particularistic relationships can be found in formally institutionalized polyarchies, of course. I am pointing here to differences of degree that seem large enough to require conceptual recognition. One important indication of these differences is the extraordinary leniency with which, in informally institutionalized polyarchies, political leaders, most of public opinion, and even courts treat situations that in the other polyarchies would be considered as entailing very severe conflicts of interest.
21. For a discussion of neopatrimonialism, see my "Transitions, Continuities, and Paradoxes," in Mainwaring et al., *Issues in Democratic Consolidation*, 17–56. An interesting recent discussion of neopatrimonialism is Jonathan Hartlyn's "Crisis-Ridden Elections (Again) in the Dominican Republic: Neopatrimonialism, Presidentialism, and Weak Electoral Oversight," *Journal of Interamerican and World Affairs* 34 (Winter 1994): 91–144.
22. By "regime" I mean "the set of effectively prevailing patterns (not necessarily legally formalized) that establish the modalities of recruitment and access to governmental roles, and the permissible resources that form the basis for expectations of access to such roles," as defined in my *Bureaucratic Authoritarianism: Argentina, 1966–1973, in Comparative Perspective* (Berkeley: University of California Press, 1988), 6.
23. Adam Przeworski, *Democracy and the Market: Political and Economic Reforms in Eastern Europe and Latin America* (Cambridge: Cambridge University Press, 1991).
24. See, among many others that could be cited (some transcribed in Shin, "On the Third Wave of Democratization"), the definition of democratic consolidation proposed by Gunther, Diamandouros, and Puhle in *Politics of Democratic Consolidation*, 3: "the achievement of substantial attitudinal support for and behavioral compliance with the new democratic institutions and the rules which they establish." A broader but equivalent definition is offered four pages later.
25. Przeworski, *Democracy and the Market*, 26.
26. In another influential discussion, Philippe C. Schmitter, although he does not use this language, expresses a similar view of democratic consolidation; see his "Dangers and Dilemmas of Democracy," *Journal of Democracy* 5 (April 1994): 56–74. Schmitter begins by asserting, "In South America, Eastern Europe, and Asia the specter haunting the transition is . . . nonconsolidation. . . . These countries are 'doomed' to remain democratic almost by default." He acknowledges that the attributes of polyarchy may hold in these countries—but these "patterns never quite crystallize" (pp. 60–61). To say that democracy exists "almost by default" (i.e., is negatively defined) and is not "crystallized" (i.e., not formally institutionalized) is another way of stating the generalized view that I am discussing.
27. An exception is Gunther et al., *Politics of Democratic Consolidation*, where Italy is one of the four cases studied. But the way they deal with recent events in Italy is exemplary of the conceptual problems I am discussing. They assert that in Italy "several important partial regimes . . . were challenged, became deconsolidated, and entered into a significant process of restructuring beginning in 1991" (p. 19). On the same page, the reader

learns that these partial regimes include nothing less than "the electoral system, the party system, and the structure of the state itself." (Added to this list later on is "the basic nature of executive-legislative relations" [p. 394].) Yet the "Italian democracy remains strong and resilient"—after practically every important aspect of its regime, and even of the state, became "deconsolidated" (p. 412). If the authors mean that, in spite of a severe crisis, the Italian polyarchy is likely to endure, I agree.

28. Actually, the authors are ambiguous about this first "test." Just before articulating their list of tests with this one at its head, they assert that they "reject [peaceful alternation in government between parties that were once bitterly opposed] as a *prerequisite* for regarding a regime as consolidated." See Gunther et al., *Politics of Democratic Consolidation*, 12 (emphasis added).
29. I may have sounded naive in my earlier comments about how individuals performing public roles are supposed to be guided by universalistic orientations to some version of the public good. Now I can add that, as the authors of the *Federalist Papers* knew, this is not only, or even mostly, a matter of the subjective intentions of these individuals. It is to a large extent contingent on institutional arrangements of control and accountability, and on expectations built around these arrangements, that furnish incentives (including the threats of severe sanctions and public discredit) for that kind of behavior. That these incentives are often insufficient should not be allowed to blur the difference with cases where the institutional arrangements are nonexistent or ineffective; these situations freely invite the enormous temptations that always come with holding political power. I wish to thank Adam Przeworski and Michael Coppedge for raising this point in private communications.
30. The reader has surely noticed that I am referring to countries that have presidentialist regimes and that, consequently, I am glossing over the arguments, initiated by Juan J. Linz and followed up by a number of other scholars, about the advantages of parliamentarism over the presidentialist regimes that characterize Latin America. Although these arguments convince me in the abstract, because of the very characteristics I am depicting I am skeptical about the practical consequences of attempting to implant parliamentarism in these countries.
31. For analyses of some of these situations, see Paulo Sérgio Pinheiro, "The Legacy of Authoritarianism in Democratic Brazil," in Stuart S. Nagel, ed., *Latin American Development and Public Policy* (New York: St. Martin's, 1995), 237–53; and Martha K. Huggins, ed., *Vigilantism and the State in Modern Latin America: Essays on Extralegal Violence* (New York: Praeger, 1991). See also the worrisome analysis, based on Freedom House data, that Larry Diamond presents in his "Democracy in Latin America: Degrees, Illusions, and Directions for Consolidation," in Tom Farer, ed., *Beyond Sovereignty: Collectively Defending Democracy in the Americas* (Baltimore: Johns Hopkins University Press, 1995). In recent years, the Freedom House indices reveal, more Latin American countries have regressed rather than advanced. For a discussion of various aspects of the resulting obliteration of the rule of law and weakening of citizenship, see Guillermo O'Donnell, "On the State, Democratization, and Some Conceptual Problems: A Latin American View with Glances at Some Post-Communist Countries," *World Development* 21 (1993): 1355–69.
32. There is a huge adjacent theme that I will not discuss here: the linkage of these problems with widespread poverty and, even more, with deep inequalities of various sorts.
33. Obviously, we need analyses that are more nuanced, comprehensive, and dynamic than the one that I have undertaken here. My own list of topics meriting much further study includes: the opportunities that may be entailed by demands for more universalistic and public-oriented governmental behavior; the odd coexistence of pervasive particularism with highly technocratic modes of decision making in economic policy; the effects of international demands (especially regarding corruption and uncertainty in legislation and adjudication) that the behavior of public officials should conform more closely to the formal rules; and the disaggregation of various kinds and institutional sites of clientelism and particularism. Another major issue that I overlook here, raised by Larry Diamond in a personal communication, is locating the point at which violations of liberal rights should be construed as cancelling, or making ineffective, the political freedoms surrounding elections. Finally, Philippe C. Schmitter makes an argument worth exploring when he urges that polyarchies be disaggregated into various "partial regimes"; most of these would surely look quite different when comparing formally versus informally

institutionalized cases. See Schmitter, "The Consolidation of Democracy and Representation of Social Groups," *American Behavioral Scientist* 35 (March–June 1992): 422–49.

34. This is the title of the reports of the commissions that investigated human rights violations in Argentina and Brazil. For further discussion of what I call a dominant antiauthoritarian mood in the transitions, see my "Transitions, Continuities, and Paradoxes," in Mainwaring et al., *Issues in Democratic Consolidation*, 17–56; and Nancy Bermeo, "Democracy and the Lessons of Dictatorship," *Comparative Politics* 24 (April 1992): 273–91.

35. Symptomatically illustrating the residues of the language and the hopes of the transition as well as the mutual influences between political and academic discourses, on several occasions the governments of the countries that I know more closely (Argentina, Brazil, Chile, and Uruguay) triumphantly proclaimed that their democracies had become "consolidated."

14.2

TOWARD CONSOLIDATED DEMOCRACIES

Juan J. Linz and Alfred C. Stepan

Juan Linz, professor emeritus at Yale University, has conducted extensive research on the politics of both authoritarian and democratizing regimes. In particular, his groundbreaking research has focused on the causes of democratic collapse. Alfred Stepan is professor of government and director of the Center for the Study of Democracy, Toleration, and Religion at Columbia University. His work focuses on the processes of democratization in Latin America, Southern Europe, and postcommunist Europe. In this article, Linz and Stepan attempt to define a "consolidated democracy." While most scholars distinguish between consolidated and nonconsolidated democracies, defining the difference empirically is an extremely complicated task. Linz and Stepan, using a wealth of real-world examples, argue that to be consolidated, a country must be a state that has successfully completed a democratic transition and has a government that rules democratically. Without these characteristics, a country cannot claim to be a consolidated democracy. When reading this article, students should carefully consider what exactly these criteria mean. For example, what exactly is a state? Why is a state necessary for a consolidated democracy? Also, students should consider why having experienced a democratic transition is not sufficient to be a consolidated democracy.

It is necessary to begin by saying a few words about three minimal conditions that must obtain before there can be any possibility of speaking of democratic consolidation. First, in a modern polity, free and authoritative elections cannot be held, winners cannot exercise the monopoly of legitimate force, and citizens cannot effectively have their rights protected by a rule of law unless a state exists. In some parts of the world, conflicts about the authority and domain of the *polis* and the identities and loyalties of the *demos* are so intense that no state exists. No state, no democracy.

Second, democracy cannot be thought of as consolidated until a democratic transition has been brought to completion. A necessary but by no means sufficient condition for the completion of a democratic transition is the holding of free and contested elections (on the basis of broadly inclusive voter eligibility) that meet the seven institutional requirements for elections in a polyarchy that Robert A. Dahl has set forth.[1] Such elections are not sufficient, however, to complete a democratic transition. In many cases (e.g., Chile as of 1996) in which free and contested elections have been held, the government resulting from elections like these lacks the de jure as well as de facto power to determine policy

Juan J. Linz and Alfred C. Stepan, *The Global Divergence of Democracy,* ed. Larry Diamond and Marc Plattner (Baltimore: Johns Hopkins University Press, 2001), 93–112.

in many significant areas because the executive, legislative, and judicial powers are still decisively constrained by an interlocking set of "reserve domains," military "prerogatives," or "authoritarian enclaves."[2]

Third, no regime should be called a democracy unless its rulers govern democratically. If freely elected executives (no matter what the magnitude of their majority) infringe the constitution, violate the rights of individuals and minorities, impinge upon the legitimate functions of the legislature, and thus fail to rule within the bounds of a state of law, their regimes are not democracies.

In sum, when we talk about the consolidation of democracy, we are not dealing with liberalized nondemocratic regimes, or with pseudo-democracies, or with hybrid democracies where some democratic institutions coexist with nondemocratic institutions outside the control of the democratic state. Only democracies can become consolidated democracies.

* * *

In most cases after a democratic transition is completed, there are still many tasks that need to be accomplished, conditions that must be established, and attitudes and habits that must be cultivated before democracy can be regarded as consolidated. What, then, are the characteristics of a consolidated democracy? Many scholars, in advancing definitions of consolidated democracy, enumerate all the regime characteristics that would improve the overall quality of democracy. We favor, instead, a narrower definition of democratic consolidation, but one that nonetheless combines behavioral, attitudinal, and constitutional dimensions. Essentially, by a "consolidated democracy" we mean a political regime in which democracy as a complex system of institutions, rules, and patterned incentives and disincentives has become, in a phrase, "the only game in town."[3]

Behaviorally, democracy becomes the only game in town when no significant political group seriously attempts to overthrow the democratic regime or to promote domestic or international violence in order to secede from the state. When this situation obtains, the behavior of the newly elected government that has emerged from the democratic transition is no longer dominated by the problem of how to avoid democratic breakdown. (Exceptionally, the democratic process can be used to achieve secession, creating separate states that can be democracies.) Attitudinally, democracy becomes the only game in town when, even in the face of severe political and economic crises, the overwhelming majority of the people believe that any further political change must emerge from within the parameters of democratic procedures. Constitutionally, democracy becomes the only game in town when all of the actors in the polity become habituated to the fact that political conflict within the state will be resolved according to established norms, and that violations of these norms are likely to be both ineffective and costly. In short, with consolidation, democracy becomes routinized and deeply internalized in social, institutional, and even psychological life, as well as in political calculations for achieving success.

Our working definition of a consolidated democracy is then as follows: *Behaviorally,* a democratic regime in a territory is consolidated when no significant national, social, economic, political, or institutional actors spend significant resources attempting to achieve their objectives by creating a nondemocratic regime or by seceding from the state. *Attitudinally,* a democratic regime is consolidated when a strong majority of public opinion, even in the midst of major economic problems and deep dissatisfaction with incumbents, holds the belief that democratic procedures and institutions are the most appropriate way to govern collective life, and when support for antisystem alternatives is quite small or more-or-less isolated from prodemocratic forces. *Constitutionally,* a democratic regime is consolidated when governmental and nongovernmental forces alike become subject to, and habituated to, the resolution of conflict within the bounds of the specific laws, procedures, and institutions sanctioned by the new democratic process.

We must add two important caveats. First, when we say a regime is a consolidated democracy, we do not preclude the possibility that at some future time it could break down. Such a breakdown, however, would be related not to weaknesses or problems specific to the historic process of democratic consolidation, but to a new dynamic in which the democratic regime cannot solve a set of problems, a nondemocratic alternative gains significant supporters, and former democratic regime loyalists begin to behave in a constitutionally disloyal or semiloyal manner.[4]

Our second caveat is that we do not want to imply that there is only one type of consolidated democracy. An exciting new area of research is concerned with precisely this issue—the varieties of consolidated democracies. We also do not want to imply that consolidated democracies could not continue to improve their quality by raising the minimal economic plateau upon which all citizens stand, and by deepening popular participation in the political and social life of the country. Within the category of consolidated democracies there is a continuum from low-quality to high-quality democracies. Improving the quality of consolidated democracies is an urgent political and intellectual task, but our goal in this essay, though related, is a different one. As we are living in a period in which an unprecedented number of countries have completed democratic transitions and are attempting to consolidate democracies, it is politically and conceptually important that we understand the specific tasks of "crafting" democratic consolidation. Unfortunately, too much of the discussion of the current "wave" of democratization focuses almost solely on elections or on the presumed democratizing potential of market mechanisms. Democratic consolidation, however, requires much more than elections and markets.

Crafting and Conditions

In addition to a functioning state, five other interconnected and mutually reinforcing conditions must be present, or be crafted, in order for a democracy to be consolidated. First, the conditions must exist for the development of a free and lively *civil society.* Second, there must be a relatively autonomous *political society.* Third, throughout the territory of the state all major political actors, especially the government and the state apparatus, must be effectively subjected to a *rule of law* that protects individual freedoms and associational life. Fourth, there must be a *state bureaucracy* that is usable by the new democratic government. Fifth, there must be an institutionalized *economic society.* Let us explain what is involved in crafting this interrelated set of conditions.

By "civil society," we refer to that arena of the polity where self-organizing and relatively autonomous groups, movements, and individuals attempt to articulate values, to create associations and solidarities, and to advance their interests. Civil society can include manifold social movements (e.g., women's groups, neighborhood associations, religious groupings, and intellectual organizations), as well as associations from all social strata (such as trade unions, entrepreneurial groups, and professional associations).

By "political society," we mean that arena in which political actors compete for the legitimate right to exercise control over public power and the state apparatus. Civil society by itself can destroy a nondemocratic regime, but democratic consolidation (or even a full democratic transition) must involve political society. Democratic consolidation requires that citizens develop an appreciation for the core institutions of a democratic political society—political parties, legislatures, elections, electoral rules, political leadership, and interparty alliances.

It is important to stress not only the difference between civil society and political society, but also their complementarity, which is not always recognized. One of these two arenas is frequently neglected in favor of the other. Worse, within the democratic community, champions of either civil society or political society all too often adopt a discourse and a set of practices that are implicitly inimical to the normal development of the other.

* * *

The Need for a *Rechtsstaat*

To achieve a consolidated democracy, the necessary degree of autonomy of civil and political society must be embedded in, and supported by, our third arena, the rule of law. All significant actors—especially the democratic government and the state apparatus—must be held accountable to, and become habituated to, the rule of law. For the types of civil society and political society we have just described, a rule of law animated by a spirit of constitutionalism is an indispensable condition. Constitutionalism, which should not be confused with majoritarianism, entails a relatively strong consensus regarding the constitution, and especially a commitment to "self-binding" procedures of governance that can be altered only by exceptional majorities. It also requires a clear hierarchy of laws, interpreted by an independent judicial system and supported by a strong legal culture in civil society.[5]

The emergence of a *Rechtsstaat*—a state of law, or perhaps more accurately a state subject to law—was one of the major accomplishments of nineteenth-century liberalism (long before full democratization) in continental Europe and to some extent in Japan. A *Rechtsstaat* meant that the government and the state apparatus would be subject to the law, that areas of discretionary power would be defined and increasingly limited, and that citizens could turn to courts to defend themselves against the state and its officials. The modern *Rechtsstaat* is fundamental in making democratization possible, since without it citizens would not be able to exercise their political rights with full freedom and independence.

A state of law is particularly crucial for the consolidation of democracy. It is the most important continuous and routine way in which the elected government and the state administration are subjected to a network of laws, courts, semiautonomous review and control agencies, and civil-society norms that not only check the state's illegal tendencies but also embed it in an interconnecting web of mechanisms requiring transparency and accountability. Freely elected governments can, but do not necessarily, create such a state of law. The consolidation of democracy, however, requires such a law-bound, constraint-embedded state. Indeed, the more that all the institutions of the state function according to the principle of the state of law, the higher the quality of democracy and the better the society.

Constitutionalism and the rule of law must determine the offices to be filled by election, the procedures to elect those officeholders, and the definition of and limits to their power in order for people to be willing to participate in, and to accept the outcomes of, the democratic game. This may pose a problem if the rules, even if enacted by a majority, are so unfair or poorly crafted and so difficult to change democratically that they are unacceptable to a large number of citizens. For example, an electoral law that gives 80 percent of the seats in parliament to a party that wins less than 50 percent of the vote, or an ideologically loaded constitution that is extremely difficult to amend, is not likely to be conducive to democratic consolidation.

Finally, a democracy in which a single leader enjoys, or thinks he or she enjoys, a "democratic" legitimacy that allows him or her to ignore, dismiss, or alter other institutions—the legislature, the courts, the constitutional limits of power—does not fit our conception of rule of law in a democratic regime. The formal or informal institutionalization of such a system is not likely to result in a consolidated democracy unless such discretion is checked.

* * *

A Usable Bureaucracy

These three conditions—a lively and independent civil society; a political society with sufficient autonomy and a working consensus about procedures of governance; and constitutionalism and a rule of law—are virtually definitional prerequisites of a consolidated democracy. However, these conditions are much more likely to be satisfied where there are also found a bureaucracy usable by democratic leaders and an institutionalized economic society.

Democracy is a form of governance in which the rights of citizens are guaranteed and protected. To protect the rights of its citizens and to deliver other basic services that citizens demand, a democratic government needs to be able to exercise effectively its claim to a monopoly of the legitimate use of force in its territory. Even if the state had no other functions than these, it would have to tax compulsorily in order to pay for police officers, judges, and basic services. A modern democracy, therefore, needs the effective capacity to command, to regulate, and to extract tax revenues. For this, it needs a functioning state with a bureaucracy considered usable by the new democratic government.

In many territories of the world today—especially in parts of the former Soviet Union—no adequately functioning state exists. Insufficient taxing capacity on the part of the state or a weak normative and bureaucratic "presence" in much of its territory, such that citizens cannot effectively demand that their rights be respected or receive any basic entitlements, is also a great problem in many countries in Latin America, including Brazil. The question of the usability of the state bureaucracy by the new democratic regime also emerges in countries such as Chile, where the outgoing nondemocratic regime was able to give tenure to many key members of the state bureaucracy in politically sensitive areas such as justice and education. Important questions about the usability of the state bureaucracy by new democrats inevitably emerge in cases where the distinction between the communist party and the state had been virtually obliterated (as in much of postcommunist Europe), and the party is now out of power.

Economic Society

The final supportive condition for a consolidated democracy concerns the economy, an arena that we believe should be called "economic society." We use this phrase to call attention to two claims that we believe are theoretically and empirically sound. First, there has never been, and there cannot be, a consolidated democracy that has a command economy (except perhaps in wartime). Second, there has never been, and almost certainly will never be, a modern consolidated democracy with a pure market economy. Modern consolidated democracies require a set of sociopolitically crafted and accepted norms, institutions, and regulations—what we call "economic society"—that mediate between the state and the market.

No empirical evidence has ever been adduced to indicate that a polity meeting our definition of a consolidated democracy has ever existed with a command economy. Is there a theoretical reason to explain such a universal empirical outcome? We think so. On theoretical grounds, our assumption is that at least a nontrivial degree of market autonomy and of ownership diversity in the economy is necessary to produce the independence and liveliness of civil society that allow it to make its contribution to a democracy. Similarly, if all property is in the hands of the state, along with all decisions about pricing, labor, supply, and distribution, the relative autonomy of political society required for a consolidated democracy could not exist.[6]

But why are completely free markets unable to coexist with modern consolidated democracies? Empirically, serious studies of modern polities repeatedly verify the existence of significant degrees of market intervention and state ownership in all consolidated democracies.[7] Theoretically, there are at least three reasons why this should be so. First, notwithstanding certain ideologically extreme but surprisingly prevalent neoliberal claims about the self-sufficiency of the market, pure market economies could neither come into being nor be maintained without a degree of state regulation. Markets require legally enforced contracts, the issuance of money, regulated standards for weights and measures, and the protection of property, both public and private. These requirements dictate a role for the state in the economy. Second, even the best of markets experience "market failures" that must be corrected if the market is to function well.[8] No less an advocate of the "invisible hand" of the market than Adam Smith acknowledged that the state is necessary to perform certain functions. In a crucial but neglected passage in the *Wealth of Nations,* Adam Smith identified three important tasks of the state:

> First, the duty of protecting the society from the violence and invasion of other independent societies; secondly, the duty of protecting, as far as possible, every member of the society from the injustice or oppression of every other member of it, or the duty of establishing an exact administration of justice; and, thirdly, the duty of erecting and maintaining certain public works and certain public institutions which it can never be for the interest of any individual, or small number of individuals, to erect and maintain; because the profit could never repay the expense to any individual or small number of individuals, though it may frequently do much more than repay it to a great society.[9]

Finally, and most importantly, democracy entails free public contestation concerning governmental priorities and policies. If a democracy never produced policies that generated government-mandated public goods in the areas of education, health, and transportation, and never provided some economic safety net for its citizens and some alleviation of gross economic inequality, democracy would not be sustainable. Theoretically, of course, it would be antidemocratic to take such public policies off the agenda of legitimate public contestation. Thus, even in the extreme hypothetical case of a democracy that began with a pure market economy, the very working of a modern democracy (and a modern advanced capitalist economy) would lead to the transformation of that pure market economy into a mixed economy, or that set of norms, regulations, policies, and institutions which we call "economic society." [10]

Any way we analyze the problem, democratic consolidation requires the institutionalization of a politically regulated market. This requires an economic society, which in turn requires an effective state. Even a goal such as narrowing the scope of public ownership (i.e., privatization) in an orderly and legal way is almost certainly carried out more effectively by a stronger state than by a weaker one. Economic deterioration due to the state's inability to carry out needed regulatory functions greatly compounds the problems of economic reform and democratization.[11]

* * *

Two Surmountable Obstacles

Two of the most widely cited obstacles to democratic consolidation are the dangers posed by ethnic conflict in multinational states and by disappointed popular hopes for economic improvement in states undergoing simultaneous political and economic reform. These are real problems. Democratic theorists and crafters alike must recognize that there is often more than one "awakened nation" present in the state, and that there can be prolonged economic reversals after democratic transition begins. Nonetheless, we are convinced, on both theoretical and empirical grounds, that democracy can still make significant strides toward consolidation under such conditions. We are furthermore convinced that if democratic theorists conceptualize what such obstacles mean and do not mean, this may lessen the dangers of democratic disenchantment and help to identify obstacle-reducing paths. That is our task in the rest of this essay.

Under what empirical conditions do "nation-states" and "democratization" form complementary logics? Under what conditions do they form conflicting logics? If they form conflicting logics, what types of practices and institutions will make democratic consolidation most, or least, likely?

Many political thinkers and activists assume that Weberian states, nation-states, and democracy cohere as part of the very grammar of modern polities. In a world where France, Germany, Portugal, Greece, and Japan are all Weberian states, nation-states, and democracies, such an assumption may seem justified. Yet in many countries that are not yet consolidated democracies, a nation-state policy often has a different logic than a democratic policy. By a nation-state policy we mean one in which the leaders of the state pursue what Rogers Brubaker calls "nationalizing state policies" aimed at increasing cultural homogeneity. Consciously or unconsciously, the leaders send messages that the state should be "of and for" the nation.[12] In the constitutions they write and in the politics they practice, the dominant nation's language becomes the only official language and occasionally the only acceptable language for state business and for education; the religion of the nation is privileged (even if it is not necessarily made the official religion); and the culture of the dominant nation is privileged in state symbols (such as the flag, national anthem, and even eligibility for some types of military service) and in state-controlled means of socialization (such as radio, television, and textbooks). By contrast, democratic policies in the state-making process are those that emphasize a broad and inclusive citizenship that accords equal individual rights to all.

Under what empirical conditions are the logics of state policies aimed at nation-building congruent with those aimed at crafting democracy? Empirically, conflicts between these different policies are reduced when almost all of the residents of a state identify with one subjective idea of the nation, and when that nation is virtually coextensive with the state. These conditions are met only if there is no significant irredenta outside the state's boundaries, if there is only one nation existing (or awakened) in the state, and if there is little cultural diversity within the state. In these circumstances (and, we will argue, virtually *only* in these circumstances) leaders of the government can simultaneously pursue democratization policies and nation-state policies. This congruence between the *polis* and the *demos* facilitates the creation of a democratic nation-state; it also virtually eliminates all problems of "stateness" and should thus be considered a supportive condition for democratic consolidation. Under modern circumstances, however, very few states will begin a possible democratic transition with a high degree of national homogeneity. This lack of homogeneity tends to exacerbate problems of "stateness."

Democracy is characterized not by subjects but by citizens; thus a democratic transition often puts the question of the relation between *polis* and *demos* at the center of politics. From all that has been said thus far, three assertions can be made. First, the greater the extent to which the population of a state is composed of a plurality of national, linguistic, religious, or cultural societies, the more complex politics becomes, since an agreement on the fundamentals of a democracy will be more difficult. Second, while this does not mean that consolidating democracy in multinational or multicultural states is impossible, it does mean that especially careful political crafting of democratic norms, practices, and institutions is required. Third, some methods of dealing with the problems of "stateness" are inherently incompatible with democracy.

Clear thinking on this subject demands that we call into question some facile assumptions. One of the most dangerous ideas for democracy is that "every state should strive to become a nation-state and every nation should become a state." In fact, it is probably impossible for half of the territories in the world that are not now democratic ever to become both "nation-states" and "consolidated democracies," as we have defined these terms. One of the reasons for this is that many existing nondemocratic states are multinational, multilingual, and multicultural. To make them "nation-states" by democratic means would be extremely difficult. In structurally embedded multicultural settings, virtually the only democratic way to create a homogeneous nation-state is through voluntary cultural assimilation, voluntary exit, or peaceful creation and voluntary acceptance of new territorial boundaries. These are empirically and democratically difficult measures, and hence are exceedingly rare.

The other possibilities for creating a homogeneous nation-state in such settings involve subtle (or not-so-subtle) sanctions against those not speaking the language, wearing the attire, or practicing the religion of the titular nation. Under modern circumstances—where all significant groups have writers and intellectuals who disseminate national cultures, where communication systems have greatly increased the possibility for migrants to remain continuously connected to their home cultures, and where modern democratic norms accept a degree of multiculturalism—such sanctions, even if not formally antidemocratic, would probably not be conducive to democratic crafting.[13] If the titular nation actually wants a truly homogeneous nation-state, a variant of "ethnic cleansing" is too often a temptation.

Another difficulty in the way of building nation-states that are also democracies derives from the manner in which humanity is spatially distributed across the globe. One building block for nations is language. But as Ernest Gellner observed, there are possibly as many as eight thousand languages (not counting important dialects) currently spoken in the world.[14] Even if we assume that only one out of every ten languages is a base for a "reasonably effective" nationalism, there could be as many as eight hundred viable national communities.[15] But cultural, linguistic, and religious groups are not neatly segmented into eight thousand or eight hundred nationalities, each occupying reasonably well-defined territories. On the contrary, these groups are profoundly intermixed and overlapping.

We are not arguing against democratically crafted "velvet divorces." We should note, however, that relatively clear cultural boundaries facilitate such territorial separations. Latvia would like to be a nation-state, but in none of its seven most-populous cities is Latvian spoken by a majority of the residents.

In Tallinn, the capital of Estonia, barely half the people of this aspiring nation-state speak Estonian. For these and many other countries, no simple territorial division or "velvet divorce" is available.[16]

Democracy and Multinational States

Some analysts were happy when the separate nationalities of the USSR became 15 republics, all based on "titular nationalities," on the assumption that democratic nation-states might emerge. In fact, many political leaders in these republics sounded extreme nationalist (rather than democratic) themes in the first elections. One possible formula for diminishing conflict between titular nationalities and "migrants" is what David Laitin calls the "competitive-assimilation game." That is, it becomes in the best interests of some working-class migrants to assimilate in order to enhance the life chances of their children in the new environment. This may happen to Spanish working-class migrants in culturally and economically vibrant Catalonia, but is it likely to occur among Russians in Central Asia? In 1989 in Almaty, the capital of Kazakhstan, Russians constituted 59 percent of the population, and the Kazakhs, the titular nationality, only 22.5 percent. Less than 1 percent of the Russians spoke the titular language. In Bishkek, the capital of Kyrgyzstan, the comparable percentages were virtually identical. In such contexts, shaped by settler colonialism, it is utterly implausible that a nation-state would emerge voluntarily through a process of competitive assimilation.[17]

So how can democracy possibly be achieved in multinational states? We have a strong hypothesis about how *not* to consolidate democracy in multinational settings. The greater the percentage of people in a given state who either were born there or arrived without perceiving themselves as foreign citizens, and who are subsequently denied citizenship in the state (when their life chances would be hurt by such denial), the more unlikely it is that this state will consolidate democracy. Phrased more positively, our hypothesis is that in a multinational, multicultural setting, the chances of consolidating democracy are increased by state policies that grant inclusive and equal citizenship and give all citizens a common "roof" of state-mandated and state-enforced individual rights.

Such multinational states also have an even greater need than other polities to explore a variety of nonmajoritarian, nonplebiscitarian formulas. For example, if there are strong geographic concentrations of different groups within the state, federalism might be an option worth exploring. The state and the society might also allow a variety of publicly supported communal institutions—such as media and schools in different languages, symbolic recognition of cultural diversity, a variety of legally accepted marriage codes, legal and political tolerance for parties representing different communities, and a whole array of political procedures and devices that Arend Lijphart has described as "consociational democracy."[18] Typically, proportional representation, rather than large single-member districts with first-past-the-post elections, can facilitate representation of geographically dispersed minorities. Some strict adherents to the tradition of political liberalism, with its focus on universalism and individual rights, oppose any form of collective rights. But we believe that in a multinational, multicultural society and state, combining collective rights for nationalities or minorities with individual rights fully protected by the state is the least-conflictual solution.[19]

Where transitions occur in the context of a nondemocratic, multinational federal system, the crafting of democratic federalism should probably begin with elections at the federal level, so as to generate a legitimate framework for later deliberations on how to decentralize the polity democratically. If the first competitive elections are regional, the elections will tend to favor regional nationalists, and ethnocracies rather than democracies may well emerge.[20] However, the specific ways of structuring political life in multinational settings need to be contextualized in each country. Along these lines, we believe that it is time to reevaluate some past experiments with nonterritorial autonomy such as the kinds of partially self-governing ethnic or religious communities exemplified by the Jewish Kabal of the Polish-Lithuanian Commonwealth, the millets of the Ottoman Empire, or the "national curias" of the late Habsburg Empire. These mechanisms will not eliminate conflict in multinational states, but they may moderate conflict and help make both the state and democracy more viable.

We also believe that some conceptual, political, and normative attention should be given to the possibility of "state-nations." We call "state-nations" those multicultural or even multinational states that nonetheless still manage to engender strong identification and loyalty from their diverse citizens. The United States is such a multicultural and increasingly multilingual country; Switzerland is another. Neither is strictly speaking a "nation-state," but we believe both could now be called "state-nations." Under Jawaharlal Nehru, India made significant gains in managing multinational tensions by the skillful and consensual use of numerous consociational practices. Through this process India became, in the 1950s and early 1960s, a democratic "state-nation"; but if Hindu nationalists win power in the 1990s and attempt to turn India (with its 115 million Muslims) into a Hindu nation-state, communal violence would almost certainly increase and Indian democracy would be gravely threatened.

Multiple Identities

Let us conclude with a word about "political identities." Many writings on nationalism have focused on "primordial" identities and the need for people to choose between mutually exclusive identities. Our research into political identities, however, has shown two things. First, political identities are not fixed or "primordial" in the *Oxford English Dictionary*'s sense of "existing at (or from) the very beginning." Rather, they are highly changeable and socially constructed. Second, if nationalist politicians (or social scientists and census-takers with crude dichotomous categories) do not force polarization, many people may prefer to define themselves as having multiple and complementary identities.[21] In fact, along with a common political "roof" of state-protected rights for inclusive and equal citizenship, the human capacity for multiple and complementary identities is one of the key factors that makes democracy in multinational states possible. Because political identities are not fixed and permanent, the quality of democratic leadership is particularly important. Multiple and complementary political identities can be nurtured by political leadership, as can polarized and conflictual political identities. Before the conscious use of "ethnic cleansing" as a strategy to construct nation-states in the former Yugoslavia, Sarajevo was a multinational city whose citizens had multiple identities and one of the world's highest interfaith-marriage rates.

Our central proposition is that, if successful democratic consolidation is the goal, would-be crafters of democracy must take into careful consideration the particular mix of nations, cultures, and awakened political identities present in the territory. Some kinds of democracy are possible with one type of *polis*, but virtually impossible if political elites attempt to build another type of *polis*. Political elites in a multinational territory could initiate "nationalizing policies" that might not violate human rights or the Council of Europe's norms for democracy, but would have the effect, in each of the five arenas of the polity, of greatly diminishing the chances of democratic consolidation.

* * *

A final point to stress concerns timing. Potentially difficult democratic outcomes may be achievable only if some preemptive policies and decisions are argued for, negotiated, and implemented by political leaders. If the opportunity for such ameliorative policies is lost, the range of available space for maneuver will be narrowed, and a dynamic of societal conflict will likely intensify until democratic consolidation becomes increasingly difficult, and eventually impossible.

Problems of Simultaneous Reform

The widely held view that market reform and privatization can legitimate new democracies is based on the dubious assumption that economic improvement can be achieved simultaneously with the installation and legitimation of democratic institutions. We believe that, in countries with imploded command economies, democratic polities can and must be installed and legitimized by a variety of other appeals before the possible benefits of a market economy fully materialize. Many analysts and political advisors dismiss the case for giving priority to state restructuring because they assume that, due to people's demands for material improvements, economic and political gains must not only be pursued but occur simultaneously. Some even argue that simultaneous economic and political reforms are necessary, but that such simultaneity is impossible.[22]

We can call the two opposing perspectives about the relationship between economics and democratization the "tightly coupled" hypothesis and the "loosely coupled" hypothesis. By "loosely coupled," we do not mean that there is no relationship between economic and political perceptions, only that the relationship is not necessarily one-to-one. For at least a medium-range time horizon, people can make independent, and even opposite, assessments about political and economic trends. We further believe that when people's assessments about politics are positive, they can provide a valuable cushion for painful economic restructuring.[23] Let us look at the evidence concerning the relationship between economic growth and democratization in the first five years of postcommunist Europe. Certainly, if we look only at relatively hard economic data, none of the 27 countries in postcommunist Europe except Poland experienced positive growth in 1992. Indeed, in 1993 all postcommunist countries were still well below their 1989 industrial-output levels.[24]

If we look at subjective impressions of economic well-being in six East Central European countries, the mean positive rating (on a +100 to a –100 scale) among those polled between November 1993 and March 1994 was 60.2 for the communist economic system, but was only 37.3 for the postcommunist economic system—a drop of almost 23 points. The tightly coupled hypothesis would predict that attitudes toward the political system would also drop steeply, even if not by the full 23 points. What does the evidence show? The mean positive ranking of the communist political system was 45.7. Thus a one-to-one correlation between the political and economic evaluations would have yielded a positive evaluation of the political system of 22.6. Yet the mean positive ranking for the postcommunist political system, far from falling, rose to 61.5—or 38.9 points higher than a "perfectly coupled" hypothesis would have predicted.[25]

How can we explain such incongruence? First of all, human beings are capable of making separate and correct judgements about a basket of economic goods (which may be deteriorating) and a basket of political goods (which may be improving). In fact, in the same survey the respondents judged that, in important areas directly affected by the democratic political system, their life experiences and chances had overwhelmingly improved, even though they also asserted that their own personal household economic situations had worsened.[26]

We do not believe such incongruence can last forever; it does indicate, however, that in a radical transformation like that occurring in East Central Europe, the deterioration of the economy does not necessarily translate into rapid erosion of support for the political system. The perceived legitimacy of the political system has given democratic institutions in East Central Europe an important degree of insulation from the perceived inefficacy of the new economic system. Indeed, most people in East Central Europe in 1994 had a fairly long time horizon and expressed optimism that by 1999 the performance of both the new democracy and the new economic system would improve significantly.[27]

Thus the evidence in East Central Europe is strongly in favor of the argument that deferred gratification and confidence in the future are possible even when there is an acknowledged lag in economic improvement. Simultaneity of rapid political and economic results is indeed extremely difficult, but fortunately the citizens of East Central Europe did not perceive it as necessary.

Democracy and the Quality of Life

While we believe that it is a good thing for democracies to be consolidated, we should make it clear that consolidation does not necessarily entail either a high-quality democracy or a high-quality society. Democratic institutions—however important—are only one set of public institutions affecting citizens' lives. The courts, the central bank, the police, the armed forces, certain independent regulatory agencies, public-service agencies, and public hospitals are not governed democratically, and their officials are not elected by the citizens. Even in established democracies, not all of these institutions are controlled by elected officials, although many are overseen by them. These institutions operate, however, in a legal framework created by elected bodies and thereby derive their authority from them.

In view of all this, the quality of public life is in great measure a reflection not simply of the democratic or nondemocratic character of the regime, but of the quality of those other institutions.

Policy decisions by democratic governments and legislators certainly affect the quality of life, particularly in the long run, but no democracy can assure the presence of reputable bankers, entrepreneurs with initiative, physicians devoted to their patients, competent professors, creative scholars and artists, or even honest judges. The overall quality of a society is only in small part a function of democracy (or, for that matter, a function of nondemocratic regimes). Yet all of those dimensions of society affect the satisfaction of its citizens, including their satisfaction with the government and even with democracy itself. The feeling that democracy is to blame for all sorts of other problems is likely to be particularly acute in societies in which the distinctive contributions of democracy to the quality of life are not well understood and perhaps not highly valued. The more that democrats suggest that the achievement of democratic politics will bring the attainment of all those other goods, the greater will be the eventual disenchantment.

There are problems specific to the functioning of the state, and particularly to democratic institutions and political processes, that allow us to speak of the quality of democracy separately from the quality of society. Our assumption is that the quality of democracy can contribute positively or negatively to the quality of society, but that the two should not be confused. We as scholars should, in our research, explore both dimensions of the overall quality of life.

Notes

1. See Robert A. Dahl, *Polyarchy: Participation and Opposition* (New Haven: Yale University Press, 1971), 3.
2. We document the incomplete status of the Chilean democratic transition in chapter 13 of our book. For military prerogatives, see Alfred Stepan, *Rethinking Military Politics: Brazil and the Southern Cone* (Princeton: Princeton University Press, 1988), 68–127. For the electoralist fallacy in Central America, see Terry Lynn Karl, "The Hybrid Regimes of Central America," *Journal of Democracy* 6 (July 1995): 72–86. Dahl in his *Polyarchy* has an eighth institutional guarantee, which does not address elections as such, but rather the requirement that "[Institutions] for making government policies [should] depend on votes and other expressions of preference," (p. 3). This addresses our concern about reserve domains.
3. For other discussions about the concept of democratic consolidation, see Scott Mainwaring, Guillermo O'Donnell, and J. Samuel Valenzuela, eds., *Issues in Democratic Consolidation: The New South American Democracies in Comparative Perspective* (Notre Dame: University of Notre Dame Press, 1992).
4. In essence, this means that the literature on democratic breakdown, such as that found in Juan J. Linz and Alfred Stepan, eds., *The Breakdown of Democratic Regimes* (Baltimore: Johns Hopkins University Press, 1978), would be much more directly relevant to analyzing such a phenomenon than this essay or related books on democratic transition and consolidation. This is not a criticism of the transition literature; rather, our point is that the democratic-transition and democratic-breakdown literatures need to be integrated into the overall literature on modern democratic theory. From the perspective of such an integrated theory, the "breakdown of a consolidated democracy" is not an oxymoron.
5. On the relationships between constitutionalism, democracy, legal culture, and "self-bindingness," see Jon Elster and Rune Slagstad, eds., *Constitutionalism and Democracy* (Cambridge: Cambridge University Press, 1988), 1–18.
6. Robert A. Dahl, in a similar argument, talks about two arrows of causation that produce this result; see his "Why All Democratic Countries Have Mixed Economies," in John Chapman and Ian Shapiro, eds., *Democratic Community, Nomos XXXV* (New York: New York University Press, 1993), 259–82.
7. See, for example, John R. Freeman, *Democracies and Market: The Politics of Mixed Economies* (Ithaca, N.Y.: Cornell University Press, 1989).
8. For an excellent analysis of inevitable market failures, see Peter Murrell, "Can Neoclassical Economics Underpin the Reform of Centrally Planned Economies?" *Journal of Economic Perspectives* 5 (1991): 59–76.
9. Adam Smith, *The Wealth of Nations*, 2 vols. (London: J.M. Dent and Sons, Everyman's Library, 1910), 2:180–81.
10. Robert A. Dahl's line of reasoning follows a similar development. See his "Why All Democratic Countries Have Mixed Economies," cited in note 7 above, 259–82.
11. In postcommunist Europe, the Czech Republic and Hungary are well on the way to becoming institutionalized economic societies. In sharp contrast, in Ukraine and Russia the writ of the state does not extend far enough for us to speak of an economic society. The consequences of the lack of an economic society are manifest everywhere. For example, Russia, with a population 15 times larger than Hungary's and with vastly more raw materials, only received 3.6 billion dollars of direct foreign investment in 1992–93, whereas Hungary received 9 billion dollars of direct foreign investment in the same two years.
12. See Rogers Brubaker's "National Minorities, Nationalizing States, and External National Homelands in the New Europe," *Daedalus* 124 (Spring 1995): 107–32.
13. See, for example, the outstanding monograph by Eugen Weber, *Peasants into Frenchmen: The Modernization of Rural France, 1870–1914* (Stanford: Stanford University Press, 1976), which analyzes in extensive detail the wide repertoire of nation-state mandated policies in the schools, the civil service, and the military that were systematically designed to repress and eliminate multilingualism and multiculturalism and to create a nation-state. From today's perspective, similar endeavors of modern states appear far from admirable and represent a cost

that many of us would not like to pay. However, it is not just a question of how we evaluate such efforts of state-based nation-building, but of how feasible these efforts are in the contemporary context.

14. See Ernest Gellner, *Nations and Nationalism* (Ithaca, N.Y.: Cornell University Press, 1983), 44.
15. This conjecture is developed by Gellner in *Nations,* 44–45.
16. See the excellent, and sobering, book by Anatol Lieven, *The Baltic Revolution: Estonia, Latvia, Lithuania and the Path to Independence* (New Haven: Yale University Press, 1993), 434.
17. For David Laitin's analysis of what he calls a "migrant competitive-assimilation game" in Catalonia, and his analysis of a possible "colonial-settler game" in the Central Asian republics of the former Soviet Union, see his "The Four Nationality Games and Soviet Politics," *Journal of Soviet Nationalities* 2 (Spring 1991): 1–37.
18. See Arend Lijphart's seminal article "Consociational Democracy," *World Politics* 21 (January 1969): 207–25.
19. For interesting arguments that some notion of group rights is, in fact, necessary to the very definition of some types of individual rights and necessary to the advancement of universal norms in rights, see the work by the Oxford philosopher Joseph Raz, *The Morality of Freedom* (Oxford: Oxford University Press, 1986), 165–217. Also see Will Kymlicka, *Multicultural Citizenship: A Liberal Theory of Minority Rights* (Oxford: Oxford University Press, 1995), 107–30.
20. We develop this point in greater detail in our "Political Identities and Electoral Sequences: Spain, the Soviet Union and Yugoslavia," *Daedalus* 121 (Spring 1992): 123–39; and in our *Problems of Democratic Transition and Consolidation* in the chapters on Spain, on "stateness" in the USSR, and on Russian speakers' changing identities in Estonia and Latvia.
21. In our *Problems of Democratic Transition and Consolidation,* we show how in Catalonia in 1982, when respondents were given the opportunity to self-locate their identities on a questionnaire offering the following five possibilities—"Spanish," "more Spanish than Catalan," "equally Spanish and Catalan," "more Catalan than Spanish," or "Catalan"—the most-chosen category, among respondents with both parents born in Catalonia, as well as among respondents with neither parent born in Catalonia, was the multiple and complementary category "equally Spanish and Catalan." We also show how identities in Catalonia were becoming more polarized and conflict-ridden before democratic devolution.
22. The title of a widely disseminated article by Jon Elster captures this perspective; see "The Necessity and Impossibility of Simultaneous Economic and Political Reform," in Douglas Greenberg, Stanley N. Katz, Melanie Beth Oliviero, and Steven C. Wheatley, eds., *Constitutionalism and Democracy: Transitions in the Contemporary World* (Oxford: Oxford University Press, 1993), 267–74.
23. The voters might, due to negative economic performance, vote incumbents out of office, but the overall economic policies of their successors might well continue to be roughly the same. Poland in 1993–95, and Hungary in 1994–95 come to mind.
24. See our *Problems of Democratic Transition and Consolidation.*
25. See Richard Rose and Christian Haerfer, "New Democracies Barometer III: Learning from What is Happening," *Studies in Public Policy* No. 230 (1994), questions 22–23, 32–33. Percentages rounded off.
26. Rose and Haerfer, "New Democracies," questions 26, 35, 36, 39, 40, and 42.
27. Rose and Haerfer, "New Democracies," questions 24, 26, 35, 36, 39, 40, 42, and 34.

Chapter 15

ARE THERE CULTURAL REQUISITES FOR DEMOCRACY?

With the advent of modern comparative analysis, some of the most prominent bodies of research in the field are concerned with issues surrounding the impact of culture and other contextual factors on political outcomes. In particular, comparativists are concerned with the nature, causes, and consequences of cultural change, especially in the Western world, and with the question of whether certain cultural or other contextual attributes are required for the establishment and maintenance of democracy. Ronald Inglehart, in some of the most influential and oft-cited research in the last three decades, has been at the cutting edge of both of these questions.

Because cultural factors are necessarily "soft" concepts that cannot be directly measured, they are inherently difficult to apply consistently within the modern research standards of rigorous testability. That means that there is necessarily a measure of inference or interpretation in moving from direct observation (such as responses to a questionnaire or a test score) to a conclusion about the extent to which the concept is presumed to be present. Cultural factors refer to individual dispositions to react in a certain way to a given stimulus, dispositions such as tolerance or trust that cannot be directly observed.

From the above example, one can see how cultural factors include attitudes, beliefs and belief systems, feelings, values, and knowledge. Attitudes refer to a psychological orientation toward political objects, such as an egalitarian, authoritarian, or deferential conception of authority. Beliefs refer to conceptions of how things are, which may be either true or false. The factor of beliefs also refers to the disposition to make choices and to behave consistently within the standards of a closed, comprehensive system of ideas; in other words, to be guided by an ideology. The opposite of that disposition is to make choices and behave according to what works on a trial-and-error basis; in other words, to take a pragmatic approach. Feelings can include a sense of belonging to, identification with, and feeling a personal stake in the fortunes of a system or society, as opposed to feeling apart from or alienated from such a system or society. Values include preferences or the setting of goals and priorities, such as, for example, the choice between the maintenance of order and the pursuit of some conception of social justice, a goal that may necessitate a disruption of the existing order. Knowledge refers to the population's grasp of reality and awareness of the world about them. For example, to what extent are people in less-modern societies aware of the actual lifestyle of people in the West?

The subject of cultural change at the heart of the controversy in this chapter has been the focus of "modernization theory," which has guided inquiry about less-industrialized nations for much of the postwar era. This perspective questions whether certain social and cultural attributes must be in place to permit the establishment and the maintenance of a democratic political format. The issue of the cultural requisites of democracy argument has been a central concern to students of comparative politics at least since the publication of a landmark five-nation study in 1963 by Garbriel Almond and Sidney Verba, the first major cross-national survey of attitudes and other cultural factors in relation to the establishment and maintenance of successful democracy and the data basis of their oft-cited book, *The Civic Culture.*[1]

The piece by Ronald Inglehart and Christian Welzel (reading 15.2) is, among other things, the most recent example by prominent scholars of the cultural requisites of democracy argument, that is, the claim that modernization generates the spread of the education, literacy, and participation positively associated with successful democracy. Edward Friedman's piece (reviewed and summarized by Eric Dowling in reading 15.1) is an oft-cited demurral to that position. His argument centers on the idea that elites may successfully opt to install democratic political formats in various sociocultural contexts; hence, democracy may successfully operate in contexts outside of the modern Western institutions once thought to be necessary for democracy. Students should ask whether the establishment of democracy in Asian contexts, such as Japan and South Korea, belies the cultural requisite argument or whether such non-Western democracies still possess some key cultural requisites.

Note

1. Gabriel Almond and Sidney Verba, *The Civic Culture* (Boston: Little Brown, 1961).

15.1

REVIEW OF EDWARD FRIEDMAN, ED., *THE POLITICS OF DEMOCRATIZATION: GENERALIZING EAST ASIAN EXPERIENCES*

Eric Dowling

The following selection is an excellent, manageable summary and critique of a long essay by University of Wisconsin–Madison political scientist Edward Friedman. In the introduction to his book on the politics of democratization in East Asia, Friedman rejects the argument that certain cultural attributes need to characterize a given setting in order for a democratic format to function effectively. This principle had almost attained the status of conventional wisdom in comparative politics: in 1959, for example, the esteemed scholar Seymour Lipset published *Some Social Requisites of Democracy,* which went on to become one of the most cited works on democracy. Conversely, Friedman notes the successful installation of a democratic format in the clearly non-Western Japan, South Korea, and Taiwan, and he argues that democracy can be installed and consolidated by the decisions of elites. He contends that a democratic format will cause the necessary cultural attributes to evolve. Since their democratic constitution was imposed on the country by the victorious Allies despite a long history of authoritarian cultural attributes, students should consider whether the success of democracy in the reunited Federal Republic of Germany, a country in which democratic values and attitudes only began to dominate that country's culture two decades after the establishment of the democratic format, supports Friedman's positions.

* * *

I: Summary Survey

The book's editor, Edward Friedman, takes the lion's share of this book with over sixty pages which aim to give a frame of reference in which to place the other contributors. They are Masanori Nakamura, David Arase, and Yasunobu Sato on Japan (54 pp.); Tun-jen Cheng and Eun Mee Kim, and Heng Lee on Korea (33 pp.); Ming K. Chan on Hong Kong (20 pp.); Hung-mao Tien and Hsin-Huang Michael Hsiao on Taiwan (33 pp.); and Su Shaozhi and Stephen Manning on China (27 pp.).

In his Introduction and "Theoretical Overview" (which has the same title as the book), Friedman seems to conceive democracy as a state in which accountable governments are institutionally and peace-

Eric Dowling, "Review of Friedman, Edward; ed., The Politics of Democratization: Generalizing East Asian Experiences," H-Japan, H-Net Reviews, March 1998, URL: http://www.h-net.org/reviews/showrev.php?id=1868.

fully chosen "without fear" and by "fair rules" to deliver a transparent administration. I think he also regards judiciary independence, due process of law, and "human and civil rights" as of the essence of democracy (p. 3), but since he doesn't clearly distinguish democracy itself from either its pre-conditions (if any) or its outcomes, I may be wrong.

I may be wrong because, in his Introduction, Friedman repeatedly emphasises that in his view, there are *no* "unique historical, cultural, and class preconditions" for democracy (p. 4), and there's nothing in Europe or the West that was peculiarly conducive to democracy. What *does* lead to democracy says Friedman, is politics. Politics themselves, however (the *only* "preconditions" of democracy) have no preconditions at all; for politics lie in "a contingent realm" (p. 41). Rather than focusing on inherited historical preconditions, he writes,

> the universal political approach of the authors [is to] investigate political actions, leadership, alliances, programs, trade-offs, and the like. Democratization is then understood as the building of political institutions, common interests, and new forms of legitimation. Consolidating a democracy requires building political parties and alliances capable of establishing credible national agendas and control of the military, making the security forces accountable to electoral representatives, and crafting a constitutional arrangement. . .that will seem fair, open, and in the interests of all major social sectors, including old and new elites [p. 5].

There's nothing at all distinctive about the West's democratic achievements. Anyone can do it, anywhere, any time: "In contrast to the lesson derived from theories premised on unique historical, cultural and class preconditions that people must wait for democracy. . .the lesson from a focus on ordinary politics in Japan or anywhere is that democrats can learn and then act more wisely in the here and now to secure democracy" (p. 4). What is needed for democracy is not "unique preconditions" but "generalizable politics," for "[d]emocracy in the West was not the consequence of a purported culture of Protestant individualist consciences" (p. 7). All of which is illustrated, according to Friedman, by his contributing authors. History has shown that "unique" culture has nothing at all to contribute to democracy: to the contrary, "democratic cultures are the consequences, not the causes, of democratization" (p. 20). Although Friedman nowhere elaborates a definition of democracy, he regards its definition as of such impact that influential and "narrowly self-serving" Eurocentric theorists with their "[h]istorical cultural blinders" have so grievously *misdefined* democracy as actually to conclude that Japan is not a democracy at all: "[i]n this view that mythologizes the Western experience, democracy means a clash of opposing interests resulting in the voting of 'ins' out of power. Democracy is defined so that Japan is not democratic" (p. 19).

Friedman regards this as misconceived since, by his criteria, Japan *is* democratic. Those criteria are given on page 21: 1) fair rules, 2) the possibility of peaceful challenge to existing rule, 3) the possibility of eventual compromise between government and opposition. In less than two pages (pp. 22-23) Friedman summarises the U.S.-Japanese reaction to the Cold War to serve as an example of *how* Japan then "consolidated" its democracy.

If I properly grasp him here, he claims that Japanese democracy was consolidated during that period because (and only because) Japan's socialists succeeded in "preventing Japan from military action on the side of U.S. Cold War policies. The socialists won on this agenda because. . .the ruling Yoshida faction and bureaucrats of the powerful Ministry of Finance were willing to forego a global politico-military role for Japan. The resultant compromise, diagnostic of democratic consolidation, was itself the result of the government's concessions to left-wing challengers" (p. 23), *i.e.*, the result of party politics. Such political compromise in Japan did in fact reveal a general political pattern for the consolidation of democracy which, in the case in question, had nothing to do with any cultural or historical disposition to social harmony. It was contemporary politics, not historical culture.

The post-WW II outcome in Japan was a "grand conservative coalition, usually treated by Western analysts as so strange as to be beyond the pale of democratic mores..." (p. 46). He calls it a coalition, I think, not because the conservatives formed a coalition of parties or factions but rather because, as I understand him, the LDP formed a *de facto* coalition with the socialists to isolate the extremes of the left and right. There is a hint of a suggestion, on page 47, that Japan's "grand conservative coalition" (an oft-repeated phrase) actually constituted a *socialist* victory since, had the established middle and upper classes been isolated, they'd have been strong enough to stop any democratic consolidation. (He thinks the same happened in England in and after 1688, and in America's Federalist success.)

Friedman concludes that "[t]o understand democratization, it is useful to abandon a misleading opposition of consensual Asia versus individualistic Europe and to rethink Western experience in terms of generalizable lessons of consensus building" (p. 25).

Briskly moving from Japan in the Cold War to China's history from Confucius to the present day (pp. 24 ff.) Friedman suggests that Deng Xiaoping was much mistaken not to have foreseen that his "1989 suppression of democratic forces" would lose him a place in which "his name and fame would resound happily to Chinese ears for centuries to come" (p. 25). And an equally curt glance at Mencian Confucianism's doctrine of popular support as the only basis for legitimate rule, and Confucius's concept of the educability of everyman, and Daoism's focus of freedom, the Legalists' concept of universal equality before the law, and Mohism on egalitarianism and "the yin-yang school on compromise and dialogue...[shows that] China seems replete with tendencies favorable to democratization" (pp. 27–8).

Friedman actually says, on page 28, that in the light of the foregoing "[o]ne might expect that Chinese *culture* [my italics]...would lead Chinese intellectuals...to take the lead against...Leninism;" and, he adds, "[t]hat is precisely what happened in China's 1989 democracy movement" (p. 28). He therefore feels able to conclude that "all [*sic*] people and all [*sic*] cultures are alive with a democratic potential."

However, on page 31, having said that "[a]ny society tends to be rich in multiple possibilities," he immediately and in the next sentence adds that "in actuality, most cultures are largely authoritarian." Whence I infer that his position, if coherent, is as intricate as these words suggest.

He repeatedly asserts or implies that democracy is a good thing. It has always been "the simple truth that democracy was humanly attractive and dictatorship inhumanly repellent" (p. 33), and "the universal attractiveness of democracy and human rights" (p. 34) should need no demonstration.

But lest they do, he gives such demonstration, saying that democracy "can appeal to any society because democracy helps bar the evils of a permanent succession crisis that, in despotisms, continually threatens chaos;" it "offers public accountability that can limit...corruption;" and blocks "arbitrary arrest, degrading treatment, internal exile, slaughter,and torture...Whether the culture values face, pride, or individual dignity, only political freedom can offer a life fit for human beings" (p. 34), for such freedom "is a facilitator of continuous progress" (p. 35).

Yet, alas, the universal appeal of these obvious truths *was* concealed from Marx, Weber, *et al.*, who "slight the East Asian experience that the authors of this volume stress, moral legitimacy, the politics of social equity, and democratic consensus building" (p. 35).

Friedman considers the widely held view that first, since it was individualism in the West which led to its democratic achievements and, secondly, since such individualism is lacking in East Asia, therefore East Asia will have difficulty in developing democracy. On page 36, he simply denies the two premises, and claims that the observable fact of successful East Asian democracies prompts reassessment:

> In the conventional wisdom, democracy in Europe is related to a rise of self-interested individuals. In East Asia, successful democracy is linked to the rise of a patriotic people willing a common, better destiny. *But that is how it actually was in the West, too.* The East Asian experience calls attention to almost buried Western essentials. Democracy succeeds best when it ends archaic humiliations imposed on a long-suffering people. Even when one looks at the revolutions of 1688, 1776, and 1789, one finds in England, America, and France, as in East Asia, an emerging group solidarity that defined the old despotic system as outmoded, traitorous, and beyond the pale of the true national community. To look back at Western experience with a vision sharpened by East Asian glasses focused on nationalistic identities permits one to see both East and West more clearly. . . .The East Asian experience thus permits the uncovering and recovering of the West's actual political path to democracy [my italics].

In this connexion he considers Japan (p. 37f.):

> National survival required political democracy and social equity. . . . In Japan, the democratic constitution, social equity, land reform, and legalization of labor unions facilitated a prodemocracy consciousness. . . . [W]ithin a democratic consensus, conservatives, needing a regular popular mandate, offered the Shinto-Buddhist-Confucian people of Japan a social equity pact that could facilitate national consensus [for]. . .[c]ommon identity does [!] matter. Democracy is not easy to consolidate in a nation-state era if there is no shared national identity. . . [and] the conventional wisdom that dismisses East Asia because people there are supposedly homogeneous could not be more wrong. It is *wrong everywhere* because, when closely examined, *all* constructed national identities are replete with an almost endless diversity of particularisms from histories of conquest, sectarian religious conversions, regional affections, and speech differences. . . . In the chapters on democratization in Taiwan and Korea the authors correct the error of dismissing East Asia's achievement with the misleading assertion that it is uniquely homogeneous.
>
> That surely is not how the feudatories of Tokugawa Japan conceived each other. A politics replete with regionalisms, particularisms, and conflicting interest is *ubiquitous*. . . . That divisive danger was softened during democratization in Japan, Taiwan, and Korea because of political mobilization against a common threat to all in the nation and because of governmental policies fostering greater equity among diverse social groups. Politics can encourage local communalisms to find a fair stake in a national democratic community, a compacted patriotism [my italics].

Contrary to the "Occidentalism" of "self-serving" and "blinkered" Eurocentrics that there is something "culturally peculiar about the West," the West is not that different from the East for, as in the East, democracy is also under threat in the West, where

> [r]eligious or *cultural* fundamentalism, racist nativism, and military chauvinism still threaten democracy. As with those French forces backing fascism in the Nazi era, as with the racism that facilitated America's civil war, as with the embrace of local ethnonationalisms against the United Kingdom, political threats to democratic consolidation persist . . . *The politicization of ethnic, regional, religious, and other cultural identities can challenge democracy anywhere* [p. 38f, my italics].

Such Eurocentric Occidentalism is also invoked by Orientalist Asian "dictators to legitimate their anti-democratic cause by contending that their people are not yet ready for democracy," as did the old French counter-revolutionary monarchists. Such "super patriots" as "Korean reactionaries, Taiwan militarists, or Mainland Chinese xenophobes" also pretend that democratic movements will cause national disintegration. They claim that Western "individualism" is "hostile to virtually all *cultural* communities" whereas, in fact, "the actual creation of national culture in the democratizing West was also in conflict with the West's subsequent mythos of rational secular individualism" (p. 40 my italics).

Democracy was first said to be confined to Calvinists, then to all Protestants, then to all Christians:

> But by the end of the twentieth century, after lengthy eras of democracy in Hindu-Muslim-Sikh-Buddhist India and Shinto-Buddhist-Confucian Japan and its spread to Confucian East Asians, Muslim Albanians, animistic Pacific Islanders, and Buddhist Mongols, one might think that this diversity would discredit all notions of peculiar cultural, value or socioeconomic prerequisites of democracy [p. 40].

Friedman, however, still allows some connexion between the economy and democracy. While on page 2 he rejects the "conventional wisdom" that "a large middle-class socioeconomic foundation" is a "precondition" of democracy (repeated on p. 12 and 32), he also says, on page 33, that economic growth can "help" democratization. And on page 51 he remarks that "Japan's grand conservative coalition actually has much to teach about. . .a linkage of a legitimate polity to economic growth." However he immediately, on the same page, claims that in [China] and Taiwan "democratization was made possible not by economic growth but by political struggles," and that "[p]olitics. . .is not an immediate reflection of some deeper economic reality. Democracy is not determined by economic preconditions."

* * *

> The Japanese experience after the occupation reveals *mutual* support between democracy and development. The democratization of economic reward was only delayed, not denied. In the era of high-speed economic growth, movements for wage increases, social welfare, and social security policies were institutionalized. In contrast, in the post-oil shock years when economic growth was sluggish, people tended toward conservatism, and the movement for further democratic progress receded [p. 70, my italics].

That passage, which continues his identification, on page 62, of democracy with "progressivism" and of conservatism with anti-democracy, also continues his claim that there are indeed economic and ideological "mainstays" for political structures (p. 64).

David Arase's chapter, on "Japan's Foreign Policy and Asian Democratization," explores Japan's shift from the "Yoshida doctrine" of "low-cost, low-risk" dependency on America to an independent international influence consistent with its economic power. Japan, "without being selfish or crudely interventionist, can link its resources to the promotion of democracy and human rights in the countries of democratizing Asia. . .[but] has not grasped the opportunity to lead Asia toward democracy despite the many gains and modest costs involved, due to domestic factors" (pp. 83 and 96). The *reason* for this woeful dereliction is obvious to Arase:

> The insulated, autonomous bureaucracy serving primarily the interest of the dominant conservative coalition keeps Japan from embracing democracy in foreign policy. This gap can hurt Japan's search for

> an appropriate set of values that are classically "political," that is, having to do with defining those moral and spiritual values that accompany the good life not just for Japanese but for all of humanity (p. 97).

In this connexion he is particularly severe on Motofumi Asai's claim that "the true nature of the Tiananmen incident is unclear," since the participants "interpreted democracy as all democrats do, and no one credits the Li Peng government's account of the massacre, of peaceable soldiers responding to violent attacks by hoodlums" (p. 91).

As with Friedman, Arase offers no extended examination of the nature of democracy, or of what he takes democracy to be, although at one point he explicitly recognises the possibility of a different view from that presupposed by Friedman:

> . . .Ardath Burks notes that Japanese democracy "opts in favour of the individual person rather than for individualism. The person often achieves security in the group. . . . To the Japanese, it is the right to belong to a group and to become involved in a demanding but protective world of duties that is the core of human rights." *Equating democracy with individualism may be problematic.* Nevertheless, calls for human rights and government accountability are compatible with *all* Asian systems and portend continued democratic development in ways suitable to these Asian societies [p. 96, my italics].

Yasunobu Sato's "New directions in Japanese foreign policy. . ." considers the Tiananmen incident, Japanese promotion of human rights and democracy in Asia, and ODA. His consideration of these topics is little (if anything) more than a repetition of standard and well-known slightly left of center critics such as Asia Watch, Amnesty International, *et al.*

* * *

15.2

A REVISED THEORY OF MODERNIZATION

Ronald Inglehart and Christian Welzel

This essay introduces a larger piece of research that links modernization with cultural changes that facilitate democratization by diminishing constraints on human choice and bringing about emancipation from authority. As such, it explores the likelihood of establishing and consolidating democratic institutions and whether there are cultural attributes that facilitate or support the effective functioning of such institutions. Carrying on his large volume of research on value change (see reading 4.2), Ronald Inglehart works with German political scientist Christian Welzel to modify classic modernization theory—which views modernization as linear, inevitable, and universal—by suggesting that these attributes may not characterize all settings. They argue that the values promoted by modernization are modified by the persistence of traditional values in particular settings. Students should think of the universe of less-developed systems of which they are aware and ask themselves if they can identify countries that do not seem to be developing toward the Western direction by either stagnating or moving away from Western values.

The Controversy over Modernization Theory

People in different societies see the world differently and have strikingly different values. In some countries, 95 percent of the people say that God is very important in their lives; in others, as few as 3 percent say so. In some societies, 90 percent of the people believe that if jobs are scarce, men have more right to a job than women; in others, only 8 percent think so. These cross-national differences are robust and enduring. But. . .these and many other important values are gradually changing in developed countries throughout the world.

These changes are roughly predictable, for they are closely linked with socioeconomic development. They are occurring in virtually all modern societies, and they have important consequences. Changing values are reshaping religious beliefs, job motivations, fertility rates, gender roles, and sexual norms and are bringing growing mass demands for democratic institutions and more responsive elite behavior. As we will demonstrate, socioeconomic development brings roughly predictable cultural changes—and beyond a certain point, these changes make democracy increasingly likely to emerge where it does not yet exist, and to become stronger and more direct where it already exists.

Ronald Inglehart and Christian Welzel, *Modernization, Cultural Change and Democracy* (New York: Cambridge University Press, 2005), 15–47.

Modernization theory is based on the idea of human progress (Carneiro, 2003). Historically, this idea is relatively new. As long as humans did not exert significant control over their natural environment, and agrarian economies were trapped in a steady-state equilibrium where almost no perceptible change took place from one generation to the next, the idea of human progress seemed unrealistic (Jones, 1985; McNeill, 1990). The situation began to change only with the occurrence of sustained economic growth (North, 1981; W. Bernstein, 2004).

Economic growth began to outpace population growth in a sustained way when the Commercial Revolution gave rise to preindustrial capitalism in the urban areas of late medieval Western Europe (Hall, 1989; Lal, 1998; Landes, 1998). As this happened, the philosophies of humanism and enlightenment emerged. The idea that technological innovations based on systematic research would enable humans to overcome the limitations nature imposes on them gained credibility, contesting the established view that human freedom and fulfillment can come only in the afterlife. Science began to provide a source of insight that competed with divine revelation, challenging the intellectual monopoly of the church, which fiercely defended feudal society as an unchangeable eternal order (Landes, 1998). The idea of human progress was born and with it modernization theory began to emerge.

Modernization theory originated in the Enlightenment era, with the belief that technological progress will give humanity increasing control over nature. Antoine de Condorcet (1979 [1795]) was among the first to explicitly link economic development and cultural change, arguing that technological progress and economic development will inevitably bring changes in people's moral values. The idea of human progress had a massive impact on social philosophers, but from its origins to the present, it has been opposed by notions of social decay that saw humanity heading toward a dark age. Edmund Burke (1999 [1790]) formulated such an antimodern view in his *Reflections on the Revolution in France*. In a similar vein, Thomas R. Malthus (1970 [1798]) developed a scientific theory of demographic disasters that is echoed in contemporary theories of growth limits and ecological risks (Meadows et al., 1972; U. Beck, 1992).

The most influential version of modernization theory was propounded by Karl Marx (1973 [1858]). The Marxist version provided a penetrating critique of the harsh exploitation that characterized early industrial society and proposed a utopian solution that allegedly would bring peace and an end to exploitation. Many of Marx's predictions were flagrantly wrong. Today, virtually no one believes that a proletarian revolution is about to take place that will abolish private property and bring an end to history. But the insight that technological changes and socioeconomic development have predictable cultural and political consequences remains valid. When Marx and Engels published *The Communist Manifesto* in 1848, industrialization was limited to a handful of countries, and the working class was small, powerless, and ruthlessly exploited. Marx and Engels argued that industrialization was the wave of the future and that industrial workers would become increasingly numerous and seize power. Although Marx failed to foresee the rise of the service class and the knowledge society, which aborted the numerical preponderance of workers he predicted, industrial workers have become a major political force in most societies, and today most of the world's population lives in countries that are either industrialized or industrializing (Rowen, 1996; Barro, 1997; Estes, 1998; Hughes, 1999).

Adam Smith (1976 [1776]) and Karl Marx (1973 [1858]) propagated competing versions of modernization, with Smith promoting capitalism and Marx advocating communism. But apart from their sharply contradictory views about the best pathway into modernity, both thinkers saw technological innovation and its socioeconomic consequences as the basis of human progress, with pervasive implications for culture and political institutions. Marx was most explicit on this point, arguing that socioeconomic development determines subsequent cultural changes in people's value orientations: a society's prevailing value orientations and moral standards form the "ideological superstructure" that reflects a society's "socioeconomic basis," and ideology necessarily changes as the socioeconomic basis changes. Consequently, the abolition of private property will bring the end of history—a classless society in which people no longer define their identity along the divisive lines of class distinctions but see themselves and others throughout the world as equals. This egalitarian classless society will make humanistic values dominant.

Competing versions of modernization theory enjoyed a new resurgence after World War II when the capitalist and communist superpowers espoused opposing ideologies as guidelines concerning the best route to modernity. Although they competed fiercely, both ideologies were committed to economic growth, social progress, and modernization, and they both brought broader mass participation in politics (Moore, 1966). Furthermore, because both sides believed that the developing nations of the Third World would seek modernization through either the communist path or the capitalist path, the two superpowers struggled to win them over. But industrialization and economic growth turned out to be far more difficult than anticipated (Randall and Theobald, 1998). Rather than modernizing, most of the new nations remained poor and ruled by corrupt regimes. Although these regimes gave lip service to capitalist, communist, or "nonaligned" visions of modernization, in reality most of them were run by rent-seeking elites who created "rogue states" to enrich themselves, doing little to modernize their countries (Rueschemeyer, Stephens, and Stephens, 1992).

In the postwar United States, a version of modernization theory emerged that viewed underdevelopment as a direct consequence of a country's internal characteristics, especially its traditional economies, traditional psychological and cultural traits, and traditional institutions (Lerner, 1958; Almond and Coleman, 1960; Pye and Verba, 1963; Almond and Powell, 1966; Weiner, 1966; Binder et al., 1971; Inkeles and Smith, 1974). From this perspective, traditional values not only were mutable but could—and should—be replaced by modern values, enabling these societies to follow the (virtually inevitable) path of capitalist development. The causal agents in this developmental process were seen as the rich, developed nations that stimulate the modernization of "backward" nations through economic, cultural, and military assistance.

These arguments were criticized as blaming the victim, because modernization theorists assumed that underdeveloped societies needed to adopt "modern" values and institutions to become developed societies (e.g., Bradshaw and Wallace, 1996). Modernization theory was not only criticized; it was pronounced dead (Wallerstein, 1976). Neo-Marxist and world-systems theorists argued that rich countries exploit poor countries, locking them in positions of powerlessness and structural dependence (e.g., Frank, 1966; Wallerstein, 1974; Chirot, 1977, 1994; Chase-Dunn, 1989). Underdevelopment, Frank claimed, is *developed*. This school of thought conveys the message to poor countries that poverty has nothing to do with internal problems: it is the fault of global capitalism. In the 1970s and 1980s, modernization theory seemed discredited (O'Donnell, 1973), and dependency theory came into vogue (Cardoso and Faletto, 1979). Adherents of dependency theory claimed that the Third World nations could only escape from global exploitation if they withdrew from the world market and adopted import-substitution policies.

In recent years, it became apparent that import-substitution strategies have been less successful. Rather than being the most successful, countries that were least involved in global capitalism actually showed the *least* economic growth (Firebaugh, 1992, 1996). Export-oriented strategies were more effective in bringing sustained economic growth and even, eventually, democracy (Barro, 1997; Randall and Theobald, 1998). The pendulum swung back: dependency theory fell out of favor, while the Western capitalist version of modernization regained credibility (Pye, 1990). The rapid development of East Asia and the subsequent democratization of Taiwan and South Korea seemed to confirm its basic claims: producing low-cost goods for the world market initiates economic growth; reinvesting the returns into human capital qualifies the work force to produce high-tech goods, whose export brings even higher returns and enlarges the educated urban middle classes; and once the middle class becomes large enough, its pressure for liberal democracy can no longer be resisted (L. Diamond, 1993a; Lipset, Seong, and Torres, 1993). World-systems theory came under heavy criticism. Evans (1995) argues that the structure of the global division of labor offers opportunities, enabling developing nations to transform themselves and change their positions in the global economy. The involvement of multinational corporations in underdeveloped nations does not seem to be as harmful as world-systems theorists claim. In fact, foreign investment seems to stimulate growth (Firebaugh, 1992) and to improve national welfare, benefiting the masses and not just the elites (Firebaugh and Beck, 1994). Hein (1992), Dollar (1992), and Firebaugh (1996) have demonstrated that nations that traded most and had the most investment from capitalist countries showed *higher*, not lower, subsequent rates of economic growth than other countries.

But it is clear that any simplistic version of modernization theory has serious shortcomings. Modernization theory needs to be revised for a number of reasons. One of the most obvious is the fact that, although the classic modernization theorists in both West and East thought that religion and ethnic traditions would die out, they have proved to be surprisingly resilient throughout the world. Indeed, with the close of the Cold War, Huntington (1996) has argued that future political conflicts will be based primarily on enduring cultural cleavages, largely reflecting a society's religious tradition.

The Persistence of Traditional Cultures

Huntington (1996), Putnam (1993), and Fukuyama (1995) argue that cultural traditions are remarkably enduring and shape the political and economic behavior of their societies today.[1] But modernization theorists from Marx and Weber to Bell and Toffler have argued that the rise of industrial society is linked with coherent cultural shifts away from traditional value systems.[2] Surprising as it may seem, *both* claims are true. . .

In recent years, research and theory on socioeconomic development have given rise to two contending schools of thought. One side emphasizes the *convergence* of values as a result of modernization—the overwhelming force that drives cultural change. This school predicts the decline of traditional values and their replacement with modern ones (e.g., Meyer, Boli, Thomas, and Ramirez, 1997; Stevenson, 1997). Another school of thought emphasizes the *persistence* of traditional values despite economic and

---

1. For the autonomous influences of culture, see, among others, Gibson, Duch, and Tedin, 1992; Putnam 1993; DiMaggio, 1994; Gibson and Duch, 1994; Miller, Hesli, and Reisinger, 1994; Gibson, 1997; Fleron and Ahl, 1998; Dalton, 1999, 2000; Crothers and Lockhard, 2000; Fukuyama, 2000; Inglehart and Baker, 2000; Lipset and Lenz, 2000.
2. For the impact of economic development on culture, see, among others, Abramson, 1989; Inglehart, 1990, 1997; L. Diamond, 1993c; Putnam, 1993; Dalton, 1994; Reisinger, Miller, Hesli, and Maher, 1994; Gasiorowski and Power, 1998; Rohrschneider, 1999; Inglehart and Baker. 2000.

political changes and assumes that values are relatively independent of economic conditions (e.g., DiMaggio, 1994). Consequently, it predicts that convergence around some set of "modern" values is unlikely; traditional values will continue to exert an independent influence on the cultural changes caused by socioeconomic development.

The central claim of modernization theory is that socioeconomic development is linked with coherent and, to some extent, predictable changes in culture as well as political life (Deutsch, 1963; Pye and Verba, 1963; Stinchcomb, 1965; Huntington, 1968). As we shall see, evidence from around the world indicates that socioeconomic development *does* tend to propel various societies in a roughly predictable direction. Socioeconomic development starts from technological innovations that increase labor productivity; it then brings occupational specialization, rising educational levels, and rising income levels; it diversifies human interaction, shifting the emphasis from authority relations toward bargaining relations; in the long run this brings cultural changes, such as changing gender roles, changing attitudes toward authority, changing sexual norms, declining fertility rates, broader political participation, and more critical and less easily led publics.

But cultural change is path dependent. The fact that a society was historically Protestant or Orthodox or Islamic or Confucian manifests itself in coherent cultural zones with distinctive value systems that persist even when one controls for the effects of socioeconomic development. These cultural zones are robust. Although the value systems of different countries are moving in the same direction under the impact of powerful modernizing forces, their value systems have not been converging, as simplistic notions of cultural globalization suggest (Meyer et al., 1997; Stevenson, 1997).

This may seem paradoxical, but it is not. If the world's societies were all moving in the same direction at the same rate of speed, the distances between them would remain as great as ever, and they would never converge. The reality is not that simple, of course, but this illustrates an important principle: postindustrial societies *are* changing rapidly and are moving in a common direction, but the cultural differences between them were empirically as great in 2001 as they were in 1981.[3] Although socioeconomic development tends to produce systematic changes in what people believe and want out of life, the influence of cultural traditions does not disappear. Belief systems have a remarkable durability and resilience. While values can and do change, they continue to reflect a society's historical heritage. Cultural change is path-dependent.

Nevertheless, it seems clear that socioeconomic development brings predictable long-term changes. One indication of this is the fact that the worldviews and behavior of the people living in developed societies differ immensely from those of peoples in developing ones. Another indication is the fact that the value systems of developed societies are changing in a consistent and roughly predictable direction. These changes do not reflect a homogenizing trend—they cannot be attributed, for example, to the impact of a global communications network that is said to be transmitting a common set of new values throughout the world. If this were the case, the same value changes would occur in all societies that are exposed to global communications. But this is not what has been happening, as we will demonstrate. For these value changes are *not* taking place in societies that have been experiencing sharply declining standards of living, such as the Soviet successor states, even though these societies are integrated into the global communications network. These changes occur only when the people of a given society have

3. Empirical evidence supporting this claim is presented in Chapter 2.

experienced high levels of economic prosperity for long periods of time. Socioeconomic development brings predictable cultural and political changes, and economic collapse tends to bring changes in the opposite direction.

These changes are probabilistic. They are not deterministic laws, like the Scientific Socialism that Karl Marx propounded. Moreover, cultural change is not linear, continuously moving in one direction as economic development takes place, until one reaches the end of history. Instead, industrialization brings a shift from traditional to secular-rational values; with the rise of postindustrial society, however, cultural change starts to move in another direction. The shift from traditional to secular-rational values becomes slower and stagnates, while another change becomes more powerful—the shift from survival to self-expression values, through which people place increasing emphasis on human choice, autonomy, and creativity. This change was moving slowly during the transition from preindustrial to industrial societies, but it becomes the dominant trend when industrial society gives way to postindustrial society. Modernization theorists foresaw value changes linked with the process of socioeconomic development, but they focused on the rise of secular-rational values, not anticipating a later wave of change—the rise of self-expression values. The classic modernization theorists, quite understandably, did not foresee the emancipative impulse that emerges in the later stages of modernization. This impulse is incompatible with the technocratic authoritarianism that many modernization theorists (and such writers as George Orwell) thought would be the outcome of political modernization. In contrast with these expectations, self-expression values make democracy the most likely outcome of political development.

Moore (1966) correctly pointed out that the industrial phase of modernization does not necessarily lead to democracy but follows different paths that allow for authoritarian, fascist, and communist versions of mobilizing the masses into politics. But in the postindustrial phase of modernization, rising self-expression values provide a social force that questions authority and operates in favor of genuinely mass responsive democracy, not only electoral democracy, as we will demonstrate.

Progress is not inevitable. The value changes linked with the various stages of modernization are reversible. Socioeconomic development brings massive and roughly predictable cultural changes, but if economic collapse occurs, cultural changes will tend to move in the opposite direction. Nevertheless, development has been the dominant trend of recent centuries: most countries are considerably more prosperous today than they were two hundred years ago. A powerful logic links high levels of socioeconomic development; cultural changes that emphasize human autonomy, creativity, and self-expression; and democratization. Through this process, democracy itself evolves to become increasingly responsive. With rising self-expression values, even long-established democracies become more responsive to mass preferences, and politics becomes less and less a game restricted to elites who pay attention to the masses in elections only.

Different societies follow different trajectories even when subject to the same forces of modernization, because specific factors, such as the cultural heritage of a given society, also shape how this society develops. Weber (1958 [1904]) argued that traditional religious values have an enduring influence, and scholars from various disciplines have observed that distinctive cultural traits endure over long periods of time and continue to shape a society's political and economic performance. For example, Putnam (1993) shows that the regions of Italy where democratic institutions function most successfully today are those in which civil society was relatively well developed in the nineteenth century and even earlier. According to Fukuyama (1995), societies with a cultural heritage of "low-trust" are at a competitive disadvantage in global markets because they are less able to develop large and complex social institutions. Hamilton (1994) argues that, although capitalism has become an almost universal way of life, civilizational factors continue to structure the organization of economies and societies. "What we witness with the development of a global economy is not increasing uniformity, in the form of a universalization of Western culture, but rather the continuation of civilizational diversity through the active reinvention and reincorporation of non-Western civilizational patterns" (Hamilton, 1994: 184). Thus, there are striking cross-cultural variations in the organization of capitalist production and associated managerial ideologies (DiMaggio, 1994; Guillén, 1994).

* * *

The fact that a society was historically shaped by a Protestant or Confucian or Islamic cultural heritage leaves an enduring impact, setting that society on a trajectory that continues to influence subsequent development—even if the direct influence of religious institutions is modest today. Thus, although few people attend church in Protestant Europe today, the societies that were historically shaped by Protestantism continue to manifest a distinctive set of values and beliefs. The same is true of historically Roman Catholic societies and historically Islamic or Orthodox or Confucian societies. The secularization thesis is only half true. In the industrialization phase, the role of religion does become less important, and even in postindustrial societies the ability of established religious authorities to dictate to the masses is rapidly crumbling away. But spiritual concerns, broadly defined, are not disappearing—they are becoming more widespread. Thus, while support for the old hierarchical churches is eroding in postindustrial societies, spiritual life is being transformed into forms that are increasingly compatible with individual self-expression.

The Causal Primacy of Socioeconomic Development

The urge to survive is common to all creatures, and normally survival is precarious. This reflects a basic ecological principle: the population of any organism tends to rise to meet the available food supply; it is then held constant by starvation, disease, or predators. Throughout most of history, the survival of all organisms, including humanity, was precarious (Birch and Cobb, 1981).

Humans developed cultures that helped soften the competition for survival. Virtually all traditional societies had cultural norms that repressed aspirations for social mobility. They justified acceptance of the existing social order by the poor. Moreover, cultural norms limiting reproduction softened the ruthless competition for survival brought by overpopulation.

Apart from disasters and wars, no other phenomenon affects people's daily lives more massively and brings changes that are more immediately felt than socioeconomic development (Nolan and Lenski, 1999; Carneiro, 2003). Socioeconomic development changes a society's basis of material subsistence and its social fabric (Sen, 1999). It directly affects people's sense of existential security, determining whether physical survival is uncertain or can be taken for granted. Economic threats concern people's most basic needs and are immediately felt. Its relevance to survival itself places socioeconomic development at the root of key causal chains in the development of societies (Jones, 1985).

Thus, the values and beliefs found in developed societies differ strikingly from those found in developing societies. Some of the most profoundly important cross-cultural differences involve religion, and the importance people attach to religion varies immensely. In agrarian societies, religion tends to be central to people's lives; in industrial societies, it tends to become a relatively peripheral concern. Another major dimension of cross-cultural variation involves gender roles, self-expression, and quality-of-life concerns, and here too the variation is enormous. In some low-income societies, fully 99 percent of the people say that men make better political leaders than women; in rich postindustrial societies, only a small minority agrees with this proposition.

Value orientations set standards for desirable and undesirable goals. This goal-setting function makes value orientations a powerful motivational regulator of human behavior (Rokeach, 1960, 1968, 1973). Cultural anthropologists (Durham, 1991; Barkow, Cosmides, and Tooby, 1992) argue that the function of different value orientations lies in their "cultural fitness": values change is an evolutionary process in which those values that are best suited to cope with life under given existential conditions have a selective advantage over values that are less suited to these conditions. This selection reflects an evolutionary principle, making those values most likely to survive and spread that are most effective in coping with given conditions. This evolutionary principle has two implications. First, prevailing value orientations reflect prevailing existential conditions. Second, if existential conditions change, value orientations are likely to change correspondingly—but only after a significant time lag that is needed to react to the impact of existential changes and to experiment with new life strategies that fit the new conditions better.

Moreover, new life strategies are more likely to be adopted by the young than by the old, who find it more difficult to abandon deeply inculcated habits and worldviews. But once a new life-style has emerged, succeeding generations have a choice between different role models and will adopt those that best fit their existential experiences.

Socioeconomic development is crucial because it impacts powerfully on people's existential conditions and their chances of survival. This is particularly true in societies of scarcity. Survival is such a basic human goal that when it is uncertain, one's entire life strategy is shaped by the struggle to survive. Whether people grow up in a society with an annual per capita income of $300 or $30,000 has more direct impact on their daily lives than whether they grow up in a country that has free elections or not. Throughout history, survival has been precarious and human choice has been restricted for most people. In recent decades, the publics of postindustrial societies have experienced unprecedented levels of existential security: real income levels are many times higher than they ever were before World War II, and welfare states have emerged that provide comprehensive safety nets for most people. Life expectancies have risen to unprecedented levels: in 1900, even in the United States—then the world's richest country—life expectancy was only forty-nine; a century later, it was seventy-eight. Today, most people in rich countries have grown up taking it for granted that they will not starve. These developments have changed people's lives fundamentally. Contemporary events such as the crisis of the welfare state, volatile stock markets, and the risk of unemployment are important but not life-threatening.

Socioeconomic development diminishes objective constraints on human autonomy, creativity, and choice in three ways. First, reduction of poverty diminishes material constraints on human choice and nourishes a sense of existential security. Second, socioeconomic development tends to increase people's levels of formal education and to give them greater access to information through the mass media (Lerner, 1958; Inkeles and Smith, 1974; Inkeles, 1983). In the same vein, the requirements of the emerging knowledge society mobilize people's cognitive abilities (Bell, 1973; Inglehart, 1990). Thus, the second major effect of socioeconomic development is that it diminishes cognitive and informational constraints on human choice, fueling a sense of intellectual independence.

The third important consequence of socioeconomic development is the fact that it increases occupational specialization and social complexity, diversifying human interactions. Growing diversity of human interactions liberates people: it frees them from ascriptive communal ties and closed social circles, bringing them to interact with others on a bargaining basis. These tendencies were recognized by early sociologists who identified a shift from "mechanical solidarity" to "organic solidarity" (Durkheim, 1988 [1893]) and from "community" to "association" (Tönnies, 1955 [1887]). In the same vein, Simmel (1984 [1908]) emphasized the individualizing and liberating effect when people begin to develop ties that bridge social circles (see also Granovetter, 1973). Diversification of human interaction frees people from prefixed social roles and social ties, making them autonomous in defining their social roles themselves and in shaping their social ties to other people. As U. Beck (2002) puts it, there is a shift from "communities of necessity" to "elective affinities" to others. Socialization and socializing become a matter of choice: people are free to connect and disconnect with whomever they want; and rigidly fixed roles for such categories as gender and class are eroding, giving people more room to express themselves as individuals. In short, the third effect of socioeconomic development is to diminish social constraints on human choice, nurturing a sense of social autonomy.

By reducing economic insecurity, by cognitive mobilization, and by diversifying human exchanges, socioeconomic development diminishes objective constraints on human choice. People become materially more secure, intellectually more autonomous, and socially more independent. Thus, people experience a greater sense of human autonomy.

Table 1 summarizes this emancipative effect of socioeconomic development.

Table 1 The Emancipative Effects of Socioeconomic Development

	Socioeconomic Development	
⇩	⇩	⇩
Economic growth and the welfare state increase people's economic resources.	Rising levels of education, expanding mass communication, and increasingly knowledge-intensive work widen people's intellectual resources.	Growing social complexity and diversification of human interactions broaden people's social resources.
⇩	⇩	⇩
People become materially more secure.	People become cognitively more autonomous.	People become socially more independent.
⇩	⇩	⇩
	Diminishing constraints on human choice	
	⇩	
	Growing emphasis on human autonomy	

Two Dimensions of Cultural Change

The impact of socioeconomic development on cultural change operates in two phases. Industrialization gives rise to one major process of cultural change: bringing bureaucratization and secularization. The rise of postindustrial society leads to a second major process of cultural change: instead of rationalization, centralization, and bureaucratization, the new trend is toward increasing emphasis on individual autonomy and self-expression values. Both cultural changes reshape people's authority orientations, but they do it in different ways. The industrial stage of modernization brings the *secularization* of authority, whereas the postindustrial stage brings *emancipation* from authority.

Industrializing societies focused on maximizing material output, at any cost, as the best way of maximizing human well-being. This strategy has been dramatically successful in alleviating starvation and raising life expectancies, but it produces diminishing returns in postindustrial societies. Postindustrial modernization brings a fundamental shift in economic strategies, from maximizing material standards of living to maximizing well-being through life-style changes. The "quality of experience" replaces the quantity of commodities as the prime criterion for making a good living (Florida, 2002). The rise of self-expression values has changed the political agenda of postindustrial societies, challenging the emphasis on economic growth at any price by an increasing concern for environmental protection. It has also brought a shift from political cleavages based on social class conflict toward cleavages based on cultural issues and quality-of-life concerns.

Thus, socioeconomic development produces not one but two major dimensions of cross-cultural variation, one linked with industrialization and the other linked with the rise of postindustrial society. Both dimensions reflect changes in people's authority orientations. Rising secular-rational values bring a secularization *of* authority, which shifts from being legitimized by traditional religious beliefs to being legitimized by secular-rational ones. But these secular beliefs are no less dogmatic than religious ones. Secular beliefs and doctrines do not necessarily challenge unlimited political authority; they usually legitimize it, as did fascist and communist ideologies. By contrast, rising self-expression values bring an emancipation *from* authority: people increasingly tend to reject external authority that encroaches on individual rights. Authority becomes internalized within people themselves.

Industrialization and Rising Secular-Rational Values

Sustained economic growth starts with industrialization as productivity begins to outpace population growth (Landes, 1998; W. Bernstein, 2004). In agrarian societies, humanity was at the mercy of inscrutable and uncontrollable natural forces. Because their causes were dimly understood, people tended to attribute events to anthropomorphic gods. The vast majority of the population made its living from agriculture and depended on things that came from heaven, like the sun and rain. One prayed for good weather, for relief from disease, or from plagues of insects.

In industrial society, production moved indoors into a man-made environment. One did not wait for the sun to rise and the seasons to change; when it got dark, one turned on the lights, and when it got cold, one turned on the heating. One did not pray for good crops because production came from machines that were built by human ingenuity. With the discovery of germs and antibiotics, even disease ceased to be seen as a divine visitation; it became a problem within technological control. As technology gave people increasing control over their environment, God became less central.

The shift from preindustrial to industrial society brought profound changes in people's daily experiences and prevailing worldviews (Bell, 1973; Spier, 1996; Inglehart, 1997). Preindustrial life, Bell (1976: 147) argues, was a "game against nature" in which "one's sense of the world is conditioned by the vicissitudes of the elements—the seasons, the storms, the fertility of the soil, the amount of water, the depth of the mine seams, the droughts and the floods." Industrialization brought less dependence on nature, which had been seen as ruled by inscrutable forces or anthropomorphic spirits. Life now became a "game against fabricated nature" (Bell, 1973: 147), a technical, mechanical, rationalized, bureaucratic world directed toward creating and dominating the environment. As technological control of the environment increased, the role ascribed to religion and God dwindled. Praying to God for a good harvest was no longer necessary when one could depend on fertilizer and insecticides. Materialistic ideologies arose, offering secular interpretations of history and secular utopias to be attained by human engineering operating through rationally organized bureaucratic organizations. But these ideologies were as dogmatic as religion, reflecting the rigidly disciplined and standardized way in which industrial societies organize the work force and life in general (Whyte, 1956; Florida, 2002). Accordingly, the rise of secular-rational values does not bring a decline of authority: it only shifts the basis of authority from traditional religious sources to secular-rational sources. Rational science and its belief in technological progress becomes the new source of authority in a highly mechanical world.

One reason for the decline of traditional religious beliefs in industrial societies is that an increasing sense of technological control over nature diminishes the need for reliance on supernatural powers. In the uncertain world of subsistence societies, the belief that an infallible higher power will ensure that things ultimately turn out well filled a major psychological need. One of the key functions of religion was to provide a sense of certainty in an insecure environment. Physical as well as economic insecurity intensifies this need: the old saying that "there are no atheists in foxholes" reflects the fact that wartime dangers increase the need for faith in a higher power. But as industrial production outpaces population growth and as scientific progress prolongs life expectancy, there is a dwindling need for the reassurance that religion traditionally provided.

In the preindustrial world, humans have little control over nature. They seek to compensate for their lack of physical control by appealing to the metaphysical powers that seem to control the world: worship is seen as a way to influence one's fate, and it is easier to accept one's helplessness if one knows the outcome is in the hands of an omnipotent being whose benevolence can be won by following rigid and predictable rules of conduct. These are important functions of religion in a world where humans have little or no control over their environment. Industrialization vastly increases humans' direct physical control over the environment in which they live and work. This process undermines the traditional function of religion to provide reassurance in an uncertain world.

But industrialization does not increase people's sense of individual autonomy because of the disciplined and regimented way in which industrial societies are organized. In industrial societies, people—and especially factory workers—are embedded in uniform social classes with rigid social controls and conformity pressures. Life in industrial society is as standardized as its uniform mass products. The disciplined organization of uniform masses in industrial societies, which marches armies of workers from their barracks to the assembly line and back, creates a need for rigid codes of conduct. Although it tends to replace religious dogmas with secular ones, industrialization does not emancipate people from authority. The industrial standardization of life discourages self-expression values.

Postindustrialization and Rising Self-Expression Values

The emergence of postindustrial society brings another wave of cultural change, moving in a different direction. In the United States, Canada, Western Europe, and a growing share of East Asia, the majority of the labor force no longer works in factories. Instead of living in a mechanical environment, ever more people now spend their productive hours dealing with people, symbols, and information. Human efforts are no longer so much focused on producing material objects as on communicating with other people and processing information; the crucial products are innovation, knowledge, and ideas. Human creativity becomes the most important production factor (Florida, 2002). In the nineteenth-century United States, 80 percent of the work force was still engaged in agriculture; today, only 2 percent is. By the early twentieth century, industrial production dominated American society; today, the United States has become a knowledge society that spends far more on computers alone than on all industrial equipment combined. One of the most crucial aspects of this shift in economic activities is the fact that people experience far more individual autonomy in doing their jobs than industrial workers did. Routine tasks increasingly are taken over by computers and robots. Instead of being cogs in a huge machine, workers in the knowledge sector exercise individual judgment and choice. Even in the periphery of menial services, people have more flexibility in performing their tasks than did assembly-line workers in the industrial age.

The postindustrial age diminishes objective constraints on human choice in three major ways. First, postindustrial societies attain unprecedentedly high levels of prosperity and have welfare states that make food, clothing, shelter, housing, education, and health service available to almost everyone. Even in the United States, with a relatively limited welfare state, more than one-quarter of the national product is redistributed through the state for public welfare. Despite recent retrenchment of welfare benefits, never before in history have the masses experienced levels of existential security comparable with those that have emerged in postindustrial societies. Physical survival, a minimum living standard, and an average life expectancy of nearly eighty years can be taken for granted by most people living in these societies. This unprecedentedly high degree of existential security enables people to focus increasingly on goals beyond immediate survival.

Second, although mass literacy became widespread with industrialization, postindustrialization launches a massive process of cognitive mobilization. Modern service activities increasingly involve cognitive skills. Researchers, engineers, teachers, writers, lawyers, accountants, counselors, and analysts all belong to the "creative class" (Florida, 2002), whose members work with knowledge, perform analytical tasks, and use information technology. They have a high degree of autonomy in doing their work, even if they work within organizational hierarchies. Moreover, the need for cognitive skills increases the demand for higher education, and educational levels have risen dramatically in all postindustrial societies. Education makes people intellectually more independent because they no longer depend on other people's interpretations of the world. Increasingly, one's formal education and job experience help develop the potential for autonomous decision making (Bell, 1973, 1976). The prevalence of rigid manual routines in the typical factory required (and allowed) very little autonomous judgment. Service and knowledge workers deal with people and concepts, operating in a world where innovation and the freedom to exercise individual judgment are essential. Creativity, imagination, and intellectual independence become central. In addition, the evolution of mass media and modern information technology gives people easy access to knowledge, increasing their informational autonomy. Thus, rising levels of education, increasing cognitive and informational requirements in economic activities, and increasing proliferation of knowledge via mass media make people intellectually more independent, diminishing cognitive constraints on human choice.

Third, postindustrial society has a socially liberating effect. For service-based economies reverse the disciplined, standardized ways in which industrial societies organize people's daily activities. In the industrial age, the mass-production system subjected the labor force to rigid centralized control, and workers were embedded in closely knit groups with strong conformity pressures. By contrast, postindustrialization destandardizes economic activities and social life. The flexible organization of service-based economies and the autonomy they give workers radiate into all domains of life: human interaction is increasingly freed from the bonding ties of closely knit groups, enabling people to make and break social ties readily. The welfare state supports this individualization trend (U. Beck, 2002). Formerly, children's survival largely depended on whether their parents provided for them, and children took care of their parents when they reached old age. Although the role of the family is still important, the life-or-death nature of this relationship has been eroded by the welfare state. Maintaining family relations is nowadays a matter of choice, not of necessity. One-parent families and childless old people are far more viable under contemporary conditions than they once were. What Durkheim (1988 [1983]), Tönnies (1955 [1887]), and Simmel (1984 [1908]) once anticipated is becoming more and more a reality: social ties shift from "communities of necessity" to "elective affinities" (U. Beck, 2002). This makes people personally more independent, diminishing social constraints on human choice.

Postindustrialization brings even more favorable existential conditions than industrialization, making people economically more secure, intellectually more autonomous, and socially more independent than ever. This emancipative process gives people a fundamental sense of human autonomy, leading them to give a higher priority to freedom of choice and making them less inclined to accept authority and dogmatic truths. The shift from traditional to secular-rational values linked with industrialization brings a secularization *of* authority. But the shift from survival to self-expression values linked with postindustrialization brings emancipation *from* authority.

Industrialization gives humans increasing control of their environment, diminishing their deference to supernatural power and encouraging the rise of secular-rational values. But industrialization does not nourish a sense of human autonomy or lead people to question absolute authority, which persists in secular ideologies. By contrast, postindustrialization gives people a sense of human autonomy that leads them to question authority, dogmatism, and hierarchies, whether religious or secular. And because survival comes to be taken for granted, people become increasingly critical of the risks of technology and appreciative of nature. Spiritual concerns about humanity's place in the universe regain prominence. This does not bring a return to dogmatic religiosity, but it does bring the emergence of new forms of spirituality and nonmaterial concerns.

Table 2 contrasts the ways in which the industrial phase and the postindustrial phase of modernization bring cultural changes. Economic growth and growing material prosperity are common to both phases of modernization, which tends to increase people's sense of existential security. Existential security is conducive to both secular-rational values and self-expression values. Accordingly, both sets of values tend to rise throughout both phases of modernization. But apart from their common tendency to increase existential security, the two phases of modernization differ in how far they promote individual autonomy, which makes them promote the two sets of values to varying degrees.

* * *

Table 2 Differences between the Impact of the Industrial and Postindustrial Phases of Modernization on Human Values

Industrialization		Postindustrialization	
Intensifying exploitation of natural resources	Regimented organization of human activities	Continuing exploitation of nature increases ecological risks	Individualized organization of human activities
Sense of technological control over natural forces	Weak sense of individual autonomy in society	Revival of spiritual concerns about the protection of Creation	Sense of individual autonomy in society
Massively growing emphasis on secular-rational values	Slowly growing emphasis on self-expression values	Slowly growing emphasis on secular-rational values	Massively growing emphasis on self-expression values

In the postindustrial phase, economic scarcity continues to recede, strengthening people's sense of existential security even more. In addition, the destandardization of economic activities and social life that occurs in the post-industrial age diminishes social constraints in unprecedented ways. In this phase, people's sense of existential security *does* translate into a broader sense of human autonomy. As this happens, the secular dogmas that arose in the industrial age erode with the spread of self-expression values. Thus, at the same time as postindustrial society accelerates the emergence of self-expression values, it slows down the trend toward secular-rational values.

Individualized Forms of Spirituality

With the rise of the knowledge society, the mechanical world of the factory shapes the daily lives of fewer and fewer people. One's life experience deals more with people and ideas than with material things. The computer becomes the dominant tool, and computers verge on magic, creating an almost limitless number of virtual realities. In the knowledge society, productivity depends less on material constraints than on ideas and imagination. This creates a climate of intellectual creativity and stimulation in which spiritual concerns again become more central. Although the authority of the established churches continues to decline, during the past twenty years the publics of postindustrial societies have become increasingly likely to spend time thinking about the meaning and purpose of life. Whether one views these concerns as religious depends on one's definition of religion, but it is clear that the materialistic secularism of industrial society is fading. There is a shift from institutionally fixed forms of dogmatic religion to individually flexible forms of spiritual religion. Even one's religious ideas become a matter of choice, creativity, and self-expression.

A sense of insecurity has never been the only factor motivating religion. The desire to understand where we come from and where we are going and why we are here is inherent in humanity, and philosophers and theologians have been concerned with these questions throughout history. But throughout most of history existential insecurity dominated the lives of most people, and the great theological questions were of central concern to only a small minority. The vast majority of the population needed reassurance and a sense of predictability in a world where humans had little control over their environment—and this was the dominant factor underlying the grip of traditional religion on mass publics.

Although the traditional churches (like most bureaucratic organizations from labor unions to political parties) continue to lose members in postindustrial societies, we find no evidence that spiritual concerns, broadly understood, are losing ground. Quite the contrary, comparing the results of the 1981 Values Surveys with the results from 1989–91, 1995–97, and 1999–2001, we find that people in postindustrial societies are spending more time thinking about the meaning and purpose of life than they used to. Religion does not vanish. What we observe is a transformation of religion's function, from institutionalized forms of dogmatic religiosity that provide absolute codes of conduct in an insecure world to individualized spiritual concerns that serve the need for meaning and purpose in societies where virtually no one starves to death.

Religious thought seems to have become superfluous as industrial society demonstrates seemingly unlimited human control over nature and secular ideologies promise a scientifically certain route to utopia. But the publics of postindustrial societies manifest a growing awareness of the risks and limitations of science and technology, and initially religious questions about the relationship of human civilization and natural life again become central. This is most obvious in the debates about the ethical dimensions of genetic engineering, biotechnology, and other new technologies (Gaskell and Bauer, 2001).

Growing individual autonomy undermines the need for dogmatic guidelines and rigid authority, whether religious or secular. Spiritual concerns regain salience. This revival is linked with an increased awareness of the risks of civilization (Giddens, 1990, 1991; U. Beck, 1992). A growing number of people have the time, the information, and the education to understand that modernization has given humanity so much power over its environment that it can destroy life on this planet. This insight propagates respect for life and the limitations of human ingenuity. This has led to the blossoming of new forms of spirituality, many of which focus on a new balance between humans and nature. Postindustrialization makes modernity increasingly "self-reflexive," as Giddens puts it (1991). Postindustrialization replaces the lost ground of institutionalized dogmatic religiosity with individualized spiritual concerns. Whether or not we define this as religion, its function has changed—from providing absolute rules of conduct to providing a sense of the meaning of life.

Humanistic Risks and Egocentric Threats

Uncertainty is part of the human condition, and risks persist in postindustrial society, as U. Beck (1992) has convincingly pointed out, and the risk perceptions on which the ecological movement focuses represent a new form of concerns. But the risk perceptions of postindustrial society are fundamentally different from the survival concerns of the preindustrial and industrial phases of development. In these earlier phases, hunger and economic scarcity present an immediate threat to individual survival that is a direct firsthand experience. It does not require specialized knowledge or intellectual insight to perceive them: hunger is immediately felt.

The risks of postindustrial society, by contrast, are abstract. They are not based on firsthand experience but require cognitive insights. Even full-time specialists disagree about how rapidly global warming is occurring and what its consequences will be. The risks of new technologies, such as genetic engineering, are long-term risks to humanity, not immediate risks to the individual. These risks are not immediately felt but have to be understood, which requires high levels of information and a grasp of complex argumentation. Thus, the related risk perceptions are socially constructed. This makes it possible for much of the population to ignore these risks or view them as hypothetical. No immediate threat forces people to take into consideration the risks of global warming or genetic cloning in their daily activities. But precisely this relief from immediate threats also enables people to focus on problems that are not of an immediate concern to themselves. High levels of existential security and autonomy allow people to widen their horizons, allowing for a higher degree of risk awareness. This risk awareness is the product of cognitive insights among people who—as individuals—are relatively safe and free to devote energy to concerns that do not immediately threaten them. As individual safety and autonomy reduce egocentrism, they increase homocentrism (Maslow, 1988 [1954]).

The best-documented aspect of this process is the shift from materialist to postmaterialist priorities—a shift from giving top priority to economic and physical security, to self-expression and the quality of life. This shift from materialist to postmaterialist values has been measured annually from 1970 to the present, in surveys carried out in a number of Western societies... Postmaterialists are economically more secure than materialists, but much more sensitive to environmental risks. Individual security increases empathy, making people more aware of long-term risks. The rise of self-expression values fuels *humanistic* risk perceptions. These risk perceptions are fundamentally different from the *egocentric* threat perceptions that underlie survival values.

Value Change as a Cultural Process

People have always needed to eat, and they always will. Rising emphasis on self-expression values does not put an end to material desires. But prevailing economic orientations are gradually being reshaped. People who work in the knowledge sector continue to seek high salaries, but they place equal or greater emphasis on doing stimulating work and being able to follow their own time schedules (Florida, 2002). Consumption is becoming progressively less determined by the need for sustenance and the practical use of the goods consumed. People still eat, but a growing component of food's value is determined by its nonmaterial aspects. People pay a premium to eat exotic cuisines that provide an interesting experience or that symbolize a distinctive life-style. The publics of postindustrial societies place growing emphasis on "political consumerism," such as boycotting goods whose production violates ecological or ethical standards. Consumption is less and less a matter of sustenance and more and more a question of life-style—and choice.

People's worldviews and value orientations reflect their basic life experiences. Value orientations are functional: they provide guidelines that allow people to master life under given existential conditions (Durham, 1991; Mark, 2002). Cultural norms tend to be internalized at an early age and reinforced by nonrational sanctions. The power of these sanctions does not lie in their rationality; it lies in their emotionality, so that violations of norms cause feelings of guilt and shame, which is a much more reliable regulator of human behavior than sheer legal sanctions (Lal, 1998).

People's aversion to divorce does not simply reflect rational cost calculations. Instead, traditional value systems tend to make divorce so deeply anchored in people's emotions that it becomes a question of good and evil. Norms that can constrain people's behavior, even when it is in their rational interest to do something else, are norms that are taught as absolute rules and inculcated so that their consciences torture them if they are violated. Such societal norms have considerable momentum. The mere fact that the function of a given cultural pattern has weakened or disappeared does not mean that the norm itself disappears.

But if the original reason behind a given norm vanishes, it does open the way for that norm to weaken gradually. People begin to experiment with new ideas and norms, creating new life-styles. New generations then face a confrontation between old and new norms and life-styles, which offer them alternative role models among which they can choose. Insofar as the new worldview fits the new generations' firsthand formative experiences, they tend to adopt it. Thus, new values, life-styles, and role models can replace older ones in a gradual process of generational replacement.

Norms linked to the maintenance of the two-parent heterosexual family clearly are weakening for a variety of reasons, ranging from the rise of the welfare state to the drastic decline of infant mortality rates, meaning that a couple no longer needs to produce four or five children in order to replace the population. In these realms, one would expect experimentation to take place; gradually, new forms of behavior would emerge that deviate from traditional norms, and the groups most likely to accept these new forms of behavior are the young more than the old, the relatively secure more than the insecure, the educated more than the uneducated, and those having diverse human interactions more than those embedded in closely tied networks.

* * *

Cognition and Experience as Sources of Value Change

Classic modernization theory needs to be modified in another respect: we need to correct its one-sided emphasis on cognitive factors in shaping cultural change. Weber attributed the rise of a secular, rational worldview to the spread of scientific knowledge. Scientific discoveries had made traditional religious explanations obsolete; as awareness of scientific interpretations spread, religion was inexorably giving way to rationality. God was dead, and science had killed him—or, at least, it was doing so. Similarly, such modernization theorists as Lerner (1958), Inkeles and Smith (1974), and Inkeles (1983) argued that education drives the modernization process: within any given country, the most educated tend to have modern worldviews, and as educational levels rise, traditional religious worldviews inevitably give way to secular-rational ones.

This emphasis on cognitive forces captures an important part of the story but only part. Experiential factors, such as whether people feel that survival is secure or insecure, are at least equally important in shaping people's worldviews. Higher levels of formal education tend to be linked with the presence of secular-rational values and self-expression values. But higher education is not just an indicator of the extent to which one has absorbed scientific knowledge, rationality, and humanistic ideals. It is, at least equally, an indicator of the extent to which one has experienced relatively secure conditions during one's formative years, when formal education takes place. Throughout the world, children from economically secure families are most likely to obtain higher education.

A high level of education is an indicator that an individual grew up with a sufficiently high level of existential security to take survival for granted—and therefore gives top priority to autonomy, individual choice, and self-expression. In virtually every society that has been surveyed, people with a university education place stronger emphasis on self-expression than the public in general. This reflects the fact that the highly educated tend to be recruited from the more privileged strata and have grown up under relatively favorable existential conditions, experiencing more security and autonomy than other citizens of their society. But not only a person's own security and autonomy make a modern worldview more likely. A society's general social climate also helps shape people's sense of security and autonomy. Thus, although there is a universal tendency for higher education to encourage people to place more emphasis on self-expression values, there is much more difference in the degree of emphasis on self-expression values *between* the highly educated people of different nations than between the highly educated and the general public within the same nations (see Figure 1).

Figure 1 Self-expression values among the university-educated and among the rest of the public.

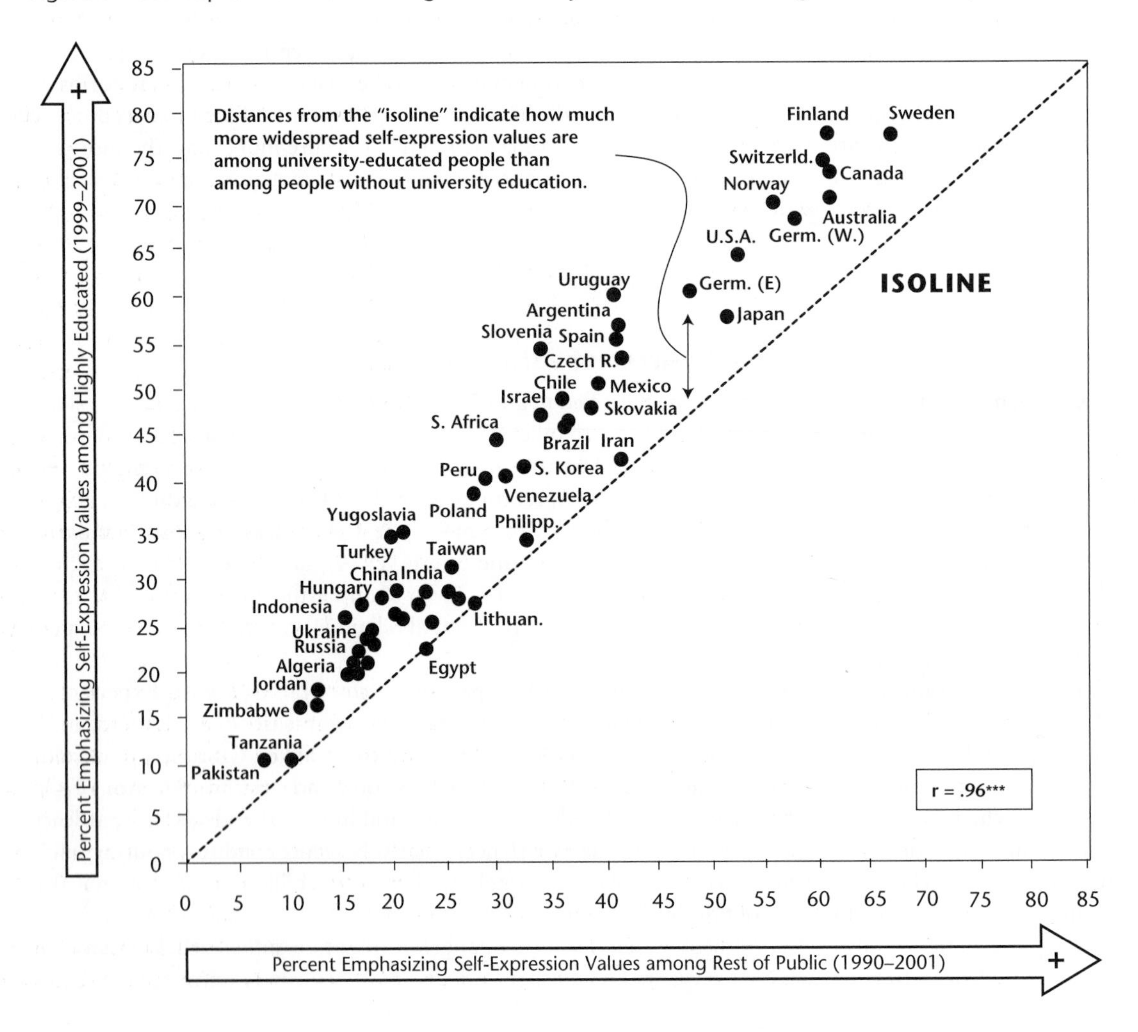

Thus, we can distinguish between education as an indicator of the extent to which people have experienced a sense of security and education as an indicator of the extent to which people have become familiar with scientific thought and humanistic ideals. Because the highly educated in all countries are relatively familiar with scientific thought and humanistic ideals, cross-national value differences among the highly educated do not reflect differential exposure to scientific thought, so much as they reflect differences in a society's prevailing sense of existential security and human autonomy.

The cognitive component of education is, for all practical purposes, irreversible, whereas one's sense of security and autonomy is not. The feeling that the world is secure or insecure is an early-established and relatively stable aspect of one's outlook. But these feelings can be eroded by short-term period effects and, even more so, by catastrophic events such as the collapse of one's entire society and economy. Such catastrophic events are rare, but an entire group of societies experienced them during the period covered by the Values Surveys. In 1989–91 communism collapsed throughout Central and Eastern Europe. In the Soviet successor states, this event brought drastic decreases in standards of living, stagnant or falling life expectancies, and the traumatic experience of the collapse of the social and political systems and also the belief systems under which these people had lived for many decades. Scientific *knowledge* did not disappear—it continued to grow—and educational levels remained as high as ever in these societies. But the prevailing sense of existential security and individual control over one's life fell sharply. If the emergence of modern values were solely determined by cognitive forces, then self-expression values would have continued to spread. But insofar as these values are shaped by feelings of security or insecurity and a sense of autonomy or heteronomy, we would expect to witness stagnation or a regression toward traditional values and survival values in the ex-Soviet societies. As we will see, this is exactly what happened.

Although the past decade has been a period of slow economic growth, the rich democracies have not experienced anything like the catastrophic changes felt in the ex-Soviet world. Moreover, the relative stagnation since 1990 has been offset by the momentum of intergenerational population replacement, which continues to push the rich democracies toward increasingly modern values. Cultural modernization has continued there, as one would expect. The cognitive interpretation implies that cultural modernization is an irreversible process as knowledge continues to increase. Our interpretation implies that it is reversible, and under the conditions that have prevailed since 1989, we would expect it to be reversing itself in recent years in most ex-Soviet societies. The empirical evidence indicates that it has. A society's prevailing sense of existential security is more important than cognitive factors.

In conclusion, cultural change is determined not simply by cognition and rational choice but by people's exposure to different existential conditions (Mark, 2002). Yet cultural change is not illogical. Quite the contrary, there is an evolutionary logic behind it, driving people to adopt those values that fit given existential conditions.

Cultural Change and Its Institutional Manifestations

Major changes in cultural values at the individual level are reflected in changes at the societal level, but there is rarely a one-to-one relationship between underlying cultural change and its societal-level manifestations. For example, starting in the mid-1960s, birthrates declined throughout postindustrial societies. By 1990 fertility rates were below the population replacement level in almost all postindustrial societies. Cultural change played a significant role in this shift (see Inglehart and Norris, 2003).

From 1960 to 1990 divorce rates rose sharply in almost all postindustrial societies except one: the Republic of Ireland, where divorce remained illegal until 1995. In Italy and Spain, divorce had become legal in the 1970s, and legalization was followed by a surge of divorces. One might attribute this sudden increase in divorce rates to the legal changes that preceded them. This interpretation is true but superficial, focusing only on the immediate cause. If one probes deeper, the first question that arises is, *Why* did divorce suddenly become legal in these countries? Divorce had been illegal for centuries because it violated deeply held religious norms. This remained true in the Republic of Ireland, where a majority of the public voted against legalizing divorce as recently as 1987. But, as our data indicate, these norms have gradually been weakening over time. Public support for legalizing divorce became increasingly widespread and articulate in Italy and Spain, until the laws themselves were changed in the 1970s. By 1995 even the Irish finally accepted divorce in a national referendum. One consequence was a sudden surge of divorces immediately after the laws were changed. Although the behavioral change was sudden and lumpy, it reflected a long process of incremental value change.

The rise of the pro-environmentalist Green Party in West Germany provides another illustration of the disparity between the incremental pace of cultural change and the abrupt emergence of its institutional manifestation. In 1983 the Greens suddenly achieved prominence when they won enough votes to enter the West German parliament for the first time, bringing a fundamental change in German politics. But this abrupt breakthrough reflected a gradual intergenerational rise of mass support for environmentalist policies. Institutional barriers, such as the fact that a party must win at least 5 percent of the vote to gain seats in the German parliament, made the party's breakthrough to prominence sudden and dramatic. But its rise reflected long-term processes of incremental change. If one focuses only on the immediate causes, a society's electoral rules seem to be the decisive factor: the Greens had little visibility until they surmounted the 5 percent threshold; and in societies without proportional representation, such as the United States and Great Britain, ecology parties may never play an important role. But even in these countries, a rising concern for environmental protection has transformed the agendas of existing parties. In most societies, the Green activists are mainly postmaterialists, and it seems unlikely that Green parties or environmentalist movements would have emerged without the intergenerational cultural changes that gave rise to a postindustrial worldview that reflects an increased awareness of ecological risks. Starting from obscurity in the early 1980s, the Green parties have come a long way. At this writing, environmentalist parties were part of the governing coalitions in Germany and seven other European countries.

Similarly, in 2001 the Netherlands experienced a sudden surge in same-sex marriages, starting from a zero base. The immediate cause of this shift was the fact that the Dutch parliament had just legalized same-sex marriages—which had been not merely illegal but virtually unthinkable for centuries. The root cause of this societal-level change was the fact that a gradual shift had taken place in the Dutch public's attitudes toward homosexuality. In this case, the societal change is so recent that the four waves of the Values Surveys provide detailed information about the cultural changes that preceded the societal-level change. It is by no means coincidental that the Netherlands was the first country in the world to legalize same-sex marriages: the Values Surveys demonstrate that the Dutch public has consistently been more tolerant of homosexuality than any other public in the world. But even in the Netherlands, prevailing attitudes were still unfavorable to homosexuality until recently. In the 1981 Values Survey, 22 percent of the Dutch public said that homosexuality was never justifiable, selecting point 1 on a 10-

point scale on which "1" meant that homosexuality was never justifiable, and point 10 indicated that homosexuality was always justifiable. At that time, 40 percent of the Dutch selected points 1 through 5, indicating relative disapproval. Disapproval of homosexuality was still widespread in the Netherlands in 1981, although the Dutch were more favorable than any other public. In most countries, disapproval of homosexuality was expressed by overwhelming majorities, ranging from 75 to 99 percent of the public.

These attitudes have changed markedly since 1981 throughout postindustrial societies, as part of a broad intergenerational value shift toward more tolerant values. Throughout postindustrial societies, the younger birth cohorts are much more tolerant of homosexuality than are their elders. In the Netherlands, for example, in 1981 fully 52 percent of those older than sixty-five years felt that homosexuality can never be justified, placing themselves at point 1 on the scale. Among those who were eighteen to twenty-four years old, only 11 percent took this position. By 1999 only 7 percent of the Dutch public was still at point 1, registering absolute disapproval, and only 22 percent at points 1 through 5. Disapproval had fallen to less than half its 1981 level. A year later, in 2000, the Dutch parliament legalized same-sex marriages. In 2002 the German constitutional court legalized same-sex marriages, followed by Canada in 2003 and Spain in 2004. Not surprisingly, the Dutch public had the most favorable attitudes toward homosexuality of any country in the world, and the Germans, Spanish, and Canadians also ranked among the most favorable, as Table 3 shows. In only nine countries did less than half of the public disapprove of homosexuality, and all four of these countries fell into that group.

Table 3 Disappraval of Homosexuality in the Ten Most Permissive Societies (percentage at points 1 to 5 on a 10-point scale)

Country	Disapproval (%)
Netherlands	22
Sweden	26
Iceland	32
Denmark	41
Switzerland	43
Germany[a]	45
Spain	47
Canada	49
Luxembourg	49
Czech Republic	51
Norway	52

Note: These are the only societies (among 77) in which less than 53 percent of the population disapproved of homosexuality in the latest available survey, as indicated by selecting points 1–5. In the United States in 2000, 60 percent disapproved of homosexuality—but it ranked among the 18 most tolerant societies. In 24 societies, fully 95 percent or more of the public disapproved.

[a] German data are based on the combined results from the surveys in the eastern and western regions of Germany in 1997 and 1999.

Cumulative Changes and Sudden Breakthroughs

It is commonly assumed that only change measures can explain social change. This assumption seems convincing until one examines it more closely. In many cases, especially those involving cross-level linkages such as the impact of cultural change on its institutional manifestation, a society's absolute *level* on a given variable is a much stronger predictor of institutional change than recent changes on that variable. To illustrate, let us assume that in 2000, 78 percent of the Dutch public was at least moderately tolerant of homosexuality (somewhere to the right of point "5," the midpoint of the scale). At the same time, only 8 percent of the Nigerian public was equally tolerant. But the amount of change observed in Nigeria from 1995 to 2000 was actually greater than that in the Netherlands: in 1995, only 4 percent of the Nigerian public was on the right half of the scale, a figure that doubled in 2000, rising to 8 percent. During the same period, tolerance of homosexuality in the Netherlands only rose slightly, from 76 to 78 percent.

These figures are hypothetical but close to reality, and they illustrate an important point: both in absolute and relative terms, the amount of attitudinal change observed in Nigeria from 1995 to 2000 was larger than in the Netherlands; but the Netherlands was much likelier to manifest institutional change. Unlike Nigeria, the Netherlands had passed the threshold at which a majority of the public was tolerant of homosexuality. Accordingly, institutional change occurred in the Netherlands, in the form of legislation legalizing same-sex marriages. This change is very unlikely to take place in Nigeria in the foreseeable future. The crucial difference lies in the fact that the Dutch public has a much higher *level* of tolerance than the Nigerian public: the absolute "stock" of tolerance is far more important than the short-term fluctuations or "flows" of tolerance.

The Dutch public's relatively high level of tolerance represents a stock that had been built up gradually, through a process of intergenerational value change that took place during the past fifty to sixty years. If one attempted to use standard time series methods to analyze this relationship, one would conclude that the attitudinal changes that took place in the Dutch public from 1940 to 1995 had no impact whatever on same-sex marriages and that the short-term attitudinal changes from 1995 to 2000 were *negatively* correlated with subsequent changes in the rate of same-sex marriages. The relatively high level of tolerance observed among the Dutch public in recent surveys is robust, shows large intergenerational differences, and has been growing gradually—and this relatively high level provides a far better predictor of institutional breakthroughs than do short-term fluctuations, which are relatively small and can fluctuate in either direction, so they may even have the wrong sign when change occurs.

A similar pattern applies to the relationship between cultural change and democratization. As we will demonstrate, there was a gradual intergenerational shift toward growing emphasis on autonomy and self-expression among the publics of Poland, Hungary, Czechoslovakia, East Germany, and other Central European countries during the decades before 1989. But another crucial factor occurred in 1988, when Gorbachev announced that Soviet troops would no longer be used to prop up unpopular communist regimes in Eastern Europe. Within a year communist regimes began collapsing throughout the region. Mass demands for liberalization had built up gradually over many years in these countries; but this cumulating factor could not manifest itself in an institutional breakthrough until the blocking factor—in this case, the Red Army—was removed. When cultural change leads to institutional change, the overcoming of thresholds or blocking factors is the rule, rather than the exception.

There is rarely a one-to-one correspondence between changes at the individual level and the system level. Accordingly, a society's *level* of economic development is a much better predictor of democratization than its economic growth rate. In fact, economic growth rates at any given point in time are misleading as a predictor of democracy—and they may even have the wrong sign (Doorenspleet, 2004). They tend to be highest in low-income countries such as China that are in the early phase of industrialization but have not yet reached a level of development where democracy becomes likely. If high growth continues, we expect that China will eventually make the transition to democracy—*not* because it has high growth rates at that time but because it has reached a high *level* of development.

We reject both economic and cultural determinism. It is clear that given elites, leaders, institutions, and situation-specific factors play crucial roles. The immediate cause of institutional change can virtually always be found at the elite level, almost by definition, because the people who negotiate political changes are *defined* as elites (even if they did not fall into that category a year earlier). But underlying cultural changes also play a major role in the emergence of important institutional changes, from changing legislation concerning gays and lesbians to the massive shift toward democracy that took place from 1985 to 1995.

If one believed that cultural changes alone determined institutional change, one would assume that there must have been a sudden surge of support for democracy among East European publics in 1989, and a massive surge of approval for homosexuality in the Netherlands in 1999. This was not true in either case: instead, a slow but steady intergenerational value change took place during the decades preceding both of these institutional breakthroughs. The precise timing of when the institutional breakthrough occurred was determined by elite-level factors. But gradual underlying value changes were the root cause of the fact that East Germany suddenly democratized in 1989–90, and that same-sex marriage finally became legal in the Netherlands in 2000.

Intergenerational cultural changes have been gradually transforming the value systems of people in many countries, bringing a shift from survival values to self-expression values. . . . [T]he extent to which a given public placed high priority on self-expression values when a window of opportunity opened in 1988 (when Gorbachev announced that the Soviet army would no longer prop up communist regimes in Central and Eastern Europe) was crucial in determining how far toward democracy their society would subsequently move—and how well democratic institutions flourished once they were adopted.

Consequences of Cultural Change

The shift from industrial to postindustrial values is eroding many of the key institutions of industrial society. In the political realm, the rise of postindustrial values brings declining respect for authority and growing emphasis on participation and self-expression. These trends are conducive to democratization in authoritarian societies and to a more elite-challenging, issue-oriented, and direct form of democracy in already-democratic societies. In any case, rising self-expression values push for more genuine democracy. Self-expression values are inherently emancipative and people-centered, giving rise to a new type of humanistic society that promotes human freedom and autonomy on numerous fronts.

Respect for authority is eroding, and the long-term trend toward increased mass participation has taken on a new character. In large-scale agrarian societies, political participation was limited to a narrow minority. In industrializing societies, the masses were mobilized by disciplined, elite-led political parties. This was a major advance for democratization, and it resulted in unprecedented numbers of people taking part in politics by voting; however, mass participation continued to be guided by elites, in keeping with the Iron Law of Oligarchy (Michels, 1962 [1912]).

In postindustrial society the emphasis is shifting from voting to more spontaneous, issue-specific, and elite-challenging forms of civic action. New forms of political self-expression extend the boundary of politics from the narrow domain of elite-led electoral campaigns into increasingly autonomous forms of public self-expression. The traditional representative form of elite-centered democracy transforms into a people-centered form of democracy (Cain, Dalton, and Scarrow, 2003). Contrary to often-repeated claims that social capital and mass participation are eroding, the publics of postindustrial societies are intervening in politics more actively today than ever before; however, they are changing the ways in which they participate.

Elite-led forms of participation are dwindling. Mass loyalties to long-established hierarchical political parties are weakening. No longer content to be disciplined troops, the public has become increasingly autonomous and elite-challenging. Consequently, though voter turnout is stagnant or declining (Dalton and Wattenberg, 2000), people are participating in politics in more active and issue-specific ways (Dalton, 2001; Norris, 2002). In many countries, demonstrations against American military intervention in Iraq in 2002–3 were the largest in history. Increasingly, people are using the public sphere as a stage for expressing commitments to alternative life-styles (Cain et al., 2003). As the leaders of political machines are losing their ability to mobilize voter turnout, the publics of postindustrial societies are engaging in new, largely self-organizing and self-expressive forms of participation (Welzel, Inglehart, and Deutsch, 2004). People engage in these activities even if they think it is unlikely to change official decisions. Political self-expression becomes a value in itself and not just a way to attain specific goals.

Antimodern Reactions to Modernity

Rapid changes linked with postindustrialization stimulate defensive reactions among marginalized parts of the population. Postindustrialization brings increasing individual freedom and growing opportunities for self-actualization for large parts of society, but substantial minorities—particularly the less educated and the unemployed—still feel existential threats. In terms of relative deprivation, they may be even worse off than poor people in poor societies. Education is the most important form of capital in the knowledge society, which puts the less educated in a worse position than they had in the industrial age.

In the industrial age, disciplined mass organizations were a tremendous asset to the lower classes because they enabled them to translate their sheer numbers into political power. They could exert pressure to redistribute wealth from the rich to the poor, bringing an increasing degree of income equality (Esping-Andersen, 1990). The individualizing tendency of postindustrial societies has partly reversed this trend. The working class has declined in numbers and lost the cohesion that gave it political power; labor unions are weakening. In addition, the working classes in postindustrial societies are under increasing economic pressure from globalization and immigration; the high-cost labor force of rich countries is now competing with that of low-income countries. The equalizing trend in income distribution has been reversed since the 1980s (Goesling, 2001). This nourishes threat perceptions and defensive reactions, providing a social base for new dogmas, including right-wing populism and new forms of religious fundamentalism. Contrary to widespread belief, religious fundamentalists have not become more numerous in Western societies, but they *have* become more active and more salient (Norris and Inglehart, 2004). Formerly a relatively quiescent segment of the public, in recent years they have come to believe (accurately) that some of their most basic norms are rapidly eroding, which has galvanized those with traditional religious beliefs into heightened political activism, opposing such things as abortion and same-sex marriage. Consequently, the postindustrial phase of modernization is not conflict-free. On the whole, postindustrialization brings individualization, more autonomy, and more freedom of choice, but it also brings new conflicts. It stimulates anti-modernist reactions among marginalized parts of the population, feeding the ranks of right-wing parties (U. Beck, 2002).

Existential Security, Individual Autonomy, and the Knowledge Society

Socioeconomic development brings rising levels of existential security, which is its most basic contribution to human development. This process relieves people from material constraints on their life choices. This contributes to rising self-expression values because it allows people to move beyond sheer survival and focus on other goals. But providing existential security is not the only way through which socioeconomic development is conducive to self-expression values. The growing experience of autonomy linked with the rise of the knowledge society, and its social complexities, cross-cutting networks and diverse human interactions, is also important.

Some oil-exporting countries, such as Bahrain and the United Arab Emirates, are rich and have maximized their population's existential security through extensive transfer programs. As Barro (1997), M. Ross (2001), and others have demonstrated, however, these societies have not evolved the occupational diversification, social complexity, and knowledge-intensity that characterize the creative economies of postindustrial societies. The availability of vast natural resources made it unnecessary to make major investments in human capital, or to establish a knowledge society. Instead, they established rent-seeking economies based on the revenues of state monopolies in oil exports. Rentier economies can become very rich, but they do not show the massive individualization trend that occurs in postindustrial economies. Although their populations enjoy high levels of existential security, the publics of rich oil-exporting countries do not show an emphasis on self-expression values comparable with that found in postindustrial societies. Existential security gives rise to self-expression values if it is coupled with individualization and the experience of autonomy. This experience arises from the destandardization and diversification of economic activities, social roles, and human interactions typical of postindustrial economies. The experience of existential security evolves into a broader sense of human autonomy in postindustrial economies far more than in rentier economies or in industrial economies.[4]

Conclusion

Modernization, Cultural Change, and Democracy presents a massive body of evidence supporting the central insight of modernization theory: socioeconomic development brings systematic changes in political, social, and cultural life. But it is clear that earlier versions of modernization theory need revision. We propose the following modifications:

---

4. Landes (1998) discusses a historical example of this contrast in comparing the Spanish and Dutch colonial empires. The Spanish empire established a rent-seeking economy based on the exploitation of Latin American silver mines. The Dutch empire was based on an innovative commercial economy. Accordingly, the sense of individual autonomy, liberty, and freedom of expression was far more pronounced in Dutch society than it was in Spanish society in colonial times.

1. Although socioeconomic development tends to transform societies in a predictable direction, the process is not deterministic. Many other factors besides socioeconomic development are involved, so our predictions are probabilistic: other things being equal, socioeconomic development tends to make people more secular, tolerant, and trusting and to place more emphasis on self-expression, participation, and the quality of life. But socioeconomic factors are not the only significant influences.
2. Religion and other aspects of a society's traditional cultural heritage are not dying out and will not disappear with modernization. Contrary to Marxist expectations, a society's historical cultural heritage continues to shape the values and behavior of its people. Although the publics of industrializing societies are becoming richer and more educated, we are not moving toward a uniform global culture: cultural convergence is not taking place. A society's cultural heritage is remarkably enduring.
3. Cultural modernization is not irreversible. It results from socioeconomic development and protracted economic collapse can reverse it, as was happening during the 1990s in most of the Soviet successor states.
4. The process of cultural change is not linear. The prevailing direction of change has shifted repeatedly in history. Industrialization gives rise to one major process of cultural change, bringing bureaucratization and secularization. But the rise of postindustrial societies leads to *another* major process of cultural change that moves in a different direction: instead of rationalization, centralization, and bureaucratization, the new trend is toward increasing emphasis on individual autonomy and self-expression values. Thus, economic development produces not one but two major dimensions of cross-cultural variation, one linked with industrialization and the other linked with the rise of postindustrial society.
5. An ethnocentric early version of modernization interpreted the process as Westernization. It is not. Historically, the process of industrialization began in the West, but during the past few decades East Asia has led the world in many aspects of modernization. Similarly, these changes do not constitute Americanization. The United States is not leading the world in cultural change; it is a deviant case, exhibiting much more traditional and religious values than other rich societies. The United States is not the model for the cultural changes that are taking place, and industrializing societies in general are *not* becoming like the United States, as a popular version of modernization theory assumed.
6. Most important, emerging self-expression values transform modernization into a process of human development, giving rise to a new type of humanistic society that promotes human emancipation on many fronts, from equal rights for homosexuals, handicapped people, and women to the rights of people in general. This process reflects a humanistic transformation of modernization.

Throughout history, cultural change has repeatedly changed course. In postindustrial societies in recent decades, rising emphasis on self-expression values has become the key cultural manifestation of modernization. Human choice and emancipation have become the leading themes in all domains of life from politics to child care to gender relations to work motivations to religious orientations and civic engagement. Self-expression values and rising emphasis on freedom of choice emerge as increasingly favorable existential conditions allow the universal desire for autonomy to take priority. Rising emphasis on human choice has immensely important consequences, generating pressures for female empowerment, more responsive elites, effective civil and political liberties, and democratic institutions.

In the postindustrial stage, socioeconomic development, rising self-expression, and effective democracy work together, providing the means, values, and rights that make people increasingly able, willing, and entitled to shape their lives according to their autonomous choices—relatively free from external constraints. This process constitutes "human" development because it emphasizes the most distinctively human ability: the ability to make decisions and actions based on autonomous choices. The process of human development leads to the emergence of increasingly strong societal demands for democracy. Culture alone does not determine the outcome: these changes are probabilistic. World events, wars, depressions, institutional changes, elite decisions, and even specific leaders can influence what happens; but cultural change is a major factor in the emergence and survival of democracy, and one that has generally been underestimated.

References

Almond, Gabriel A., and James S. Coleman (eds.). 1960. *The Politics of the Developing Areas.* Princeton: Princeton University Press.

Almond, Gabriel A., and G. Bingham Powell. 1966. *Comparative Politics: A Developmental Approach.* Princeton: Princeton University Press.

Barkow, Jerome, Leda Cosmides, and John Tooby. 1992. *The Adapted Mind: Evolutionary Psychology and the Generation of Culture.* Oxford: Oxford University Press.

Barro, Robert J. 1997. *Determinants of Economic Growth: A Cross-Country Empirical Study.* Cambridge, MA: MIT Press.

Beck, Ulrich. 1992. *Risk Society.* London: Sage.

———. 2002. "Losing the Traditional: Individualization and 'Precarious Freedoms.'" In Ulrich Beck and Elisabeth Beck-Gernsheim (eds.), *Individualization.* London: Sage, pp. 1–21.

Bell, Daniel. 1973. *The Coming of Postindustrial Society.* New York: Basic Books.

———. 1976. *The Cultural Contradictions of Capitalism.* New York: Basic Books.

Bernstein, William J. 2004. *The Birth of Plenty.* New York: McGraw Hill.

Binder, Leonard, et al. (eds.). 1971. *Crises and Sequences in Political Development.* Princeton: Princeton University Press.

Birch, Charles, and John B. Cobb Jr. 1981. *The Liberation of Life: From the Cell to the Community.* Cambridge: Cambridge University Press.

Bradshaw, York W., and Michael Wallace. 1996. *Global Inequalities.* Thousand Oaks, CA: Pine Forge.

Burke, Edmund. 1999 [1790]. *Reflections on the Revolution in France.* Oxford: Oxford University Press.

Cain, Bruce E., Russell J. Dalton, and Susan E. Scarrow. 2003. *Democracy Transformed? Expanding Political Opportunities in Advanced Industrial Democracies.* Oxford: Oxford University Press.

Cardoso, Fernando Henrique, and Enzo Faletto. 1979. *Dependency and Development in Latin America.* Berkeley: University of California Press.

Carneiro, Robert. 2003. *Evolutionism in Cultural Anthropology.* Boulder, CO: Westview Press.

Chase-Dunn, Christopher. 1989. *Global Formations: Structures of the World-Economy.* Cambridge, MA: Basil Blackwell.

Chirot, Daniel. 1977. *Social Change in the Twentieth Century.* New York: Harcourt Brace Jovanovich.

———. 1994. *How Societies Change.* Thousand Oaks, CA: Pine Forge.

Condorcet, Jean-Antoine-Nicolas de Caritat. 1979 [1795]. *Sketch for a Historical Picture of the Progress of the Human Mind.* Westport, CT: Hyperion Press.

Dalton, Russell J. 2001. *Citizen Politics: Public Opinion and Political Parties in Advanced Western Democracies* (3rd ed.). Chatham, NJ: Chatham House.

Dalton, Russell J., and Martin P. Wattenberg (eds.). 2000. *Parties without Partisans: Political Change in Advanced Industrial Democracies.* Oxford: Oxford University Press.

Deutsch, Karl. 1963. *The Nerves of Government.* New York: Free Press.

Diamond, Larry. 1993. "The Globalization of Democracy." In Robert O. Slater, Barry M. Schutz, and Steve R. Dorr (eds.), *Global Transformation and the Third World.* Boulder, CO: Lynne Rienner, pp. 31–69.

DiMaggio, Paul. 1994. "Culture and Economy." In Neil J. Smelser and Richard Swedberg (eds.), *The Handbook of Economic Sociology.* Princeton: Princeton University Press, pp. 27–57.

Dollar, David. 1992. "Outward-Oriented Developing Economies Really Do Grow More Rapidly: Evidence from 95 LDCs, 1976–1985." *Economic Development and Cultural Change* 13: 523–44.

Doorenspleet, Renske. 2004. "The Structural Context of Recent Transitions to Democracy." *European Journal of Political Research* 43: 309–36.

Durham, William H. 1991. *Coevolution: Genes, Culture, and Human Diversity.* Stanford: Stanford University Press.

Durkheim, Émile. 1988 [1893]. *Über soziale Arbeitsteilung* [On Social Division of Labor]. Frankfurt am Main: Suhrkamp.

Esping-Anderson, Gøsta. 1990. *The Three Worlds of Welfare Capitalism.* Princeton: Princeton University Press.

Estes, Richard J. 1998. "Trends in World Social Development, 1970–1995: Development Challenges for a New Century." *Journal of Developing Societies* 14: 11–39.

Evans, Peter. 1995. *Embedded Autonomy: States and Industrial Transformation.* Princeton: Princeton University Press.

Firebaugh, Glenn. 1992. "Growth Effects of Foreign and Domestic Investment." *American Journal of Sociology* 98: 105–30.

———. 1996. "Does Foreign Capital Harm Poor Nations?" *American Journal of Sociology* 102: 563–75.

Firebaugh, Glenn, and Frank Beck. 1994. "Does Economic Growth Benefit the Masses? Growth, Dependence, and Welfare in the Third World." *American Sociological Review* 59: 631–53.

Florida, Richard. 2002. *The Rise of the Creative Class.* New York: Basic Books.

Frank, Andre Gunder. 1966. "The Development of Underdevelopment." *Monthly Review* 18: 17–30.

Fukuyama, Francis. 1995. *Trust: Social Virtues and the Creation of Prosperity.* New York: Free Press.

Gaskell, George, and Martin Bauer. 2001. *Biotechnology: The Making of Global Controversy.* Cambridge: Cambridge University Press.

Giddens, Anthony. 1990. *The Consequences of Modernity.* Cambridge: Polity Press.

———. 1991. *Modernity and Self-Identity: Self and Society in the Late Modern Age.* Cambridge: Polity Press.

Goesling, Brian. 2001. "Changing Income Inequalities within and between Nations: New Evidence." *American Sociological Review* 66: 745–61.

Granovetter, Mark S. 1973. "The Strength of Weak Ties." *American Journal of Sociology* 78: 1360–80.

Guillén, Mauro. 1994. *Models of Management: Work, Authority, and Organization in a Comparative Perspective.* Chicago: University of Chicago Press.

Hall, John A. 1989. "States and Societies: The Miracle in Comparative Perspective." In Jean Baechler, John Hall, and Michael Mann (eds.), *Europe and the Rise of Capitalism.* Oxford: Basil Blackwell, pp. 20–38.

Hamilton, Gary G. 1994. "Civilizations and Organization of Economies." In Neil J. Smelser and Richard Swedberg (eds.), *The Handbook of Economic Sociology.* Princeton: Princeton University Press, pp. 183–205.

Hein, Simon. 1992. "Trade Strategy and the Dependency Hypothesis: A Comparison of Policy, Foreign Investment and Economic Growth in Latin America and East Asia." *Economic Development and Cultural Change* 13: 495–521.

Hughes, Barry B. 1999. *International Futures: Choices in the Face of Uncertainty* (3rd ed.). Boulder, CO: Westview Press.

Huntington, Samuel P. 1968. *Political Order in Changing Societies.* New Haven: Yale University Press.

———. 1996. *The Clash of Civilizations and the Remaking of the World Order.* New York: Simon and Schuster.

Inglehart, Ronald. 1990. *Culture Shift in Advanced Industrial Societies.* Princeton: Princeton University Press.

———. 1997. *Modernization and Postmodernization: Cultural, Economic, and Political Change in 43 Societies.* Princeton: Princeton University Press.

Inglehart, Ronald, and Pippa Norris. 2003. *Rising Tide: Gender Equality and Cultural Change around the World.* Cambridge: Cambridge University Press.

Inkeles, Alex. 1983. *Exploring Individual Modernity.* New York: Columbia University Press.

Inkeles, Alex, and David Smith. 1974. *Becoming Modern: Individual Changes in Six Developing Societies.* Cambridge, MA: Harvard University Press.

Jones, Eric L. 1985. *The European Miracle: Environments, Economies and Geopolities in the History of Europe and Asia* (3rd ed.). Cambridge: Cambridge University Press.

Lal, Deepak. 1998. *Unintended Consequences: The Impact of Factor Endowments, Culture, and Politics on Long Run Economic Performance.* Cambridge, MA: MIT Press.

Landes, David S. 1998. *The Wealth and Poverty of Nations: Why Some Are So Rich and Some So Poor.* New York: W.W. Norton.

Lerner, Daniel. 1958. *The Passing of Traditional Society: Modernizing the Middle East.* New York: Free Press.

Lipset, Seymour Martin, Kyoung-Ryung Seong, and John C. Torres. 1993. "A Comparative Analysis of the Social Requisites of Democracy." *International Social Science Journal* 45: 155–75.

Malthus, Thomas R. 1970 [1798]. *An Essay on the Principle of Population.* Harmondsworth: Penguin.

Mark, Noah P. 2002. "Cultural Transmission, Disproportionate Prior Exposure, and the Evolution of Cooperation." *American Sociological Review* 67: 323–44.

Marx, Karl. 1973 [1858]. *Grundrisse.* Harmondsworth: Penguin.

Maslow, Abraham. 1988 [1954]. *Motivation and Personality* (3rd ed.). New York: Harper and Row.

McNeill, William. 1990. *The Rise of the West: A History of the Human Community.* Chicago: University of Chicago Press.

Meadows, Donella H., et al. 1972. *The Limits to Growth.* New York: Universe Books.

Meyer, John W., John Boli, George M. Thomas, and Francisco O. Ramirez. 1997. "World Society and the Nation-State." *American Journal of Sociology* 103: 144–81.

Michels, Robert. 1962 [1912]. *Political Parties.* London: Collins Books.

Moore, Barrington. 1966. *The Social Origins of Democracy and Dictatorship: Lord and Peasant in the Making of the Modern World.* Boston: Beacon Press.

Nolan, Patrick, and Gerhard Lenski. 1999. *Human Societies: An Introduction to Macrosociology* (8th ed.). New York: McGraw-Hill.

Norris, Pippa. 2002. *Democratic Phoenix: Political Activism Worldwide.* Cambridge: Cambridge University Press.

Norris, Pippa, and Ronald Inglehart. 2004. *Sacred and Secular: Religion and Politics Worldwide.* Cambridge: Cambridge University Press.

North, Douglas C. 1981. *Structure and Change in Economic History.* New York: W. W. Norton.

O'Donnell, Guillermo. 1973. *Modernization and Bureaucratic Authoritarianism: Studies in South American Politics.* Berkeley: University of California Press.

Putnam, Robert D. 1993. *Making Democracy Work: Civic Traditions in Modern Italy.* Princeton: Princeton University Press.

Pye, Lucian W. 1990. "Political Science and the Crisis of Authoritarianism." *American Political Science Review* 84: 3–19.

Pye, Lucian W., and Sidney Verba (eds.). 1963. *Political Culture and Political Development.* Princeton: Princeton University Press.

Randall, Vicky, and Robin Theobald. 1998. *Political Change and Underdevelopment* (2nd ed.). Durham: Duke University Press.

Rokeach, Milton. 1960. *The Open and Closed Mind: Investigations into the Nature of Belief Systems and Personality Systems.* New York: Basic Books.

———. 1968. *Beliefs, Attitudes and Values.* San Francisco: Jossey-Bass.

———. 1973. *The Nature of Human Values.* New York: Free Press.

Ross, Michael L. 2001. "Does Oil Hinder Democracy?" *World Politics* 53: 325–61.

Rowen, Henry S. 1996. "World Wealth Expanding: Why a Rich, Democratic, and (Perhaps) Peaceful Era is Ahead." In Ralph Landau, Timothy Taylor, and Gavin Wright (eds.), *The Mosaic of Economic Growth.* Stanford: Stanford University Press, pp. 93–125.

Rueschemeyer, Dietrich, Evelyn Huber Stephens, and John D. Stephens. 1992. *Capitalist Development and Democracy.* Chicago: University of Chicago Press.

Sen, Amartya. 1999. *Development as Freedom.* New York: Knopf.

Simmel, Georg. 1984 [1908]. *Das Individuum und die Freiheit* [The Individual and Freedom]. Berlin: Duncker & Humblodt.

Smith, Adam. 1976 [1776]. *An Inquiry into the Nature and Causes of the Wealth of Nations.* Chicago: University of Chicago Press.

Spier, Fred. 1996. *The Structure of Big History: From the Big Bang until Today.* Amsterdam: Amsterdam University Press.

Stevenson, Mark. 1997. "Globalization, National Cultures, and Cultural Citizenship." *Sociological Quarterly* 38: 41–67.

Stinchcomb, Arthur L. 1965. "Social Structure and Organization." In J. G. March (ed.), *Handbook of Organizations.* Chicago: Rand McNally, pp. 142–93.

Tönnies, Ferdinand. 1955 [1887]. *Community and Association.* London: Routledge and Kegan Paul.

Wallerstein, Immanuel. 1974. *The Modern World System I.* New York: Academic Press.

———. 1976. "Modernization: Requiescat in Pace." In Lewis A. Coser and Otto N. Larsen (eds.), *The Uses of Controversy in Sociology.* New York: Free Press, pp. 131–35.

Weber, Max. 1958 [1904]. *The Protestant Ethic and the Spirit of Capitalism.* New York: Charles Scribner's Sons.

Weiner, Myron (ed.). 1966. *Modernization: The Dynamics of Growth.* New York: Basic Books.

Welzel, Christian, Ronald Inglehart, and Franziska Deutsch. 2005. "Civil Society, Social Capital and Collective Action: Which Type of Civic Activity is Most Democratic?" Paper presented at the HPSA annual meeting, Chicago, 11 April.

Whyte, William H., Jr. 1956. *The Organization Man.* New York: Simon and Schuster.

INDEX